DOS 6.0 POWER TOOLS®

DOS 6.0 POWER TOOLS®

Techniques, Tricks, and Utilities

John M. Goodman
John Socha

BANTAM BOOKS
NEW YORK • TORONTO • LONDON • SYDNEY • AUCKLAND

DOS 6.0 Power Tools:® Techniques, Tricks, and Utilities
A Bantam Book/April 1993

ISBN 0-553-37190-8

Published simultaneously in the United States and Canada

Bantam Books are published by Bantam Books, a division of Bantam Doubleday Dell Publishing Group, Inc. Its trademark, consisting of the words "Bantam Books" and the portrayal of a rooster, is Registered in U.S. Patent and Tradmark Office and in other countries. Marca Registrada, Bantam Books, 1540 Broadway, New York, New York 10036.

PRINTED IN THE UNITED STATES OF AMERICA

0 9 8 7 6 5 4 3 2

Contents

PART One

GETTING UP TO SPEED

CHAPTER

1

Your PC and DOS — An Overview

You and every other PC user want to have power—power to make your PC do what you want, when you want, and the way you want. If you already view yourself as a DOS power user, this book will make you a better and more powerful one. If you don't yet think of yourself in this way, this book can give you the skills and confidence to change your perspective.

What Is DOS, Anyway?

When you buy a copy of DOS, you get a lot in the box: some of it is packaging material, explanatory material, and advertising for other products. And somewhere deep in the package you will also find some diskettes. Of all this, what really is DOS? Answer: none of these things.

DOS is the software *contained* on the diskettes. (Remember, software is just information.) But even that is not the whole answer because DOS is *not* all of the software on those diskettes. The DOS program is contained in just one of the files on any bootable DOS diskette. It is one that you don't normally see when you do a directory listing because it has been given *hidden* and *system attributes.* This is the file Microsoft calls MSDOS.SYS and IBM calls IBMDOS.COM. The other hidden system file, IO.SYS, (called IBMBIO.COM by IBM) contains mainly the default device drivers and the program code to build DOS in the PC, a process called SYSINIT. One new hidden system file in MS-DOS 6 is DOUBLESPACE.BIN. This is a special device driver that does on-the-fly file compression. (Interestingly, it gets loaded into RAM by IO.SYS along with the usual default device drivers, but it gets moved to a different location in RAM later on, after the CONFIG.SYS processing is complete.) The only other essential part of DOS is a command interpreter, and COMMAND.COM is the one shipped with DOS by both Microsoft and IBM.

These are the essential components of the actual DOS operating system. They get loaded into memory when you boot your computer, and they stay there all the time, doing their jobs of managing and allocating resources for the benefit of whatever other programs you choose to run.

All the rest of the files on the diskettes that come in the DOS package are utility programs that get shipped with DOS. You may need them, but they are not directly a part of the disk operating system, DOS. The DOS utility programs are like third-party utility programs such as Norton Utilities. The only difference is that Microsoft chose to bundle some utilities with DOS and not others. (Of course, that also means that you got the bundled ones at no extra charge, whereas you normally have to pay for third-party utilities.)

Third-party utilities are developed by people who see a gap between what the Microsoft-provided utilities do and what they want to have. So they write (and then sell to others) programs to do those additional tasks. The DOS Power Tools contained on the diskettes accompanying this book are some of the cream of the crop of third-party DOS enhancers. (We must caution you about one thing, however. Many of the DOS Power Tools are *shareware* programs, which means that you are free to *try them out* and *share them with your friends.* But, if you decide that they are really useful to you, and you plan to go on using them, you *must pay* a registration fee directly to the author. (This is discussed in more detail in Chapter 16.)

Throughout this book, you will be told what the utility programs that come bundled with DOS can do. You will also be told when one of the DOS Power Tools can do an even better job of that task. At other times, you will also be told about some of the very best of the commercial third-party utility packages that you may wish to add to your toolkit, especially when they can do certain things that the DOS-provided tools and the DOS Power Tools cannot.

Logical PC Layers

Viewed abstractly, there are three main layers in your PC. The lowest level is the hardware, which is composed of the pieces that do the actual computing,

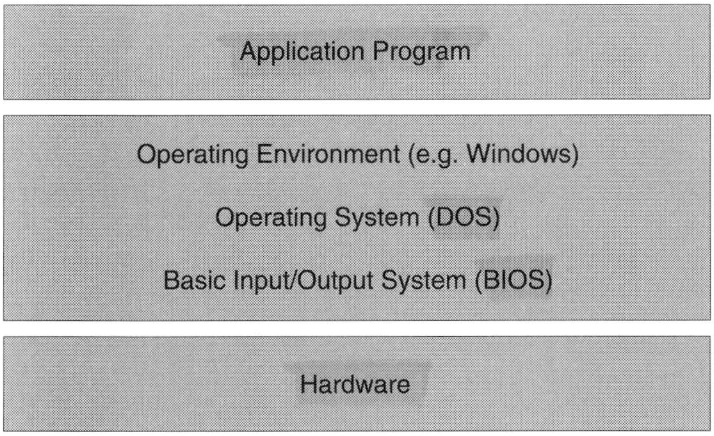

Figure 1-1 The logical layers

printing, and so forth. The highest level is your application program, which is what you interact with when you are using your PC.

Between those two levels is the operating system and, often, a host of other helper programs. Figure 1-1 shows these three logical layers: the big picture. The middle layer deserves a much closer look. You need to know the sub-layers that it contains, both to better understand your PC and, even more importantly, to manipulate it as a true power user.

Physical Layers

Figure 1-2 shows an image of the computer's memory. To see what most of the layers in this diagram would look like in your PC, run the command `MEM /D /P`. The sizes of the layers are given in hexadecimal numbers, but you need not worry about that. (Hexadecimal numbers are explained in the last section of this chapter.) Just notice what all the layers are called and the relative size of each layer. (Also notice that this diagram puts the lowest memory addresses at the bottom, while the output of the MEM command shows the lowest addresses first, at the top of your monitor screen.)

> ***Note:*** The drawing in Figure 1-2 has been carefully created to show the relative size of the portions of memory occupied by each of the layers in one particular PC. Some of the layers may be of drastically different sizes in different PCs or even in the same PC when it has been configured differently; others are the same in all PCs running the same version of DOS.

The figure in the foreground shows DOS 6 with a typical assortment of default and installed device drivers. The CONFIG.SYS file in this PC included a line reading DOS=HIGH.

The figure in the background shows DOS 6 with a much larger assortment of device drivers (including ones to support networking). In this case, no DOS=HIGH line was used. Those two differences explain all the variations in layer thicknesses you will see there.

The very lowest level is a data table (called the *Interrupt Vector Table*) that is of central importance to your PC's functioning. Its use is explained in the next section, and how it (and the other layers) is created is explained in the section after that. The second layer (the *DOS and BIOS data area*) is a storage space used by both the DOS and BIOS program pieces to keep track of many things about your PC.

The third layer holds a collection of device driver programs, some of which are built into DOS and are called the *DOS default device drivers.* Others are loaded into memory in response to some lines in your CONFIG.SYS file and are called *installable device drivers.* Between the two groups is a layer containing some of the program that is actually DOS.

The distinction between the two groups of device drivers is that the default drivers do things almost every PC user needs. The installable drivers are loaded only when a PC user has certain special hardware or needs some of the standard hardware to be handled in a special way. Both kinds of device drivers are explained in more detail in the next section.

Directly above the installable device drivers is a layer containing some key DOS data tables: the *system file table,* the *file control block table,* the *DOS disk buffers* the *current directory structure,* and the "public" *stacks.* The size of these objects is controlled by the FILES=, FCBS=, BUFFERS=, LASTDRIVE=, and STACKS= lines in your CONFIG.SYS file. If you use DOS=HIGH, most of the system file table and DOS disk buffers will be loaded into the high memory area (HMA) along with some of the DOS program.

The only DOS file that shows up in a simple DIR listing of a bootable DOS disk's root directory is COMMAND.COM. This file is called the *command interpreter*; it is also known as a *shell.* Only a portion of COMMAND.COM occupies the next layer in Figure 1-2. This is referred to as the permanent part, for reasons that will shortly become clearer. The rest of COMMAND.COM is put high in memory, just under the video image storage area; it is called the transient part.

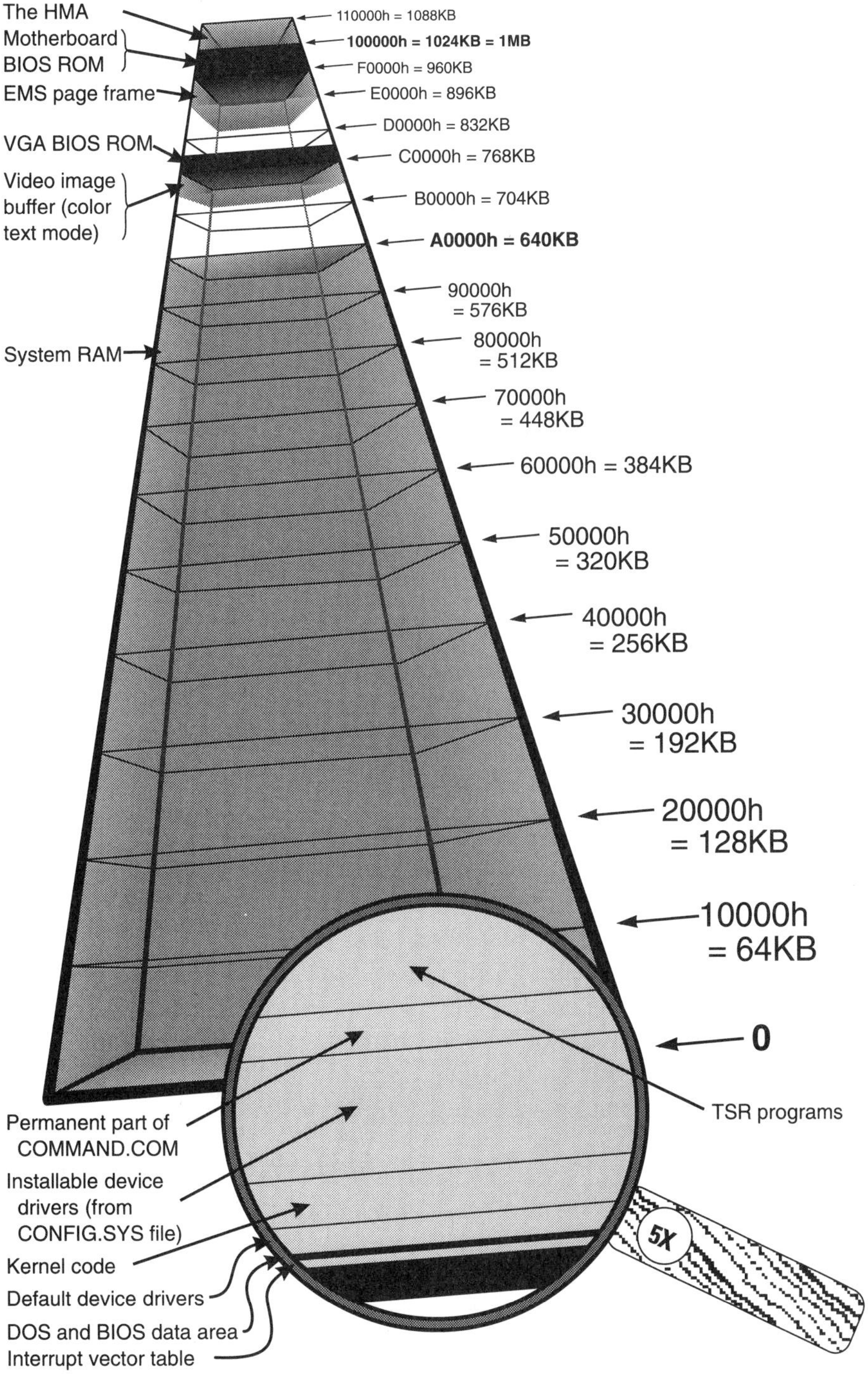
The HMA
Motherboard BIOS ROM
EMS page frame
VGA BIOS ROM
Video image buffer (color text mode)
System RAM
110000h = 1088KB
100000h = 1024KB = 1MB
F0000h = 960KB
E0000h = 896KB
D0000h = 832KB
C0000h = 768KB
B0000h = 704KB
A0000h = 640KB
90000h = 576KB
80000h = 512KB
70000h = 448KB
60000h = 384KB
50000h = 320KB
40000h = 256KB
30000h = 192KB
20000h = 128KB
10000h = 64KB
0
TSR programs
5X
Permanent part of COMMAND.COM
Installable device drivers (from CONFIG.SYS file)
Kernel code
Default device drivers
DOS and BIOS data area
Interrupt vector table

Figure 1-2 The many layers of software in a PC

These two layers are responsible for giving you the DOS prompt. They also "listen" to what you type on the keyboard and display it on the screen. When you press the Enter key, COMMAND.COM is the program that attempts to interpret your command and then "makes it so."

A minimal DOS system would have free memory right above this point. But any PC that is doing something useful has at least one more program (and often many) loaded right above the command interpreter. Figure 1-2 has a layer marked TSRs (*terminate-and-stay-resident* programs). They may do things similar to device drivers, or they may be what are sometimes called *desktop accessories,* such as a pop-up calendar program.

Above the TSRs is a large layer marked "Your Application Program." This is where your word processor, for example, would be loaded. The application program is initially given the use of all the rest of the RAM in your PC up to the bottom of the video image storage area. If it did not use all of that memory, some of the memory may now be in a layer marked as "free," which means that DOS is able to allocate that memory to other programs when necessary.

Notice the layer labelled "Transient part of COMMAND.COM." This is where the largest portion of that program resides. But that memory region is not reserved for its use. In fact, any application program may be put there instead. If that happens, the permanent part of COMMAND.COM will notice this fact the next time it is about to give you a DOS prompt, and will first reload itself from the disk, thereby refreshing the transient part of itself in memory.

The dividing line between where application programs live and the video image storage area is normally at address A0000h, 640KB above the bottom of memory. The region below that point is called *lower memory;* the region from that point up to 1MB is called *upper memory.*

The broad layer called "Video Image Storage Area" is used to hold information about the image that is on your screen. These addresses refer to RAM chips that are physically located on the video display adapter. The video display circuitry on that card is constantly looking at these RAM chips in order to know what image to repaint on the screen at least sixty times each second.

Some hardware pieces that you can add to your PC come with what is called an *option ROM* on them. That is a memory chip containing programs to supplement those in the motherboard BIOS ROMs. Specifically, they are programs that are needed to activate that hardware piece. One common example is a VGA or EGA video display card. Although the option ROM is physically located on the option card you plug into your PC's bus, it shows up in memory address space in the layer marked "Option ROMs and UMBs" in Figure 1-2. That region is often shared by many ROMs. In many PCs, however, much of that region is not used by any ROMs, and any such free space is available for other purposes, but only if something special is done first. The reason for that is simple: If there is literally nothing at an address, that address is not usable for anything. So the necessary first step is to make some RAM appear in those otherwise unused spaces. This is easy to do if your PC is built around a 386 or 486 CPU chip. It is harder to do, but still often possible, with some of the earlier designs based on the 8088 or 80286 CPU chips (more commonly called XTs and ATs).

If you can put RAM in those empty spaces, it can be put to good use in two ways: first as an expanded memory (EMS) page frame, and second as upper memory blocks (UMBs) into which TSR programs and device drivers can be loaded. (You will learn more about how UMBs can be made in just a few paragraphs.)

> ***Expanded memory*** is available to programs that ask for access to it according to a special protocol called the Expanded Memory Specification (or EMS). The EMS page frame is a 64KB region of upper memory space that is dedicated to use by the expanded memory manager (EMM) program for four 16KB chunks of RAM that it can evoke at any given time. When a program needs access to some other section of EMS memory, it normally asks the EMM to make it appear in one of the four page frame slots. (We'll discuss the various types of memory further in Chapter 6.) The EMM can also, in many PCs, make some EMS memory appear in part of lower memory. This is very useful if you wish to do task swapping using a program like DESQview.

The top layer in the first megabyte of a PC is the motherboard BIOS ROM. This contains the POST (Power On Self Test) program, the boot program that loads DOS and a collection of hardware-activating programs. DOS was originally designed for a PC built using an 8088 CPU chip. That chip can address only one megabyte of memory, so for that sort of PC the memory map ends at this point.

Starting with the AT, the memory map got extended, first to 16MB, and later on to 4GB (that is 4 gigabytes, or 4,096 megabytes). If you have more than a megabyte of RAM in your PC, the excess shows up here and it is called, not too surprisingly, *Extended memory.*

Extended memory (not to be confused with expanded memory) is memory that is physically present at memory addresses above 1MB. By loading the device driver called HIMEM.SYS (or a third-party equivalent), you will convert the first 64KB of the memory into the *high memory area* (or HMA). The rest of the extended memory is converted by HIMEM into what is called *XMS memory* (for eXtended Memory Specification).

Any program that can access HIMEM (or another XMS memory manager) can make use of the HMA. But only the first program will be allowed in there. If you put the directive `DOS=HIGH` in your CONFIG.SYS file, then DOS gets the HMA and everybody else gets locked out. DOS will put a portion of its actual program code there, along with the DOS disk buffers (but only if all of them will fit), thus reducing the size of DOS in lower memory.

Some programs can use extended memory, but only if it has not been converted to XMS memory; others can use it only if it has been converted. The vast majority of PC programs can't use extended memory in either form, although more and more modern programs are being made XMS-memory aware.

One very important DOS program that can use XMS memory is EMM386.EXE. This program is designed to take some of the XMS memory and convert it into expanded memory and/or take some XMS memory and make it appear as RAM in one or more regions of upper memory called upper memory blocks (UMBs). This program, which can be run only on a 386- or 486-based PC, is what makes it easy to have UMBs in upper memory wherever there are no option ROMs. You will learn all about how to use EMM386 in Chapters 6 and 10.

Interlayer Communication

With over a dozen layers, each containing a different program (or a set of programs), how can they all work without interfering with one another? How does DOS control them, and how can they communicate with each other? The short answer is that only one program is in control of the PC at any one time. There is a single *register* inside the central processor unit (CPU) called the *instruction pointer* (IP). The number stored in that location (in conjunction with another register called the *code segment*, or CS, register) points to the place in memory that is currently in control of the PC.

Control is passed back and forth between the many programs loaded in the CPU's memory address space in three different ways: through *direct transfers*, by using *interrupts*, and by calling for *service from a device driver.*

DIRECT TRANSFERS

Conceptually, the simplest way to hand off control from one program to another is for the first one to simply CALL the second one. That means it sets up a place marker to show the CPU where to come back to, then it directs the instruction pointer at the second program. This works, but only if the first program knows exactly where in memory the second program is located.

Because of its limitations, this strategy is normally used only to transfer control between different pieces of a program that have been written by the same programming team. It is fast and effective, but is severely limited in its applicability in a PC that is filled with many programs from many different companies.

INTERRUPTS

The most common method of communication between the different layers of software in PCs is by use of interrupts. Interrupts, as Intel implemented them, are very flexible and get used in several quite different ways. Interrupts are used to provide basic services on the PC , without you having to worry about the exact details of how the service is performed. Let's look at a typical event that gets handled this way: putting some information on the PC's display screen.

First, the program sets a pointer to the information that is to be displayed in a special place. Then it declares a particular kind of "magic" event—an `INT 10h` instruction which stands for an interrupt of type 10h (or, in decimal, type 16). When the CPU executes an INT instruction, the special design of the CPU takes over. It notices what kind of interrupt was declared by the program. The INT instruction is 2 bytes long. When the CPU reads the first byte of the INT instruction, it automatically assumes that the next byte will tell it just what kind of interrupt this one is.

Tip: If you are snooping in memory inside a program, you will see the hexadecimal value CDh (which in binary is 11001101) stored wherever there is an interrupt instruction. That is the first byte of an INT instruction. The binary number stored in the next byte tells what kind of interrupt that one is.

Once the CPU knows what kind of interrupt it is dealing with, it does several things. First, it saves a pointer to the next instruction. Then it looks in a special place near the bottom of its memory address space where it finds an address. It then begins reading instructions at that address and doing whatever they say to do. Eventually, it comes to a special instruction in the second program that tells it to stop reading there and to go back to the original program. This process occurs in five steps:

1. The first step, remembering where to come back to, is pretty easy. The CPU simply saves the address of the next instruction in the program it was executing when it came across the INT instruction. The place it saves this address is called the *stack.*
2. The next step, looking up the address of the *interrupt service routine* it is now going to *execute,* is also pretty simple. The type of interrupt is a 1-byte number, which means it can have any value from 0 to 255. The CPU automatically multiplies that number by 4 and reads the number at that memory location and the 3 bytes after that. In our example, the interrupt type was 10h (which is 16 decimal), so the address of the interrupt service routine will be found in memory locations 40h (64 decimal) through 43h (67 decimal).
3. The CPU assumes that the four numbers it finds in those four locations are the 4-byte address (in segment:offset form) of the location at which the appropriate interrupt service routine begins. (Don't worry if the phrase "segment:offset form" means nothing to you. It is explained in Chapter 6.)
4. Next, the CPU simply reads and executes the instructions in this new program, one after another just as it had been doing in the original program.
5. Eventually, it will come across the special instruction called an IRET (Return from Interrupt or Interrupt RETurn). When it sees that instruction, the CPU knows it is time to return to reading and executing the original program. Notice that by the time the CPU resumes its work in the original program the interrupt service routine will have done whatever was necessary to make the required "magic" happen.

Why is this particular convoluted way of doing things necessary, and why is it so important to PC program design? The key to the answers is found where the addresses of the interrupt service routines get stored. Interrupt service routines (ISRs, for short) are programs that have been crafted each to handle a certain type of situation. The type of situation for which each one is appropriate is signaled by the interrupt number and, therefore, the address in low memory where the address of the ISR is stored. This collection of addresses of ISR programs is called the *interrupt vector table*. (Remember, this is the lowest of the physical layers of software described in the previous section.)

Key Features of Intel's Interrupt Strategy The first important thing to notice is that the CPU knows where to go looking for the relevant ISR. It just looks in the right slot in the interrupt vector table to find out where the ISR program is. The program writer desiring some help from another program no longer needs to know where that second program is located in memory space. The first program's author need merely call for that kind of "magic" and it will happen (assuming, of course, that the needed second program is in memory somewhere and has had its address put into the proper place in the interrupt vector table).

The second important point is that the interrupt vector table is located in a region of the CPU's memory address space that is populated with RAM chips. That means that any program can, at any time, change one or more of the pointers in the interrupt vector table. In so doing, it will force different ISR programs to be used the next time those kinds of interrupts are called for by any other program.

Third, the Intel design for the x86 family also spells out a way to extend this whole notion of interrupts to include responses to outside events. For example, if you press a key on the keyboard, that fact is signalled to the CPU via an externally generated interrupt (of type 9). In addition, Intel made the CPU so it can interrupt itself whenever it senses an error condition.

The independence between calling and called programs granted by the interrupt strategy means that the ISR programs can be written by different teams of programmers than the application programs that use the services of those ISR programs.

Key Features Advantages The first feature—all the ISR addresses in a fixed set of locations—means that all programs can call for interrupt services totally without regard to where the ISR programs that will service them may be loaded in memory. Furthermore, those ISR programs can do what is needed independent of where the program that caused the interrupt is located.

The second feature—ISR addresses stored in RAM—means that any program can alter which ISR will serve a given interrupt. Typically, when you load a TSR utility program or device driver it will "hook" several of the interrupts; that is, it will plug into the table at those locations addresses within itself. This assures the TSR program that when the next interruption of any of those types occurs, the TSR program will get control of the PC instead of the original ISR.

The third feature—hardware and error conditions outside the CPU that can trigger interrupts—means that programs need not anticipate all the external events or error conditions that might arise. The program can simply assume there is nothing else going on and that all its actions are performed perfectly. Then, when some important outside event does occur, or when an error crops up, the program that is running at the time will be interrupted, and the appropriate ISR will be invoked to handle that "crisis" in a suitable manner. This makes writing PC programs much easier.

THE DEVICE DRIVER CHAIN

There is a third way that the programs in the different layers can communicate among themselves: via the device driver chain. Any operating system has to know how to manipulate the various devices that are attached to the computer it is running. The first operating systems were written to have that knowledge firmly built in from the start. That works, but it is an inflexible approach. Each time some new device is added to the computer, its operating system has to be rewritten to accommodate that new hardware piece.

Beginning with version 2.0, DOS has used a much more flexible way of dealing with devices. It has the notion of device drivers as separate entities built deeply into it. (This separation between device drivers and the operating system they serve is much like that between ISR programs and the application programs that use their services. A key difference is that Intel designed the interrupt strategy into the x86 microprocessors, while the device driver strategy was built into DOS by Microsoft.) One important feature of the DOS concept of devices is that all of them accept or generate streams of information. There are two classes of devices: character and block. *Character devices* supply or accept a single character at a time. The keyboard is an example: When you press a key you want the PC to notice that fact and not to wait until you have typed a whole sentence. *Block devices,* on the other hand, only handle information in full blocks. Usually a block contains 512 bytes; a disk drive is an example. (It would be very inefficient to ship data to or from a disk drive a single byte at a time.)

A file on a disk drive looks to DOS in many ways just like any other device. This is why you can copy files from one name to another or, with equal ease, from a name to a device, such as LPT1:. In the first case you get two copies of your file; in the second, you get a hard copy printout of the file. (Watch out: This works, but only if the file contains all printable characters.)

Tip: Another use for the apparent similarity of files and devices is as a power user's trick for batch file programming. You can test for the existence of files, but not directories, in a batch file. But you can check on the existence of a subdirectory simply by checking for the existence of any of the DOS devices in that subdirectory. For example:

```
IF EXIST \MYDIR\NUL GOTO OPTION1
```

will let you branch (change what gets done) on whether or not \MYDIR exists, regardless of whether MYDIR is empty, itself contains only subdirectories, or contains files. You will learn more about this technique in Chapter 12.

DOS comes with a default set of device drivers. It includes the all-important CON, or console device, the name for the keyboard and screen. Without this one you'd have a hard time telling your PC what to do, and a hard time finding out what it had done. Other default devices are NUL, CLOCK$, AUX, COM1, COM2, COM3, COM4, LPT1, LPT2, LPT3, and one block device driver for all your floppy and hard disks.

These device drivers are specialized programs that know how to initialize the devices they serve, how to convert information from the stream of bytes flowing from DOS into whatever form the device may need, and how to convert information in the other direction, from the device back into a DOS-style stream of bytes.

The device driver programs get linked into DOS in an interesting way. The NUL device (also known as the "bit bucket" because it simply discards any information sent to it) is built into the DOS program itself. The NUL device also contains a pointer to the next device in the device chain. Each device in the chain has a pointer to the next one, except the last one, which has a special number (FFFFh) as its pointer to indicate that it is the last one in the chain. As you will learn in more detail in the next section, additional drivers may be easily added to this chain. When they are added, the pointers from device to device get altered to include the new drivers. In this way an installed device driver may get put into the chain ahead of some of the default drivers.

When DOS wants to send or receive some information to or from a device, it first sends a message down the linked device driver chain asking the driver for that device to "listen up." The first driver on the chain whose device name matches that in the message will respond. After that, DOS sends (or receives) its stream of information directly to (or from) that device driver, ignoring all the rest.

Because installed drivers can have the same name as a default driver and can be installed in front of the default drivers (other than NUL), an installed driver can preempt one of the default drivers. This is the mechanism by which, for example, ANSI.SYS can take over the CONsole device so you can get the benefit of its improved processing of keystrokes and handling of screen output. Other installable device drivers have names that are unlike any other drivers previously installed. They serve to extend the operating system to allow it to manage new hardware. Examples of these drivers include the driver for a CD-ROM player or a SCSI host adapter. Finally, some installable device drivers have new names because they are going to be used to provide some altered form of access to one of the existing devices. The DoubleSpace disk compression program is one of these.

> ***Note:*** The names of device drivers, as they get installed into the device driver chain, are often not the same as the file name of the driver as it lives on the disk drive. Use the DOS command `MEM /D /P` to see both names. You will see some lines in the output that end in `DEVICE=`. Those lines start with the file name of the device driver. In the preceding column you will find the name of the device driver as it is installed in the device driver chain.

How the Layers Get There

The layers shown in Figure 1-2 come in two kinds: those that are always there, and those that get rebuilt each time you reboot your PC. The former are always the same size and in the same place (of course); the latter may vary dramatically with changes in your configuration (which mainly means changes in your CONFIG.SYS and AUTOEXEC.BAT files).

THE PERMANENT LAYERS

Intel designed two special address ranges into their x86 microprocessors. One is hexadecimal address FFFF0h, just 16 bytes below the 1MB mark, the address at which all those processors start reading instructions when they first are turned on. The other is the location of the interrupt vector table, which is the first 1KB of the processor's memory address space.

Because the startup address is near the top of the first megabyte, it is a natural place to put some ROM with the appropriate startup program in it. And that is where a PC's motherboard BIOS ROM always is put. Since the interrupt vector table is most flexible when it is in RAM, the bottom of the address space is all RAM.

The only other layers whose size and location cannot be changed from one work session to another are the ones created by option ROMs, which are ROM chips mounted on various option cards that you have added to your PC. Not all option cards have ROMs. Usually the only ones that do are those that have hardware pieces that must be accessed during the boot process. Most of what each of these option ROMs contains is either an interrupt service routine or a device driver program to activate the hardware on the option card or that is meant to be attached to that card. The way these interrupt service routines and device drivers get linked into DOS is explained in the next section.

> **Note:** Not every option card whose hardware is involved in the boot process will have an option ROM. For example, an IDE/ATA "paddle card" need not have an option ROM even though it is connected to your hard disk and maybe to your floppy disk drives, because IDE/ATA drives are specifically designed to emulate precisely the standard drive and controller of an AT. The device driver program code for that (and the floppy disk drives) is included in the motherboard BIOS ROM and in the default DOS block device.

All the rest of the layers shown in Figure 1-2 get rebuilt each time you restart your PC. The process of building them is called the boot process. (The name is a whimsical reference to the notion of "pulling oneself up by one's bootstraps," since any computer that could start itself seemed, not so many years ago, about that unlikely.)

THE BOOT PROCESS

The boot process has many steps, and what follows is a recounting of most of them. Figure 1-3 shows these steps in flowchart form. First, if the boot is a *cold boot* (starting the computer from power down or by pressing its reset button), the startup program in the motherboard BIOS ROM does a quick check of the PC's health and a survey of its component parts. Neither check is comprehensive, but passing the Power On Self Test (POST) does give you a fair level of confidence that your PC is functioning correctly—at least mostly—and the system survey lets the PC have a pretty good idea of how many disk drives, serial ports, and printer ports it has.

The opposite of a cold boot is, of course, a *warm boot,* which is what happens when you use the "three finger salute"—pressing the Ctrl, Alt, and Delete keys simultaneously. The two kinds of boots differ only in whether or not they include the self test and keyboard initialization.

Next is the option ROM prescan. This is very special purpose perusal of a region of upper memory (normally the 16KB just above the video image storage area, at addresses C0000h through C7FFFh). The goal in this step is

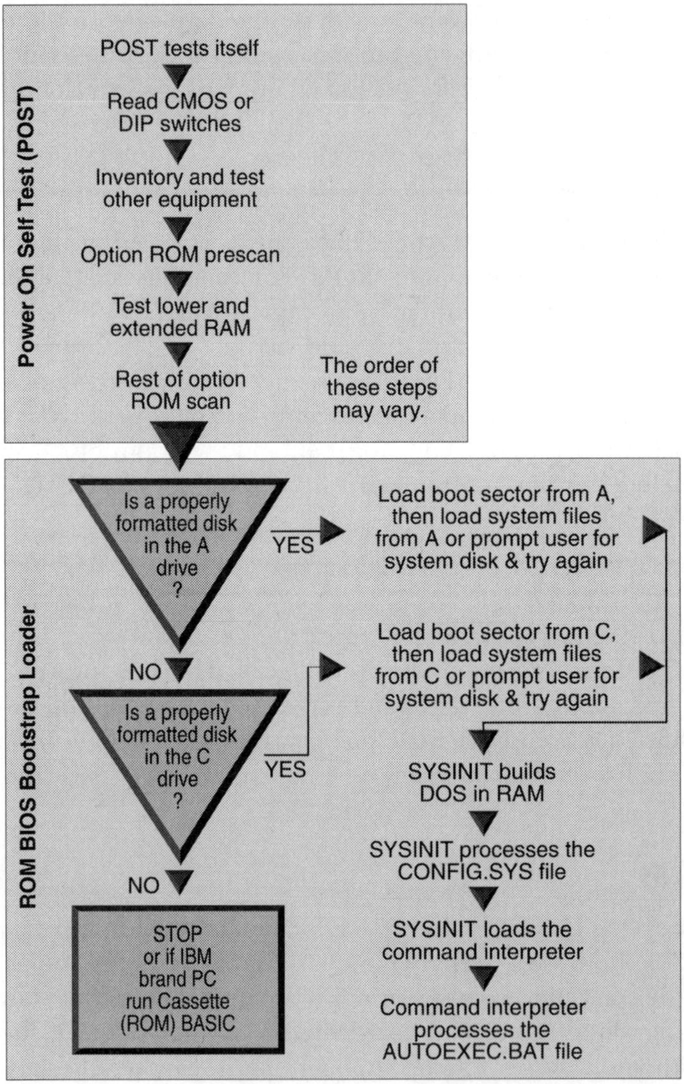

Figure 1-3 The major steps in PC boot process

to find out if this PC has an EGA, VGA, or other advanced video display adapter. If it does, the device driver in that display adapter's option ROM must be linked into DOS before any messages can be made to appear on the screen. You know the option ROM prescan is in progress when you see the message on your PC screen identifying the kind of video card you have.

Linking in the video option ROM mainly means replacing the pointer in the interrupt vector table for INT 10h which is, you will recall, the particular interrupt that is used to send information to the screen. The default device driver loaded by DOS can be used without change, as the only significant differences all get handled in the INT 10h interrupt service routine.

After the video display is properly initialized and activated, the POST has a few more steps to do (if it is a cold boot). Most significantly, it tests the RAM both to find out how much you have and to be sure it is working correctly. At this time, the POST will also initialize the keyboard controller and the keyboard. (You will learn more about the keyboard and its controller in Chapter 4.) The startup program at this time also fills in the first sixteen entries in the interrupt vector table. The interrupt service routines that are pointed to by those entries are all located in the motherboard BIOS.

The boot process next returns to the option ROM scan. It checks every memory address in the range C8000h through E0000h that is a multiple of 2KB. If it finds a valid option ROM at that location, it allows a portion of the program code in that ROM to execute, which causes that option ROM to be linked into DOS properly. The linking is accomplished primarily by taking over one or more interrupts, as was the case for the video display adapter. If the option ROM in question has a device driver in it, it would be added to the device driver chain as well.

Once the option ROM scan is finished, it is time to go looking for an operating system. (Incidentally, notice that no matter what operating system or operating environment you run on a PC, be it DOS, Windows, UNIX, OS/2, Pick, or whatever, all the steps in the boot process up to this point will be exactly the same.) The startup program normally looks first at the A: floppy disk drive. If it finds a properly formatted floppy diskette in that drive, it checks to see if the rest of some PC operating system is on that diskette. If so, it will load it and let it initialize itself.

Note: A properly formatted floppy is one that has as its first sector something called a boot record, which is a program and a small data table that describes that diskette.

If the startup program finds a properly formatted floppy, but doesn't find a valid operating system on that diskette, then it displays on the screen the message

```
Non system disk. Replace and press any key.
```

(This is a typical wording; the exact phrasing depends on which version of DOS was used to format that diskette.) If the startup program sees no properly formatted floppy in the A: drive, it normally goes to the C: drive next.

(This order can sometimes be altered, or the search of the A: drive even omitted, by a setting in the configuration CMOS memory of the PC. To do that, you must run the setup program for your PC, either from a diskette or by pressing a special *hot key* such as *Del*, or a combination such as *Ctrl-Alt-Ins*. Machines with a hot key or combo will generally put a message on screen to that effect as part of their boot process, either warm or cold.)

The startup program does basically the same things on the C: drive that it did on the A: drive. The only difference is that the first sector on the hard drive is what we call the Master Boot Record and it contains both a Partition Table and a program to read that table and act on what it finds there.

The partition table points to a portion of the disk (the active partition), and the startup program next looks inside that partition for a boot sector very much like that on a floppy diskette, and in turn the program in that boot sector looks for an operating system. If the boot sector program finds the DOS hidden system files (usually called IO.SYS and MSDOS.SYS), it will load them into memory and let them take over control of the PC. These programs fill in the rest of the interrupt vector table, define the DOS and BIOS data area, load the DOS default device drivers, and load the essential DOS program code. Then they process the CONFIG.SYS file. The official name for all this initial building-DOS-in-RAM effort is the SYSINIT process.

The CONFIG.SYS file is a text file of instructions to DOS on how it will customize this PC for this work session. If it is a properly created file, you can use the DOS command TYPE CONFIG.SYS to display it on your monitor. You should be able to read everything in that file, which is to say it should not contain any nontypeable characters. (You can read it; whether or not you can understand what you read is an entirely different issue!) Each line of the CONFIG.SYS file is a separate instruction. There are six kinds of lines that can be put in a CONFIG.SYS file:

1. REMarks: Use these to help you know why the other lines are there.
2. Menuing commands: These are new in DOS 6. See Chapter 9 for details on how to use them.
3. Directives to DOS: Mostly, these specify the size of various DOS data structures, such as the system file table and the DOS disk buffers. Other directives set various DOS variables. One particularly significant directive in terms of what gets loaded where is the line DOS=HIGH. (This directive is only available in DOS 5 or later versions.)
4. Lines to load device drivers: These can load device drivers either into lower or upper memory.
5. Lines to install TSR programs: Normally, TSR programs are run from your AUTOEXEC.BAT file, but some of them can be loaded through an

INSTALL line in your CONFIG.SYS file. (TSRs loaded this way must not need any of the services of COMMAND.COM, and they can be loaded only into lower memory.)

6. A SHELL statement: This specifies what command interpreter to use (and, optionally, to give some directions to that interpreter on how it will do its job).

Once the SYSINIT process is through reading and acting on the lines in the CONFIG.SYS file, it loads COMMAND.COM or any other command interpreter that may have been specified in a SHELL= statement in CONFIG.SYS. The first thing the command interpreter does is link itself into DOS and relocate much of itself (the so-called transient part) up near the top of lower memory, just under the video image storage area. Next, it reads the AUTOEXEC.BAT file and acts on each of the lines in it. When it finishes processing that file, the command interpreter presents its famous DOS prompt.

The AUTOEXEC.BAT file, like the CONFIG.SYS file, is a pure text file. Each line specifies one action. As with lines in the CONFIG.SYS file, there are six kinds of lines in an AUTOEXEC.BAT file:

1. REMarks: Once again, use these liberally or you may never be able to make sense of your AUTOEXEC.BAT file once you have been away from it for long.

2. Directives to tell DOS how to do its work: Two examples are BREAK and VERIFY.

3. Lines to load TSR programs: From the AUTOEXEC.BAT file, any TSR can be loaded, including some of them into upper memory.

4. Running programs that do things you want to occur each time you start your machine: Not all programs that are run from the AUTOEXEC.BAT file are TSR programs. Many just do their job, then exit, leaving no trace of themselves in memory.

5. Presenting a menu or running an operating environment on top of DOS: Examples include the DOSSHELL program and Windows.

6. Change the order in which other lines are run or the way in which some line is interpreted: This includes the new DOS command, CHOICE, that lets you make decisions about how the AUTOEXEC.BAT file will be processed as it is running.

Chapter 9 is all about how to customize your PC through use of the CONFIG.SYS and AUTOEXEC.BAT files. Until you master the tricks described there, you won't be a true DOS power user.

HOW DOUBLESPACE CHANGES THE BOOT PROCESS

The new DOS 6 program, DoubleSpace, is a special block device driver that does on-the-fly file compression and decompression. It gives you the illusion that your disk drives have a larger capacity than they really do. In Chapter 7 you will learn how it works (and how to set it up to greatest advantage). Right now it is necessary only to understand how the boot process is changed when DoubleSpace is involved.

DBLSPACE.BIN is a new, third system hidden file (in addition to IO.SYS and MSDOS.SYS). It gets loaded into memory as a part of the SYSINIT process. Initially, it is loaded fairly high up in lower memory. Its job is to mount any *compressed volume files* (CVFs) that it is directed to mount by lines in another hidden system file, DBLSPACE.INI. Mounting a CVF file means to create a fictitious disk drive whose contents are the uncompressed version of the information stored in the CVF file. In the process of mounting those files, it may also swap some drive letters if it is directed to do so by DBLSPACE.INI

In particular, if your C: drive was compressed, a CVF file will become your C: drive, and what was your C: drive will assume some new identity. All this happens before any of your CONFIG.SYS file is read. That means that your CONFIG.SYS file and all the device drivers it specifies and your AUTOEXEC.BAT file will, in this case, be located inside the CVF file that is to become your working C drive. You won't be able to see them at all until DoubleSpace has done it magic on that file.

If you have a line in your CONFIG.SYS file that reads

```
DEVICEHIGH = C:\DOS\DBLSPACE.SYS
```

assuming C:=\DOS is where you have your DBLSPACE.SYS file, then at the time this line is interpreted, DBLSPACE.BIN will be moved from the upper end of lower memory into a location in upper memory (if there is room there).

If there is not enough room for DBLSPACE.BIN in upper memory (around 57KB) or if you don't have that DEVICEHIGH= line in your CONFIG.SYS file, then at the end of processing the CONFIG.SYS file and before loading the command interpreter, SYSINIT moves DBLSPACE.BIN down to just on top of the other installable device drivers loaded in lower memory.

THE LAYERS THAT GET REBUILT

Now let's review the layers that get rebuilt each time you boot your PC. The first is the interrupt vector table. Its location and size are always the same, but its contents get refreshed at each boot. The DOS and BIOS data areas are also fixed in size and location. Again, their contents are rewritten at each boot.

This allows DOS to record such things as how many disk drives and serial or parallel ports it found during the POST.

> **Note:** Many of IBM's PS/2 models and some clone PCs need more room than is provided in the standard DOS and BIOS data area. The solution is to create a region called the *extended BIOS data area* (EBDA). To determine if you have an EBDA, peek at locations 40Eh and 40Fh in the main DOS and BIOS data area. If those locations contain zeros, you probably don't have an EBDA. If those locations hold a number, it is (in hexadecimal) the segment address of the EBDA. To convert it to an actual (hexadecimal) memory address, take the number at 40Fh, tack the number at 40Eh on the end of it, and then tack a 0 on the end of that.
>
> Ordinarily, if you have an EBDA, it will be 1KB in size and will start at address 9FC00h. Naturally, this means you have 1KB less of lower memory available for programs (639KB instead of 640KB), and it means that the transient part of COMMAND.COM will be moved down 1KB.
>
> A way to check for the presence of an EBDA on a PS/2 is to use your reference diskette. If it reports only 639KB of available DOS memory, the missing 1KB piece is your EBDA.
>
> Yet another way to check for the existence and find the location of an EBDA is through the use of some BIOS interrupt calls. INT 15h, Function C0h will return an address in ES:BX of a configuration table. If the byte at offset 5 has bit 2 turned on, you have an EBDA. In that case, you can use INT 15h, Function C1h to find out where the EBDA is located. This interrupt call returns with the segment of the EBDA in ES. (In both cases, if the carry flag is set, the function call did not succeed and no significance should be attached to the numbers returned in the registers.)

The layer for the DOS default device drivers will, of course, have a fixed size for any given version of DOS. The region used by the installable device drivers will vary in size both according to the number and size of those drivers and by which ones get loaded into upper memory instead of in lower memory.

The size of the DOS data tables is set by the numbers you put in your CONFIG.SYS directives FILES=, FCBS=, BUFFERS=, LASTDRIVE=, and STACKS=. If you also specified DOS=HIGH and if BUFFERS= a number less than about 45, all of the DOS disk buffers will go into the high memory area (along with much of the DOS program code); otherwise, they will bloat this next layer in memory.

If you have used any INSTALL= lines in your CONFIG.SYS file, those TSR programs will come next, followed by the permanent part of the command interpreter (usually COMMAND.COM). The layer for the command processor is always the same size for a given version of DOS. The layer for TSR programs loaded through the AUTOEXEC.BAT file will, of course, vary depending on which ones you load. Again, they might go into upper memory and not show up here at all.

The application program layer's size depends totally on what application program you run. The transient part of COMMAND.COM comes next (unless it was overlaid by the application program), but it doesn't show up in the `MEM /D /P` listing, so you cannot easily see just how large it is.

The video image storage area is nominally the whole 128KB from memory address A0000h to BFFFFh. Actually, only a part of that is used in most PCs most of the time. If you have only a monochrome video adapter, you are only using the region B0000h to B7FFFh. If you have only CGA or if you use either EGA or VGA strictly in text mode (and have it attached to a color monitor), then you are using only the region from B8000h to BFFFFh. But if you use EGA or VGA in any graphics mode, you will be using the region from A0000h to AFFFFh; and if you use some super-EGA or super-VGA modes, you may also be using the B0000h to BFFFFh range as well.

The option ROMs share the next 128KB (from C0000h to DFFFFh) with upper memory blocks and possibly an EMS page frame. UMBs and the EMS page frame only happen if you loaded a memory management program like EMM386 or if you have a hardware EMS board and have loaded its special EMM device driver.

You will learn more about memory and the different kinds of PCs, based on different members of the Intel x86 family (or their clones), in Chapter 6.

Computer Languages vs. Human Languages

If you have ever tried using the DOS command TYPE on an executable PC program file (one with an EXE or COM extension), you already know that PCs don't use the same language you do. What you saw on your screen resembled nothing more than gibberish.

The True, Native Language of Your PC

Your PC doesn't "speak" (or understand) English. Nor is fluent in French. The true, native language of any modern computer is strictly a lot of binary numbers. For example, we have spoken several times of the INT instruction. But to the CPU that construction is not an I, N, and a T; rather, it is a single byte binary number, 11001101 (or CD in hexadecimal and 205 in decimal).

Making Life Simpler for People

It is possible for people to program computers using only those binary numbers. But it is tedious and difficult, and programmers who use this approach are likely to make many errors. Fortunately, there is a better way. We can use the power of the computer to translate from some pseudo-human language into the true computer language. In this way, people can do what they do best (analyze difficult problems and decide on the best approach to solve them), and computers can do what they do best (tedious, exacting detail work). This is a very powerful and appropriate way to use both people and computers to best advantage.

COMPILERS AND INTERPRETERS

There are two quite different approaches to machine translation of pseudo-human language into binary computer language: interpreters and compilers. An *interpreter* is a program that takes one line of the pseudo-human language program and translates it into an equivalent set of machine instructions, then actually executes those instructions. When it finishes with one line, it goes on to the next line and both translates and executes it. This works well enough for program development, but it takes a lot of unnecessary time to do the translation over again each time you want to rerun the same program.

Compilers are programs that just translate pseudo-human language into machine code. They can be used to make the translation once, and the translated code can then be run any number of times without incurring the overhead of translation each time. The PC programs you buy in stores are all compiled. DOS itself was compiled, as were all the external DOS commands (the utility programs that come with DOS).

PSEUDO-HUMAN COMPUTER LANGUAGES (HIGH- AND LOW-LEVEL)

Many different pseudo-human languages have been developed to help people write computer programs. Every one of them was intended to be the very best possible language for some purpose; none, however, is ideal for all purposes. A useful way of classifying these languages is to determine how closely they mimic the underlying computer's native language. Those that mimic it very closely are called *low-level languages*; those that are far more abstract are called *high-level languages.*

A low-level language is especially good for controlling what the computer does with exquisite accuracy. The lowest level language in which people normally program is called an *assembly language*, and it allows you to specify exactly what sequence of machine instructions the program will be turned into by the compiler (which, in this case, is more often called an *assembler*).

A high-level language is normally adapted more to the needs of the humans who will work with it and to efficiently communicating the ideas relevant to some set of problems to be solved. In general, each command in such a high-level language will be turned into many instructions in the final machine code, and the programmer has little control over exactly how that is done. Programming in a high-level language, like BASIC or C, can be done much faster than in an assembly language, but more of the decisions about exactly how things will get done by the computer are left to the compiler (and its designers).

THE THREE LANGUAGES DOS SUPPORTS

You may have thought of language compilers and assemblers only as products bought by programmers. In fact, you have some that came with DOS. There are three languages supported directly by the tools that come with DOS. They are an assembly language, Basic, and a special, DOS-specific batch language.

Assembly Language Support in DOS The program DEBUG includes a mini-assembler and mini-disassembler. Skilled programmers can use it to create quite complex programs with all the power of those created using the latest and greatest macro assemblers. The only difference is that using DEBUG makes the job much harder, as it doesn't include all the niceties of those larger programs. This book will not teach you to program in assembler, but in Chapter 13 you will find out how to use DEBUG to create and modify programs.

Basic Support in DOS DOS used to include programs called BASIC, BASICA, or GWBASIC. Starting in DOS 5, these programs were dropped from the Microsoft version of DOS (though IBM kept BASICA.EXE in its version). Instead, DOS 5 introduced QBASIC.EXE. This is a program that provides an editing environment in which you can easily write Basic programs, and then when you are ready to run them, it will do so interpretively.

Microsoft also sells a stand-alone version of this product called QuickBasic that includes a compiler in addition to the editing environment and the interpreter. Another version of that language, called Visual Basic, is available both for Windows and DOS.

Tip: If you don't plan to do any Basic programming, you may have thought you could delete QBASIC.EXE from your hard disk to save some room. Don't do it. At least don't do it unless you also are willing to give up the MS-DOS command EDIT and the MS-DOS HELP program. These EDIT and HELP programs simply invoke the QBASIC editing environment without the program interpretation features. So, if QBASIC.EXE is missing, EDIT and HELP will fail to work at all.

DOS Batch Language Support The third programming language supported by DOS is its batch file language, which is implemented through the command interpreter, COMMAND.COM. Chapter 12 teaches the essentials of batch file programming. It also gives power users many tips that go beyond the rules of batch file programming.

If you use an alternative command interpreter, such as NDOS or 4DOS, you will find that you have access to a batch file language that includes everything the DOS batch file language does and then some. Prior to DOS 6, the differences were very significant. Now, with the improvements in the DOS batch language, these third-party alternatives have less to offer in the way of enhancements.

Demystifying Hex Codes

The dictionary defines a *hex* as something to do with witchcraft. And most dictionaries don't define *hexadecimal* at all. Many PC users think of hex numbers as some sort of evil scheme by computer engineers to keep normal people from understanding what is where in their PCs. If that describes you, then this section is what you need to get rid of that fear and to learn to recognize and read (if not to love or to do arithmetic in) hexadecimal numbers.

What Is Hexadecimal?

Hexadecimal stands for the base sixteen numbering system. It is a placc value system, just like decimal numbers, but instead of the ten numbers 0–9, hexadecimal uses sixteen numerals. They are usually represented by the normal ten decimal numerals plus the first six letters of the alphabet (usually in their uppercase form): A–F.

Figure 1-4 shows the first 256 numbers in each of three forms (all the possible values of a byte, which is an 8-bit binary number). First, the values are shown in decimal, then in binary, and, finally, in hexadecimal. In this book,

DEC	HEX	BINARY	DEC	HEX	BINARY	DEC	HEX	BINARY
0	00	0000 0000	43	2B	0010 1011	86	56	0101 0110
1	01	0000 0001	44	2C	0010 1100	87	57	0101 0111
2	02	0000 0010	45	2D	0010 1101	88	58	0101 1000
3	03	0000 0011	46	2E	0010 1110	89	59	0101 1001
4	04	0000 0100	47	2F	0010 1111	90	5A	0101 1010
5	05	0000 0101	48	30	0011 0000	91	5B	0101 1011
6	06	0000 0110	49	31	0011 0001	92	5C	0101 1100
7	07	0000 0111	50	32	0011 0010	93	5D	0101 1101
8	08	0000 1000	51	33	0011 0011	94	5E	0101 1110
9	09	0000 1001	52	34	0011 0100	95	5F	0101 1111
10	0A	0000 1010	53	35	0011 0101	96	60	0110 0000
11	0B	0000 1011	54	36	0011 0110	97	61	0110 0001
12	0C	0000 1100	55	37	0011 0111	98	62	0110 0010
13	0D	0000 1101	56	38	0011 1000	99	63	0110 0011
14	0E	0000 1110	57	39	0011 1001	100	64	0110 0100
15	0F	0000 1111	58	3A	0011 1010	101	65	0110 0101
16	10	0001 0000	59	3B	0011 1011	102	66	0110 0110
17	11	0001 0001	60	3C	0011 1100	103	67	0110 0111
18	12	0001 0010	61	3D	0011 1101	104	68	0110 1000
19	13	0001 0011	62	3E	0011 1110	105	69	0110 1001
20	14	0001 0100	63	3F	0011 1111	106	6A	0110 1010
21	15	0001 0101	64	40	0100 0000	107	6B	0110 1011
22	16	0001 0110	65	41	0100 0001	108	6C	0110 1100
23	17	0001 0111	66	42	0100 0010	109	6D	0110 1101
24	18	0001 1000	67	43	0100 0011	110	6E	0110 1110
25	19	0001 1001	68	44	0100 0100	111	6F	0110 1111
26	1A	0001 1010	69	45	0100 0101	112	70	0111 0000
27	1B	0001 1011	70	46	0100 0110	113	71	0111 0001
28	1C	0001 1100	71	47	0100 0111	114	72	0111 0010
29	1D	0001 1101	72	48	0100 1000	115	73	0111 0011
30	1E	0001 1110	73	49	0100 1001	116	74	0111 0100
31	1F	0001 1111	74	4A	0100 1010	117	75	0111 0101
32	20	0010 0000	75	4B	0100 1011	118	76	0111 0110
33	21	0010 0001	76	4C	0100 1100	119	77	0111 0111
34	22	0010 0010	77	4D	0100 1101	120	78	0111 1000
35	23	0010 0011	78	4E	0100 1110	121	79	0111 1001
36	24	0010 0100	79	4F	0100 1111	122	7A	0111 1010
37	25	0010 0101	80	50	0101 0000	123	7B	0111 1011
38	26	0010 0110	81	51	0101 0001	124	7C	0111 1100
39	27	0010 0111	82	52	0101 0010	125	7D	0111 1101
40	28	0010 1000	83	53	0101 0011	126	7E	0111 1110
41	29	0010 1001	84	54	0101 0100	127	7F	0111 1111
42	2A	0010 1010	85	55	0101 0101			

Figure 1-4a All possible values of a byte, shown in three number bases

and in many of the computer manuals you will read, hexadecimal numbers (or "hex" for short) are distinguished from decimal numbers by an "h" at the end of the hex numbers. You will also see it as an uppercase H, but this book will consistently use a lowercase h. Basic language programs indicate hexadecimal numbers a little differently. They put &H in front of the number.

Often you can tell if a number is in hexadecimal just by noticing that it contains letters as well as the usual numerals. To further keep from confusing people, many authors precede any hexadecimal number that starts with a

DEC	HEX	BINARY	DEC	HEX	BINARY	DEC	HEX	BINARY
128	80	1000 0000	171	AB	1010 1011	214	D6	1101 0110
129	81	1000 0001	172	AC	1010 1100	215	D7	1101 0111
130	82	1000 0010	173	AD	1010 1101	216	D8	1101 1000
131	83	1000 0011	174	AE	1010 1110	217	D9	1101 1001
132	84	1000 0100	175	AF	1010 1111	218	DA	1101 1010
133	85	1000 0101	176	B0	1011 0000	219	DB	1101 1011
134	86	1000 0110	177	B1	1011 0001	220	DC	1101 1100
135	87	1000 0111	178	B2	1011 0010	221	DD	1101 1101
136	88	1000 1000	179	B3	1011 0011	222	DE	1101 1110
137	89	1000 1001	180	B4	1011 0100	223	DF	1101 1111
138	8A	1000 1010	181	B5	1011 0101	224	E0	1110 0000
139	8B	1000 1011	182	B6	1011 0110	225	E1	1110 0001
140	8C	1000 1100	183	B7	1011 0111	226	E2	1110 0010
141	8D	1000 1101	184	B8	1011 1000	227	E3	1110 0011
142	8E	1000 1110	185	B9	1011 1001	228	E4	1110 0100
143	8F	1000 1111	186	BA	1011 1010	229	E5	1110 0101
144	90	1001 0000	187	BB	1011 1011	230	E6	1110 0110
145	91	1001 0001	188	BC	1011 1100	231	E7	1110 0111
146	92	1001 0010	189	BD	1011 1101	232	E8	1110 1000
147	93	1001 0011	180	BE	1011 1110	233	E9	1110 1001
148	94	1001 0100	181	BF	1011 1111	234	EA	1110 1010
149	95	1001 0101	182	C0	1100 0000	235	EB	1110 1011
150	96	1001 0110	193	C1	1100 0001	236	EC	1110 1100
151	97	1001 0111	194	C2	1100 0010	237	ED	1110 1101
152	98	1001 1000	195	C3	1100 0011	238	EE	1110 1110
153	99	1001 1001	196	C4	1100 0100	239	EF	1110 1111
154	9A	1001 1010	197	C5	1100 0101	240	F0	1111 0000
155	9B	1001 1011	198	C6	1100 0110	241	F1	1111 0001
156	9C	1001 1100	199	C7	1100 0111	242	F2	1111 0010
157	9D	1001 1101	200	C8	1100 1000	243	F3	1111 0011
158	9E	1001 1110	201	C9	1100 1001	244	F4	1111 0100
159	9F	1001 1111	202	CA	1100 1010	245	F5	1111 0101
160	A0	1010 0000	203	CB	1100 1011	246	F6	1111 0110
161	A1	1010 0001	204	CC	1100 1100	247	F7	1111 0111
162	A2	1010 0010	205	CD	1100 1101	248	F8	1111 1000
163	A3	1010 0011	206	CE	1100 1110	249	F9	1111 1001
164	A4	1010 0100	207	CF	1100 1111	250	FA	1111 1010
165	A5	1010 0101	208	D0	1101 0000	251	FB	1111 1011
166	A6	1010 0110	209	D1	1101 0001	252	FC	1111 1100
167	A7	1010 0111	210	D2	1101 0010	253	FD	1111 1101
168	A8	1010 1000	211	D3	1101 0011	254	FE	1111 1110
169	A9	1010 1001	212	D4	1101 0100	255	FF	1111 1111
170	AA	1010 1010	213	D5	1101 0101			

Figure 1-4b All possible values of a byte, shown in three number bases *(continued)*

letter with an additional zero. Thus, they would write the hexadecimal number for the INT command as 0CDh instead of merely CDh. That convention is not, however, used in this book.

Why Is Hex Important to Computer Engineers?

Look again at Figure 1-4. Notice that the binary column has eight symbols for each value; the hexadecimal column has just two symbols, and the decimal column has up to three. Notice further that each of the hexadecimal symbols directly encodes four bits of the corresponding binary number. This means that if you memorize just the first sixteen lines of that figure and this rule, you will be able to reconstruct the whole diagram any time you want. (For example, what is the number A4h expressed in binary? The Ah converts to 1010 binary, the 4h converts to 0100: The result is A4h = 10100100.) It also means that any binary number can be efficiently expressed in hexadecimal and that the hex number can be turned back into binary with hardly any effort by anyone who knows the rules.

This is in sharp contrast to the difficulty one has in converting binary numbers into decimal ones, or vice versa. That can be done, but the process is about as difficult as the one you may have learned in junior high school for doing square roots longhand.

Everything in most modern computers (including your PC) is binary. All the memory is addressed by low and high voltages (which are interpreted as binary zeros and ones) on a bunch of address wires. The data flows in or out of the CPU and the memory chips as low and high voltages (thus as zeros and ones). The ability to easily write binary numbers as hexadecimal is a great convenience when describing the inner workings of a PC. You'll see why later, in Chapter 6.

Why Is Hex Important to You?

This economy of effort has lead most computer hardware and software manufacturers to use hexadecimal numbers almost exclusively in describing their products, which means that you at least ought to be able to recognize and read hex numbers. If you can roughly translate the more commonly encountered ones into decimal, so much the better, but that is frosting on the cake.

You also will find that things look much simpler when viewed in hexadecimal. For example, the size of the total memory address space for an XT is 1 megabyte, which in decimal is 1,048,576 bytes. In hex that is 100000h. The boundary between lower and upper memory comes at 640KB, which is 655,360 bytes above the bottom of memory address space. In hexadecimal that is A0000h bytes.

Must You Learn Hexadecimal Arithmetic?

In a word: no. We have computers that can do hexadecimal arithmetic for us! It would be nice if you could do a few simple sums in hexadecimal and, indeed, that is not very hard. All you have to remember is that next number after 9h is not 10h, but Ah. You have to get all the way up to Fh and add one before you get to 10h (which is 16 in decimal).

But remember: The real payoff comes simply in being able to recognize hex numbers for what they are, and to occasionally convert one of them into a binary number. For anything else, rely on a calculator or computer to do the hard work for you.

C H A P T E R

2

◆ ◆ ◆ ◆ ◆

A Brief History of DOS

The PC is the most successful computer in history. Over 100 million PCs have been sold worldwide, including all models of the IBM PC, PS/1, and PS/2 lines, and all the "clones" and "closely compatible" competitive models. And since the vast majority of those PCs run DOS as their operating system, DOS has become the most successful software product in history.

The IBM PC was not the first computer, nor even the first personal computer, and DOS was not the first personal computer operating system. But these products were, at the time of their introduction, such significant innovations in an industry that was filled with a wide variety of similar, yet markedly different products that they quickly gained acceptance. In fact, one of the most striking aspects about the PC was how quickly it came to dominate the market. The result was that the huge PC market was standardized to a degree not previously seen.

Prehistory of the PC

The IBM PC and DOS did not break altogether new ground, but were instead evolutionary improvements to earlier developments. Their design reflects the common practices used in developing the products that had preceded them, and a quick review of that context will help explain certain of the sometimes puzzling aspects of the PC and of DOS.

Electronic digital computers date from the 1940s. Personal electronic digital computers are a much more recent invention. The first "mass market" example was the MITS Altair 8800 computer introduced in a cover story in the January, 1975 issue of *Popular Electronics* magazine, which accounted for its relatively large sales, despite the facts that it was a do-it-yourself kit, had no keyboard, no screen, a tiny amount of RAM, and no long-term storage mechanism at all. To use the Altair, one had to enter instructions by flipping switches on the front panel. The only output it provided was via some blinking lights on that panel.

The central processing unit (CPU) in the Altair was an Intel 8080 microprocessor chip. That same chip was used at the heart of another microcomputer introduced later that year, the IMSAI 8080. This computer was a vast improvement on the Altair: It used a keyboard and screen, and it could read and write information on floppy diskettes.

Initially the hobbyists who bought Altairs programmed them in machine code. That is, they directly entered each binary number that the machine would later read and execute. That was okay for learning about computers, but it certainly didn't make them practical machines for business automation.

The IMSAI 8080 was the first small computer that had enough hardware to do some interesting things for a small business. Of equal importance, it came with some software to help the user take advantage of its hardware power. Most importantly, it came with an operating system called Control Program for Microcomputers, or CP/M for short. This was the first of a large number of CP/M computers that were introduced in the 1970s, all aimed at the small business market. Since all these machines used essentially the same microprocessor (either the Intel 8080 or the Zilog Z-80, which was an enhanced version of the 8080), they could all run much of the same software. Each model came with a customized version of CP/M, one that took into account the ways in which that particular brand of microcomputer differed from its peers of other brands. This common operating system presented a relatively constant computing environment for application software and utility programs.

This near-uniformity among different models of microcomputer helped make the CP/M market large enough to attract many software developers. By the end of the 1970s, CP/M machines were firmly entrenched as the de facto standard for small business computing in the U.S.A. This standard was limited in its scope, however. For example, nearly every CP/M machine used a unique format for putting information on diskettes. That meant that one could not easily save information on a diskette on one brand of CP/M computer and expect to be able to read it on another. This severely fragmented the marketplace for CP/M programs, as each one had to be offered in multiple versions—one for each brand of CP/M computer.

But there was one thing that virtually all microcomputers made in the 1970s shared: They all came with a version of the BASIC computer programming language. It was true for all CP/M machines, for the Apple II, and for a number of otherwise incompatible micro computers.

BASIC, which stands for Beginners All-Purpose Symbolic Instruction Code, is the name of a programming language developed in 1964 at Dartmouth College. It was created there as an experiment. Every Dartmouth undergraduate student was required to learn to program a computer, no matter what major subject that student was planning to study. That meant that BASIC had to be as easy a computer language to teach and learn as possible. It also made it an ideal language to put on microcomputers to save their owners from having to do all their programming in machine code.

A couple of Harvard undergraduates from Seattle, Washington—Bill Gates and Paul Allen—had this insight about BASIC. Paul first challenged Bill to write a version of BASIC for a microcomputer when the Intel 8008 was the most capable microprocessor on the market. Gates thought about it carefully and decided it was simply not possible. The 8008 had too many limitations. When Gates and Allen heard about the Altair 8080-based computer they reconsidered the idea and decided that, finally, it was a feasible project.

They wrote and sold a version of a BASIC language interpreter, first to MITS and later to nearly all the manufacturers of microcomputers. Their company, which eventually was named Microsoft, became the de facto industry standard source for BASIC interpreters.

Such was the small computer scene in 1979 when IBM decided to enter the market. There were dozens of brands of "personal" computers, all to some degree incompatible with one another, all sporting their own version of BASIC (usually written by Microsoft), and many of them (especially those targeting the small business market) offering a version of the CP/M operating system.

IBM wanted to achieve a presence in the small business market, but they did not want to spend a lot of time or money on what they regarded as mainly an interesting experiment—the creation of the first IBM microcomputer for general home and business use. So their development team was directed to use off-the-shelf hardware as much as they could. In what was a truly radical departure from IBM's previous practices, they also were told to use off-the-shelf software whenever possible.

IBM settled upon Intel's latest microprocessor chip, the 8088, as the CPU in its new machine. This chip and its sibling, the 8086, processed information internally 2 bytes (16 bits) at a time (in contrast to the 8080, Z-80, and 6502, all of which were able to process only a single byte at a time). The 8086 also exchanged data with the outside world 2 bytes at a time, but the 8088 shipped data in or out only a single byte at a time (as did the 8080, Z-80, and 6502). Using the 8088 meant that IBM would get the computational speed advantage of computing 16 bits at a time, but without having to pay any more for the circuitry that they would have to build around the CPU chip had they used the slower Intel 8080 microprocessor chip.

The story of how IBM came to choose Microsoft to create the operating system for its new personal computer has grown to mythical proportions. Like all myths, it contains elements that are factual and some that are apocryphal. Still the story is worth retelling, for, overall, it conveys some truths about its participants that may be more important than exactly how factual it is in all its details. A recent attempt to tell this story with a maximum of fact can be found in *Gates,* by Steven Manes and Paul Anderson, Doubleday, 1993. What follows is a very brief summary of that version.

The marketplace IBM chose to enter imposed one clear requirement for any new personal computer. It must have an operating system and a suite of programming languages. IBM was not sure where to get the operating system, but they knew that Microsoft had become the most likely source for programming languages for microcomputers, and in particular for ones using the Intel 8086 (or 8088) as the CPU.

A delegation of IBM representatives went to Microsoft to see what sort of deal they could arrange. They began the conversation in a very typical IBM fashion, by insisting on having a signed agreement about confidential material before they would even say exactly what they had in mind for the actual business deal. The agreement they proposed that Gates sign was very one-sided in favor of IBM. Nonetheless, Gates signed it without complaint.

IBM shared its plans with Microsoft and reached a tentative deal for a suite of programming languages that Microsoft would provide. Then they turned to the question of an operating system. They knew that Microsoft had a SoftCard add-on product for the Apple II that allowed it to run CP/M programs. Microsoft licensed the CP/M operating system from Digital Research to sell with this product.

CP/M was created by Gary Kildall when he worked at Intel. Since Intel did not see fit to develop and market it, they gave all rights to CP/M to Kildall who then left Intel and started a company he called initially Intergalactic Digital Research (later shortened to simply Digital Research). A primary business of Digital Research was the creation of custom versions of CP/M for most of the new brands of microcomputer.

One of IBM's representatives asked Gates if they could sub-license CP/M from him. "No," he was told. The problem was not simply a legal one. CP/M was only an operating system for 8080- and Z80-based microcomputers. It could not be used with the 8088 CPU chip that IBM wanted to use in their new computer. Gates was aware, however, that Digital Research was developing an operating system for 8088- and 8086-based microcomputers. Called CP/M-86, it had been scheduled for completion some months earlier. So he called Digital Research and set up an appointment for the IBM team for the next day.

What happened that next day, and the events that followed, had enormous repercussions. They set the stage for Microsoft to become the dominant force in PC software, but exactly what happened to lead to this result is less clear.

Apparently, the major problem IBM encountered at Digital Research was a conflict of corporate cultures. The DR team simply would not do business with IBM in IBM's normal fashion. The problems began with the confidentiality agreement. This was not all that stood in the way, however. CP/M-86 simply was not ready and might not be ready in time to meet IBM's deadline.

IBM was about to give up on building a computer around the 8086, and instead go back to the then-standard 8080 as the CPU. In a last effort to save the original plan, it asked Gates for help. This time it was Paul Allen who found the solution. Allen knew Tim Patterson, another Seattle area computer entrepreneur. Patterson had developed a PC motherboard built around the 8086, and in desperation—since Digital Research was unable to deliver CP/M-86 for it any time soon—Patterson wrote his own 16-bit operating system. He made it nearly a clone of CP/M, both for his own convenience and to help other programmers translate their programs to run on his computer running his operating system. The result he christened QDOS, for Quick and Dirty Operating System. Later on Patterson gave QDOS a new name: 86DOS.

Microsoft and Seattle Computer Products (Patterson's company) quickly reached a deal that benefited both of them. Under this deal, Seattle Computer Products could sell Microsoft languages, and Microsoft could sell 86-DOS. Microsoft renamed 86-DOS as Microsoft DOS and sold it to IBM. Microsoft also retained the rights to sell this operating system to others, which they soon did as PC clones began to appear.

The similarities between CP/M and the new Microsoft DOS were substantial. For example, CP/M used three system files, one to handle input and output (called the Basic Input/Output System or BIOS in CP/M machines), one to handle file access (called the Basic Disk Operating System, or BDOS), and one to handle communication with the user (called the Console Command Processor or CCP). DOS also uses three files for these purposes; IBM's names for these three files are IBMBIO.COM, IBMDOS.COM, and COMMAND.COM. Microsoft calls these same files IO.SYS, MSDOS.SYS, and COMMAND.COM, and these are the names that most of the PC clone makers use as well.

DOS used most of the same basic notions of file management as CP/M. It was not so compatible with CP/M that one could exchange files directly, but close enough that it did not seem too strange to CP/M programmers. And it was close enough that they could "port" (translate) their programs from the CP/M world to the new DOS world simply and quickly.

> **Note:** Some of the most annoying things about DOS also come directly from CP/M. The limitation of file names to eight characters with a three-character extension is one. The default DOS prompt (either A> or C>) is another. The brevity of error and other messages from the operating system is a third.

A major advantage of Gates and Allen using DOS was that it existed, and it would work with the Intel 8088 as the CPU chip, so they were guaranteed to be able to meet their deadline for IBM. Also, the many ways in which DOS resembled the dominant small business computer operating system of the day would make this an especially attractive operating system for IBM. In addition to DOS, Microsoft sold IBM a number of computer programming languages: BASIC, FORTRAN, Pascal, COBOL, and an 8086/8088 Assembler.

IBM called its new computer simply the IBM "Personal Computer," and its operating system simply "DOS." But soon everyone in the industry was calling the computer the IBM PC and its operating system PC DOS. (To this day IBM literature—unlike all the other industry sources—never refers to its personal computer operating system as PC DOS, but simply as DOS.)

IBM later offered two other PC operating systems: CP/M86 and the UCSD p-system. Neither one caught on. DOS was entrenched and it remains so today. (Much more recently IBM offered a new alternative: OS/2. It is still unclear if that one will catch on sufficiently to endure or not.)

Microsoft retained the right to sell their languages and their new 8086 operating system to whomever they chose. Thus, when the clone PC market began to develop, Microsoft became the operating system supplier to all the clone manufacturers. Microsoft named their version of the product Microsoft DOS, or MS-DOS for short.

What Microsoft sold was called the OAK, or Original Equipment Manufacturer's Adaptation Kit, and they sold it only to makers of PC clones (called original equipment manufacturers, or OEMs for short), not to end users of PCs. Microsoft expected each OEM to modify the BIOS portion of MS-DOS to properly support the particular hardware design of the PCs they were building. The DOS portion was to stay the same from machine to machine.

Some OEMs did modify DOS, occasionally quite extensively. But many others did not, especially once it became common to build true clones of the IBM design. Therefore, many PC owners, especially those who bought "no-name" clone PCs, got an essentially unaltered copy of the MS-DOS Microsoft sold to its OEM customers.

There wasn't a retail version of MS-DOS available officially until version 5, and then only as an upgrade package. Prior to that, you could only buy MS-DOS bundled with a computer system. At least, that is what Microsoft would have told you. In fact, MS-DOS was readily available through normal retail channels. But, Microsoft steadfastly refused to give support directly to people who bought it, claiming that they should instead "call the computer system dealer who sold you your system."

Creating a New Standard of Computing

The IBM team that created the PC threw it together from existing parts with only a few things designed for it from scratch. They bought diskette drives from standard industry suppliers. They contracted with Epson for printers. They used a keyboard previously designed and built by another division of IBM for a small scientific computer.

In another radical departure from previous IBM practices, they also published nearly all the technical specifications for its new computer right away. This was done to help any company that might wish to make add-on parts for use with the new IBM PC. This move was very important. When IBM first offered its PC, it had only a modest number of hardware options and a tiny library of available software to sell. The only video options were a monochrome text display adapter and a grainy graphics display adapter with fewer colors than the better CP/M machines of the day sported.

The PC had two key advantages over all its competition. One was that it computed inherently faster (because it internally handled data 16 bits at a time). The second was that, while it only came with somewhere between 16KB and 64KB of RAM, you could in theory increase its total RAM to as much as 544KB. (Only with the introduction of the second model of PC was it possible to expand RAM to 640KB.) But without programs that took advantage of the speed and with RAM costing so much that most people could not afford even 128KB, these advantages were more potential than real at that time.

If IBM had kept the design "closed" (as it traditionally had on its mainframe and minicomputers), its PC simply would not have been very attractive to businesses, and it would likely have failed to gain much market share. However, as things turned out, the PC became an absolute phenomenon. Many computer hardware companies looked at it and decided that the PC was a very powerful computing engine and that it was badly in need of some added parts, which they then proceeded to make and market. Soon it became possible to buy a customized PC that would do almost anything anyone would want a small computer to do. Sales surged. The PC became both the most popular and the most customized computer in history.

With a large market of highly compatible machines to sell for, programmers started writing software for it. At first these were almost all simple ports of CP/M applications, but soon programs appeared that took advantage of the ways in which the IBM PC was a superior computing engine to any CP/M machine.

Just as VisiCalc had guaranteed the success of the Apple II, the emergence of Lotus 1-2-3 in 1983 assured the success of the IBM PC. That program, and the PCs to run it on, sold like hot cakes. Now sales really boomed. With vast increases in the quantity of PCs being sold, and therefore of the amounts of RAM being made and sold, prices for RAM fell. Financial analysts and other business people used 1-2-3 to build ever larger spreadsheets and so kept clamoring for more RAM in their PCs. Soon RAM was considered "cheap," and the fully packed PC with 640KB of RAM became the norm. The PC revolution was off and running.

The openness with which IBM published the technical specifications for the PC led directly to its success. It also was IBM's downfall. While it allowed others to enhance the basic PC and thus insured much greater PC sales than would otherwise have been the case, it also allowed some manufacturers to make copies of the PC itself.

At first, these "clone PC" makers were afraid to copy the PC's design too exactly. So, their copies only "sort of" worked the same, and they did their best to compensate with clever modifications to the BIOS programs built into the ROMs on the motherboards of their clone PCs. This strategy worked well enough so that many of those makers, including COMPAQ, AST, and Tandy, thrived. In time the clone makers settled on either of two strategies. Some of them actually licensed IBM's designs. Others simply copied them wholesale. Clone models included copies of all the popular models of IBM PC (the PC, XT, AT, and most recently some of the PS/2 models). Either way, they made PC clones that were really clone-like (except that they left off the clearly IBM-copyrighted BASIC ROMs). These PCs worked every bit as well as the IBM brand and usually they cost a lot less.

That made PC sales (now counting clones as well as IBM brand units) go through the roof, but it cut IBM's market share dramatically. Around 1986, with IBM's share of new PC sales having fallen to about 25 percent, IBM decided it was time for a change. Some IBM staff sniffed: "They are even selling PCs in K mart. We don't want to be a part of that sort of commodity marketplace." So, IBM announced it was stopping production of PCs. What it introduced instead was its new line of PS/2 computers. And later on, it introduced its PS/1 line. Both of these turned out to be merely enhanced versions of the PCs it had been building all along.

Note: The high-end PS/2 computers did sport an entirely new input/output bus, the Micro Channel. In response, the clone makers came up with another new input/output bus design. Machines with the new IBM bus design are called MCA machines (for Micro Channel Architecture). Those using the alternative enhanced bus are called EISA machines (for Extended Industry Standard Architecture). All other PCs are called ISA machines (for Industry Standard Architecture.) Further complicating the picture is the emergence of two new *local bus* standards, VESA (from the Video Electronics Standards Association), and Intel's PCI (for Peripheral Component Interconnect), which allow high-speed peripherals to run at the CPU clock speed. Local bus slots can be designed into motherboards using any of the three existing standards and may eventually offer a direct challenge to all of them.

It is fair to say that IBM clearly established a new standard for small computers when it introduced its PC in August of 1981 (and its big brother the IBM PC/AT in August of 1984), but by the end of the decade IBM equally clearly had lost control of that standard. No longer does one ask of a PC, "Is it IBM compatible?" Now the question is simply, "Which industry standard does it adhere to?"

Evolutionary Steps from Then to Now

What was happening to DOS during all this ferment? It was growing up too. Each new model of IBM PC saw the introduction of some new piece of PC hardware or functionality. Most of them required new features in the operating system. Thus, when the PC/XT was introduced, it included a hard disk. The PC/AT came with the first high-density (1.2MB) diskette drives. Soon PCs were being offered with local area network (LAN) connections. The PS/2 computers used 3-1/2" diskette drives. The list goes on.

It became traditional that with each new PC model IBM would ship a new version of DOS, one that "knew about" and could support the newest PC hardware features. (Typically, Microsoft would shortly release a new version of MS-DOS with the same new capabilities.)

DOS Versions 1.x

DOS 1.0 understood only single-sided diskettes, which was fine, since the earliest PCs were only sold with disk drives capable of reading only one side of a diskette. In mid-1982, IBM introduced double-sided diskette drives and released DOS 1.1, which had been upgraded to understand the new diskette format. (The Microsoft MS-DOS upgrade with this feature was version 1.25.)

DOS Versions 2.x

DOS 2.0 was introduced with the XT. In order to accommodate the new hard disks with their vast (for the time) storage capacity of 10MB, DOS was enhanced in two very significant ways. The first was the notion of disk subdirectories. The second, and even more significant, new notion was that of installable device drivers. Both of these features were borrowed from UNIX, a popular mainframe and minicomputer operating system developed by AT&T. (The idea of subdirectories is a very powerful and important one, which you will learn more about in Chapter 7. It often is just as useful on floppy diskettes as it is on large hard disks.)

Starting with DOS 2.0, it was possible to define the DOS PATH, a list of subdirectories that DOS checks when you tell it to execute a program. This makes it possible to give commands without saying where the program you have named is located. If it is in the current directory or a directory anywhere along the DOS PATH, it will be found and run.

Installable device drivers were initially added to simplify the process of upgrading DOS to support new hardware; they are now used for all manner of things, including connecting to local area networks and CD-ROM drives, modifying how DOS views data stored on a local hard disk, and modifying how DOS treats the screen and keyboard.

DOS Versions 3.x

DOS 3.0, introduced with the IBM PC/AT in August of 1984, was a major upgrade to DOS, which was appropriate, as the AT was a major upgrade to the PC standard. The principal reason that the AT was so significant was that it used a new Intel microprocessor, the 80286, for its CPU. This meant that the AT was the first personal computer that not only did its internal computations 16 bits at a time, but also transferred data externally in the same size chunks. The other major change was that the AT could address an unprecedented 16MB of RAM. (The modern industry standard for PCs is often called the AT standard. One example of this usage is in the name ATA, [AT Attachment] standard for IDE disk drives.)

One of the new features of the AT, and thus of DOS 3.0, was the introduction of the 5-1/4" high-density (1.2MB) diskette drives. At this point, DOS understood five distinct formats for 5-1/4" floppy diskettes: 160KB, 180KB, 320KB, 360KB, and 1.2MB.

A different sort of change was the introduction of 16-bit FAT tables. The FAT, or file allocation table, is a data structure DOS uses to keep track of which files "own" which portions of a disk drive. Before DOS 3.0, all FATs used 12-bit numbers for their entries. The 16-bit FAT tables allowed specifying disk ownership to about one four-thousandth of the disk's capacity. Those units are called *clusters* or *allocation units.* It also means that, on average, one must waste at least one eight-thousandth of the disk's capacity, as each file stored will have some *slack space* at its end to fill out the last allocation unit. When the largest disk drives were 10MB, that was acceptable. With PCs now sporting 1–gigabyte hard drives, the idea of wasting as much as 128KB is more painful to contemplate.

To minimize storage space usage inefficiencies and still accommodate the larger disk drives that were becoming available and affordable for PCs, DOS 3.0 allowed the use of either 12-bit or 16-bit entries in a FAT. The new, larger size for FAT entries lowered the minimum waste space to around a hundred-thousandth of the total capacity. All the entries in any one disk's FAT would be the same size, but the size to use was decided by DOS in a way that most users never figured out.

Warning: If you upgrade a hard disk from DOS 2.x to DOS 3.x (or to any later version), be sure to back up all of your files first. Make two copies, just for safety's sake. Then check that you can restore them successfully. You may find that after you have done the upgrade, DOS will have changed its idea of the size of the FAT entries from 12 to 16 bits. In that case, all the files on your disk will mysteriously disappear and DOS will declare your disk's FATs a disaster zone! Many power users had become accustomed to merely using the SYS command to upgrade to a new version of DOS and they were horrified when they did this with DOS 3.0 and saw all their files go away. The good news is that if you have done this, you need merely boot the PC from an old DOS 2.x floppy disk. Then you will be able to save your files to backups even after SYSing the hard disk with version 3+. Then reformat the disk using your new version of DOS and restore all your files from your backups.

DOS 3.0 also introduced new versions of the BACKUP and RESTORE programs. Although they were modestly improved over their predecessors, they also introduced a new way to ruin your data.

Warning: If you back up files from a PC that is running DOS version 3.x, 4.x, or 5.x and try to restore them on a machine running DOS version 2.x, you will fail because the form in which backed up files are stored on the backup diskettes changed with version 3.0. The solution to this quandary (if you choose not to upgrade the machine with the older DOS to a more modern version) is to be sure to take with your backups a bootable DOS diskette created under the version of DOS that you used to do the backups. Be sure to include on that diskette the RESTORE program from the same version of DOS. Boot the old computer on the newer DOS diskette and then restore your files. This works, since DOS 3+ "understands" the DOS 2.x disk format, while DOS 2.x does not understand the new disk format introduced with DOS 3.0.

One annoying inconvenience in DOS versions 2.x was that if you knew a program was not in a directory on the PATH, but you knew where it was, you weren't able to simply type in the full path name of the file and have it execute. You had to change the current DOS directory on the disk drive where the program lived to the home directory of the program. Then you could run it either from that directory or from another logical drive (if you preceded the command name with the disk drive letter and a colon). Thus, the command `C:WHATSIT` would work if WHATSIT.COM were in the C:\ODDONES directory, and only if you first issued the command `CD C:\ODDONES` (and it wouldn't matter if your current DOS drive was C or D). DOS 3 finally removed this limitation. At last, it became possible to use the command `C:\ODDONES\WHATSIT` directly no matter what the "default DOS directory" might be on the C drive.

Version 3.0 of PC DOS and MS-DOS were supposed to include support for local area networks (LANs), but that support was not ready in time for IBM's rollout of the AT. So Microsoft disabled that code until version 3.1, released in November of 1984. Version 3.1 also introduced the SUBST command, which can be a real boon if you like using a DOS PATH with very many subdirectories in it. (It also can be a problem if you misuse it from within a DOS window of Windows. Chapter 15 gives some precautions to follow to avoid trouble.) This version of DOS was the first to allow one to change the size of the Master environment (in which the PATH definition, among other things, is stored).

Version 3.2 brought us one of the most useful of all the DOS external commands, XCOPY. It also introduced support for 3-1/2" 720KB capacity diskette drives.

Version 3.3 added 1.44MB 3-1/2" diskette drive support, a new APPEND command, augmented the ATTRIB command, and completely redid the DOS mechanisms for supporting foreign languages. (The APPEND command can also cause problems with Windows. See Chapter 15 for details.) Also new in this version of DOS was a good idea that was badly implemented. FASTOPEN was meant to speed up access to your files. Unfortunately, all too often it also damages them. (The good news is that you no longer have to use FASTOPEN to get the speed it was designed to provide.) Use a good disk cache program instead. Many good commercial ones are available, and with DOS 6, SmartDrive has finally become a satisfactory disk cache program as well.

Another welcome change with DOS 3.3 was that for the first time DOS was smart enough to check your hardware before deciding how many disk buffers to assign. Earlier versions always assumed that PC and XT owners wanted only two buffers, and AT owners wanted three. You could override that default by specifying a BUFFERS= line in your CONFIG.SYS file, but many users did not know what value to choose. (The right answer is probably to reduce the number back to the pre-DOS 3.3 AT default of 3, but only if you also use a good disk cache program. Otherwise, you will want to use at least the new DOS default values of up to 50 for the latest versions of DOS and very large hard drives.)

With version 3.3 the DOS batch file language became noticeably more friendly. The additions were little things, like being able to suppress the echoing of any line by starting it with a commercial "at" sign (@) and being able to CALL one batch file from within another one and return to the first one when the second one finished. They were little steps, but very much appreciated. (For more on batch file programming, see Chapter 12.)

One of the biggest changes in DOS version 3.3 was support for larger than 32MB hard disks. Until that version anyone with a disk larger than 32MB had to resort to some third-party disk partitioning scheme or else forgo using the rest of the disk. DOS 3.3 also introduced the idea of a *primary DOS partition* and an *extended DOS partition*. The former could not be any larger than 32MB, and it would become just one drive letter logically. The latter could be any size you wanted (at least up to 504MB), and it could then be subdivided into as many *DOS logical drives* as you liked, as long as each of them was no larger than 32MB.

Several of the clone makers came out with enhancements to this scheme to allow even the primary DOS partition and the logical drives to be larger than 32MB. Only the scheme used by COMPAQ in its DOS 3.31 has survived, as it was developed in conjunction with Microsoft who used the opportunity to try out a new idea they were readying for DOS 4.

DOS Versions 4.x

DOS 4.0 was a big mistake. Even Microsoft and IBM now admit that. They introduced it with insufficient testing, and it contained an unacceptable number of bugs for the amount of new help it offered users. Microsoft brought out a fixed version, 4.01. IBM never officially did that, but it did send Corrective Service Diskettes to its dealers (and to end users who asked for them). The dealers were supposed to upgrade any user's DOS 4 diskettes for free. The official version number stayed at 4, but those in the know were aware that at least five different versions called 4 existed, and they would insist on getting the latest one.

DOS 4 was bloated. CP/M had accomplished all of the tasks anyone thought a microcomputer operating system ought to do in a mere 4KB of RAM. DOS 1.0 used about twice that much. Every subsequent version, with all its new bells and whistles plus continuing support for all the old features, kept getting bigger. DOS 4 was a lot bigger than even DOS 3.3—nearly 70KB total. This was so large that many users found it hard to run their favorite (RAM-hungry) application programs with just DOS loaded, let alone any useful TSR programs or a network driver.

What did DOS 4 offer that anyone wanted? The most obvious thing was support for very large disk drives. At last, it was possible to have a single DOS logical drive (in a primary or an extended partition) of any size you wanted up to at least 504MB and maybe even up to 2GB (1GB = 1024MB = 1,048,576KB = 1,073,741,824 bytes). It was also possible to treat your whole disk as a single logical volume, but it has never been a particularly good idea (for many users). So this merely permitted users to do something that was apparently convenient but ultimately did not serve them very well. (See Chapter 7 for more on this point.)

DOS 4 also included the DOSSHELL program, which has been described by one pundit as "a baroque and somewhat Rube-Goldberg-like arrangement involving a batch file, a COM file, an EXE file, a number of MENU files, and a near-total lack of documentation." (Tim Kyle in A. Schulman, et. al., *Undocumented DOS*, Addison-Wesley, 1990, page 412.)

DOSSHELL offered users two potentially valuable things. One is a better way of viewing files and directories on their disk drives and an easier way of manipulating those files. The other is a convenient way of launching and swapping between multiple applications. There is nothing that DOSSHELL does, however, that cannot be done by using various batch files or third-party "DOS shell" programs. And most of those alternatives did those things better than DOSSHELL did. So while some users loved it, most saw it as another unfortunate kludge—and one best forgotten about. (The good news is that Microsoft got this right in DOS 5. You can learn more about it in Chapter 3.)

In the end, DOS 4 was mostly ignored by PC users. At the time of the introduction of DOS 5 in April of 1991, most PC users were still booting their machines on some version of DOS 3.x, many using DOS 3.0, which at the time, was nearly seven years old.

DOS Version 5

Microsoft learned an important lesson from the DOS 4 fiasco. It was determined not to repeat the same mistakes with DOS 5, so it conducted the largest beta test of any software product released up to that time. More than 7,000 companies and individuals tested copies of the software for many months before its official release in June of 1991.

Microsoft also took pains to be sure that this new release incorporated some really useful features. In addition to the hew and cry of the unhappy DOS 4 users, Microsoft may have been encouraged to add new features by its awareness that Digital Research had gotten back into the PC operating system game in a serious way, introducing its own DR DOS, version 5, as a retail product almost a full year before Microsoft released MS-DOS 5 (and IBM released PC DOS 5).

MAKING MORE MEMORY AVAILABLE TO PROGRAMS

The loudest cry Microsoft heard from users was "give us more memory," so it engineered into DOS 5 several things that were aimed at doing just that. First, it reduced the resident size of DOS itself. This was accomplished in several ways, most significantly by making it possible to move a big chunk of the DOS program code and (in many cases) the DOS disk buffers into a memory region called the high memory area (HMA). This is a 64KB region of RAM with addresses starting at 1MB. (Since PCs and XTs only have 1MB of possible addresses, they cannot have an HMA. And while any AT, 386, or 486 computer can potentially have an HMA, it won't have one unless it has enough RAM installed.) Assuming your PC has an HMA, by putting the line `DOS=HIGH` into your CONFIG.SYS file you can free up more than 40KB of lower memory for other, better uses.

Next, Microsoft provided some tools for taking advantage of formerly unused regions of upper memory. Chapter 1 described the various layers of programs in a typical PC and explained that in many PCs there are holes in upper memory between the video image storage area, the option ROMs, and the motherboard BIOS ROM.

For many years, the cognoscenti had been using QEMM, 386MAX, Netroom, or some other of the third-party memory managers to fill those holes with RAM and put them to good use storing device drivers and TSR programs. Now Microsoft brought that capability to any user of DOS 5—well, to any user who owned a 386 or 486 computer and who was willing to do a bit of studying to learn what was possible and just how to achieve it. No one said Microsoft made it really easy to manage memory efficiently in a PC with DOS 5; they just made it possible for the first time using only DOS-provided tools.

The tools that came with DOS 5 included HIMEM.SYS, EMM386.EXE, the DOS=UMB directive, and the DEVICEHIGH and LOADHIGH commands, plus an enhanced MEM command to let you see more of what is going on in the memory usage in your PC. HIMEM.SYS is an extended memory manager used to create the HMA, turn the rest of the extended memory in something called XMS memory, and manage both XMS and upper memory. EMM386.EXE is called a LIMulator. It is used to turn some of the XMS memory into upper memory blocks and some other XMS memory into simulated EMS (expanded) memory conforming to the Lotus-Intel-Microsoft Expanded Memory Specification (LIM EMS). The DOS=HIGH line tells DOS to take control of any upper memory that HIMEM is managing. The DEVICEHIGH and LOADHIGH commands tell DOS to attempt to put the device drivers and TSR programs named after those commands into upper memory, if it can.

All of this can get quite complex and confusing. Chapter 6 goes into considerable detail on how memory gets used in your PC and how you can use the DOS 5 or DOS 6 tools to help you manage your PC's memory.

NEW COMMANDS

In addition to the memory management tools, DOS 5 included a number of new commands. Many of these were Microsoft developments, but for the first time it also included some programs that had been licensed from another company.

HELP The most welcome new command in DOS 5 for many users was HELP. Simply by typing `HELP` and then pressing Enter one could see many screens of information telling (briefly) what all the DOS commands do. In addition, most DOS commands had some internal help information added to them. Type either `DEBUG /?` or type `HELP DEBUG`, for example, and you will get substantially more helpful information than if you typed simply `HELP` and read what it displayed about DEBUG.

EDIT and QBASIC Creating ASCII text files (such as CONFIG.SYS and AUTOEXEC.BAT) with only the DOS-provided tools formerly meant either using the COPY CON trick (explained in Chapter 7) or the line-oriented DOS editor, EDLIN. The first technique is fine for small files, but it can be annoying to have to start over each time you make a mistake. The second technique is fine, too, if you like line-oriented editors. But most of us have come to depend on full-screen editors and find EDLIN to be nearly unbearable. So, DOS 5 introduced EDIT. You could still use EDLIN, but the full screen editor, EDIT, was a much friendlier way to go. Not only was it a full-screen editor, but it also supported the use of a mouse and offered on-screen help.

Actually, the EDIT program was just an incidental benefit of Microsoft's inclusion of another newcomer. For the first time, DOS did not include the customary BASIC programming language interpreter. Instead, Microsoft adapted its very popular QuickBASIC editor/interpreter/compiler product for inclusion with DOS. The resulting QBASIC.EXE did not have the ability to compile programs, but it did provide all the other features of QuickBASIC. EDIT is merely the editor portion of that program. Both of these programs, which have not substantially changed in MS-DOS 6, are explained further in Chapter 7.

> ***Note:*** The Microsoft BASIC interpreter had been called GWBASIC; IBM's PC DOS included two versions, BASIC and BASICA. BASICA was still included in PC DOS 5, as well as QBASIC. In PC DOS 6, neither QBASIC nor BASICA will ship with DOS.

DOSKEY Another welcome addition to DOS with version 5 was the DOSKEY program. Once this TSR program is loaded, it modifies how COMMAND.COM processes commands in two different and equally useful ways. The first is that it stores up old commands so you can easily edit and reissue them. The second is that it allows you to define "macros" with which you can replace designated strings of characters with other, possibly longer strings. The latter feature can even be used to make one short command issue several DOS commands. Again, this program has not been markedly changed in DOS 6. You will learn what it does and how to use it in Chapters 4 and 12.

SETVER SETVER is a command that should never have had to exist. Its sole job is to insert itself between your application and utility programs and DOS so that, when those programs ask DOS what version it is, SETVER can lie to them. Why is this ever necessary? Because certain programs were badly written.

Typically, these programs check the DOS version number and if it doesn't begin with a 3 they think it must mean the version is older than 3.0. If that were true, the operating system would not be able to provide some of the services that the program requires. So, the program simply declines to run, which is unfortunate, since DOS 4 and 5 do supply those services. (Do you wonder how a programmer could possibly make such a "dumb" mistake? Remember, DOS versions 1.0 through 2.x were the current versions for about three years. DOS 3.x was the current version, or at least the most popular one, for nearly seven years.) Other programs are looking for DOS 4.x and they also don't allow for DOS 5 or later versions. For all these cases, SETVER provides a solution, albeit a fairly clunky one.

There are two major difficulties with SETVER. First, it takes up some valuable RAM any time you have it loaded. Second, it doesn't make your applications compatible with DOS; it merely lies to the application about what version of DOS your PC is using. So, if you know you have some applications that won't work with DOS 5 simply because of its version number and not because of some feature in DOS 5, you can use SETVER to trick the application into running. But don't use SETVER otherwise, since by running it you at least will be wasting RAM and you might be outsmarting yourself as well by tricking an application into running when it really is *not* DOS 5-compatible. Forcing a DOS 5-incompatible program to run can have terrible consequences, like destroying some of your data.

The badly written programs that "inspired" SETVER are still around and so, therefore, is the SETVER command. (Invoke SETVER at the DOS prompt and it will show you a list of 41 programs it is preprogrammed to lie to. You can add to this list as necessary.)

LOADFIX This is another program that should never have had to exist. In this case, the problem is that some programs were written in the secure knowledge that DOS would fill up at least the first 64KB of RAM. With use of DOS=HIGH and all the other memory management tricks, that isn't necessarily so. Some programs, when they are loaded below the 64KB line, fail with a message saying `Packed file corrupt`. This happens most often with EXE files that have been compressed by use of the Microsoft EXEPACK program.

The LOADFIX solution is very simple and not very useful. When you run LOADFIX, it simply uses up enough memory to force the next program to load after the 64KB address boundary. The memory that LOADFIX uses is simply taken away from what all your other resident programs can use. The correct response to this message is to redo your memory management so you have at least 64KB of DOS, device drivers, and TSR programs in lower memory. LOADFIX is the wrong way to go! But, for folks who did not understand memory management, Microsoft included this gem with DOS 5, and it, too, is present in DOS 6.

MIRROR, UNDELETE, and UNFORMAT MIRROR, UNDELETE, and UNFORMAT are three commands that Microsoft licensed from Central Point Software. They had previously been available as a part of the Central Point Product PC Tools.

MIRROR does three different things. It takes a snapshot of the partition table and master boot record on your hard disk. It also takes a snapshot of the FAT and directory structure. Third, it keeps track of the clusters that had been owned by files that you delete.

If you use MIRROR, UNDELETE, or UNFORMAT judiciously, you often can recover from some pretty bad messups (hardware failures and people-caused mistakes, mostly). Unfortunately, you can make bad things worse, if you aren't careful. In particular, the MIRROR strategy for saving partition table information was incomplete, and under certain circumstances UNDELETE or UNFORMAT could claim to have recovered information that was not, in fact, recovered accurately.

In DOS 6, MIRROR is gone (and with it both the problems with its partition table saving and the benefits you could get if MIRROR did it right), but UNDELETE and UNFORMAT have been substantially improved. See Chapter 15 for details on both the dangers and the wonders of these programs and some tips on how to use them safely. In Chapter 16 you will learn about a couple of DOS Power Tool programs that will correctly do what MIRROR tried to do.

ENHANCED COMMANDS

As mentioned above, the DOSSHELL program finally worked right in DOS 5. The DIR command was extended in many ways, as was the ATTRIB command.

Competing Brands of DOS for the PC

Microsoft created the first DOS for the very first PC, and it has been the best-known supplier of every succeeding version of DOS. But it is not the *only* developer of a DOS that can be used on your PC.

In the beginning, IBM took each new version of DOS that Microsoft provided, did some additional development in its own laboratories, and then released the result as PC DOS. Microsoft generally released the same numbered version of MS-DOS a few months later. Sometimes Microsoft adopted for MS-DOS some of the things IBM had added. (The XCOPY command is perhaps the most wonderful addition to DOS that can clearly be credited to IBM.)

That camaraderie was back when Microsoft and IBM were partners, however. Now they are acting more like the participants in a rather messy divorce. Their parting of the ways came over a dispute about OS/2 versus Windows and the about-to-be-released Windows NT. IBM believes the future of PCs means OS/2. Microsoft believed that once, but now it is betting on Windows NT.

When MS-DOS 5 was introduced, IBM felt that it would be best served by making PC DOS identical to MS-DOS 5. This was largely so it and Microsoft could present a unified front to the world of PC users and convince them to upgrade from DOS 3.3 or whatever other version they might be using far more successfully than they had done with DOS 4.

Thus, IBM released PC DOS 5 at the same time that Microsoft released MS-DOS 5, and the two products are almost identical. Both companies saw their self-interests diverging after that time. Now they are very much interested in separating their products in the marketplace.

The contract between IBM and Microsoft allows IBM access to and use of all the source code for MS-DOS, but it doesn't require IBM to use any of it. This means that IBM knows all about what Microsoft is doing and how. Competitive pressures ensure that IBM will offer comparable (or better) functionality in PC DOS, but they may elect to do it in a different way from that chosen by Microsoft.

The first evidence of the diverging paths of PC DOS and MS-DOS came in the fall of 1992 when IBM—very quietly—released PC DOS 5.02. With a version number like that, you might reasonably expect it to be merely a slight tweak on PC DOS 5—fixing some bugs, perhaps. In fact, it introduced some major differences and foreshadowed some of the features in MS-DOS 6.

This discussion is not meant to imply that the only players are Microsoft and IBM. Remember Digital Research—the company that produced CP/M? They may have declined to make the first DOS for PCs, but shortly after it became apparent that the PC was going to be a success, Digital Research began making a version of DOS for PCs, called DR DOS (pronounced "Dee Arr DOS," not "Doctor DOS").

Initially, Digital Research focused on a niche market, creating versions of DR DOS that could be permanently installed in ROM chips for use mainly in portable PCs. Just as Microsoft had done (and unlike IBM), it sold its product only to original equipment manufacturers.

In August, 1990, Digital Research did something unusual: It released the new DR DOS 5, marketed directly to end users of PCs. Microsoft did not get around to releasing version 5 of MS-DOS until June, 1991. (IBM released PC DOS 5 at the same time.) Since that time, Digital Research and DR DOS have been acquired by Novell, the leading vendor of LAN system software. In August, 1991, Digital Research released DR DOS 6. Once again, it was a full version number ahead of Microsoft, and this time it held that lead for over a year.

How They Are Alike

Are all these different DOS brands (PC, MS, and DR) identical? No; but they are close enough for many people. At the very least, all three brands offer the same basic functionality.

After each new generation of MS and PC DOS (which, up through version 5.0, were almost identical in their capabilities), Digital Research created a version of DR DOS with the same version number and with nearly identical functionality. Then, with DR DOS 5, Digital did something brand new. It upped the ante by coming out with DR DOS 5 well before Microsoft and IBM and gave its new DOS version many features that users loved.

DR DOS 5 included memory management strategies very much like those later included in MS-DOS 5 and PC DOS 5. DR DOS 5 included a task switcher (which many people still regard as better than DOSSHELL), support for large disk partitions, password protection for files and directories, a full-screen editor, and on-line help for all the external commands.

That all of these features, with the exception of password protection, were ultimately included in MS-DOS 5 and PC DOS 5, is pretty clear evidence of how well Digital had assessed the market and of how much Microsoft was pressured by Digital's competition.

When DR DOS 6 was introduced, it continued this tradition of offering more features than the then-current MS-DOS version. Principally, DR DOS 6 added on-the-fly disk compression and a better disk cache program. The former was a version of the commercial program SuperStor (licensed from AddStor). The latter was a version of SuperPCKwik (licensed from what was Multisoft and is now the PCKwik Corporation). The next section describes how Microsoft responded to this challenge with MS-DOS 6, and something of how IBM may respond with its PC DOS 6.

How They Differ

Make no mistake: DR DOS is not a clone of MS-DOS. It does some of the same things in different ways, it fails to do a few things that MS-DOS and PC DOS do, and it does some things neither of the others have yet matched.

Perhaps the worst failing of DR DOS is simply that it was not written by Microsoft's engineers, and Digital Research—unlike IBM—did not have access to Microsoft's source code. Despite Microsoft's proud claim that its applications and operating system developers work totally independently, time and time again we have seen cases where Microsoft products seem to work better with Microsoft operating systems, almost as though the programmers in the two groups were sharing some inside secrets.

One example of this occurred when Windows 3.1 was announced. It would not work with DR DOS 6 (which had reached the market eight months previously). Many people accused Microsoft of building something into Windows 3.1 specifically to ensure that it would not work with DR DOS. Within a few weeks Digital Research released a patch to DR DOS 6 to enable it to work with Windows 3.1. But the experience left many users more than a little apprehensive over which DOS applications may turn out to be incompatible with DR DOS in the future.

Principal New Features in MS-DOS 6

Now we have Microsoft's answer to DR DOS 6. MS-DOS 6 includes many new features, some of which may be answers to corresponding features in DR DOS 6 (although Microsoft won't publicly say so) and others that are simply wonderful extensions to a popular standard.

The theme of MS-DOS 5 was "more memory." There are several themes to MS-DOS 6, but they can mostly be subsumed under the overall theme of "more, better, and easier." Figure 2-1 presents a tabular listing of the news in MS-DOS 6.

More Disk Space with DoubleSpace

DoubleSpace is Microsoft's answer to both DR DOS 6's inclusion of SuperStor and the popularity of SuperStor's rivals, including the industry leader Stacker, and also Expanz, DoubleDisk, Xtradisk and others. But DoubleSpace is not a licensing of one of those products, nor is it merely another implementation of the technology exemplified by them. DoubleSpace goes well beyond that. It is based on something Microsoft has christened the MRCI (Microsoft Real-Time Compression Interface), which is intended to be a new standard way of extending DOS's way of dealing with disks, much as the EMS and XMS standards have expanded DOS's ways of dealing with memory.

By incorporating the compression strategy into the very core of DOS—it gets invoked before the beginning of CONFIG.SYS processing—Microsoft neatly side-stepped many of the problems that have vexed users of Stacker,

NEW IN VERSION 6	SIGNIFICANTLY IMPROVED	MISSING
Antivirus programs MSAV and VSAFE	EMM386	ASSIGN
Clean Boot Strategy	HELP	BACKUP
CHOICE command for batch files	SMARTDRV	COMP
CONFIG.SYS menus and %config% parameter	SWITCHES	CV (CodeView)
DELTREE	UNDELETE	EDLIN
DoubleSpace disk compression		EXE2BIN
INTERLNK and INTERSRV file		GRAFTABL
MemMaker automated memory management		MIRROR
MSBackup		MSHERC
MSD diagnostics		PRINTER.SYS and 4201.CPI, 4208.CPI, 5202.CPI, and LCD.CPI
POWER management program		PRINTFIX
Windows version of UNDELETE		RECOVER
Windows version of MSAV and VSAFE		The *.BAS sample programs
Windows version of MSBackup		

Figure 2-1 The news in MS-DOS 6

SuperStor, and similar products. Finally, if they do succeed in making MRCI a new industry standard, many developers will create hardware and software compression products to work alongside or instead of DoubleSpace. Competition in that market should give end users the usual benefits of the free market: better products at lower prices.

DoubleSpace has several parts:

- DBLSPACE.BIN is the device driver that gets loaded by IO.SYS even before the CONFIG.SYS file is processed.
- DBLSPACE.SYS is used to control where in memory the device driver ends up.
- DBLSPACE.INI controls how DBLSPACE does its job at boot time.
- DBLSPACE.EXE gives a full-screen user interface for control and reports.

Chapter 7 includes all the details you need to know about how DoubleSpace works. It also explains some limitations of DoubleSpace that you need to be aware of and how to work around them.

Better Disk Caching with SMARTDrive

The SMARTDrive disk caching program, when it was first introduced, was not the best way to speed up your disk accesses. Almost any of the third-party cache programs could run circles around SMARTDrive. Indeed, it earned the scorn of many in the industry who came to call it "DumbDrive." Now, at version 4.1, SMARTDrive is able to hold its head high. It now is essentially as fast as any of its competitors, and it has nearly enough features to please the most critical power user.

It achieves its increase in speed in two ways. First, it now supports write caching in addition to read caching (but defaults to read caching only on floppy disks and Interlnk drives); second, it reads the disk beyond the sectors you have requested, in hopes of having more data waiting for you in the cache when you ask for it. Also, it now loads itself into upper memory by default. All of these actions can be altered or turned off if you wish. Finally, it allows the user to control the size of the elements it moves in a single operation. (While the speedup of SMARTDrive is most welcome, you should be aware of some dangers that go along with it. Chapter 12 explains them in detail and makes some recommendations on how to use SMARTDrive.

The version of SMARTDrive included with MS-DOS 6 was enhanced to be sure it caches *host volumes* and other uncompressed disks, but it does not attempt to cache *compressed volume files* (CVFs). What this means and why it is important are explained more fully in Chapters 3 and 17. In the latter discussion, you will also learn about some important precautions you need to observe with any caching program and removable media drives.

Better Windows Connectivity

DOS is the most popular PC operating system, and Windows (working on top of DOS) is the most popular operating environment enhancement to DOS. If you use Windows, you will be happy to learn that MS-DOS 6 has made it possible for you to stay inside Windows even while doing such essential chores as file backup, file undeleting, and virus checking. The programs to do these tasks are some of the new utilities Microsoft licensed from Central Point Software and Quest Development, and they are included in both DOS command line and Windows application versions. In Chapter 17, you will learn about all six of these programs (three functions in both DOS and Windows versions).

Easier Memory Management with MemMaker

DOS 5 first brought memory management utilities down to the operating system level, but they were not particularly easy to use. Furthermore, unless you really knew what you were doing, you could not get nearly as much upper memory space for programs using the DOS tools as you could with many of the popular third-party memory management utility programs.

New in MS-DOS 6 is MemMaker, a memory usage optimization utility program. You run MemMaker after you have fully installed DOS, including building your AUTOEXEC.BAT and CONFIG.SYS files. MemMaker will modify those files in an attempt to maximize your free memory, while guarding the upper memory that Windows needs for its best performance. Like all such programs, MemMaker will do its job best if you learn how to help it. DOS memory management remains a difficult field, and one in which a collaborative approach between user and utility software yields the greatest rewards. Just how to engage in this collaboration most fruitfully is explained in Chapter 3.

More Connectivity with the Workgroup Connection

The world is becoming networked. More and more PCs are being used not simply as stand-alone machines, but as links to other PCs or mainframe and minicomputers. In Chapter 14, you will learn about the many ways this can be done and about the MS-DOS 6 programs that support this. Specifically, if you have a network that is compatible with the Microsoft LAN Manager strategy (and many of them are), you can use the Workgroup Connection program to make your PC a client station on that network. (You will need at least Windows for Workgroups before you can make your PC a server.) Once you are on the network, you can take advantage of Microsoft Mail. MS-DOS 6 includes two programs, MICRO and MAIL, for this purpose. See Chapter 14 for some tips on using them.

Better Disk Management with DEFRAG and MSBACKUP

After a lot of hard use, most PCs slow down. They are not wearing out, but the information stored on their hard disks has simply become too jumbled. DOS can still find each and every piece, but it takes longer than when the information was first placed on the disk in a nice, tidy fashion.

Until now there was no DOS tool for remedying this situation. Now there is. The new MS-DOS 6 program DEFRAG, licensed from the Peter Norton division of Symantec, fills this need quite nicely. Chapter 7 explains both what it does and when to use it.

Another aspect of good file maintenance is backing up at least your critical files. Earlier versions of DOS included the commands BACKUP and RESTORE, which did the job, but they didn't make it easy or fun. Too many people simply ignored them and worked without the safety net of having good backups. (And all too many of them paid a huge price when their hard disks died!)

Third-party file backup utilities have been around for years. A version of the Norton Backup program is now included with MS-DOS 6 under the name MSBACKUP. It comes in both DOS and Windows versions. Chapter 17 tells you all about both versions.

Easier Configuration Management

DOS has always been readily customizable by the end user. The CONFIG.SYS and AUTOEXEC.BAT files are the key to this capability. Unfortunately, it is all too easy to get something in one of those files wrong and then find you cannot get your computer started at all.

There are ways to deal with this problem. Now MS-DOS provides one of the most elegant. In an approach they call "Clean Boot," they have given us some simple ways to prevent DOS from processing either the entire CONFIG.SYS file or any line within it, and a way to suppress the processing of the AUTOEXEC.BAT file as well.

In a related development, MS-DOS 6 also provides a means for creating menus (in color!) in your CONFIG.SYS file. You no longer have to maintain a host of alternative CONFIG.SYS and AUTOEXEC.BAT file pairs. Nor must you choose one and then reboot before it takes effect. Once you choose an option from one of these new CONFIG.SYS menus, your choice can be used to control what happens in the rest of the processing of the CONFIG.SYS and AUTOEXEC.BAT files. This means you can build one simple menu—or a hierarchical arrangement of multiple menus—that will be presented to you each time you boot your PC. In Chapter 11 you will learn all about both the Clean Boot approach and how to build CONFIG.SYS menus and their associated AUTOEXEC.BAT files.

Finally, MS-DOS 6 includes a long-awaited new batch file command, CHOICE, to accept user input. Now you don't have to build a separate batch file for every possible option: Simply build a multipurpose one and get user input to specify one of many options when the batch file is run. Chapter 14 explains how to do this. You will also learn that there some important precautions you must take if you choose to use both menus in your CONFIG.SYS file and MemMaker.

Greater File Safety

The new Sentry method of protection provides absolute protection for deleted files (or only specified ones of them) by moving them to a special directory. These saved files are kept until either they are older than some specified number of days or until the space occupied by the saved files exceeds a specified fraction of your total disk space. In addition to command line parameters, UNDELETE can be controlled by entries in an UNDELETE.INI file. Also new in this version is the Windows UNDELETE program mentioned above.

Greater Safety Overall

There is no 100-percent way to detect or prevent harm from absolutely all computer viruses without severely reducing your PC's efficient performance. Still, a lot can be done to make your PC work safer. For the first time, Microsoft has included with DOS some tools (licensed from Central Point Software) to help in this fight. Chapter 17 explains what computer viruses are and how to guard against them. It also details what the new DOS programs MSAV and VSAFE do and how best to use those protections.

Easier Integration of Portable Computers

Many PC users have more than one computer. Often, they have a desktop machine (which may be linked to others over a network), plus a portable or laptop computer that they take on trips. A chronic problem for these folks is making sure they are working on only the most current version of all their files.

It is possible to hook a portable computer to a network (and Chapter 14 will tell you how), but often all you need is a link between your portable and your desktop machine. Also, you may need to link your portable temporarily to another user's PC somewhere away from your office.

In both cases, the new DOS program, INTERLNK, can be the solution. (Incidentally, this program—which was licensed from Sewell Development—first appeared in DOS with PC DOS version 5.02.) With that program and a suitable cable, you can easily access and update your portable's files from your desktop machine or vice versa. Chapter 16 gives you all the details, including exactly how to wire the needed cable (three choices).

Longer Battery Life for Certain Portables

Speaking of portable computers, one of the most annoying habits they have is dying just when you are getting into your work. Then you have to stop working while you either recharge the battery or, if you can, replace it with a freshly charged one.

Microsoft can do nothing to repeal the law of conservation of energy, but it can and has done something to help reduce the appetite of portable computers for energy. Many manufacturers are now building into their portable computers a mechanism whereby a program can make the computer power down some or all of its parts. (For example, it may be possible to turn off power to the serial ports as long as they are not needed without affecting any other part of the PC.)

If power to a part is reduced to the "Standby" state, it is not working at the moment but can resume working at an instant's notice. If the whole computer is powered down to the ultra-low-power "Suspend" state, then it can be awakened by a program but may take a moment to get ready to work again.

The new device driver, POWER.EXE, provides a manufacturer-independent way for programs to command these power control functions. The syntax for invoking POWER is explained in Chapter 12.

Other News in MS-DOS 6

In addition to those major new features in MS-DOS 6, there are several minor improvements. These include a new NUMLOCK directive for your CONFIG.SYS file, the ability to put SET statements in a CONFIG.SYS file, and a new DELTREE command.

DELTREE allows deleting whole directory subtrees, files and all. The directory undelete feature of UNDELETE can be used to bring back a subdirectory that has been deleted (but not all the files and subdirectories under it).

Warning: Use DELTREE with extreme caution. You could do much more than you intend and not know it. And recovering from such a slip of the finger could be tough.

Also new is MSD, a diagnostic program that provides many detailed screens of information on your PC's hardware and its software configuration.

Some of the news in MS-DOS 6 did not come in the form of new programs or commands, but simply as much improved versions of older ones. In addition to SMARTDrive, which we already discussed, these include EMM386 and

HELP. EMM386 has been enhanced in several ways. It has seven new command line parameters, allowing it to do many new things. For the first time, EMM386 is able to create from XMS memory a pool of memory that is made available for programs to access either via EMS/VCPI standard calls or via the XMS calls. It can shadow ROMs in a system that either has no ROM shadowing or has that feature turned off. EMM386 now supports both EMS and VCPI or only EMS standard access to expanded memory. It can load all of itself in lower memory or put part of itself into upper memory. You can control in a new fashion where in upper memory it creates UMBs, and you can tell it to reserve space there for the Windows translation buffers.

The MS-DOS 6 HELP is not just a minor upgrade. It is actually a whole new program. Modeled on EDIT, it uses the file display capabilities of the QBASIC editing environment. Menu-driven and mouse-aware, HELP has entries for both concepts and programs (e.g., EMM386 and EMM386.EXE), and has multiple screens of information under each entry (syntax, examples, and notes).

The program, GRAPHICS, has been substantially enhanced in MS-DOS 6, too. In recognition of Hewlett-Packard's market leadership in PC printers, the GRAPHICS command now supports several HP models and continues to provide support for several IBM models.

Missing Pieces

Not all the news items in MS-DOS 6 are about additions to its capabilities. Some tell of the disappearance of features or programs that were in MS-DOS 5. RECOVER is gone. Hurray! This was the most dangerous DOS program every devised, and it has been obsolete for many years. Finally, Microsoft has essentially acknowledged these facts and taken away this time bomb for the unwary. (One can only imagine with terror how many users have confused RECOVER and RESTORE with tragic results.)

Warning: If you upgrade to DOS 6, you may still find RECOVER in your DOS directory. It is a leftover from your previous version of DOS. Get rid of it now, before it causes any mischief.

EDLIN is gone from MS-DOS 6, but it will not be missed by many. The new full-screen EDIT program is generally far nicer for creating or modifying ASCII text files, and if you need a really small editor, the DOS Power Tools program LIST will do the job nicely.

BACKUP is gone, but not RESTORE. MSBACKUP replaces the functionality of BACKUP (and offers much more). RESTORE is still included to permit restoring files backed using a previous version of DOS.

MIRROR is gone, but its functionality has largely been moved to UNDELETE. The one part not moved (saving the partition table) can be done better by the DOS Power Tool program MHSAVE.

MSHERC.COM and PRINTFIX.COM have been removed. The first of these programs gave support for a Hercules monochrome graphics card. The latter program allowed you to disable verification of a printer's status line.

ASSIGN is gone. Use the SUBST command instead. The GORILLA, MONEY, NIBBLES, and REMLINE sample Basic programs have also been removed.

Support for extended graphics characters on a CGA display (via GRAFTABL) has been removed. Unless you have a CGA display and wish to use PrtScrn to print screens with the line draw and other extended graphics characters, you will not miss this one.

CV and EXE2BIN have been removed. Most people who need these programmer's tools have gotten copies with their language compiler programs. (A related tool, LINK, that used be bundled with DOS was removed in version 5.)

The file compare program, COMP, has been eliminated. Originally developed by IBM, COMP has now been replaced by the Microsoft version, FC. In what may be a related move, much of the special support for certain IBM printers (the files PRINTER.SYS, 4201.CPI, 4208.CPI, and 5202.CPI) has been removed. This is an interesting contrast to the GRAPHICS command, in which IBM printer support has been retained and support for Hewlett-Packard printers added. The one area where PC DOS will probably differ from MS-DOS the most is in the support of IBM-brand hardware.

If you had MS-DOS 5 installed on your system and upgraded to DOS 6, all these pieces will still be right where they were, and they all will continue to work with DOS 6 just fine. If you did not have DOS 5 and you want to get these programs, Microsoft offers a Supplementary Disk with them, plus some programs to facilitate access to PCs by persons with various handicaps.

File Size Changes

Naturally, the programs that have had a lot of new features added tend to be larger than they were before. What is surprising in MS-DOS 6 is that some of the programs got markedly smaller, in some cases despite many added features! This happened because those programs (FDISK is the most dramatic example) have been compressed using the Phil Katz compression utility PKLITE.

How PC DOS 6 May Differ

IBM has made it clear that they intend to be a major player in the DOS market, and that no longer will they simply clone Microsoft's MS-DOS. At this writing, IBM has not officially announced PC DOS 6, but sources close to them have given us an inside peek at IBM's plans. We can say with some assurance that there will be a PC DOS 6 and that it will be released sometime in mid-1993. Further, we have learned some of the ways in which it will be the same as or very likely different from MS-DOS 6.

First, IBM plans to have only one PC DOS 6. It is dropping the distinction formerly made between the "Base" DOS product (intended for use on a new PC) and the "Retail Upgrade Package." PC DOS 6 will come on several diskettes (each holding either 1.2MB or 1.44MB), and the first will be a bootable diskette with enough uncompressed DOS files to allow you to FDISK, FORMAT, and CHKDSK a disk, install national language support, and install DOS.

The IBM installation program will encourage you to backup your old DOS floppy diskettes, but it will not require this nor take up hard disk space for an OLD_DOS directory, as the MS-DOS SETUP program does. It will be possible to uninstall PC DOS 6, provided you have made the suggested floppy disk backups of your prior DOS and have not yet installed file compression for your boot drive. As is the case with MS-DOS 6, installing on-the-fly disk compression can make uninstalling DOS 6 impossible, without deleting much of what you have stored on your hard disk and nearly starting over from scratch. The installation program will permit you to install PS DOS 6 to a hard disk volume other than C. It will also integrate the setup of disk compression into the installation routine. MS-DOS 6, in contrast, has the user run a separate program, DBLSPACE, to install disk compression.

Finally, the installation program will understand both DBLSPACE and Stacker compressed volumes, and it will correctly sense into which volume it should install the system files. Even if you have "Stacked" or "DoubleSpaced" your C drive, you will be able to install PC-DOS 6 successfully without uninstalling Stacker first.

IBM has not made final decisions on many features of PC DOS 6. Still, it seems pretty certain that it will offer on-the-fly disk compression in a fashion that very closely resembles what Microsoft did with DoubleSpace. However, IBM is likely to use its own compression engine—one name it is toying with is COMPRESS.BIN. The IBM compression engine will be loaded by IBMBIO.COM (the hidden system file that corresponds to IO.SYS in MS-DOS), just as DBLSPACE.BIN is loaded by IO.SYS. This will happen before the CONFIG.SYS file is read.

An important distinction between the two compression engines is that COMPRESS is apparently going to be able to mount Stacker compressed volumes as well as create and mount its own compressed volumes. If this is the case, and if Stac comes out with its promised Stacker for OS/2, this could provide a means for both OS/2 and PC DOS 6 to access the same compressed volume files—something that is not yet possible for OS/2 and MS-DOS 6.

IBMBIO.BIN will load COMPRESS.BIN if it finds it, or will load DBLSPACE.BIN if that is present. This will allow an easy means of converting a PC that is running MS-DOS 6 and has DoubleSpace compressed volumes to one that is running PC DOS 6. What is not quite clear yet is whether COMPRESS.BIN will also be able to access DoubleSpace volumes. If it can, then you don't need DBLSPACE.BIN on your system.

IBM's PC DOS 6 will also have several wonderful new features that will improve its memory usage and performance. One is that SETVER will load totally in the HMA, so you need not worry about the modest, yet significant, amount of space SETVER used to take in lower or upper memory. IBM has also tuned the kernel code and ANSI.SYS so that when you load EMM386 (or any other protected mode memory manager) and then run DOS programs in a virtual 8086 mode session, many interrupts that formerly caused faults and then had to be handled by the virtual control program (EMM386, or whichever one you have loaded) will now be handled directly and without the overhead of fault processing.

PC DOS 6 will include device drivers to provide upper memory blocks (utilizing what is sometimes wasted memory) on low-end PCs that use the 8088, 8086, or 80286 as the CPU chip. These drivers will be able to "borrow" unused video memory in PCs with two video cards or convert hardware EMS (on a plug-in EMS card) into upper memory blocks in which programs can be loaded.

If you have a Monochrome display adapter (MDA), Hercules graphics card, or clone (MGC), plus a Color Graphics Adapter (CGA), Enhanced Graphics Adapter (EGA), or Video Graphics Array (VGA) display card, you will be using one of them to display images on your screen. If you wish, you may choose not to use the second card as a video card. Just load the IBM-supplied UMB provider, and it will turn most of the memory on your unused video card into upper memory available for programs to use.

The UMBCGA.SYS driver that is designed to borrow memory from a CGA card may also be able to borrow memory from an EGA or VGA card. IBM has also designed some clever protections into the device drivers it supplies for this video memory borrowing to prevent you from accidentally trying to use the same memory for both program code and video image data. The mechanism by which PC DOS 6 will be able to borrow EMS memory is very similar, and the protections against misuse of that type of memory are even stronger.

Almost all the MS-DOS 6 commands will be supported. One notable exception is that PC DOS 6 will not include the QBASIC compiler, nor will it have BASIC or BASICA interpreters. Partially as a consequence, IBM will have to include a different help engine, a different full-screen text editor called E, and EDLIN.

Two totally new features in PC DOS 6 will be extensive support for PEN computing as well as programs and peripherals that use the PCMCIA (credit card size) 68-pin slots. PC DOS will include a device driver that provides Card Services in a fashion that complies with the Release 2.00 PCMCIA specification.

Beyond DOS 6—The Power Tools Programs

MS-DOS 6 is a substantial improvement over all previous versions. It gives you added power to manage and manipulate your PC. But, it doesn't do everything you might like it to do, so this book is about giving you added power. In addition to facts, tips, and warnings, it gives you some programs that go beyond DOS, adding significant functionality that Microsoft left out.

The DOS Power Tools programs on the enclosed diskettes are a mixture of shareware and freeware utilities. Some have been written especially for this edition of *DOS Power Tools*. Others have been culled from the many thousands of shareware programs available on bulletin boards around the world. Chapter 16 introduces you to each of these programs. Every other chapter points out which of the *DOS Power Tools* programs are most relevant to the subject matter of that chapter.

CHAPTER

3

Getting Started with DOS 6

Obviously, before you can use DOS 6, it must be installed on your PC. While DOS 6 greatly simplifies the installation procedure for the benefit of new users, there are still a few places where you could trip yourself up.

How to Install DOS 6

With each new version, DOS has become more complex. Fortunately, the installation process has been getting easier. Microsoft has designed a SETUP program to walk you through all the steps of at least a minimal DOS installation. If you wish to install all of the DOS 6 features and programs, however, there are some other steps you'll have to take after SETUP is finished, such as running MemMaker, the new memory optimizer, and installing DoubleSpace, which provides on-the-fly data compression for your files. The details of those features are described in Chapters 9 and 17. You will especially want to read the discussion of DoubleSpace in Chapter 9 if you have been using a third-party disk compression product, such as Stacker or SuperStor. You might want to convert from the non-Microsoft compression program to DoubleSpace, but then again, there are some very good reasons why you may not.

Because most people will get DOS 6 by buying either the upgrade package or a new computer with DOS 6 installed, this section will cover only the steps needed for a DOS 6 upgrade. Installing the full version of DOS is no more difficult, however; in fact, the main thing to note is that you won't have to do the first step (booting your PC from a previous version of DOS) before inserting the SETUP disk in one of your PC's floppy disk drives.

The DOS 6 upgrade includes a feature meant to reassure you. SETUP forces you to create an "uninstall" diskette, unless your PC has a data compression program such as Stacker already installed. You can use either the A: or the B: drive for the setup disks, or you can run SETUP across a network. Whichever way you run it, SETUP will insist that you put a diskette in the A: drive when it is ready to create the uninstall diskette. The whole idea is to create an uninstall diskette that you can use to boot your computer, in case you decide you don't like DOS 6 and you want to go back to whichever version of DOS you were using before. If your A: drive is a 360KB drive, you must have two diskettes handy to be turned into the uninstall diskettes. These diskettes may be formatted or not, but whatever files they contain will be erased. If your A: drive is any higher-capacity model—720KB, 1.2MB, or 1.44MB—you will need only one uninstall diskette.

Installing to a Hard Disk

Boot your computer (either from DOS of some version on the hard disk or by using some bootable DOS diskette). Insert the DOS 6 disk labeled "Disk number 1" in either your A: or B: drive; make that drive the DOS default drive. (That is, if you put the diskette in the A: drive, type `A:` and press the Enter key.) Now type `SETUP` and press Enter. Follow the directions on the screen—that is all there is to it!

Tip: You can use the DOS 6 upgrade package as long as you have *any* bootable DOS diskette. You don't have to have DOS installed on your PC's hard drive—you don't even have to have a hard drive. The DOS 6 upgrade works as long as your PC can be booted to DOS; any version of MS-DOS, PC DOS, or DR DOS will do.

There are really only three times in the setup process that you have to enter or confirm some information. After two informational screens, SETUP will show you a list of the system configuration you have, as it sees it. This is a list with only three items on it: your DOS type, DOS path, and Display type.

The options for the DOS type are a bit curious. You can specify MS-DOS, COMPAQ, ZENITH, or Other; PC DOS is not an option. If you have PC DOS on your machine currently, simply choose the MS-DOS option at this point (choosing OTHER will also work).

The DOS path means the directory in which your current version of DOS is installed. For most people it will be `C:\DOS`. This directory is also where DOS 6 will be installed. All of the files that DOS 6 is planning to replace will be saved to another directory, normally called `C:\OLD_DOS.1` and any files in your DOS directory that are not going to be updated will be left in place, such as other utility programs you may have copied into the DOS directory for convenience, or files that came with DOS 5 that you may wish to continue using, even though they do not come with DOS 6. This is rather important, as with most prior versions of DOS, the external commands would refuse to run unless they came from the same version as the hidden system files.

You have nine choices for the Display type. Usually, SETUP will have figured out the correct one, but if you know it got that entry wrong, you can correct it. Next comes a screen that lets you choose which of the optional programs to install. The programs this screen offers are the new MSBACKUP, Microsoft Antivirus, and UNDELETE programs. Each comes in a DOS version and a Windows version.

Provided you have Windows installed on your PC, for each of the three optional programs you can choose to install the DOS version, the Windows version, both, or neither. Watch this screen carefully for its report of the number of bytes that will be required to install DOS and these optional programs, versus the number of bytes you have free. If you are unsure about which of the optional programs to install, you need not install any at this time. You can rerun SETUP (with the /E switch) any time you want to install those components.

Finally, SETUP will ask you to confirm your Windows directory. Naturally, it only does this if it found that you had Windows installed on your hard disk.

Once you have finished with those three screens of information entry or confirmation, you can sit back and let SETUP do the work. You will have to swap diskettes several times, but that is all. Oh yes, there are a few very important warnings you need to heed, which are listed in the following Warning box.

If you have a system without DOS on it, you'll need to get a full, retail version of DOS 6. You may be able to buy a copy at your local computer store, but it might be harder to find a full version than the upgrade package. Since you don't need to have installed DOS on your PC's hard disk, you could buy an older copy of DOS plus the DOS 6 upgrade. Just insert the older DOS diskette in the A: drive and turn on your PC; when it is finished booting, take out that diskette and install DOS 6 by running SETUP.

Warning:

1. When the DOS 6 SETUP program finishes, it suggests that you reboot. If you had some disk caching software installed, you could be in for a rude surprise. Normally SETUP will install SMARTDRV without telling you or asking you anything. It will not notice if you have some other disk cache (such as SuperPCKwik or the Norton Cache). Having two disk caches is an almost certain formula for disaster. As soon as SETUP finishes, it is a good idea to exit the program without rebooting, then look around to see what SETUP did. Examine your CONFIG.SYS file and your AUTOEXEC.BAT file. Only once you are pretty sure SETUP did not set up any unfortunate booby traps is it safe to reboot.
2. During the setup process, the boot record on your C: drive is altered. If something goes awry during the process you may find that the next time you reboot you get the message `Insert your uninstall disk now`. If SETUP had gotten far enough to create that diskette completely, you can do that and whatever work SETUP had finished will be completely undone. If, however, SETUP bombed before it got quite far enough to create a workable uninstall diskette you may be in deep trouble. If you have a bootable DOS diskette with the prior version of DOS on it and if it also has the SYS command on it, you can simply reboot on that diskette and SYS your C: drive. That will at least let you access your hard disk so you can see what, if any, mess SETUP may have left there.
3. You can rerun SETUP at any time. You might need to do so if you wanted to add the optional components of DOS any time after the initial installation. Normally, you will do that by using the command `SETUP /E`. If, however, you are attempting to reinstall all of DOS, and therefore use the simple command `SETUP`, and if the SETUP program you use is a later release than the one used to initially install DOS 6 on that PC, there is a potentially serious problem you need to be careful to avoid. The problem arises because the SETUP program puts only the system files on your C: drive. If you had used the DBLSPACE compression program to compress the files on that drive, what appears to be C: is really just the contents of a compressed volume file; the real, original C: drive is now some other drive letter. You have to SYS that other drive with the exact same version of hidden system files and COMMAND.COM as those put on what appears to be the C: drive by using SETUP.

Tip: (For network users only!) There is an alternative way to install DOS 6 that may come in handy, if you happen to have only a 3-1/2" diskette drive on your computer and only have a DOS 6 package for 5-1/4" drives. Your PC must be connected to a network before you can apply this trick. Here it is: Simply copy all the files from all the installation diskettes to a subdirectory on your hard disk or network file server. Then make that directory the DOS default directory and run SETUP from there. (Don't put the contents of the separate diskettes into separate directories. That won't work, even if you try to tell SETUP where to look for each of the diskettes.)

Optional Switches

There are several optional switches you can put on the command line after the word SETUP to modify how it will do its job. Here is a quick rundown of what they do.

/B tells SETUP that you have a monochrome monitor. (Normally, it will detect this fact, so you only need to tell it this if you find that the screens presented are unreadable.)

/E tells SETUP to install the DOS and Windows optional programs. This is useful if you already have DOS 6 installed and simply want to add those programs.

/F tells SETUP to install a very minimal subset of DOS 6 onto floppy diskettes. The floppies you create this way need not be in the same drive as the DOS installation diskettes. Thus, if your computer normally boots from the A: drive, which is a 5-1/2" drive and if you happen to have gotten the DOS installation package for 3-1/2" drives, you can set up DOS on your hard disk and create a bootable 5-1/4" DOS diskette using those 3-1/2" installation diskettes.

/I says you don't want SETUP to try to figure out what hardware your PC has. Use this only if SETUP fails to run. If it runs and gets a wrong view of what hardware you have, you will have a chance to set it straight during the setup process.

/M forces a minimal installation. When you specify /F (for install to floppies) you are implying a /M as well.

/Q copies the DOS files to the hard disk; that is, it expands all of the files on the installation diskettes and places those expanded files in a subdirectory on the hard disk. This is *not* the same as installing DOS. You would use this switch only if SETUP failed to complete a normal installation.

/U forces the installation to proceed even if SETUP reports that it found one or more disk partitions that might be incompatible with the DOS 6 setup program. As always, when you overrule a program, be quite sure you really do know more than it does about your system!

Warning: Far too many people fail to make a bootable DOS floppy when they upgrade their PC. Don't repeat that error. Either run SETUP /F switch, or after you have installed DOS 6 on your hard drive, use FORMAT /S or SYS to create a bootable DOS 6 diskette that will work in your PC's A: drive. Having such a *safety boot diskette* is a vital piece of protection if something should happen to the system files on your hard disk. The new DOS 6 "Clean Boot" strategy (explained in Chapter 9) will save the day for you if the only problem is with the contents of your CONFIG.SYS or AUTOEXEC.BAT files, but it will do nothing for you if the hidden system files get messed up. A full-fledged safety boot diskette contains a good deal more than what is on a simple bootable DOS diskette, but that simple bootable DOS diskette is the essential starting point for creating the full safety boot diskette, and it can do the most essential of the things that a safety boot diskette is meant to do. Chapter 9 explains why you probably should create a more complex version of the safety boot diskette and how to do that.

IF DOS 6 IS ALREADY INSTALLED

If your system came with DOS 6 installed, you may still have to worry about setting up DOS 6. Before you start using it, poke around a bit. Learn more about how it is set up. Compare what you read here with what you find in your computer. The time you spend doing this will be amply repaid. Here are some things to look for:

1. Do you have a legal copy of DOS? Do you have a set of original DOS distribution diskettes, the DOS 6 manuals, and a registration card? If not, you probably don't actually own a copy of DOS 6 no matter what has been put on your new PC's hard disk. If you are in this boat, the first thing to do is ask your dealer for the missing materials. If you don't get them, get a better dealer, then buy a real, legal copy of DOS and install it following the steps in this chapter.
2. Make sure DOS was installed correctly. Perhaps the most common error people make is to install only some of DOS. The second most common error is to install all of the DOS files in the hard disk's root directory. If

you find that you are missing some DOS files, you will have to get them from the installation floppy diskettes. One way to do this is to rerun the SETUP program. Another way, if you are missing only a few files, is to use the DOS command EXPAND. (You cannot simply copy the files you want from the installation diskettes, as most of them only exist there in a compressed form.) You will find a list of all the DOS files and commands in the Command Reference. The second most common setup error, putting all the DOS files in the root directory, makes quite a mess of your hard disk. Fortunately, you can recover from that mess fairly easily. First, make sure you have a directory for DOS, or, if not, create one by typing:

```
MD \DOS
```

Then MOVE all the DOS files (except for COMMAND.COM and the .386 files) to that subdirectory. Double-check your CONFIG.SYS and AUTOEXEC.BAT files to make sure the DEVICE, INSTALL, and LOADHIGH pathnames are correct—you may need to add `C:\DOS` as a prefix to many of the driver or executable filenames—and make sure your PATH statement includes the DOS directory. Alternately, it may be simpler to get rid of almost all the files in the root directory of your hard disk, leaving just enough to boot the computer (the hidden system files and COMMAND.COM), then run the SETUP program from the DOS 6 diskettes.

3. Was DOS installed completely? With DOS 6 there are some new ways in which your DOS installation may or may not be complete. Depending on the choices made by whoever installed the DOS files originally, your memory configuration may not have been optimized with MemMaker, your disk might not have been compressed with DoubleSpace, or you may not have the Microsoft Antivirus utilities, and the MSBACKUP and UNDELETE programs. And finally, you may or may not have the Workgroup Connection files installed.

4. The SETUP program will offer to install the DOS 6 support for Windows and the Windows application programs if it finds that you have Windows installed on your hard disk. If you don't yet, you will have to install Windows first, and then go back and rerun SETUP to install the Windows-related aspects of DOS 6.

5. MemMaker is not automatically run by the SETUP program, and offers a vast improvement in memory utilization on 386-or better hardware.

6. The antivirus and MSBACKUP programs (in DOS and/or Windows versions) can be installed as options by the SETUP program. If all you are missing are the Antivirus, MSBACKUP, and UNDELETE program, you can install them by using the command `SETUP /E`.

7. The SETUP program does not automatically invoke the DoubleSpace on-the-fly disk compression program. If you find that you don't have enough room on your hard disk and it is not DoubleSpaced, you may want to use this file compression technique. In Chapter 7 you will find all the details you need to know about how to do this.
8. The Workgroup Connection files are installed by use of a totally separate program, WCSETUP. You will learn more about it in Chapter 14.

IF OS/2 IS INSTALLED

If you have OS/2 installed on your hard disk, Microsoft's DOS 6 SETUP program will give you many opportunities to remove it. You will see several stern warnings that you might not be able to access your OS/2 files once you have run the DOS 6 SETUP program. Don't worry about these messages. Presumably, since Microsoft and IBM are so at odds, Microsoft would love to get you to stop using the IBM alternative operating system.

You don't have to follow Microsoft's advice. You can run both OS/2 and DOS 6 on the same PC, with the usual caveats and precautions. If your OS/2 installation is in an HPFS partition, then DOS 6 will not be able to access any of the files in that partition. This is no different from what was true with DOS 5. If you use the OS/2 version 2 dual-boot strategy, you may have to manually modify the DOS CONFIG.SYS and AUTOEXEC.BAT files after SETUP is through before you can boot back to OS/2.

IBM's OS/2 Boot Manager is a program that lives in a 1MB partition of your hard disk all by itself. Normally that partition is specified as the active one. The primary DOS partition and the logical volume that contains the OS/2 system files are both marked in the partition table as not bootable. When you boot your PC in this configuration, Boot Manager gets control, then it presents a menu of possible systems it can boot. You choose one, and it goes to the right place on the disk and loads the boot sector from the beginning of that partition.

Tip: The safest way to install DOS 6 in a system like this is to first create a bootable OS/2 diskette with the OS/2 FDISK program on it. Then use the OS/2 FDISK to make the primary DOS partition active (thus making the Boot Manager partition inactive). Now if you reboot your PC, it will boot directly into DOS, ignoring both Boot Manager and OS/2.

Next, do a normal DOS 6 installation. SETUP will not see Boot Manager and it may not see your OS/2 installation (if you have OS/2 in an HPFS formatted logical volume), or it may see it and suggest you remove it. Simply ignore those suggestions.

Finally, boot from the special bootable OS/2 diskette you prepared. Use the OS/2 FDISK to reset the Boot Manager partition to the active state. When you reboot the next time, you should get the usual Boot Manager menu and everything should work just as it did before, except that when you choose DOS, you will get DOS 6.

Warning: There is one way you can seriously interfere with your OS/2 installation with MS-DOS 6: if you DoubleSpace your disk. OS/2 understands the normal DOS FAT structured logical volumes, but it will be completely baffled by a DoubleSpace compressed volume. (You may safely use DoubleSpace on any logical volumes that you don't mind having inaccessible while you are running OS/2.)

One solution to this problem is to augment OS/2 so that it can understand the DOS compressed volume file format. IBM is aware of this problem and the possible solutions. Stac Electronics is scheduled to release a version of Stacker for OS/2 sometime in 1993. PC DOS 6 may include the ability to mount Stacker compressed volume files in a fashion similar to the way that MS-DOS 6 mounts DoubleSpace volumes. (These could be Stacker volumes created using Stacker for DOS—or using Stacker for OS/2 if the resulting compressed volume files are stored in a FAT volume.)

Preparing Additional Bootable DOS Disks

Once you have installed DOS 6 on the C: drive of your PC, you may need to install it on additional hard or even floppy disks. You could run SETUP for each such installation, but there is a much easier way.

First, however, any new hard disk requires a two-step preparation before it is ready to accept DOS. The first step, called the low-level format (or the physical format), is often done at the factory (for IDE or SCSI drives). But, if you have an MFM, RLL, or ESDI drive that you bought separately from the disk controller, you must do this step yourself. Check with the controller manufacturer or your dealer for instructions. The process generally involves using DEBUG to run a program in ROM on the controller card and is decidedly something you don't want to learn by trial and error. Chapter 7 explains in more detail just what a low-level format is and why it is needed.

FDISK FOR HARD DISKS

The second step in preparing a new hard disk, partitioning, can be done by using the DOS program FDISK. You can use FDISK from any version of DOS you have handy, but if it is pre-version 4, you will be limited in the size of the disk volumes you can create. A pre-version 3.3 FDISK will be unable to fully utilize any hard disk with than 32MB total capacity. Whatever version of FDISK you use, however, you will most likely have to boot your PC from a DOS diskette of the same version as the FDISK program before you can use it, since FDISK—like most of the DOS external commands—checks the DOS version number before it will run.

Tip: If you don't have an installed hard drive on your PC and need to run FDISK to install one, you can use the DOS 6 version of FDISK by running SETUP /F to create a set of bootable DOS 6 diskettes, then boot from one of them and run FDISK.

As a safety feature, DOS 6 has a new /STATUS switch for FDISK. Use this if you are not sure whether or not your disk has been partitioned. This will cause FDISK simply to report the partitioning that exists, without any possibility of changing it, which makes it a very nice, safe first step before you try anything that could possibly disrupt an existing partition with data in it. Run the command `FDISK /STATUS > {filename}` to create a disk file of that report. (The notation {filename} means that you are to type at that location in the command any filename you like. You also can include a disk drive letter and/or path with that filename if you wish. An example of the total command might be:

```
FDISK /STATUS A:\HD1STATS.TXT
```

if you wanted the report to go to a file on a floppy diskette in your A: drive's root directory and have the name HD1STATS.TXT.)

This disk file can be a very useful future reference item if your hard drive's partitioning gets corrupted. (Naturally, you should store this file on a floppy diskette or on some other hard drive, because you will need it most when you cannot access any of the files on this hard drive.)

Note: There are some important issues to consider when partitioning a hard disk. If you are uncertain what size partitions and how many of them you should create, read the section "Organizing Disk Information" in Chapter 7 before you do this step.

> ***Warning:*** If you use FDISK to repartition a drive that's already in use, all data will be irretrievably lost!

FDISK allows you to create, view, activate, and delete partitions on a physical hard drive. You may define more than one logical drive per physical drive, if for example, you are running more than one operating system (OS/2 or UNIX, for example), or if you want to segregate all your business documents onto your C: drive and your personal applications onto a D: drive. Normally, though, you'll probably want to devote the entire disk space to a single bootable DOS drive and use directories to keep applications or data separate. To handle this most common case, a single partition on a single, new drive, follow these steps:

1. Type FDISK (and press Return.)
2. Select choice 4, Display partition information, to be sure you're not clobbering an existing partition(s). This is especially important if you think the drive may have been used previously. If you find established, but inactive partitions, you may want to activate them before proceeding to see what's there. Once you're sure you can dispense with any existing partitions, use choice 3 to delete them. All data on the disk will be lost at this point, so be very sure before deleting any existing partitions.
3. If you find no existing partitions or have deleted any you found, select choice 1, Create DOS partition or logical drive. Tell FDISK that you want to allocate all the available cylinders to the DOS partition.
4. Use choice 2 to make the partition you've just created the active partition.

Once you have your hard disk partitioned you are ready to apply the high-level, or logical format. That is what you will be doing when you use the DOS program FORMAT.

FORMAT AND SYS

You may have already used the FORMAT command, perhaps many times. Still, there are some quirks to this program and some clear and present dangers that you might not remember. Read this section to learn (or review) them.

Before DOS can store and retrieve data on a disk, there must be some placemarkers written there. Think of them as marking the row and seat numbers in a theater. Once they are in place, DOS can put your data in a well-defined location on the disk and keep track of that location in a directory table.

The FORMAT program puts all the necessary markers and locator tables on a floppy diskette. It puts only the locator information on a hard disk; the position markers are put on a hard disk during the low-level formatting process.

To create a bootable disk on the active partition, use the command:

```
FORMAT drive: /s
```

where *drive:* would typically be, for the first hard drive on a system, C:. This command both formats the disk and installs the necessary system files to allow the system to boot from this disk. Note that the command works for both hard and floppy disks; but, in the case of a hard drive, it will squawk at you and let you change your mind before deleting your files.

Starting with version 5 of DOS, the FORMAT program was given some valuable new features. No longer is every format totally destructive. In fact, unless you explicitly specify the /U switch on the command line or there are no files on the disk being formatted, FORMAT will attempt to save a copy of the FAT and root directory information. Then, if you decide *before you write any information to this disk* that you want to undo the format process, you can usually do so by using UNFORMAT. (There are some limitations to UNFORMAT's abilities, which will be discussed in Chapter 15.)

WHEN TO USE THE SYS COMMAND

If you have a diskette that is already formatted, and you simply want to add DOS to it, you can use the SYS command. In DOS versions prior to 5, the SYS command copied only the two hidden system files (IO.SYS and MSDOS.SYS, or IBMBIO.COM and IBMDOS.COM). Starting in version 5 the SYS command also copies COMMAND.COM, thus saving you the necessity of copying the command interpreter to the newly-SYSed diskette in a separate step. Notice, however, that if you use an alternative command interpreter (perhaps 4DOS or NDOS), the SYS command will not copy that file to the diskette.

What if you have some files already on the diskette? Unlike the FORMAT command, which will erase those files, SYS just adds the DOS system files and COMMAND.COM. Some earlier versions of DOS could do this only if the diskette previously had some version of DOS on it or had been specially prepared to leave space for DOS. Version 6, however, needs only enough empty space on the diskette for the files it has to transfer.

There are two features new to SYS in DOS 6: First, you can specify a source drive as well as a target drive (up to this point you had to make the drive that had the system files your DOS default drive, or else put a DOS diskette into the A: drive or SYS would fail to work); second, the SYS command now also copies a third hidden system file, DBLSPACE.BIN, to the target disk. Of course, if you do not have DBLSPACE.BIN on the source disk, SYS cannot do this.

The DBLSPACE.BIN file is new with DOS 6. Its function is to provide on-the-fly file compression and expansion. It is loaded by IO.SYS at an early stage in the boot process. It looks for any *compressed volume files* (CVFs) on any of your drives and, if it finds them, converts them into what appear to you and your programs as additional disk drives. Chapter 7 explains this technology in detail.

You may be surprised to learn that if SYS doesn't find DBLSPACE.BIN, it will not give you an error message. DOS 6 accepts disks with or without this file as being complete system disks. Since you cannot see if SYS has copied this file to the diskette simply by using the DIR command, be sure to check by using the DIR /A or the ATTRIB command. You can also check the diskette using CHKDSK (see Figures 3-1 and 3-2). Remember that the volume label (if you specified one) is counted by CHKDSK as one hidden file.

Since you can easily add the system files to already formatted diskettes, and since you don't want the system files on any diskettes that you use only to hold data (no reason for wasting the space on them), you might as well format several diskettes at one time without using the /S switch. Then SYS only those diskettes you need to make bootable.

It is also possible to buy preformatted diskettes. This can save you a lot of time otherwise spent in that boring task. Preformatted diskettes do not have DOS on them, however, so you will have to use the SYS command if you want to make them bootable.

```
C:\ >chkdsk a:
Volume Serial Number is 3553-17E7

   1457664 bytes total disk space
     78336 bytes in 2 hidden files
     53760 bytes in 1 user files
   1325568 bytes available on disk

       512 bytes in each allocation unit
      2847 total allocation units on disk
      2589 available allocation units on disk

    655360 total bytes memory
    554528 bytes free

C:\ >attrib a:
  A  SHR      A:\IO.SYS
  A  SHR      A:\MSDOS.SYS
  A           A:\COMMAND.COM

C:\ >
```

Figure 3-1 A 1.4MB floppy disk that has been formatted with DOS 6, but that does not have DBLSPACE.BIN on it. Both CHKDSK and ATTRIB command outputs are displayed.

```
C:\ >chkdsk a:
Volume Serial Number is 18ED-0D30

   2375680 bytes total disk space
    147456 bytes in 3 hidden files
     57344 bytes in 1 user files
   2170880 bytes available on disk

      8192 bytes in each allocation unit
       290 total allocation units on disk
       265 available allocation units on disk

    655360 total bytes memory
    554528 bytes free

C:\ >attrib a:
     SHR      A:\IO.SYS
     SHR      A:\MSDOS.SYS
  A           A:\COMMAND.COM
     SHR      A:\DBLSPACE.BIN

C:\ >
```

Figure 3-2 The same floppy diskette with DBLSPACE.BIN and after using DBLSPACE.EXE to mount it. Notice the increase in apparent disk capacity.

Warning: Buying preformatted diskettes can save you a lot of time, but they could end up costing you dearly. Check at least a random sample of those diskettes for viruses before you use any of them. Unfortunately, even some of the major brands of preformatted diskettes have come from the factory complete with boot sector viruses!

Volume Labels and Serial Numbers

Volume labels is something else you can ask the FORMAT command to do: Add a volume label to the disk after it finishes formatting it. This is often a very good idea. You will see the volume name each time you use DIR or CHKDSK on that disk. Some software can read volume labels as well. This is simply an electronic label, similar to the paper one you probably apply to the outside of the diskette jacket. DOS stores the volume label as an entry in the root directory, which means that you don't use any of the diskette's data storage capacity by adding a label. You can also add a label later by using the DOS command, LABEL. The VOL command just displays the volume label (if any).

Beginning with version 4.0, the DOS command, FORMAT, automatically puts a unique serial number on each disk it formats. DISKCOPY will make a faithful copy of a diskette, complete with its volume label, but will also put a unique serial number on the diskette it is creating. DISKCOMP will report that two diskettes are identical if they differ only in their serial numbers.

Optimizing Memory Usage

One of the most exciting aspects of DOS 5 was the introduction of some memory management tools. DOS 6 introduces a new program, MemMaker, which makes it easier for you to use the DOS memory management tools introduced in DOS 5 (for the most part, little changed in DOS 6).

Basic Ideas

Chapter 1, in the "Physical Layers" section, explains that a PC running DOS has several different regions of memory. Chapter 6 explains these regions in more detail. Without using any memory management tools, DOS and most DOS programs can only take advantage of the first 640KB of the CPU's memory address space, the region called *lower memory.*

If you have an AT (80286-based PC) or better and you load the HIMEM.SYS device driver, you will have converted your extended memory to XMS memory, and you will have created a special 64KB region just above the 1MB mark called the *high memory area* (HMA). The DOS=HIGH directive in your CONFIG.SYS file tells DOS to load as much of itself as it can into the HMA.

If yours is a 386- or 486-based PC and you load the EMM386 device driver, you can convert some of your XMS memory into *upper memory* and/or into *expanded memory.* The LOADHIGH and DEVICEHIGH commands put resident programs and device drivers into upper memory. Doing so will give you more room in lower memory for your application programs.

That is the basic idea of memory management. The trick is in deciding which of these tools to use and exactly how to use them. Prior to DOS 5 you were on your own. Now you can use MemMaker.

Using MemMaker

MemMaker is easy to use—intentionally. If you choose the Express Setup option, you will have only one question to answer: Do your programs use expanded memory? Answer that and away it goes.

Conversely, the Custom Setup option allows you to participate in the process, at least to a degree, which can help MemMaker a lot. We strongly recommend that whatever memory management program you use, you don't simply let the optimizing aspect of that program work in its fully automatic mode. Almost always you can improve matters if you get involved.

One of the most important things you can do to get involved is to decide what parts of DOS you'll load on a regular basis. SETUP has its own ideas as to what you'll need, which may or may not correspond to your priorities.

Tip: Review the contents of your CONFIG.SYS and AUTOEXEC.BAT files *before* running MemMaker. There's no point optimizing something you're going to change later! Add or delete whatever device drivers and TSRs you need, test to make sure everything works, and then run MemMaker.

Pieces to Load Every Time

There are a number of pieces of DOS that you may well want to install in your CONFIG.SYS and AUTOEXEC.BAT files so that they are loaded into RAM every time you start or restart your PC. Here is our suggested list. You may not choose to install all of them, but we think you should at least give careful consideration to using each one.

- VSAFE—INSTALL this first in your CONFIG.SYS file and it will have the maximum chance at catching nasty programs before they hurt you. Note, though, that it will take up 23K of conventional memory, so remember to put it on the uncompressed volume if you're running DoubleSpace. For a slightly lower level of protection, LOADHIGH this file in your AUTOEXEC.BAT. Chapter 15 explains how and why to use VSAFE. Be aware, please, that not all the alarms that this or any other virus program sounds indicate actual computer viral infection. The discussion in Chapter 15 explains the trade-off that must be made between false positive and false negative reports.
- HIMEM and EMM386—Normally, these go very early in your CONFIG.SYS file as they set up the RAM environment (XMS and upper memory) into which you will be loading other files. Remember to also specify `DOS=HIGH,UMB` to let DOS use the HMA and to ask it to manage upper memory.
- SETVER—*Don't* load this one unless you really need it. If you do, at least make sure it goes high—there's really no reason to load it before the memory managers.
- SHARE—*Do* load this one. *Every* power user needs it. Users of networked PCs know about this one; too many others do not. Most DOS power users will do some task swapping or, at least, occasionally "drop to DOS" from within an application program. Those are the exact situations in which you really want to have SHARE loaded.

- SMARTDRV—Load either this or some other disk caching program. If you use SMARTDRV, you need to be aware that it can get mentioned twice. The first time is by a line in your CONFIG.SYS file that reads

  ```
  DEVICE={path}SMARTDRV.EXE /DOUBLE_BUFFER
  ```

  and the next time is in your AUTOEXEC.BAT file where the line will read simply

  ```
  {path}SMARTDRV
  ```

  with, possibly, some additional command line options after the file name in the second case. The first line is necessary only if you use a protected mode memory manager (EMM386 and Windows are two such programs) and you have a hard disk controller that uses a DMA strategy for moving information to and from the disk drive.

Tip: You can determine whether or not your system will benefit from the /double_buffer switch by adding the DEVICE={path}SMARTDRV.EXE /double_buffer line to your CONFIG.SYS file, rebooting, and then running SMARTDRV.EXE from the DOS prompt. If the column marked buffering is filled with "no" entries, then the /DOUBLE_BUFFER switch isn't accomplishing anything, and you should remove the line from your CONFIG.SYS to save some conventional memory.

Warning: If you are upgrading from a considerably older version of DOS, be aware that the older versions of this program were called SMARTDRV.SYS and were installed only through a `DEVICE=` line in the CONFIG.SYS file. If your CONFIG.SYS file has such a line, remove it and get rid of the SMARTDRV.SYS file.

- DOSKEY—This useful macro program and command line editor occupies a place of honor in many users' AUTOEXEC.BAT files. There are, as usual, many third-party alternatives, some of which offer even more goodies. Choose one, but do use something that lets you replay and edit old commands and create macro definitions. This will greatly ease your workday. Chapter 12 explains all you need to know about this program; for now, just note that it too can be loaded high.

- ANSI—This device driver is loved by some, hated by others, and ignored by most. It extends the way in which a PC handles the keyboard and screen to more closely approximate the American National Standards Institute specified way a computer terminal should behave. If you run programs (which could include some fancy batch files you write) that use the ANSI-supported features, you will need to include a line loading ANSI.SYS in your CONFIG.SYS file.
- DBLSPACE—This is the new Microsoft on-the-fly file compression program. Using it can make your hard disk seem about twice as large as it really is. But before you install this program, please read Chapter 7 carefully. You must know what you are getting into here, as getting back out is not very easy.
- SWITCHES = /F—There are other options for this command, which you may or may not find useful, but this one cuts two seconds out of every reboot. That may not sound like much, but while you're tweaking your system configuration, it gives you an easy psychological victory at the very least.
- UNDELETE—As a *terminate-and-stay-resident* (TSR) program, UNDELETE can be used to keep track of files you delete, making them much easier to recover if you discover that you deleted them in error. Read the discussion in Chapter 15 to decide which version of deleted file protection (tracking or Sentry), if either, you wish to use.

Once you've decided what to use and what to discard, run MemMaker with the Express Setup option. You should see an immediate improvement in the amount of free memory in the first 640Kb DOS memory area. Additional improvement may be possible via the Custom Setup option, but this will involve a close analysis of your system configuration and may require that you set up several different task-specific configurations. We'll cover the fine-tuning in Chapter 11.

Other Ways to Go

Although this is a new area for DOS, there have been some very good third-party memory management utility programs available for many years; QEMM and 386MAX are the most well known of these. Some others that have earned a good reputation include Netroom, Memory Commander, and QMAPS. These are very sophisticated programs and have developed a great deal over many generations.

If you are already using a memory manager, you will very likely find that it does at least as good a job of tuning your system as MemMaker can. The main reason to use MemMaker is that you don't have to buy an alternative program. Even so, you might wish to consider one of the third-party memory managers.

If you want to use any utility programs from a third-party vendor, you would be wise to check with that vendor to see if they have an upgraded version recommended for use with DOS 6. This is doubly true for something as critical as a memory manager.

Optimizing Disk Space

Now that you've cleaned up your RAM, let's see what we can do to make the best possible use of that other scarce commodity, disk space. DOS 6 provides a new built-in tool in the DBLSPACE utility, but there are some old-fashioned techniques that will also help you gain back some space—and maybe even protect you from trouble.

Installing DBLSPACE

Like the SETUP and MEMMAKER routines, Microsoft made DBLSPACE easy to install. After you've installed DOS 6 with SETUP, you only need to type DBLSPACE to start the disk compression process on your C: drive, then follow the instructions on screen. Other DBLSPACE options, which we'll cover in Chapter 9, will let you check the status of compressed disks, create and reconfigure compressed drives on either hard drives or floppies, or optimize the performance of compressed disks by defragmenting a drive. If you're using Stacker, DBLSPACE will offer to convert your Stacker volumes to Microsoft's disk compression format.

Because the DBLSPACE install procedure invokes the time-consuming defragmentation option as a mandatory part of the process, you'll want to schedule DBLSPACE's installation to take place when you won't need to use the PC. Typically, installing DBLSPACE takes several hours, depending on the size and speed of your disk, so starting it before you quit for the evening is a good idea if you don't enjoy watching the "percent complete" figure crawl from 1 to 100.

Once DBLSPACE is installed, you won't notice any major difference in the way your PC operates, until you type DIR and wonder where all that space came from. If you type DBLPACE /LIST, you'll also find that your PC has acquired a new drive—the *host drive,* which bears a previously unused drive letter. It actually corresponds to the old physical drive in your system, plus the CVF file created by DBLSPACE; the CVF file responds as if it were your old C: drive. Doing a DIR on the host drive will show only COMMAND.COM (and any files you've intentionally installed on the uncompresssed drive, such as the partition information for a Windows permanent swap file), but poking around with either ATTRIB or DIR /A:H will show four DBLSPACE.* files (as well as the normal IO.SYS and MSDOS.SYS boot files); the one named DBLSPACE.000 is the CVF file.

Once DBLSPACE is installed, you can resume reclaiming a bit more space the old-fashioned way—by trashing files you don't need.

DOS Files You Can Safely Discard

Some of the programs that come with DOS are not necessary. A few are actually dangerous. You may as well delete these files, and doing so has two advantages: One is that you can reclaim the disk space they occupied; the other is that you won't make a mistake and run one of those programs when you have already decided it doesn't do anything you want.

Almost everyone knows that FORMAT can be a dangerous program. But you need to have it around in order to format diskettes. But you do have some alternatives. If you spend most of your day in Windows or another operating environment that works on top of DOS, you may be able to format diskettes using a feature of that environment. Then you could remove the DOS FORMAT program from your hard disk. This is not, however, necessarily a wonderful idea. For one thing, the Windows format routine, even in its latest version, doesn't offer the safe format option. For another, you probably need to have the FORMAT program around for those rare occasions when you need to format a hard disk.

A much more dangerous DOS program is RECOVER. Finally, with DOS 6, this program is no longer installed on your hard disk automatically. Now it is available only on a supplemental diskette, along with other pieces removed from DOS 5 in the creation of DOS 6. Don't, however, be complacent. Since DOS 6 did not install RECOVER, it also did not remove an older copy you may have. Look in your DOS directory and if you find RECOVER.COM or RECOVER.EXE, delete it.

FASTOPEN is another bad actor you might as well delete from your hard disk. Other programs you may wish to get rid of are not intrinsically dangerous; you simply don't think you'll need or want to use them. But be a bit careful about deleting files whose purpose you don't understand. Some are essential helper files, such as the WINA20.386 and DSVXD.386 files in the root directory of your C: drive. Both of these files must be there for Windows to work correctly on a 386- or 486-based PC. (It is possible to relocate them, but to do so means adding a special flag to the SWITCHES directive in your CONFIG.SYS file and some special entries to the SYSTEM.INI file in your Windows directory.)

When you delete a DOS program that implements one of the DOS external commands, you probably should also delete all its helper files. The table in the Command Reference shows these helper file names indented under the corresponding command name in the first column.

The following list enumerates a couple of categories of other programs that you might consider sacrificing if you are short on disk space. Remember, you can always get them from the DOS installation diskettes (by using the EXPAND command) if you ever need them.

1. DOSSHELL—This is the DOS equivalent of training wheels: If you use it, you'll outgrow it, and if you find it in the least appealing, you might as well bite the bullet, upgrade your hardware as needed, and go straight to Windows. Likewise for any of the third-party alternatives.
2. The files that are left over from DOS 5—They include 4201.CPI, 4208.CPI, 5202.CPI, ASSIGN.COM, BACKUP.EXE, COMP.EXE, CV.COM, EDLIN.EXE, EXE2BIN.EXE, GORILLA.BAS, GRAFTABL.COM, JOIN.EXE, LCD.CPI, MIRROR.COM, MONEY.BAS, MSHERC.COM, NIBBLES.BAS, PRINTER.SYS, PRINTFIX.COM, and REMLINE.BAS.
3. The files used to change international settings and foreign language support—They are COUNTRY.SYS, DISPLAY.SYS, KEYB.COM, and NLSFUNC.EXE. Before you toss these files, though, read what they can do for you in Chapter 4. You may decide that even though you live in the United States and type only in English, these programs can benefit you significantly.

And finally, look over the full list of DOS commands and files in the table in the Command Reference and read the descriptions of any you don't recognize. This may help you identify many more files you can safely clear off your hard disk.

Avoiding Dangerous DOS Tools

In addition to dangerous DOS programs, some other parts of DOS are either dangerous or not particularly helpful. Most of the time this is not a serious problem. You can have lots of programs in your DOS directory that you will never use and they will never harm your data. They just take up space you might better use for something else.

What *can* be a real problem are the pieces of DOS that get installed in your CONFIG.SYS or AUTOEXEC.BAT file by the DOS SETUP program, possibly without your knowledge. You need to ferret out the changes SETUP makes and scrutinize each one. Some are good for you; others you will want to remove.

SETUP is quite sure that you want to have SETVER.EXE and SMARTDRV.EXE installed in your CONFIG.SYS and AUTOEXEC.BAT files, respectively. Earlier versions of DOS installed FASTOPEN.EXE routinely. MemMaker will add DEVICE statements to your CONFIG.SYS file to load HIMEM.SYS and EMM386.EXE, plus it will add the directive `DOS=HIGH,UMB`. These could all be useful—well most of them could, anyway—but often you should not have them installed.

SETVER is necessary only if you run one of the programs that needs to be fooled into working with DOS 6. If you don't have any programs that complain of a `Wrong DOS version`, then you can save some memory by removing the `DEVICE=SETVER.EXE` line from your CONFIG.SYS file—or at the very least, you can make sure that SETVER loads high by changing the line to DEVICEHIGH and moving it to a position after the HIMEM, EMM386, and DOS=HIGH,UMB lines in your CONFIG.SYS.

SMARTdrive is a pretty good disk caching program. But if you are presently using some other disk cache program you will have to make a choice. It is never a good idea to have two disk cache programs fighting over which one will help speed up your disk. Far too often the result is data loss. SETUP makes no attempt to see if you are already using a disk cache program; it just adds SMARTDRV.EXE to your AUTOEXEC.BAT file (and may also add it to your CONFIG.SYS file with the /DOUBLE_BUFFER option) if it was not already installed in those files.

As already noted, FASTOPEN is a dangerous program. Any good disk cache will give you all the benefits FASTOPEN is supposed to provide, and much more. SETUP will not put FASTOPEN into your AUTOEXEC.BAT file, but if you had it there from some previous version of DOS, it may not have been taken out. Look for it and remove it.

HIMEM.SYS and EMM386.EXE are the principal DOS memory management tools. They are fine, unless you are already using some other memory manager. As with SMARTDRV, you must choose whether to use the DOS tools or some others. Just don't try using both the DOS tools and a program like QEMM, 386MAX, Netroom, Memory Commander, or QMAPS.

Tip: **Dealing with a Stuffed Hard Disk:** If you try to install DOS 6 on a really full hard disk, you are in for a shock. You may not have anticipated just how much DOS has grown in the past couple of years. If you were running MS-DOS 5, your C:\DOS directory probably contained less than 3MB of files. After the DOS 6 upgrade, if you had SETUP install all of the optional parts, your C:\DOS directory will boast more than 6MB in files. Don't forget that

SETUP also creates an OLD_DOS.1 subdirectory to store the DOS 5 files it overwrote. That adds roughly another 1.75 million bytes. In all, your disk will have a little more than 8MB of DOS files on it when you finish—if you finish without running out of space!

If you think you might run out of space, first go through every subdirectory on your C: drive (or wherever you are going to install DOS 6) and mercilessly weed out all unnecessary files. Save them to a backup just in case you were wrong, but get rid of anything you can. In this way, you might be able to open up enough space for the full DOS 6 installation.

If that doesn't do it, your next step is to tell SETUP not to install any of the optional programs. That will cut things down a lot. Still, you may find that you are unable to complete the SETUP, even though you are sure you had room on your C: drive for all of the new and old DOS files you planned to have installed. This can happen because SETUP writes some temporary files as it is uncompressing the files from the installation diskettes. The combination of the new, the old, and the temporary files might exceed your disk's capacity.

The solution to this, if you have either a second physical or logical drive, is to set an environment variable called TEMP before you run SETUP. Make it point to the drive other than the one on which you are installing DOS (and be sure that drive has several megabytes of free space). SETUP will use that location for its temporary files. If you have a large RAM disk, that is an ideal place, as you will keep SETUP from running out of room and speed the process as well.

Optional Components

Several times in this chapter you have read about the "optional components" of DOS 6. This refers to the DOS and Windows versions of three programs: Antivirus, MSBACKUP, and UNDELETE. You need to load only the versions you are going to use (of course). Obviously, not loading the ones you don't need can save you a good deal of precious disk space. (The exact numbers of bytes needed are shown on the second of the three screens in SETUP where you get to make a decision.)

Tools to Check Your Work

How do you know if you have done a good job of setting up your PC? DOS provides several programs that are useful to determine this.

1. Perhaps the most important is CHKDSK. This program verifies the integrity of the file allocation table and directory structure on a disk. It also can be used to check on total free (lower) memory, and to discover

which files are fragmented. Chapter 7 explains what these terms mean and why you need to check on them regularly.

2. Checking on memory usage is the special domain of MEM. Its /C, /D, and new /M options can tell you just about all you need to know about what is where in your RAM. A good way to keep score on memory management tweaks is to run MEM /C /P to see what you've gained or lost. Read Chapter 6 to learn more about RAM in your PC.
3. FC and COMP (if you still have them around from DOS 5) let you compare the content of files. Here is one way to make these files very useful as you tune your PC: Keep copies of your CONFIG.SYS, AUTOEXEC.BAT, WIN.INI, and SYSTEM.INI files in a special directory. Then, whenever you do something that might have changed one of those files, check the current copies in your C:\ and Windows directories against those backup copies. That will alert you to what has been changed.
4. DOSSHELL provides an easy way to study the contents of all your subdirectories, if you're not running Windows. This is a necessary step in weeding out unneeded files, and thus is an important part of setting up your PC optimally and in discovering just how well you have done it.

DOS Commands for Setting Up Your System

Not all of the DOS commands are useful for setting up your system, but many of them are. Here is a list of the ones you are most likely to use. If you don't recognize one or more of these names, read all about them in the Command Reference.

COPY	RESTORE
DOSSHELL	SETUP
FDISK	SYS
FORMAT	VER
MSBACKUP	XCOPY
REPLACE	

These are just the DOS commands. Some of them, like DOSSHELL and SETUP, also have several associated files. You can discover what files are associated with any DOS command in the table in the Command Reference.

DOS Power Tool Programs for Setting Up Your System

There are always some clever programmers seeking to improve on DOS. Many of them have made some very useful tools that go beyond what DOS 6 offers. On the DOS Power Tools diskette you will find some of the cream of this crop. Of particular relevance to setting up your system are these files:

ADDCOMM and **PORTTEST**	helps you troubleshoot and configure I/O ports.
DMM	dynamic memory map, which shows you how memory is being allocated.
SHO and **SIZE**	displays disk space used versus free space.
ZIP	helps you transfer programs and data onto a newly-installed machine.

CHAPTER

4

◆ ◆ ◆ ◆ ◆

The Keyboard

Keyboards—every PC has one (just about). Most users assume that keyboards simply come with system units. Power users know that they have choices. This chapter is all about the choices you have, both in terms of keyboard hardware and in what you can do with the keyboard.

The Function and Importance of the Keyboard

The keyboard is the primary tool for putting information into your PC. Later, this chapter describes some alternative input devices you can use. Keyboards also return some information to you in several different ways. You can feel the keys move on almost all keyboards. Sometimes when it passes a critical point in its motion, the key will suddenly lunge forward; eventually, the key runs into a stop. When your fingertips feel the key lunge forward and later when you feel it hit bottom, you are receiving what is called tactile feedback. Normally, the keyboard will also emit a click at about the same point as the lunging motion.

Ideally, three events will coincide exactly: the key lunge, the click, and the computer reacting to the key press. In practice, they almost coincide, but not quite. A measure of the quality of a keyboard is how well all three of these events coincide and how clearly you can sense the two that are directed at you (the key lunge and click).

There is one other kind of feedback you can get from your keyboard. In all but the original, 83-key version, IBM's PC keyboards have included a group of three lights to show the state of the three shift locks: Caps Lock, Num Lock, and Scroll Lock. Nearly all clone keyboards also include these lights.

Many keys on a PC keyboard have two symbols printed on their key caps. The one in the lower left is the normal, or unshifted meaning of that key; the one in the upper left is its shifted representation. (Some keys have more than two symbols printed on their key caps. Others have an extra symbol or word printed on the front face of the key cap. What these mean is described later in this chapter.)

Each of the letter keys has only one symbol printed on its key, but those keys also can be used to type either of two characters, namely the lowercase and uppercase versions of their letter. With all the locks (Caps Lock, Num Lock, and Scroll Lock) off, you get the unshifted meaning of each key when you press it. If you hold down either the left or right Shift key and press some other key, you'll get the shifted representation of that other key. For the letter keys, and only for them, these denotations are reversed if Caps Lock is on; the same is true of the number keys in the 10-key array at the right end of the keyboard.

> ***Note:*** Scroll Lock is different. The BIOS keeps track of the Scroll Lock state, but it does nothing with that information. Most new PC users assume that Scroll Lock has something to do with stopping the screen from scrolling text out of sight. This is not at all the case. The way to do that is explained later in this chapter in the section "Surprising Uses for Certain Keys."
>
> Early PC technical documentation notes that the BIOS maintains a record of the Scroll Lock state, but then both the BIOS and DOS ignore that state. Think of the screen as a window onto a document. Normally, the cursor control keys move the cursor around in the document. (The cursor is the blinking line that shows where the next character you type will appear.) When Scroll Lock is on, according to IBM, the cursor control keys move the window instead of the cursor. This function has been implemented in some programs, including Microsoft's Word for DOS and Borland's Quattro Pro. Other programs use Scroll Lock in very different ways, or they simply ignore it.

Table 4-1 Memory Locations That Hold Shift and Shift Lock States

Meaning of the bits in the byte at 0417h

Bit number	If value is 0			If value is 1		
MSB 7	INSERT MODE			OVERSTRIKE MODE		
6	Caps Lock is		OFF	Caps Lock is		ON
5	Num Lock is		OFF	Num Lock is		ON
4	Scroll Lock is		OFF	Scroll Lock is		ON
3	Both	Alt	UP	Either	Alt	DOWN
2	Both	Ctrl	UP	Either	Ctrl	DOWN
1	Left	⇧	UP	Left	⇧	DOWN
LSB 0	Right	⇧	UP	Right	⇧	DOWN

Meaning of the bits in the byte at 0418h

Bit number	If value is 0			If value is 1		
MSB 7	Insert	is	UP	Insert	is	DOWN
6	Caps Lock	is	UP	Caps Lock	is	DOWN
5	Num Lock	is	UP	Num Lock	is	DOWN
4	Scroll Lock	is	UP	Scroll Lock	is	DOWN
3	System NOT paused			System IS paused		
LSB 2	Sys Req	is	UP	Sys Req	is	DOWN
1	Left Alt	is	UP	Left Alt	is	DOWN
0	Left Ctrl	is	UP	Left Ctrl	is	DOWN

The BIOS in a PC maintains a record of the shift lock states in 3 bits of the byte at address 417h (see Table 4-1). In this and the next byte are also kept the present state of the many shift keys and the state of the Insert/Overstrike toggle, which is described in the section "Special Computer Keys" later in this chapter.

Ordinarily, the shift lock indicators on the keyboard accurately reflect the actual shift lock state as it is stored in that special low memory address.

Sometimes, though, the keyboard gets out of sync. This usually happens when a program just reaches down into the low memory address and changes the keyboard shift lock state in RAM without bothering to tell the keyboard about it.

Commands can be sent to a PC keyboard through the PC's input/output port at address 60h. (This is true for all the IBM PC and compatible keyboards, except the original 83-key IBM PC version.) If you first send a byte whose value is EDh, the keyboard will interpret the least significant 3 bits of the next byte as the shift lock states and set its lights to match. The least significant bit sets the state of the Scroll Lock light; the next most significant bit sets the Num Lock light; the bit after that sets the Caps Lock light.

There is a small program that lets you see how those lights can be controlled on the DOS Power Tools Diskette. You run it by typing the command

```
KBTEST
```

Now for something a bit more practical. There is a second program that will read the shift lock state from the proper byte in low memory, then command the keyboard to set its lights to correspond to that reality. A copy of this program is included on the DOS Power Tools Diskette. You can run this program by typing `KBSYNC`. Any time you notice that your keyboard lights have gotten out of sync, just run this resynchronizer.

Why the Keyboard Matters

The job of the keyboard is to respond when you press a key and send a message to the system unit telling it which key you pressed. It also has to tell the system unit each time you release a key. If you hold almost any key down long enough, the keyboard will repeat the key-has-been-pressed message a fixed number of times per second. This is called the *typematic* function.

Sometimes what you type is data. For example, writing this book involved typing each character that you see on the page. At other times, the keystrokes are intended as a means of controlling what the PC does. Some control keystrokes result from pressing the cursor keys to move the blinking underline around in a document; others are letters or numbers that are part of a DOS command.

Using the keyboard is the way most people control their PCs most of the time. It is pretty hard to use a PC without a keyboard, but it can be done if you set up the PC properly. (This is often done for exhibits and point-of-sale terminals, etc., in which case some alternative input device, such as a touch screen, is used instead of a keyboard, and a special switch or flag bit is set in the PC to tell it that there is no attached keyboard.)

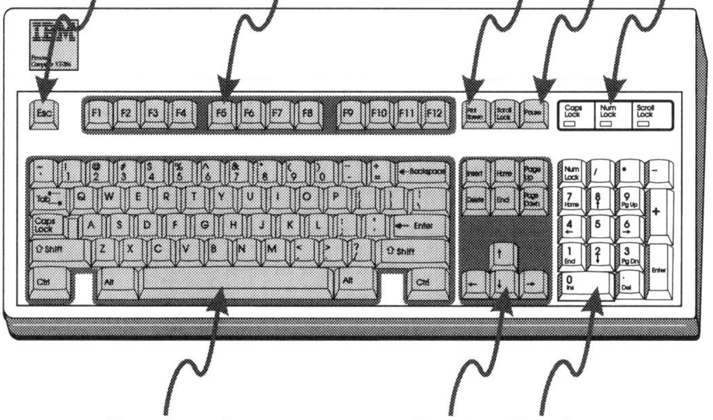

Figure 4-1 The standard IBM enhanced (101-key) keyboard layout

Keyboard Layout

A PC keyboard resembles a typewriter keyboard, more or less, although you need more keys on a computer since you have more things to control. Also, many PC keyboards have some of the keys duplicated for convenience.

IBM's PC keyboards have gone through a multistep evolution, although there have been no new keyboard layouts in the past several years. Figure 4-1 shows the now-standard IBM enhanced keyboard. (IBM also manufactures some variations on this keyboard for special-purpose personal computers, such as its 3270 terminal emulator PS/2s and for terminals for its mainframe machines. All of them bear a clear family resemblance to this design.) Many other manufacturers also make PC-compatible keyboards. Some of them are mentioned in the section "Optional Key Arrangements" later in this chapter.

Basic Groups of Keys

TYPEWRITER KEYS

The largest section of the keyboard contains the keys you would find on any typewriter: letter keys, numerals, common punctuation symbols, plus the Shift keys (one on each end of the next to bottom row and marked with a hollow arrow pointing up). The Caps Lock key is here too. Because of the resemblance of the key arrangement in this region to the keys found on an ordinary typewriter, this is called the *typewriter section* of the keyboard. The largest single key on the keyboard is in this section; it is the Spacebar. (When a program prompts you to `Press any key`, this is a very good choice for the "any" key.)

Also in the typewriter section are some keys used for control purposes. These include the Tab key, Backspace key, and Enter key (carriage return key). Enter is used to signal the end of a command or, if you are entering text into a word processor, to signal the end of a paragraph.

There are more punctuation symbols on a PC keyboard than on many typewriters: the forward slash (/), backward slash (\), and four kinds of parentheses (normal rounded ones (), square brackets [], curly brackets {}, and angle brackets <>). In addition to the usual typewriter double quote and single quote symbols (" and '), there is a reverse single quote (‘), also known as the grave accent mark, a tilde (~), and a vertical bar (¦), which in computer jargon is called the pipe symbol.

Finally, there are more shift keys on a PC keyboard than on a normal typewriter. These extra shift keys do a different kind of "case shifting" and they carry the names Ctrl (or Control) and Alt (Alternate).

Computers can use more characters than just the ones used in normal text. Conceptually, think of those extra characters as existing in one or more extra "cases." Holding down the Ctrl key makes the letter keys produce characters that signal *actions* rather than printable symbols. For example, pressing Ctrl-M usually produces the same effect as pressing the Enter key; Ctrl-H is a backspace, and Ctrl-I is a tab character. Most printers use the Ctrl-L character to signal the start of a new page (since the printer feeds a new page, or form, into the printing area, this character is called the *form feed character*).

Holding down the Alt (Alternate) key also modifies the messages the keyboard sends when you press any other key. However, with two exceptions that are described later in the chapter, there are no standard meanings to any of the Alt-shift keystrokes.

SPECIAL COMPUTER KEYS

Those key definitions account for only a little more than half the keys on a modern computer keyboard. Why do we need the rest? One reason is to create greater convenience for special uses of the keyboard. Since a PC can be used as a text processor, it is convenient to have the typewriter-like key arrangement. And because it can also be used as a calculator, it is convenient to have an additional group of keys arranged like those on a 10-key calculator: the *numeric keypad* (see Figure 4-1). Here you will find the numerals from 0 to 9, and the period, plus, minus, division, and multiplication sign keys. This section also has an additional Enter key and the Num Lock key.

Actually, the key in the numeric keypad that looks like a minus sign key is, for most purposes, just the same as the hyphen key in the top row of the typewriter section. The plus key is likewise duplicated in the top row of the typewriter section, and the multiply sign key is just another asterisk key to almost all programs.

Notice in the numeric keypad region that the number keys also have another symbol on them (except for the 5 key), and that the numbers are printed at the upper left of each key cap. The numerals are the shifted meanings of these keys; the other designations are their unshifted meanings. (Remember, when Num Lock is on, the unshifted and shifted meanings of the keys in the numeric keypad are exchanged.)

The unshifted meanings of the keys in the numeric keypad relate to cursor movement, and are, therefore, called *cursor control keys.* The 8, 2, 4, and 6 keys have arrows pointing up, down, left, and right respectively. In many programs, pressing one of them moves the cursor one space in the indicated direction. The 9 and 3 keys are labelled PgUp and PgDn, which obviously stand for page up and page down. As you would expect, many programs let you move your view up or down in a document by some distance called a page. The 7 and 1 keys are labelled Home and End. Usually, they move the cursor to the "home" position (usually the top left-hand corner of the screen or the top of a document or spreadsheet) or to the end position (usually the bottom of a document, but sometimes the right-hand end of the current line).

The 0 key carries the label Ins, short for Insert. It controls whether you are in an insert or an overstrike mode. Insert mode means the characters you type are introduced between existing ones; overstrike mode means they replace the existing ones.

The period key carries the additional label Del or Delete. Pressing this key usually deletes a character to the right of the cursor. (In some programs it deletes other, larger objects.) The Backspace key (above the Enter key in the typewriter section) also deletes a character, but it erases one character to the *left* of the cursor. The Delete key deletes the character at the cursor location (the one that the blinking cursor is directly underneath or on top of).

On an IBM enhanced keyboard, all of these cursor navigation keys are replicated without their shifted numeric key actions in a special section between the numeric keypad and the typewriter section, which is called the *alternate cursor controls.*

Tip: When the original PC was introduced, its keyboard did not have an alternate set of cursor controls. This is why IBM chose to make the numbers in the numeric keypad accessible only by shifting, while the cursor controls are available without shifting. (Except for applications like spreadsheets in which you are entering lots of numbers, you will generally find yourself using the cursor keys much more often than the number keys.)

When IBM introduced the PS/2 line with its new, enhanced keyboard, the company decided that the numeric keypad should default to numbers (since the user always had the alternate cursor controls available). That is why enhanced keyboards normally "wake up" with Num Lock on. If, however, you are among the many PC users who wish their keyboard would wake up with Num Lock *off*, DOS 6 has the answer you have been waiting for. Add a line to your CONFIG.SYS file that reads

```
NUMLOCK = OFF
```

and you won't have that problem any more.

The very top row of the keyboard has a number of special keys. At the far left, off by itself, is the *Escape key* (labelled Esc). As its name suggests, pressing this key is often a means of escaping from some program that is doing something you really don't want it to do any more. DOS (or more precisely, the command interpreter COMMAND.COM) uses it to let you cancel the current command you are typing (provided you press it before you press Enter). Other programs may use it quite different ways. One common example is as a means of retracing your steps back through a menu structure.

Most of the keys across the top of the keyboard are labelled with numbers preceded by the letter F. These are the *function keys* (F1 through F12), general purpose keys that can be programmed to do many different things. You will learn how DOS uses these keys in the section "Holding onto Inputs," later in this chapter.

The top row also has the Scroll Lock key (whose function was described earlier) and a couple of other keys with names that may not suggest what they really do. The Print Screen key is pretty straightforward: pressing this key (or pressing it while the shift key is held down) causes your printer to print a copy of whatever is on the screen at that moment—sometimes. It only works if the running program permits it to work, and some do not. For one thing, it usually won't work while you are booting your computer, at least until your AUTOEXEC.BAT file starts being processed. The Pause key is also fairly obvious. Press it and your PC will pause in its tracks. Press any other key (except the Shift, Caps Lock, and Insert keys) and the PC will resume where it left off.

What is not at all obvious about these two keys is that each can perform a totally different job. The Pause key also carries the legend, Break, on its front surface. If you press the Pause key while you have the Ctrl key pressed, you are issuing a Ctrl-Break command, which will interrupt many programs—more of them, in fact, than the Escape key can. The Print Screen key also carries the legend SysRq on its front. If you hold down the Alt key and press the Print Screen key, you will be issuing a "system request." In most PCs and with most PC programs, that means exactly nothing. This combination keystroke is included in the IBM enhanced keyboard design because some of their terminal emulation programs needed some way to signal the host computer whenever you wanted to send a command to its operating system.

Keyboard History

The earliest PC came with an 83-key keyboard that IBM had designed and built for a small scientific computer a year or so before it designed the PC. This key layout is shown in Figure 4-2. Note that the Ctrl and Alt keys, the alternate cursor control keys, and F11 and F12 are not on this keyboard. The Pause and SysRq keys are also missing, the Print Screen key (Prt Sc) is combined with the asterisk in the numeric keypad, and there is no extra Enter key in the numeric keypad region.

Although some people loved this keyboard and it certainly was better than any other personal computer keyboard in common use at the time, it had some drawbacks, including a too-small Enter key, noisy keyclicks, and keys in unfamiliar prositions.

With the development of the PC/AT, IBM introduced a new keyboard with 84 keys (see Figure 4-3). The added key was labelled Sys Req and it corresponds to the SysRq key on the current enhanced keyboard. The AT keyboard had a less pronounced clicking sound than its predecessor, and some of the keys had been moved to new locations. The biggest benefit was that the Enter key was now large enough that typists only occasionally missed it. The shift keys were larger, and the new shift lock indicators alerted many people *before* they typed a lot of wrongly shifted text.

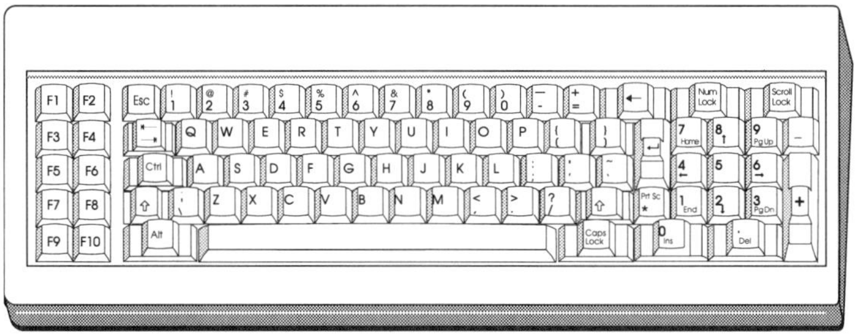

Figure 4-2 The original IBM PC 83-key layout

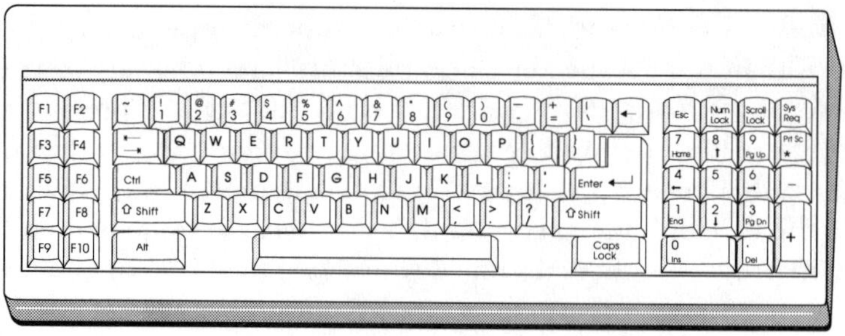

Figure 4-3 The original IBM PC/AT 84-key layout

Still, many people complained that they did not like the Escape key in the numeric keypad instead of "where it belonged" at the left end of the top row of numbers. They also complained about some of the other keys that had "roamed." The worst offenders were the tilde and backward slash keys, which had each moved almost to the diagonally opposite corner of the typewriter section from their original locations.

Another frequently mentioned problem was with the position of the function keys. This had been an issue with the original 83-key layout also. Located at the left side of the typewriter section, they could easily be reached by a touch typist, but often programs displayed what the function keys did in boxes arrayed across the bottom of the screen—far from where the function keys themselves were located.

Finally, IBM introduced the current key layout shown earlier in Figure 4-1. Among other things, the Escape key was back in its original corner, but a short distance from all the other keys. That little bit of space really helps. Now you are much less likely to hit the Escape key by mistake, possibly wiping out some lengthy command line you were typing.

This keyboard layout, nevertheless, has earned its share of complaints from some users, largely because IBM did what some other users had been demanding for a long time: It moved the function keys from the left side to the top. Now they were directly underneath the little on-screen labels that certain programs displayed, but they were now impossible to touch type (unless you are a concert pianist or professional basketball player).

To make matters worse, many programs had built in a dependence on some "natural" keystroke combinations, such as Ctrl-F6 or Shift-F8, which were very easy to strike on the 83- and 84-key keyboards. The 101-key layout made these frequently used combination keystrokes impossible for most people to type unless they stopped, looked at the keyboard, and used both hands.

A related annoyance is that IBM put the Caps Lock key where the left-hand Ctrl key had been, although there was some logic to this decision. This was the location at which the Caps Lock key had been on its famous Selectric typewriters (which, of course, had no Ctrl key). Unfortunately, by this time, most PC users were no longer using Selectric typewriters. Furthermore, this placement of the Caps Lock key ruined a number of perfectly natural combination keystrokes that had been used extensively in PC software, such as Ctrl-A.

Optional Key Arrangements

There are many clone keyboard makers. They each claim to make a better keyboard than the others. One popular innovation is the "bilingual" keyboard. The original 83-key PC keyboard (which IBM also used on the PC/XT) uses an interface to the computer that is different both electrically and logically from that used by all the later models of PC keyboard. Now it is popular for clone keyboards to have a switch that lets you tell them whether to interact with the system unit as an XT-style keyboard or as an AT-style keyboard. There even are "smart" keyboards that listen carefully to the messages sent by the system unit during the boot process, figure out which kind of PC they are attached to (XT-style or AT-style keyboard interface), and then set themselves to use that interface appropriately.

Some third-party keyboards also have function keys both up the side and across the top. The Northgate Omnikey Ultra is typical of this breed (see Figure 4-4). It has switches that allow setting many of its features, including some that let you define the top row of function keys, as exact copies of the left-hand set or as the shifted versions of those keys. (You may even choose the regular-shifted, Ctrl-shifted, or Alt-shifted function keys.) Another switch lets you reverse the Left-Ctrl and Caps Lock keys; in its default position, this keyboard has the Left-Ctrl key where the Ctrl key was on the earlier IBM keyboards. In addition, it can be set to any of four different key arrangements

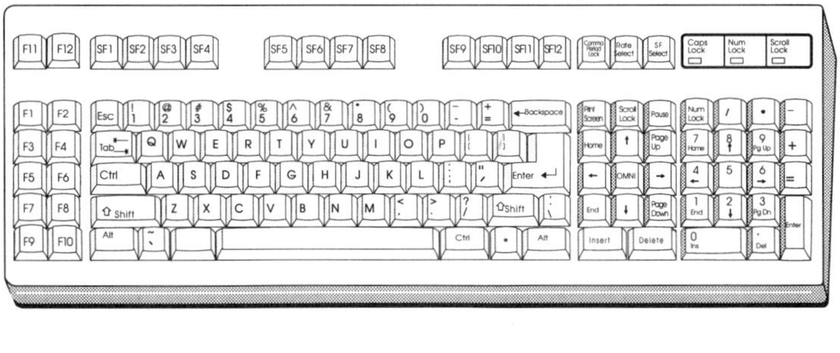

Figure 4-4 Northgate's Omnikey Ultra (119-key) keyboard layout

(and you can buy alternate key caps and install them for those other arrangements). The four arrangements are QWERTY (the usual arrangement), Dvorak (regular), left-handed Dvorak, and right-handed Dvorak.

Another switch on the Northgate keyboard makes it possible to set a "sticky keys" mode. In that mode you can type a shift key (letter shift, Ctrl, or Alt) and follow that keystroke by another key, and the keyboard will interpret them as if you had been holding down the Shift key while you typed the other key. The sticky mode and the single-handed Dvorak layouts are features intended mainly for use by people who have physical limitations that prevent them from typing normally.

Another helpful feature of Northgate's keyboards is that you have to press the Print Screen key twice in succession before it will send the Print Screen signal to the system unit. This must have saved whole forests that would otherwise have been wasted on printing screen images unintentionally.

Many laptop computers have too little room for a full PC keyboard, yet those computers must run modern software, some of which assumes you have an enhanced keyboard. These keyboards often have a special supershift key that lets some of the letter keys serve double duty as numeric keypad keys. These keys, when supershifted, respond to the shift key just as the numeric keypad ones do on an enhanced keyboard. Thus, you can get four different results from a single key, depending on what combination of shift and supershift keys you press first.

Other keyboards differ dramatically in the arrangement of their keys. The QWERTY arrangement (named for the first six letters of the next to top row in the typewriter section) is the most common, but there are advocates of at least a couple of alternatives. The Dvorak arrangement of the letter keys is claimed to enable faster touch typing. Some of the palmtop computers use a keyboard with the keys arranged in alphabetical order—almost certainly *not* an order that facilitates touch typing.

In yet another variation, some manufacturers have introduced keyboards with huge numbers of function keys. Some of these keyboards allow you to store vast quantities of text as macro definitions for each of these function keys. The memory they use is nonvolatile, so these keyboards remember those definitions even when you turn off power to your PC.

Lately, ergonomic considerations have gained in popularity. This has led to the development of some really weird looking keyboards. The vertical keyboard is one (see Figure 4-5). It may look nothing like any keyboard you have ever seen before, but if it lives up to its inventors' claims, we may be seeing many more of them in the future.

And finally, there are the keyboards that include alternate input devices such as a trackball or force transducer. At first, the inclusion of a pointing

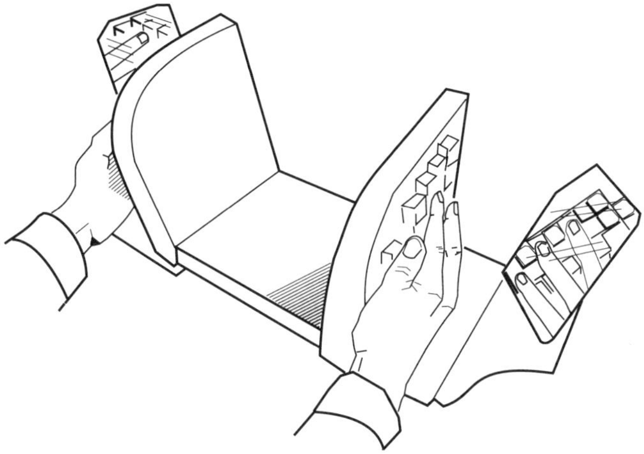

Figure 4-5 The vertical keyboard

device seemed like a very odd thing to do. Now, with the rapidly rising popularity of mobile computing and *graphical user interfaces* (GUIs) such as Windows, keyboards that incorporate pointing devices are almost becoming necessities.

Internal Workings

So far, we've only talked about how keyboards look and act from the outside. But what goes on inside them? Each PC keyboard contains an entire computer of its own. That computer runs a single program that is permanently stored in it. (Another name for computers like this that are included in some larger machine is an *embedded controller.*) The keyboard computer's program causes it to scan the keys constantly, looking for those that have changed their up or down position since the last scan; send messages to the PC system unit each time it sees a key go up or down; and send repetitions of the key-down message when appropriate for the typematic action.

Backtalk

The keyboard computer not only sends messages to the system unit, it also listens for messages coming from the system unit. One such special command resets the keyboard. This is issued by the system unit each time you reboot your PC; it activates the keyboard to start at the beginning of its program at the same time the system unit restarts its program. This is the only command the 83-key keyboard is able to understand.

Tip: The keyboard reset is issued only as a part of the cold boot process. If your keyboard gets confused, you may not be able to recover simply by pressing Ctrl-Alt-Del. You may need to do a complete restart, either by pressing a reset button—if your PC has one—or by turning off power, waiting a minute, and then turning power on again.

All the other IBM keyboard models and the clone keyboards understand a modest repertoire of commands. You read earlier in this chapter about the commands that turn the Shift Lock lights on or off. Other commands allow you to change the delay before onset and repetition frequency of the typematic action, asking the keyboard to resend the last message, etc. Thus, in these keyboards, there is a two-way dialog carried on between the keyboard and the system unit.

Scanning the Key Matrix

The keyboard sends messages to the system unit each time a key is pressed or released (plus the typematic repetitions of the keypressed messages). These messages are called *scan codes.* Most of the messages are a single byte long; some are two bytes long. The typematic repetitions of the keypressed messages are sent at regular intervals after an initial delay. The default programming of the keyboard specifies that the delay is one-half second, and the repetitions are to occur at the rate of ten per second. All but the 83-key keyboard can be reprogrammed to use different delay and repetition rate values, as noted above.

Another aspect of the keyboard computer's job is to support *N-key rollover.* This mouthful merely means that the computer must keep track of each individual keypress or release and tell the system unit about each one in the correct order. Some, less-capable keyboards (not used on PCs) are able to keep track of keypresses only if you never press two keys at once (other than, perhaps, a shift key and one other key).

DIFFERENT DIALECTS

The scan code messages that are sent when you press a particular key differ depending on which keyboard you are using. In effect, the different keyboard models speak in different dialects. As already stated, the early IBM PC and PC/XT came with keyboards that had 83 keys, and they both used the same scan code dialect. In this dialect, each scan code was a single byte. The value of that byte signaled which key had been pressed or released. One bit of that byte is 0 and signals a keypress, and another one signals a key release.

The early 83-key AT keyboard used a different dialect for its scan code messages. These messages varied in two ways from those sent by an XT keyboard. First, the scan code numbers were assigned to the keys in a different order. Second, the key release message was made 2 bytes long: the first was always F0h, and the second was the same as the keypressed message for that key.

The enhanced (101-key) keyboard can use any of three different scan code sets. Normally, it uses one that resembles the AT keyboard set (with extensions for the extra keys on the enhanced keyboard). The alternate cursor keys and the keypad Enter key on an enhanced keyboard cause the keyboard to send an E0h before the scan code for the equivalent key on an 83-key keyboard, both when you press the key and when you release it (but not before the typematic repetitions of the make scan code).

The differences among these scan code dialects is one of the reasons that an 83-key keyboard won't work on an AT, a 386, or 486 PC. Likewise, the 84- and 101-key keyboards won't work with a PC or an XT. (There also are some electrical differences in the interface and how it is used. You won't destroy a keyboard by plugging in the wrong kind, but it definitely won't work properly.)

SCAN CODES AND ASCII CHARACTERS

Scan codes are very different from the codes used to represent letters in files stored on a PC's disk drives or in RAM. Those places all use the *American Standard Code for Information Interchange* (ASCII) character set or IBM's graphic extensions to the set.

You may have wondered why PC designers developed the keyboard to send scan codes. It certainly seems simpler to have the keyboard send the ASCII codes. The problem is that we want to know more about what is typed than the ASCII code can convey. For example, the system unit needs to be informed each time you press a function key. Those keys don't have ASCII codes, nor are there ASCII codes for the cursor control keys or the Shift and Shift Lock keys.

Instead of sending different codes for a letter key depending on whether the Shift keys are up or down, the keyboard simply sends a unique scan code for every keypress and key release. That includes scan codes for the Shift keys and the Shift Lock keys. It is up to the system unit BIOS to figure out what the flow of scan codes means.

If, for example, the scan code 1Eh (30 decimal) is received from an XT keyboard by itself, the BIOS figures that you typed a lowercase letter a. If that

DEC	HEX	Screen Symbol	Scan Code	DEC	HEX	Screen Symbol	Scan Code	DEC	HEX	Screen Symbol	Scan Code
0	00			43	2B	+	78	86	56	V	S-47
1	01	☺	C-30	44	2C	,	51	87	57	W	17
2	02	☻	C-48	45	2D	-	12	88	58	X	S-45
3	03	♥	C-46	46	2E	.	52	89	59	Y	S-21
4	04	♦	C-32	47	2F	/	53	90	5A	Z	S-44
5	05	♣	C-18	48	30	0	11	91	5B	[	26
6	06	♠	C-33	49	31	1	2	92	5C	\	43
7	07	•	C-34	50	32	2	3	93	5D	]	27
8	08	◘	14	51	33	3	4	94	5E	^	S-7
9	09	○	15	52	34	4	5	95	5F	_	S-12
10	0A	◙	C-36	53	35	5	6	96	60	`	41
11	0B	♂	C-37	54	36	6	7	97	61	a	30
12	0C	♀	C-38	55	37	7	8	98	62	b	48
13	0D	♪	28	56	38	8	9	99	63	c	46
14	0E	♫	C-49	57	39	9	10	100	64	d	32
15	0F	☼	C-24	58	3A	:	S-39	101	65	e	18
16	10	►	C-25	59	3B	;	39	102	66	f	33
17	11	◄	C-16	60	3C	<	S-51	103	67	g	34
18	12	↕	C-19	61	3D	=	13	104	68	h	35
19	13	‼	C-31	62	3E	>	S-52	105	69	i	23
20	14	¶	C-20	63	3F	?	S-53	106	6A	j	36
21	15	§	C-22	64	40	@	S-3	107	6B	k	37
22	16	▬	C-47	65	41	A	S-30	108	6C	l	38
23	17	↨	C-17	66	42	B	S-48	109	6D	m	50
24	18	↑	C-45	67	43	C	S-46	110	6E	n	49
25	19	↓	C-21	68	44	D	S-32	111	6F	o	24
26	1A	→	C-44	69	45	E	S-18	112	70	p	25
27	1B	←	1	70	46	F	S-33	113	71	q	16
28	1C	∟	C-43	71	47	G	S-34	114	72	r	19
29	1D	↔	C-27	72	48	H	S-35	115	73	s	31
30	1E	▲	C-7	73	49	I	S-23	116	74	t	20
31	1F	▼	C-12	74	4A	J	S-36	117	75	u	22
32	20		57	75	4B	K	S-37	118	76	v	47
33	21	!	S-2	76	4C	L	S-38	119	77	w	17
34	22	"	S-40	77	4D	M	S-50	120	78	x	45
35	23	#	S-4	78	4E	N	S-49	121	79	y	21
36	24	$	S-5	79	4F	O	S-24	122	7A	z	44
37	25	%	S-6	80	50	P	S-25	123	7B	{	S-26
38	26	&	S-8	81	51	Q	S-16	124	7C	|	S-43
39	27	'	S-9	82	52	R	S-19	125	7D	}	S-27
40	28	(	S-10	83	53	S	S-31	126	7E	~	S-41
41	29	)	S-11	84	54	T	S-20	127	7F	⌂	
42	2A	*	55	85	55	U	S-22				

Scan codes are shown as follows: **Number alone** = key pressed without any shift
S-nn = Shift-keypress, **C-nn** = Control-keypress

Figure 4-6 ASCII code values, IBM's screen symbols, and keyboard scan codes

same scan code is received after receiving a scan code of 36h (the right shift key scan code) and before receiving a B6h (the scan code for the release of that shift key), then the BIOS figures you typed a shifted, or uppercase letter A. In the former case, the BIOS puts the ASCII value of a lowercase a (61h or 97 decimal) in the keyboard buffer; in the latter case, it puts the ASCII value of an uppercase A (41h or 65 decimal) in the keyboard buffer.

Figure 4-6 shows the ASCII codes for all the symbols that can be stored in a file on a PC's disk. Also shown are the screen images that correspond to each symbol along with the scan code of the key you would press to send that symbol to the PC. Notice that for some ASCII symbols there is no associated scan code, so you won't find a key on the keyboard with which you can type that symbol directly. (The scan codes shown in this chart are those for the XT keyboard. The keyboard controller and BIOS will translate inputs from an AT or enhanced keyboard to either an ASCII code or the scan codes shown in this figure before an application program can see them.) There is, however, a way to enter any ASCII symbol's code from the keyboard, but it sometimes requires many keystrokes. This method is described in the section "Surprising Uses for Certain Keys" later in this chapter.

What about the keys on the keyboard that don't correspond to an ASCII symbol? They have other scan codes, as shown in Figure 4-7. As you will see there, some of the non-ASCII keys generate a single byte scan code; others generate a 2-byte code. Whenever the scan code is 2 bytes long, the first byte is a 0. Again, this figure shows the scan codes for an XT-style keyboard.

Keyboard Controller

Your PC doesn't have just one embedded computer dedicated to the keyboard, it has two. The first one is the computer located inside the keyboard. The second one is located inside the system unit, and it is called the *keyboard controller.*

All the scan code messages come from the keyboard to the keyboard controller. The keyboard controller's primary job is to receive those scan codes and then alert the CPU that a message is coming in from the keyboard. Figure 4-8 shows this sequence of events. The keyboard controller causes a hardware interrupt when a scan code message is received.

Key	Scan Code DEC	Scan Code HEX	Key	Scan Code DEC	Scan Code HEX
Function keys			Alt-F4	107	6B
F1	59	3B	Alt-F5	108	6C
F2	60	3C	Alt-F6	109	6D
F3	61	3D	Alt-F7	110	6E
F4	62	3E	Alt-F8	111	6F
F5	63	3F	Alt-F9	112	70
F6	64	40	Alt-F10	113	71
F7	65	41	Alt-F11	87	57
F8	66	42	Alt-F12	88	58
F9	67	43	Left Shift	42	2A
F10	68	44	Left Ctrl	29	1D
F11	87	57	Left Alt	56	38
F12	88	58	Right Shift	54	36
Shifted-F1	84	54	Right Ctrl	* 29	* 1D
Shifted-F2	85	55	Right Alt	* 56	* 38
Shifted-F3	86	56	Caps Lock	58	3A
Shifted-F4	87	57	Space bar	57	39
Shifted-F5	88	58	Enter	28	1C
Shifted-F6	89	59	Num Lock	69	45
Shifted-F7	90	5A	Scroll Lock	70	46
Shifted-F8	91	5B	Insert	82	52
Shifted-F9	92	5C	Delete	83	53
Shifted-F10	93	5D	End	79	4F
Shifted-F11	87	57	↓	80	50
Shifted-F12	88	58	PgDn	81	51
Ctrl-F1	94	5E	→	75	4B
Ctrl-F2	95	5F	←	76	4C
Ctrl-F3	96	60	Home	71	47
Ctrl-F4	97	61	↑	72	48
Ctrl-F5	98	62	PgUp	73	49
Ctrl-F6	99	63	Ctrl-←	115	73
Ctrl-F7	100	64	Ctrl-→	116	74
Ctrl-F8	101	65	Ctrl-Home	119	77
Ctrl-F9	102	66	Ctrl-End	117	75
Ctrl-F10	103	67	Ctrl-PgDn	118	76
Ctrl-F11	87	57	Ctrl-PrtScrn	114	72
Ctrl-F12	88	58			
Alt-F1	104	68			
Alt-F2	105	69			
Alt-F3	106	6A			

(*) The keys indicated with an asterisk, like most of the keys that were added on the advanced keyboard are prefixed by 224 (E0h).

Figure 4-7 Extended scan codes

The keyboard controller also has some other tasks to perform. You won't be surprised to learn that in addition to receiving messages from the keyboard, the keyboard controller is responsible for sending messages to the

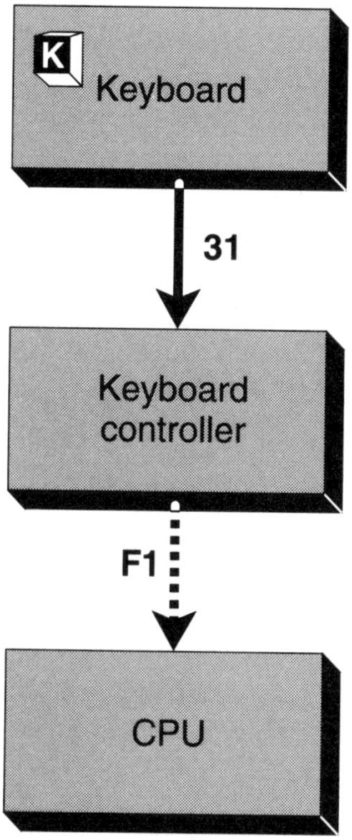

Figure 4-8 The keyboard controller receives messages from the keyboard and informs the CPU of their arrival.

keyboard (in all but XT-class computers, in which there are no messages other than reset to send). What may surprise you is that the keyboard controller in many PCs has a couple of tasks to perform that have nothing at all to do with the keyboard.

Often the keyboard controller is used to control access to the high memory area. In particular, it is used to block or pass the signal on the A20 line (the 21st address line) from the CPU to memory. When that line is blocked, any address just above 1MB will appear to be an address near the bottom of memory address space (near address 0). When that line is enabled, even in real mode, the CPU can address nearly 64KB of memory beyond the nominal 1MB limit—and that 64KB region is the high memory area.

The other oddball task the keyboard controller may be called upon to do is reset the CPU every time a program wants to change from protected mode back to real mode. These memory-related issues are discussed in Chapter 6.

THE BIOS KEYBOARD ROUTINE (INT9)

When a scan code message comes in from the keyboard, the keyboard controller receives it and immediately causes a hardware interrupt. This signal is converted by the interrupt controller into a software interrupt of type 9. When the CPU is ready to deal with this interruption, it invokes the interrupt service routine (ISR) for interrupt 9. (Interrupts and interrupt service routines are explained in Chapter 1.) The ISR for interrupt 9 reads the scan code message from the keyboard controller, does a little processing, and then deposits the results of its processing in a place called the keyboard buffer.

If the scan code indicates that a letter, numeral, or punctuation symbol key was pressed, the ISR converts the scan code to the equivalent ASCII value and puts that in the keyboard buffer. If the key that was pressed was a function key or one of the other keys with an extended scan code (see Figure 4-7), the ISR puts both the null byte (ASCII value 0) and the second byte into the keyboard buffer without change.

If the scan code message indicates the press or release of a shift key (Shift, Ctrl, or Alt) or of a shift lock key (Caps Lock, Num Lock, or Scroll Lock), it does not put anything in the keyboard buffer. Instead it updates the bits in the keyboard flag bytes at addresses 417h and 418h (see Table 4-1). Some scan codes cause very special actions. There are five cases:

1. When the ISR sees the combination of a Num Lock press while Ctrl is down or the scan code indicating the pressing of the Pause key, it goes into a special loop looking for an "unpause" key. That is the keypressed scan code for any key other than the Pause or Num Lock keys. When that unpause key is detected, the ISR leaves the loop and resumes normal processing of incoming scan code messages. Whatever keypress was used as the unpause key is effectively thrown away.
2. When the ISR sees a scan code indicating the Sys Req key (on an 84-key keyboard) was pressed or that the Print Screen key was pressed while the Alt key was down on an enhanced keyboard, it calls INT15h, function 85h. This interrupt is called again when that key is released. DOS does nothing when this interrupt is called, but if you load a terminal emulator program, it may hook this interrupt and take some appropriate action. Nothing gets added to the keyboard buffer in this case.
3. If the Print Screen key is pressed while either the left or right Shift key is down on an 83- or 84-key keyboard or the Print Screen key is pressed on a 101-key keyboard, the ISR calls INT5, which prints a copy of the screen's contents on the printer. Again, nothing is added to the keyboard buffer.
4. If the ISR detects a press of the Ctrl-Break combination (which is the Scroll Lock key pressed in combination with the Ctrl key on an 83- or

84-key keyboard, or the Pause key pressed with either Ctrl key down on a 101-key keyboard), it calls INT1Bh. What happens next is up to DOS. Whatever else happens, the ISR also puts 2 null bytes into the keyboard buffer.

5. If the ISR sees a press of the Del (Delete) key while both Alt and Ctrl are down, it puts the number 1234h in RAM at address 72h and causes the CPU to reset itself. This is what is called a *warm boot.* (When the CPU wakes up again it looks at address 72h and if it sees the flag value 1234h, it knows not to do the memory test or reset the keyboard.)

Finally, there are some scan code messages that the interrupt 9 ISR completely ignores. These include all the messages signaling the release of a key other than a shift key, any keypress message that is invalid in the present context of the shift states (for example, when Alt is down, the alternate cursor control keys do nothing). It also includes the typematic repeats of key-down messages from the Shift Lock keys, the Insert key and the Pause key. In most PCs, the ISR beeps the PC speaker for the invalid key combinations. It does not do this when it ignores a typematic repeat of a Shift Lock, Insert, or Pause key.

Holding Onto Inputs

In the last section the keyboard buffer was mentioned many times. This is an important concept. The keyboard computer, the keyboard controller, and the interrupt 9 ISR can deal with only a single keystroke at a time, and sometimes your application program is not prepared to deal with an incoming keystroke. Therefore, the PC must have some sort of holding area where keystrokes can be "parked" until they are needed.

DOS Default Keyboard Buffer

There is one standard place defined for this purpose. Starting exactly at address 41Eh, 32 bytes can hold at least sixteen keypress codes. A pointer at address 41Ch tells the interrupt 9 ISR where to put the next keystroke. A pointer at address 41Ah tells the interrupt 16h ISR where to retrieve the next keystroke to be given to an application program. (Normally, a program that wants to get input from the keyboard will call INT16h and let the ISR do the actual retrieving of the keystroke from the keyboard buffer.)

Each time a keystroke code is put in the buffer, the pointer at 41Ch is moved forward in the buffer one position, and each time a character is read from the buffer, the pointer at 41Ah is moved forward. Whenever one of the pointers reaches the end of the buffer, it automatically jumps back to the start

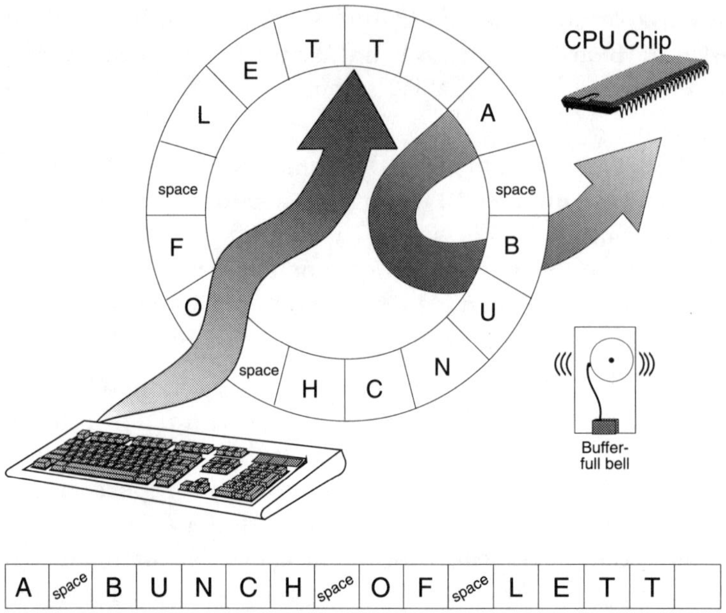

Figure 4-9 Keyboard buffer stores keystrokes temporarily.

of the buffer. Conceptually, the keyboard buffer is a circle of locations with no beginning or end. The two pointers just perpetually chase one another around this circle.

If the interrupt 16h pointer (at address 41Ah) catches up to the interrupt 9h pointer (at address 41Ch), it means that the buffer has been emptied. If a program asks for a keystroke in this case, the interrupt 16h ISR will report that there are no keystrokes waiting. If the interrupt 9 pointer catches up with the interrupt 16h pointer, it means the buffer is full. If another keystroke arrives in this situation, the interrupt 9 ISR must not put anything into the buffer. Instead, it simply beeps the PC speaker and discards the incoming keystroke.

Figure 4-9 shows this process. The upper part of the figure shows the (conceptual) circular keyboard buffer and the bell that is rung (actually a speaker beep) when the buffer is full. The lower part of the figure shows the actual physical linear array of memory locations that make up the keyboard buffer.

KEYBOARD BUFFER EXTENDERS

A fast typist can overwhelm the default keyboard buffer. Even a slow typist can do so if the application program is not picking up keystrokes very often. The solution is to make a larger keyboard buffer and modify the INT9 ISR so it uses this larger buffer.

What COMMAND.COM Does with Your Input

When you type on the keyboard, you naturally expect to see what you typed on the screen. Actually, this happens only because some program makes it happen. When you are at the DOS prompt you are really running the COMMAND.COM program (or some alterative command interpreter, such as 4DOS or NDOS). The DOS prompt is put on the screen by that program to tell you it is ready to accept commands.

When you type at the DOS prompt, COMMAND.COM reads each character you type. For most characters, COMMAND.COM just prints its symbol on the screen and keeps a copy of the character in a special command line buffer somewhere inside of itself. If you backspace, COMMAND.COM does two things: First, unless this is the first character of the new command you are creating, COMMAND.COM backs up the cursor one space, prints a space character (to wipe out whatever the last character was that you typed), and then backs up the cursor again (so the next character you type will go into the proper place on the screen). The second thing it does is to forget, in essence, the last character you typed before the backspace.

When you press the Enter key, COMMAND.COM does something completely different. It stops listening for keystrokes and starts trying to figure out what the command you typed is telling it to do. If you typed the name of an internal command (like VER, DIR, MKDIR, etc.), it will execute some code inside of itself to accomplish whatever you asked it to do. If you typed the name of an external command or any other program, COMMAND.COM will attempt to find that program, load it, and let it do its job.

If you press the Escape key before you press the Enter key, COMMAND.COM aborts the command you were creating and lets you start over. DOS prints a backslash character at the end of the line you were typing, then drops down to the next line to let you start composing your command over again.

STORED LAST COMMAND

COMMAND.COM keeps your most recent command even longer than necessary to run the program or do the action you have requested. In fact, if it can, it keeps the command until you type a new command. The old command is kept in the transient part of COMMAND.COM located high up in RAM, just under the video image buffer area. That region is sometimes used by programs, and when it is, COMMAND.COM's transient part is wiped out. Al-

Key	Function Performed by This Key at the DOS Prompt	
	Without DOSKEY	With DOSKEY
F1	Copies characters one by one from previous command line to current command line	
F2	Copies up to specified character from previous command line	
F3	Copies all remaining characters from previous command line	
F4	Skips up to specified character from previous command line	
F5	Replaces previous command line with existing one	
F6	Generates ASCII 26 end-of-file marker (^Z) (Same as Ctrl-Z)	
F7	Generates ASCII 0 null (^@)	Displays all commands stored in memory, with their associated numbers
ALT F7		Deletes all commands stored in memory
F8		Searches memory for a command you want Doskey to display
F9		Prompts you for a command number and displays the command associated with the number you specify
ALT F10		Deletes all macro definitions

Figure 4-10 Function keys at the DOS prompt

though COMMAND.COM knows how to find a fresh copy of itself on the disk so it can easily replace its program code, all memory of the command you last typed command will be gone forever.

COMMAND.COM keeps a copy of your last command, as well as the characters you have typed on your next one, in order to help you with the creation of that next command. The way you get its help is by using the function keys plus, perhaps, the Insert and/or Delete keys. Figure 4-10 shows the meaning that each of the function keys have when you are at the DOS prompt. (For the moment, focus on the left column of meanings; the right column will be explained in the next section.)

While DOS has uses for six function keys, most PC users remember to use only F1 and F3, which really are worth remembering—especially if you are a poor typist. F3 repeats the entire last command (or finishes up one you have only partially retyped). F1 copies a single character from the last command each time you press it. (You can get the same effect by pressing the right-arrow cursor control key.)

As an example, suppose you type `MD TEMP` and press Enter. You have just created a subdirectory called TEMP immediately below the current directory. Now you may want to move to that new subdirectory. The hard way is by typing `CD TEMP` and pressing Enter. The easy way is to type `C`, press function key F3, and press Enter. Three keypresses instead of eight. And that was a relatively simple example.

A more impressive example is if you type this command:

```
COPY A:ALEXANDER.TXT C:\LETTERS\PERSONAL\ALEXANDER.DOC
```

and just after you press the Enter key you suddenly remember that you were supposed to have typed

```
COPY A:ALEXANDER.TXT C:\LETTERS\1993\PERSONAL\ALEXANDER.DOC
```

instead. The hard way to fix things is to retype the whole command. A much easier way is to press F1 enough times to get up to the slash character after `LETTERS`. Then press Insert, type `1993\`, and press F3.

An even easier way, if you remember all the things DOS knows how to do with the function keys, is to press function key F2, then press P. You will see DOS retype the line up to the \ just before the word `PERSONAL` (the first occurrence of the letter P). Now press Insert, type `1993\`, and press F3. You have really saved keystrokes—50 of them in this example—as well as avoiding the possibility of mistyping them again.

That is pretty nice, but you can do even better. Starting with version 5, DOS included a program that will remember not only your most recent command, but all the commands you have typed as far back as you care to ask it to remember them. That command is DOSKEY.

DOSKEY Command Editor

DOSKEY is designed to do two different, but related jobs. One is to remember old commands so you can recall them, edit one, and reissue it. The other job is to remember macro substitutions so you can type an abbreviation for a command or a set of commands and have DOSKEY convert the abbreviation into the full command or set of commands. You can learn all about the

DOSKEY macro capability in Chapter 12. Here we will focus on the DOSKEY old command recall and editing capability.

You load DOSKEY just as you would any other TSR program, by typing its name at the DOS prompt or by having a line in a batch file that invokes it. Many people put a line to invoke DOSKEY in their AUTOEXEC.BAT file. (Editing files is discussed in Chapter 7. The AUTOEXEC.BAT file is discussed in detail in Chapter 12.)

If you just type `DOSKEY` and press Enter, you get DOSKEY in its default configuration. In this mode it has a 512-byte buffer in which it can store old commands (and macros). You can add a number of command line switches and parameters after the name DOSKEY. The one that is of most use here is `/BUFSIZE=nnn` where *nnn* is the number of bytes you'd like DOSKEY to set aside. This buffer is used both to store any macros you define as well as all the old commands that fit.

All the function keys that work at the DOS prompt *without* DOSKEY also work when DOSKEY is loaded, with one exception: F7 no longer generates an ASCII null character; instead, it displays all the commands that DOSKEY is remembering so that you can recall your last command by pressing F3. In addition, you can recall your last command by pressing the up-arrow key. If you press up arrow again, you will get the command before that. In this way, you can go back as far as DOSKEY remembers your commands.

The down arrow, of course, does exactly the opposite thing; it walks you through your old commands in the other direction; PgUp and PgDn take you to the oldest and most recent commands. This does not mean, though, that you have to scroll through your old commands, looking for one you want to reuse. You can find a stored command by content or by address. Just type the first few characters of a command and press F8. DOSKEY will immediately display the first stored command that starts with those characters. Pressing F8 again will show you the next command that starts with those characters.

You can also press F7 to see the stored commands listed for you. Each one will be preceded by a number, starting with 1 for the oldest stored command. Press F9 and enter the number of the command you want and DOSKEY will retrieve it for you.

Once you have retrieved a command you can edit it before you reissue it. In earlier versions of DOS, you could do this by using the Backspace key to erase the end of the command and then type in your modified ending. With DOSKEY, you can do much more. The left- and right-arrow keys move the cursor nondestructively back and forth. Ctrl combined with the left or right arrow will move the cursor a word at a time. Home and End move it to the start or end of the line. Pressing Insert allows you add material in the middle of the line. Pressing Delete removes it one character at a time.

If you wish, you can make DOSKEY default to insert mode by using the `/INSERT` switch when you load it. Then you have to press Insert to get to the overstrike mode. Watch the cursor as you do this. It changes size between insert and overstrike modes. (Reinvoking DOSKEY with the `/OVERSTRIKE` switch will once again make it operate in overstrike mode.)

The last switch that you need to know about is `/HISTORY` (it may be abbreviated as /H). This tells DOSKEY to list all the commands it is storing, but this time without associated numbers. If you redirect this output to a file with a BAT extension, you will have created a batch file that does whatever your last several commands did. You can edit this batch file before you use it if it isn't exactly what you want, but having this as a starting point can save you a lot of retyping.

Tip: To create a batch file quickly, invoke DOSKEY, then type the commands directly from the DOS prompt. Once you're satisfied that you've done what you set out to do, type:

```
DOSKEY /H >MYFILE.BAT
```

If you didn't make any mistakes while entering commands at the DOS prompt, you're done, and you can rerun those commands as needed by running MYFILE. If you've made the usual assortment of typing or syntax errors, you can clean up MYFILE.BAT by typing:

```
EDIT MYFILE.BAT
```

and then remove any mistakes before saving and exiting from EDIT.

There probably will be times when you don't want DOSKEY to continue to remember commands. One instance is when you are about to start some sequence you want it to remember and that later you will dump to a batch file by using the /H switch. Just press Alt-F7 before you start and you will have cleared DOSKEY's buffer of all its stored commands. Another reason for clearing the buffer is if you are about to define a macro and you suspect that there might not be room enough for it in the buffer.

Tip: Before you invest DOSKEY with some huge buffer size, remember that it places its buffer inside the first megabyte of RAM. That is precious real estate. Use only as much as you will need for DOSKEY's buffer. (The minimum buffer size is 256 bytes.)

Surprising Uses for Certain Keys

You've already seen what the function keys do at the DOS prompt in Figure 4-10. They don't always do those things, however. There are a couple of special uses for them during the boot process that are discussed in Chapter 9, but in this section you will learn some other ways the function keys can be used. In particular, you will learn about some programs that quite radically change what those (and sometimes other) keys do.

ANSI Macros

If you first load the ANSI.SYS device driver, you can reprogram just about any key on the keyboard, function keys included, so that when you press the key, it will cause programs to think the keyboard emitted a whole string of characters. One example of how that might be done is to first add a line to your CONFIG.SYS file something like this:

```
DEVICE = C:\DOS\ANSI.SYS
```

(You may have to put in a different path if your copy of ANSI.SYS is not in the DOS directory on the C drive.) Reboot your computer so it will read and act on that new line in the CONFIG.SYS file.

Next, at the command prompt type this line:

```
PROMPT $e[0;134;156p $p$g
```

and press Enter. You won't see anything happen, but it did. You told DOS to send an *ASCII escape sequence* to the console device (your keyboard and screen) each time it normally makes a prompt appear on the screen. The effect of this particular ANSI escape sequence is to reprogram the F12 function key so that when you press it, you will have typed the symbol for the British currency unit, the pound sterling. Try it.

You can restore things to their normal state by rebooting first, then issuing this command

```
PROMPT $e[0;134;0;134p $p$g
```

and then this one

```
PROMPT $p$g
```

These lines assume that you like the appearance of the prompt that `$p$g` causes (for example, C:\> if you are in the root directory of the C drive). This is the same as the default MS-DOS 6 prompt and unlike the default prompt in earlier versions of DOS (which was simply C>).

This just scratches the surface of what you can do with ANSI.SYS and how to do it. You can also reprogram keys by using special ECHO statements in batch files or by using the TYPE or COPY commands to send a file to the console. Chapter 10 describes all of what ANSI.SYS can do. It also explains why creating files with ANSI escape sequences can be a bit difficult and tells you how to get around those difficulties.

Other Ways Keys Change Their Meanings

In general, pressing keys simply sends scan code messages to the system unit. The keyboard controller and the BIOS put either the scan code itself or its ASCII equivalent into the keyboard buffer. What happens from there depends entirely on the program that retrieves those keystrokes.

Commercial keyboard macro programs, such as SuperKey or ProKey, are ordinary TSR programs that hook the keyboard interrupt. (Usually they hook both INT9 and INT16h.) They watch for key combinations that you have defined as macro names and when they see them, they emit the corresponding macro definitions.

This lets you modify keystrokes before they are seen by an application program. This strategy fails, however, if you are running some program that completely takes over keyboard input. One popular example of such a program is Windows.

DOSKEY macros are another way to modify the apparent behavior of your keyboard when you press certain special key sequences. They are really closer to batch files than to simple keyboard redefinition. Chapter 12 explains DOSKEY macros in detail.

How Applications Use Keystrokes

Any way they want! That really is true, and it is pretty much all there is to say about it. You may have thought that if you typed a letter L it would show up as a letter L. It might, but only if the program that receives the keystroke was written to make it show up that way. Alternatively, that same letter key could be a command to the program to do the first item on a menu—or the tenth. There really are no limits to what a programmer can do. Compared to all that possible diversity, DOS is pretty tame. To DOS an L is an L is an L, and it always looks like an L. Still, even to DOS, Ctrl-L is something very different—in fact it is a line feed character (and it shows up on the command line as ^L—which is only one character, despite the fact that it looks like two characters).

Special Power-User Keyboard Tricks

An important aspect of being a power user of any program is learning the tricks of the trade—the shortcuts and workarounds. The special uses for the function keys at the DOS prompt mentioned earlier are examples of the shortcut methods (see Figure 4-10).

HOW TO TYPE ANY ASCII CHARACTER

Technically, you can type only some of the ASCII characters directly on a PC keyboard (Figure 4-6 shows which ones). But there is a way to type absolutely any ASCII character from the keyboard. This trick works at the DOS prompt and also inside most application programs. It will work in even more application programs if, after you press the Alt key, you press a 0 on the numeric keypad before beginning the number you want to use. Here's how: Hold down the Alt key. Now tap out the decimal value of the ASCII character you wish to type. Then release the Alt key. Remember, you must use the numerals on the *numeric keypad*, not the ones at the top of the typewriter section. You won't see anything happen until you have finished typing the numbers and have released the Alt key. Then you will see whatever character you just typed.

One caveat is necessary here. Although you can type any ASCII character this way, it may not empower you quite as much as you might think. For example, you know that if you type the Escape key in the middle of a command line, COMMAND.COM sees that as an instruction to forget everything you have typed so far. You might like to issue a command that included an Escape character—for example if you wished to send a message to the ANSI.SYS driver that included an "ANSI Escape sequence." So maybe you thought, "Aha! I can get around COMMAND.COM by holding down the Alt key and pressing 0, 2, and 7 on the numeric keypad. That should allow me to enter an Escape character into my command." Too bad. What you will have done is produce *exactly* the same effect as pressing the Escape key. COMMAND.COM will wipe out all your efforts so far and force you to start over. You will learn in Chapter 10 how you can send ANSI escape sequences to the screen by using any of several workarounds.

The ANSI numeric keypad number trick comes in handy when you want to type a normal typewriter key—one that you usually press on the keyboard—on a keyboard that is partially broken. If, for example, the N key is broken, you can still use that keyboard. Simply type `Alt-78` for uppercase N or `Alt-110` for the lowercase n. It isn't as easy as pressing the N key, with or without the Shift key, but at least it works. This is a good example of the concept of a workaround. (If you find yourself doing this a lot, you may wish to reprogram some other key to act like the N key—or buy a new keyboard. You can do the former with ANSI.SYS as is explained in Chapter 10.)

ANOTHER SPECIAL USE OF THE ALT KEY

Earlier we said that the Alt key is a shift key, much like the alphabetic shift and Ctrl keys. We pointed out that it differs from them in that there are only two situations in which the Alt key and some other key or keys makes any special sense to DOS. You just learned about one of them: Using the Alt key and the numeric keypad to type any ASCII character.

The other special use is commonly called the "three-finger salute." Press and hold both the Ctrl and the Alt keys, then press the Delete key and you will have rebooted your computer. (If you are working in Windows 3.1 you will have issued only a "local reboot" command. Windows intercepts these keystrokes and acts on them in its preferred fashion.)

SEVERAL CTRL-KEY COMBINATIONS

You already know that the Print Screen key (by itself on an enhanced keyboard and in combination with the Shift key on an 83- or 84-key keyboard) will cause the PC to print a copy of the screen on your printer. What you may not have known is the Ctrl-Print Screen is also a meaningful key combination.

Ctrl-Print Screen and Ctrl-P [ASCII value 17] Hold down Ctrl and press Print Screen. You have just turned on *printer echo.* Do it again and you turn printer echo off. Printer echo means that every character that is sent to the screen also gets sent to your printer.

This can be a very handy way to document what you are doing. Or it can be a horrible nuisance. It is especially bad when you have your printer turned off (or simply off-line) and you accidentally hit Ctrl-Print Screen. As soon as the very next character is sent to the screen your PC will appear to freeze. What is happening is that the PC is waiting for the printer to acknowledge receipt of that character. Until it does so, the PC will do nothing other than wait.

(This presumes that you have set the printer time-out to forever, which you could have done by issuing the command

```
MODE LPT1: RETRY=P
```

Even if you have not reset the time-out interval, it may take a minute or two before the printer times out, and for that period of time your PC will seem completely frozen.)

Tip: If this happens, one way to get out of the lockup is to physically disconnect the printer from the parallel port. (This will not work on a printer connected to a serial port.)

Ctrl-P has the same effect as Ctrl-Print Screen on most PCs. This is a leftover from the CP/M days, when personal computers did not have a Print Screen key.

Ctrl-Num Lock This key combination was IBM's initial choice for a means to stop the PC from scrolling information off the screen. Even when the Pause key was introduced (on the enhanced keyboard), Ctrl-Num Lock still worked as it had before.

To pause your PC in mid-stride, either press Pause or Ctrl-Num Lock. To get it to resume its activities, press any key other than the Pause, the Num Lock key (or one of the other lock keys), or any of the shift keys. The most convenient key is usually the Spacebar or the Enter key.

Ctrl-Scroll Lock or Ctrl-Pause (also Ctrl-C [ASCII value 3]) Look at the front face of the Scroll Lock key and, if you have one, the Pause key. One of them will have the word Break printed on it. That key, in combination with the Ctrl key, is used to tell the PC you'd like it to stop whatever it is doing. The PC will not always respond, however—at least not right away. It often waits until it is good and ready before noticing that you have pressed this key combination.

Normally, the PC checks the keyboard buffer to see if there is a pending Ctrl-Break key combination just before it is about to write something on the screen or read a character from the keyboard. You can make it check more often by adding a line to your AUTOEXEC.BAT file or your CONFIG.SYS file that reads `BREAK=ON` or merely `BREAK ON`. (This is the only directive that is valid with exactly the same syntax in both the CONFIG.SYS and AUTOEXEC.BAT files.) When BREAK is ON, the PC checks the keyboard buffer just before it reads from or writes to any device, not just the console device.

Be aware that BREAK is merely another toggle that the BIOS keeps track of by the value in a bit in low memory. Any program can ask DOS to turn BREAK on or off. Most programs that turn BREAK off do so because their programmers thought it unwise to let you interrupt them in the middle of their work. Unfortunately, these programs often don't set the BREAK flag back to its original value when it's through working. Therefore, no matter what you set BREAK to in your AUTOEXEC.BAT or CONFIG.SYS file, you may have to check from time to time to see if it still is set the way you want. In particular, if you are about to start some long task that you fear may go awry, you may wish to check the status of BREAK just before you begin. To do that, simply type `BREAK` at the DOS prompt and press Enter.

In another leftover from the CP/M days, most PCs will respond to Ctrl-C in almost the same fashion as they do to Ctrl-Break, but this is not 100-percent so. There are situations in which only Ctrl-Break will do. But if you find Ctrl-C easier to remember or easier to type, try it. It may work.

Neither of these will stop every runaway PC, but they are the nearest thing to a panic button that you have, short of pressing the reset button or invoking the three-finger salute (Ctrl-Alt-Del).

Ctrl-S [ASCII value 20] Ctrl-Num Lock or Pause will stop your PC in its tracks. Pressing (almost) any other key will get it going again. You can't simply toggle the PC between running and pausing by pressing one key combination over and over. Well, you can't do it by using the officially supported Ctrl-Num Lock or Pause.

Most PCs will allow you to start and stop their screen displays by pressing Ctrl-S. If this works, pressing Ctrl-S again will very likely start it running once more. Actually, Ctrl-S to stop and Ctrl-Q to restart are the official ANSI-supported way to control a serial terminal to a mainframe or minicomputer using XON/XOFF data flow controls.

Ctrl-G [ASCII value 7] Originally, this key combination was defined for use with teletypewriters. These machines allowed one operator to type on many machines in remote locations all at the same time. Whenever the operators reached the end of a story or came to some really juicy news, they would press Ctrl-G several times. Each press of Ctrl-G would ring the bell on the teletype machine, which alerted anyone in the vicinity to come running and see what was going on.

PCs respond whenever a Ctrl-G is sent to the console (meaning it is sent to the screen) by beeping the speaker. (This is the nearest thing a PC has to a bell.) The bell code is not displayed on the screen; it is merely acted upon.

Ctrl-H [ASCII 8], Ctrl-I [ASCII 9], Ctrl-J [ASCII 10], Ctrl-L [ASCII 12], and Ctrl-M [ASCII 13] These key combinations primarily are equivalent to certain of the control keys on the PC keyboard. Thus, you could use them on a keyboard on which one of those control keys did not work. Ctrl-J and Ctrl-M are a partial exception to that rule. Ctrl-L is completely special; there is no key on the keyboard that types the equivalent of the Ctrl-L code.

Typing Ctrl-H is the same as pressing the Backspace key; Ctrl-I is like Tab; Ctrl-J is a line feed; Ctrl-M is a carriage return. Normally, when you press the Enter key you see the cursor jump back to the left side, and the screen image scrolls up one line, or the cursor drops down one line. That action is both a carriage return and a line feed. You press only one key on the keyboard (Enter), but you get the effect of two control codes. That is the partial exception to Ctrl-J and Ctrl-M just mentioned.

If you look inside any pure ASCII text file for a PC, you will find that every line ends with both a Ctrl-M and a Ctrl-J. This is not true of many document files (such as those a typical word processor creates), which may have a single Ctrl-M code to mark the end of each paragraph and nothing that is obvious to the eye to show where the lines break.

Even pure ASCII text files may not have the Ctrl-M and Ctrl-J characters at the end of every line. While it is the PC standard for such files, not every application creates them that way. Other computers, running other operating software, may use a different standard for text files. UNIX, for example, ends every line with just a Ctrl-J.

The Ctrl-L character was explained earlier in this chapter. It is called the form feed character, and tells a printer to start a new page.

Ctrl-Z [ASCII 26] The last of the useful Ctrl-letter key combinations is Ctrl-Z. In CP/M this was used to signal the end of a file. Some people still refer to it as the EOF (end-of-file) character. PCs don't need an end-of-file character, as DOS keeps track of the length of files down to the byte.

But DOS also supports some specialness about the Ctrl-Z character. If you try to TYPE a file that has a Ctrl-Z character in it, you will find that the TYPE command will stop reading the file at that point. If you copy a file with an embedded Ctrl-Z in it without telling COPY to keep going, it will stop there also. Pressing function key F6 at the DOS prompt generates a Ctrl-Z character. This can be useful when you are creating a simple text file by using of the COPY CON trick (explained in Chapter 7).

SOME WAYS TO GET SNEAKY AND ROUNDABOUT WITH DOS

DOS allows you to slip in extras and be very indirect at times, which is merely another way of saying that there are some more important keys and an important new concept to discuss—*redirection.* First we will describe the keys that let you slip in extra (and get rid of superfluous) characters; then we will explain redirection.

The Insert key allows you to toggle between insert and overstrike modes. This can be most helpful when you are replaying an old command line, and you realize you have to add some extra characters. If, on the other hand, you have to excise some extraneous characters, the Delete key will do the job.

The distinction between insert and overstrike modes is also commonly made in editors, including the DOS EDIT program. DOS tries to signal which mode you are in by the shape or size of the cursor, although unfortunately, the shapes it uses don't always seem to go with the mode they indicate. (This is discussed further in the next chapter.)

Three more special characters are the piping symbol and the two redirection characters. These allow you to make DOS commands look somewhere other than the keyboard for input and send their output elsewhere than to the screen. (Not all output can be redirected, however. Error messages, in particular, tend not to be redirectable. This is understandable, as you often will not look at the output file you create until sometime later on, and you probably need to know about any errors right away.)

If, in a DOS command line, you have a less than symbol (<), DOS understands the command to be only the part you type before that symbol. It assumes that whatever follows that symbol will be a valid file or device from which it can take input when the commands looks for data. The greater than symbol (>) tells DOS to send any output normally destined for the screen to whatever device or file is named after the > symbol. (Technically, the only output that gets redirected is anything that would have gone to the *standard output device*; what is not redirected is whatever might have been meant for the *standard error device*—even though both the standard output and standard error devices are normally the screen in the absence of redirection.)

Sometimes you will see command lines with two greater than symbols together (>>). This is also a way of redirecting output. The difference between > and >> only shows up when the target of the redirection is a file. Then > says to open a *new* file with the specified name. The >> symbol says that if a file of the specified name already exits, just open it up and add the redirected material to its end. The difference is sometimes described by saying that > says to overwrite, and >> says to append to a file.

The last of the redirection symbols is called the piping symbol. This vertical bar (¦), which has a small break in it on the keyboard and screen (but not always in print), tells DOS that the output of whatever precedes it is to become input to whatever follows it. Think of the piping symbol as a > followed by a <. (This does not mean that typing a command with >< in it would work. It won't.)

For a simple example of these ideas, type this command

```
ECHO. ¦ DATE ¦ FIND "is"
```

and see what happens. (Notice the period after `ECHO` and the space after it. They are significant parts of this command.) Compare what this command does with what happens when you simply type

```
DATE
```

and press the Enter key. In the first case you get the current date and are immediately returned to the DOS prompt. In the latter case, after showing you the current date, DOS prompts you to give it the correct date. Only when you answer the query, by at least pressing Enter, will you get back to the DOS prompt. (The DOS command, FIND, is one of the DOS *filter* programs discussed in Chapter 7.)

This complicated looking command works, but just how may not be clear to you. Knowing what DOS does to execute this command will help you explain some very strangely named files that may show up on your disk from time to time. If you have a command with one or more pipe symbols in it, DOS construes it as several commands. (This, and using DOSKEY are the only exceptions to the rule that a single command line can contain only a single DOS command.)

DOS takes the first part of the line, up to the first pipe symbol and executes it, redirecting its output to a file it creates (and which it names with a wonderfully obscure name like DGAGABAC). When that command is done working, DOS executes the second section of the command line, this time redirecting its input from that arbitrarily named file. The output may be supplied to the screen, or it may go into another file, which this time may be named DGAGABAH, or some such. Don't try to make sense of these names. There isn't a Da-Gaga-Bac whose file this is. DOS simply makes up names that are unique. (The names also often include numerals. Essentially any legal characters for a file name may appear in them.) Once the entire command line has been processed, all these temporary files are erased.

The only time you will find these files is when you look at the erased files in your TEMP directory (or in any directory, if you haven't defined a TEMP variable), or if somehow DOS got interrupted before it could get around to erasing those files. Actually, the latter case happens often enough that many people have seen these names and wondered about them.

Tip: If you don't have enough room on the current disk (or on your TEMP drive if you have defined a TEMP variable in your environment), DOS will simply fail to do the piped operation, and it may not give you an error message. (Environment variables and how they can be set are discussed in Chapter 11.)

Other Input Devices

There are many alternate input devices on the market. They are popular for use with programs that present graphical user interface—GUI (pronounced gooey)—kinds of programs.

Mice, Trackballs, and Graphics Tablets

Many people have found that while they can type commands very rapidly, nothing beats a pointing device for selecting a region of text or an object out of a collection. The most popular pointing device is a mouse. Trackballs and graphics tablets are a distant second and third in popularity, but their users often swear by them. Figure 4-11 shows what some of these devices look like.

Basically a mouse is a box-like input device with one, two, or three buttons on it. When you move the mouse, its circuits relay signals that move a cursor on the screen. The buttons are "clicked" to choose commands from menus, select text to edit, move objects, and much more. (One-button mice are usually used on Apple computers, but the Microsoft two-button mouse has set the standard for PCs. Logitech and others make three button mice, but very few programs take advantage of the extra button.)

There are several kinds of mice, with different mechanisms to sense motion and various shapes, with or without a wire connection to the computer. All of them do the same thing, though, and for our purposes they are equivalent.

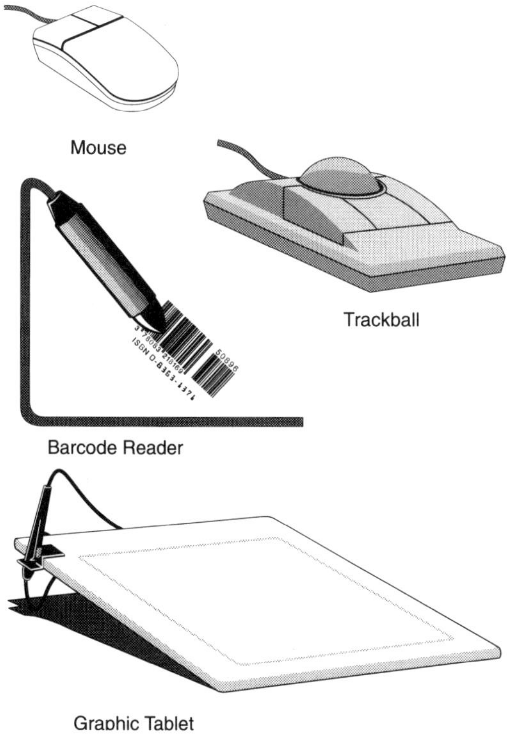

Figure 4-11 Some popular alternate input devices

A trackball is a device designed to replace a mouse and moves the mouse pointer on-screen when you rotate a ball that is embedded in the keyboard or in a box next to the keyboard.

Graphics tablets come with a pointing object, usually resembling a pen or pencil. Point somewhere on that tablet with that object and the cursor jumps to the corresponding location on the screen. This is called an absolute input device as opposed to a relative one. Usually, there is one switch in the tip of the pointing object, and pressing the tablet with the pen sends a signal to the computer just as clicking the left mouse button does. Often, there is at least one and sometimes many other buttons on the pointing object, corresponding to the other buttons on a mouse.

Many graphic tablets also offer a mode in which they emulate a mouse (thus providing a form of relative motion input). This is not their primary use, however.

Using the Keyboard As a Mouse

One purpose of a mouse is to point to and select objects or regions on the screen. You can often do these things from the keyboard as well. The cursor arrows let you move the cursor to a location. And if the program permits, you can then select either the object pointed to, or while holding the selection key, move the cursor to select a region.

Microsoft Word for DOS is typical of this behavior. Point to a character, press Shift, and move the cursor. You will see a range of characters highlighted. By changing the program's mode of operation, you can select either lines of text or rectangular regions on the screen.

Using a Mouse or Graphics Tablet instead of the Keyboard

The opposite is also possible. You can sometimes use a pointing device in lieu of a keyboard. This is usually done by providing a region in which a map of a keyboard is displayed. Keys can then be picked off that map. This is not very fast compared to typing, but it can be very convenient if you are holding a pen-like pointing device over a tablet and need to pick a single character or two to form a command.

Barcode Readers and Keyboard "Wedges"

Barcodes have become ubiquitous. Nearly everything sold in the United States is barcoded. With a suitable scanning device, you can read the bar code information automatically. Simply pass a wand over a coded page and you may be able to enter entire paragraphs of prose or, more likely, some important data that must not be mistyped.

Most barcode readers connect to a PC's serial port. Some are called *keyboard wedges*. These latter devices connect between the keyboard and the PC system unit. The data read off the barcode labels is inserted as if that information had been typed on the keyboard. This is a very convenient way to enter certain kinds of data with very high reliability and accuracy.

DOS Keyboard and Other Input-Related Commands

DOS provides many functions that affect input. COMMAND.COM is the most important DOS program in this connection, as it is the one that provides the DOS prompt and interprets your keystrokes.

The device driver ANSI.SYS and the TSR program DOSKEY both modify how COMMAND.COM "sees" the keyboard. The device drivers, DISPLAY.SYS and PRINTER.SYS, and the TSR program, NLSFUNC, in combination with the CONFIG.SYS directive, COUNTRY, and the DOS external commands, MODE (with the CP PREP option), CHCP, and KEYB, provide foreign language and country-specific support.

One more DOS program is available that affects input. It is not often used, but when you need it nothing else will do. This is the CTTY command. Its purpose is to make DOS treat one of the alternate input/output devices as if it were the console. Type the command

```
CTTY COM1:
```

and from the instant you press Enter until this command has been rescinded, your PC will ignore the keyboard and display nothing on the screen. (This does not erase what is already showing on the screen; it merely prevents any new information from going there. Other programs may write to the screen, but DOS won't.)

If you have used the MODE command to set up COM1: to an appropriate baud rate and other communications parameters, you can hook any teletype-like device (which could be another PC) to the first serial port and DOS will treat it as if it were your keyboard and screen.

There are only two ways to undo the CTTY command. One is from the remote terminal. Type the command

```
CTTY CON
```

which returns control to the normal console. The only other way is to reboot your PC.

One of the principal uses for the CTTY command is to allow a remote PC to send a copy of a file transfer program over a serial link to your PC. Use this if you need that program and don't yet have a copy. Thereafter, you can use the file transfer program instead of CTTY. You will learn more about file transfer programs in Chapter 14.

The DOS Power Tools Keyboard Programs

In addition to the KBTEST and KBSYNC programs, KEYS lets you assign up to four sets of character strings to each of the twelve function keys. KEYSCOPE shows you the make and break key scan codes for any key.

C H A P T E R

5

◆ ◆ ◆ ◆ ◆

The Screen

While keyboards may be used or ignored, all PC users are very aware of the computer screen. It is, after all, what you look at most of the time. It's obvious that some PCs have monochrome screens and others can display things in color, but this is not the only difference between PC video setups. Power users need to know what their options are and how to get the most from the video display hardware they already have. That is what you will learn in this chapter.

The most important issues involve performance and memory management. Before you can understand the issues, let alone the solutions, however, you have to know something about how your *video display subsystem* works. (For starters, we will define this term in just a couple of paragraphs.)

Function and Importance of the Screen

The screen and keyboard (what programmers call the console device) form the link from you to your PC. Nearly all information you put into and receive from your PC goes via this link. The only other output channel that gets much use on the typical PC is the printer, which we discuss in Chapter 8.

A distinction can be made between the central portion of your PC and its video subsystem. The latter has three parts: the screen (monitor), the circuitry that forms the images (the video adapter), and the cable that connects the two. In some PCs the video adapter is built onto the motherboard. Many more have a video adapter on a plug-in card. There are many different kinds of video display adapters, ranging from the super-simple monochrome text displays to the fanciest super-VGA and XGA cards and a number of even fancier, proprietary video cards. The amount of RAM on these display adapters ranges from a measly 4KB to several megabytes.

The monitor works closely with the display adapter, and the two must be closely matched to work properly. Later in the chapter, we'll give you a quick overview of the different choices you have in this marketplace, but first you need to know exactly what the crucial jargon means.

IBM set the tone for the future when it first introduced the PC. Instead of simply having a standard video display, it offered buyers two alternatives. One was a very nice monochrome text display with crisp, stable, well-formed characters. The other offered a state-of-the-art (for small computers) color graphics display. Both are archaic by today's standards, although there are still plenty of them being used.

Text Mode vs. Graphics Mode

Basically, text mode works faster and is less expensive to implement; graphics mode is able to show more information on the screen. As a result, you must choose between these virtues: speed and low cost, or greater information display capacity at a higher cost. The key difference between these two modes of image creation is the way the computer constructs and stores the image on the video display adapter. For both text and graphics screen images, the video display adapter stores information about what appears where on the screen in its image buffer RAM. Another section of the circuitry on the display adapter is constantly reading the information stored in the image buffer and sending the necessary signals to the screen to cause it to display the stored image.

Once an image has been loaded into the image buffer RAM on the video card, that image can be displayed indefinitely with no further work on the part of the CPU. The output circuitry on the video display adapter, on the other hand, is constantly busy, redrawing the entire screen image many times each second.

In text mode, the screen is divided into character cells. The most common arrangement is 25 rows with 80 characters in each row. A display adapter that is operating in text mode, therefore, must store information on what to display in each of 2,000 character cells.

A text mode video display adapter stores 2 bytes of information for each character cell. The first byte tells which character (symbol) will appear there;

the second byte stores the attributes of that character. Thus, an entire text mode screen image can be stored in only 4KB of RAM.

Monochrome text images store effectively just four bits of attribute information for each character cell, but a whole byte is used for each cell's attributes anyway. These 4 bits determine if the character is extra-bright or of only regular intensity, if it is to be displayed in *reverse video* (a black character on a light background), if it will blink, and if it is to be underlined. There are fourteen combinations of these effects that can be displayed.

The color text attribute byte stores four bits of foreground color information (these bits specify the color of the symbol itself), three bits of background color information (to specify the color of the rest of the character cell), and one bit to specify if the character is to blink. (This use of the attribute byte is the same for all PC color text displays, from the earliest CGA to the latest XGA. For text images, these display adapters differ only in how well formed the characters are and how many screenfuls of text information they can store.)

Figure 5-1 shows how the bits of the attribute bytes are used in both monochrome and color text display adapters. The middle chart ("Monochrome text possibilities") shows only half of the possibilities. The other half are exactly the same as those shown, but with the character blinking. The binary numbers at the right side have an x in place of some of the bits, which can be either a 1 or a 0 without affecting the visual appearance of the character being displayed. The bottom table shows the foreground and background colors that correspond to all the possible bit patterns on a color card.

In graphics mode the video display adapter must store information about each dot (called a *pixel*) on the screen. The amount of information that must be stored depends, therefore, on the number of dots on the screen, which is also called the screen resolution.

The original MDA used a 9 × 14 matrix for its characters. To display 80 columns and 25 rows of characters of this size, the MDA had to be able to draw 720 pixels on each of 350 rows. About a year after the PC was introduced, the Hercules company introduced a clone of the MDA with a difference: It was able to generate the same 25 rows of crisp, stable text, and it was able to generate graphic images at the same screen resolution as the MDA. The Hercules Graphics Card (HGC) actually used only 348 rows of 720 pixels; they did not need the last two scan lines.

IBM was able to get away with putting only 4KB of RAM on the MDA, as that was sufficient to store one entire text mode (80 × 25 row) image with 2 bytes (character and attribute) for each location. Hercules had to put a lot more RAM on their HGC card. It needed to have 2 bits for each of the 720 × 348 locations so they could have the dot off, on, or bright. This works out to 31,200 bytes. They actually put 64KB of RAM on the card, allowing it to store two full bit-mapped graphic images. (This design has become so popular that

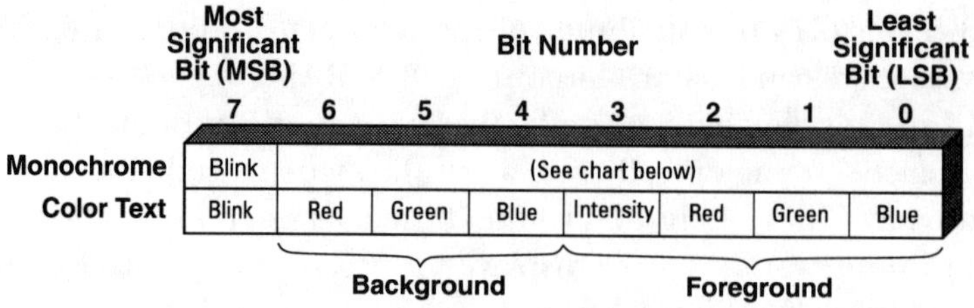

Monochrome text possibilities

Visual effect	Attribute values for which this effect occurs (shown in hexadecimal and binary)	
Black on black (invisible text)	0 or 8	
Underlined normal text on black	1	
Normal text on black	2 3 4 5 6 7 A B C D E F 18 19 1A 1B 1C 1D 1E 1F 28 29 2A 2B 2C 2D 2E 2F 38 39 3A 3B 3C 3D 3E 3F 40 41 42 43 44 45 46 47 50 51 52 53 54 55 56 57 60 61 62 63 64 65 66 67 71 72 73 74 75 76 77	x000 0xxx x000 1xxx x001 1xxx x010 1xxx x011 1xxx x100 0xxx x101 0xxx x110 0xxx x111 0xxx
Underlined high-intensity text on black	9	
High-intensity text on black	10 11 12 13 14 15 16 17 20 21 22 23 24 25 26 27 30 31 32 33 34 35 36 37 48 49 4A 4B 4C 4D 4E 4F 58 59 5A 5B 5C 5D 5E 5F 68 69 6A 6B 6C 6D 6E 6F 79 7A 7B 7C 7D 7E 7F	x001 0xxx x010 0xxx x011 0xxx x100 1xxx x101 1xxx x110 1xxx x111 1xxx
Reverse-video, normal intensity	70	
Reverse-video, high-intensity	78	

Color text possibilities

Bit Pattern R	G	B	Background Color	Foreground Color (I = 0)	Foreground Color (I = 1)
0	0	0	Black	Black	Dim White
0	0	1	Blue	Blue	Bright Blue
0	1	0	Green	Green	Bright Green
0	1	1	Cyan	Cyan	Bright Cyan
1	0	0	Red	Red	Bright Red
1	0	1	Magenta	Magenta	Bright Magenta
1	1	0	Brown	Brown	Bright Yellow
1	1	1	White	White	Bright White

Figure 5-1 Character attributes for text mode screen displays

many clone video card makers supply them. The generic name for them is a *monochrome graphics adapter,* or MGA. It is no longer possible to buy a simple text-only monochrome card like the original MDA.)

IBM's CGA card also had 2 bits per dot in order to form graphic images (called the medium resolution mode). This was done to allow those images to be displayed in four colors. To save RAM, IBM designed the CGA display adapter to have fewer on-screen dots than the MDA. The character cell was set at 8 × 8 (instead of 9 × 14). This works out for an 80 column, 25 row screen at 640 pixels per row and 200 rows. The RAM required was exactly 16,000 bytes, so IBM put 16KB (16,384 bytes) of RAM on the CGA card. That was four times as much RAM as on the MDA, but IBM thought its customers could probably afford it. If the company had tried to make the CGA card display text as well as the MDA card *and* do bit-mapped graphics, it would have had to use twice as much RAM on the card and that would have priced it right out of the market.

But times have changed (and RAM prices fallen). Now, the standard entry-level business PC has a video card with at least a quarter megabyte of RAM on it. Still, if you don't need graphics, you can buy a really inexpensive video card that does only monochrome text and Hercules-compatible monochrome graphics. These MGAs have totally replaced the original IBM monochrome text-only cards.

It takes a lot more memory to store a graphics screen image than a text-based one, and graphic images also require the CPU to work harder creating them, which is one reason that any graphical user interface runs slower than a pure text application.

> **Note:** Not all text-only screen images are actually text mode images. It is possible to use a video card in one of its graphics modes and make the image come out pure text. From the point of view of the CPU and video card, this is a graphics screen. The PC is not able to draw such a screen any faster than it can draw any complicated graphic image.

Colors and Palettes

Color displays easily pay for themselves in improved productivity in many applications. This was not always the case, however. The early CGA displays were rejected because of hard-to-read typefaces. Users were willing to put up with single-color characters to get the crisply formed, rock solid letters of an MDA display.

Now that EGA and the even better VGA video display subsystems are so inexpensive, there is little reason not to have color, and many reasons to have it. Most program designers, especially for Windows programs, expect you to have a color system.

For all the advantages of color, one disadvantage is that storing color images can take more memory than monochrome ones—sometimes a lot more. A black-and-white image requires storing 1 bit of information for each pixel on the screen. (If the bit is a 0, the corresponding pixel will be black; if the bit is 1, the pixel will be white.) But as soon as the pixels take on additional colors, the video card must store more than 1 bit for each pixel. The rule is: Raise 2 to the power of the number of bits your video card stores per pixel. The result is the number of simultaneous on-screen colors that video card can display. Therefore, cards that store 2 bits per pixel can display four-color images, cards that store 4 bits per pixel can display sixteen-color images, and cards with 8 bits per pixel can display images with 256 colors. The most advanced video cards store 24 or even 32 bits per pixel. These cards can make each pixel display any one of an astounding 16,777,216 colors.

If you use a modern video card (an EGA, VGA, or a more advanced model), it is able to send color information to the screen. The image may be formed in its image buffer with only 1 bit per pixel, 4 bits per pixel, etc., and that number determines the number of different colors that you can include in the image at one time. But it does not determine what those colors are.

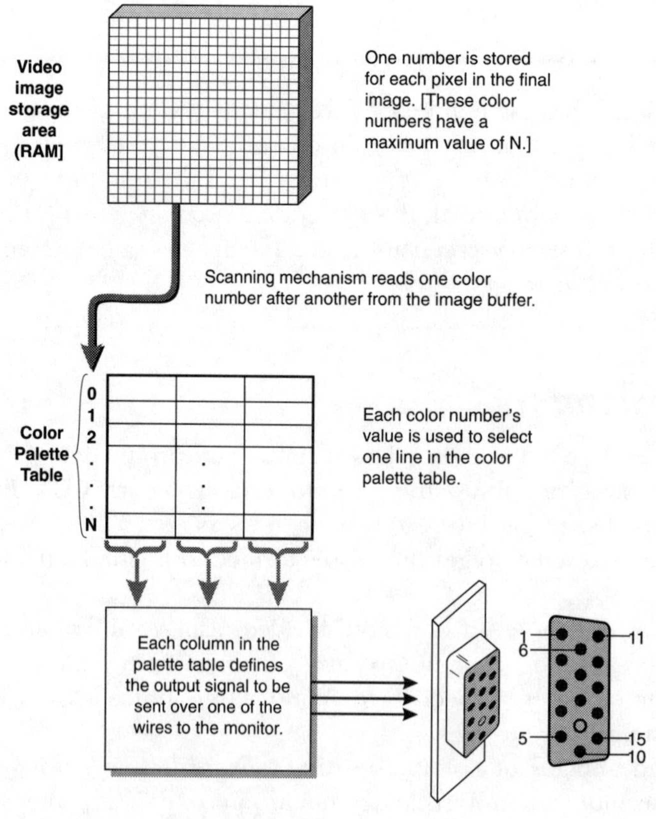

Figure 5-2 Pixels and palettes

The circuitry that scans the image buffer, generates the signals, and sends them to the monitor forms graphic images in this way: It reads the color number at each pixel location; then, in most cases, it uses that number as an index into a table called the *palette lookup table*. In the specified row of the table the circuitry finds several more numbers, each of which describes the signal to put on a particular wire to the monitor. Figure 5-2 shows this process conceptually.

Figure 5-2 shows the process in a general way, but it does not show the details for any of the popular video cards. We will go into those details shortly; first there is one more important aspect of any computer display system that we need to discuss.

Cursors

There are many forms of cursors, and it is possible to encounter more than one kind on the screen at once. One cursor is merely a highlighted line of text, often used in a menu to indicate which option you are about to select. A text cursor points to the place where your next character will appear, and a mouse cursor points to the place on the screen to be affected if you click the mouse button.

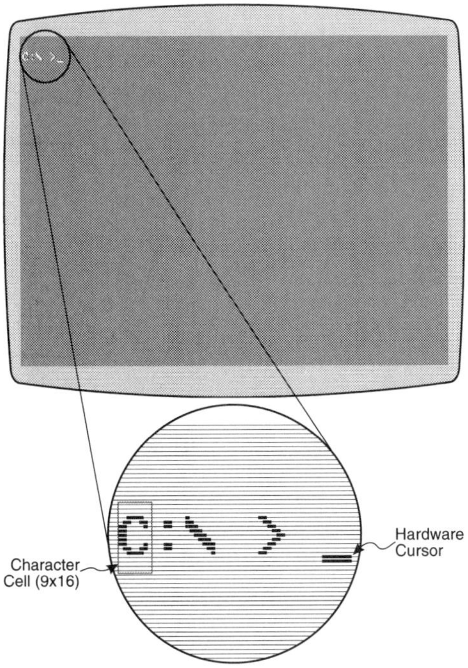

Figure 5-3 The DOS prompt and default hardware cursor

Hardware Cursor

Figure 5-3 shows the usual DOS prompt cursor. This figure is a negative image; normally, you see white letters on a black screen. The fine horizontal lines indicate the path followed by the electron beam as it traces out the raster on the tube face. The wider black bars represent where the beam is turned on; thus, the pixels are shining brightly. This figure can't, however, show that the cursor is blinking on and off two times per second.

The dot prompt cursor is also called the hardware cursor because it is created by some special circuits on the video display adapter. The other cursors discussed in this section are considered software cursors. They get added to the image by the CPU.

Software Cursors

Figure 5-4 shows a variety of cursors. The upper portion of this figure is a close-up view of a few character cells, and in some of them are examples of the text cursor. Again, the thin horizontal lines represent the path of the electron beam. The black regions show where the beam is turned on. The large grey boxes outline the character cells. The lower-left portion of the

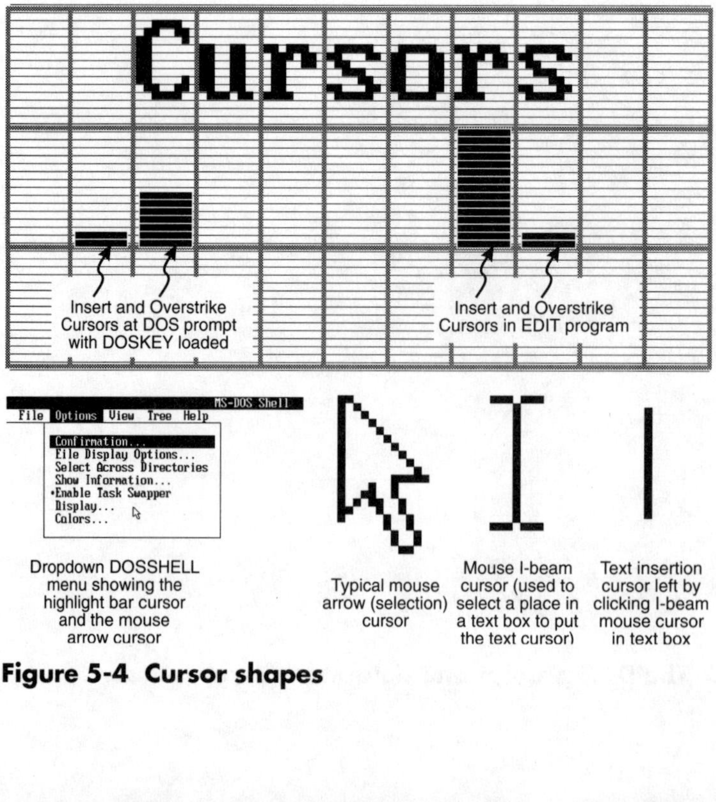

Figure 5-4 Cursor shapes

figure shows, at a much lower magnification, a text menu with a highlight bar cursor. The lower-right shows some typical graphical cursors.

You can change the appearance of the hardware cursor somewhat by using a third-party utility program like the Norton Control Center (a component of the Norton Utilities), but not very many people bother because about all you can do is make it taller or shorter. On some video displays you can make it into two bars: one near the top of the character cell and one near the bottom.

GUI Cursors

The mouse cursor on a GUI screen can take many forms. Usually, it is a small arrow angled either to the left or the right. When the mouse cursor is used to resize a window it generally turns into a two- or four-headed arrow. While dragging handles on an object in a drawing program, it often becomes a large plus sign. When entering text into a dialog box, the text cursor usually is either a vertical bar or a bar with serifs on top and bottom (called the I-beam cursor).

TEXT MODE MOUSE CURSORS

In text mode, creating a mouse cursor is a bit of a problem because you want an indicator that looks different from the hardware (text) cursor. The popular solution has been to make the mouse cursor a full character cell of reversed video. Recently, though, a number of programs have been very cleverly programmed so that on EGA and VGA video systems the arrow mouse cursor closely resembles that used on a graphics screen. This cursor even moves smoothly, and does not jump a character cell at a time. But not many programs use this strategy, because it adds so much programming complexity. Done well, however, it is very effective.

Two or More Cursors On Screen

One typical case of two cursors appearing on the screen at once is in a text-based program that incorporates mouse usage. One cursor is for the keyboard (the typing insertion point); the other cursor is for mouse pointing actions. Another case is in a spreadsheet program, in which, typically, the cell you are editing is highlighted in some way. You move that highlight using the cursor keys or the mouse.

On a GUI screen, you will often have both a text cursor (usually an I-beam) and the mouse cursor. Often, you can reprogram the shapes of these cursors quite radically. (For example, in Windows, by use of a third-party utility such as Magic Cursor, you can make your mouse cursor resemble a bomber, turn the hourglass cursor into a calendar, and alter other cursors in still other ways.)

Two Monitors

Although most PCs have only one screen, some have two independent screens. Usually, this is done so that one screen can show an image being edited while the other screen shows a menu of image editing commands. Often, the first screen is a very high-resolution color screen, and the second is a monochrome screen.

If both monitors are connected to typical PC video cards (one to a VGA and one to an MGA card, for example), then only one monitor will be active at any moment. The active monitor will have an active (blinking) text cursor and a mouse cursor. The inactive screen will have a static image (possibly including a text cursor, but one that is no longer blinking).

In this situation, the DOS `MODE` command can be used to switch between the two screens. The `MODE MONO` command activates the monochrome screen, and `MODE CO80` activates the color screen (in its default 80-column text mode).

Another arrangement of two monitors uses one standard PC video card and one proprietary, nonstandard one. In this case, both monitors may be active, but only when running special programs that are capable of communicating with both screens. At the DOS prompt only the standard PC video display will be active.

Video Subsystem

The next sections describe some key parameters of a computer video system, and they must be considered in order to make wise choices of video cards and monitors and to know what is reasonable to expect any given system to do.

Graphic Image Resolution

As already explained, graphic images consist of dots. The resolution most commonly quoted describes the number of dots per scan line and the number of scan lines inside the active image area. In this language, EGA images have resolutions up to 640 × 350; VGA has a standard resolution of 640 × 480; and super EGA and super VGA can have higher resolutions, with a maximum of 1024 × 768. XGA starts at 1024 × 768 and goes as high as 1280 × 1024. Some proprietary video display systems go all the way up to 4096 × 3072.

Whether or not you can actually see all those dots is determined by several things: first is the size of the dots as they are drawn on the screen. If they are too large, each dot will partially overlap its neighbors. Conversely is the dot pitch, which is the size of the smallest dot that a monitor can display on screen. Finally, there is the video bandwidth of the monitor, which determines how quickly the electron beam can be turned on and off. That, too, puts a limit on how many distinct dots you can see on a line, no matter how many the video card may be trying to draw. If you try to display an image with more pixels than can be resolved by the monitor, you will see your picture, but it will look blurry or smeared.

In addition to the image area described by the number of pixels per line and the number of active scan lines, there is a border area in which no image information can be written, but which, nonetheless, may be illuminated if the border color is anything other than black. Few VGA systems have their border color set to anything other than black.

Text Mode Resolution

In text mode, the relevant resolution numbers are the number of characters per row and the number of rows. There is, of course, a close relationship between the graphic resolution, the size of the character cell, and the text mode resolution.

For example, on an EGA screen with 640 × 350 pixels, it is possible to draw 80 columns and 25 rows with each character cell 8 pixels wide and 14 pixels high. VGA uses a different pixel resolution in text mode. The character cell is 9 × 16 in text mode, leading to a pixel resolution of 720 × 400 for the usual 80 columns and 25 rows.

Interlace

Another feature of video display systems is that some are interlaced and some are not. In a non-interlaced system, the electron beam paints the image a dot at a time across each row, and row after row until it reaches the bottom of the screen. Then it starts over again at the top. An interlace system separates the rows into two groups (the odd-numbered and even-numbered ones). The beam traces all the even-numbered lines first, then the odd ones, then the even ones again, which is to say that it paints only half the screen with each pass (see Figure 5-5).

The advantage to interlace is that you achieve higher resolution, but because images are not refreshed quickly, rapidly moving images streak and/or flicker.

If the image has little vertical contrast from one scan line to the next, interlace is a good strategy. If, however, you are doing a CAD drawing or

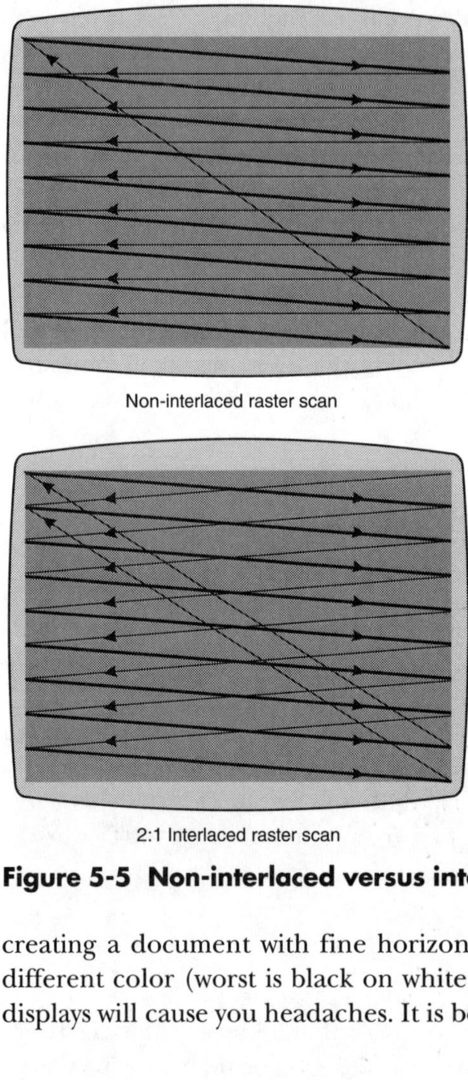

Figure 5-5 Non-interlaced versus interlaced raster scans

creating a document with fine horizontal lines on a background of a very different color (worst is black on white or white on black), then interlaced displays will cause you headaches. It is best to buy a non-interlaced monitor.

Color Depth and Palette Size

Earlier in this chapter, in the section "Colors and Palettes," a general description of how color numbers get turned into actual, on-screen colors was given (Figure 5-2). This section goes into greater detail of this process for four of the most popular video display system designs.

Color depth simply means how many bits are used to define the color of a single pixel. Think of the map of numbers used to describe the entire screen as a set of single-bit maps with one bit in each map for each pixel on the screen. The number of these maps is the number of bits of information stored per pixel, and it is called the color depth.

Usually, the color numbers specify the color of the dot that will appear on the screen somewhat indirectly. The color number is used as in index into a table, called the *palette lookup table*, whose contents specify the actual color that will appear on the screen. The original IBM color graphics adapter (CGA) operating in its medium resolution mode is a simple example (see Figure 5-6).

The outputs from the palette table are bits that tell the display circuitry which of the output lines to turn on or off. CGA cards have four TTL outputs

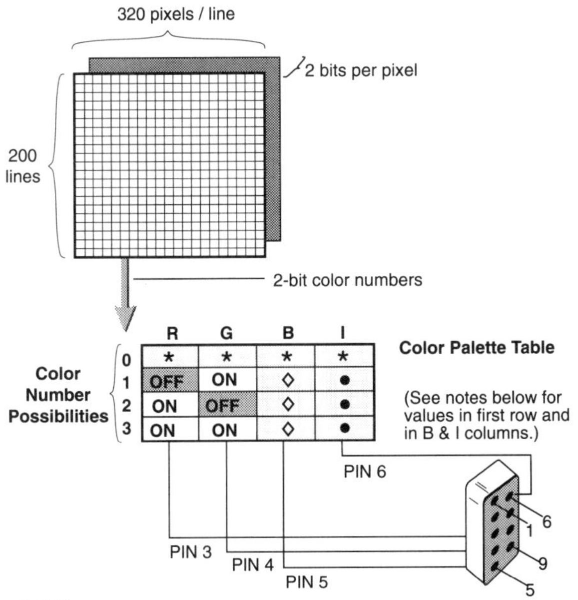

Notes:

[★] Color number zero [backround] can be any one of the sixteen possible colors.

[◇and ●] There are four different color sets available with this adapter and video mode.

Color Set	B [◇]	I [●]	Color Number 1	2	3
A	OFF	OFF	GREEN	RED	BROWN
B	ON	OFF	CYAN	MAGENTA	WHITE
C	OFF	ON	BRIGHT GREEN	BRIGHT RED	BRIGHT YELLOW
D	ON	ON	BRIGHT CYAN	BRIGHT MAGENTA	BRIGHT WHITE

Color Graphics Adapter - Medium Resolution Graphics Mode

Figure 5-6 A simple example of color numbers and palette lookup table (CGA)

(for red, green, blue, and intensity) that are always either on or off. Notice that the blue and intensity lines are not directly controlled by the color number. They are set at the outset when you (or your program) choose which of four color schemes to use.

The enhanced graphics adapter (EGA) video card also has TTL outputs, but it has more of them (six wires). This allows a larger number of possible colors (64 colors). But since the color depth is at most 4 bits, there can be no more than 16 colors on screen at once (see Figure 5-7).

A PC with a VGA (video graphics array) display system creates analog output signals. This means that the voltage on those wires can have any value

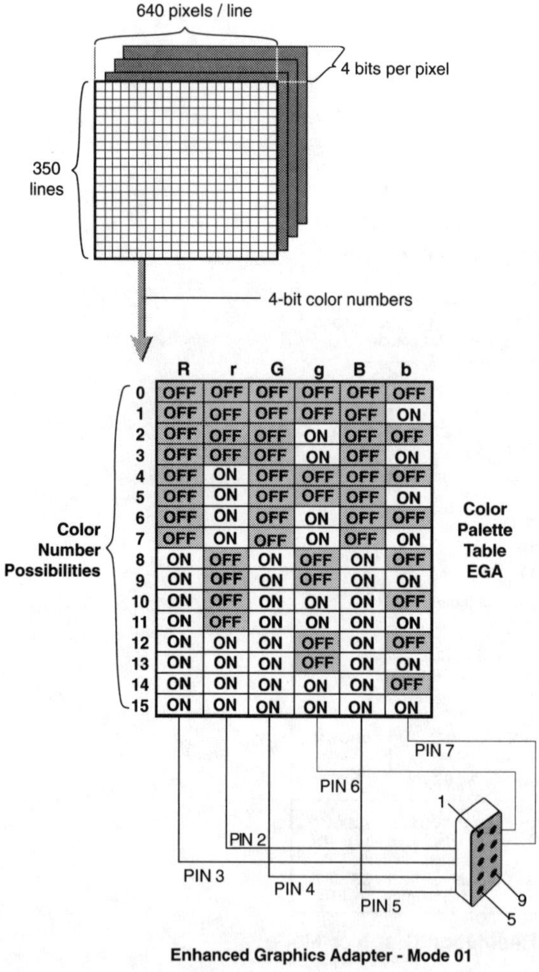

	R	r	G	g	B	b
0	OFF	OFF	OFF	OFF	OFF	OFF
1	OFF	OFF	OFF	OFF	OFF	ON
2	OFF	OFF	OFF	ON	OFF	OFF
3	OFF	OFF	OFF	ON	OFF	ON
4	OFF	ON	OFF	OFF	OFF	OFF
5	OFF	ON	OFF	OFF	OFF	ON
6	OFF	ON	OFF	ON	OFF	OFF
7	OFF	ON	OFF	ON	OFF	ON
8	ON	OFF	ON	OFF	ON	OFF
9	ON	OFF	ON	OFF	ON	ON
10	ON	OFF	ON	ON	ON	OFF
11	ON	OFF	ON	ON	ON	ON
12	ON	ON	ON	OFF	ON	OFF
13	ON	ON	ON	OFF	ON	ON
14	ON	ON	ON	ON	ON	OFF
15	ON	ON	ON	ON	ON	ON

Figure 5-7 A more complex example of color numbers and palette lookup table (EGA)

between 0 and 1 volt, with higher voltage resulting in greater brightness of that color on the screen, which allows an almost arbitrary number of possible colors to be generated.

The actual limit on the number of colors is set by the size of the numbers stored in the palette table. Each of them is a 6-bit number, specifying one of 64 possible levels for the corresponding color (red, green, or blue). In all, this means you may choose any 16 colors (or in the 320 × 200 mode, which has a color depth of 8 bits, any 256 colors) from a total palette of 262,144 colors. The color depth of the VGA's main image buffer area limits the number of simultaneous colors on screen to 4, 16, or 256, depending on the mode in which it is operating (see Figure 5-8).

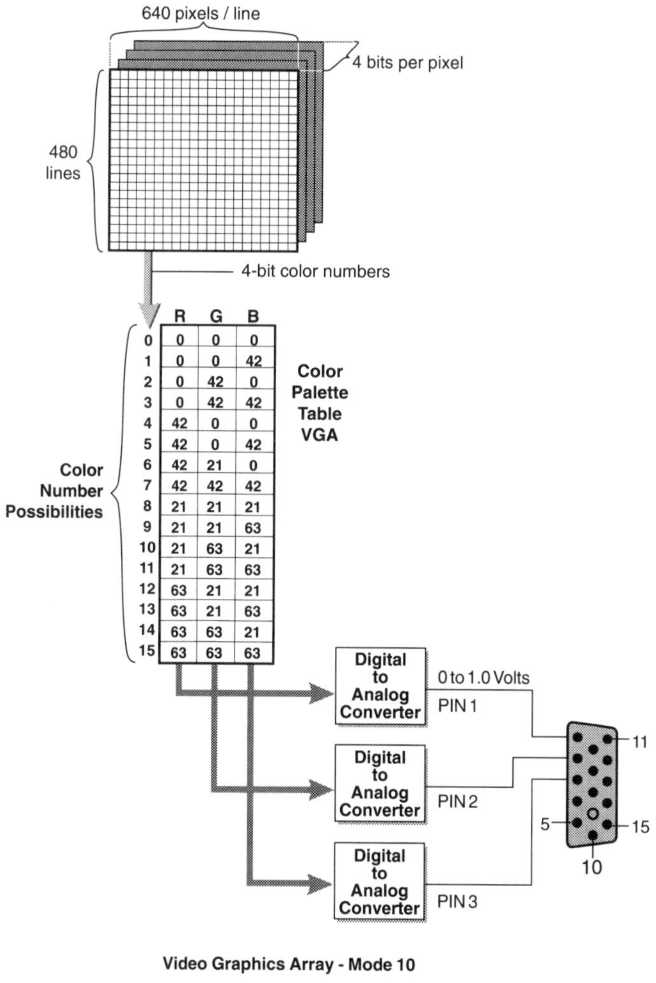

	R	G	B
0	0	0	0
1	0	0	42
2	0	42	0
3	0	42	42
4	42	0	0
5	42	0	42
6	42	21	0
7	42	42	42
8	21	21	21
9	21	21	63
10	21	63	21
11	21	63	63
12	63	21	21
13	63	21	63
14	63	63	21
15	63	63	63

Figure 5-8 A 16-color VGA generates three analog output signals.

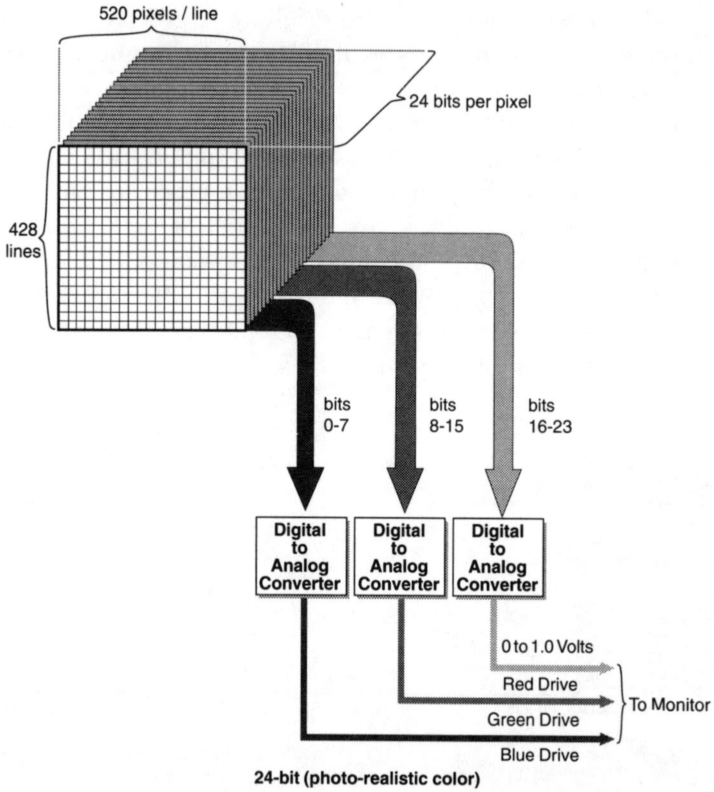

Figure 5-9 Photo-realistic (24-bit) color needs no palette table

Recently, "photo-realistic" video boards have become quite popular. These boards store 24 bits per pixel of color information. (Some of them also store an additional 8 bits of so-called "alpha channel" information, used to control video overlays, masking, and other special effects.) This works out to 256 shades of red, 256 of green, and 256 of blue, for a total palette of 16,777,216 possible colors, which is much more than the number of pixels on the screen. In this case, it makes no sense to have a palette lookup table. The desired color values are loaded directly into the image buffer (see Figure 5-9).

Extra Video "Pages"

A typical video card can operate in several different modes. In particular, you can use any but the original MDA video card in a text or graphics mode. When the card is running in graphics mode, it is probably using all of the RAM it has (or nearly all of it) to store color numbers for the pixels in the screen image, but because feasible amounts of RAM always come in integral powers of two numbers of bytes, there may be some RAM left over after the image buffer is allocated. For example, a VGA 16-color 640 × 480 graphic image requires 4 bits per pixel, which works out to 153,600 bytes. This means that a VGA card has to have at least 256KB of RAM, since the next smaller feasible amount would be 128KB, and that is not enough to hold this image. The extra RAM is often put to good use. A small amount of it is used to store the palette lookup table. More of it is usually used for caching fonts and icons.

But what about when the card is running in text mode? As stated earlier in this chapter, any text mode screen image requires only 4KB (for 80 columns by 25 rows). Even if you run the VGA card in some strange text mode with many more than the usual number of rows and columns, you still won't need anything close to the amount of RAM you have on the card. Even the original CGA card had 16KB of RAM, which just sufficed for the graphic images it could create. But in text mode that amount was four times more than necessary.

The common use of the extra memory is to store additional screen images. These are sometimes referred to as extra *video pages*. A program can be drawing an image on one page (the *active page*) while the display circuitry is showing you the image previously drawn on another page (the *visible page*).

CGA cards operating in 80-column mode can hold four pages (screensful) of text. EGA cards or VGA cards can have as many as eight pages. You may have thought that with a 1MB RAM allotment, a super-VGA card could hold a whopping 256 pages of text; unfortunately, that is not so. DOS will use only the first 32KB of RAM for text mode screen images. The rest of your video memory is simply ignored until you put your video card into a graphics mode.

Figure 5-10 shows how a color graphics card (CGA, EGA, or VGA) divides the memory address space normally used for one graphic screen image into multiple text pages. In the figure, you see the CPU transferring information into text page #1 (currently the "active page") while the display circuitry is transferring information from text page #2 (currently the "visible page") to the screen.

Virtual Screens

Multitasking and task swapping programs like the DOSSHELL task swapper, DoubleDOS, DESQview, Windows, and GeoWorks all manage screen memory a bit differently than a PC running a single program. A single-tasking PC can devote the entire screen to the single program that currently has control. In a multitasking or task swapping environment, the control program must manage the screen and only allow the individual programs to write to the

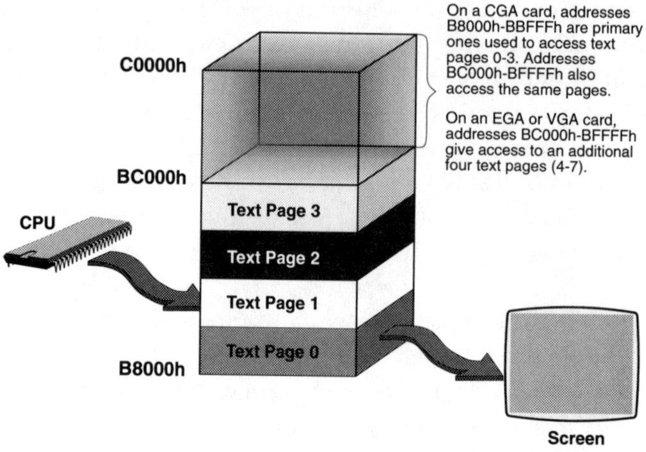

Figure 5-10 Image buffers for multiple text screens

screen when (and where) it is their turn to do so. This is managed by using *virtual screens* for the individual programs.

A simple task swapping system (typical of DOSSHELL and DoubleDOS) simply sets aside enough space somewhere outside the first megabyte in which to store each of the tasks and a copy of what was in the video image buffer the last time that program was running. This space might be in extended memory, in expanded memory, or on a disk. As each program is loaded into memory for its turn to run, its screen contents are also loaded into the video card's image buffer.

A more complex situation is a multitasking or task swapping environment that uses windows on screen to show you simultaneously either all or a portion of the screen image generated by each of the programs that are sharing the PC. DESQview and Windows are two popular examples of this sort of environment. Again, the supervisor program sets aside space for each program. It also allocates space for a virtual video image buffer for each of those programs. The programs are then "tricked into thinking" of that virtual image buffer as if it were the actual video card's image buffer. This means that each of the programs can write anything to any place on what it "thinks" is the screen.

Several times a second, the supervisor program copies information from each of the virtual image buffers to corresponding windows within the overall screen image in the video card's image buffer. In this way it is able to control which program gets to draw on each portion of the real screen. This also allows a program to continue running (and continue updating its virtual image buffer) while it is totally invisible on the actual, physical screen (See Figure 5-11).

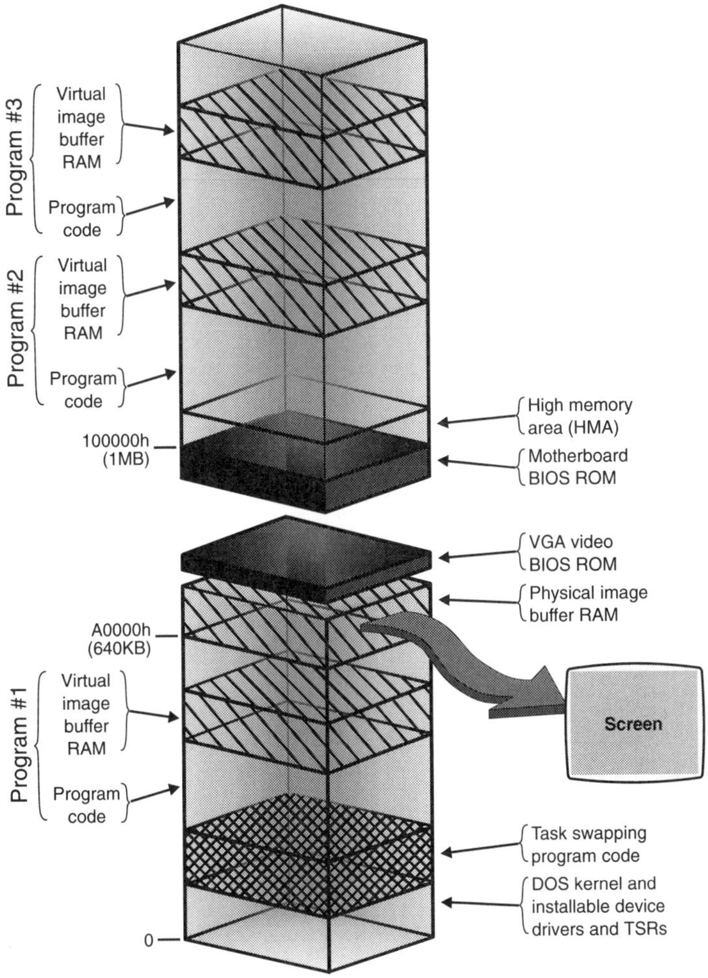

Figure 5-11 Multiple programs, each with its own virtual screen image buffer, share memory in a PC

Matching Video Cards and Monitors

It is important to remember that the monitor and the video display circuitry must be matched to one another. You cannot just choose a monitor and then choose a video card and expect them to work together. Some monitors are more flexible than others, however. If you buy an EGA monitor, it will work with either a CGA or EGA video card because the EGA card can emulate the CGA card; but it will not work with a VGA card.

Monitors advertised as multiscanning or multifrequency are usually designed to work with many different video modes and possibly with several different kinds of video card. Watch out, though. The monitor may work with a video card (meaning it can display images) and still not let you see all the dots the card is generating. Look at the dot pitch and dot size; compare them to the length of a scan line and the number of pixels you propose to display on that line. Then look at the video bandwidth. Dividing that number by the horizontal scan frequency in the highest resolution mode should yield a number at least as large as the number of pixels you wish to see distinctly on one scan line.

Using ANSI.SYS

DOS provides several useful tools that enable you to modify how it deals with your PC's video system. The one that offers the most possibilities is the ANSI.SYS device driver. Chapter 4 explained how ANSI.SYS could be used to redefine your keys. Here you'll learn how to make fancy versions of the DOS prompt, complete with colors, the date and time, the current drive and directory, happy faces, or a host of other things. ANSI.SYS can also be used to clear the screen—or only a portion of the screen—and position the cursor anywhere you like.

But before you can get ANSI.SYS to do anything for you, you have to load it through a line in your CONFIG.SYS file, the same way you load most device drivers. If you keep the file in your C:\DOS directory, the line you need in your CONFIG.SYS file looks like this:

```
DEVICE = C:\DOS\ANSI.SYS
```

Reboot your computer with this line in the CONFIG.SYS file and you will have much closer to full American National Standards Institute video terminal screen support. (You still won't have full ANSI support, but close enough for most purposes.)

Once you have ANSI.SYS loaded, you send it commands by including in your screen output certain strings of characters. All of the ANSI command strings start with the escape character (a byte whose value is 27), so naturally they are called *ANSI escape sequences.*

You can't type an ANSI escape sequence as a part of a DOS command. The reason, as explained in Chapter 4, is that COMMAND.COM sees the escape character as a command instructing it to forget everything you have typed up that point in the command. You *can* embed escape characters in files you create with various editors, and the discussion of ANSI.SYS in Chapter 10 includes examples of how to command some popular editors to do this.

Once you have a file with some embedded escape sequences, you can send its contents to the screen—and thus to the ANSI.SYS driver—by using the DOS TYPE command or by copying the file to CON:. Any ANSI escape sequences you have in the file will not appear on the screen; instead, ANSI.SYS will intercept them and act on them.

The easiest way to create and send ANSI escape sequences is to modify the DOS prompt string, the string of characters that COMMAND.COM puts on the screen each time it is ready to receive another command. All early versions of DOS just put the current drive letter and a greater than symbol on screen as a prompt; for example, the infamous `C>` prompt. While this told you what drive you were on, it failed to tell you where on the drive (in which subdirectory) you were. Finally, with version 6, DOS has remedied that oversight. Now the default prompt shows you both the current drive and the current path and then the greater than symbol.

For years many people have included in their AUTOEXEC.BAT files a line that read

```
PROMPT $P$G
```

to make COMMAND.COM remind them of this crucial information. If that is all you want, you don't need this line any more. The combination of a dollar sign and certain letters or other symbols is interpreted by COMMAND.COM when it is constructing a command prompt as a *metacharacter*. COMMAND.COM does not include metacharacters in the prompt; instead it replaces them with other characters according to these rules:

$E is replaced with the escape character
$N is replaced with the current drive letter
$P is replaced with the current drive and path
$D is replaced with the current date
$T is replaced with the current time
$V is replaced with the version of DOS you are running
$G is replaced with the greater than symbol (>)
$L is replaced with the less than symbol (<)
$B is replaced with the pipe symbol (¦)
$H is replaced with a backspace
$_ is replaced with a carriage return and a line feed
$Q is replaced with an equal sign
$$ is replaced with a dollar sign ($)

As usual, uppercase and lowercase letters are treated as equivalent by COMMAND.COM. (The earlier, less informative DOS default prompt was equivalent to NG.) One thing that is not obvious is that you can include an

```
PROMPT $e[0;33;40m $d at $t$h$h$h $e[0m  $e[7;34m Directory $q $p $e[1;32;40m$_$g
```

```
Thurs 02-04-93 at 10:35:20  Directory = E:\BOOKS\DOSPWR\WORK
> _
```

Figure 5-12 A fancy prompt string and the DOS prompt that it produces

equal sign in a prompt string and it will appear in the prompt as an equal sign. The $Q metacharacter is, therefore, not really necessary. Figure 5-11 shows what one of the authors of this book uses as his standard DOS prompt. Also shown is what that prompt string produces on his PC screen (but only if the ANSI.SYS device driver is loaded).

The PROMPT command must be entered all on one line (like all DOS commands). Whatever you specify each time you enter a PROMPT command replaces the former DOS prompt string. As you see in Figure 5-12, you can easily type PROMPT strings that include ANSI escape sequences. Just begin each one with `$e[` followed by whatever you need to achieve your desired effect. Chapter 10 includes a full description of the syntax of ANSI escape sequences.

Using EGA.SYS

If you have an EGA video card and you are going to run a task swapping program (such as DOSSHELL's task swapper) or use a multitasking environment (such as Windows), you must load the EGA.SYS device driver first. This is necessary because of a subtle, but important difference between EGA and VGA video cards.

Programs send instructions to your video card to set the card into any of several modes. In order for this to work correctly when you are doing task swapping, the task swapper must be able to set the mode correctly each time it restarts a task.

With VGA cards, the job is quite simple. The task swapper reads the VGA *registers* (places on the video card that receive the instructions) and saves the values it gets with each task it is swapping out. Then it resets those registers to whatever values they had when last running the task it is about to swap into memory.

EGA cards present task swappers with a problem. The task swapping program cannot read registers on an EGA card; those registers are write-only. This was done to save a small amount of cost in the construction of EGA cards, and is no longer an appropriate way to build a video card, but it is a standard part of the design of all EGA cards.

The purpose of EGA.SYS is simply to store a copy of all the EGA registers' contents in RAM where any program may inspect them. You load EGA.SYS by adding a line to your CONFIG.SYS file that reads

```
DEVICE=C:\DOS\EGA.SYS
```

where it is assumed you keep the EGA.SYS file in your C:\DOS subdirectory.

If you are going to load both EGA.SYS and a mouse driver, you will save a small amount of memory by loading EGA.SYS first. If your mouse driver is a TSR program, that is not an issue, because all TSRs get loaded after all device drivers. The only time you need to be concerned is if you use a MOUSE.SYS (or other similarly named file) and load it by using a DEVICE statement in your CONFIG.SYS file. In that case, be sure the line comes later in the CONFIG.SYS file than the line mentioning EGA.SYS.

Using GRAPHICS.COM and GRAFTABL.COM

The TSR programs GRAPHICS and GRAFTABL each do a single task, and either you need them or you don't. Microsoft decided that enough people need the GRAPHICS program, so it not only kept it in DOS 6, it enhanced it substantially. On the other hand, the company decided that GRAFTABL is needed by so few users that it has been removed from DOS 6. You can use an old copy from a previous DOS version, or you can get a copy from Microsoft simply by asking for it (or actually, by asking for the supplemental DOS programs diskette).

If you have ever tried doing a screen dump when your video system was in graphics mode and the screen had a mixture of text and graphical objects drawn on it, then you know that normally a PC will dump only the text objects to the printer, and the way those objects get printed may not resemble what appears on the screen. If you want to be able to print accurate copies of what appears on your screen when it is in graphics mode, simply load the GRAPHICS program first.

Until version 6, the only printers that GRAPHICS supported were various models of IBM brand printers. Now, with the parting of the ways between IBM and Microsoft, GRAPHICS has been enhanced to support many other, more popular printers. In fact, the latest version has command line parameters for six groups of IBM brand printers and ten groups of Hewlett-Packard printers. Prominently missing is any support for PostScript printers.

The syntax for GRAPHICS is very simple: include a line in your AUTOEXEC.BAT file (or type it at the DOS prompt) that says

```
GRAPHICS LASERJETII
```

if you have an HP LaserJet II. Change the parameter name to the one that best fits your printer. Type `HELP GRAPHICS` to see a list of all the printers it supports.

Now, when you press Print Screen (or Shift Print Screen if your computer uses that combination), you will get an accurate copy of your screen output to your printer. Everything will be there, and each object will be printed as it shows up on the screen—to the pixel.

GRAFTABL solves a different, but related problem. If you have tried screen dumps of screen images that included the IBM extended ASCII characters (for example, the line draw characters often used to form menu boxes), you may have seen those high-bit set characters turn into an odd-looking mess of letters and other symbols. There are two reasons that this happens.

If, for example, you have an HP LaserJet printer, its normal definition for the extended ASCII characters is different from IBM's. You can tell the printer to use its PC8 character set (by using the front panel controls or by sending it an appropriate command sequence), and then it will use IBM's definitions for those characters. No need for GRAFTABL in this case.

The other possible cause is that you are using a CGA video display adapter. It uses a ROM on the card to define the characters, and that ROM is not accessible to the screen dump routine. So any high-bit set characters will be printed as some fairly arbitrary garbage. Loading GRAFTABL will solve this problem.

There is one other situation in which GRAFTABL may be useful: If you have loaded an alternate character set (for national language support). In this case also, you may need to load GRAFTABL to get accurate screen dumps.

Both GRAPHICS.COM and GRAFTABL.COM are TSR programs. Run either of them only once until after the next time you reboot your computer.

Using the MODE Command

The DOS command MODE has many jobs. One of them is helping you set up your video system the way you want it to work. In Chapter 4 you saw how it is used to set up devices for alternate character sets. In Chapter 8 you will learn how it is used with printers. Here we are going to discuss its other uses with video devices. There are three different syntactically valid ways to use MODE with a display adapter. They are:

```
MODE display_adapter [,n]
MODE display_adapter, shift [,T]
MODE CON[:] COLS=c LINES=n
```

where, as usual, the items in square brackets are optional. (Whether or not you choose to include those items, don't type the square brackets.) In place of `display_adapter`, you must put one of these values: `MONO`, `CO40`, or `CO80`. If you include a `shift` value, it must be either `L` or `R`. The only valid numbers for `c` are `40` and `80`, while the only valid numbers for `n` are `25`, `43`, or `50`.

The first syntax is the most commonly used one. With it you can switch from a color display (which could be CGA, EGA, or VGA) to a monochrome (MDA or MGC), or you can switch a color display between its 80-column and 40-column modes.

The second syntax is rarely used anymore. It was primarily needed on very old CGA cards and monitors. It allows you to shift the image left or right by one or two characters. The `T` option stands for test and causes MODE to display a test pattern that will help you see if the beginnings or ends of lines are falling off the screen.

The third syntax is the newest one. It allows you to change the video subsystem from the standard 25-line screen to one with 43 or 50 lines per screen. This version of MODE works only if you have the ANSI.SYS device driver loaded.

Finally, you can simply type `MODE` at the DOS prompt, which will give you a status report on all devices it knows about except for any redirected printers. To see a similar status report on them, add the command line switch `/STATUS` (or `/STA` for short) after the word `MODE`.

Video Modes and Memory Issues

One of the principal things you can do to enhance your PC's performance is correctly manage its use of memory within the first megabyte of the CPU's memory address space. At last, with version 6, DOS provides a tool to help you do this (MemMaker). However, it will only do a so-so job unless you pitch in and help.

Before you can do anything helpful, though, you have to know what uses your PC is making of memory already. Your PC's video card is one very important user of memory space, and knowing what it needs is often the most critical key to deciding how to manage the rest of memory address space.

Note: If you find yourself confused by some of the terms or issues discussed in this section, turn to Chapter 6 and read all about the general issues. Then return to this section for the details on memory usage by video cards.

Video cards use memory in two ways. They store image information in a region of RAM, and many of them also have an option ROM that uses some more address space. All monochrome cards (MDA and MGC and EGA or VGA cards when they are emulating an MGC) use memory in the region from B0000h to B7FFFh. They may use only a portion of that space, or they may use all of it, but either way no other program can use any of that space if a monochrome card is there.

All color cards use the space from B8000h to BFFFFh when they are operating in color text mode. This includes a VGA card that is hooked to a monochrome VGA monitor. A Hercules Graphics card (HGC and the clone MGCs) can also operate in a mode that uses the whole of the B page (addresses from B0000h to BFFFFh) as long as there is no other video card in that PC.

EGA and VGA cards use the A page (addresses from A0000h to AFFFFh) to store information for graphic images. Some super-EGA and super-VGA cards will use all of the A page and some or all of the B page at the same time when they are operating in one of the "super" (non-IBM defined) modes.

Except for IBM PS/2 Models 50 and above and a few clone PCs that have VGA circuitry on the motherboard, any PC with EGA or VGA video will have an option ROM located somewhere in the upper memory space. Usually, its address range starts at C0000h. Some of these option ROMs are as small as 24KB; others use a full 32KB. So the end of the option ROM may come at C5FFFh or at C7FFFh. Just a few VGA cards use the space from C8000h to CFFFFh as well.

A few PCs put the VGA option ROM in the E page. This is possible only if their motherboard BIOS ROM knows to look there for the VGA option ROM.

If you don't have a monochrome video card, the memory management folk will want to use the B0000h to B7FFFh address range for upper memory blocks (UMBs) in which they can put programs. (You will find this suggestion in the Microsoft literature that comes with Windows and the Windows Resource Kits, as well in the DOS MemMaker program). The Qualitas memory manager 386MAX, and its associated MAXIMIZE program, proudly declare that it will move your VGA option ROM to the B0000h to B7FFFh addresses. These could be good moves, and they will certainly seem to increase your available memory. Taking these steps could, however, get you into a lot of trouble.

If you are using a super-EGA or super-VGA card and *ever* plan to use them in their extended video modes, don't let your memory manager use the B page at all. If you were to let a memory manager put some UMB memory there and load a program into it, once your video card switched into one of its extended video modes, it would trash that program. Then, the next time you have occasion to call that program, there is no telling what would happen. And the *best* thing would be to have your PC simply hang!

Windows does a lot of memory management on its own, mostly without asking for your opinions on where it should do what. You can, and probably should, influence its choices by putting EMMExclude and EMMInclude lines in the [386Enh] section of your SYSTEM.INI file. Tell it to stay out of places you know are needed by something else, and tell it to use regions you know are okay, even though Windows might not be sure.

Tip: Here is a subtle point that is easily missed: In this book all memory addresses are given as full, linear addresses, or they are given as an explicit segment:offset number pair. When putting values on an EMMInclude or EMMExclude statement in SYSTEM.INI you must use only the segment value. This is equivalent to dropping the last character in the linear addresses as we have been using them. You must also give addresses in the segment-only form to most memory management programs, including EMM386.EXE. Thus, the proper form of the EMMExclude statement to tell Windows to keeps its paws off your video RAM space is

```
EMMExclude=B000-B7FF
```

or, if you wish to protect yourself more fully, use

```
EMMExclude=A000-C7FF
```

if you have an EGA or VGA card. A very similar form is useful on your DEVICE=EMM386.EXE line (see Chapter 10 for the details).

The DOS Power Tools Programs for Video

BL is a useful tool for LCD displays. BLANKS will prevent screen burn-in. ANSCOLOR and ANSICTRL will let you set screen colors and modes, while ICK! will let you restore your screen and cursor to normal appearance if you or one of your programs put things awry.

C H A P T E R

6

◆ ◆ ◆ ◆ ◆

Memory and CPUs

PCs have a complicated memory architecture, with many similar terms that describe very different physical realities (such as extended versus expanded memory and UMBs versus EMBs). This chapter explains what memory management is, and how to use the tools DOS provides to explore and manage the memory in your PC.

To understand the memory architecture issues, it is first necessary to explain the differences between the various processors in Intel's product line, which are either used or imitated in all IBM-compatible PCs.

The Intel "x86" Family

The first member of Intel's x86 family of microprocessors was named the 8086. It was very similar to the earlier 8080, but it varied significantly in that it did computations on data 16 bits at a time. (Presumably the 6 at the end of its name somehow reflected that.)

The 8086 also had a much expanded *memory address space,* and it used a novel means of pointing to places in that space: a process called *segment: offset addressing.* Pointing to addresses essentially means constructing the 20-bit address numbers that are to appear on the address pins. Why this is useful is explained later in this chapter.

Not only did the 8086 process information internally 16 bits at a time, it also used 16 pins to transfer 2 bytes of data in and out of the microprocessor in parallel. This was a radical departure from the 8080 design (doubling the number of data pins), and it meant that a computer designed to use it would require roughly double the amount of support circuitry. Unfortunately, the cost, too, doubled. This, needless to say, was not very appealing to the designers of systems that might use such a microprocessor.

Therefore, Intel brought out a sibling to the 8086, called the 8088. The final 8 in its name signifies that this version passes information in or out of the chip only 8 bits at a time. Otherwise, it was identical to the 8086. But that one change meant that while the 8088 did computations internally 16 bits at a time, and it had all the memory addressing power of the 8086, it would be possible for manufacturers to build computers using the 8088 as the CPU for almost the same cost as the earlier generation CP/M machines. The similarities also meant that programmers would not have to concern themselves with the difference between the 8088 and 8086.

IBM used the 8088 as the CPU in its new personal computer, so naturally the 8088 chip became a huge success. Intel then decided to offer an improved model chip, but one so closely related to the original 8088 and 8086 that manufacturers could use it with very few changes in the designs of new models of their computers; programs written for the 8088 or 8086 would all run on the new chip totally unchanged. This next x86 family member was called the 80186. (This chip was never very popular with PC manufacturers, as it cost more than the 8086 and did not offer enough additional power to be worth that extra cost.)

Intel tried again a couple of years later with the 80286. Now the naming sequence was becoming clear. The overall pattern was going to be 80x86, with the x first missing, then a 1, then a 2, and so on. For awhile, that was what this family of chips was called: the 80x86 family. More recently, because the former 80386 was called the 386, and its newer sibling the 486, the family became known simply as the x86 family.

IBM chose to use the extra power of the 80286 chip as the core of their new PC/AT. Again, Intel made sure this new chip would run all the programs that worked with computers built around the earlier 8088, 8086, and 80186 chips—a group that included all the earlier IBM PC and XT computers and their clones.

The 80286 would "wake up" acting exactly like a fast 8086, but if a programmer knew how, it was possible to put the 80286 into a different mode of operation with greatly enhanced capabilities. All the modes of the x86 CPU chips will be described later in this chapter.

Intel, in time, brought out another generation of microprocessor chip, the 80386, and made sure that all programs that worked on an 8088 or 80286-based PC would also run on an 80386-based PC. But the 80386 offered some important new capabilities. It had four modes of operation and its memory space was radically enlarged. It finally made it relatively easy to do some of the things that the 80286 had promised, but was not quite able to deliver.

In short, with the 80386, Intel had finally fleshed out the promise of the 8086. The architecture of this chip family was essentially completed. According to Intel, all future enhancements in the x86 family will be only elaborations on the theme that was defined in the 80386.

COMPAQ introduced an 80386-based PC before IBM, and other clone manufacturers followed COMPAQ's lead. Suddenly, the industry had a personal computer for which there was no really good name. The 8088-based machines were PCs or XTs, and 80286 systems were ATs, but what should you call a machine that had no IBM equivalent? People began to use a shorthand version of the Intel part number for the CPU—simply "386 computers." Intel naturally loved that and officially changed the name of the chip to 386, then applied for trademark protection on that name. When the next member of the family was introduced, it was called the 486; Intel again applied for legal protection, but did not succeed in its legal efforts. The court ruled that numbers could not be granted trademark protection. As a result, there are now many competing brands of 386 and 486 chips on the market.

Consequently, Intel's newest chip design, which everyone was sure would be called the 586, was instead officially dubbed the Pentium Processor in an attempt to give it a better shot at trademark protection. (The information on the Pentium Processor is based on rumors, as Intel has not yet officially announced the technical details on its latest chip.)

Figure 6-1 shows drawings of the most commonly used package for each of the key members of the x86 family. Also shown are some important numbers about each of these chips.

Note: The 80286 has 24 address pins and the 386SX has 23, yet both are listed as able to address up to 16MB of memory. Similarly, the 386DX and 486 chips have only 30 address pins, yet they can address 4GB of memory, which would seem to imply 32-bit address values.The explanation is simple enough: The data bus is 2 bytes wide in the 80286 and 386SX, and 4 bytes wide for the 386DX and 486, which means that the CPU can supply only the most significant 23 or 30 bits of the full 24- and 32-bit addresses. The least significant bits would discriminate among only the bytes that are fetched in parallel. Apparently, the Intel designers of the 80286 either did not have this insight, or they had a spare pin. The least significant bit address line on that chip is really redundant.

Variations on a Theme

Intel has not been content to make just these generational improvements in its chips. The company also found it very profitable to produce a number of variations on each new generation, first with the 8086 and 8088 and next with the 386, which was renamed the 386DX when the 386SX was introduced. (DX stands for "Double-word eXternal data bus" and SX for "Single-word eXternal data bus.") There are only two differences between the 386SX and the 386DX: Both process data internally 32 bits at a time, but only the 386DX has a full 32-bit data bus to the external world; the 386SX is put into a smaller package and has only 16 pins to carry data in and out. The other difference is that the 386DX has 30 address lines while the 386SX has only 23 address

Name	Package	Pins used for Data	Pins used for Address	Maximum memory	Pins used for Control Signals	Total Number of Pins
8088		8	20	1MB	20	40
8086		16	20	1MB	21	40
80286		16	24	16MB	18	68
386SX		16	23	16MB	19	100
386DX		32	30	4GB	21	132
486DX 486SX		32	30	4GB	37	168
Pentium	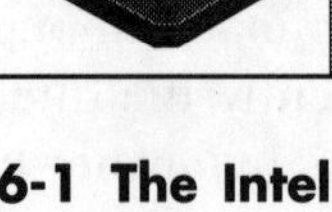	64	28	4GB	76	273

Figure 6-1 The Intel x86 family's key members. Pin totals may not match the sum of each row because some pins are used for more than one purpose or support pins such as power and ground.

lines, which means that the 386DX can address a full 4GB of physical RAM chips, and the 386SX can address only 16MB.

The 386SX was very successful because it offered manufacturers a way to build a real 386-based PC, complete with all the delightful memory management tricks a 386-based computer can perform; thus, it was able to run all of the latest PC software, but at only the cost of building an AT clone. Since the external data paths were only 16 bits wide, a 386SX motherboard is very much like that for an AT; the only real changes are the CPU chip and the BIOS programming in the ROM chips. Note that while a 386SX will run almost all the same programs as the 386DX, some of them will run more slowly—it takes twice as long to read or write information to memory when you can do it only 2 bytes instead of 4 bytes at a time.

Intel priced the 386SX chip almost as inexpensively as the 80286 chip and far below the price of 386DX chips at the time. Intel saw its market share threatened by the *second source* vendors of 80286 chips, while it had a 100-percent monopoly on 386 chips. As a result, Intel launched a massive advertising campaign to convince PC users to get rid of their old ATs and upgrade to 386-based PCs, more specifically the 386SX.

Shortly after the 486 was introduced, Intel tried the same maneuver. The 486 was renamed the 486DX and a closely related product was introduced called the 486SX. Unfortunately, this time the difference made a lot less sense. Both the 486DX and 486SX are full 32-bit computers internally and in their connections to the outside world. The only real difference is that the 486SX doesn't have the math coprocessor functionality that is built into the 486DX.

Given that the two chips are essentially equally complex and difficult to manufacture, you'd expect their prices to be quite close. And because the rest of a PC built using them is going to be about the same, you'd expect those prices to be close, too. Not so. Intel decided to "aggressively" price the 486SX, and PC makers passed the savings to their customers.

Note: Actually, a 486SX-based PC is usually a tad more complicated and expensive for the manufacturer to build, as it almost always has an extra, empty socket on the motherboard that is not needed with the 486DX. In the better machines, this socket is a fancy (and quite costly), "zero insertion force" socket that can accept a 487 chip, which is not merely a math coprocessor, but a full-fledged 486DX chip with one extra pin. When a 487 chip is plugged into the extra socket, the extra pin deactivates the original 486SX for the duration.

When Intel first introduced the 486SX (and its associated 487 chip), the industry thought it was a ridiculous idea. (Nevertheless, the marketplace gobbled up the new machines.) Then, Intel did something to redeem itself by introducing the OverDrive series of chips and the DX/2 chips. These chips can, in some cases, be plugged into the 487 socket on a 486SX motherboard to enhance speed on the PC. This speed is achieved in several ways. One is by adding the math coprocessor functionality; another is by having more internal complexity that can be used for extra instruction pipelining and other neat tricks. Another of these new chips—the speed-doubling DX/2 chip—is intended as either replacements for 486DX chips or for use in newly designed motherboards.

In a 486, most of the processing is done on the chip with little need to refer to anything outside, although the CPU occasionally has to retrieve more data or instructions from memory or insert results there. In the meantime, though, it is able to crunch along all by itself.

Intel believed that it could speed up the overall performance of a PC without making it any harder for motherboard manufacturers, if only it could speed up the chip's internal processing, but keep its transactions with the external world (the rest of the motherboard) down to a more modest pace. Consequently, we now have 486DX/2 chips operating with 50MHz and 66MHz internal clocks that are plugged into what are essentially standard 25MHz and 33MHz motherboards. Part of what makes this approach feasible are the on-chip memory cache and the on-chip math coprocessor. (Note that since 386 chips have neither of these features, speed-doubled 386s don't make much sense.)

Another variation on the theme from Intel is the 386SL. This is a set of two chips designed for use in low-power PCs (for example, in a portable, laptop, or palmtop unit). One of these chips is basically a 386 microprocessor, but with a few extra features built in. The other chip integrates most of what is needed on the motherboard to support the 386. Therefore, all a manufacturer has to add to the two of them is some RAM, a bunch of connectors, and a power supply.

The 386SL chip set also incorporates some special features that make it possible for portions of the system—the hard disk, serial and parallel ports, and even the CPU—to be powered down whenever they are not needed for actual computing or for performing some input or output operation. To fully benefit from a PC built around this chip, you need a PC that has been designed to take advantage of its features. Such PCs are finally becoming affordable, and thus popular. You also need software support for these power-saving features. Starting with PC DOS 5.02, and now with MS-DOS 6, we have POWER.EXE as the main DOS program to help you in this regard.

The developments in this industry are testimony to the benefits of vigorous competition. The products (x86-compatible microprocessors) have been rapidly getting more powerful and less expensive. And there is no end in sight.

Computer Architecture

Let's look at how the CPU connects with other parts of the PC in a little more detail. At the first level, wiring up a computer based on a particular CPU chip is determined by the design of that chip. The Intel x86 processors are no exception. The computer manufacturer is responsible for the rest. A portion of what the computer manufacturer adds to the architecture is the motherboard chip set. Another portion is the programming included in the BIOS ROM chips on the motherboard. (The chip set also implies a choice of input/output bus. Presently, the options for the bus include ISA, MCA, and EISA, possibly augmented by some VESA or PCI local bus slots.)

An x86 processor classifies everything into two realms: The CPU considers the RAM and ROM chips that fill up its memory space to be an internal part of the PC; the CPU regards the rest of the hardware in your PC as external. The CPU reads or writes information to locations in either of these two realms. *Reading* means data is flowing into the CPU. *Writing* means data is flowing out of the CPU and into either memory or the external world.

A variable number of address pins are used to signal the circuits around the CPU as to which particular memory or external address it is to read data from or write data to. (See Figure 6-1 for the exact number of data and address pins for each member of the x86 family.)

In addition to the data and address pins, the CPU has a number of pins that carry *control* signals, which include several devoted to distinguishing between times the CPU brings information in from the world (reads), and times it sends information out (writes). These control signals also determine whether the information exchange is to be with memory or the external realm.

The external realm is addressed through *input/output ports* (also called *I/O ports*). Figure 6-2 shows these distinctions between memory and I/O ports, as well as between reading and writing. It also shows that control signals are used to govern which event takes place. The exact number of pins shown in this figure represents the 8086. All members of the x86 family have exactly 65,536 (64K) input/output ports. Thus, only the least significant sixteen address bits are used to select an I/O port; all of them are needed to select a memory address.

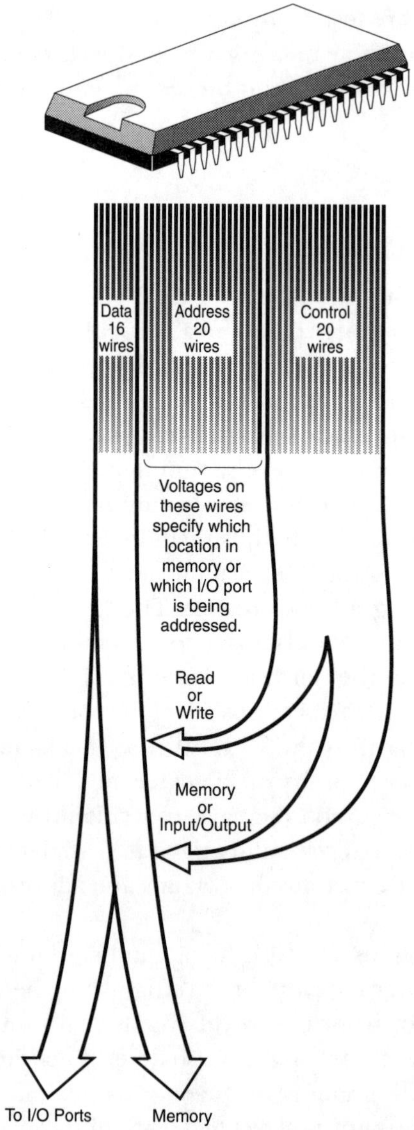

Figure 6-2 Control signals govern whether data flows in or out of the CPU and whether the CPU is connected to memory or to its input/output ports.

x86 CPU Modes

As already noted, one of the improvements in the 80286 over the 8088 was that the 80286 could operate in two modes; the 386 and 486 can operate in any of four modes.

REAL MODE

The one mode that all x86 processors have in common is called *real mode*. This is the mode in which every member of the family "wakes up." After a reset, all x86 processors also return to real mode operation.

In order to accurately emulate the "elderly" members of the family, all the "younger" (advanced) members have to forgo using most of their special features when running in real mode. For example, starting with the 80286, more pins are devoted to addresses than the 8088; therefore, these more advanced chips can address much more memory than can an 8088. But when operating in real mode, they simply ignore those extra address pins and operate as if they have only 20 address pins—just like an 8088 or 8086.

> ***Note:*** Sometimes the 21st address line is used in real mode, but not to double the memory that can be accessed—just to increase the amount by about 6 percent. That will be explained in a moment.

The predecessor to the 8086 was the 8080. In that microprocessor there were a number of 16-bit *registers*, meaning there were places inside the chip to temporarily store binary numbers up to 16 bits long. One of those places was used to store the address to which the CPU was next going to write, or from which it would next be reading. Another held the location of the next instruction in the program that the CPU was currently processing. That worked well, as the 8080 had exactly 16 pins used for address information.

When Intel designed the 8086, it wanted to make it as compatible with the 8080 as possible, yet increase the size of the address space. Twenty address pins were built in, but all the registers on the chip were only 16 bits wide (as on the 8080). This gave the Intel engineers an interesting problem to solve: how to use 16-bit numbers to point to arbitrary locations in a memory space so large that a 20-bit number was necessary to specify each location.

There is one obvious way this problem could be solved: Use two of those 16-bit numbers and tack them together end-to-end. This gives you a 32-bit number. Then, simply ignore all but the lowest 20 bits of that number, and you will have your memory address. While this worked, it seemed a waste to have 12 out of 32 bits unused. So Intel did something very clever by using two 16-bit numbers to generate each 20-bit memory address. But this was accomplished in a curious way, and ever since then programmers have either praised or damned Intel.

Intel specified that one of the two 16-bit numbers used to generate an address should be multiplied by 16. This number (named the *segment* value) after it had been multiplied by sixteen, could have any value that was a multiple of 16, from 0 to 1,048,560.

The other number, which Intel called the *offset* value, was to be added to 16 times the segment value. The sum could be any number (any integer) from 0 to 1,114,095, which was just a little more than needed to span the range of memory address values.

The logic of this rather arcane memory addressing strategy is revealed when you learn that 16 times the segment value is often called the *base address.* This product points to a place in memory that marks the start of a group of 64K consecutive locations called a segment. You indicate a particular segment by choosing a particular segment value, and you point to a particular place within that segment by choosing a particular offset value to be added to the base address.

> **Note:** At first, these numbers may seem odd and arbitrary; they are not. If re-expressed as hexadecimal values, their specialness becomes apparent. For example, a 16-bit number in hexadecimal is anything from 0 to FFFFh. (And FFFFh is just one less than the very "round" number 10000h.) The 20-bit memory addresses in an 8088 can be written in hexadecimal as numbers from 0 to FFFFFh. Multiplying by 16 in hexadecimal simply means adding a 0 on the end. So the range of segment values becomes any number from 0 to FFFF0h, with the restriction that the number must end in 0. Finally, the full range of addresses you can compute by the rule "segment value times 16 plus offset value" is from 0 to 10FFEFh, or just 16 bytes less than 1MB plus 64KB. (This last number is also the sum of FFFF0h and FFFFh.)

Any time you run across two four-symbol hexadecimal numbers separated by a colon (e.g., A103:0045), you can be sure you are looking at a memory address expressed in *segment:offset* form. The number before the colon is the segment value; the number after the colon is the offset value, and both are expressed in hexadecimal. (See Chapter 1 for an explanation of hexadecimal numbers.)

Now, about that 21st address line: If you add a large segment value to a large offset value, the answer can be slightly more than will fit into a 20-bit number. There are exactly 65,520 possible sums that exceed that maximum. Remember, the chip itself has only 20 address pins, so if you point to such an address, the carry bit (which would be the 21st bit of the resulting sum) is simply discarded. That means that a large segment value combined with a large offset value actually points to a memory location near the bottom of memory (which is address 0). This phenomenon is called *address wrapping.*

When IBM designed the AT, it was aware that since the AT actually has 24 address lines, it was possible to add large segment and offset values and actually point to a memory address just beyond 1MB. If IBM had allowed the AT to do this, it wouldn't have been able to accurately emulate the PC; some programs that worked on a PC wouldn't run on the AT. As a result, IBM engineered into its new PC/AT a special circuit that does only one thing: Whenever the CPU is operating in real mode, this circuit clamps the 21st address line to its 0 state. (The names of the address lines are A0 through A19 in an 8088, so this 21st address line carries the name A20.)

Years later, Quarterdeck, and later Microsoft, realized that if it were possible to turn off that special circuitry (and only then), it would be possible to store almost 64KB more data over the 1MB line, even when the processor was running in real mode. (That 64KB is 6.25 percent of 1MB, which is the "about 6 percent" mentioned earlier.)

This trick works on any PC that has one of the more advanced processors (which means it won't work on the original PCs or XTs, but it will on all ATs, 386s, and 486s), as long as the CPU is operating in real mode and provided the PC has some memory installed at addresses beyond 1MB. This extra region of real-mode accessible memory is now called the *high memory area* (*HMA*).

286-PROTECTED MODE

Intel called the extra mode in which an 80286 could operate *protected mode.* Since it later enabled the 386 and 486 chips to use both this mode and a slightly different one, it is now customary to refer to the protected mode that an 80286 can use as *286-protected mode.* (Naturally, protected modes used only by 386 and 486 chips are respectively called *386-* and *486-protected modes.*)

After the processor is put into 286-protected mode it can address the full range of memory addresses that its 24 address pins permits. Addresses can be up to 24 bits long, so that the 80286 can "talk" to 16MB of memory. Obviously, in order to do this, the chip must be able to generate 24-bit long address numbers. How does it do this? Certainly not by using the same "segment value times 16 plus offset value" rule used in real mode.

Intel decided to continue using two 16-bit numbers, but to use one of them in a slightly different way. What was called the segment value now became the *selector value.* Most of this number (all but the three least significant bits) is used as an index into a *descriptor table.* The entry in the table to which this number points is called the *segment descriptor,* which consists of three parts. The first part is the memory address of the beginning of a segment. The second part is the size of that segment. Unlike real mode, in which every segment is 64KB, segments in 286-protected mode may be any size, from a single byte to a maximum of 64KB. The third part is a collection of bits used to control access to this segment. (The 3 bits of the selector value that aren't a part of the index into the descriptor table are also used in controlling access to the segment.)

Controlled access is the reason this mode is called protected. Programs access only regions of memory to which they have rights. Other regions are protected against alteration by programs that do not have access rights to them, and a program can access input/output ports only if it is given permission to do so. Futhermore, because the strategy for accessing memory locations in protected mode is totally different than in real mode, programs must be completely rewritten before they can run in protected mode.

In fact, Microsoft and IBM had plans to rewrite DOS to take advantage of all these access controls, making it possible to run multiple programs in a PC without fear of the system crashing and without enabling any program to harm any other program or its data. Unfortunately, writing that new operating system was very difficult. Before that 286-specific operating system (called OS/2) was finally completed, Intel had introduced another two generations of x86 processors.

386-PROTECTED MODE

Both the 386 and 486 microprocessors operate in real mode when they "wake up." They can operate in 286-protected mode when a program directs them to, or in an extended version (386-protected) of that mode.

386-protected mode differs from 286-protected mode in that it allows segment addresses and sizes to be much larger. Both the maximum segment size and the maximum memory address in this mode are 4GB (4,096MB); in addition, the offset values can be 32-bit numbers.

The other major difference is that in 386-protected mode a program may be given permission to use some, but not all, input/output ports. No longer is it necessary to grant a program either total or no I/O freedom. Different ports can be allocated to different programs simultaneously.

VIRTUAL 8086 MODE

The other new mode for the 386 and 486 chips is called *virtual 8086 mode*. In this mode the chip behaves in many ways just like an 8086, but with some very important differences. Normally, virtual 8086 mode is used by an operating system as a way of providing application programs with an even safer working environment than is possible using 286-protected mode. In particular, this mode allows very safe multitasking.

Programs running in virtual 8086 mode can be exactly the same as programs that would run on a real 8086, i.e., they don't have to have been written to run in protected mode. Any such program will see only 1MB of accessible memory (or 1MB plus an HMA of almost 64KB). Any attempt by the program to access an I/O port will cause a special interrupt, and the supervisor program (which must be running in 386-protected mode) will intervene to ensure that only permitted programs actually do any I/O activity.

Each program running in a virtual 8086 session has its own *virtual video image buffer* area. The supervisor program (operating system) copies appropriate portions of that buffer's contents to the actual video image buffer, which is how multiple programs display their output in separate windows on your screen simultaneously.

Multitasking *can* be done using only 286-protected mode, but it requires emulating a lot of features that the 386 and 486 chips offer directly as hardware features in virtual 8086 mode. When provided in hardware, these features work much more reliably and quickly.

Why Modes Matter

DOS was first written for the original PC to run only in real mode—the original DOS had no knowledge of protected mode. When the AT was introduced, DOS could not access any memory beyond the first megabyte—what we now call *extended memory*.

Then, IBM included VDISK.SYS with PC DOS 3.x to permit its customers to make use of their new AT's extended memory, and Microsoft put RAMDRIVE.SYS in its MS-DOS 3.x. Each of these programs simulates a disk drive using extended memory. For several years, all the ATs and AT-clones in the world were acting like very fast XTs with, perhaps, a super-fast electronic "disk drive." Eventually, DOS was upgraded to include tools for working with extended memory. (You will learn what they are and how to use them later in this chapter.)

Any application program written to run in real mode can work only if the CPU is in real mode or virtual 8086 mode. The only way to use those programs in a multitasking environment is to get an operating system (such as OS/2) or operating environment (such as Windows) that runs the processor in protected mode. When that supervisor program decides to let an application program run, it must either put the CPU back into real mode temporarily, or else put it into virtual 8086 mode. Of these two choices, the safer is to use virtual 8086 mode.

Fundamentally, this is why you want to have a PC that uses a 386 or better processor as its CPU. It can then run the best of modern PC software, which requires that the CPU be able to run in the most advanced modes.

Memory Maps

A memory map helps keep track of which addresses in your PC's memory address space refer to locations in RAM chips and which refer to locations inside ROMs. Further, such a map can show you which RAM chips are physically located on which circuit card. Finally, these maps can indicate which programs occupy which memory address ranges.

Therefore, you need to know how to read PC memory maps. The good news is, this is easy to learn. The bad news is, not all memory maps are drawn the same way, so you have to closely examine each one to see how it has been drawn.

How to Read a Memory Map

One element to look for in memory maps is how the locations are designated. Some people use decimal values, others use hexadecimal numbers, still others use both. The memory maps in this book are labelled with hexadecimal addresses on one side and decimal addresses on the opposite side.

Another factor in reading memory maps is determining which way is up. Geographical maps are almost always drawn with North at the top. Similarly, all the memory maps in this book (except one) have been drawn with larger memory addresses higher on the page. This is the not the case with memory maps from some other sources, however, so be sure to check out that aspect of each map you want to read before you try deciphering whatever else it is trying to tell you.

Figure 6-3 shows a simple memory map for the first megabyte of a PC's memory address space. This is about as simple as a PC memory map can get. It shows five regions. At the lowest memory address is the RAM in which DOS and the BIOS reside. Next is available RAM, extending up to 640KB. Just above that is a region for video image buffers. Most PC video subsystems don't use all of this space—at least not at one time. (See Chapter 5 for details on how PC video subsystems use memory.)

Right above the video image buffers is an empty space. Literally, it is empty in many PCs. If you try to write data to locations in that range, you are simply throwing those bits away. If you try reading from one of those addresses, what you get has no meaning. This space, however, may get filled up with video and other option ROMs, the EMS page frame, and upper memory blocks.

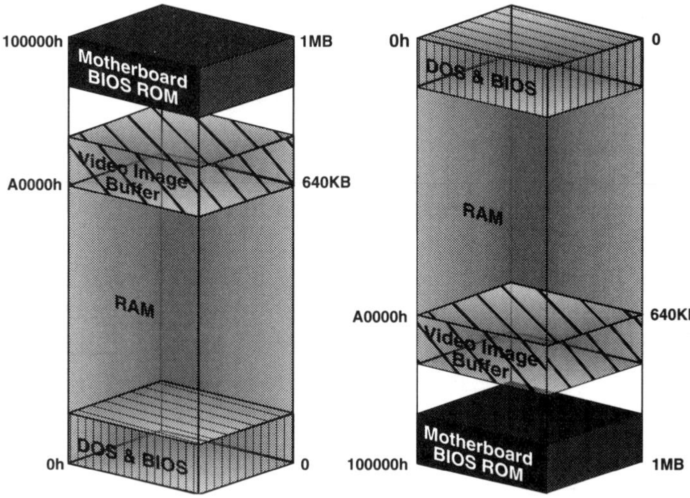

Figure 6-3 The "right" and "wrong" ways to draw a memory map

Finally, there is a region marked "Motherboard BIOS ROM," which indicates that this region is occupied by ROM chips, which reside on the PC motherboard and hold the permanent and unchanging portions of your PC's BIOS programs. (Not all PCs use all of this space for that purpose. You can also use additional UMBs to fill any leftover space.)

If your PC uses an 8088 or 8086 as its CPU, this first megabyte is all the memory address space it has. If yours is a higher-level PC—one that uses an 80286, 386, or 486 for its CPU—you have additional memory addresses beyond 1MB, whether or not you have memory chips located at those addresses.

The left half of Figure 6-3 shows what is called a right-side-up memory map. Address 0 is at the bottom; the maximum address is at the top. The right half of this figure shows what this map looks like when drawn upside-down.

One argument for defining a memory map with address 0 on the bottom as the "right" way is that programs tend to be loaded one on top of another, in lower addresses first and then in higher ones. Stacking objects in this manner is natural; stacking them down "from the ceiling" is unnatural.

A counter argument is that when you issue the DOS command `MEM /D` you are asking DOS to list all the programs that are resident in your PC's RAM. It will do so starting with the lowest addresses, but because of the nature of your PC's video system, this means that the MEM display puts the lowest memory addresses at the top of its display. This is true for all the screen images you will see in this book as well as what you will experience on your own PC. Still, we think it better to draw memory maps as diagrams with address 0 at the bottom. Be warned, though, not everyone agrees.

Intel Order for Data

Small binary numbers (integers from 0 to 255) can fit into a single byte. Usually, though, binary numbers in PCs are stored in more than 1 byte. A *word* refers to 2 bytes; four bytes are called a *double-word.* (You'll also run across references to half a byte, which is commonly called a *nibble.*) Many programs store binary numbers in words, double-words, and occasionally even in quadruple words (8 bytes).

When you fit a number into 2 or more bytes, a question arises as to which part of the number goes into each byte. There are two contradictory industry conventions. Intel order specifies that the least significant byte of a multibyte binary number goes into the lowest memory address; succeeding bytes go into the following, higher addresses. Motorola order is exactly the reverse. Another name for Intel order is *Hebrew notation* because written Hebrew reads from right to left. Converting from one order to the opposite has become such an issue that the latest versions of microprocessors from both Intel and Motorola (the 486 and 68040) each include special order-conversion instructions.

Most PC memory-peeking programs use a display convention that was established by the earliest versions of the DOS DEBUG program. (An example of DEBUG's output is shown later in this chapter, in Figure 6-8.) DEBUG's "dump" display shows the contents of memory in two forms: hexadecimal and ASCII. The hex display shows you what is actually in each byte. The ASCII display shows what those bytes correspond to, if anything, as ASCII characters. Because character strings are stored one character per byte with the first character at the lowest address (an ordering that is used both on PCs using an Intel CPU chip and those using a Motorola CPU chip), DEBUG shows memory in the same order, which means that it shows you all numbers in a reverse order of the bytes within each binary number.

To make things even more confusing, DEBUG shows the contents of each byte as two hexadecimal symbols side by side. And here it uses the more "natural" order, putting the least significant symbol on the right. Thus, the four-symbol hexadecimal number ABCDh, in which the A nibble is the most significant and the D nibble is least significant, is displayed by DEBUG this way: `CD AB`. Not quite what you'd expect, is it? Reading numbers from the DEBUG dump display is something you have to get used to in order to be comfortable using DOS power-user functions.

The Five (or Six) Kinds of DOS-Accessible Memory

PCs running DOS have five or six distinct kinds of memory they can access. The distinction between these is based partly on the memory addresses at

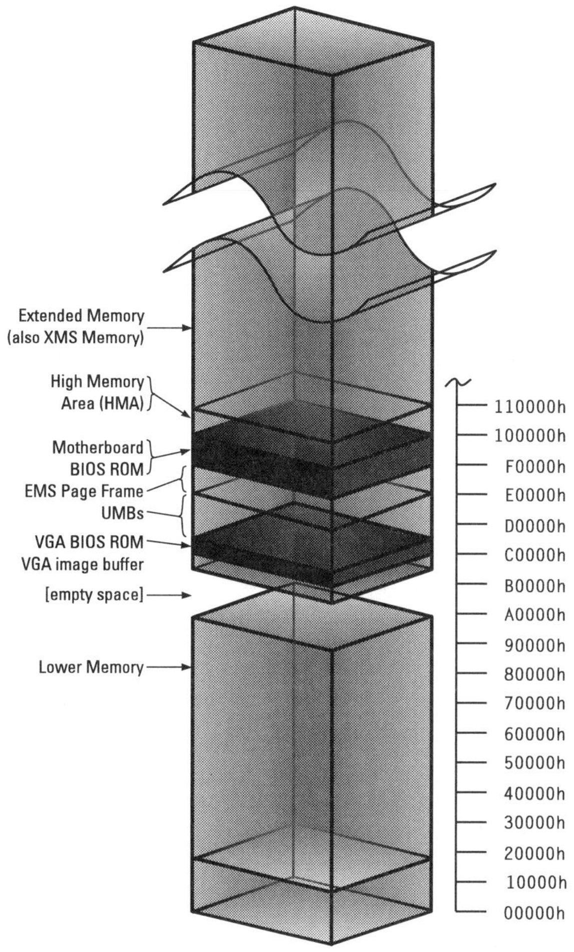

Figure 6-4 DOS-accessible memory types

which each kind of memory resides and partly on the protocols that must be followed by programs seeking to access memory at those addresses. Figure 6-4 shows all these memory varieties graphically. The following sections describe each one and what distinguishes it from the others.

Lower Memory

The first 640KB of the memory address space is very special. Originally, in the first PCs and XTs, it was all the RAM in which programs could be placed. Even today, it is the most convenient place to load a program. Much of PC memory management revolves around keeping as much of this space as possible open and available for application programs. This space is called *lower memory*, but is also referred to as *system memory* and *conventional memory*.

Upper Memory

The rest of the first megabyte was originally reserved by IBM for system uses, such as video image buffers in the region from address A0000h to BFFFFh and BIOS ROMs in the region from E0000h to FFFFFh); the remainder was called *reserved memory*.

Reserved memory (from C0000h to DFFFFh) is the only place where option ROMs can be put to be activated during the boot process. It is also where the expanded memory page frame normally resides. (Expanded memory is discussed shortly in more detail.) Early PCs had gaps in this region of the memory address space. In modern PCs those patches often get filled in with RAM that has been remapped.

The entire region from A0000h (640KB) to FFFFFh (1MB) is called *upper memory*. When a portion of that space is filled with RAM and made available for the storage of programs, that portion is called an *upper memory block* (UMB).

EXTENDED MEMORY

Memory locations with addresses in excess of 1M are considered *extended memory*. Any PC that uses an 80286 or higher-level x86 chip can have extended memory, and any program that can put the PC into protected mode can access that memory. Until recently, however, PCs running DOS have not had any really good ways to control the use of that memory. There are well-defined ways that DOS manages lower memory, because when DOS first was written, lower memory was the only place a PC could have any RAM. But DOS was not built to manage any other kind of memory. Usually, a program acquires extended memory through an *XMS memory manager* (*XMM*), which is designed to implement and conform to the eXtended Memory Specification.

Note: The problem with extended memory is not really due to a lack of standards, since today there are at least three "standard" methods of gaining control of some extended memory. The original method, called the VDISK method after the program that first used it, is to look in memory just beyond the 1MB address. If you don't see a "flag" there proclaiming that region as occupied (by another copy of VDISK), then you put *your* flag there and stake your claim. The data structure that VDISK installs (as its "flag") not only says it is resident, it also proclaims how much extended memory it is going to consider as its turf.

By the VDISK rules, no checking is done to see if any other program is using any extended memory other than looking for the VDISK "flag in the sand" just past 1MB. If that flag is found, but the associated numbers do not indicate that all of extended memory has been claimed, VDISK will skip over the portion that has been claimed and then set its flag in memory just beyond that region. This method keeps only one copy of VDISK from trashing the area claimed by another copy of VDISK. Any other program that wants to use extended memory has to check first to be sure that a copy of VDISK is not using it.

Microsoft improved on the VDISK strategy by what has been called the "white lie" technique for acquiring extended memory. Its RAMDRIVE.SYS program (which is otherwise a RAM disk program very much like VDISK.SYS) asks the BIOS how much extended memory the PC has. The program takes for itself however much extended memory it wants from the region just under the top of extended memory.

Next, RAMDRIVE.SYS hooks the interrupt that is used by programs that want to ask the BIOS for the amount of memory in the PC. Thereafter, if any program asks the BIOS (by that interrupt call) how much extended memory the PC has, the request will be intercepted by RAMDRIVE.SYS, which simply will lie to the requesting program. The lie it tells hides the extended memory that RAMDRIVE is using from all other programs' view. This strategy is more formally called the INT15h way of acquiring extended memory. For safety's sake, any program using this technique must first check by the VDISK rules to be sure it doesn't intrude on space claimed by that means.

Both of these methods allow multiple programs to acquire portions of extended memory. Neither one, however, is very good at letting a program relinquish memory it no longer needs.

An XMS memory management program is a device driver that, once loaded, examines extended memory and grabs all of it that is unclaimed. (You can direct it to leave some amount of extended memory available for acquisition by the INT15h strategy, but by default, an XMS memory manager will take over all of extended memory for its exclusive use and control.)

Again, for safety's sake, the XMS manager must look first for any memory that has been claimed according to the VDISK rules. Then it can grab whatever is left after that.

Once an XMM is loaded, other programs can ask it for any of the memory it is holding. This strategy supports both allocation and deallocation of memory. The memory acquisition protocol is, however, quite different from either the VDISK or INT15h method—so much so, that memory acquired by that alternate method is often called XMS memory, instead of extended memory.

Expanded Memory

Originally, there was no more than 1MB of memory address space in any early PC, but many programmers coveted more. A number of companies came up with a strategy variation called *expanded memory*, which is a way to make as much as 16MB of RAM show up, a piece at a time, in the PC's memory address space. To do this, 64KB of the memory address space must be dedicated to use as a "window" into the larger RAM space. This also means that only 64KB of expanded memory can be accessed by the CPU at any one time. But with appropriate fast footwork on the part of the *expanded memory manager*, the pieces of expanded memory can be juggled in and out of the PC's memory address space so rapidly that programs can be given the illusion that they can have unlimited expanded memory. The expanded memory manager is an installable device driver (like the XMM), and is often called an *EMS memory manager* or *EMM*, because it operates according to a protocol defined in the Expanded Memory Specification.

The most important thing to know about expanded memory is that it is an available option in *any* PC. If your PC has only an 8088 as the CPU, you may still install an EMS memory board, add a line to your CONFIG.SYS file to load its EMM, and away you go.

After several generations, the EMS standard is now at version 4.0, and all good EMS hardware and software should support most of the features described in this document. All of them will claim "compatibility" or "compliance" with the EMS 4.0 standard, but be aware that this doesn't insure that

Warning: Use only the EMM driver that comes with the hardware. The same thing will work with any PC up to the very latest and greatest 486. But once you get to the 386 level (including the 386SX), there is a better way to achieve the same result. It is discussed in the section "Fundamental DOS Memory Managers" later in this chapter.

they support all of its features. Often all the product can do with respect to some feature is recognize what a program is asking for and tell the program, "Sorry, I don't do that."

The High Memory Area (HMA)

The first 64KB beyond address 1M can be accessed two ways. It is the first 64KB of extended memory (accessible only when the CPU is operating in protected mode), and it also is accessible in real mode as the high memory area (HMA).

The RAM chips that are at those memory addresses can serve only one of these two purposes at a time, and some memory management program must decide which purpose that will be at any particular time. When you load an XMM in accordance with the XMS document's requirements, that program not only manages extended memory, it also creates and controls the HMA. The XMM is built with the knowledge of how to control the A20 gate that permits or denies real-mode programs access to the HMA. The XMM also manages upper memory, if you have any available RAM in that region.

XMS Memory

Lower, upper, extended, and expanded memory, and the HMA are the five kinds of DOS-accessible memory. XMS memory is really just another name for extended memory, but since the access protocols are quite distinct, it may be (and sometimes is) considered a sixth kind of memory.

Management of Memory and Other Resources

An operating system's primary responsibility is to take control of the computer's resources and then parcelling them out to whatever program may need them on a first-come, first-served basis, subject only to some possible restrictions on what resources certain programs are allowed to use. DOS provides allocation and deallocation services over both memory and disk space. Allocation means assigning a given patch of memory or disk space to a particular program. Deallocation is when the program gives back some or all of what it was granted, so other programs may use that same resource later on.

The other key role that an operating system performs is *conflict arbitration.* DOS does this in some respects, but not all. The design of DOS assumed that every program running in a PC would be a responsible program, and that only one would actually be executing at a time. This is part of the reason DOS is described as a *single-tasking, single-user operating system.*

The principal resource for any program in any computer is memory in which to load the program code and the data that is to be processed. Disk space on which to store the program and its data files is another vital resource. Every input/output port is a resource, as are interrupts, IRQ levels, and DMA channels. One region of memory has a dedicated function above and beyond that of merely storing information and so deserves to be thought of as a separate resource. This is the video image buffer. Information stored there shows up on your screen.

Any program might need to use any of these resources. If you never let more than one program run in your PC at a time, each program could just grab whatever resources it wanted. But few people run only one program at a time these days—power users often run many programs simultaneously.

It is not important that the programs actually be executing instructions at the same time; in fact, that cannot happen in a PC. What does matter in terms of resource allocation is whether or not each program ends its use of all resources before another program begins using some. You may well have some programs that take turns running, but that also hold onto resources while they are idle, waiting for their next turn to execute.

The only sane way to handle this sort of situation is to empower one central arbiter of requests for each of the PC's resources. DOS is normally the designated arbiter, at least for memory and disk space. But the designated arbiter can allocate only those resources of which it is aware.

If you have expanded memory, the EMM (EMS memory management device driver) will be the gatekeeper over all requests for use of EMS memory. If you have loaded an XMM (XMS memory manager), it will serve a similar role with respect to extended memory, the high memory area, and any available blocks of memory in the upper memory region. (The last regions are those called upper memory blocks, or UMBs).

If you run an operating environment on top of DOS, especially one that allows for multitasking or task swapping, that program will have to assume much of the duties of the operating system with respect to conflict arbitration. This is especially true for resources like input/output ports and the video image buffer. For example, Windows or DESQview must be allocated some memory by the appropriate memory manager. Then, as each task is launched, Windows or DESQview will suballocate a portion of that memory for program code and data areas; plus it will allocate some memory for use as a virtual video image buffer. The task manager (DESQview or Windows, in our example) is responsible for keeping the real video image buffer updated with information from the task that "owns" each individual window on the screen. (The issues of memory management and video are discussed further in Chapter 5.) Likewise, any tasks that want to use the printer or a communications port will be allowed to do so only if the task manager has allocated that resource to that task.

The DOS Memory Tools

Any modern PC operating system must be prepared to handle this diversity of memory and other resources effectively. MS-DOS and PC DOS have been upgraded many times for just this purpose. With version 5, DOS acquired a number of new tools for managing memory. In version 6 these tools have been strengthened and supplemented with some additional tools. In the following sections we'll cover those tools and how they work.

DOS Memory Reporting Tools

In many ways, the most crucial tool is the one that lets you see what is where in memory. From the outset, DOS has included a programmer's tool, DEBUG, which has the capability to display the contents of any specified region of memory.

DEBUG is valuable, but it's not for everyone—DEBUG can be dangerous to your data if you don't know what you are doing. So, starting with version 4, both Microsoft and IBM included a memory usage reporting tool with DOS called the MEM program, which has been significantly improved in DOS 6.

MEM

When you type `MEM` at the DOS prompt and press Enter, you'll see a quick summary of how much memory you have and how much you are using of four of the DOS-accessible kinds of memory. (Extended memory and XMS memory are lumped together. The only memory not fully reported on is expanded.)

If you were accustomed to the MEM command in DOS 5, you may be surprised by what you see when you first use the DOS 6 MEM command. The reporting style has changed quite a bit, giving considerably more information about the breakdown of available memory. (Only the amount of information on expanded memory is less than it was.)

Furthermore, if you type `MEM /D`, you will get considerably more information. Figure 6-5 shows a sample of the output it generates. (This output is actually too much to fit on a single screen. Figure 6-5 was crafted to look as if it were a single screen capture, but it wasn't.) Another change from the DOS 5 version is that MEM now supports a /P command line switch to make it pause after each screenful of information has been displayed. (In DOS 5, the /P switch gave almost the same information as /D—just a few items were omitted in the /P version.)

You certainly can learn a lot about what is where in memory by studying the MEM /D output. The only drawbacks are that you get almost too much detail, and the numbers are all in hexadecimal. If MEM /D gives you a report on

```
C:\ >MEM /D

Conventional Memory Detail:

  Segment         Total           Name          Type
  -------    ----------------  -----------   --------
   00000         1039     (1K)                Interrupt Vector
   00040          271     (0K)                ROM Communication Area
   00050          527     (1K)                DOS Communication Area
   00070         3120     (3K)  IO            System Data
                                   CON        System Device Driver
                                   AUX        System Device Driver
                                   PRN        System Device Driver
                                   CLOCK$     System Device Driver
                                   A: - C:    System Device Driver
                                   COM1       System Device Driver
                                   LPT1       System Device Driver
                                   LPT2       System Device Driver
                                   LPT3       System Device Driver
                                   COM2       System Device Driver
                                   COM3       System Device Driver
                                   COM4       System Device Driver
   00133         5424     (5K)  MSDOS         System Data
   00286        54144    (53K)  IO            System Data
                 1136     (1K)     XMSXXXX0   Installed Device=HIMEM
                 3104     (3K)     EMMQXXX0   Installed Device=EMM386
                44240    (43K)     DBLSBIN$   Installed Device=DBLSPACE
                 1488     (1K)                FILES=30
                  960     (1K)                FCBS=16
                  512     (1K)                BUFFERS=30
                  704     (1K)                LASTDRIVE=H
                 1856     (2K)                STACKS=9,128
   00FBE           80     (0K)  MSDOS         System Program
   00FC3         2640     (3K)  COMMAND       Program
   01068           80     (0K)  MSDOS         -- Free --
   0106D          272     (0K)  COMMAND       Environment
   0107E          224     (0K)  MEM           Environment
   0108C        88368    (86K)  MEM           Program
   0261F       499200   (488K)  MSDOS         -- Free --

Upper Memory Detail:

  Segment  Region     Total           Name          Type
  -------  ------  ----------------  -----------   --------
   0CD3A     1        3136    (3K)  MSDOS         -- Free --

   0CF01     2          48    (0K)  MSDOS         -- Free --
   0CF04     2       27264   (27K)  SMARTDRV      Program
   0D5AC     2          96    (0K)  MOUSE         Environment
   0D5B2     2       10608   (10K)  MOUSE         Program
   0D849     2          96    (0K)  MSDOS         -- Free --
   0D84F     2        5248    (5K)  SHARE         Program
   0D997     2         192    (0K)  MSDOS         -- Free --
   0D9A3     2         560    (1K)  FBPSCHED      Program
   0D9C6     2       91040   (89K)  MSDOS         -- Free --

Memory Summary:

  Type of Memory        Total        =       Used        +       Free
  ----------------  ----------------   ----------------   ----------------
  Conventional        655360  (640K)      67712   (66K)     587648  (574K)
  Upper               138288  (135K)      43776   (43K)      94512   (92K)
  Adapter RAM/ROM     254928  (249K)     254928  (249K)          0    (0K)
  Extended (XMS)     4194304 (4096K)    1150976 (1124K)    3043328 (2972K)
  ----------------  ----------------   ----------------   ----------------
  Total memory       5242880 (5120K)    1517392 (1482K)    3725488 (3638K)

  Total under 1 MB    793648  (775K)     111488  (109K)     682160  (666K)

  Memory accessible using Int 15h             0    (0K)
  Largest executable program size        587552  (574K)
  Largest free upper memory block         91040   (89K)
  MS-DOS is resident in the high memory area.

  XMS version 3.00; driver version 3.09
```

Figure 6-5 Typical output from MEM /D

```
C:\ >MEM /C

Modules using memory below 1 MB:

  Name          Total       =   Conventional   +   Upper Memory
  --------  ----------------   ----------------   ----------------
  MSDOS       16077    (16K)     16077    (16K)          0     (0K)
  HIMEM        1152     (1K)      1152     (1K)          0     (0K)
  EMM386       3120     (3K)      3120     (3K)          0     (0K)
  DBLSPACE    44256    (43K)     44256    (43K)          0     (0K)
  COMMAND      2912     (3K)      2912     (3K)          0     (0K)
  SMARTDRV    27264    (27K)         0     (0K)      27264    (27K)
  MOUSE       10704    (10K)         0     (0K)      10704    (10K)
  SHARE        5248     (5K)         0     (0K)       5248     (5K)
  FBPSCHED      560     (1K)         0     (0K)        560     (1K)
  Free       682160   (666K)    587648   (574K)      94512    (92K)

Memory Summary:

  Type of Memory        Total       =      Used        +       Free
  ----------------  -----------------   -----------------   -----------------
  Conventional         655360   (640K)     67712    (66K)     587648   (574K)
  Upper                138288   (135K)     43776    (43K)      94512    (92K)
  Adapter RAM/ROM      254928   (249K)    254928   (249K)          0     (0K)
  Extended (XMS)      4194304  (4096K)   1150976  (1124K)    3043328  (2972K)
  ----------------  -----------------   -----------------   -----------------
  Total memory        5242880  (5120K)   1517392  (1482K)    3725488  (3638K)

  Total under 1 MB     793648   (775K)    111488   (109K)     682160   (666K)

  Largest executable program size       587552   (574K)
  Largest free upper memory block        91040    (89K)
  MS-DOS is resident in the high memory area.
```

Figure 6-6 Typical output from MEM /C

upper memory, pay attention to whether you have multiple regions in upper memory that say they contain programs. If you do, you may be able to improve the management of upper memory by merging some of them. This point is further discussed later in this chapter.

If you want a summary of how much memory each program uses and are willing to forgo knowing exactly where each one is, there is another way to invoke the MEM command that will give you just what you want: Type `MEM /C`. Figure 6-6 shows you what the output of this command looks like. Not only does this command pull together multiple entries per program, it also reports everything in both decimal numbers of bytes and decimal numbers of KB.

If you want to know more about how one particular program uses memory, enter the command `MEM /M:modulename`. What might not be obvious at first glance is that the module name you have to use is the name listed in the output of the `MEM /C` or `MEM /D` command in the Name column. Figure 6-7 shows a couple of examples of this output.

DEBUG

Many people are scared of using DEBUG, and rightfully so. It is necessary to know how to use this program safely. In Chapter 15 all the ins and outs of DEBUG will be covered. For now, we want to show you only how it can be used to peek at memory.

The major problem with DEBUG is its terse interface. If you type `DEBUG` and press Enter, you will get a simple hyphen as the prompt. You are supposed to know what to do next. Of course, the most important thing to know

```
C:\ >MEM /M:SMARTDRV

SMARTDRV is using the following memory:

  Segment  Region       Total          Type
  -------  ------  ----------------  --------
   0CF04      2     27264    (27K)   Program
                   ----------------
  Total Size:       27264    (27K)

C:\ >MEM /M:MSDOS

MSDOS is using the following memory:

  Segment  Region       Total          Type
  -------  ------  ----------------  --------
   00133             5424     (5K)   System Data
   00FBE               80     (0K)   System Program
   01068               80     (0K)   -- Free --
   0261F           499200   (488K)   -- Free --
   0CD3A      1      3136     (3K)   -- Free --
   0CF01      2        48     (0K)   -- Free --
   0D849      2        96     (0K)   -- Free --
   0D997      2       192     (0K)   -- Free --
   0D9C6      2     91040    (89K)   -- Free --
                   ----------------
```

Figure 6-7 Samples of the output from MEM /M

(about any program) is how to quit. In DEBUG, any time you are at the hyphen prompt, just type `Q` and press Enter to get out of DEBUG and back to the DOS prompt. Fortunately, the DOS HELP program has a lot of information on how to use DEBUG. Also, whenever you are at the hyphen prompt you can type `?` and press Enter to get a quick reminder of all the legal commands.

To show the contents of a region of memory, start DEBUG, and at the hyphen prompt type `D segment:offset`. The D stands for dump; the address is where you want DEBUG to start showing you the contents of memory. (Naturally, you need to put in explicit numbers for the segment and offset.) All numbers you enter in DEBUG must be in hexadecimal. Figure 6-8 shows a sample DEBUG memory dump.

Another useful DEBUG trick shows you not only the hexadecimal numbers stored in memory, but what those numbers mean to the CPU as instructions. This is done using the U (unassemble) command. See Chapter 13 for details.

There is one very important limitation to DEBUG as a memory-snooping tool, and this limitation also applies to many other memory snoopers. DEBUG (and those other tool programs) operates only in real mode, which means it can snoop only inside the first megabyte. (If you manage to open the

```
C:\ >DEBUG
-D 40:0
0040:0000  F8 03 F8 02 00 00 00 00-78 03 00 00 00 00 00 00   ........x.......
0040:0010  21 44 C0 80 02 02 00 40-00 00 2C 00 2C 00 44 20   !D.....@..,.,.D
0040:0020  20 39 34 05 30 0B 3A 27-30 0B 0D 1C 4C 26 53 1F    94.0.:'0...L&S.
0040:0030  0D 1C 44 20 45 12 42 30-55 16 47 22 0D 1C 01 00   ..D E.B0U.G"....
0040:0040  F6 00 00 00 00 00 00 02-02 03 50 00 00 10 00 00   ..........P.....
0040:0050  00 08 00 00 00 00 00 00-00 00 00 00 00 00 00 00   ................
0040:0060  07 06 00 D4 03 29 30 76-07 8C 19 00 75 CA 0E 00   .....)0v....u...
0040:0070  00 00 00 00 00 01 00 00-14 14 14 34 01 01 01 01   ...........4....
-Q
```

Figure 6-8 Sample DEBUG memory content display

A20 gate, you could also snoop inside the HMA, but doing so requires knowing either how to operate the specific A20 gate hardware on your PC [which is truly arcane knowledge], or how to ask your XMM to open the gate for you.)

Fundamental DOS Memory Managers

You may need to simultaneously load as many as four different memory managers in your PC. How many and which ones you load depend on what class of CPU your PC uses, whether you have a hardware EMS board installed, whether you have extended memory installed, and what it is you wish to accomplish. The four memory managers are listed below:

1. There is one memory manager you must load—DOS itself, which is the memory manager for lower memory. It can also manage upper memory, but it does so only after another memory manager (an XMM) has initially taken control of that memory.
2. The second memory manager is the XMM. Microsoft and IBM supply HIMEM.SYS (discussed later in this chapter) with DOS as their XMM. This program manages upper and extended memory and the HMA.
3. The third memory manager you might load is actually a combination program for converting XMS memory into simulated EMS memory and/or into upper memory and an EMM. The DOS-bundled version of this program is EMM386.EXE, also discussed later in this chapter.
4. The fourth memory manager you may need is an EMM. This is the only way to manage expanded memory on a hardware plug-in card.

Figure 6-9 shows the different regions of memory that are managed by each of these memory managers.

DOS AS A MEMORY MANAGER

Initially, as DOS is loading, there is no memory manager. There is only one program running—the SYSINIT portion of IO.SYS. Once that program has loaded MSDOS.SYS, it relinquishes control of the rest of lower memory to DOS.

DOS exerts its control by putting small data structures called *memory control blocks* (MCBs) or *memory arena headers* in memory at the lowest address of each distinct memory region it has allocated. Each of these control blocks is 16 bytes long (called a *paragraph*), and each one starts at a memory address that is an exact integer multiple of 16 (a *paragraph boundary*.) The contents of a memory control block indicate essentially three things: which program has

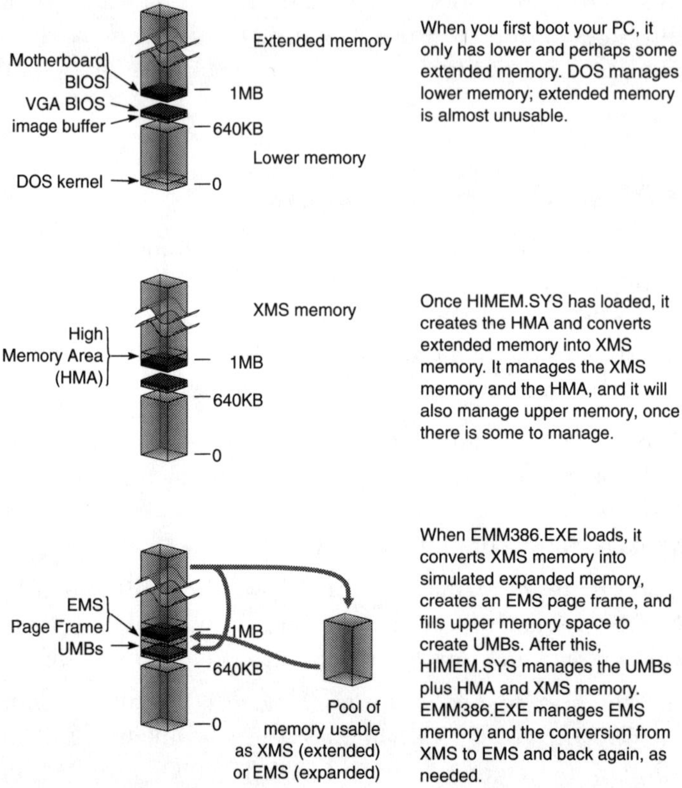
Extended memory
Motherboard BIOS
VGA BIOS
image buffer
1MB
640KB
Lower memory
DOS kernel
0
When you first boot your PC, it only has lower and perhaps some extended memory. DOS manages lower memory; extended memory is almost unusable.
XMS memory
High Memory Area (HMA)
1MB
640KB
0
Once HIMEM.SYS has loaded, it creates the HMA and converts extended memory into XMS memory. It manages the XMS memory and the HMA, and it will also manage upper memory, once there is some to manage.
EMS Page Frame
UMBs
1MB
640KB
0
Pool of memory usable as XMS (extended) or EMS (expanded)
When EMM386.EXE loads, it converts XMS memory into simulated expanded memory, creates an EMS page frame, and fills upper memory space to create UMBs. After this, HIMEM.SYS manages the UMBs plus HMA and XMS memory. EMM386.EXE manages EMS memory and the conversion from XMS to EMS and back again, as needed.

Figure 6-9 Memory regions and their managers

been given the use of that region, how big the region is, and what type of memory control block this one is.

If you move up in memory address space from the MCB by the size of the memory region it controls plus the size of the control block itself, you will come to the next memory control block. Keep doing this and you will be "walking the memory control block chain" until you come to a block that is marked as the end of the chain (see Figure 6-10).

The first byte in a memory control block signifies its type. There are only two main types: the last one in a chain is always of type Z; all the others in that chain are of type M. Some blocks, however, have subchains within them. These are always blocks that are allocated to the operating system. These subchains are called device chains because some of the sub-blocks they define are used to load device drivers. Other sub-blocks are used for other important DOS data structures such as the DOS disk buffers, system file table, file control blocks, public stacks, and the current directory structure.

Memory Control Block (MCB) Structure

Byte Position	Contents
0	Block Type M for most MCBs Z for final MCB in chain Other values for device sublocks: D = Device Driver (from DEVICE line in CONFIG.SYS) E = Device Driver appendage I = Installable file system (currently not used in DOS) F = System file table extension (if FILES > 5 in CONFIG.SYS) X = File Control Blocks (from FCBS line in CONFIG.SYS) B = DOS disk buffers (from BUFFERS line in CONFIG.SYS) L = Current Directory Structure (holds current DOS directory for each drive; size set by LASTDRIVE line in CONFIG.SYS) S = Code and data area for DOS stacks (size set by STACKS line in CONFIG.SYS)
1 and 2	Process ID 0000h for free space 0008h for system block = address of Program Segment Prefix (PSP) for all other MCBs (third-party memory managers use other values as well)
3 and 4	Size in paragraphs (bytes / 16)
5 through 7	-- reserved --
8 through 15	Owner name The name only appears here if this MCB controls the memory containing the PSP of the program that owns it. (This is shown by the value in Process ID being one greater than the segment portion of the address of this MCB.) The name is terminated with nulls or spaces.

Figure 6-10 Memory control blocks

When you use `MEM /D`, you are asking the MEM program to walk the memory control block chain and report what it finds. MEM does some translating for you, but basically each MCB corresponds to one entry in the MEM /D output. (The sizes reported by MEM /D don't include the associated memory control block, but those reported by MEM /C do.)

Prior to version 5, DOS always built and maintained exactly one chain of memory control blocks. Later versions of DOS still create that primary memory control block chain, but they may create others as well. The primary chain must remain unbroken, and it must account for all of lower memory above the address at which it starts. If that chain is ever corrupted (so DOS cannot successfully walk it from end to end), DOS will issue a chilling message that says either: `Memory allocation error` or `Memory control blocks destroyed`, and then DOS halts your PC.

Other memory control block chains can exist in other regions of memory. Third-party memory managers typically create their own private chains in upper memory. The chains they create are very similar to those DOS creates, but since only the third-party memory program knows where these chains start, only it can use them.

MEM cannot see chains created by third-party managers, but the DOS Power Tools MCB-walking program, MCBS, can sometimes find and display them for you. To try this, invoke it with the command line `MCBS a`, or, if you know or even suspect where a memory control block chain might start in upper memory, use

```
MCBS u aaaa
```

where *aaaa* is the segment portion of the upper memory address, expressed in hexadecimal, you want to check. If there is a chain starting there that has at least a couple of blocks, MCBS will display it. You can even check two addresses at once with this form of the command:

```
MCBS u aaaa bbbb
```

where *aaaa* and *bbbb* are the two upper memory segment values to check. The complete syntax of MCBS is

```
MCBS [d] ¦ [b aaaa] ¦ [u aaaa [bbbb]] ¦ a
```

If you have no command-line arguments, MCBS will display the ordinary lower-memory, DOS-managed memory control block chain. If you use the `d` command-line parameter, you are asking MCBS to show you that chain plus the device sub-block chain in lower memory. The `u` parameter shows only one or two chains in upper memory at addresses you must specify in hexadecimal as segment values. The `b` parameter shows both the lower memory chain and one upper memory chain (whose address you must specify). Parameter `a` tells MCBS to sniff out and show you any memory control block chains it finds. (It won't always find every one, which is why it can be useful to have the `u` and `b` options. Also, be aware that MCBS does not pause when the screen fills. If you want to see all of a long chain or a listing of multiple chains, you will have to either pipe MCBS through the FIND filter

```
MCBS a ¦ MORE
```

or send the output to a file

```
MCBS a > file-specification
```

or to your printer

```
MCBS a > PRN
```

After you have sent the output to a file, it is suggested you use the LIST program (from the DOS Power Tools disk) to look at the contents of that file.

Starting with version 5, DOS gained the ability to maintain more than one chain of memory control blocks. It always uses just one chain in lower memory, however; it may use several in upper memory.

If you have specified `DOS=UMB` in your CONFIG.SYS file, you are telling DOS that you want it to manage upper as well as lower memory. Once DOS has been told to manage upper memory, it will look for an XMM program that might have some upper memory under its control. DOS will ask the XMM to allocate to DOS any available upper memory the XMM has. DOS does this after any program runs, just in case that program created or freed up some upper memory.

If DOS finds some upper memory, it usually will do two things with it. First, it builds a "private" chain of memory control blocks that describe all of that memory and all the other space in the upper memory region from the start of the upper memory obtained from the XMM to the start of the motherboard BIOS ROM. Some of the memory control blocks in this chain describe regions of RAM into which programs may be loaded (upper memory blocks). The other memory control blocks in this chain will include any option ROMs and the EMS page frame, if you have one. The second thing DOS does is put a memory control block at the top of lower memory (normally, at address 9FFF0h). This memory control block is marked as belonging to the system, and its size is at least large enough to span the entire video image buffer area plus any video option ROM that you may have starting at C0000h.

> **Note:** If you have created upper memory blocks in the monochrome video display buffer area (between B0000h and B7FFFh), then the memory controlled by the memory control block at 9FFF0h will span only across the A page. The next memory control block in that chain will be at B0000h and will control the UMB that extends to B7FF0h. At B7FFF0h is another memory control block to span the video buffer for color text and the EGA or VGA option ROM, if you have one.

The memory control block at 9FFF0h is the start of a "public" upper memory block chain maintained by DOS. It uses this chain to allocate memory to programs and device drivers that you have asked DOS to load high. The second block in the chain that starts at 9FFF0h is put in the first paragraph of an upper memory block described by one of the MCBs in the DOS private upper memory block chain. From that location DOS extends its public chain of memory control blocks to the end of the available upper memory.

This placement of the MCBs means that the MCB for the private chain is immediately followed by the MCB in the public chain. The memory controlled by the MCB in the private chain includes all of the memory controlled by the MCB in the private chain, and sometimes even more.

Whenever you type `MEM /D`, if you have specified `DOS=UMB`, you will see a report on both lower and upper memory. The first part comes from walking the lower memory chain; the second part comes from walking the public upper memory chain that starts at 9FFF0h. MEM will never tell you anything about DOS's private upper memory block chain (except that the memory it controls will be included in the totals provided by MEM /C.

Look carefully at Figure 6-5. Notice that the upper memory chain is reported as starting at CD3A0h. (MEM reports the segment addresses; just add a 0 on the end to get the full, hexadecimal linear address.) In this computer there is a video option ROM that extends from C0000h to CBFFFFh. Therefore, upper memory could start at CC000h. Actually, in this PC, it does. If you were to look with DEBUG at that location (use the command `D CC00:0` at DEBUG's hyphen prompt), you would see a line that reads

```
CC00:0000  4D 01 C0 38 01 00 00 00-55 4D 42 20 20 20 20 20   M.......UMB
```

which is the first memory control block in DOS's private upper memory block chain. The letter M with which this MCB starts tells us that there is at least one more block in the chain. The size indicated in the fourth and fifth bytes tells where that next block is located.

The next memory control block in this chain is at CD390h (the paragraph just before the first upper memory MCB in DOS's public chain). The MCB at CD390h will have the name "UMB   " just like the block at CC000h.

The first memory control block (the one at CC000h) controls the region of memory from CC010h to CD138Fh. This is a UMB that contains a portion of the program code for the program EMM386.EXE. The rest of the private chain has a number of blocks in this machine to span the EMS page frame and some other obstacles in the upper memory region. Each of those other blocks will have one of three uses. If it spans a region that cannot be used for UMBs, it will be marked as allocated to the system. This keeps DOS from trying to put any programs there. Other blocks will, like the first one, contain program code indicating that DOS loaded "privately" and, therefore, will not show up in a MEM report. The third kind of block in DOS's private upper memory chain contains a number of smaller UMBs, each of which starts with an MCB that describes it. These blocks are reported by MEM (in Figure 6-5) as located in upper memory, and are where DOS loads programs into upper memory "publicly."

HIMEM.SYS AS MEMORY MANAGER

HIMEM.SYS is an installable device driver provided by Microsoft with DOS and Windows. It implements version 2.0 of the XMS standard. As such, it takes control of the A20 gate hardware in your computer, and it takes control of all of the extended memory that is available when it loads. Subsequently, it will make that memory available to any program that knows how to ask for it in accordance with the XMS 2.0 protocol.

Installing HIMEM You install HIMEM through a DEVICE line in your CONFIG.SYS file, the syntax of which is

```
DEVICE=[path]HIMEM.SYS [switches]
```

where [*path*] is the full path to where you have the HIMEM.SYS file stored on your disk (normally, C:\DOS). The Command Reference lists all the possible switches; in Chapter 12 we explain the more important ones in detail. Here, we will cover only the two that most people have to use, `/INT15=` and `/MACHINE:`.

> ***Note:*** Because HIMEM itself has to be installed before upper memory blocks can be created, you can't use the DEVICEHIGH option to load HIMEM high.

By default, HIMEM takes all of the extended memory, but you may request that it not do so. To exit simple extended memory, you must invoke HIMEM with the `/INT15` switch set to a value 64KB larger than the largest block you want to use as simple extended memory. For example, suppose you want to run an older disk-cache program—one that must be able to access extended memory by the INT15h protocol for its data buffer. Suppose you decide to reserve half a megabyte (512KB) for that program. The command line you need in your CONFIG.SYS file is

```
DEVICE=C:\DOS\HIMEM.SYS /INT15=576
```

(The extra 64KB is needed to allow for the HMA.)

The only other switch most people ever use with HIMEM is the /MACHINE switch. This tells HIMEM not to attempt to figure out how to control the A20 address line in your computer, but instead to look in a table of strategies it has and use the one that you are specifying through the /MACHINE switch. The proper syntax for using this switch is either

```
DEVICE=[path]HIMEM.SYS /MACHINE:17
```

or

```
DEVICE=[path]HIMEM.SYS /MACHINE:DELL
```

where we have shown as an example the setting for the Dell computerss with XBIOS. If you have a PS/2 computer, you might think you need to specify a machine type of PS2 or a code of 2, and you can, but it is almost never necessary; HIMEM usually figures out those computers by itself. (The switch `/MACHINE:` can be abbreviated `/M:` if you prefer; we like to use the full name as a reminder why that switch is there.)

If you're not sure that you need to use the /MACHINE switch, note what HIMEM tells you when you boot your PC. If HIMEM is unable to manipulate the A20 line successfully, you will get the message

```
Unable to control A20 line!
```

followed by

```
HMA not available; loading DOS low
```

if you had specified `DOS=HIGH` in your CONFIG.SYS file.

Microsoft says to put the DEVICE line that loads HIMEM.SYS first in your CONFIG.SYS file, but its SETUP program usually puts the one invoking SETVER.EXE there. You can save about three-quarters of a kilobyte of lower memory by moving the SETVER line after the HIMEM and EMM386 lines and changing it to read

```
DEVICEHIGH=C:\DOS\SETVER.EXE
```

DEVICEHIGH tells DOS to load SETVER into an upper memory block, but none are available until after both HIMEM and EMM386 have been loaded. (If you use PC DOS 6 and specify `DOS=HIGH` you don't need to use DEVICEHIGH; that version of DOS will automatically load SETVER into the HMA. You do have to have a DEVICE line for it, though.)

HOW HIMEM WORKS

HIMEM looks at the memory addresses just past 1MB. If it doesn't see the characteristic VDISK flag structure there, it will permit the first 64KB of extended memory to be accessed either as XMS memory or as the HMA (but not both). Which of these alternatives it chooses depends on which way a program first asks for it.

Once one program has asked for access to that region as the HMA, that region will remain the HMA until you reboot. Likewise, if a program uses that space as XMS memory before any program requests access to the HMA, then

HIMEM will not permit any program to access it as the HMA—until you reboot. These statements hold even if that first user of the region has already finished with it and relinquished the memory back to HIMEM.

HIMEM has another job. It is the primary memory manager for all the RAM that may be used for loading programs high. (HIMEM, however, has nothing to say about the RAM on your video card, nor about any RAM buffer that might be on a network interface card (NIC).) If you have asked DOS to manage upper memory (by using the `DOS=UMB` directive, then HIMEM will relinquish control of all upper memory RAM to DOS, and DOS will do the allocating and deallocating of that memory for other programs. If you don't use the `DOS=UMB` directive in your CONFIG.SYS file, then any program that wants to use some upper memory must ask HIMEM for it, following the XMS 2.0 protocol.

Note: Certain programs may locate and try to gain control of some RAM in upper memory. This can happen in a PC running in real mode, and nothing can prevent it. Just hope all your programs are sufficiently well behaved not to do this; otherwise, since HIMEM has not been informed that someone is using that space, it may well load yet another program on top of the first one. Or the first program may destroy a program HIMEM had previously loaded there.

HIMEM manages upper memory RAM if there is any. HIMEM does not create upper memory. That job is left to other programs, such as EMM386.EXE.

EMM386.EXE AS MEMORY MANAGER

Microsoft included its EMM386 program with Windows version 3.x, and both Microsoft and IBM include it with DOS, starting with version 5. This program has two, fundamentally different jobs to perform. One is to transform memory; the other is to manage it. In this section we'll describe its memory management role. In the next section we will describe its memory transforming role. First, though, we will explain how to install the EMM386 device driver (and why you might *not* want to load it in some situations).

Installing EMM386.EXE EMM386 is two programs in one. It is an installable device driver that you load through a DEVICE line in your CONFIG.SYS file, and it is an executable program you can run at the DOS prompt. As its name suggests, EMM386 is designed for 386- and 486-based PCs. In fact, it won't work on any other PCs. If you have a 386 or a 486, and if you ever run programs other than Windows and Windows applications, you probably will want to have EMM386 installed through a DEVICE line in your CONFIG.SYS file. Most people never need to use it at the DOS prompt. Furthermore, if you have not installed it in your CONFIG.SYS file, EMM386 will not do anything for you at the DOS prompt.

The syntax for EMM386 is

```
DEVICE=[path]EMM386.EXE [options]
```

where [*path*] is the full path to where you have the EMM386.EXE file stored on your disk (normally C:\DOS). There are many possibilities for the options. The Command Reference lists all of them; in Chapter 12 we explain the more important ones in detail. Here we will only discuss the ones that directly relate to memory conversion and allocation.

The most important thing to know about EMM386 is that if you install it with no switches, it does the following:

- creates an EMS page frame (which takes up 64KB) in upper memory
- converts at least 256KB of that XMS memory into EMS (and more likely 640KB)
- provides as much EMS memory as any program wants, up to the total amount of XMS memory that HIMEM.SYS has created

EMM386.EXE can create EMS memory only out of XMS, and it can manage (act as the EMM for) only the expanded memory it has created. The biggest news in DOS 6 is that EMM386 no longer irrevocably converts a specified amount of XMS memory into EMS. It is almost totally flexible in this regard. Thus, where formerly you had to specify how much EMS memory you wanted (unless you were content with the default of 256KB), now you have to specify only if you don't want it taking all of your memory, or if you want to be sure it converts at least some limited amount. You specify the maximum memory it may convert by putting that amount (specified in KB) in the command line as one of the options. You specify the minimum amount it will convert with the `MIN=yyyy` switch (*yyyy* is expressed in KB).

One obscure point about EMM386 is that, by default, it will replace the lower memory from 256KB through 640KB with EMS memory it has created. The RAM that was there simply disappears. When you read that EMM386 converts a minimum of 256KB, it is referrring to the amount it converts in addition to what it needs for this lower memory remapping. (This mapping is done to make progams like DESQview work with maximum effectiveness.)

EMM386.EXE will place the EMS page frame it creates in upper memory in a location it "thinks" is okay. Because it makes fairly conservative assumptions about what constitutes an okay place, most likely that location really is okay, but it may not be the *best* place for the EMS page frame from your perspective.

Without your instructions, EMM386 will *not* create any upper memory blocks. Therefore, the main choices you need to make at the outset are whether you want EMS memory and whether you want upper memory blocks. Then you must decide where to place the EMS page frame and any UMBs it creates.

The answer to the first question depends substantially on what programs you will be running, as many programs cannot take advantage of EMS memory. Windows and Windows applications, for example, use only extended memory (actually XMS memory). If all the programs you run are of this type, then you clearly will want to specify that EMM386 not make any EMS memory. The command line option to do this is `NOEMS`. And even if you do run DOS programs that need EMS memory, but you run them only from within a DOS window of Windows and you do so only when Windows is running 386-enhanced mode, you don't need to have EMM386 create any EMS memory; Windows will do it for you. If you are not sure, it might be best to let EMM386 create an EMS page frame and provide some EMS memory. However, if you find that you want to load more programs into upper memory than can fit there, you can access 64KB more space for UMBs by telling EMM386 not to create the page frame.

The answer to the second question—whether or not you want EMM386 to create upper memory—is simpler: It is hard to think of a situation in which the owner of a 386 or 486 would *not* want to have UMBs. Loading programs there frees up more lower memory so you can run more and larger DOS programs. Doing this also makes the DOS windows in Windows larger.

On the other hand, it is possible to get carried away creating UMBs. You don't want to use up every last scrap of upper memory for UMBs. If you run Windows, be sure to reserve at least 24KB of upper memory address space for its use. Also, leaving a small amount of "excess" upper memory free goes a long way toward making your system more stable.

To make EMS memory and UMBs, you must put the parameter `RAM` on the command line after EMM386.EXE; to make only UMBs, put `NOEMS` there; to make only EMS memory, put nothing there.

How much upper memory to make and where to put it (along with where to put the EMS page frame if you are going to have one) are the next questions to be answered. This is more complicated and is the reason many people found the optimization of memory use with DOS 5 so hard to do.

DOS 6 has a new program, MemMaker, designed to help you make all these choices. However, like any automatic program, its decisions are not always the best ones. You will do much better in managing your PC's memory if you take the time to learn what MemMaker does and how you can do it yourself. Here we will explain what the memory placement options are for EMM386 and how to select the appropriate ones to use. Later, we will provide some tips on running MemMaker. (Even if you already know how to do the job yourself, MemMaker can give you some welcome assistance.)

There are two ways to control EMM386's use of upper memory: One is by telling it what upper memory addresses it may use; the other is to tell it what portions of that space it may *not* use. Naturally, before you can tell EMM386 which memory regions it should or should not use, you have to know which ones are in use for some other purpose. If you omit these specifications, EMM386 will try to figure out for itself where it may or may not put UMBs. Its perception is, however, not always the best.

The A and B pages (addresses A0000h through BFFFFh) are designated by IBM for video image buffers, but not all of that space is necessarily in use, most notably the following:

- If you use either a monochrome video card or a CGA card.
- An MGA or MDA will use only the addresses from B0000h to B7FFFh (in full page Hercules emulation mode, an MGA card may use up to BFFFFh).
- The CGA card uses addresses from B8000h to BFFFFh.
- In any case, the entire A page (A0000h to AFFFFh) is available, and it makes perfect sense to let EMM386 put upper memory there.

VGA and EGA cards use the same range of addresses as CGA for color text, and they also use the entire A page for graphics. At most that means you could use the monochrome video region for an upper memory block, but often that is not advisable. If you have a super VGA card and use it in its most advanced graphics modes (those sporting the highest resolution and maximum numbers of colors), you definitely should not let EMM386 use any of the A or B pages.

Many memory optimizing programs tell you to use the range B0000h through B7FFFh, and MemMaker will ask you if you want to use it (if you choose Custom Setup), but our advice is "just say no."

If you are certain that you will never use your VGA card for anything but color text and the ordinary VGA graphics, you may be able to use the B000h to B7FFFh range for an upper memory block. We don't recommend this, however, as all too often you are unaware of what your video card needs. Some of the clone VGA cards use that region to store fonts even when they are in the standard VGA modes modeled after IBM's VGA design.

At the opposite end of upper memory, your PC's motherboard BIOS ROM occupies some or all of the range from E0000h to FFFFFh. But exactly how much is not always an easy question to answer. Many third-party diagnostic and memory utility programs attempt to answer it for you. Manifest is one of the best of this genre. (It comes bundled with QEMM, or you can buy it as a separate program.) CheckIt is another good program to use.

In the middle of upper memeory is a great, grey, hard-to-define region. The C and D pages are the designated places for optional, add-on BIOS ROMs. If you have an EGA or VGA video plug-in display card, it will almost certainly have an option ROM that occupies addresses starting at C0000h. EGA option ROMs often end at C5FFFh. VGA option ROMs usually go to C7FFFh. Rarely, a video option ROM may extend some or all of the way up to CFFFFh.

Many option cards have BIOS ROMs that can be placed at any of several locations in the C and D pages. You set the card to use by some jumpers, or perhaps by running a software setup program. Those with software setup programs often include a pretty good diagnostic tool that can find safe places with fairly high certainty. Those with jumpers rely on your knowing what else is where and then choosing a location to avoid all of those other users.

Your goal is to push every use of upper memory other than the EMS page frame and upper memory blocks to either the top or the bottom of the upper memory address range. If you succeed, you will have one unbroken open space in the middle. Then you can put the EMS page frame at one end of that space and use all the rest for upper memory. Often, however, you cannot do this, and you must accept having several nonadjacent regions of upper memory, which is better than not having that memory, but it is a bit less efficient way to use upper memory space, and it definitely takes more work to figure out which programs to load into each of the separate upper memory block regions.

Following are some typical cases and the memory that is available for each. Also shown in each case is the DEVICE line to use to load EMM386.EXE to best advantage:

1. Consider first a PC with a monochrome graphics card, network adapter (NIC), and a 64KB motherboard BIOS ROM. The MGA card requires addresses B0000h through B7FFFh (we are assuming it will not be used in full page mode). The NIC has a ROM that takes up 16KB and can be put at C8000h, D0000h, or D8000h. In this instance, we will assume it is put at D0000h. The motherboard BIOS ROM extends from F0000h to FFFFFh. You are not going to run Windows and you don't want an EMS page frame. In this example, you can create upper memory in the

following regions: A0000h through AFFFFh, B8000h through CFFFFh, and D4000h through EFFFFh, for a total of 272KB. The DEVICE line you need reads:

```
DEVICE=C:\DOS\EMM386.EXE /I:A000-AFFF /I=B800-CFFF /I=D400-EFFFh
```

Notice that the included (and excluded) regions are specified to EMM386 in terms of segments. Omit the last hex symbol in the total linear address at the beginning and end of a range when using them on the EMM386 command line.

2. With the same PC, you may wish to have an EMS page frame. In that case, you want the page frame located where it will not create yet another region for upper memory. You cannot have the EMS page frame start any lower than C0000h (unless you put it in lower memory, which is not a good idea), nor any higher than E0000h. The best choice here is to put it at C0000h so the NIC ROM is just above the EMS page frame. The DEVICE line now reads:

```
DEVICE=C:\DOS\EMM386.EXE /I:A000-AFFF /I=B800-BFFF /I=D400-EFFFh
/FRAME=C000
```

Again, you will have three regions in which upper memory blocks are created. However, now they only total 208KB.

3. Consider next a PC with a super VGA card, the same NIC, and a motherboard BIOS ROM that occupies only 32KB (with an additional 32KB used for the hardware setup program). This means that we must not use the addresses from F8FFFh to FFFFFh, but we may use F0000h through F7FFFh, even though there is ROM there. (We explain why mapping upper memory on top of the setup ROM may be an actual virtue in "The DOS Memory Creation Tool" section later in this chapter.) The video card we have specified means that we must exclude all the memory addresses in the A and B pages. The VGA option ROM is, we assume, 32KB in size; thus, it extends from C0000h to C7FFFh. The best choice for the NIC card is just above the VGA option ROM at C8000h.

   In this case, we will get only one region in which the EMS page frame and upper memory blocks may be placed, running from CC000h through F7FFFh. This spans a rather healthy 176KB, but you can't use it all for upper memory. We assume this PC will be used to run Windows, at least some of the time, so we choose to allocate 24KB for its use. The EMS page frame will take another 64KB. That still leaves 88KB for upper memory blocks. Not nearly what we got in the previous cases, but still enough to load a number of device drivers and TSR programs.

Where should we reserve memory for the Windows translation buffers, and where should we put the EMS page frame? Again, our goal is to avoid fragmenting whatever region we have left for upper memory blocks. In this case we would choose to put the Windows space right above the NIC, at addresses CC000h through D3FFFh, and the EMS page frame immediately after that. Now the DEVICE line reads:

```
DEVICE=C:\DOS\EMM386.EXE /X=A000-D3FF /I=E400-EFFFh /FRAME=D400
/WIN=CC00-D3FF
```

Notice the exclude specification `/X=A000-D3FF`. This might not be necessary, but it never hurts to explicitly tell EMM386 where you don't want it trying to put upper memory, especially if that region includes some spaces it normally likes to use, like the lower half of the B page.

There are other options for EMM386 that affect memory usage, but most users will not find it necessary to use them. If you think you might benefit from using them, you can read all about these options in Chapter 12 and the Command Reference.

Tip: You might benefit more from *not* loading EMM386. There are two reasons for this. When you load EMM386, you are putting your PC into protected mode, which causes a slight performance decrease and prevents you from running certain DOS programs. Second, you are using up a considerable amount of memory for which you might have better uses. Putting your PC into protected mode is usually a virtue, but it can be a problem if you are running some of the older, DOS-extended applications that want to do that job themselves. Also, your PC will run just a tad slower when it must constantly be switching between real and protected mode, as it does while EMM386 is running.

Finally, there is the issue of memory consumption. From the `MEM /D` display, you can see that EMM386 takes about 3KB of your lower memory. What that display fails to disclose is that EMM386 is also using at least 3.5KB of upper memory in one or more of DOS's private memory blocks. EMM386 is also using around 100KB of extended memory for its program code. Then, if it supplies any UMBs, all of that memory is taken out of the XMS memory pool, as is any expanded memory you get.

Now that EMM386 does not irrevocably convert XMS memory to EMS memory until it is used, you might think that you weren't wasting any XMS if you allow EMM386 to load and do its default thing, even though you aren't currently running any EMS applications. Actually, that is not quite correct. EMM386, by default, creates an EMS page frame, and it maps EMS memory into the top 384KB of lower memory (from 40000h to 9FFFFh).

All of these factors mean that just by loading EMM386 (with its default behavior), you will use more than half a megabyte of extended memory (100KB for the program, 386KB for lower memory, and 64KB for the EMS page frame). You can minimize its use of extended memory by specifying `NOEMS`. Of course, the ultimate way to decrease EMM386's memory consumption is not to use it at all, which is what you should do if you run only Windows and Windows programs. You also shouldn't load EMM386 if you will be running Windows all the time, even though you plan to run some DOS programs that need EMS memory in a DOS window within Windows. As long as you are running Windows in 386-enhanced mode, Windows will provide simulated EMS memory to any DOS programs that need it.

How EMM386 Manages Memory As a memory manager, EMM386 is an expanded memory manager (an EMM) conforming to the EMS standard, version 4.0. Notice, however, that EMM386 can manage only expanded memory that it has created out of XMS memory. It cannot be used to manage EMS memory on a hardware expanded memory board, nor any motherboard shadow RAM that may have been converted to EMS memory.

EMM386 is a full implementation of the LIM 4.0 EMS standard, lacking mainly the (seldom used) feature of aliasing of expanded memory blocks. This feature refers to the possibility that exists with some hardware expanded memory boards of putting the same chunk of RAM into the CPU's memory address space at two locations. The memory mapping capabilities of the 386 (and 486) chip that EMM386 uses don't permit emulating this feature.

The first version of this program was called EMM386.SYS. All later versions have been called EMM386.EXE. Be sure you erase the old SYS file version if you still have it on your disk. Indeed, you should be very careful to use only the latest version of this program (and any other, similar programs that you may get in various versions as you upgrade your DOS and Windows installations).

Note: EMM386 is useful only if you have a PC whose CPU is a 386 or 486. It won't run on ATs and XTs with 80286 and 8088 CPUs. If you have one of those PCs and want expanded memory, your best bet is probably to add a hardware expanded memory board and then use the EMM that comes with that board. Your only other option with MS-DOS is to try converting shadow RAM to EMS memory. This can be done for some PCs with certain chip sets by using a third-party memory manager such as QRAM, 386MAX, or UMBPro.

THIRD-PARTY MEMORY MANAGERS

In addition to the three DOS memory managers (DOS, HIMEM, and EMM386), you may need to load a fourth memory management program. That program would be an expanded memory manager, which you must use if you have a hardware expanded memory board or have converted some shadow RAM to EMS memory.

Another reason to load a third-party memory manager is if you use it in place of HIMEM and EMM386. Some popular choices for this use are QEMM, 386MAX, Netroom, Memory Commander, and QMAPS. In each case, the single program from the third-party vendor replaces both HIMEM and EMM386 (and replaces EMM386 in both memory management and memory transforming roles).

The MS-DOS documentation clearly specifies that if you choose to use a third-party memory manager you will have to use it both for providing and managing upper memory and for loading programs there. This is not true. The current versions of most third-party memory managers so faithfully mimic the DOS way of handling upper memory that you can use `DOS=UMB` and both the `DEVICEHIGH` and `LOADHIGH` commands with them.

There is only one possible advantage to using the third-party loaders, and there are some (minor) disadvantages. If you have an EMS page frame located immediately above a UMB, some of the third-party loaders can use the EMS page frame temporarily to let them load a TSR program that has a large load size, but a smaller run size. This can be useful if that program could not be loaded into the UMB without this help. On the other hand, LOADHIGH, which may be abbreviated as LH, is an internal DOS command, which means you don't need an additional program to accomplish what this does; COMMAND.COM already contains the needed code.

The version 5 DEVICEHIGH and LOADHIGH commands were more limited than many of the third-party loaders. You could not specify a region into which you wished to have them load a particular device driver or program. In version 6 these commands have that ability. (But LH still cannot borrow the EMS page frame for those situations when that could be helpful.) More about using the flexibility to load devices or TSR programs into specific upper memory regions will be explained shortly.

The DOS Memory Creation Tool

EMM386.EXE is more than just an expanded memory manager. It is almost a magical memory transformer. Many users invoke it only for this purpose; they ignore its EMM capabilities. EMM386's "magic" comes from the memory mapping power inherent in any 386 or 486 CPU chip. Once HIMEM has created a lot of XMS out of extended memory, EMM386 is able to take that memory and further transform it. Some of that memory may become simulated expanded memory, and some may become blocks of upper memory (UMBs). The resulting expanded memory may be mapped into much of lower memory space to facilitate task swapping with programs like DESQview, as well as showing up in an EMS page frame in upper memory.

Whenever XMS memory is mapped into a region of lower or upper memory address space, any memory that previously was at that location simply disappears. There is never a conflict, and you don't have to worry about removing memory chips or disabling memory address decoding as you do when installing a hardware expanded memory board. You do, however, have to be sure that you won't miss whatever disappears. If it was an important ROM, your PC could be disabled by its absence.

Starting with DOS 6, EMM386 has greater flexibility. With all earlier versions you had to decide at the outset how much XMS memory to let EMM386 convert to EMS memory (and upper memory). It would make that conversion, and thereafter, until you rebooted with a different set of parameters on the EMM386 line in your CONFIG.SYS file, that memory would no longer be available as XMS memory. Now, EMM386 can be given all of your XMS memory to play with. It will convert only what is actually needed as upper or expanded memory, leaving the rest for use as XMS memory. Any program asking how much memory is available as XMS or as EMS memory will get the same response, and that program can have whatever memory it wants from the EMM386 pool in either form the program chooses.

EMM386 has been able, for several versions, to place the EMS page frame more flexibly than most hardware EMS boards. The original intent of IBM's architecture would have forced you either to place the 64KB EMS page frame somewhere in the region C0000h to DFFFFh, sharing that space with all your option ROMs, or to put the page frame somewhere in lower memory. EMM386 allows all of those possibilities (although it almost never is a good idea to use lower memory for the page frame). In addition, EMM386 can make the EMS page extend from E0000h to EFFFFh, provided you don't have a motherboard BIOS ROM at that location. Some PCs, however, have a ROM at that location that can safely be ignored, and with these PCs you can tell EMM386 to put the EMS page frame there despite the ROM's presence. EMM386 will warn you each time it loads if it notices a ROM where you have told it to put the EMS page frame, but if you already know it is a safe location, simply ignore the warning message.

Tip: A ROM can be ignored when it is the location of your PC's setup program. In that case, not only is it very likely that you can safely ignore it and put the EMS page frame in its place, you positively will benefit if you do so. Principally, you won't ever inadvertently activate the setup program while you are in the middle of some other program and lose any unsaved work in that other program.

MemMaker

While there are significant improvements to EMM386 in MS-DOS 6, the real news in memory management in this version is MemMaker, the memory management assistant it includes. MemMaker automatically configures your system by making changes to the CONFIG.SYS and AUTOEXEC.BAT files. This feature was introduced in Chapter 3, where the basics were covered. But if you really want your PC to use its memory optimally, you will have to get involved. You can't leave this decision to MemMaker's defaults.

The material already presented in this chapter explained how EMM386 works and how to configure it. Therefore, you know most of what you need to become an effective partner with MemMaker. All you need to learn is how programs get loaded into upper memory blocks, how much free space they need to do so, and how MemMaker decides these things and communicates its decisions to you and DOS.

Tip: With MS-DOS or PC DOS, either version 5 or 6, you can save a significant amount of lower memory by using `DOS=HIGH` and judiciously choosing the number of BUFFERS. The main purpose of the `DOS=HIGH` line is to move the essential kernel code of DOS into the HMA. Not all of it can be moved there, and when all that can be has been, there is still quite a bit of room left in the HMA. Since only one program can use the HMA at a time, that extra memory would ordinarily go to waste. If, however, you have set the BUFFERS line in your CONFIG.SYS file to no more than 35 or 40, all of the DOS disk buffers (except one) will be put into the HMA along with the DOS kernel. Beware, though, that if you try to cram in even one too many buffers, DOS will move all of them back down to lower memory. Use `MEM /D` to check how much lower memory it says BUFFERS is using. If you see only 512 bytes, you know that most of the buffers are in the HMA. If you see many KB for BUFFERS, you know you asked for too many of them and that they could not, therefore, fit into the HMA. It is recommended that you use fewer than the most you can fit; `BUFFERS=35` is usually a good choice, and you may actually need far fewer if you're using SMARTDRV. DR DOS 6 is better in this regard. It will put as many buffers as can fit in the HMA and put the rest into upper memory. MS-DOS and PC DOS don't have that ability yet.

Most COM programs use exactly as much memory as space on your disk. Invoke DIR in the directory where these programs are, and the size that DIR reports tells you how much memory they will need. This is not true for all COM programs, but it is a good place to start your planning.

Many EXE programs, on the other hand, use a different amount of memory than their file size on disk. There may be as many as four different amounts of memory required by a program at different times: First is its file size; second is the minimum amount of memory into which they can be placed without DOS telling you there is too little memory to load this program; third, the program may well expand its memory usage during its initialization phase of operation; fourth, when it is done initializing, the program may shrink itself down to a final run size that is considerably smaller than any of the other three sizes.

RUNNING MEMMAKER

When you use MemMaker it will ask you some questions, do some things you cannot easily see, reboot your PC a couple of times, and then say it is done. Very mysterious and very easy, with surprisingly good results in many cases. (Which is not to say you cannot help it do even better.)

What is MemMaker doing? First, it asks you if you want EMS memory. If you do, it will load EMM386.EXE (assuming you are using a 386 or 486) and tell it to create an EMS page frame. This is the only question it will ask, if you use MemMaker in its Express Mode. If you wish to exercise more control, you can ask MemMaker to run in its Custom Mode, which will be discussed in a moment.

Next, MemMaker examines your CONFIG.SYS and AUTOEXEC.BAT files to see whether you have already loaded HIMEM and EMM386, and what options (if any) you specified on the EMM386 line. It also looks to see if your computer has an extended BIOS data area (EBDA) located near the top of lower memory. If it finds that you have already installed EMM386, it will preserve whatever options you put on the DEVICE line after the program's name. (If, however, you asked for EMS memory and previously specified `NOEMS`, MemMaker will replace that option with RAM.) If it finds an EBDA, MemMaker will move it to upper memory so that it can open up the maximum amount of free lower memory. If it finds that you did not load EMM386, it ensures that both HIMEM and EMM386 are loaded, that `DOS=HIGH` and `DOS=UMB` are specified (it doesn't combine these two into one line, but you can do so if you wish), and it will make sure that EMM386 has been instructed to provide EMS memory.

Next, MemMaker needs to find out how much RAM is required by each device driver and TSR that you have called for in your CONFIG.SYS and

AUTOEXEC.BAT files. MemMaker does this by adding the word SIZER on each DEVICE line just after the equal sign and before the device name. It will also use SIZER to help it determine the amounts of RAM your TSR programs need. How SIZER works and how it communicates its results to MemMaker is not documented. If you try to run SIZER yourself, it simply will inform you that it is only meant to be used by MemMaker. Still, it is clear what SIZER must be doing. It loads each device driver or TSR program and notices as it does so the maximum amount of memory used by that program at any point in the loading and initializing process, plus the minimum amount retained by that program when its initialization phase is complete. It passes this information back to MemMaker, which uses it to decide how to arrange programs in upper and lower memory.

After MemMaker has collected that information, it does some serious calculating. Essentially, it tries all the possible ways to put things into upper memory. For each possibility it makes sure that at the time each device driver or TSR program is loaded into an upper memory block it will have enough space in that block for any initialization activities it needs to do.

MemMaker tells you how many different configurations it tries. It may try as few as one (if it succeeds in putting everything it wants into upper memory on the first try) or many thousands. The more different regions your upper memory space is broken into, the more possible arrangements there are for your device drivers and TSRs, and the more combinations MemMaker will have to try.

Finally, MemMaker returns to your CONFIG.SYS and AUTOEXEC.BAT files and changes them again. This time it includes DEVICEHIGH and LOADHIGH (LH) commands in those lines that load the device drivers and TSRs it has decided should go into upper memory. When you next reboot, your system will be optimized, according to MemMaker.

THE DOS LOADHIGH (LH) AND DEVICEHIGH COMMANDS

The syntax of the DEVICEHIGH command is

```
DEVICEHIGH [options]=[path]drivername.type [dd-parms]
```

where, as usual, `[path]drivername.type` is the full file specification of the device driver program to load; `[dd-parms]` is any parameters that driver needs to do its job. The special part about DEVICEHIGH is in the `[options]` that may be used in front of the equal sign. An explanation of what they are and what each of them does follows.

The detailed syntax of the DEVICEHIGH options section is:

```
[/L:region1[,minsize1][;region2[,minsize2]... [/S]]
```

This really is only two switches, with some parameters you can specify for the first one. The /L switch lets you specify which of several upper memory regions you wish to have DEVICEHIGH use when loading this device driver. Some programs can use two or more separate regions of memory, and for them you can specify multiple regions into which the device driver is to be loaded. The program is loaded into the first one, but as it asks for more memory, DOS knows to give it what it asks for out of the other regions.

The regions are numbered consecutively, starting with 1 for the lowest region containing UMBs. For example, in our previous discussion of the EMM386 command line, in the first case we described, the final result of loading EMM386 was to create three separate regions with UMBs. The first one (number 1 for DEVICEHIGH purposes) extended from A0000h to AFFFFh. The second one went from B8000h to CFFFFh. The third one went from DC000h to EFFFFh. To specify that you want to load your MOUSE.SYS device driver into region 3 you would use the line

```
DEVICE /L:3=[path]MOUSE.SYS
```

or, if you wanted the driver also to have access to region 2 for any additional memory it might need, you would replace `/L:3` with `/L:3;2`.

To find out if a driver or TSR uses more than one patch of memory, issue the `MEM/D` command after you have loaded the device driver or TSR in lower memory. Look down the list and find the program you are interested in. Note its module name as reported by MEM. Next, use `MEM /M:`*`modulename`* to see how many regions (and of what sizes) are presently being used by this program. It is possible that more or larger regions were used in initialization, but that is harder to determine. Usually, although some of the regions might have been larger during initialization, there would not have been more of them.

The *`minsize1`*, *`minsize2`*, and other similar values are used to tell DEVICEHIGH not to try loading this program into any UMB that doesn't have at least the *`minsize`* specified amount of free RAM. If any of the specified regions has less than the amount of free RAM specified on the DEVICEHIGH line for that region, DOS will load the device driver into lower memory.

The `/S` option can be used only if you have also specified `/L:`*`region-number,minsize`*. It makes DOS reduce the UMB to the specified minimum size during loading, which Microsoft claims makes the loading more efficient. Normally, only MemMaker uses this command; it is not intended for use by end users (even power users).

The only difference between using DEVICEHIGH and LOADHIGH for loading device drivers into UMBs is that DEVICEHIGH gets used in the

CONFIG.SYS file while LOADHIGH gets used in the AUTOEXEC.BAT file or at the DOS prompt. You have all the same options with LH that you have with DEVICEHIGH, they are invoked the same way, and they do the same things.

> **Warning:** Not every device driver or TSR program can safely be loaded high. Some will crash your machine simply because they end up using an unpredictable amount of RAM during intialization; others will load just fine, but they won't work right. One example is if you load the MODE command into upper memory and ask it to redirect some ports and then run Ventura Publisher. Ventura will not notice the redirections MODE supposedly put into effect.

MEMMAKER'S CUSTOM SETUP

If you invoke MemMaker and choose Custom Setup you will be first asked the same question about EMS memory as in Express Setup. After that, you will be given six options to choose (see Figure 6-11). (Alternatively, you can tell it your choices ahead of time by modifying the MEMMAKER.INF file in the DOS directory.) The first option instructs MemMaker to ask which TSRs and device drivers you don't want it to load high.

The next three options let you tell MemMaker how aggressively you want EMM386 to search for upper memory spaces it can use for UMBs (the default is yes), whether it should save room in upper memory for the Windows

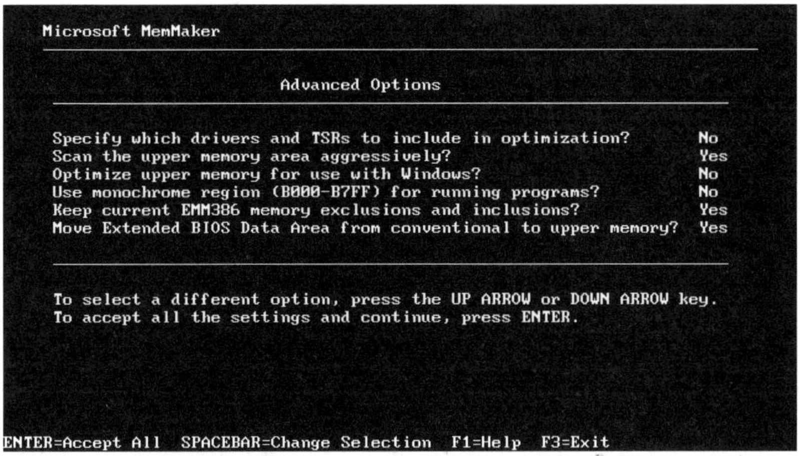

Figure 6-11 The MemMaker Custom Setup Advanced Options screen

translation buffers (the default is no), and whether it should use the monochrome video image buffer area (the default is no). The fifth option lets you tell MemMaker to keep whatever it finds on your EMM386 line. Finally, you can instruct MemMaker whether or not to tell EMM386 to move the EBDA to upper memory.

After you have decided on these options, MemMaker will look for your Windows directory, prompt you to confirm its location; then, it will resume its functions without much feedback about what it is doing at each stage.

Tip: There is one glaring problem with the MemMaker and SIZER approach to determining how much memory a device driver or TSR will need in order to be loaded into an upper memory block. (Most memory optimizing programs have the same difficulty.) MemMaker assumes that the programs will take the same maximum amount of memory when they are loaded low and when they are loaded high, but for a number of popular TSRs this simply is not so.

SuperPCKwik, for example, tends to take all of lower memory (temporarily) when you load it low. That seems to say it never could fit in any modest sized UMB. Actually, though, it can fit into almost any UMB that is any amount larger than its final size, so long as you let it load itself high, but not if you try to have LOADHIGH load it high.

The reason for the difference is that when SuperPCKwik loads itself high it can use lower memory to do its initialization and then just load high the final, initialized resident module. If you attempt to use LOADHIGH (or any other high loader) to do this, SuperPCKwik will try to get along with only a restricted amount of upper memory in which it can initialize itself. It may succeed, but it certainly will (temporarily) use more upper memory than if you had let it load itself high.

The correct approach to loading any programs high that know how to do so themselves is to let them. (Or, force them to load low if you know you have a better use for that region of upper memory.) Don't use LOADHIGH or any other high-loader on them. DOS programs that know how to load themselves high include DEFRAG, INTERLNK, and SMARTDRV. A few DOS programs (such as MSCDEX and VSAFE, and the PC DOS 6 version of SETVER) can load some or all of themselves into expanded or extended memory. VSAFE defaults to loading into extended memory, but you can direct it to load into conventional memory, low or high; and, if you deny it extended memory, it will attempt to load into expanded memory. MSCDEX loads in conventional memory, but you can tell it to use expanded memory for its sector buffers. PC DOS's SETVER loads all of itself into the HMA.

CONFIG.SYS file before and after MemMaker

```
DOS=HIGH
DEVICE=C:\DOS\HIMEM.SYS
FILES=30
BUFFERS=30
SHELL=C:\DOS\COMMAND.COM C:\DOS\  /p
```

```
DEVICE=C:\DOS\HIMEM.SYS
DEVICE=C:\DOS\EMM386.EXE NOEMS HIGHSCAN
BUFFERS=30,0
FILES=30
DOS=UMB
LASTDRIVE=H
FCBS=16,0
DOS=HIGH
SHELL=C:\DOS\COMMAND.COM C:\DOS\  /p
```

AUTOEXEC.BAT file before and after MemMaker

```
@ECHO OFF
C:\DOS\SMARTDRV.EXE
C:\MOUSE\MOUSE
C:\QUICKENW\BILLMIND.EXE C:\QUICKENW
C:\DOS\SHARE
C:\NU\NDD C:/Q
C:\NU\IMAGE C:
PATH C:\DOS;C:\NU;C:\WINDOWS;C:\FB;C:\MTEZ;C:\WORD
PROMPT $P$G
set SYMANTEC=C:\SYMANTEC
set NU=C:\NU
set FASTBACK=C:\FB
set FBP_EXT=500
C:\FB\FBPSCHED
set MTEZ=C:\MTEZ
set TEMP=C:\WINDOWS\TEMP
VER
ECHO
```

```
@ECHO OFF
LH /L:0;2,42384 /S C:\DOS\SMARTDRV.EXE
LH /L:2,14912 C:\MOUSE\MOUSE
C:\QUICKENW\BILLMIND.EXE C:\QUICKENW
LH /L:2,13984 C:\DOS\SHARE
C:\NU\NDD C:/Q
C:\NU\IMAGE C:
PATH C:\DOS;C:\NU;C:\WINDOWS;C:\FB;C:\MTEZ;C:\WORD
PROMPT $P$G
set SYMANTEC=C:\SYMANTEC
set NU=C:\NU
set FASTBACK=C:\FB
set FBP_EXT=500
LH /L:2,65536 C:\FB\FBPSCHED
set MTEZ=C:\MTEZ
set TEMP=C:\WINDOWS\TEMP
VER
ECHO
```

Figure 6-12 Changes made by MemMaker

Figure 6-12 shows the CONFIG.SYS and AUTOEXEC.BAT files for one computer before and after running MemMaker. Notice that MemMaker added some lines to CONFIG.SYS, modified some other lines, and added some LH (LOADHIGH) commands to AUTOEXEC.BAT. Figure 6-13 shows the output of MEM /C before and after those changes. There has been an increase in the available lower memory, but not by nearly as much as the amount of upper memory that was used. The difference shows the overhead required by the memory managers loaded by DOS.

The good news is that MemMaker can and will try literally thousands of combinations of programs to load high in its attempt to find the optimum mix. The bad news is that it can get confused and start with some wrong assumptions, thus making all its conclusions suspect, at best.

Recommendations

Should you use MemMaker? Absolutely, but don't rely on it totally. Use it intelligently: Keep a copy of what your CONFIG.SYS and AUTOEXEC.BAT files looked like before and after each run of MemMaker. Take note of the sizes MemMaker puts in the DEVICEHIGH and LOADHIGH lines. These tell you what SIZER reported regarding the memory needs of those programs. You also can force MemMaker not to load high by putting entries in MEMMAKER.INF or by running MemMaker's Custom Setup, to see if it will put other programs into upper memory. Then you can see how much memory they require.

Output from MEM /C before running MemMaker

```
Modules using memory below 1 MB:

  Name           Total       =   Conventional   +   Upper Memory
  --------  ----------------   ----------------   ----------------
  MSDOS       15357    (15K)     15357    (15K)          0    (0K)
  HIMEM        1152     (1K)      1152     (1K)          0    (0K)
  DBLSPACE    44256    (43K)     44256    (43K)          0    (0K)
  COMMAND      2912     (3K)      2912     (3K)          0    (0K)
  MOUSE       10704    (10K)     10704    (10K)          0    (0K)
  SMARTDRV    28800    (28K)     28800    (28K)          0    (0K)
  SHARE        6208     (6K)      6208     (6K)          0    (0K)
  FBPSCHED      560     (1K)       560     (1K)          0    (0K)
  Free       545216   (532K)    545216   (532K)          0    (0K)

Memory Summary:

  Type of Memory       Total       =      Used        +       Free
  ----------------  ----------------   ----------------   ----------------
  Conventional         655360   (640K)    110144   (108K)    545216   (532K)
  Upper                     0     (0K)         0     (0K)         0     (0K)
  Adapter RAM/ROM      393216   (384K)    393216   (384K)         0     (0K)
  Extended (XMS)      4194304  (4096K)   1900544  (1856K)   2293760  (2240K)
  ----------------  ----------------   ----------------   ----------------
  Total memory        5242880  (5120K)   2403904  (2348K)   2838976  (2772K)

  Total under 1 MB     655360   (640K)    110144   (108K)    545216   (532K)

  Largest executable program size       544832   (532K)
  Largest free upper memory block            0     (0K)
  MS-DOS is resident in the high memory area.
```

Output from MEM /C after running MemMaker

```
Modules using memory below 1 MB:

  Name           Total       =   Conventional   +   Upper Memory
  --------  ----------------   ----------------   ----------------
  MSDOS       16077    (16K)     16077    (16K)          0    (0K)
  HIMEM        1152     (1K)      1152     (1K)          0    (0K)
  EMM386       3120     (3K)      3120     (3K)          0    (0K)
  DBLSPACE    44256    (43K)     44256    (43K)          0    (0K)
  COMMAND      2912     (3K)      2912     (3K)          0    (0K)
  SMARTDRV    27264    (27K)         0     (0K)      27264   (27K)
  MOUSE       10704    (10K)         0     (0K)      10704   (10K)
  SHARE        5248     (5K)         0     (0K)       5248    (5K)
  FBPSCHED      560     (1K)         0     (0K)        560    (1K)
  Free       682160   (666K)    587648   (574K)      94512   (92K)

Memory Summary:

  Type of Memory       Total       =      Used        +       Free
  ----------------  ----------------   ----------------   ----------------
  Conventional         655360   (640K)     67712    (66K)    587648   (574K)
  Upper                138288   (135K)     43776    (43K)     94512    (92K)
  Adapter RAM/ROM      254928   (249K)    254928   (249K)         0     (0K)
  Extended (XMS)      4194304  (4096K)   1150976  (1124K)   3043328  (2972K)
  ----------------  ----------------   ----------------   ----------------
  Total memory        5242880  (5120K)   1517392  (1482K)   3725488  (3638K)

  Total under 1 MB     793648   (775K)    111488   (109K)    682160   (666K)

  Largest executable program size       587552   (574K)
  Largest free upper memory block        91040    (89K)
  MS-DOS is resident in the high memory area.
```

Figure 6-13 Results of MemMaker changes

Feel free to alter the order of device drivers in your CONFIG.SYS file and TSR lines in your AUTOEXEC.BAT file. If you know you want a certain TSR to load low, and if it doesn't need to have the services of COMMAND.COM, you can load it through an INSTALL line in your CONFIG.SYS file.

The worst mistake that MemMaker may make is to fragment upper memory needlessly. This really is a problem with EMM386 and its scanning of upper memory. If it determines that there are a lot of isolated elements that it must not tread upon, these two programs together may create a flock of excludes for the EMM386 command line. Therefore, examine that line carefully. See what regions of memory are included (with `I=` parameters) and which are excluded (with `X=` and `WIN=` parameters). Think about what you know is in the upper memory in your computer.

If you see many small blocks included or excluded, be very sure that MemMaker knows what it is doing. If you believe MemMaker got confused and needlessly excluded some regions it could have used—and especially if including them will bridge the gap between other included regions—edit the EMM386 line in your CONFIG.SYS file to specify the correct regions to include and exclude. The `WIN=` parameter is important, but only if you are planning to run Windows. Be sure to include 24KB of space with this parameter.

Warning: Don't overlap the include, exclude, and Windows regions. If you do overlap them, the `X` parameter will override the `WIN` parameter, which in turn will override the `I` parameter with respect to any overlap regions.

If it appears that MemMaker and EMM386 have reasonably assigned upper memory blocks to the available spaces, the next thing to check is where programs were placed. This you can do two ways: One is to look at the MEM reports (`/D` and `/C`, but also `/M` if you wish to explore the RAM usage of any specific module). The second way is to examine the CONFIG.SYS and AUTOEXEC.BAT lines for the `/L:`*`n,minsize`* entries after `DEVICEHIGH` or `LH`.

In order to handle the programs that can load themselves high, you must first identify them. Do this by editing your CONFIG.SYS and AUTOEXEC.BAT files to remove all references to the LOADHIGH or LH commands and converting all DEVICEHIGH lines to DEVICE lines. Then, reboot your computer and use `MEM /D` to see which programs made it to upper memory. The ones that did are those that can load themselves high. Then, determine how much room they took up in upper memory by using `MEM /M:`*`modulename`*. Now, temporarily mark out those lines that invoke programs that load themselves high and edit the EMM386.EXE line to reduce the amount of upper memory it will create to accommodate loading all those programs high.

Rerun MemMaker, using the Express Setup; or, if you choose Custom Setup, tell it to accept whatever it finds on the EMM386.EXE line of CONFIG.SYS. This time, it should figure out which other programs can be loaded high and what their optimal locations are. (Look over what it has done, though. You may want to reorder your device drivers or TSRs and/or enter some of them in MEMMAKER.INF per the instructions in that file; then rerun MemMaker to see if it can do better.) Finally, reedit your EMM386 line to get all the upper memory you safely can. Reedit your CONFIG.SYS and AUTOEXEC.BAT files to reenable the device drivers and programs that can load themselves high. Reboot and see how well you have done.

When Menus Are the Answer

To this point, we have acted as if there is one best configuration for your PC. This may or may not be so. If you have a standard set of things that you do and if all of them require essentially the same set of resident programs and device drivers, then you may find that one "best" configuration serves you very well.

If, on the other hand, you sometimes do one thing and sometimes another, and the two require very different sets of resources and supporting programs, you might want to create a custom menu in your CONFIG.SYS file and make your AUTOEXEC.BAT file vary in its effect, depending on the choices you make during the menu presentation at each bootup. In this way, you can have only those devices and resident programs loaded that you need for the current task. A simple reboot, with a different set of answers to your menu options, and your PC becomes a totally different animal, ready to do a totally different task and optimized for that purpose.

Unfortunately, using MemMaker with menus must be done very carefully because MemMaker was built with the assumption that there was no menu in CONFIG.SYS and only one way the AUTOEXEC.BAT file could run. Therefore, the only way to be really safe is to create a lot of different CONFIG.SYS and AUTOEXEC.BAT files, one pair for each possible path through your menu tree. No matter how complex your menu, make one menu block with no includes for each configuration. Make any multiple paths through your AUTOEXEC.BAT file similarly nonoverlapping. This will let you extract from these master files the several pairs of files you need to have one set per configuration. It also will let you optimize your PC for each of those sets and then recombine them to get a globally optimized master CONFIG.SYS and AUTOEXEC.BAT file pair. Then you are done. (Menus and flexible configurations are discussed in general in Chapter 11.)

DOS TOOLS TO CHECK YOUR WORK

To check your work, use MEM /D, MEM /C, and MEM /M (for looking at a given module's memory use if you suspect it may be other than you had anticipated). If you follow all these steps you should get the best memory usage possible, short of using a memory manager that knows a more aggressive way of obtaining upper memory. (QEMM with its Stealth strategy and 386MAX with its ROM Search strategy are two examples of that sort of memory manager.)

DMM, LDEVICE, NOTE, and FREENOTE offer you some simple tools for loading and releasing both device drivers and TSRs without rebooting. MAM offers some similar capabilities, with much more capacity for snooping at system vectors and interrupts, if that's your cup of tea. LASTBYTE.SYS and its accompanying drivers are included to give you a chance to experiment with an alternative to HIMEM and EMM386 that works in non-protected mode and actually lets you load HIMEM high. We do suggest that you try this out from a floppy before tearing up your system configuration.

LOADFIX, THE MEMORY TOOL TO AVOID

LOADFIX is a kludge. There is no nicer word for it. This program offers to help you out when you have too much free memory for an application program to tolerate. It simply takes away the "excess" memory. LOADFIX does nothing with the memory; it just hides it.

It may seem impossible for there to be too much free memory for a program to tolerate. Usually, it isn't a problem, but strangely enough, it can be. Some programmers were so sure that DOS would always use up the first 64KB of lower memory before loading their programs, that they wrote these programs to assume and even demand that they not be loaded with a starting address lower than 10000h. If you try loading them lower, you will get the obtuse message `Packed file corrupt`. The file is not corrupt; you simply tried to load it too low in memory.

Although you *can* use LOADFIX to "solve" this problem, you will be wasting valuable memory if you do. Presumably, you did not go through the effort of loading device drivers into upper memory, DOS into the HMA, and perhaps TSR programs in upper memory for no reason. What's the point in now throwing away perfectly good (in fact extremely precious) lower memory?

The correct solution to this problem is to force some device driver or TSR program to load low and use up at least the first 64KB before you load the offending program. Normally, that is easy to do. You can use the upper memory you free up in this way on some other TSR or device driver you load later on. If you had been using all of your upper memory, and if you run Windows, you may want to leave the space you created empty. Windows can take good advantage of 24KB of upper memory for its translation buffers.

The only situation in which LOADFIX may be the right solution is if you have a program that needs it and also needs such a "cleanly" configured PC that you have no device drivers or TSRs to load low. Even in this case, though, you probably can fill up the first 64KB or more simply by not including the line `DOS=HIGH` in your CONFIG.SYS file.

CHAPTER

7

◆ ◆ ◆ ◆ ◆

Disks

This chapter details how disks maintain information and how DOS organizes information on them. This knowledge can help you organize your own work better. You also will learn in this chapter how to recover from some of the most common disk disasters and how to prevent some of them.

Forms of Information Storage

Most disks in PCs are magnetic storage devices, which means that they store information as patterns of magnetization in some medium. The most common medium forms are flat, round disks of plastic, metal, or glass coated on both sides with a magnetizable material. (Tapes wound on spools are also used, but much less frequently than disks, primarily because it takes longer to find a given patch of tape than it does a given spot on the surface of a disk.)

Figure 7-1 shows three ways of looking at disks: The first is the physical appearance of the disk (its case); Figure 7-1(a) shows that appearance for both small and large floppy disks and for a typical hard disk drive. The second way to look at a disk is from the viewpoint of the disk drive, i.e., the disk that is inside the case. Figure 7-1(b) shows that for each of

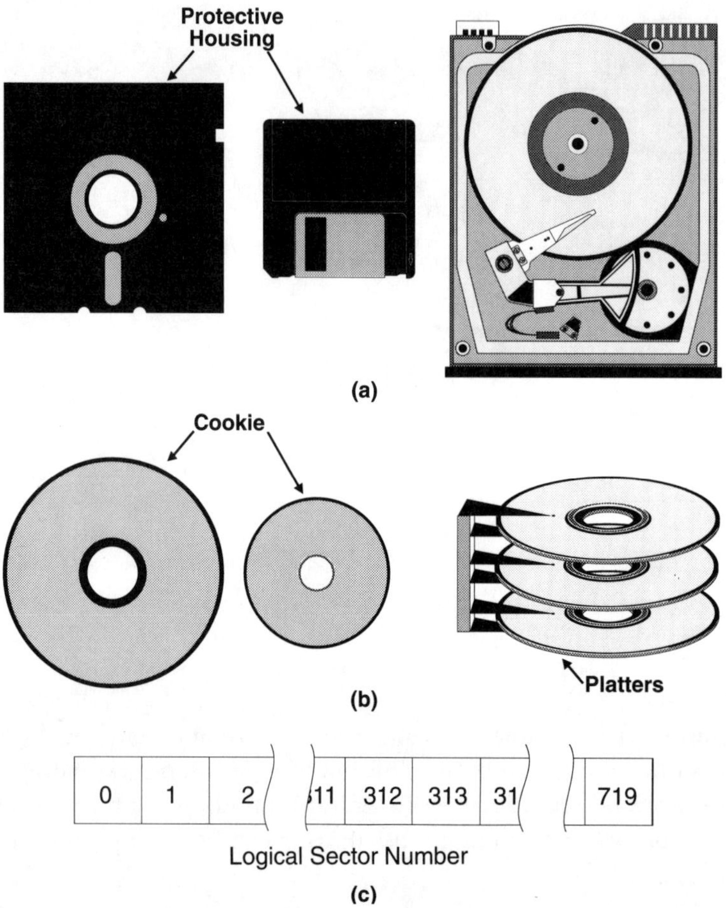

Figure 7-1 Different views of disks: (a) their physical appearance, (b) as seen by the drive, and (c) as seen by DOS

the same three cases. Finally, when DOS looks at a disk drive, it sees only a string of logical sector addresses and the data that is stored at those addresses. That view is indicated in Figure 7-1(c). The number of logical sectors indicated there is that of a 360KB floppy diskette.

Floppy Diskettes

Floppy diskettes contain plastic disks that are called "cookies" by the industry that makes them. The cookie you ultimately buy is encased in a plastic housing. Most users call these diskettes floppies. (Some people wonder why they are called floppy disks, when—in their protective housing—they seem quite rigid. In fact, the cookie inside is limp and will flop quite satisfyingly if it is removed from the housing.

Floppies come in two sizes (5-1/4" and 3-1/2" diameters), and in a confusing array of designated densities. The first PCs had only single-sided diskette drives, and with them and DOS 1.0 you could put only 160KB on a 5-1/4" diskette. Now, with a state-of-the-art version of DOS and double-sided drives, you can put 360KB on that same diskette. A high-density 5-1/4" diskette can accept up to 1.2MB of data. The 3-1/2" size diskettes come in three distinct varieties: One holds 720KB of data, another holds twice that (1.44MB), and the newest type holds 2.88MB.

When you insert a floppy into a floppy diskette drive, the drive clamps the cookie around its central hole and spins it at 360 revolutions per second. Two arms reach in from the outer edge of the disk on either side of the cookie, each bearing a read/write head. The arm can move in toward the spindle or out toward the outer edge of the cookie. It moves to a position and stops for awhile each time you wish to read or write data to the diskette. This means that information is recorded in a number of separate concentric circles, called tracks. Low-density, 5-1/4" diskettes have 40 tracks on each side; high-density 5-1/4" and all 3-1/2" diskettes have 80 tracks per side.

Data is stored on a floppy diskette in regions called *sectors.* Each sector holds 512 bytes of data plus some other bytes used to ensure the integrity of the data and to help the drive know which sector it is on. A 360KB diskette has 9 sectors per track; high-density (1.2MB) diskettes have 15 sectors per track. The 3-1/2" diskettes (720KB and 1.44MB) have 9 and 18 sectors per track, respectively; the extra-high-density, 2.88MB diskettes have 36 sectors per track.

These details aside, there is one important thing you must know about floppy diskettes: *There really is a difference between low-density and high-density floppies*Low-density disksHigh-density disks (and an even greater difference in extra-high density floppies). Don't try to save money by buying cheaper, low-density floppies and trying to use them as high-density floppies. This might seem to work at first, but your data are significantly less safe on a disk that has been formatted beyond its rated capacity than on a diskette that is used within its specifications.

Hard Disks

Hard disks work by the same physical principles as floppy disks. They differ from floppies primarily in the precision with which they are built and the design sophistication of their head positioning mechanisms. These design differences result in a higher storage capacity as well as a much greater speed of access to the data stored on them.

Hard disks are so called because the platters (which serve the same purpose as a floppy disk's cookie) are hard. They are usually made of aluminum, although some now are made of glass. The platters are permanently sealed inside a metal housing to keep them clean. Some hard disks have only a couple of platters, while others have up to a dozen with a head on each side of each platter. (Sometimes one or two of these surfaces are not used for data storage.) More surfaces means, of course, more data storage capacity.

Two other facts are even more important to the data storage capacity of a hard disk: One is that these disks use a rigid medium that doesn't change size markedly with temperature and humidity (as a floppy's cookie does); second, is that the head positioning mechanisms in most hard disk drives are much more sophisticated than those in floppy diskette drives. These facts mean that a hard disk can have many more tracks per surface and many more sectors per track than a floppy. Typical numbers for modern hard disks are several hundred up to a few thousand tracks on each platter surface, with each track having anywhere from 17 to 75 sectors of data (with 512 bytes of data in each sector).

Hard disks turn much faster than floppies; most complete 3600 revolutions per second, and some go as fast as 5400 rpm. This, and the higher density of information stored on a hard disk platter, are the primary reasons that you can access your data more quickly when it is kept on a hard disk.

PC hard disk subsystems come in a number of variations, but to DOS, they are all just disk drives. Some are bigger or faster than others, but that is about the only difference you or the operating system notice when using them.

RAM Disks

Hard disks are fast, but not fast enough for some folks who want *really* fast disk drives. The fastest ones are not made with rotating machinery; they are made, instead, using silicon integrated circuits—RAM chips, called *RAM disks* or *solid-state disks.*

A RAM disk can be a separate cabinet with a huge number of RAM chips and a power supply, etc., or it can be merely an aspect of how you use the main memory in your PC. Separate RAM disks are quite expensive, but they have certain advantages. It is much more common, however, and certainly a lot less expensive, to create a RAM disk out of your PC's main memory by running a RAM disk program.

Regardless of how it is physically created, a RAM disk must appear to DOS as if it were a standard, magnetic, rotating machinery disk drive because DOS and the BIOS were designed to deal only with disks that look to them like the original PC disk designs. This means that the program that creates the RAM disk must create data structures in the RAM that directly parallel those on a normal magnetic disk, and the program must also translate addresses on the RAM disk to the three-dimensional form demanded by the BIOS in your PC.

The least expensive RAM disk is one you create by loading the VDISK or RAMDRIVE device driver that comes with DOS. Just add a line to your CONFIG.SYS file to invoke that driver and add some parameters on the line to tell it how big you want your drive to be, then reboot, and you'll discover that you have a new disk drive. (The exact syntax for doing this is explained in Chapter 10.) If you have not played with a RAM disk before, you will probably find it hard to believe how fast it is.

Speed is wonderful, but beware: There is a dark side to RAM disks. They typically forget everything you have stored on them the instant you shut down or reboot your PC. The external solid-state disks in a box (with their own separate power supply) are almost the only RAM disks that don't have this characteristic. The fact that a RAM disk wipes itself clean each time you boot your PC can, however, be a blessing. If you store only temporary files on the RAM disk, this will keep you from having to remember to clean up any leftover temporary files.

Usually, people use RAM disks to store data and programs that they want to keep. The programs are not usually a problem, as they are copied to the RAM disk from somewhere on your hard disk. The original copy on the hard disk won't disappear just because the RAM disk copy vanishes when you reboot or power down.

Data files, on the other hand, can be a big problem. You have to be very disciplined to remember to copy your data files back to the hard disk *every* time before you shut down your PC. Furthermore, if your PC should happen to get "hung," you will lose whatever was on the RAM disk that was not yet saved to the hard disk. If you are worried that you might lose data this way, there is only one guaranteed solution: Keep only programs and temporary files on your RAM disk, and always keep your data files on a real, magnetic medium.

As is often the case with the utility programs bundled with DOS, better RAM disk programs than RAMDRIVE or VDISK are available if you want to spend the money on them. As a rule, these other programs are not going to be much faster or more capable of creating larger RAM disks than VDISK or RAMDRIVE. Their advantages come, typically, in the special features they support. For example, some third-party RAM disks can borrow memory from a disk cache program, and only borrow as much as they need to store the files presently on the RAM disk. In this way, you can avoid choosing how much RAM to devote to the RAM disk and how much to the disk cache. The program chooses the optimum amount for each at every moment in time.

Other Disk-Like Entities

As stated, to DOS, every hard disk is like any other. And RAM disks look the same to DOS also. (Even floppies look only slightly different.) It is even possible to make other devices that act, as far as DOS is concerned, like a disk drive. Technically, all of these objects are called *block devices.* Their essential quality is that you can write information to them and read information from them in blocks of a fixed size (usually 512 bytes). And you can address those blocks in a fashion much like that used to address locations on a disk drive.

To fully emulate a disk drive for DOS, the device must be capable of having its locations addressed by use of *logical sector numbers,* and it must implement a *file allocation table* (FAT) and *directory structure* similar to that on a DOS disk. We will explain just what each of these is later in this chapter.

Some of the ersatz disk drives in common use with PCs are network drives, optical drives (CD-ROM, WORM [write-once read-many], and read/write optical), and some Flash RAM cards. It is even possible to make a tape drive look to DOS just like any other block device (except that it will be painfully slow).

The original design of DOS assumed that the A and B drives were always floppy disks and that all other drives were fixed disks. Now we have Bernoulli boxes, Floptical drives, and Passport and Megadrive removable hard drives, just to name a few of the removable disks commonly used with PCs. DOS and the BIOS need help in order to deal with these objects correctly. In particular, they won't know when you change disks unless you augment the BIOS with an installable device driver or option ROM.

Organizing Disk Information

The best thing about DOS and disks is that DOS takes care of the details for us. We don't have to worry about where our data is. We (and our application programs) merely hand off to DOS a file full of data. We expect DOS to put it away on the disk wherever it wishes. And we expect DOS to be able to retrieve our data whenever *we* wish by merely telling it the name of the file we want.

DOS, on the other hand, must keep track of all the locations on the disk, so that it knows which ones are in use and by what files, which regions are flawed and thus unsafe to use, and which are available for more data storage.

Nitty-Gritty Disk Details

Actually, DOS keeps track only of the data in your files in blocks of 512 bytes. These bytes are stored in regions on the disk called sectors. The BIOS keeps track of how many sectors there are per track, how many tracks per surface, and how many surfaces there are in each of your disk drives.

DOS doesn't care about or need to know the physical details. DOS works, instead, with *logical drives* (also called *DOS volumes*), each of which contains some number of sectors that DOS numbers starting with 0 up to some maximum value. DOS logical volumes are more commonly referred to as drive letters.

Each sector has two parts. The first is a sector header, which contains information about where on the disk this sector is located; it also contains a flag declaring whether the sector can be relied on for data storage. (Most disks have some bad spots, but flagging each one prevents storage on them, and thus, we almost never notice those bad regions.) The second part is where the data for this sector are placed.

Magnetic media are fallible. If you haven't yet experienced a disk failure, it is only because you either have not dealt with disks long enough, or you have been extraordinarily lucky—so far. You probably *have* experienced some disk failures, but didn't realize it, a phenomenon that occurs because the manufacturers of disk drives go to great lengths to make their products appear more reliable than they are.

A minimal amount of protection is offered for data stored on a floppy diskette; much more is provided on hard disks. How sophisticated the protection mechanism is depends a lot on how large the drive's capacity is; larger drives get more protection.

Every sector header contains the full, three-dimensional address of the sector. One number specifies which surface of the drive this sector lives on. A second number specifies the track number (with track 0 at the outside of the disk and higher numbers closer to the spindle). The third number is called the physical sector number and tells which sector is in a particular track.

Physical sector numbers usually start at 1 and renumber from this point on each track. Logical sector numbers, on the other hand—which is all that DOS uses—start with 0 at the beginning of each DOS logical volume (drive letter) and proceed from there, never starting over again until you go to the next logical volume.

The first level of protection you have against errors in accessing your data is the address in the sector header, so you must look there to get the right information. To ensure that the address numbers in a sector header are not corrupted, a CRC (*cyclical redundancy check*) number is also stored in the header. Essentially a complicated way of adding up all the other numbers in the sector header, this CRC value makes it easy to detect any alteration of the numbers it protects. If the CRC value is inconsistent with the rest of the information in the sector header, you can be sure that something is amiss.

If a sector header in the file you wish to access is corrupted, DOS will report that it cannot find the file with the message `Sector not found`, or one similar. In addition to the CRC value stored in each sector header, another CRC value is used to protect the data in each sector on a floppy. If the data area of a sector in your file becomes corrupted, DOS will report it as a data error reading from that drive.

On a hard disk, a better protection scheme is used for the data area of each sector (but not for the sector headers)—an *error correction code* (ECC). Like a CRC, this scheme allows the disk controller to detect at any time that the data it is reading from a sector differ from what was written there. (The error could have occurred in writing or in reading; to distinguish which, the controller typically reads several times any sectors whose data it suspects.)

ECCs are more cleverly constructed than CRC values. They allow the controller to know not only if there is an error in the data being protected, but in most cases they also allow reconstruction of those data as originally written.

Only a tiny amount of the disk's storage capacity is taken up with ECC values—typically, less than a sixth of 1 percent. But because most disk errors have some predictable qualities (for example, they generally occur in a single small region of a sector), and thanks to the clever design of the ECC strategies, these few bytes of data suffice to let the controller almost always deliver data either unflawed or corrected to the point that they look unflawed. These ECC strategies are also the reason that about 99 percent of all disk read errors get corrected without your knowledge. Still, glitches do happen. Any DOS power user should expect to have to go in and do "data surgery" on a disk drive some day. In order to do that, you need to know in some detail just how DOS keeps track of your files and the data they contain.

Building the Logical Structure of a Disk

DOS can't interpret a disk until it has been properly formatted, which is done by using the FORMAT command. FORMAT does somewhat different things to a floppy diskette and a hard drive. On a floppy diskette, the FORMAT program first lays down the low-level format. (It does this only if you have specified the /U switch or if the diskette you are processing was not formatted previously.) For each track on both the top and bottom surface it writes a string of 9, 15, 18, or 36 sectors, depending on the disk capacity. These sectors have their addresses and CRC values (and good or bad sector flag) written in them, and the data area of each one is filled with 512 bytes of E5h (plus the appropriate ECC numbers).

Next, the FORMAT program creates some vital information structures to help DOS keep track of your files on this disk—*file allocation tables* (FATs) and the *root directory*. FORMAT also puts a program and special data table called the *DOS boot record* in the very first sector. The program in this sector is used whenever you boot your PC from this disk. The data table is used the first time you access the disk to inform DOS of some key numbers it needs to properly use this disk.

The file allocation table (FAT) is a map of the disk. Usually, there are two identical FATs on a disk. The design of DOS allows more or fewer, but all current versions of DOS put two FATs on all disks. (Some RAM disk programs put only one FAT on the disks they create.)

DOS creates two FATs per disk to provide a modicum of protection against physical damage to the disk in that area. If one of the FATs contains a sector that is unreadable, DOS will use the corresponding sector from the second FAT. It does this without informing you what it is doing.

Sometimes the disk is not actually damaged, but will appear to be. This can happen if the two FATs hold different information. When DOS detects the fact, it usually quits. Often, if you are familiar enough with the proper form of information in the FAT, you can discover which FAT has the erroneous information and then copy the good FAT over the bad one. This will fix the most common FAT content errors. The only time this won't work is if both FATs are damaged, or if you cannot tell which one is the good one.

The only DOS-bundled utility program that checks to be sure the two FATs are the same is CHKDSK. If it discovers that they are different, it will report its finding; often, however, it makes no attempt to fix anything.

The sectors on a disk are grouped in *allocation units*, also called *clusters*. One of the numbers in the DOS boot record refers to the number of sectors in each cluster on this disk. The allowed values are 1, 2, 4, 8, and other integral powers of 2. A hard disk volume with between 16MB and 127MB capacity has four sectors per cluster, which means that DOS stores and retrieves information 2,048 bytes at a time in these volumes.

DOS keeps track of the status of each cluster on the disk, through the FAT. Each entry in the FAT is a number that describes one cluster. That number tells DOS if the described cluster is available for new information storage, if it is flawed; for clusters that are in use, this number indicates if this cluster contains the end of the file, and if not, where the file information continues. This last point is worth amplifying. DOS may have to allocate many clusters to a single file, and it may end up choosing clusters that are not next to one another on the disk. DOS records in the FAT for each file a chain of numbers, each one of which points to the next number in the chain, except for the last one, which is a special end-of-file number. This chain-per-file concept is central the FAT approach to disk space management.

The second critical information structure DOS keeps on the disk is the root directory. This table has 32 bytes per entry for a fixed number of entries. The maximum number of entries depends on the size of the disk and the version of DOS. A 360KB or 720KB floppy diskette can have at most 112 entries in its root directory. A 1.2MB or 1.44MB floppy can have 224 entries. Typical hard disk volumes (and many RAM disks) have a maximum of 512 entries in the root directory.

Tip: **Avoiding Common Errors in Disk Formatting** Most problems with FORMAT arise when preparing floppy diskettes. There are now eight different DOS formats for floppies. Five of them are for 5-1/4" diskettes (160KB, 180KB, 320KB, 360KB, and 1.2MB), and three are for 3-1/2" diskettes (720KB, 1.44MB, and 2.88MB). The 160KB, 180KB, and 320KB formats are now obsolete. The 360KB and 720KB formats are often called the *low-density* formats for 5-1/4" and 3-1/2" diskettes, respectively. The 1.2MB and 1.44MB are the corresponding *high-density* formats. The new 2.88MB format is *extra-high-density* and comes only in 3-1/2" diskettes.

1. The first kind of problem comes from using the wrong diskettes for your purpose. Manufacturers of diskettes carefully formulate the surface coating according to the intended use for the diskette. This means that no matter what drive you use or how you fool the FORMAT program, you cannot reliably format low-density diskettes as if they were high-density.

   You might seem to succeed in formatting low-density (720KB) 3-1/2" diskettes (labeled as 1MB diskettes, which refers to their capacity before the formatting overhead is written to the diskette) as if they were high-density (1.44MB diskettes, which are labeled 2MB capacity on the box) by putting those low-density diskettes into some high-density 3-1/2" diskette drive and simply running FORMAT. The diskettes will *say* that they have the high-density format on them. In fact, you can often load them with a full 1.44MB of information. The problem arises, however, when you try to *read* that information back. In time, those diskettes will not be reliable, no matter how well they seem to perform initially. Furthermore, they will be much more likely to give read errors in another PC than the one in which they were recorded.

2. If you're willing to waste some of the potential capacity, you can format high-density diskettes as low-density ones. This allows you to exchange information with someone who has only low-density diskette drives even though your PC has only high-density. But don't think that low-density formatting of a high-density diskette will make your data ultra-safe. It will be exactly as safe as if you had used the full potential of that diskette, and no more.

3. While all high-density floppy diskette drives can write lower-density formats onto low-density diskettes, they are not as reliable as when you use the type of diskettes the drive was really designed to handle.
4. The FORMAT command uses three ways to determine what format to write to a diskette. First, if you don't tell it otherwise, it will attempt to format the diskette to the maximum capacity of the drive. This is a very bad idea unless the diskette you put in the drive was meant to hold that capacity of format. The second way is to tell FORMAT what size to use by explicitly saying how many sectors per track and how many tracks you want it to record on the diskette. You do this with the /N and /T switches. For example, the command `FORMAT A: /N:9 /T:80` specifies a 720KB format for a 3-1/2" drive. This method used to be the only way to specify which format to record. Now it is only included in FORMAT's capabilities for backward compatibility. The third, and preferred way to tell FORMAT which pattern to record is to use the /F switch instead of /N and /T. (You cannot use both methods at the same time.) The proper syntax is `FORMAT A: /F:nnn` where *nnn* is one of these values: 160, 180, 320, 360, 720, 1200, 1.2, 1440, 1.44, 2880, or 2.88. You can add K, KB, M, or MB to any of those values as appropriate and DOS will still understand that, for example, 720 = 720K = 720KB.

Figure 7-2 shows this logical organization of a DOS disk volume. This figure was drawn to depict a 360KB floppy diskette, but except for such details as how many sectors there are in a cluster (2 in this case), in a FAT (also 2 for this size disk), and in the root directory (7 for 360KB floppies), the figure could represent any DOS logical volume. All the sectors of the disk are shown lined up according to their logical sector numbers down the left side of the figure. In addition to the logical sector numbers, this diagram also shows the cluster numbers. (Note that cluster numbers start at the beginning of the data area, instead of at the beginning of the volume, and begin with the number 2. In the FAT there are two numbers that would seem to correspond to cluster numbers 0 and 1, but they are special numbers with a different use.)

The first FAT is shown in greater detail in the lower-right corner. Each of the sections into which the tower on the left is divided represents a region that holds 2,048 bytes, with three exceptions: the boot sector is only 1 sector, or 512 bytes; the 2 FATs each span 2 sectors, or 1,024 bytes; and the broad section for the root directory, which contains 7 sectors, or 3,584 bytes). Each small box in the FAT represents one 12-bit number—just 1 1/2 bytes. (Larger disks now commonly use 16-bit entries in their FAT tables; all floppies still use FATs with 12-bit entries.)

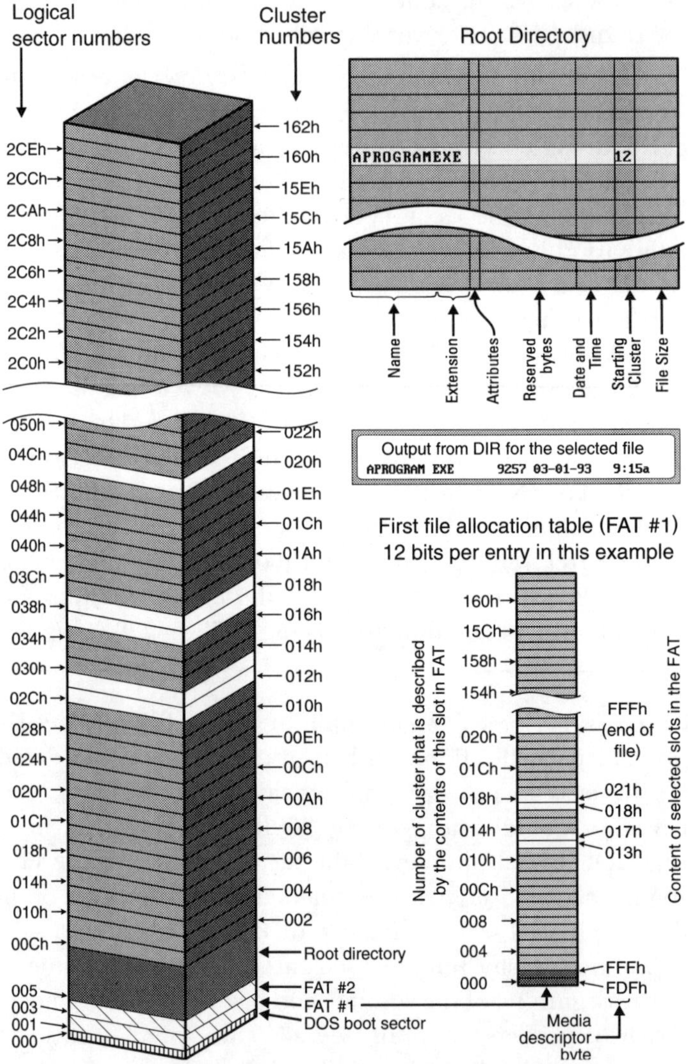

Figure 7-2 The logical structure of a DOS disk volume showing the logical sectors, clusters, root directory, and file allocation table

Each box in the FAT (except the first two) corresponds to one cluster in the data area on the disk. The first two entries (which correspond to clusters 0 and 1) are used to store a special code value indicating what kind of disk this one is.

In the upper-right corner of the figure is a detailed view of a portion of the root directory contents. The information shown is for only one file, so that you may more clearly see the chain of clusters that contain that file's data and the sequence of entries in the FAT that record where those clusters are. Just below the root directory map is one line from the output of DIR showing how it would display the illustrated file.

Each entry in the root directory contains a file name (8 characters), file extension (3 characters), information on the file's size (4 bytes), date and time of the last modification (4 bytes), and some attributes (1 byte). We will describe what each of these mean in a moment. Notice that each entry also has a starting cluster number (2 bytes), which records where on the disk DOS began storing the data for the file named in that entry. (This is the start of the chain of entries in the FAT for this file.) If the file contains more bytes than one cluster can hold, you (and DOS) must consult the FAT to find out where the rest of the file is located. The file shown in detail in Figure 7-2 has its data stored in three noncontiguous regions of the disk. Such a file is called *fragmented.* How fragmented files get created, the problems they can cause, and how file fragmentation may be eliminated are issues discussed in Chapter 9.

In addition to the file name and extension, file size, attributes, date and time of the last modification, and starting cluster, each directory entry also contains 10 reserved bytes that each are an ASCII null character (value = 0). When CHKDSK finds lost chains of clusters, it reports that it found some entries in the FAT that look like they map out chains of clusters that are in use, but that it was unable to find any directory entries pointing to the start of those chains.

The FAT plus root directory strategy discussed so far works well if you don't have too many files on a disk. But it breaks down as soon as you want to put more files on the disk than there are spaces for entries in the root directory. If you attempt to write a file to the disk when the root directory has something in each of its entries, DOS will tell you that the disk is full, which may not be true. Consider a couple of cases: A 360KB floppy diskette can have up to 112 entries in its root directory. The cluster size on that type of diskette is two sectors, or 1KB. If you write several files that are all less than 1KB in size to such a floppy diskette, you will run out of room as soon as you have written the 112th file. At that point you will have exhausted less than one-third of the disk's data capacity, but you cannot add any more files. What about a hard disk? With the typical 2KB per cluster and 512 maximum root directory entries, you could get the message `disk full` from DOS with only 512 files and less than 1MB of data on the disk. Clearly, this is not a satisfactory situation. Fortunately, there is an easy way around the problem.

Subdirectories

Starting with version 2.0, DOS has supported *subdirectories.* Although subdirectories are actually just files on the disk, DOS creates and uses them in a very special way. The content of a subdirectory file is structured identically to the root directory; that is, each 32 bytes in the file represents a directory entry for another file. The big difference is that, like any file—but unlike the root directory—a subdirectory file grows as large as necessary to hold whatever information is added to it. You even can make a subdirectory file that is too large to fit into a single cluster on your disk. (With a 2KB cluster size typical of a hard disk, this means any directory that contains more than 64 entries.) The subdirectory file will then spill over into another cluster, possibly one located on the disk far away from its first cluster. Fragmented subdirectory files are commonplace.

The way around the limited size of the root directory is simply to put one or more subdirectory files in the root directory, and then put information describing all the rest of the files on your disk into those subdirectory files.

WHAT BELONGS IN THE ROOT DIRECTORY?

In practice, you cannot move all of the files other than subdirectories out of the root directory, because there are a few files that must be described directly in the root directory. On any bootable DOS disk these include three or four hidden system files used to boot your PC and the CONFIG.SYS and AUTOEXEC.BAT files that are used to control how your PC gets customized as it is booting. If you use DoubleSpace, the `DBLSPACE.000` compressed volume file (CVF) must be in the root directory of the boot volume, and there may be some other CVF files that need to be there as well. In addition, some utility programs put files into the root directory and insist that they stay there. For example, the DOS 6 program UNDELETE does this. It puts the file `PCTRACKR.DEL` in the root directory of each volume for which you have told UNDELETE to keep track of deleted files.

Several other files may get put in the root directory as a default location, but you may move them as long as you inform the programs that use those files where they are. One example is the command interpreter (normally COMMAND.COM). You may put this file in any directory, as long as you include a `SHELL` statement in your CONFIG.SYS file that points to the command interpreter.

Every other file on your disk can be described to DOS only indirectly, through the use of subdirectories. Not only is it possible to put almost all your files in subdirectories, it is highly desirable. Any DOS power user should know to keep almost every file out of the root directory if at all possible. To do that, you must create subdirectories. Then put your files in them (or move them there if they started out somewhere else).

Note: DOS version 6 includes a MOVE command. This is long overdue. Previously, unless you had some third-party file moving utility program, you could only move a file from one directory to another by copying it from the first location to the second, and then deleting it from the first location. Not only did this waste effort, it risked fragmenting files. Now a file can be moved from one directory to another on the same disk drive (logical volume) merely by creating a new directory entry in the target directory that points to the start of the FAT chain for that file; then you delete the directory entry in the source directory. The file's data don't have to be copied or moved at all. (You do have to copy the data if you are moving a file from one disk drive to another, but the DOS 6 MOVE command will do that when necessary.

CREATING SUBDIRECTORIES

Subdirectories are created by using the `MKDIR` command, or its shorthand equivalent, `MD`. For example, to make a directory called USEFUL on your C drive, simply type

```
MD C:\USEFUL
```

and press the Enter key. DOS will create a file called USEFUL and put it in the root directory of the C drive. Furthermore, it will give that file a special *attribute* of "directory-ness." From then on, whenever you issue the DIR command in the root of C you will see one line that reads

```
USEFUL        <DIR>      03-23-93   9:59a
```

(with, of course, the date and time when you created this subdirectory).

The `C:\` portion of the command line shown in the preceding paragraph is not always necessary. `C:` tells DOS you want it to make a directory on the C drive; the `\` tells DOS to put the subdirectory file in the root directory. But if the DOS default drive and directory happen to be `C:\`, you're telling DOS to do something it would do anyway. But if you are in another directory or drive, then you must tell DOS explicitly where to create this new subdirectory file.

Note: The concepts of the *DOS default drive* and the *current DOS directory* indicate that DOS keeps track of the last time you typed a command consisting only of a valid drive letter and a colon; that drive is the DOS default drive. Similarly, it keeps track of the latest directory you changed to, using a command like that shown below. Any time you enter a DOS command that assumes a drive letter and a subdirectory, it will use the DOS default values unless you explicitly tell it to use other values. The DOS prompt will show you what those default values are (unless you changed your PROMPT command in the manner described in Chapter 11). Most PC users quickly fall into the habit of speaking of the current DOS directory on the DOS default drive as "where they are" on the disk.

Now you can change directories to your newly created one. To do this, type the command

```
CD C:\USEFUL
```

and press the Enter key. Again, we are using you the shorthand version of the command. The full name is CHDIR, but why type five letters when two will do? This command tells DOS to change the default directory on the C drive to \USEFUL. If you happen to be on a different drive at the time, you can access the C:\USEFUL directory by issuing this command, then typing C: and pressing the Enter key.

If, after typing this command, you type DIR—assuming you are on the C drive at the time—you will get a display that resembles this:

```
 Volume in drive C is MYBIGDRIVE
 Volume Serial Number is 1981-5ABA
 Directory of C:\USEFUL

.            <DIR>      03-23-93   9:59a
..           <DIR>      03-23-93   9:59a
        2 file(s)            0 bytes
                       3469312 bytes free
```

THE IMPORTANCE OF THE . AND .. "FILES"

Many PC users are puzzled by the two file names "." and "..". Some have tried deleting one or both of them, thinking that they didn't need those files. The file name ".." in this instance is actually a pointer to the root directory. (In general, the ".." entry points to the directory in which this subdirectory file resides. In this case, it is the root directory.) The file name "." points to the contents of this subdirectory file, which is another way of saying it points to this subdirectory itself.

If you delete ".", you will be deleting all the files in this directory. If you delete "..", you will be deleting all the files in your root directory!

THE RMDIR AND DELTREE COMMANDS

There are two other DOS commands for managing subdirectories. One is the remove directory command, RMDIR or RD for short. The other is the DELTREE command, which is new in version 6.

If you issue the command

```
RD C:\USEFUL
```

DOS will erase the \USEFUL directory—the file it created in the root directory of C to represent the subdirectory. DOS won't let you erase the current directory, which is reassuring when you think about it. You also can't remove a directory that has files in it. Finally, you can't remove a directory that DOS is using as a synonym for another drive letter. (This occurs only if you set it up by using the SUBST command.)

The Power and Danger of DELTREE The DELTREE command is very powerful. It allows you to delete subdirectories that are not empty, which means all the files in those subdirectories including files that are nominally protected against deletion by the read-only attribute or with the system and/or hidden attributes turned on.

DELTREE won't, however, delete the current DOS directory or any directory that contains the current directory as a subdirectory. Be warned, though; it will delete all the files in any of those directories. DELTREE also does not let you know when it is unable to delete one or more subdirectories.

DIRECTORY TREES

You can create subdirectories within subdirectories, as many levels deep as you need, provided that the total path from the root to the deepest subdirectory can be written in 64 characters or less. (Remember to count the backslash character that separates each subdirectory name from the next.) Thus, a fifth level subdirectory named FIFTH and the full path to it from the root might read:

```
\FIRST\SECOND\THIRD\FOURTH\FIFTH
```

which is a 32-character path.

```
C:\
└──LA-TIMES
     ├──LETTERS
     ├──INVOICES
     ├──REVIEWS
     └──ARTICLES
```

Figure 7-3 A DOS tree

The directories in a single DOS logical volume are usually called trees. The metaphor is an apt one if you think of the trunk as the root directory and each subdirectory as a branch, with some branches growing directly off of the trunk and others off other branches. Sometimes the subdirectories that have no additional subdirectories within them are called leaves. Figure 7-3 shows a very simple DOS directory tree resulting from issuing the DOS command TREE (on a C: drive with the particular structure shown).

NAVIGATING AMONG SUBDIRECTORIES

When you issue the command `CD C:\USEFUL` you are specifying both the drive and the exact directory you want to become the current DOS directory for that drive. If you leave off the drive designation, the change will be made on the DOS default drive. (You can leave off the initial backslash and still get the same effect, but only if you were in the `C:\` (root of C) directory at the time.) There are two ways to issue the CD command: One is with the initial backslash and one is without it. With the initial backslash (and perhaps a preceding drive letter and colon) you are using an "absolute" directory reference method. Otherwise, you are using "relative" directory addressing.

For example, suppose the directory tree looks like that shown in Figure 7-4. Two of the subdirectories have the same name: `MISC`, which is okay since each is located within a different directory. (You can have as many files or subdirectories as you like all with the same name, as long as each one is located within a different subdirectory.) If you issue the command `CD C:\UTIL\MISC`, you will be directing DOS to one of these directories. If you say `CD C:\DOCS\MISC`, you will be telling it to go to a different one. If the current directory is `C:\DOCS`, you could just say `CD MISC` and get to `C:\DOCS\MISC`. If you were in `C:\DOS` at the time, though, you would receive the error message `Invalid directory`.

You can combine the relative form of the change directory command with the special "file" names . and .. that occur in each subdirectory. Thus, you can say `CD ..` to tell DOS to move one directory closer to the root. On the other hand, `CD .` won't accomplish anything, because the command tells DOS to make the current directory the current directory.

```
C:\
├──DOS
├──UTIL
│   └──MISC
├──WORD
└──DOCS
    ├──RESUME
    ├──INVOICES
    │   ├──1991
    │   ├──1992
    │   └──1993
    ├──LETTERS
    │   ├──1991
    │   ├──1992
    │   └──1993
    └──MISC
```

Figure 7-4 A more complex example of a directory tree

A more complex example assumes you are in the `C:\DOCS\MISC` subdirectory. Then the command

```
CD ..\..\UTIL\MISC
```

would take you from that `MISC` directory to the other `MISC` directory. (The first .. says to go back from `C:\DOCS\MISC` to `C:\DOCS`. The next .. says to go back to `C:\`. The command continues from there, telling DOS to go to the directory named `UTIL` and then into the subdirectory `MISC` within `UTIL`. Therefore, your final destination is `C:\UTIL\MISC`.

Tip: DOS commands are like sentences. Each one must contain a verb. Many of them also must include one or more objects or adverbs. As is true for any English sentence, each "word" is separated from the next one by some space. But since \ and . are not valid characters in a command word (verb), COMMAND.COM knows that one of these special characters must signal the start of the next word in the command. This means that you can get away with typing `CD\DOS` instead of `CD \DOS`, and `CD..` instead of `CD ..` (but don't try it with other commands, because DOS will not be able to decipher your intentions).

ORGANIZING FILES INTO YOUR SUBDIRECTORIES

Once you know how to create subdirectories, the natural question is what to put in them. This is really a question about organizing files, and the answer is as variable as the people who use those files. Most users have a directory for all the files that come with DOS. Sometimes they include utility programs in that directory, while others keep their utility programs in a C:\UTIL directory.

Figure 7-4 illustrates a separate directory for a word processing program, which is a typical construction, as such programs usually have many files. (For example, Word for DOS, version 5.5, has 88 files in its subdirectory. Word for Windows, version 2.0 has 90, plus 72 in its tutorial subsubdirectory; WordPerfect 5.1 has 152 files in its subdirectory and an additional 54 files in its tutorial subsubdirectory.)

Figure 7-4 also shows a subsubdirectory under the word processor's main directory in which to keep the documents you create. Another strategy is to keep documents in a variety of subdirectories on various disk drives, organized according to topic or project.

Subdirectories are appropriate not only for hard disks; all the reasons for separating files by project, topic, or function also apply when stored on floppies.

Hard Disk Partitions

Every PC hard disk has a data table called the *partition table*, which has room for four entries. Most disks in PCs today have only one or two actual entries in this table; the others specify a partition of 0 size.

A partition that has a size other than 0 must also be identified as belonging to some operating system. Prior to version 3.3, there could be at most two partitions marked as belonging to DOS; and, if you had two, only one of them could be a DOS primary partition. Version 3.3 made it possible to have a second partition on a disk accessible to DOS. Such a partition is called an *extended DOS partition.*

If you have an extended DOS partition on your hard disk, it may be further subdivided into several logical volumes by putting additional partition tables (*extended partition tables*) inside the extended DOS partition. DOS will assign one drive letter to the DOS primary partition and another letter to each of the logical volumes within the extended partition.

The master partition table is kept in the first sector on every PC hard disk. This sector also contains a program that reads that table and decides which partition to access when booting your PC. This sector's contents (the program and the data table) are called the *master boot record* (MBR). Figure 7-5 shows how the master partition table in the MBR and the extended partition tables within the extended DOS partition are used to divide a disk drive. In this example the disk has been divided into three logical drives (which DOS will refer to as the C, D, and E drives). Each of these logical drives has an associated partition table, DOS boot record, FATs, root directory, and data area.

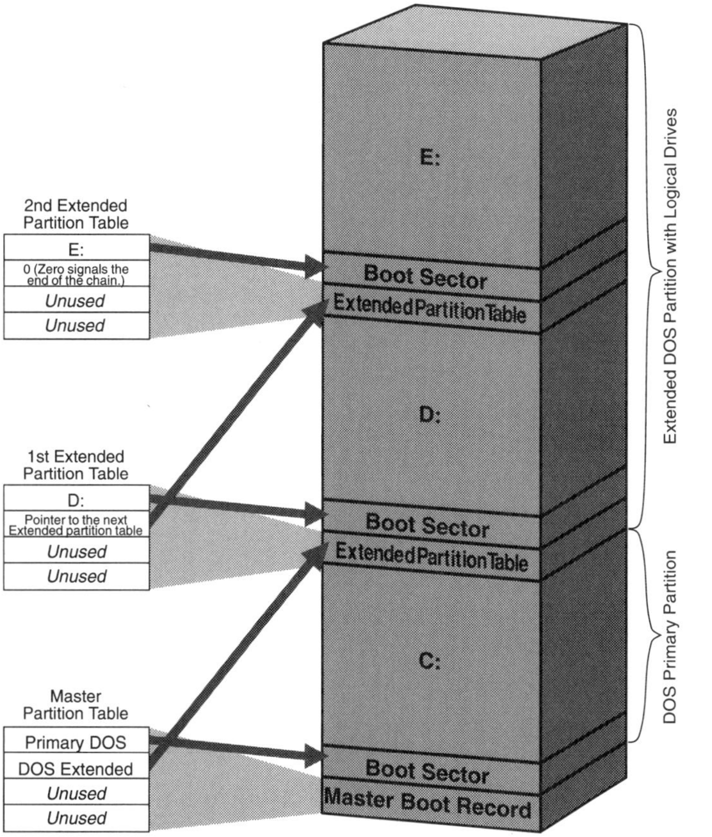

Figure 7-5 Dividing a hard disk into partitions and logical volumes

CREATING AND MAINTAINING PARTITION TABLES

The DOS program FDISK creates the master boot record, complete with its partition table. FDISK also creates the extended DOS partition and the extended partition tables within it that define the logical drives. Running FDISK is the usual way to alter the partition table data.

Warning: Be very careful when using FDISK on a disk that has valuable data on it. Most versions of FDISK don't confine their actions to the master boot record. They also wipe out all the information on several cylinders of any DOS partition they are establishing. It is safe to let FDISK tell you about the partitions that are on the disk; just don't tell it to reaffirm the present settings, or you may have to start all over again.

Tip: With the introduction of version 5, FDISK gained an important new capability. An undocumented command line switch `/MBR` tells FDISK to rewrite the master boot record program, but not alter the data table at all. This can be very useful, as one class of computer virus, the master boot record infectors, attacks computers by modifying the MBR program. The best way to rid your computer of such an attacker is by booting from an uninfected DOS floppy diskette and issuing the command `FDISK /MBR`.

With DOS version 6, FDISK becomes more useful. If you issue the command `FDISK /STATUS` it will show you the partitioning of your hard disks without actually starting the FDISK program. Thus there is no possibility of making a mistake. This command shows you a tabular listing of your physical hard disk drives, listing the total size in megabytes of each one and the amount that has been allocated to partitions. It also shows what percentage of the disk volume is unallocated, which it calls `Free`. Don't confuse this with the free space on your DOS drives, however. The free space on a DOS drive indicates how much room you have on that drive in which to create new files. The `Free` number reported by `FDISK /STATUS` only tells you if you have not allocated all of your hard disk to some partition. Finally, `FDISK /STATUS` shows you all the drive letters DOS has assigned to this drive and how large each logical volume is.

If you have any compressed volumes (accessed by use of DoubleSpace, Stacker, or some other equivalent program), `FDISK /STATUS` will ignore them. To FDISK, the compressed volume files that the file compression program uses to create additional logical drives are merely files. FDISK is concerned only with the real, physical hard disk drives and the logical volumes created within partitions on those drives. This, unfortunately, can lead to some confusion. The drive letters reported by `FDISK /STATUS` are the drive letters DOS would have assigned to those volumes if the compression software had not been loaded. For example, if you have just one primary DOS partition, FDISK will tell you about only what it sees as a C drive. But once you boot your system, that drive assumes a new identity as some other drive letter. (It is called the host volume and might, for example, have become your K drive.)

This change in drive letters referring to the same physical volume probably will not confuse Stacker and SuperStor users; they always have had to deal with the changing drive letter designations because those compressors load only during the processing of the CONFIG.SYS file. DoubleSpace users, however, may be confused, since they never get to see their host volumes with the original drive letters DOS assigns. By the time they first see a drive letter,

DoubleSpace has already mounted the compressed volume files and reassigned the drive letters.

USING FDISK

FDISK is invoked by typing the command `FDISK` at the DOS prompt. It clears the screen and gives you a menu of options. The first thing to do is be sure that FDISK is about to act on the physical drive that you want. Some versions of FDISK call the first physical hard disk drive number 0; the version included with DOS 6 calls that drive number 1. If FDISK notices that you have more than one physical drive, it will present you with menu option #5 instructing you to select which physical drive to operate on. This option displays the same information as `FDISK /STATUS`, plus gives you the opportunity to enter your choice of drive.

After you have selected the drive, confirm what you think you know about it by asking FDISK to display the current data in the partition table on that drive (menu option #4). In addition to the information in the /STATUS display, this option shows you the volume label and file system in use for each volume. (The file system for any DOS volume is always either FAT12 or FAT16.) Selecting menu option #4 also shows you which of the partitions, if any, is flagged as active, which is the same as identifying the one that the MBR program will attempt to read a boot record from when you boot your PC.

Once you are sure FDISK is focused on the disk you wish to modify, you may select one of the other menu options. Option #1 lets you create a DOS primary or extended partition or create a DOS logical drive within an extended partition. Option #2 is for making one of the partitions active. Option #3 is for deleting DOS partitions or logical drives.

Partition Sizes

How to partition a hard disk is not a question with one simple answer that applies to everyone. You need to look at how large your hard disk is and what you will be using it for. If you have what is now considered a modest-size disk (anything less than 128MB), there is little, if any reason for dividing it into partitions. If you have a larger hard drive, you may wish to partition it.

The primary argument for keeping everything in one partition is to maintain simplicity. Partition sizes are fixed. Once you have created them you cannot expand or contract them without re-creating them, which requires that you back up all your data, delete and re-create the partitions, reformat the partitions, and then restore your data. If you have only one large partition, you don't have to make any advance decisions about how often you will engage in any activity or the volume of files that activity will entail.

There are several arguments for using multiple partitions. One is a different kind of simplicity. If you partition your hard disk and put into each partition only one kind of file (DOS and your utility programs in one, word processors and documents in another, graphics programs in a third, etc.), when you want a certain kind of program or data file, you will know to which partition to go. And once you get there you will have fewer directories and files to browse through to find the file you want.

A second argument for partitioning is that it makes DOS work more efficiently. Any time you write a file to the disk, DOS must return to the file allocation table to record each new cluster it is going to use just before writing data to that cluster. On large files located far from the FAT this forces DOS to spend most of its time positioning the disk heads. Since each partition has its own set of FATs, on smaller partitions the distances traveled become much shorter.

A third argument for multiple partitions is that the cluster size can be smaller than for huge partitions. Once a partition gets over 128MB in size, the cluster size jumps from 2KB to 4KB. Over 256MB and the cluster size jumps to 8KB. This pattern continues, with the maximum size partition FDISK can create (2GB) having a cluster size of 32KB. On average, every file wastes about half a cluster of disk space in what is called the file's *slack space* (space from the end of the file to the end of the cluster). With many thousands of files and very large clusters, you could waste a substantial amount of disk real estate.

The DoubleSpace file compression program (or Stacker or SuperStor) provides a third option: You can make your entire hard disk a single DOS primary partition, then use your preferred on-the-fly file-compression program (DoubleSpace, Stacker, or SuperStor) to divide that one large volume into multiple compressed logical volumes. With each of these products it is possible to increase or reduce volumes whenever you wish. Furthermore, these programs use the disk space more efficiently than DOS alone is able to do, so you don't need to worry about slack space and the large cluster sizes associated with very large disk volumes. The distance from FAT to file is reduced, since both reside within the same *compressed volume file* (CVF). (These programs are explained in detail in Chapter 9.)

Disk-Based Components of DOS

Here is a list of the essential DOS components you'll find on your hard or floppy disks, indicating where each one resides and what it does. (The Command Reference has a table that lists all the components of DOS plus all the internal commands that don't have corresponding command program files. You also will find a brief description of each of these components and commands in that reference.)

1. The master boot record (MBR) with its partition table is essential for access to any hard disk in a PC: This program plus data table occupies the first sector on the disk (at physical address cylinder 0, head 0, physical sector number 1). You must have one of these for each physical hard disk in your system.
2. The DOS boot record and its data table. This program is also essential for access to a DOS logical volume. There is one for each DOS logical volume in your system; that is, one for the DOS primary partition on each physical hard drive, plus one for each logical drive within the extended DOS partition on each physical disk drive.) The DOS boot record's data table describes the volume in logical terms. (The contents of this table are mostly copied to the BIOS parameter block for this DOS logical drive.) The DOS boot record is located in the first sector within each DOS logical volume.
3. The BIOS program on the disk (usually called IO.SYS or IBMBIO.COM): This program file includes the SYSINIT module plus all the DOS default device drivers. SYSINIT builds DOS in memory. The default device drivers extend the BIOS code in the motherboard ROM chips to support the standard set of DOS devices. This is one of at least two hidden system files on every bootable DOS disk. In earlier versions of DOS this had to be the first file listed in the root directory and its contents had to be located at the beginning of the data area and be in one unbroken piece. Since version 5 it has been possible to physically place this file anywhere on the disk, but it still must be described in the root directory.
4. The DOS program (usually called MSDOS.SYS or IBMDOS.COM): This program contains the core portions of DOS that manage lower memory and organize disk accesses. Like the BIOS program, this is a hidden system file. In earlier versions of DOS this had to be the second file listed in the root directory, and it had to have its contents begin on the disk immediately following the BIOS program (but it did not need to be unfragmented). Starting with version 5 it, too, can be located anywhere on the disk, but it must still be listed somewhere in the root directory.
5. DBLSPACE.BIN, DBLSPACE.INI, DBLSPACE.000, DBLSPACE.SYS, DBLSPACE.EXE, and DBLSPACE.INF: These files provide support for Microsoft's on-the-fly file compression and expansion. DBLSPACE.BIN is considered a new, third, essential hidden system file of the operating

system (along with IO.SYS and MSDOS.SYS), if the disk is to support compressed volume files.

6. The command interpreter (normally COMMAND.COM, though there are alternatives available from third parties, such as NDOS and 4DOS): This is the only way to communicate with DOS. Without this shell program you'd never see a DOS prompt and never be able to enter a DOS command. Even if you have another shell program wrapped around this one (such as DOSSHELL), that program probably depends on the command interpreter to provide the interface it needs to the underlying DOS and BIOS programs. The command interpreter may be put anywhere on any of your PC's disk drives. However, unless it is named COMMAND.COM and is located in the root directory of the boot drive, you must specify its name and residence in a SHELL statement in your CONFIG.SYS file. (If you have DoubleSpaced your boot drive, then COMMAND.COM's default location is the root directory of the logical volume created from DBLSPACE.000.)
7. Key operating environment support modules (DSVXD.386 or WINA20.386): These modules are virtual device drivers needed by different versions of Windows in order to operate properly in 386-enhanced mode. They normally are installed in the root directory of the boot disk. If you are not going to run Windows 3.0 in enhanced mode, you don't need WINA20.386. If you are, you can move this file to another directory or drive, provided you add a `SWITCHES /W` line to your CONFIG.SYS file and an entry in SYSTEM.INI specifying where you have put WINA20.386. If you have upgraded to Windows 3.1 (or Windows for Workgroups), you will not need WINA20.386, but you will need the DSVXD.386 file to support enhanced mode.
8. Other loadable, installable modules: These include various device drivers and TSR programs necessary for support of any hardware you have in your PC that goes beyond the "vanilla PC" that is understood by DOS.

CONFIG.SYS and AUTOEXEC.BAT are not included in this list because they are not essential DOS components. They are very useful, and you doubtless will want to have them, but DOS will operate perfectly well without them. Furthermore, they are not programs, but rather lists of instructions to IO.SYS and COMMAND.COM, respectively, telling those programs how you want DOS customized as your PC is booting. Chapter 9 explains what to put in those files and why.

DOS Power Tools for Disks

CPYDSK lets you copy disks exactly without the famous "Insert Target Disk"/"Insert Source Disk" shuffle that the DOS DISKCOPY command requires. For hard disks, the Micro House utilities (MH-SAVE and MH-RESTR) and the ancillary programs (MH-ESDI, MH-IDE, and MH-SYS) provide additional security in the case of a hard disk malfunction, by allowing you to backup and restore vital system information, such as the master boot record, partition tables, and file allocation tables. OPTICOPY and OPTIMOVE aid in getting the most information onto floppies, while QUADRIVE lets you get around some 5 1/4- to 3 1/2-inch disk exchange problems (where it's necessary that a drive see the data on disk as coming from a given format). PARK and TIMEPARK are useful for putting the read/write heads in a safe place for moving or powering down your system. SIZE and SHO let you see how much room is left on your drives.

C H A P T E R

8

◆ ◆ ◆ ◆ ◆

Files

This chapter explains the DOS file naming rules and gives some useful suggestions on how to name your files. File attributes and the ways that files can be created and their contents examined are also explored.

Files Names

All DOS files must have names. A valid DOS file name consists of two parts: the file name and the file extension or file type. The file name can be one to eight characters long; the file extension must be no more than three characters long. When used in a command, a file name is typed first, followed by a period, and then the file extension, with no intervening spaces. This format will be referred to as the **8.3** file name rule.

The *Microsoft DOS User's Guide* tells you that there are only 52 characters that may be used in a file name. It lists the uppercase letters A through Z, the numerals 0 through 9, and these 16 symbols:

_ ^ $ ~ ! # % & - { } @ ' ' ( )

The Guide explicitly says no other symbols are permissible. This is not accurate.

Of the 256 possible values for a byte, all but 45 are acceptable to DOS as characters to be used in a DOS file name. Of the 45, the first 32 ASCII values are control characters (like the carriage return, line feed, backspace, and bell characters), and can't be used in a file name. Fourteen special punctuation marks also are off limits because they have other meanings for DOS. These include the space character (20h), colon, semicolon, period, comma, plus and equal signs, the double quote symbol ("), forward and backward slash symbols (/ and \), and both angle and square bracket symbols (< >, [ ]).

With those conventions in mind then, the name `ALEX(OR).SUE` is a valid file name. So is `MY{VERY}.OWN`, as is `12345678.901`. Even `AL&MARY` is a valid DOS file name. (This last example has a zero-length file extension. Whenever you type a file name with no extension, you can omit the period. The only exception to this is in connection with programs that presume all files have a file extension if you don't explicitly tell them otherwise. In order to let such a program know a file has no extension, you must include the trailing period after the main portion of the file name.)

Conversely, `AND/OR.ANY` is not a valid file name (it includes the forward slash character). The name `.XXX`, too, would be invalid. (Remember, the file extension may have no length, but the file name must be at least one character long). The file name `AVERYLONGNAME.WHATEVER` exceeds the normal eight- and three-character rule for a file name. Ordinarily, though, DOS will accept such a name and simply truncate it to `AVERYLON.WHA`.

The lowercase alphabet may be used in file names, but DOS normally regards them as uppercase letters. In addition, DOS uppercases some of the high-bit set characters, which reduces the number of allowable and distinct characters for file names by another 25 characters.

Note: Certain of the upper ASCII characters are accented lowercase letters and are sometimes translated into their like-accented uppercase equivalents. But other times, the translations make less sense. Table 8-1 lists the high-bit set characters and their translated values. This table shows the hexadecimal ASCII value before and after capitalization. Only for those that have high-bit reset (real ASCII) translations is the translated character shown. Refer back to Figures 4-6 and 4-11 to see which symbols are associated with each of these ASCII values in the standard IBM extended graphics character set. This table has 26 entries, but only 25 of them always get translated by DOS. The character E5h is a special case. When COMMAND.COM encounters it as the first character in a file name, it replaces it with 05h (but only in this position). It does so, not because E5h is an invalid character for a file name, but precisely because it *is* valid! COMMAND.COM does this because E5h has another role to play in connection with directory entries on the disk. If the first character in a file name in the root directory or any subdirectory on the disk is E5h, it is understood by DOS to mean that the file has been erased. When you name a file with the E5h character in the first position, DOS actually stores a 05h in that location on the disk (so it won't think the file is erased). This means that any time you enter a command with E5h as the first character in the command name, COMMAND.COM must do the same translation in order for it to find a match with the correct entry in the directory.

DOS will uppercase all the letters that you type at the DOS prompt, but it will accept lowercase letters in a file name, if you manage to get them into a directory entry unchanged. You can enter lowercase letters, or even spaces, into file names in directory entries by using DEBUG, the Norton Disk Editor, or any other program that allows direct disk-sector editing, but it is not generally a good idea.

Lowercase letters and spaces are problematic in file names because COMMAND.COM automatically capitalizes all letters in the first "word" in the command line. (COMMAND.COM doesn't change the case of the rest of the command line, as some programs must see lowercase parameter or switch values.) Next, COMMAND.COM checks to see if it knows how to do whatever action the verb implies. If it does (which means that you have specified an *internal command*), COMMAND.COM simply does what you requested. Otherwise, it looks for a file whose name is the same as the verb and whose extension is COM, EXE, or BAT. If the actual file name contains any lowercase letters, there will never be a match with the capitalized version of the command you typed. Similarly, if there is a space in the name, you can't type that into a command line and expect COMMAND.COM to understand it. COMMAND.COM assumes the first space in a DOS command line marks the end of the first word, so it only looks for a file whose name matches up to the space.

Tip: There is a way to deal with files containing lowercase letters or spaces. You could simply rename the file, or use DEBUG or the Norton Disk Editor to fix the file name. DOS, however, provides an easier way. Suppose the name is `ABC xy.FOO` (the fourth character in the name is a space). Further suppose that no other file in the same subdirectory fits all three of these criteria: `ABC` as its the first three letters, six or fewer letters in the name, and the file extension `FOO`. If none of the other files fits all three of these conditions, then you can issue the command

```
REN ABC?XY.FOO ABC_XY.FOO
```

and your problem file will be renamed to a perfectly legal `ABC_XY.FOO` without any other file being affected at all. (The role of the question mark in this command will be explained shortly.)

Finally, the actual number of acceptable symbols for file names is 186. Later in this chapter, some suggestions are given for getting the most from the DOS 8.3 file name format and describe some of the most common names and file extensions you will encounter. First, though, you need to be aware of an alternative way to specify a file name to COMMAND.COM or any other program.

Table 8-1 High-Bit Characters and Translated Values

Original Character	Translated Value	ASCII Symbol	Original Character	Translated Value	ASCII Symbol
81h	9Ah		91h	92h	
82h	45h	E	93h	4Fh	O
83h	41h	A	94h	99h	
84h	8Eh		95h	4Fh	O
85h	41h	A	96h	55h	U
86h	8Fh		97h	55h	U
87h	80h		98h	59h	Y
88h	45h	E	A0h	41h	A
89h	45h	E	A1h	49h	I
8Ah	45h	E	A2h	4Fh	O
8Bh	49h	I	A3h	55h	U
8Ch	49h	I	A4h	A5h	
8Dh	49h	I	E5h	05h	[only sometimes translated]

File Specifications and Wildcards

Any time you want COMMAND.COM or any other program to do something to a file or group of files, you must tell it which file or files you have in mind. The obvious way to specify a file is to give its name and DOS allows several variations for doing this.

A *fully qualified file specification,* which is the complete name of a file, consists of four parts:

- the drive specifier (a drive letter followed by a colon)
- an explicit path from the root directory to the particular directory in which the file can be found
- the file name (1 to 8 characters)
- the file name extension (the file type)

A fully qualified file specification reads as follows:

```
D:\LA-TIMES\REVIEWS\93MAR07.DOC
```

and its four parts are

```
D:
\LA-TIMES\REVIEWS\
93MAR07 and
.DOC
```

The last two parts of a fully qualified file specification make up the *fully specified file name.*

You don't always have to give all four parts, however. There are two ways to be more concise and still let COMMAND.COM and many other PC programs know what you mean. The first way is to just leave some elements out, in which case, DOS will make some assumptions about the missing parts of the file name. If you don't specify a drive, for example, DOS will assume you mean the current drive. If you don't specify a path, DOS will assume you mean the current DOS directory for the specified (or implied) drive.

Therefore, if you are asking COMMAND.COM to run a program, you don't need to specify the extension (but it must be COM, EXE, or BAT). Many other programs also will allow you to omit the file extension, in which case they will assume that it is their default file type. Microsoft Word (for DOS or Windows) will assume you wish to edit a file of type DOC unless you tell it otherwise.

A minor and useful variation on this is the behavior of the DIR command. You can omit the file type altogether, and DIR will assume you want to see information on files with every possible extension. If you have been in the habit of typing `DIR *.*` you can merely type `DIR`. You can also use a single * in situations where you otherwise would add `.*` at the end of some other file specification (for example, `DIR 934Q*` would produce the same results as `DIR 93Q4*.*`). Alternatively, since a single period is a synonym for the current directory, you could use the command `DIR .` in lieu of `DIR *.*`. Note that, as a safeguard, DOS does not work under the same assumptions with DEL.

Wildcards provide the second type of flexibility. There are two wildcard characters available for your use. One is the question mark, which may stand in for any single character, legal or otherwise, in a file name. The other is the asterisk, which is equivalent to one or more question marks. The exact number it stands for depends on where you use it in the file name or in the file type. Wherever you put it, the asterisk implies a question mark in that position and all subsequent positions in that part of the file name. When you use wildcards in a file name you are only partially specifying the name—you are leaving the rest of the specification open. This is called an *ambiguous file specification.*

> ***Note:*** Wildcards don't work with all DOS commands. The DOS internal command TYPE, for example, demands that you explicitly tell it what file name and file type you wish to have it display on the screen.

With the above in mind then, the wildcard file specification `B?LL.TXT` could result in `BALL.TXT`, `BELL.TXT`, `BILL.TXT`, `BULL.TXT`, and `B5LL.TXT` (not to mention `B&LL.TXT` and `B~LL.TXT` and 179 other possibilities). If you ask DIR to list information about these files by issuing the command `DIR B?LL.TXT`, it will show information for all of them that are in the current directory. In a similar fashion, the command `DIR B*.T*` will display information on all files in the current directory that have B as the first letter of the file name and T as the first letter of their file type.

You can mix the two wildcards. `DIR ABC*.D?M` asks the DIR command to display information on all files whose names begin with `ABC` and whose file type starts with `D` and ends with `M`. This would include `ABC.DIM`, `ABCDEF.DOM`, `ABCDEFGH.D_M`, and a host of other possibilities.

Before any program tries to find one or more files that match what you have ambiguously specified, any asterisks are converted into one or more question marks—enough to fill out that part of the 8.3 full file name. An asterisk in the fifth position of the file name is equivalent to four question marks; in the third position of the file type it is the same as a single question mark. Therefore, in the example command given above, `DIR B*.T*`, is the same as `DIR B???????.T??`. DOS discards any characters following the asterisk—most of the time. Occasionally, you will encounter a DOS command or program that will complain if you add letters after an asterisk or if you enter two asterisks in a row.

Notice that in all these cases the space is an acceptable match for a question mark. A legal DOS file name may not have spaces embedded in it, but any file name that is fewer than eight characters long is implicitly padded with enough spaces to make it eight characters long. Similarly, the file type is padded with enough spaces to make it three characters long. Since wildcards will match even illegal characters (or ill-advised ones in the case of lower-case letters), you can use the REN command to modify a file with the ill-formed name.

Reserved DOS File Names

A few of the innumerable possible file names are reserved by DOS. These are not actually names of files, however; they are names of devices that DOS treats almost as if they were files. There are twelve of them: AUX, CLOCK$, COM1, COM2, COM3, COM4, CON, LPT1, LPT2, LPT3, NUL, and PRN.

The AUX device is the same as COM1. The CLOCK$ device is (as you may have guessed) the program by which DOS keeps track of time. The devices COM1 through COM4 are reserved for serial communication ports, which are sometimes used for serial printers, but more commonly for modems, mice, graphics tablets, and plotters. The CON device is the mechanism through which the CPU sends messages to the screen and receives input from the keyboard. The devices LPT1 through LPT3 are reserved for communicating with parallel printer ports (usually by sending output to those ports). The PRN device is the same as LPT1.

In all twelve cases you may add a colon after one of these reserved names, and DOS will treat it the same way with or without the colon. But get in the habit of adding the colon to remind you that you are referring to a device and not to a normal file. You won't see these files when you use the DIR command, but if you try any allowable file operation on one of them, that operation will never fail unless you specify the subdirectory or drive that does not exist.

Other Files DOS Recognizes

DOS, or more precisely, COMMAND.COM, is built to recognize three kinds of files. Any other file it regards as unknown to its data file. The three file types that are special to COMMAND.COM are all executable files, and their full file names end with the extensions COM, EXE, or BAT. Executable means that they are programs that contain instructions describing how the computer is to perform an action. When you want to invoke an action, you simply name that action's executable file in a command line, and COMMAND.COM finds and runs that program. (This is not the only way to cause a program to run, but it is the simplest and most commonly used one.)

The first type of executable file, a COM file, is simply an image on disk of the contents of memory that exists when this program is loaded and ready to run. COMMAND.COM reads that file from the disk into memory and then lets it take control of your PC.

The second kind of executable file, one whose file extension is EXE, is somewhat more complex. An EXE program may have several elements to it, all in the same file. In addition to the instructions and data it needs to perform the action it was designed for, this file type also has a 512-byte header—the *relocation header*—that tells COMMAND.COM where in memory to put each of the elements that comprise the total file. COMMAND.COM reads this kind of file from the disk, computes where to put each portion of it in memory, does some internal adjustments to the program as necessary, and then lets it take control of your PC.

The third kind of executable file is the batch file, which has the extension BAT. This is a file containing nothing but printable ASCII characters, plus carriage return characters that mark the end of each line. Each line in a batch file is a DOS command. Usually, they are commands you could have typed at the DOS prompt, but some are special and can be used only within a batch file. Chapter 12 explains all about batch files and how to write them. COMMAND.COM reads this sort of file from the disk one line at a time, after which it interprets what that line is telling it to do, and does that. Then it returns to the disk file to read the next line.

There is a sequence to the way COMMAND.COM executes COM, EXE, and BAT files that are entered without a period and file extension. If the verb in the command is not an internal command, COMMAND.COM looks for a program file with that verb as its name and COM as its extension. If it fails to find such a program in the current directory, it will next look for a program with the same root name, but with the extension EXE. If it still fails to find your program, it looks one more time, this time for a file with that same name but with the extension BAT.

If all three of these searches in the current directory fail, COMMAND.COM repeats those steps in each directory named on the DOS PATH. (Chapter 13 explains what the PATH is, where it is stored, and how it is set.) If it still can't find a program to run, COMMAND.COM returns the message

`Bad command or file name`, and reissues the DOS prompt, ready for your next command.

COMMAND.COM responds differently, however, if you do type the name, a period, and the extension. In early versions of DOS the extension would be stripped off and discarded. More recent versions (starting at least with DOS 5) do not ignore what you type. If you type `MYPROG.EXE`, and there is both a `MYPROG.EXE` and a `MYPROG.COM` in the current directory, COMMAND.COM will follow your explicit instructions and load and run `MYPROG.EXE`. You can force it to read and interpret a batch file in the same way even though there is a COM or EXE file with the same name in the same directory.

Similarly, if you add a path in front of the program's name, COMMAND.COM will not follow its normal search order. Instead it will go directly to the location you have specified and run the command you named from that directory. You can use either the absolute or relative forms of path construction (starting with or without a backslash character, respectively).

If COMMAND.COM fails to find the specified file in the specified directory, it does not search in the current directory and all the directories on the PATH. You can't run a program if its name matches one of the internal commands that COMMAND.COM knows how to execute by itself because, before COMMAND.COM looks for a program to execute, it first checks your command's verb against its internal list of commands.

Tip: You can trick COMMAND.COM into executing a program called `DIR.COM` by taking advantage of the fact that COMMAND.COM follows your explicit directions when you give them. In this case, you simply need to preface your command with the path to `DIR.COM`. If the current DOS directory and drive is where you have put the `DIR.COM` program, a suitable command would be

```
.\DIR
```

plus whatever objects and adverbs you wish to specify after the verb in this command.

Note: COM and EXE files don't have to have the correct extension. COMMAND.COM will search first for a COM file, then for an EXE file of the specified name, and once it finds a match, it will load that file and process its relocation header if it has one. COMMAND.COM looks at the first two characters of the file,

> and if it sees the ASCII symbols M and Z, it assumes the file is an EXE file no matter what the actual file extension is. If COMMAND.COM doesn't find that "signature" at the start of the file, it will assume the file is a COM file.

Other Common File Types

DOS, and COMMAND.COM in particular, "know about" only COM, EXE, and BAT files. But there are many other common file types, and usually the file extension indicates what kind of file it is, which is the reason that *file extension* is also referred to as *file type.*

Files with extensions TXT or ASC, usually are text files containing only printable ASCII characters (plus a pair of characters at the end of each line: a carriage return [ASCII value 13] and a line feed character [ASCII value 10]). File type PRN often signals an ASCII text file that was produced by "printing to a file" from some application program. Other times, those files contain formatting information intended for your printer.

The extension DOC is another file type sometimes used for an ASCII text file, but more often it signals a word processing document. Such a file will have text in it, but it may also contain lots of formatting information.

Spreadsheet data files from Lotus 1-2-3 or Symphony carry extensions WK1, WK3, or WKS. Quattro Pro uses WQ1 and WB1. Excel spreadsheets are given the file type XLS. Excel macros are put in files of type XLM, while WordPerfect macro files are given the extension WPM.

Database files often carry the DB or DBF extensions and have associated DBX, NDX, or MDX index files (Paradox uses DB and DBX; DBASE, FoxPro, Clipper, and other XBASE programs use DBF with NDX or MDX).

Graphics files come with extensions that include BMP, CDR, DRW, EPS, GEM, GIF, PCX, TIF, and WPG. Some very popular programs—WordPerfect, for one—don't have a default type that they give their data files. A WordPerfect document is simply whatever you name it, and if you fail to give it an extension, it simply won't have one.

Sane Naming Conventions

One of the most common complaints about DOS has to do with its restrictions on file names. But with some simple planning, you can come up with naming strategies that make sense (at least to you) and that will help you find any file you want later on. There also are ways you can supplement the DOS name to make finding elusive files easier.

Getting the Most from 8.3 Possibilities

No, you can't name a DOS graphics image file "Camel with two riders" or a data file "1993 3rd Quarter Financials." But you could call the first file CAMEL+2R.GIF and the second one 93Q3FINS.WK3. The latter names are not as easy to read and understand, but they come pretty close, especially if you develop some of your own customs and standard abbreviations.

Namimg conventions can change to match the situation. Spreadsheets that deal with quarterly or annual financial statements, for example, might have one naming pattern (similar to that suggested above). Letters to movie studios should have a very different pattern (perhaps a three-letter studio abbreviation followed by a two-letter director code and a three-number sequence—MGMDL001.DOC, for example). Book reviews could be given a file name composed of two numerals for the year, plus three letters for the month in which they are to appear, followed by sequence number (93MAR01.REV).

Use the Uncommon (but Legal) Symbols

As stated, there are 186 different symbols that you may use in each of the eleven positions in a full DOS file name. This means that there are approximately $9.1\text{x}10^{24}$ choices for such a file name! And that only takes into account the file names that have eight characters for the file name and three for the extension. When you add the file names that are shorter in either part, there are even more possibilities.

Certainly there are enough possible file names. Of course, some of the possible combinations are virtually unintelligible and therefore useless. The filename %&${!###.&%! is perfectly legal, but unless the file is filled with swear words, most people would not consider this a very mnemonic name. Even worse is a name filled with high-bit set characters (those with ASCII values from 128 to 255).

Most people use about 40 different characters in file names: letters of the alphabet (26), numerals (10), the underscore (_), hyphen (-), and dollar sign ($). The parentheses, the tilde (~), and curly braces {} are also used frequently. Whatever you use for your file names, it is a good idea to set and follow some simple rules so that your file names always have meaning for you.

Many programs put information into temporary files with an extension of $$$, which is distinctive enough that it is not likely to conflict with other file names, and you can see those files at a glance if they are left around after the program completes its work. Other programs use the tilde as the first character in the file name and TMP for the extension for their temporary files.

One legal character to use sparingly is ASCII value 255. This character is not a space to DOS, but it shows up on your screen looking exactly like a space. There *are* times it makes sense to use it, however, but those times are rare. One such example is to add it at the end of a name for a subdirectory with personal information—say, C:\PRIVATE. If the command is entered exactly as shown

```
CD C:\PRIVATE or DIR C:\PRIVATE
```

DOS will respond `Invalid directory`. To be granted access, you must type `CD C:\PRIVATE` and then hold down the Alt key while tapping out 255 on the numeric key pad. Release the Alt key and press the Enter key. This is your password to enter your private directory.

> **Note:** ASCII 255 works only on systems that don't use a graphical user interface. With a GUI it is possible to navigate to that directory and access files by simple mouse operations.

File Typing for Clarity

As already defined, the three-letter extension to a file name is also known as the file type, and that extension should indicate what kind of information the file contains. That could mean simply letting your application programs apply their default file extensions. If an application program has a default file extension for its data files, then its File Open dialog box (or equivalent) will usually show only files with that extension. Once you are that dialog box you may have two ways to select a file to open. One way is to type in just the name portion of the total file name and let the application assume the extension is its default one. The other option, available in GUI programs, is that you may be able to "point and shoot" to select the file off of the displayed list.

Sometimes you can override an application's assumptions. For example, you could name a Microsoft Word document `LETTER2.SAL`, and you wouldn't see it listed in the File Open dialog box. But if you change the default specification (which is shown in that dialog box) from `*.DOC` to `*.SAL`, then it will show up, and you can select it. Alternatively, you could simply type in the full file name, including the extension and Word will open it. Other programs, however, do not permit this. Ami Pro documents, for example, must have the extension SAM.

If you are using DOSSHELL, Windows, or a similar user interface, you can set up file associations, which in effect determine such things as "any file ending in .DOC is a document created by Microsoft Word; any file ending .WK1 is a Lotus 1-2-3 spreadsheet file." The shell program then knows that whenever you select a data file, it is to load the corresponding application program and have the application open the selected data file.

Another Way to Use the File Type

Using an application program's default file types is not always the way to go. Suppose you put a mixture of data files all of one type, but with different kinds of contents into one subdirectory. One easy way to differentiate among them is by using distinct file extensions that reflect the files' contents.

For example, you might have several word processing documents all created by Microsoft Word. By default, they would all have the extension DOC; instead, you choose to keep them all in a D:\LA-TIMES subdirectory, since they all were documents you created for the *Los Angeles Times.* Other documents that are letters, invoices, book reviews, and magazine articles could be distinguished by giving each file a distinct extension based on its content (LTR, INV, REV, and ART are obvious extensions for these examples).

Going Against Type

A different strategy is to create subdirectories to differentiate your data files by content, project, or application program that created them. Remember: Use subdirectories within subdirectories. To store the files cited in the previous example, you could have created under the D:\LA-TIMES directory subdirectories called LETTERS, INVOICES, REVIEWS, and ARTICLES (see Figure 8-1). All of the files could then be placed in the appropriate subdirectory and be left with their default file extension of DOC. That would allow you to use DOSSHELL or Windows and its file association method of launching applications and loading data files by simply clicking on the data file name with your mouse.

```
C:\
└──LA-TIMES
    ├──LETTERS
    ├──INVOICES
    ├──REVIEWS
    └──ARTICLES
```

Figure 8-1 Organizing Files with Subdirectories

File Name Extension Strategies

If, even with the rules, mnemonic devices, and subdirectories, you still have trouble keeping track of all your files, at least three strategies are available to you:

- Use a file name extender program.
- Catalog your files.
- Use a text search and/or indexing program.

FILE NAME EXTENDERS

The first approach is typified by a program that used to be included with the Norton Utilities called File Info. This program creates a data file (which it marks as hidden) in each directory where you use it. (Keep the program file in a directory on your DOS PATH; change the directory to the one where you want to use File Info, and then execute the program.) In this data file you may put up to 60 characters of description for each file in that directory by using File Info in its Edit mode. Thereafter, you run File Info instead of DIR and you will see a normal DOS DIR listing, plus the comments you added for each file.

Many applications keep extra information about a file inside the file. For example, Microsoft Word (both Windows and DOS versions) and Ami Pro each include a section in their document files in which you can store a brief description of the file, plus some keywords. These word processors then let you search through the information in that section of all its document files in a given directory as a means of helping you find a file.

GeoWorks doesn't go that far, but it does allow very long file names for data files created by each of its application programs. It does this by putting those long names inside the data files. Then it assigns DOS names to the files that are the same as the first several characters of the internal name, plus some numerals, if they are needed to distinguish among identically named files. A shareware program, GEODIR, can be run from the DOS prompt to display a normal DIR listing, plus the first 40 characters of the GeoWorks name of any files that contain such a name.

CATALOG PROGRAMS

Cataloging files involves running a catalog program to create a central database of information on all your files. The information could be only file names, or it could include comments you add for any that you feel need additional identification. (You also could create several databases, each encompassing special groups of your files.)

One good cataloging program is CATDISK by Rick Hillier. In addition to cataloging all or some select subset of the files on your hard disk, CATDISK can be instructed to search inside of ZIP, LHA, ARC, ZOO, and other compressed collections of files (commonly called archives) and list each of the files it finds in the catalog it is creating. Further, you can add descriptive comments for the files on the disk and for each file within an archive file. Besides helping you find files on your hard disk, this can be a superb tool for keeping track of the files on your backup disks.

TEXT SEARCH AND INDEXING PROGRAMS

Another way to keep track of your files is by using an indexing program or one with good text search capabilities. Perhaps the premiere program of this kind is Magellan, which can index all the text that occurs in all of the files on your disk. Once it has done this, you can use it to find any file by either its name or its actual text content in a matter of seconds. If you don't let it index the files (or if your index is not up to date), Magellan can simply search for the file you want, which it does efficiently, although not as quickly as if it had an up to date index.

The Norton Utilities includes File Find, File Locate, and Text Search. File Find resembles the text search abilities of Magellan, although it is a much smaller program that searches for files by a partial file specification. (Use it when you remember some or most of the file name.) If you remember the beginning characters, you could use `DIR \pattern /S`, of course.) Text Search, as its name implies, looks through the files you specify for a specified word or text fragment. Many similar programs exist, both commercial and shareware.

File Attributes

DOS keeps track of several pieces of information about each file. In the directory entry it stores the file's name, size, date and time of last modification, starting cluster number, and the *attribute byte.* DOS uses 6 of the 8 bits as flags to tell it if a file is part of a class of files. (Some networks use one or both of the remaining 2 bits.)

If the first bit is a 1, the file is protected against alteration, which is called a *read-only attribute.* Any time you try to delete or alter a read-only file DOS will respond with `Access denied`. Although the protection this offers is real, it is hardly absolute. You can change this attribute by using the ATTRIB command in the syntax

```
ATTRIB +|- attribute filename
```

where the plus or minus has one of the following attribute values:

A Archive
H Hidden
R Read-only
S System

You replace *filename* with the specific file (or wildcard file specification) that you wish to protect.

Just as you can change the read-only attribute, so can any program that knows how to ask DOS to make the change on its behalf, which is the reason the protection is limited; a program could come along and change the attribute, then change your supposedly protected file.

The second and third bits in the attribute byte are called the *hidden* and *system* attributes. Hidden files do not appear on the disk directory, and you cannot display, erase, or copy them. Many DOS commands will ignore hidden files. When the system attribute set, it indicates a file that is a part of the operating system. (We say an attribute it *set* when its bit has the value 1. It is *reset* when that bit has value 0.) Usually, a file that has the system attribute set also will have the hidden, and perhaps the read-only attribute, set as well. The system files IO.SYS, MSDOS.SYS, DBLSPACE.BIN, DBLSPACE.INI, and the compressed volume files DBLSPACE.nnn (nnn = 000, 001, 002, etc.) all have their read-only, hidden, and system attribute bits set. The Windows permanent swap file 386SPART.PAR has its system and hidden bits set, but not the read-only. The PCTRACKR.DEL file has only the system bit set. (Any of these files may or may not also have their archive attribute bit set as well. That bit is described later.)

The fourth bit in the attribute byte is called the *volume attribute.* Normally, only one entry in the root directory (and none in any other directory) will have this attribute set. That entry is called the volume label. You can give a volume a label by using the LABEL command, or you can label it when you FORMAT it. The volume label entry in the directory is further distinguished by indicating a file of no length whose starting cluster is 0. Actually, there is no file associated with this directory entry. All of the data in a volume label is contained in the letters of its name.

There are good reasons to put a volume label on every disk you format. Giving a volume a descriptive name can help you figure out what that disk contains, and on hard disks you will give yourself a little protection from accidentally formatting that logical volume or deleting that hard disk partition.

When the FORMAT command sees a volume label on a hard disk volume you ask it to format (beginning with DOS version is 3.2 or greater), it will ask you to type in the volume name. If you cannot do so (or if you realize that this wasn't the disk you meant to format), FORMAT will not do its job, thus, not causing any damage. Similarly, FDISK will ask you to tell it the volume label on a partition before it will let you delete that partition.

The fifth attribute bit is the *directory attribute.* An entry marked with this attribute is a file that is to be interpreted by DOS as a subdirectory.

The sixth attribute bit is the *archive attribute.* Any time DOS opens a file for a program to use and the program asks for *read/write access,* DOS sets the archive attribute for that file. Programs can ask to open a file for read-only access and then DOS will not change this attribute bit. DOS doesn't set this bit based on whether or not the file's contents were changed; it doesn't wait to see if that occurs. DOS merely records all the files that might have changed.

Many backup programs, including MSBACKUP and the DOS command XCOPY, can be told to act selectively, working only on files that have the archive bit set. They may be directed further to leave that bit alone or to reset that bit once they have copied or backed up each file. This provides a facility both for backing up all the files that may have changed and not backing up the ones that could not have changed. (Note that these programs will err on the side of caution, backing up some files that did not change, but could have. The only way to be sure to back up *only* changed files is to inspect all the files with their archive bits turned on and manually reset the archive bit on any you know have not changed.)

The different attribute bits are independent, and you can set or reset any combination you like. The ATTRIB command lets you set or reset only the archive, read-only, hidden, and system bits, but with a disk sector editor you can alter the other bits as well. Some combinations are frequent; we've already mentioned the combinations system+hidden and system+hidden+read-only, both of which occur often. The archive bit may be set or reset totally independent of the settings of the other bits.

Initially, the seventh and eighth bits in the attribute byte are reset to 0s. DOS never inspects them, and it never changes them. No DOS programs tinker with them, althoug some network software does use one or both of them.

Making New Files

Using the COPY Command

The easiest way to create a new file is by using the COPY command. There are two distinct ways to do this. The first one is to COPY an existing file of the correct format, but which may have different contents than you want. You then edit the resulting file's contents.

The second way is to COPY from a device to a file. DOS treats devices such as the printer, keyboard, screen, and modem very much the same way it treats files. Each can be a source or a destination of a stream of bytes. The syntax for the COPY command is

```
COPY source destination
```

where you replace `source` and `destination` with the actual device or file names that you intend to be the source or recipient of the stream of bytes. COPY then transfers all the bytes it gets from the source to the destination.

The most common version of this method is the command

```
COPY CON: NEWFILE.TXT
```

to create a small text file called `NEWFILE`. CON is the DOS name for the console device; the colon is optional. For input that means the keyboard; for output it means the screen. Thus, the command shown says to copy information from the keyboard to a file named NEWFILE.TXT. (If you reverse the order of the command to read `COPY NEWFILE.TXT CON:` you would be asking DOS to display the contents of that file, just as if you had issued the command `TYPE NEWFILE.TXT`.)

Normally, COPY will copy bytes from the source file until it comes to the end of the file. With this command COPY is accepting whatever you type at the keyboard. You must type a special end-of-file character to instruct it to quit taking in bytes and end the copying process. Press the F6 function key, and you will see `^Z` on the screen. Now press the Enter key. At this point COPY decides the file is complete, and you will see the message `1 file(s) copied`.

> ***Note:*** You must press the Enter key after pressing F6 because the console device normally "buffers" inputs a line at a time. That is, it accepts your typed characters, but it will not pass them along to the COPY command until you press Enter. This has an important benefit: You can correct mistakes in what you have typed by using the Backspace key (but only up to the point at which you pressed the Enter key). Once you have pressed Enter, that line is gone from the console device and is already in the hands of the COPY command or already on the disk in the destination file.

There will be times you want to copy files that have a Ctrl-Z character embedded within them, but you don't want the copy process to stop there. If you add `/B` in front of the name of the file that you suspect has a Ctrl-Z character within it, COPY will treat it as a binary file. That means it will continue to copy bytes until it reaches the end according to the size number in the directory entry.

The following command, however, will not be completed:

```
COPY /B CON: NEWFILE.TXT
```

COMMAND.COM recognizes this as nonsense. There is no directory entry to consult to find out how many bytes to copy. So, instead of doing something nonsensical, COMMAND.COM returns the error message `Cannot do binary reads from a device` followed by `0 file(s) copied`.

If you want to create a zero-length file, don't be tempted to use the command `COPY NUL: MYFILE`. It won't work. The NUL device will return an end-of-file character as if it were the very first character it contained, and you might think that would make a zero-length file. However, the COPY command refuses to copy zero-length files, no matter what the source name is. (This fact can be used in sophisticated batch files. See Chapter 14 for some examples.)

Using EDIT

COPY should only be used to create small files because you can correct mistakes only *before* you press the Enter key. Once you have pressed Enter, that line is gone and you can do nothing to repair it.

Therefore, the practical way to create larger text files and to correct errors in them, is to use an editor. DOS no longer includes the line editor called EDLIN, which had no line wrap feature, nor any search and replace capabilities. To most people it is good riddance. (On the other hand, EDLIN can be used with script files, much as DEBUG can, and so certain users have come to depend upon it. IBM believes that EDLIN is still an important component of DOS and so it will be included in PC DOS 6, as well as a full-screen editor called simply E.)

Microsoft added EDIT in MS-DOS 5. EDIT is a full-screen editor, which means that once you have loaded a file, you may roam freely around the screen making changes until you are satisfied; then you save the file. You invoke commands by selecting items off menus (or by using the hot key combinations if you know them).

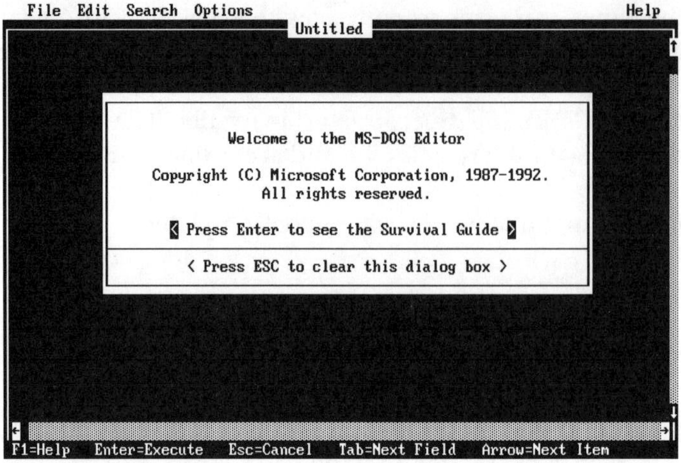

Figure 8-2 The DOS EDIT program (opening screen)

> ***Note:*** EDIT is the editor aspect of QBASIC, so if you want to use EDIT (or the MS-DOS 6 HELP program, for that matter), you must keep QBASIC on your disk, even though you may have no interest in Basic programming. When you invoke EDIT you see the screen shown in Figure 8-2. At this point you either can view their "Survival Guide" or proceed directly to the main edit screen.

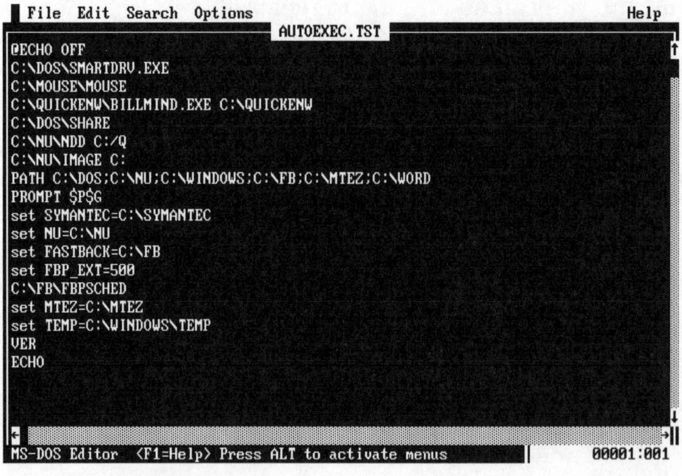

Figure 8-3 EDITing a file

Figure 8-3 shows EDIT being used on an AUTOEXEC.BAT file. This screen is called the main editing screen. You can make changes to the file by moving the cursor to the place where you want to make the change, then typing in the new text. You may use either overtype or insert modes. In overtype mode, what you type replaces the text already there. In insert mode, the new text is inserted in front of the existing text, which is pushed to the right. You also can toggle between modes by pressing the Insert key. You can delete unwanted text in front of the cursor by use of the Backspace key, or erase text to the right of the cursor by pressing the Delete key. (To delete a block of text, hold down the Shift key while you move across the text you want deleted with the cursor arrow keys, or hold down the left mouse button while you drag the mouse from the start to the end of the block, then press Delete.)

To do something other than type in new text, you must access one of the commands on the *drop-down menus*, such as that shown in Figure 8-4. You can select a menu in three ways:

1. Press the Alt key and release it and you will see the word File highlighted. Use the left or right arrow keys to move the highlight to the menu you are interested in, and press Enter. The menu will drop down.
2. Hold down the Alt key while pressing the F, E, S, O, or H key.
3. Use the mouse. Move the mouse cursor over the menu name and click the left mouse button to drop down the menu.

Once you have a menu dropped down, you may select one of its entries. In Figure 8-4 the Save As... entry is highlighted. There also are three ways to select an entry:

1. Use the cursor arrows to move the highlight to the line containing the entry you wish to select, and press Enter.
2. Press the highlighted letter in the name of that entry.
3. Position your mouse cursor on that entry and click the left button.

On the Edit menu you will notice key combinations listed at the right-hand side of the menu. You'll also find one on the Search menu. These are the hot key combinations that you can use from within the main editing screen to directly select the corresponding function. (Hot keys don't work once you have dropped down one of the menus.)

Figure 8-5 shows the Save As... dialog box that opened as a result of the selection in Figure 8-4. This is the dialog box used to tell EDIT the name of the file in which you want to save your work. If you invoke the Edit command with the name of a file on the command line, that file will be loaded, and EDIT will assume you want to save your work in that file unless you tell it otherwise.

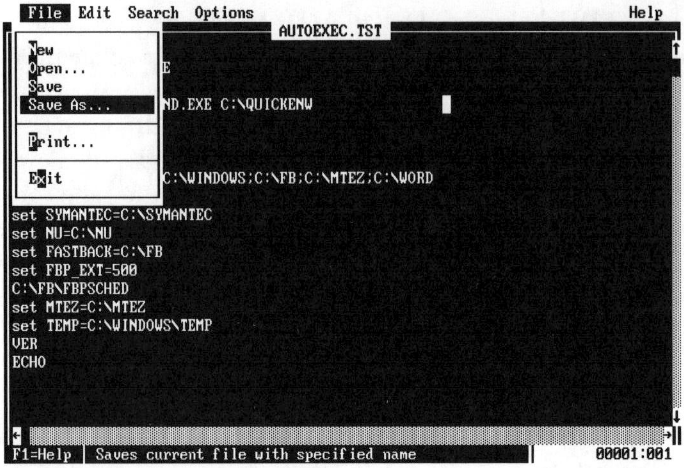

Figure 8-4 The EDIT File menu

Help is available from another drop down menu. If you are unsure how to complete a procedure, first try viewing the Survival Guide. If that doesn't clarify matters, explore the options listed on the Help menu.

Other Ways to Create New Files

It is important to understand the difference between a *text file* and a *document file.* Text editors like EDIT (and EDLIN) create only text files, in which every byte that goes into the file shows up as a character on the screen. In contrast,

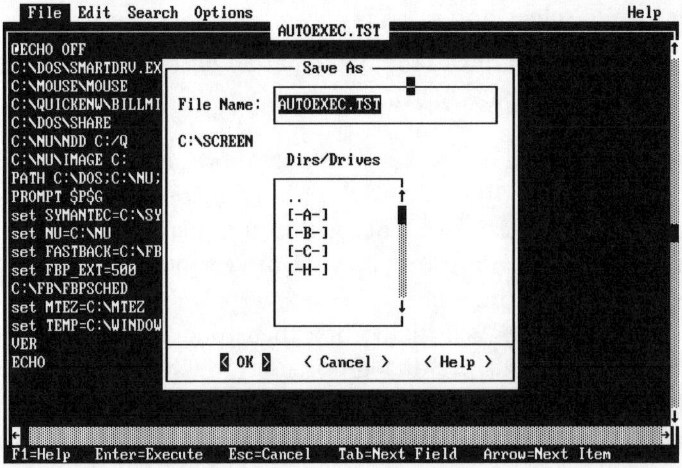

Figure 8-5 The Save As... dialog box

word processors like WordPerfect, Word, WordStar, and Ami Pro normally create document files that have many more bytes than those that appear on the screen. These extra bytes contain formatting information (and, in some cases, a summary section or other data). If you are trying to create a CONFIG.SYS file or a batch file, you must use either a text editor or instruct your word processor to save the file you create as pure text.

Not every new file you create, however, is a text file or a document. Many are data files of other sorts normally created with the appropriate application program (database files are created with a database program, for example; programs usually are created by using an assembler or a compiler).

Fancier File Finagling

There are other ways to create files. One will be discussed in Chapter 13—using a script file and the DOS program DEBUG.

This section explains how COMMAND.COM uses *file redirection* and *piping* to manipulate files.

Redirection

File redirection uses the less than (<) and greater than (>) symbols to tell COMMAND.COM *not* to look to the keyboard for input to a particular program, or to send all the output that the program would normally send to the screen to a file on disk instead.

Be aware that not all output from every program can be redirected. This capability depends on how the program was written to produce its output. If it used the DOS interrupt to send messages to the screen, redirection will work. If it went by a more direct route, bypassing DOS, then redirection will not work. Also, some programs identify two kinds of output: normal output, which you can redirect; and error messages and other critical output, which normally you cannot redirect.

Tip: You may become confused if you redirect output from a command that requires you to type some input while it is working. A simple example is the command `DIR /P`, which normally displays one screenful of file information, then prompts you to `Press any key to continue . . .` If you try to redirect its output as follows:

```
DIR /P >PRN
```

you won't see that prompt on your screen, and the command will not return you to the DOS prompt until it gets the input it is expecting. To avoid this, remember to preview any command whose output you are planning to redirect. Write down the keystrokes you must enter (and perhaps how long you must wait before entering each one). Then rerun the command, this time specifying the output redirection you want. Then input all the keystrokes you know your command requires.

Programs that typically cannot have their output redirected are those that have a full-screen display. These programs usually create and maintain that full-screen image as you work by sending information around DOS to the screen.

> ***Note:*** It is possible to have a full-screen program whose output is redirectable if you have the ANSI.SYS driver, or some equivalent console-enhancing device driver, loaded. The reason most full-screen, commercial software bypasses DOS to write to the screen is to increase speed.

Similarly, not every program can accept input redirection. Only programs that have been written to receive input from the keyboard by using the standard DOS input functions will respond to redirection instructions.

If you decide to redirect input for a particular program, be careful how you create the file from which that program's input will come. Redirection is an all-or-nothing affair. When you redirect input to a program from a file, that file must supply *all* the input that program needs until it has completed its work and exits back to DOS. Once you have started a program with its input redirected, you won't be able to give that program additional instructions.

The syntax for redirection is simple. If you want to have a program called `SOMEPROG.EXE` take input from `INFILE.TXT`, type

```
SOMEPROG < INFILE.TXT
```

and press Enter. If you want to make `SOMEPROG.EXE` send its output to `OUTFILE.LOG`, type

```
SOMEPROG > OUTFILE.LOG
```

and press Enter. You can even combine these two steps in a command that reads

```
SOMEPROG < INFILE.TXT > OUTFILE.LOG
```

which will read input from one file and insert output in the other.

There is another variation on the redirection of output. If you use the single > symbol, you are telling COMMAND.COM to create the output file if it does not exist; and if it does exist, to delete it, then create a new file by that name. If, instead, you use two >> symbols, COMMAND.COM is being told that if the specified output already exists, it should open that file and add the new information to it, starting at the end. This is called *appending* to the file.

If you use output redirection to the same file from several lines of a batch file, or if you use a `FOR...IN...DO` command with output redirection to a file, be sure to use the append operator. Otherwise, you will find that only the last line's output will actually be in your target file because each time COMMAND.COM encounters another command that involves redirection by use of the single > sign, it will throw away the contents of the indicated file before putting the new information into it. (This is not an issue when you output to a device, since there is no way a program can call back information once it has been sent to a device.)

Note: DOS assumes that any program will use at most eight files at once, unless you tell it otherwise by use of a FILES directive in your CONFIG.SYS file. This limit is actually the number of the files, plus the character devices that you are using at one time. Only after a program closes a device or file does that *file handle* become available for that or another program. Of the eight default handles provided to any program, five get taken back by the system immediately to be used for standard input, standard output, standard error output, standard printer device, and standard auxiliary (serial communication) device. The first three of these are supported by the CON default console device driver. Standard input (*stdin*) is the keyboard, unless you use input redirection (using the < symbol), in which case stdin becomes whatever source you have designated. Standard output (*stdout*) is the screen, unless you have specified output redirection (using either the > or >> symbol), in which case stdout becomes whatever destination you have specified. The file handle for standard error (*stderr*) cannot be redirected. The last two devices are PRN for the standard printer device and AUX for the standard auxiliary device. Both stdout and stderr normally show up on the screen; with output redirection only the stderr messages will appear on the screen.

BATCH FILE REDIRECTION

Be aware that you cannot redirect the output of an entire batch file. Actually, you can, but you will receive nothing. Each line in the batch file will produce output as usual; the batch file itself will not. This means that if you try to execute a batch file with its output redirected to a file name, you will find a zero-length file of that name on your disk when the batch file finishes executing. All the output you had hoped to capture in that file will show up on your screen instead. You can, of course, have each line within a batch file redirect its output as desired. If you need to write a batch file with redirectable output, use either command line parameters or environment variables within the relevant lines of the file to allow the output to be redirected to a variety of destinations. Just remember, the file is not globally redirectable.

LOCATION OF TEMPORARY FILES

During redirectin, you can determine where COMMAND.COM puts the temporary files it creates by setting an environment variable TEMP to point to the subdirectory of your choice. If you don't set TEMP, COMMAND.COM will simply create its temporary files in the current DOS directory.

If there is insufficient room on the disk you have specified for the TEMP files, or if it has been made read-only, COMMAND.COM will be unable to create those temp files. In that case, you either will get the message `Disk full` or `Unable to create file`, and the command will not be executed.

Piping

Piping is a combination of input and output redirection. (As will be explained in a moment, it occasionally is useful even with programs for which redirection of input or output is not possible.) The pipe symbol is the broken vertical bar (¦) (it may be a solid vertical bar, depending on your particular keyboard and the screen font or code page you are using).

For example, the command

```
DIR ¦ FIND "<DIR>"
```

will show you a list of only the subdirectories in the current directory. DIR's output is redirected by COMMAND.COM to a special *piping file* that it creates and gives some arbitrary name. After DIR is finished, COMMAND.COM runs the FIND command and redirects it so that it takes as its input the information in that piping file. After FIND is done, COMMAND.COM deletes the piping file. (What the FIND command is doing will be explained in the next section.)

If you ever interrupt a command in the middle of a piped command, you may find some of these piping files on your disk. Also, if you issue the command

```
DIR ¦ MORE
```

and if you either do not have a TEMP directory defined in your DOS environment or you are in the TEMP directory, you will see a couple of oddly named files of zero length in its output. They are the piping files used in connection with this command.

Piping lets you combine several DOS commands on a single command line. The actions you direct DOS to do are completed sequentially; i.e., the first command's output is put into the pipe file until it is completed. Then the pipe file is closed, then reopened so its contents can be sent to the next command.

If you issue a command line with several commands connected by pipe commands, be prepared to wait to see the results, unless you have a very fast PC. Typically, you will not see any output until the final command completes.

You may also invoke commands that are run successively by a command line with piping symbols and not actually generate any data. This means that you could issue several commands on a single line with pipe symbols in it, even though you know that none of the programs mentioned on that command line can have their input or their output redirected. COMMAND.COM will set up the piping files, even though they won't get used, and when the last command is finished, COMMAND.COM will delete the piping files. (Chapter 14 will explain how to use a DOSKEY macro to do something similar.)

There is no limit to the number of commands that may be combined using the piping symbol (other than the 128-character limit imposed by COMMAND.COM for a single command line). If, however, you have an IF command on the line, you may not have more than one pipe symbol on the same line. The workaround to this restriction is to break the command line into more than one line and include all of them in a batch file. The details of how to do this are described in Chapter 14. (For an interesting variation on piping, see the FORK utility on the Power Tools diskettes.)

Using the DOS Filters

DOS includes three special programs whose purpose is to have their inputs come via redirection or piping from a file or other program, and/or to have their output redirected to a file or piped into another program. These programs—FIND, MORE, and SORT—are called *the DOS filters.*

The DOS filters are all line-oriented text filters. These programs receive as input only streams of characters, and these streams are broken into "lines," with each line terminated by a carriage return character followed by a line feed character. These programs act only on whole lines. Each of the DOS filter programs either will pass or block each line it receives. (SORT reorders those lines, but it still acts only on complete lines. FIND and MORE may also output some extra lines, and FIND may add some text at the start of the lines. Otherwise, these three programs just pass or block the flow of the lines they receive as their input.)

FIND

Recall that FIND was used in the command `DIR ¦ FIND "<DIR>"` to display only the subdirectories in the current directory. This is a typical way to use FIND. The full syntax of a FIND command is

```
FIND options "target" filespec
```

where `options` is to be replaced by some combination of the four flags /V, /C, /N, and /I; `target` is a word to search for, and `filespec` is an optional description of a file to search. The options can be placed before, between, or after the target and the filespec, but the target must precede the filespec if you are going to use both.

Of the three items following FIND in the command line, only the target (enclosed in quotation marks) is required. If you give FIND a file specification, it will output the lines of that file that contain a string of characters that match the target. Before it begins to show you those lines, FIND will output a blank line followed by one that contains ten hyphens, a space, the file name, and a colon. After it finishes processing the file, FIND will output another blank line.

If you omit the file specification, FIND will take its input from Stdin, which could be text you type at the keyboard, although more commonly it will be text you have redirected into FIND. That redirection can be done two ways: either by using the < symbol and a file name, or by using a pipe symbol to capture some other program's output and pass it through FIND. When FIND receives input from Stdin, it doesn't output a blank line before and after the lines that it discovers contain the target (and, of course, it doesn't output a file name line, since there is no file name involved).

If you don't add any of the options flags to the FIND command, it will simply pass any line that contains the target character string and block all the rest. If you add the /V switch, FIND will reverse its actions, passing only lines that don't contain the target.

The /I switch lets FIND match the target string more flexibly. Without /I, FIND will accept only exact matches; with /I, it will consider a line a match to the target as long as it contains the correct string of letters, in any combination of upper- or lowercase.

The /N switch causes FIND to add at the front of each line it passes the number of that line in the file enclosed in square brackets. The /C switch tells FIND to block all the lines, but output a single line that tells you how many lines it would have passed if the /C switch had not been there. If you specified a file name on the command line, FIND /C will put the number of matching lines on the same line as the file name.

To illustrate how to use FIND to best advantage, suppose in your Windows subdirectory you have several hundred files, and perhaps a dozen or more directories. Also, suppose you want DIR to show you just the directory names? You can use the command

```
DIR *.
```

(the period at the end of this command is vital in this context), and it almost works. It will show you the directory names, but only those that don't have an extension. This command also will show you any files in that subdirectory that happen to have no extension, even if they aren't subdirectories.

The power user version of this command is

```
DIR | FIND "<"
```

The < symbol is not a legal part of a file name, but will occur in the DIR output for each line that is a directory. This command shows only the subdirectories, and will include those with extensions. However, it includes two extra entries you may not want to see: the two pseudo-subdirectory entries that every subdirectory has, often called "dot" and "dot-dot." To eliminate those two superfluous lines, use the command:

```
DIR | FIND "<" | FIND "." /V
```

This command says to pass only lines from DIR that have the < symbol in them and don't have a period. (Remember, DIR shows a space between a file name and its extension, rather than the period you must type when you enter that file's full name in a command. The only periods that show up in the lines of a DIR output, therefore, will be for the dot and dot-dot subdirectories.)

If you want to know how many files and subdirectories you have and which line numbers in that total hold directory entries, or you want to number the lines of output you generate and ignore the position those lines had in the original DIR listing, refer to Figure 8-6, which shows the commands to use for each of these purposes and the output generated from one PC's Windows for Workgroups directory, plus an excerpt from a normal DIR output for comparison.

Normal DIR output from a Windows for Workgroups directory (Many lines have been omitted to show both the top and bottom of the output.)

```
 Volume in drive I is MC1598-15#7
 Volume Serial Number is 1981-5ABA
 Directory of I:\WFWG

.            <DIR>        09-27-92   2:11a
..           <DIR>        09-27-92   2:11a
ENTPACK1     <DIR>        09-27-92   7:01a
SHAREWAR     <DIR>        09-27-92   6:56a
SYSTEM       <DIR>        09-27-92   2:11a
WIN      COM        53096 01-29-93   7:12a
CARDS    DLL       148528 09-14-92  12:02p
                            .
                            .
                            .
INDEXER  EXE        37271 08-24-92  12:16p
MORE-BMP ZIP       481190 02-15-93  12:05a
      258 file(s)    11932308 bytes
                     23404544 bytes free
```

Using the FIND command to print total number of files

```
I:\WFWG>DIR | FIND "<" /V | FIND "e" /V | FIND " " /C
245
```

Using the FIND command to print the total number of subdirectories (not including . and ..)

```
I:\WFWG>DIR | FIND "<" | FIND "." /V /C
11
```

Using the FIND command to print a numbered list of the subdirectories (not including . and ..) showing line number in DIR listing for each

```
C:\>DIR | FIND "<" /N | FIND "." /V
[8]ENTPACK1      <DIR>        09-27-92   7:01a
[9]SHAREWAR      <DIR>        09-27-92   6:56a
[10]SYSTEM       <DIR>        09-27-92   2:11a
[204]SKYLIGHT    <DIR>        10-08-92   3:23a
[205]WRK         <DIR>        10-05-92  10:53p
[221]FONTSHOW    <DIR>        10-09-92  11:39a
[230]FONTOG35    <DIR>        10-10-92   3:56a
[235]KIDPIX      <DIR>        10-18-92   7:46a
[237]XTREEWIN    <DIR>        10-20-92  10:41a
[239]SAVE        <DIR>        10-24-92   1:48a
[254]PACKRAT     <DIR>        12-04-92   3:13p
```

Using the FIND command to print a numbered list of the subdirectories (not including . and ..) showing line number in DIR listing for each

```
I:\WFWG>DIR | FIND "<" | FIND "." /V | FIND "<" /N
[1]ENTPACK1      <DIR>        09-27-92   7:01a
[2]SHAREWAR      <DIR>        09-27-92   6:56a
[3]SYSTEM        <DIR>        09-27-92   2:11a
[4]SKYLIGHT      <DIR>        10-08-92   3:23a
[5]WRK           <DIR>        10-05-92  10:53p
[6]FONTSHOW      <DIR>        10-09-92  11:39a
[7]FONTOG35      <DIR>        10-10-92   3:56a
[8]KIDPIX        <DIR>        10-18-92   7:46a
[9]XTREEWIN      <DIR>        10-20-92  10:41a
[10]SAVE          <DIR>        10-24-92   1:48a
[11]PACKRAT       <DIR>        12-04-92   3:13p
```

Figure 8-6 FIND commands and their output

In all but the upper-left box of this figure you see the DOS prompt (`I:\WFWG>`), followed by the DOS command that generated the output shown immediately below that prompt and command. This is what you would see on your monitor.

The upper-right command line has four commands connected by piping symbols. The first is the DIR that generates the data processed by the three FIND commands that follow. The first FIND command passes all the lines that do *not* have the < symbol in them. Thus, this will show you all the lines from the DIR output *except* those describing directories. The next FIND eliminates any lines that have a lowercase e in them, which eliminates the five lines above and below the actual list of files. Since no file name contains lowercase letters (we assume), this FIND will not block any of the lines that describe files. The final FIND command accomplishes two steps simultaneously: It blocks all lines that don't have at least one space in them, which eliminates two zero-length lines that the DIR command includes before and after the three lines of indented text at the top of its output. Then it counts the number of lines it would have, but doesn't, output. Instead, when it finishes processing all the input, it outputs just the number of lines it found that passed its test.

The command line and output shown in the middle-right box of Figure 8-6 are similar to that just discussed. The only differences are these: The first

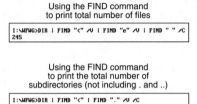

FIND command keeps the lines that the previous command line's first FIND discarded. The other FIND command filters out those that do not have a period, thereby ridding the lines of the dot and dot-dot pseudo-directory entries. That second FIND command also has the /C switch that causes it to output the number of lines instead of the actual lines that passed its test.

The lower-left command line and output show how to get a listing of all the directories, excluding dot and dot-dot, and have FIND add at the front of each line a number indicating its position among all the lines in the original output from DIR.

The final command line, at the lower-right, differs from that at the lower-left in two important ways. First, it has an extra FIND command at the end of the line, which is the location of the /N switch that tells FIND to add line numbers. Numbering after all the filtering is complete guarantees that line numbers will be added only to lines that will appear on the screen.

MORE

While FIND lets only selected lines of the input through to the output, MORE lets all of the input through, but only 23 lines at a time. After the 23rd line it adds the message `-- More --`. Press any key and MORE will output a blank line, and then output the next 23 lines. It continues until the last line of the input has made its way to the output, or until you press Ctrl-Break or Ctrl-C— which you may choose to do from time to time, to view the output more slowly.

A common use of MORE is to display long text files on the screen, one screenful at a time. There are two ways this can be done. One is by the command

```
TYPE filename ¦ MORE
```

and the other is

```
MORE < filename
```

Both do the same thing in different ways.

Previously, this capability of MORE had greater importance. Now, however, many of the DOS commands from DIR to MEM accept a command line switch that forces them to output information only one screenful at a time. Essentially, they have MORE-like capability built in.

Nevertheless, you still may run across a program that dumps its output to the screen all at once, in which case, MORE will come in handy. An even better way to look at the contents of long text files, though, is by using the LIST program, which you will find among the DOS Power Tools, and which is discussed further in the next section.

SORT

The last of the DOS filters is SORT. This is neither the fastest, nor the most capable program for doing sorting, but it works and you don't have to pay extra for it. The syntax for a SORT command is

```
SORT options filespec
```

where the `options` can be either, both, or neither of the switches `/R` and `/+n` (with `n` some number), and `filespec` is an optional file specification. If you omit `filespec`, then SORT will accept its input from stdin. In any case, it sends its output to stdout.

The /R switch tells SORT to reverse its normal order of sorting. The /+n switch allows you to tell SORT to ignore the first (n-1) characters on each line; thus, the n you specify gives the first column at which SORT examines each line to decide order.

SORT has some severe limitations. First, SORT will not handle any file larger than 64KB because it must be able to keep all of the lines of the file in memory while it is shuffling them around. Second, you can use only one *sort key* at a time, which means you cannot simultaneously sort for items that appear in two different columns in the input stream. Also, SORT does not do a stable sort; as a result, you cannot overcome the single-key limitation by doing successive sorts on progressively more significant keys. SORT usually will corrupt the results of its previous work while doing the current sort.

Another limitation is one that deals with performance. Most good sort programs allow you to specify the starting and ending characters. The DOS SORT considers *every* character from the column specified to the end of each line. Although this doesn't change the sort order, it costs in time. (Of course, since it cannot handle very large files anyway, this time penalty is limited.)

Finally, you have no control over the sequence used by SORT. Actually, SORT does respond to country settings, so using a COUNTRY directive in your CONFIG.SYS file may alter the sort order somewhat.) You cannot, however, specify a lexical sort or a strict ASCII order sort.

Lexical Sort: A *lexical sort* puts things in alphabetic order, but it also lists lowercase letters after uppercase instances of the same letter. The freeware program QSORT by Ben Baker is a generalization of SORT, which provides all three kinds of sort, plus offers multiple keys and several other features. QSORT is also blazingly fast, compared to DOS SORT. Table 8-2 illustrates the differences between the three sorts, plus a fifth column that shows the results of the MS-DOS 6 SORT command when the first column was redirected into it. The DOS SORT most closely resembles a case-insensitive sort (which is how Microsoft describes what SORT does), but the results are not quite the same as those shown in the Baker table because there is more than one way to do a case-insensitive sort.

Table 8-2 Variations of SORT

Input	ASCII	Case-Insensitive	Lexical	DOS SORT
DeLaPort	Baker	Baker	Baker	Baker
Smith	Brown	brown	Brown	brown
brown	DeAngelo	bRown	bRown	Brown
deLaPorte	DeLaPort	Brown	brown	bRown
Deangelo	Deangelo	Deangelo	DeAngelo	Deangelo
deAngelo	Deangelo	deangelo	Deangelo	deAngelo
Brown	DelaPort	Deangelo	Deangelo	DeAngelo
smith	DelaPorte	deAngelo	deAngelo	deangelo
delaPorte	Harry	DeAngelo	deangelo	Deangelo
DelaPort	Smith	delaPort	DeLaPort	DeLaPort
DeAngelo	bRown	DelaPort	DelaPort	DelaPort
DelaPorte	brown	delaPort	delaPort	delaPort
deangelo	deAngelo	DeLaPort	delaPort	delaPort
Harry	deLaPorte	DelaPorte	DelaPorte	deLaPorte
delaPort	deLaPorte	deLaPorte	deLaPorte	delaPorte
Baker	deangelo	delaPorte	deLaPorte	DelaPorte
deLaPorte	delaPort	deLaPorte	delaPorte	deLaPorte
Deangelo	delaPort	Harry	Harry	Harry
bRown	delaPorte	smith	Smith	Smith
delaPort	smith	Smith	smith	smith

Snooping Inside Files

Sometimes the only way to learn what you need to know about a file is to look at its contents. DOS provides two tools for looking inside files: TYPE and DEBUG. (You also can use EDIT, although this command is intended primarily for editing text.

TYPE

TYPE is an internal command (and is, therefore, an aspect of what COMMAND.COM does) that is useful for displaying on-screen the contents of small text files. Because its output goes to stdout, you can send it to a file by using output redirection in the form `TYPE > filename`.

There are some severe limits to what TYPE can do. It is not useful for looking at the contents of anything but a pure ASCII text file. If you try `TYPE C:\COMMAND.COM`, for example, you'll get some lines of "garbage" on your screen, hear a beep from your speaker, and be returned to the DOS prompt. TYPE stops processing input as soon at it receives a Ctrl-Z character (ASCII value 27), which is a relic of DOS's ancestry in CP/M, where the Ctrl-Z character was used as the end-of-file mark. (DOS needs no end-of-file mark, since the exact length of every file is stored in the directory entry describing that file.)

Another limitation of TYPE is that it just dumps all of the input file to the screen, nonstop. Any lines that are more than 80 characters long will be displayed 80 characters per line on successive lines on your screen. To see what is in any file beyond a screenful, you must combine TYPE with MORE. Even then, you will see the characters once, as MORE doesn't provide any way of backtracking in the file; it merely interrupts the flow every 23 lines.

One of the DOS Power Tools already mentioned briefly—LIST—is a superb extension to the TYPE command. LIST is described more later, and in depth in Chapter 18.

DEBUG

DEBUG is a marvelous, multifaceted tool. It has so many features that we have devoted a whole chapter to explaining them (Chapter 13). One of its many capabilities is displaying the contents of files. In order to do this in a way that will work for any file and be maximally useful, DEBUG uses a special display style, shown in Figure 8-7, which also shows what results when you use TYPE on COMMAND.COM for comparison with the DEBUG display.

There are three columns in the debug style display. The first column gives the address for the first byte displayed on that line. You may ignore the hexadecimal number before the colon, as it merely reflects where in memory DEBUG was able to load the copy of COMMAND.COM that it is displaying. The four-symbol hexadecimal number after the colon shows a relative address within the file; the first address is 100h.

The second, and widest, column in this figure shows the contents of 16 bytes in hexadecimal notation (two hex symbols per byte). The third column shows the printable ASCII characters corresponding to those bytes, with

```
C:\>debug command.com
-d 100
4AD8:0100  E9 5D 15 60 78 15 00 00-B7 0F 00 00 75 0E 00 00  .].`x.......u...
4AD8:0110  85 12 00 00 00 00 00 00-00 00 00 00 00 00 00 00  ................
4AD8:0120  00 00 00 00 00 00 00 00-00 00 00 00 00 00 00 00  ................
4AD8:0130  00 00 00 00 00 E8 64 00-1E 0E 2E FF 2E 04 01 FB  ......d.........
4AD8:0140  E8 59 00 1E 0E 2E FF 2E-08 01 FB E8 4E 00 1E 0E  .Y.........N...
4AD8:0150  2E FF 2E 0C 01 FB E8 43-00 1E 0E 2E FF 2E 10 01  .......C........
4AD8:0160  E8 39 00 1E 0E 2E FF 2E-14 01 E8 2F 00 1E 0E 2E  .9........./....
4AD8:0170  FF 2E 18 01 E8 25 00 1E-0E 2E FF 2E 1C 01 E8 1B  .....%..........
-
```

Figure 8-7 DEBUG displays the first sector of COMMAND.COM.

periods as placeholders for the bytes that do not have printable ASCII representations.

The first occurrence of the spurious end-of-file (Ctrl-Z) character is at relative address 1AB, which means it is the 172nd character in the file (subtract 100h from 1ABh, add 1, and convert to decimal). Often, programmers will put a jump instruction near the start of their programs and follow that with a short message (giving their copyright or some other information about the program). After that message they will put a Ctrl-Z character and then the rest of their program. Use TYPE on this sort of program and you will see just the brief message and quickly return to the DOS prompt.

The DEBUG display of a file's contents lets you see each and every byte, but it is hardly the nicest way to display all files. Further, there is one limitation to DEBUG. It is only able to hold in memory a file that is no larger than 64KB, which is not as severe a limitation as it might appear to be. While SORT simply cannot handle a file that is larger than 64KB, DEBUG's limitation only means that it cannot load more than the first 64KB of a file and let you look at that portion. Since you also can use DEBUG to explore the disk (a point covered more fully in the next chapter), you can use DEBUG to see any part of any file, no matter how large. The only issue is one of convenience.

Warning: Know the power of DEBUG. It can destroy your system almost completely if you use it carelessly. Read Chapter 15 to familiarize yourself with the DEBUG command to avoid before you start your explorations.

```
LIST      1              01-07-93 17:09 ♦ c:\screen\AUTOEXEC.AFT
@ECHO OFF
LH /L:0;2,42384 /S C:\DOS\SMARTDRV.EXE
LH /L:2,14912 C:\MOUSE\MOUSE
C:\QUICKENW\BILLMIND.EXE C:\QUICKENW
LH /L:2,13984 C:\DOS\SHARE
C:\NU\NDD C:/Q
C:\NU\IMAGE C:
PATH C:\DOS;C:\NU;C:\WINDOWS;C:\FB;C:\MTEZ;C:\WORD
PROMPT $P$G
set SYMANTEC=C:\SYMANTEC
set NU=C:\NU
set FASTBACK=C:\FB
set FBP_EXT=500
LH /L:2,65536 C:\FB\FBPSCHED
set MTEZ=C:\MTEZ
set TEMP=C:\WINDOWS\TEMP
VER
ECHO

Command▶   *** Top-of-file ***        Keys: ↑↓→← PgUp PgDn F10=exit F1=Help
```

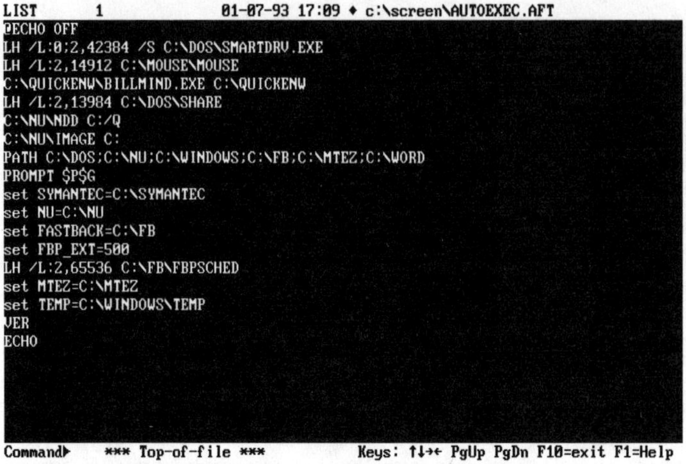

Figure 8-8 Using LIST to view an ASCII file

LIST

The DOS Power Tools program LIST is a vast improvement on the DOS TYPE command. It can display a 23-line, 80-column window on a text file or show a file's contents in DEBUG fashion. Its viewing window can be moved up, down, or sideways. LIST also can be used to search within a file for a character string and to transfer portions of one file to another file. Finally, LIST can display the contents of large files, and you can tell LIST to display a group of files and bounce back and forth among the members of that list. Among its other virtues, you can be assured that LIST will never modify a file you are viewing (unlike using EDIT for this purpose).

Figure 8-8 shows how LIST presents a text file, in this case, an AUTO-EXEC.BAT file. Figure 8-9 shows that same file displayed by LIST using its DEBUG format. You can switch between the two displays at any time.

DOS Commands Relating to Files

Handling disks and files is at the heart of what DOS does, so naturally many of the DOS commands affect files. A brief synopsis of those commands are given here, but for the full details on them, consult the Command Reference.

The special files called subdirectories are manipulated by the DOS commands MD (MKDIR), CD (CHDIR), RD (RMDIR), and DELTREE. Volume labels can be set with FORMAT or LABEL and examined with DIR, CHKDSK, and VOL. Most file attributes can be displayed or altered with ATTRIB.

```
LIST     1              01-07-93 17:09 ♦ c:\screen\AUTOEXEC.AFT
000000   40 45 43 48 4F 20 4F 46-46 0D 0A 4C 48 20 2F 4C   @ECHO OFF┘[]LH /L
000010   3A 30 3B 32 2C 34 32 33-38 34 20 2F 53 20 43 3A   :0;2,42384 /S C:
000020   5C 44 4F 53 5C 53 4D 41-52 54 44 52 56 2E 45 58   \DOS\SMARTDRV.EX
000030   45 0D 0A 4C 48 20 2F 4C-3A 32 2C 31 34 39 31 32   E┘[]LH /L:2,14912
000040   20 43 3A 5C 4D 4F 55 53-45 5C 4D 4F 55 53 45 0D    C:\MOUSE\MOUSE┘
000050   0A 43 3A 5C 51 55 49 43-4B 45 4E 57 5C 42 49 4C   []C:\QUICKENW\BIL
000060   4C 4D 49 4E 44 2E 45 58-45 20 43 3A 5C 51 55 49   LMIND.EXE C:\QUI
000070   43 4B 45 4E 57 0D 0A 4C-48 20 2F 4C 3A 32 2C 31   CKENW┘[]LH /L:2,1
000080   33 39 38 34 20 43 3A 5C-44 4F 53 5C 53 48 41 52   3984 C:\DOS\SHAR
000090   45 0D 0A 43 3A 5C 4E 55-5C 4E 44 44 20 43 3A 2F   E┘[]C:\NU\NDD C:/
0000A0   51 0D 0A 43 3A 5C 4E 55-5C 49 4D 41 47 45 20 43   Q┘[]C:\NU\IMAGE C
0000B0   3A 0D 0A 50 41 54 48 20-3A 43 5C 44 4F 53 3B 43   :┘[]PATH C:\DOS;C
0000C0   3A 5C 4E 55 3B 43 3A 5C-57 49 4E 44 4F 57 53 3B   :\NU;C:\WINDOWS;
0000D0   43 3A 5C 46 42 3B 43 3A-5C 4D 54 45 5A 3B 43 3A   C:\FB;C:\MTEZ;C:
0000E0   5C 57 4F 52 44 0D 0A 50-52 4F 4D 50 54 20 24 50   \WORD┘[]PROMPT $P
0000F0   24 47 0D 0A 73 65 74 20-53 59 4D 41 4E 54 45 43   $G┘[]set SYMANTEC
000100   3D 43 3A 5C 53 59 4D 41-4E 54 45 43 0D 0A 73 65   =C:\SYMANTEC┘[]se
000110   74 20 4E 55 3D 43 3A 5C-4E 55 0D 0A 73 65 74 20   t NU=C:\NU┘[]set
000120   46 41 53 54 42 41 43 4B-3D 43 3A 5C 46 42 0D 0A   FASTBACK=C:\FB┘[]
000130   73 65 74 20 46 42 50 5F-45 58 54 3D 35 30 30 0D   set FBP_EXT=500┘
000140   0A 4C 48 20 2F 4C 3A 32-2C 36 35 35 33 36 20 43   []LH /L:2,65536 C
000150   3A 5C 46 42 5C 46 42 50-53 43 48 45 44 0D 0A 73   :\FB\FBPSCHED┘[]s
000160   65 74 20 4D 54 45 5A 3D-43 3A 5C 4D 54 45 5A 0D   et MTEZ=C:\MTEZ┘
Command▶    *** Top-of-file ***        Keys: ↑↓→← PgUp PgDn F10=exit F1=Help
```

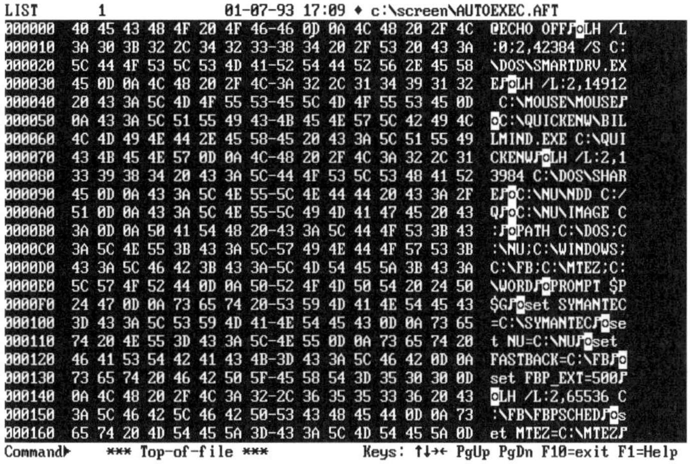

Figure 8-9 LIST also gives a hexadecimal view.

COPY, XCOPY, and DISCOPY do three different kinds of file copying. FC and DISKCOPY make it possible to check the accuracy of copies. EDIT allows you to alter a text file, and TYPE displays its contents. DEBUG can be used to display any file's contents, among other things.

FIND, MORE, and SORT are the three DOS filters. Used with input and output redirection and piping, they can modify how programs (DOS commands and some others) display their output. With the new features in the DOS commands DIR, MEM, and others, these filters are needed much less than they once were.

The REN (RENAME) command allows you to change the name of a file. The MOVE command can be used to rename subdirectories (as well as to move files from one location to another).

The DOS Power Tools Programs Relating to Disks and Files

CPYDSK, OPTICOPY, OPTIMOVE, and QUADRIVE offer a powerful ensemble of diskette-based copying facilities. NAME lets you rename directories. ! (pronounced "bang") offers a slew of file management capabilities, including searching and sorting (with options and formatting capabilities unavailable under normal DOS) duplicate and unique file name detection, and the ability to search across multiple local and network disks. FSN helps you locate lost files by name or content. FD lets you find, view, tag, and delete duplicate files. MKD combines the MD and CD functions of DOS, while PATHINC lets you adjust your path specification up or down, on the fly. NEW, in its two alternate versions, allows you to find files created or modified since a given date. MRFILTER and REFORMAT offer file stripping and formatting capabilities, while SNR lets you search and replace strings within files. SEPARATE performs the simple but sometimes-needed task of letting you create environment variables with either the file name or its extension. STF lets you compare ASCII files side by side, while VORCOMP lets you compare directories, or directory trees on a similar basis. And, of course, the PTOOL program used to launch the other Power Tools, can be used as a general purpose file browser and launcher. If you create ASCII files with an extension of .INF, you can provide your own on-line help files for programs you want to use with PTOOL.

C H A P T E R

9

◆ ◆ ◆ ◆ ◆

Working with Disks

If you have ever wanted your PC's disk drives to run faster or needed more room on those disks, or erased a file by mistake and wanted it back, then this chapter is for you. It explains why the disks in your PC slow down as you use them and how to speed them up again. It also explains what really happens when files are erased and several ways you may be able to retrieve them. Finally, it will show you more than one way to make a crowded disk roomy again—*without* removing any of the programs or data files it contains.

Keeping Disks Neat and Quick

When you keep all your paper records in order—a place for everything and everything in its place—you can retrieve any item you need quickly and easily. The same is true for DOS and the files it maintains on disk.

When an office is new and you have very few records, keeping track of them is easy. Later on, when business is booming, your file cabinets are overflowing, and you have stacks of papers waiting to be filed, it becomes more difficult to find things. Likewise, when a disk is new, DOS has no trouble placing files. It integrates them on the disk neatly, one right after another. Later on, after you have deleted and added files, or added information to others, your disk files become as disorganized as paper files.

Disorganized Disks Are Slow Disks

DOS maintains a table of numbers that describes all the places on a disk where your files may be stored. This file allocation table (FAT) has one number in it for each cluster on the disk. Clusters range in size from 512 bytes to many kilobytes; 2KB (2048 bytes) is the most common size on hard disks. DOS stores files smaller than a cluster as an entire cluster to that file; longer files are given multiple clusters.

The directory entry describing a file includes a pointer to the cluster that holds the start of that file. It also contains a number that identifies the size of that file in bytes. If the size is larger than the cluster size, DOS must consult the FAT to find where the rest of the file is stored.

When files are first written to a newly formatted disk, DOS puts them on the disk in consecutive clusters. The first file might use 16 clusters, and would be numbered 2 through 17. Suppose the next file needs only 9 clusters; it would be assigned clusters 18 through 26. A larger file might need clusters 27 through 75, and so on. This file arrangement is shown in Figure 9-1.

Over time, this neat arrangement is disrupted. Suppose, for instance, that the third file (C) was a database, and you need to add some information to it. You open it up in your database program and add several records. Then you close the file and exit the database program. On the disk the database file still occupies clusters 27 through 75, but it now also occupies clusters 165 through 170. This is now one file in *two* regions of the disk. This is called fragmentation (although this file has only two fragments).

Next, suppose you erase the sixth file (F) and the eighth file (H). That frees clusters 78 through 102, and 161 through 164, which leaves the disk in the condition shown in Figure 9-1(b). Then you write three files (I, J, and K) to the disk. If you rebooted your PC between the time you erased F and H and the time you wrote the new files, DOS will put the new files into the holes left by the erased files, which would mean—assuming the first of these new files (I) takes up 17 clusters—that clusters 78 through 94 would be assigned to it. The next file (J) takes up only 5 clusters—95 to 99. The third new file requires 14 clusters.

Now things get a little interesting. After I and J are written into the hole left by F, there will be only 3 clusters left in that hole. The next hole, created by erasing H, has only 4 clusters in it. The question is, where will DOS put K? To keep K in one location, DOS would have to put it beginning at cluster 171. Unfortunately, that's not how DOS works. DOS will put the first 3 clusters of K into the rest of the first hole (at clusters 100 through 102); the next 4

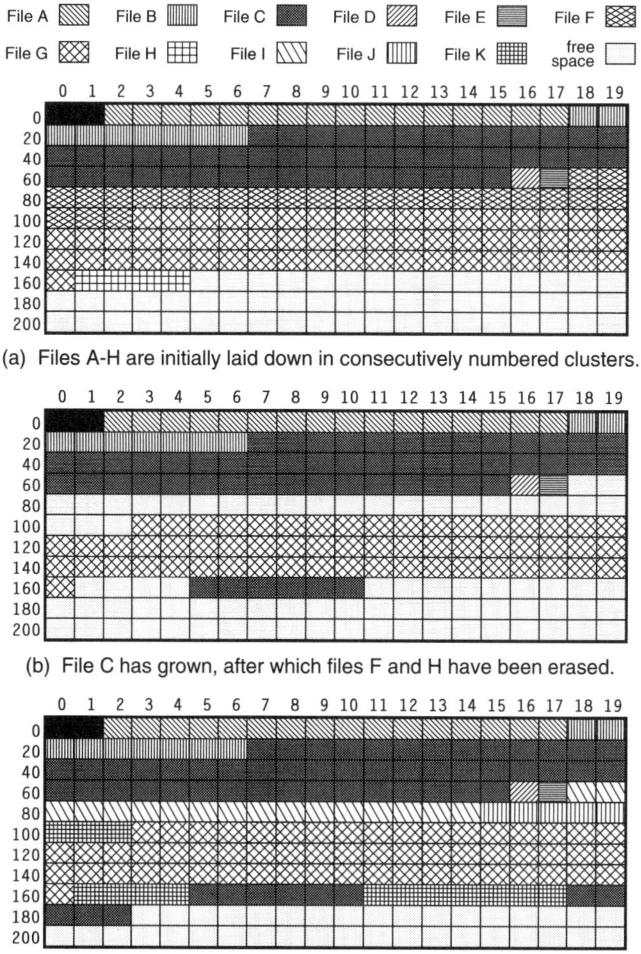

(a) Files A-H are initially laid down in consecutively numbered clusters.

(b) File C has grown, after which files F and H have been erased.

(c) New files I-K are written, then C grows some more.

Figure 9-1 How files become fragmented

clusters of K go into the hole left by H (clusters 161 to 164); and the remaining 7 clusters of K go into clusters 171 through 177.

At this point, if you go back to your database and add more records, the database file gets extended another 5 clusters, and these will have to be assigned 178 through 182. Figure 9-1(c) shows how your disk looks after these steps.

No doubt by now you can see what happens. But why should this be a problem for DOS? After all, it can consult the directory to find the start of the file and follow the chain of allocated sectors in the FAT to find the rest of the chain (see Figure 7-3). This is true, and DOS will do exactly that. But to read

K, for example, DOS must go to three separate regions on the disk and the model in Figure 9-1 has only 220 clusters. A real hard disk may have tens (or even hundreds) of thousands of clusters. To be sure, DOS can find the pieces; but each time the heads on the disk drive must be sent to a new region of the disk, lengthier times (by microprocessor standards) are involved. To the user, a PC with a badly fragmented disk will feel as if it is running noticeably slower. In fact, slowdowns of up to 75 percent are not uncommon, and all because of file fragmentation.

In order to make a PC with a badly fragmented disk run like new it is necessary to defragment all the files on the disk, a process that rearranges all the sections of files until each one is stored in one contiguous string of clusters. Ideally, all those contiguous strings of clusters would also be located as close to the front of the disk as possible. Then any new files would be placed further down the disk, past the now defragmented files, which would ensure that the new files also remain unfragmented.

One straightforward (and often used) way to accomplish this is to back up all your files. Then, erase the fragmented files from your disk and restore the files from the backup disk. Because every file is being written to an initially empty disk, they will be placed on the disk in a single, contiguous region, and no spaces will be left between the files. That is exactly what you wanted to accomplish. While this works, it is neither simple nor fast. It also is not particularly safe. Any time you have to rely on your backups you are taking the risk that the backup diskettes will run problem free. If any files cannot be restored, they are lost.

DEFRAG to the Rescue

The efficient and trustworthy way to defragment the files on your disk is to run a file defragmenting program that first examines your disk to see how many of the files are fragmented, and how many empty spaces there are. Then it moves the files, or sections of them, from one spot to another on the disk until it has rearranged all the pieces in the desired sequence.

DOS 6 now includes such a program. Called DEFRAG, this program provides the services formerly available only if you purchased commercial programs. Figure 9-2 shows ten stages of DEFRAG as it works on a floppy diskette. Screen (a) shows what you see when you start DEFRAG. After you choose a drive to analyze, DEFRAG reports how fragmented its files are and recommends an optimization strategy. At this point you could defragment your disk, but options are available by choosing Configure. When you do, you see the Optimize menu, shown in screen (c). From here you can choose Optimization Method..., which brings you to the screen shown in (d). In screen (e)

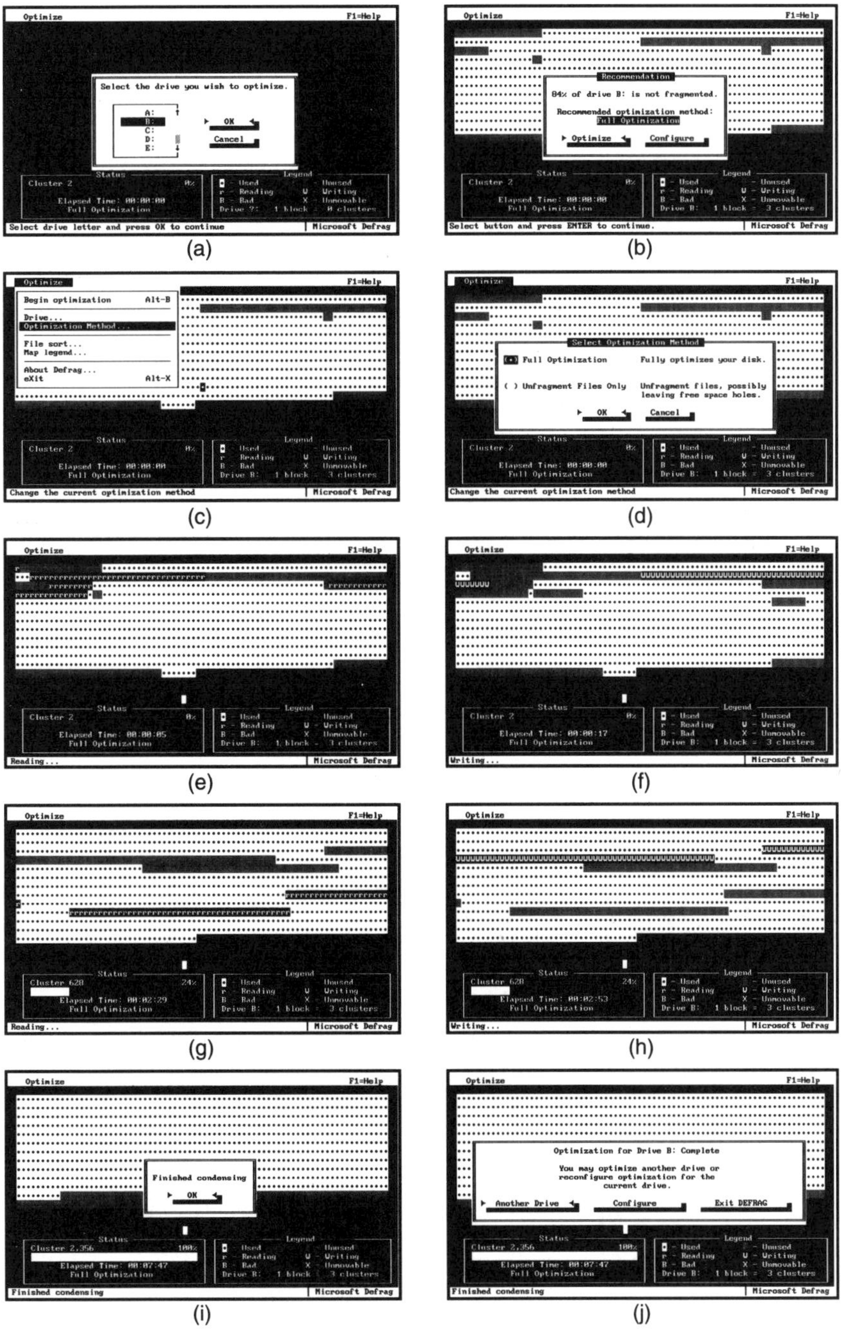

Figure 9-2 The DOS 6 file defragmenter at work

DEFRAG is reading many clusters, preparing to move the data they contain. Screen (f) shows DEFRAG writing the data just read. Screens (g) and (h) show another read-write cycle. Finally, after many of those read-write cycles, DEFRAG will complete its work. Screen (i) shows you DEFRAG's message announcing that fact. Screen (j) allows you to tell DEFRAG what you want to do next.

DEFRAG has two optimization strategies. One makes all the files contiguous, but may leave the free space in several segments among the files. The other strategy fragments all the files and puts them all as close to the front of the disk as possible, thus leaving all the free space together near the back. (By the front of the disk we mean the outermost cylinders, which are the ones with the lowest cluster numbers.) The first method is faster, but it will lead to repeat file fragmentation sooner than if you use the second method.

It is difficult to recommend how often to use DEFRAG; it really depends on how often you use your PC. But at least once a month, let DEFRAG check each of your hard disk volumes. If it reports any with more than about 10 percent fragmentation, let it defragment that volume, and consider running it more often—perhaps once a week.

Unraveling Disk Disasters

When was the last time you erased a file, then realized you shouldn't have? If it was more recent than you care to admit, this section will make that kind of mistake less painful. It explains how to build a safety net for your data.

Gone, but Not Forgotten

When you delete a file, whether you use the DOS commands DEL, ERASE, or the equivalent command in Windows or some DOS shell program, the same underlying calls are made to DOS. Two things change on the disk when you erase a file. One is that the first character in the file name in the directory entry is replaced with a lowercase Greek letter sigma (σ) (ASCII value 229, or E5h). The other change is made in the FAT where the number stored for each cluster is changed to a 0.

The first change tells the DIR command not to display that directory entry (and the File Open function in DOS to ignore that file); it also marks the directory entry as available for reuse. The second change marks the spaces on the disk where that file's data are stored as spaces which now are available for storage of new data.

Although it may not be obvious from the description above, when you delete a file, all of the data for that file actually *remains on the disk* and thus, *may be* retrieved. That's the good news; the bad news is that DOS has lost the ability to find the file because although the directory entry survives minus only the first character, that character includes the pointer to the first cluster of data. The FAT information that linked together all the clusters after the first one has been lost.

Resurrecting Lost Files

If the file was only one cluster long, or if it was unfragmented, then it can be recovered completely and with absolute certainty—*as long as you do the recovery immediately* following your erase action. All you have to do is restore the first character of the file name and replace the numbers in the FAT. You will have no trouble knowing how many of those numbers to replace or what values to use since the directory entry tells you which is the starting cluster and exactly how many bytes there are in this file. The steps in this process are:

1. Replace the first character of the file name in the directory entry.
2. Go to the indicated starting cluster entry in FAT. If it is a 0 (which it will be if you do this right after the file is erased), replace it with the correct value, which is FFFFh if the file's length is less than 1 cluster; otherwise, it is the number of the next cluster. (Use FFFh for 12-bit FAT tables.) If the file is only 1 cluster long, the retrieval process is complete.
3. If the file is more than 1 cluster long, compute how many clusters long it is. Then change that number of entries in the FAT so that each one points to the next one, and the last one is FFFFh (or FFFh for a 12-bit FAT). Now the file is restored.

You can automate the task of file recovery, at least in easy cases like this, by using the DOS program UNDELETE in its simplest mode of operation. In this default mode, UNDELETE uses only the E5h in the first character of a file name to find deleted files, and it follows exactly the strategy outlined above for recovering a file. The command to use is

```
UNDELETE [path][filename]
```

where the `path` and `filename` are optional. If you specify them, UNDELETE will tell you whether or not it can undelete the file you specified. If you leave out the path, UNDELETE will assume you mean the current DOS directory and look for the specified file. If you leave out the file name, UNDELETE will tell you about all the files it finds in the specified path (or in the current directory if you also leave out the path).

If you ask UNDELETE to show you a list of files that can be undeleted (do this by leaving out the file name), it will report any directory entries in which the first character is an E5h and the starting cluster number points to an entry

Warning: Once the FAT entries for a deleted file have been set to 0 and the first character of the file has been changed E5h, DOS sees those spaces as available. Therefore, the next time something gets written to the disk, the directory entry and/or the actual file data could be permanently lost, which is the reason it is so important to attempt to reverse an erase action immediately. Beginning with version 3.0, DOS did incorporate a degree of protection against erased files being immediately overwritten. DOS keeps a number in memory that points to the last place in the FAT where it found an available cluster. Thereafter, when it goes to the FAT for another available cluster, it starts looking at the entry following the last one it used. This strategy means that usually, within a given work session, DOS will not back up and overwrite erased files that had been written near the front of the disk. Don't count on this, however, as DOS may come back and reuse the earlier clusters if it fails to find available ones further on. Also remember that this meager protection is removed once you reboot your computer.

in the FAT whose content is a 0. UNDELETE will tell you it cannot undelete the files associated with any directory entries with a leading E5h character but whose starting cluster number points to a cluster currently in use by some other file.

Unfortunately, these facts mean that `UNDELETE` may propose to recover some files that it cannot. `UNDELETE` is certain to succeed only when the file(s) to be recovered are wholly contained within their starting clusters; or they were unfragmented, and then only if the file(s) have not been overwritten.

Note: If you delete a *single* fragmented file, you often can recover it successfully with `UNDELETE`. In such a case, UNDELETE recovers the right number of clusters, which may not be contiguous, but they comprise the next available clusters in the FAT, starting with the cluster specified as the starting cluster in the directory entry.

Once UNDELETE has told you how many files may be recoverable (and how many are not), it will ask you if you wish to undelete the next one on its list of recoverable files. If you wish to undelete a file, you must tell UNDELETE what first character to use for its file name. DOS will continue prompting you about which files you want recovered on the list; only after you have responded to each one will UNDELETE do its job.

DIFFICULT UNDELETES

When you have erased a fragmented file, or worse, several fragmented files, it is possible that the pieces of those files are all still on the disk; however, those pieces may have intermingled. If they have, you still can recover them, but the simple file recovery strategy just described is not sufficient.

Again, this process is possible manually. It involves inspecting each cluster you propose adding to a recovered file to be sure it really belongs there. This process, of course, assumes you are able to recognize the appropriate and inappropriate clusters when you see them—something that is not always easy to do.

Fortunately, there are better ways. The Norton Utilities, for one, can help you do this sort of file-recovery work. But an even better approach for protecting your files is to use the DOS protection features, *Delete Tracker* and *Delete Sentry*.

DELETE TRACKER

Obviously, the information DOS keeps about files is not sufficient to recover erased fragmented files with any certainty, even though all of the data for those files may still be safely stored on the disk. Several methods of file recovery have been tried, none to resounding success.

What was needed was a way to record—at the instant a file was deleted—exactly what its directory entry said and which clusters contained its data. And this is precisely the scheme Microsoft calls *Delete Tracker*, referred to more generically as *deletion tracking*. In DOS 5, this was done by the MIRROR program. In version 6, this responsibility has shifted to the UNDELETE program. To invoke this protection, issue the command

```
UNDELETE /Td[-entries]
```

where `d` is the drive you wish to protect and the optional `-entries` specifies the maximum number of deleted files to keep track of for that drive. If you don't specify a number of entries, UNDELETE uses a default number that depends on the size of the disk it is tracking, with a range from 25 for a 360KB floppy to 303 for a 32MB disk. (There must not be any space between the drive letter and the hyphen or between the hyphen and the number of entries you wish to specify.)

You may set up deletion tracking for as many volumes as you like, and give a different number of files to track for each one. Simply add multiple `/Td[-entries]` switches on the UNDELETE command line, one per volume for which you choose to use deletion tracking.

UNDELETE creates an UNDELETE.INI file in the same directory as its program file (usually C:\DOS). This file contains all the current specifications for how it is to do its job. Thereafter, you can simply issue the command

```
UNDELETE /LOAD
```

and it will set up whatever protections you had in effect the last time it ran.

If you have UNDELETE loaded in memory and you wish to remove it, you can do so with the command

```
UNDELETE /UNLOAD
```

This is also necessary if you wish to alter how UNDELETE is working (for example, to change from Delete Tracker to Delete Sentry operation). If you attempt to run UNDELETE with some new options, and it discovers its resident portion is already in memory, it will simply inform you of that fact and refuse to do anything.

If you are unsure if UNDELETE is resident, or which version of deletion protection it is currently implementing, you can find out by running the command

```
UNDELETE /STATUS
```

which causes UNDELETE to report not only whether it is providing Delete Tracking or Delete Sentry protection, but also which drives (logical volumes) it is protecting.

> **Note:** Deletion tracking does exact a cost. You must have the UNDELETE program resident in memory, and you must commit enough disk space to hold the PCTRACKR.DEL file. The Delete Tracker TSR portion of UNDELETE uses 9,632 bytes of RAM. The PCTRACKR.DEL file uses 182 bytes per entry.

If you have deletion tracking enabled, each time you delete a file, UNDELETE will notice this fact and make an entry in a file called PCTRACKR.DEL. This file has its system attribute turned on and is located in the root directory of the volume containing the erased file.

> **Note:** Actually, the first time that you delete a file after you invoke deletion tracking, UNDELETE will automatically set up the PCTRACKR.DEL file at the maximum size it needs to store all the entries it can contain, which is either the default number or

the number of entries you specify. All of its entries will describe the file you just deleted—over and over again. As you delete additional files, the new information will replace some of those entries. If you delete one more than the maximum number of entries in PCTRACKR.DEL, then the information about the first file you deleted will be lost.

Warning: Deletion tracking records the directory and FAT information on all files that you delete at the DOS prompt. Sometimes, however, it *will not record* that information for files that you delete through a DOS shell or application program. UNDELETE notices those deletions, but instead of recording information about them in PCTRACKR.DEL, it may sound a bell, in effect telling you that you aren't supposed to delete files that way.

When you want to recover an erased file, and deletion tracking is active, issue the command

```
UNDELETE [path][filename] /DT
```

If you specify a file to undelete, UNDELETE will report the following

- whether or not it finds the specified file in its tracker record
- whether or not it regards that file as recoverable using only the DOS approach
- whether or not it finds that file in its Delete Sentry control file

The /DT switch specifies that UNDELETE is to use the information in the PCTRACKR.DEL file to do its job.

An alternative way to find out which files may be recoverable is to issue the command

```
UNDELETE /LIST
```

which will simply tell you the numbers UNDELETE finds using its DOS, Tracker, and Sentry strategies. It also will list all the files that it could recover to the current directory using the Sentry strategy. If you add a `/DOS` or `/DT` switch after `/LIST`, UNDELETE will report the same set of numbers; but in these cases, it will list the files it thinks are recoverable in the current directory by the DOS or Tracker strategies, respectively. (In effect, not putting `/DOS` or `/DT` after `/LIST` is the same as putting `/DS` after `/LIST`.)

When UNDELETE Is Impossible Deletion tracking is totally unable to prevent DOS from overwriting erased files with new ones. Thus, with deletion tracking you can recover even badly fragmented erased files, but only if you do so before they are written over—which they will be sooner or later if you continue using the disk in a normal manner.

On occasion, you may ask UNDELETE to recover a file you erased while deletion tracking was in force and UNDELETE will report that *some,* but not all, of the file appears to be recoverable. This means that some of the clusters that formerly held that file's date are marked as available in the FAT, but others are not. In this case, UNDELETE gives you the option of recovering that portion of the file.

If you let UNDELETE recover a partial file, it will assemble the contents of all the clusters it determines belong to that file. While this may return some of your file to you, it also might give you something totally unrelated.

> ***Warning:*** Actually, when UNDELETE recovers a file using the Tracker method, there is always a chance that it will return nonsense. To see how this is possible, consider the following scenario: First, defragment your disk using DEFRAG's `Full optimize` strategy. Now all the files are packed together with no free spaces in between. Turn on Delete Tracker file protection. Next, delete a moderately large file, say one with 10 clusters of data, somewhere in the middle. This creates a 10-cluster region of free space in your mass of files.
>
> Now reboot your PC and create a new file of any size. If you stop and examine the disk, you probably will find that the new file has been put in the hole left by your earlier deletion of the 10-cluster file. If the new file is larger than 10 clusters, it will fill the hole and occupy some additional clusters beyond the end of your compacted files.
>
> Erase the new file. At this point you are again where you were before the new file was created, at least in terms of which clusters are marked as available in the FAT. Of course, the data in those clusters is not at all the same for any clusters that were overwritten by the new file.
>
> Now ask UNDELETE to recover the original 10-cluster file using deletion tracking. UNDELETE will do so, and report that you have recovered your file fully and perfectly. Obviously, this is not the case.

Because deletion tracking can't prevent your erased files from being overwritten, it is hardly perfect protection. DOS, fortunately, goes one better with Delete Sentry.

DELETE SENTRY

In the Delete Sentry scheme, which was first introduced to the PC world in Central Point's PC Tools and later was used in the Norton Desktop for Windows and the Norton Desktop for DOS, a special hidden directory is created to preserve files you think have been deleted. Each time you tell DOS to delete a file, the deletion sentry program instructs DOS to move the file to the special directory, giving it some arbitrary name as it does. The deletion sentry program also records in a control file in that directory the original file specification (path, file name, and extension) and the new name for this "deleted" file.

To the user, it does seem that the file is deleted. The directory listing will confirm that it is gone, but actually, the file is extant, in the special deletion sentry directory. Later, if you want to recover a deleted file, the file recovery program will simply undo the "erasure" process by returning the file to the directory it came from and restoring its name. This is a very quick process, and it will work every time.

This protection, too, comes at a price. First, is the memory required for the TSR deletion sentry program, and second is the amount of disk space necessary to store the "deleted" files, the deletion sentry subdirectory, and the control file. Although the memory requirement is not significantly different than that exacted by deletion tracking—13,616 versus 9,632 bytes—the disk space needed may be considerable. To control space usage, most deletion sentry schemes have some built-in limits. After your "deleted" files are more than a certain number of days old they automatically will be truly deleted. Also, as soon as your deleted files occupy more than some set fraction of your disk volume's total capacity, the deletion sentry program will delete some of those files each time you delete a new file that must be made temporarily retrievable.

To set up Delete Sentry protection using the MS-DOS 6 UNDELETE program, invoke a command line like

```
UNDELETE /Sd
```

where *d* specifies a drive to be given Delete Sentry protection. As with deletion tracking, you can set up sentry protection for as many drives as you like simply by including multiple `/Sd` switches on the command line. Alternatively, you can edit the UNDELETE.INI file to show sentry protection for those drives.

Once you have Delete Sentry active, you can recover a deleted file by using the command

```
UNDELETE [path][filename] /DS
```

where, of course, /DS specifies using the Delete Sentry copy of the specified file. Omitting the file specification will cause UNDELETE to display all the files you have deleted from the current directory that it is still holds in its Delete Sentry directory. If you see the file(s) you want, you can tell UNDELETE to proceed with the undelete procedure.

Tip: If you issue the command

```
UNDELETE [path][filename]
```

with no / parameter after it, you will get exactly the same effect as if you included a /DS switch.

Creating UNDELETE.INI The simplest way to create the UNDELETE.INI file is to invoke UNDELETE in any way that causes it to become resident in memory. Do this once, and it will create an UNDELETE.INI file. You may alter the file with EDIT or any other ASCII text editor. Like most Microsoft INI files, UNDELETE.INI has sections indicated by names enclosed in brackets (the left bracket is the first position on a line). The UNDELETE.INI file has five sections—`[configuration]`, `[sentry.drives]`, `[mirror.drives]`, `[sentry.files]`, and `[defaults]`—that allow you to specify how that aspect of UNDELETE will work.

The `[configuration]` section records how long a "deleted" file may linger in a Delete Sentry directory before it is really erased (the default is seven days), what maximum percentage of the disk volume's capacity those "deleted" files may occupy (the default is 20 percent), and whether or not UNDELETE is to save in the Delete Sentry directory a file that has its archive bit set (the default is no). This last option allows you to specify that you don't want to protect any file that is so new that you have not yet backed it up, which prevents you from cluttering your Delete Sentry directory with temporary files.

The `[sentry.drives]` section simply lists the drives currently receiving Delete Sentry protection. Each line has a drive letter followed by an equal sign.

The `[mirror.drives]` section also has a line per disk volume, indicating the volumes to be protected with Delete Sentry. Each of these lines has a drive letter, an equal sign, and the number of entries you specified that it should track for that volume.

The `[sentry.files]` section lists file specifications that Delete Sentry is to ignore. This is a second way you can protect yourself against saving temporary files. By default, UNDELETE puts in this section the line

```
sentry.files=*.* -*.TMP -*.VM? -*.WOA -*.SWP -*.SPL -*.RMG
                 -*.IMG - *.THM -*.DOV
```

to specify which files to protect (`*.*`) and which ones not to protect (those listed with preceding minus signs). You may add to or delete from this section, as you wish.

The final section, `[defaults]`, simply specifies whether Delete Sentry or Delete Tracker is currently active. You cannot have both active at once. Thus, if you have specified several drives for one kind of protection and several others for the other kind, you will be able to protect only one group or the other.

Tip: You may specify *all* your drives in each group. That way you will achieve the full effect of both Delete Tracker and Delete Sentry protection.

> **Note:** As you have probably deduced by now, the only real drawback to Delete Sentry protection is that you don't gain any disk space when you delete a file. Therefore, if you usually erase files to free up space on your disk, this protection scheme is not going to serve you very well.

You can force UNDELETE to really erase all the files in its Delete Sentry directory by using the command

```
UNDELETE /PURGE
```

but you cannot easily tell it to erase only some of them.

Tip: Microsoft doesn't talk about purging the contents of the PCTRACKR.DEL file. It could be a very useful thing to be able to do. For example, if you delete a vast number of files in some directory that you know you will never want to see again, and if you forgot and had Delete Tracker active at the time, your PCTRACKR.DEL file will be largely filled with those entries. If you later wish to recover a deleted file in the same directory but don't remember its name, you will be presented with this huge list of candidate files for possible recovery. You'll have to read the whole list and answer the "Do you want to undelete this file?" question for each one, which could take a long time.

The only way to purge the PCTRACKR.DEL file is to delete the file in its entirety. (You can enlarge the PCTRACKR.DEL file simply by telling UNDELETE to use more entries with the `/Td-entries` switch, but you cannot reduce its size in the same way.) However, you cannot delete PCTRACKR.DEL if Delete Tracker is active at the time. The Delete Tracker won't let you delete the file in which it wants to record your deletion activity. Curiously, it will not give you any error message if you try—it just will prevent DOS from deleting that file. You must set the system bit off before you can delete it. The solution is simple: Unload UNDELETE first, then use ATTRIB-S to turn off the system bit on PCTRACKR.DEL. Now erase it. If you want to use a different size tracking file, this is an excellent time to edit your UNDELETE.INI file. Finally, reload UNDELETE.

The last command line option for UNDELETE that requires description is `/ALL`. This option tells UNDELETE to recover all the files in the current directory that it can. It does this first by looking for files held in the Delete Sentry directory. Next, it looks for those specified in the Delete Tracker file (PCTRACKR.DEL). Finally, it attempts to undelete any files for which it finds a directory entry beginning with an E5h and for which the starting cluster is marked as available (a 0 in the corresponding place in the FAT). In this last case, UNDELETE must supply the missing first character in the file name, which it does arbitrarily.

Warning: UNDELETE is a complex program with a plethora of options. Its screen display is hardly a shining example of clarity. It is recommended that you read this section carefully and do some experimenting on your own until you feel comfortable with UNDELETE. Even then, you should stop and read each and every line of output from UNDELETE and think twice before you answer any of its questions.

Optimizing Disk Space

Running out of disk space—it's the one problem that every PC power user must confront sooner or later. The strategies described in this section should help you resolve most disk space crises.

File Compression

Most files stored on your PC's disk have redundancy in them, information that is not essential—the spaces between words is the best example of this. File compression is the process that removes inessential and redundant information in a file that is not in use, thereby freeing up valuable space required elsewhere. Obviously, some files can be compressed more than others, depending on their contents. Typically, approximately half of the bytes on your disk can be compressed without loss of information. DOS 6 now provides a file compression program similar to those formerly available only from third-party products.

DOUBLESPACE

In most ways, the new Microsoft DoubleSpace on-the-fly file compression program is just like third-party disk compression products such as Stacker or SuperStor. Like them, it is an optional device driver that augments how DOS deals with disks. Similarly, it uses compressed volume files (CVFs) in which to store the compressed versions of files, and it makes each of those CVFs look like a virtual disk drive. Schematically, all on-the-fly disk compression programs work as depicted in Figure 9-3.

DoubleSpace, however, also differs from those products. The fundamental difference between DoubleSpace and Stacker or SuperStor is in how the operating system loads the file compression engine. Stacker and SuperStor are typical installable device drivers; they are loaded by a DEVICE line in the CONFIG.SYS file. The DoubleSpace compression engine, DBLSPACE.BIN, gets loaded by IO.SYS before it begins reading the CONFIG.SYS file.

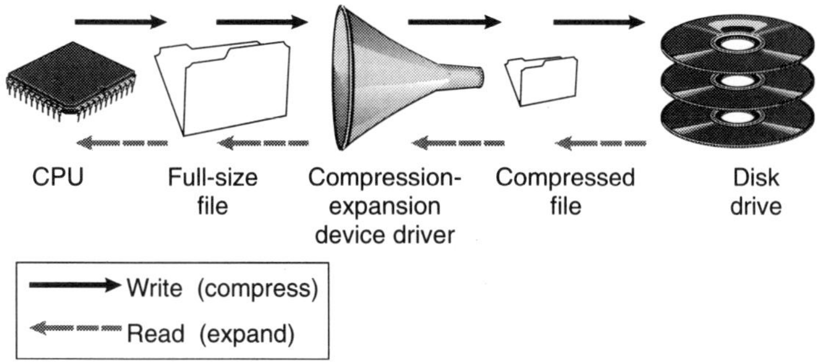

Figure 9-3 On-the-fly file compression can make a disk appear to hold more than it does.

While this may sound like a subtle difference, it's not. It creates one very obvious and important change, both in how the disks on your PC appear to you, and in how the boot process proceeds. When DBLSPACE.BIN is loaded, it looks for a file called DBLSPACE.INI. Normally, both DBLSPACE.BIN and DBLSPACE.INI are located in the root directory of the first hard drive (the C drive without DoubleSpace). Both of these files have the hidden system and read-only attributes turned on (the same as the two hidden system files, IO.SYS and MSDOS.SYS). There also will be one or more CVFs on this drive, and they too have hidden system and read-only attributes turned on. The first of these compressed volume files has the name DBLSPACE.000. The rest will have names like DBLSPACE.001, DBLSPACE.002, and so on.

Note: It is important to consider what happens if you boot your PC from a DOS 6 floppy. If you formatted that floppy diskette on a PC that had DoubleSpace installed, the floppy disk may have either two or three hidden system files: It will have IO.SYS and MSDOS.SYS, and it may have DBLSPACE.BIN. When you boot from such a floppy, all of these files are loaded into RAM, just as they would when you boot from the hard disk. You will get all three files only if you use the DOS 6 SYS command to transfer the system to the floppy disk. If you use `FORMAT /S`, you will only get the traditional two hidden system files. (This is contrary to Microsoft's documentation, but it is consistent with our observations on the DOS 6 copies we tested.)

If you formatted the floppy on some other PC that has never had DoubleSpace installed, the floppy won't have DBLSPACE.BIN on it because that PC's hard drive doesn't have it either. If the PC you are now booting has some DoubleSpace CVFs on it, the question is, will you be unable to access the files you have put inside those CVFs? The answer is that Microsoft designed IO.SYS so it looks for DBLSPACE.BIN both on the boot drive and, if the boot drive was a floppy disk, on the first hard drive (the C drive) as well. If it finds DBLSPACE.BIN and DBLSPACE.INI on the hard drive, even if there is no copy of either file on the floppy, IO.SYS from MS-DOS 6 will load DBLSPACE.BIN from the C drive and follow the directions in the DBLSPACE.INI file on C, just as it would have if you booted from that hard drive. (Any system with CVFs will have DBLSPACE.BIN and DBLSPACE.INI on it also.

DBLSPACE.000 is a very special file name to DBLSPACE.BIN. It is the file that contains in compressed form all the files that originally were on your C drive. When DBLSPACE.BIN mounts this CVF it will give the virtual drive it creates the drive letter C. The host volume will be given some other drive letter. The DBLSPACE.INI file dictates what DBLSPACE.BIN will do. If the INI file has an `ActivateDrive` entry for DBLSPACE.000, it will indicate which drive letter to give the host volume. Any other `ActivateDrive` entries in the INI file that refer to CVFs on the same host volume will tell which other drive letters to give to the virtual drives created out of those additional CVFs with extensions 001, 002, etc.

Take note that the 000 CVF is given the host volume's original drive letter. All the others are given some new drive letter. The host volume assumes a new identity as spelled out in the `ActivateDrive` line that mounts the 000 file. The other lines in the INI file affect only the virtual drive letters. (There is an exception to that statement when you have multiple host volumes. The INI file syntax is described in more detail shortly.)

Figure 9-4 shows the results of this process in a typical case. The original C drive is filled almost entirely with six hidden system, read-only files. Three are the system files, IO.SYS, MSDOS.SYS, and the new DBLSPACE.BIN; the fourth file is the INI file for DoubleSpace. The last two files, and by far the largest on the disk, are two CVFs: DBLSPACE.000 and DBLSPACE.001. (Figure 9-4 exaggerates the size of the system files and the INI file relative to the CVFs in order to make them decipherable.)

The upper part of this figure shows what you would see if you were able to examine the hard disk before the system booted DOS 6. The lower part of the figure shows what happens as soon as DBLSPACE.BIN loads. It reads its INI file and acknowledges that the 000 CVF on the C drive is to become C, and the host volume is to become G (notice the first `ActivateDrive` line ending in C0). Any 000 volume on any hard disk volume always assumes the original drive letter of the host volume and the host assumes a new drive letter indicated in the corresponding `ActivateDrive` line in the INI file. The other `ActivateDrive` line tells DBLSPACE.BIN to mount the 001 CVF (referred to as C1 in the INI file) and make it the D drive. If there were another physical disk volume, it would have begun as the D drive. If it also carried some CVFs, they would show up in yet more `ActivateDrive` lines, this time ending with D and a number. The number following the host drive volume indicates to which CVF that `ActivateDrive` line refers. The letter preceding the host's original name has one of two meanings. For 000 files, it is the new drive letter that the host will assume; for all other CVFs, it is the letter for the virtual drive to be made from that CVF.

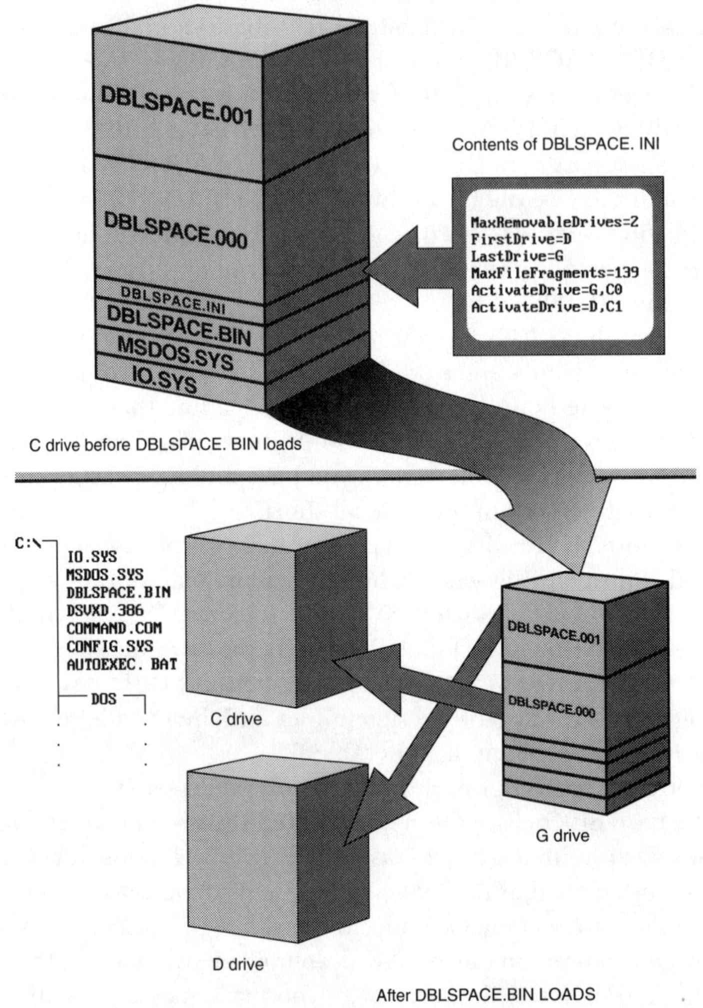

Figure 9-4 DBLSPACE.BIN converts one drive with several hidden files into three drives with greater total capacity than the original drive.

THE DOUBLESPACE ADVANTAGE

Loading DBLSPACE.BIN before processing CONFIG.SYS solved—in a single stroke—the most vexing problems faced by Stacker and SuperStor users. You no longer need to worry which files must be on the original C drive and which must be on the new virtual C drive created from the CVF. Every file, except the four hidden system files used in booting (IO.SYS, MSDOS.SYS, DBLSPACE.BIN, and DBLSPACE.INI) will be inside the DBLSPACE.000

```
Volume Serial Number is 1997-7866

  62181376 bytes total disk space
  59566080 bytes in 7 hidden files
     51200 bytes in 1 user files
   2564096 bytes available on disk

      2048 bytes in each allocation unit
     30362 total allocation units on disk
      1252 available allocation units on disk

    655360 total bytes memory
    554528 bytes free

H:\ >attrib
     SHR      H:\IO.SYS
     SHR      H:\MSDOS.SYS
  A  SHR      H:\IMAGE.IDX
  A           H:\DBLSPACE.OUT
     SHR      H:\DBLSPACE.BIN
     SHR      H:\DBLSPACE.INI
     SHR      H:\DBLSPACE.DBG
     SHR      H:\DBLSPACE.000

H:\ >
```

Figure 9-5 CHKDSK and ATTRIB listings for a host volume with one CVF

CVF on the boot drive, and thus these files will appear to the user on the virtual C drive.

Figure 9-5 shows what you would see if you boot such a system and then run CHKDSK and ATTRIB on the host volume. (In this case the host volume was given the drive letter H.) If you used DIR with no command line switches, you would see almost nothing since all but one file in this volume has its hidden system and read-only attributes set. The one file you see here without those attributes normally would not be created at all.

Figure 9-6 shows those same two programs when used on the (virtual) C drive. Unlike DIR, ATTRIB with no command line parameters shows all the files in this directory, but none of the subdirectories, which are where you find the CONFIG.SYS and AUTOEXEC.BAT file. The subdirectories also are where all of the device drivers and TSR programs mentioned in CONFIG.SYS, DEVICE, or INSTALL lines will be found. None of them is on the host volume.

DOUBLESPACE VS. STACKER OR SUPERSTOR

In contrast, the two most popular third-party disk compression programs, Stacker and SuperStor, handle things a bit differently. Ordinarily, these programs create virtual drives and then cause DOS to assign to those drives the letters originally assigned to your physical drives. The physical drives usually end up receiving new drive letters; sometimes the original physical drives are made to disappear entirely. Although this is one of the most clever things about these programs, it also is one of the most confusing and has led to most of the difficulties people have had using these products.

```
C:\>CHKDSK
Volume Serial Number is 17D1-4539

 111042560 bytes total disk space
     90112 bytes in 3 hidden files
    466944 bytes in 57 directories
  66207744 bytes in 1864 user files
  44277760 bytes available on disk

      8192 bytes in each allocation unit
     14370 total allocation units on disk
      6220 available allocation units on disk

    655360 total bytes memory
    554528 bytes free
C:\>ATTRIB
     SHR     C:\IO.SYS
     SHR     C:\MSDOS.SYS
       R     C:\COMMAND.COM
             C:\HIMEM.SYS
  A          C:\DSVXD.386
  A    R     C:\IMAGE.DAT
  A          C:\CONFIG.SYS
  A          C:\AUTOEXEC.BAT
C:\ >
```

Figure 9-6 CHKDSK and ATTRIB listings for logical volume created from CVF in Figure 9-5

Suppose, for example, that you have two physical hard disk volumes—your C and D drives. (It doesn't matter if they are two volumes on one physical hard drive or two separate hard drives.) Now install Stacker or SuperStor. You can tell the file compression program to create a virtual drive (a large hidden file) on your D drive. If you want, it will become your E drive. You could create another virtual drive (another large hidden file), also on D, which could become your F drive. You can make as many additional drives as you like. As you create these virtual drives, you can have Stacker or SuperStor move files from the uncompressed disk space into the virtual disk volume. This is all very convenient, but there is one way it also may cause trouble for you. For example, you may have built various batch files to identify which programs are on what disk drives. They will be "broken" by the drive letter changes when your files move from D to E or F or G. Similarly, many application programs get installed, and in the process, they "learn" where their key files have been placed. These applications will fail to work once the drive letters are swapped.

To circumvent this, both Stacker and SuperStor normally do some pretty fancy footwork. When you have them move files from a real disk volume into a virtual one, the virtual disk appears to have the drive letter that the host volume used to have, and the host volume assumes a new identity. Then, as far as your batch files are concerned, the files didn't move—the disks did. (Or, since a batch file can't identify what kind of disk it is dealing with, it notes instead that the disk suddenly seems to have gotten larger.) This works very well most of the time. When the host volume is your C drive, however, it doesn't because you boot from your C drive.

Since the Stacker device driver (STACKER.COM) or the SuperStor driver (SSTORDRV.SYS) is loaded into memory through a DEVICE line in your CONFIG.SYS file, it obviously cannot open up the CVFs and create virtual drives or do any drive letter swapping until after it is loaded. By that time, the hidden system files (MSDOS.SYS and IO.SYS, or IBMBIO.COM and IBMDOS.COM) have both been loaded from the disk into memory, and they are reading and processing the CONFIG.SYS file. Therefore, those files (the two hidden system files), CONFIG.SYS and STACKER.COM or SSTORDRV.SYS, must all be placed on the host volume—the volume that is your real, physical C drive. In addition, there must be on the uncompressed host volume any other device drivers that are loaded before the file compression program. Typically, this will include HIMEM.SYS and EMM386.EXE (or a third-party equivalent such as QEMM or 386MAX). It may also include other drivers, depending on how you set up your CONFIG.SYS file.

SuperStor normally swaps drive letters shortly after loading its block device driver. Stacker may do this for some drives, but will wait and do the rest of the needed swapping through the use of SSWAP statements in the AUTOEXEC.BAT file. Thus, by the time the SHELL statement in your CONFIG.SYS file is processed and the command interpreter loaded, the boot drive may have been swapped to a new drive letter with the original C designation assigned to one of the virtual drives. If that happens, the CONFIG.SYS file must also be inside the compressed virtual drive file, along with the command interpreter (COMMAND.COM, usually), and your AUTOEXEC.BAT file.

If the boot drive letter doesn't change until after the start of AUTOEXEC.BAT file processing, you may get away without a copy of CONFIG.SYS inside the virtual drive, but you must have a copy of your AUTOEXEC.BAT file in the uncompressed host volume. Either way, you must have at least some of the files duplicated both places. They must be exact duplicates. Stacker will notice when you reboot if there is any difference between the two copies of both CONFIG.SYS and AUTOEXEC.BAT and ask you to let it make them equal. Stacker advises you to let it do so every time.

In order for application programs that don't know about compressed volumes and drive letter swapping to do their usual installation or SETUP procedures, you really must have both CONFIG.SYS and AUTOEXEC.BAT in the logical C drive (thus, inside the compressed volume). And anytime either of them gets changed, be sure the other copy in the host volume is changed to match.

Initially, before you installed the file compression program, your hard disk was bootable; therefore, you normally will have all of these critical files on the host volume (the real, physical C drive). In addition, you must have exact copies of them inside the CVF so they will be present on the new C drive after the drive letter swapping has taken place. In particular, maintaining the CONFIG.SYS file and COMMAND.COM in those two locations is critical to making these file compression products work smoothly.

In general, the problems users encounter with the Stacker or SuperStor fall into four categories:

1. You have to keep much of the same directory tree on both the host and compressed volumes. Creating a new directory on the host every time a new directory is created on the compressed volume is a nuisance and often will be forgotten, as will the copying of key files in this new directory to both the compressed and host volumes. (The duplication of files and directories also wastes space—exactly the wrong thing to do with a product whose purpose is to achieve maximum usefulness from the disk space.)

2. You have to keep the CONFIG.SYS file or the AUTOEXEC.BAT file, or perhaps both of them, in both places, and the two copies of each file must always be the same.

3. If an installation program attempts to modify the CONFIG.SYS file to add a new device driver, the process will fail unless it happens to load the new driver after the line that loads the file compressor, because the installation program will be run when the file compressor is already loaded. As a result, it will identify the CONFIG.SYS file on the virtual drive as C, will modify that file, and may ask for a driver to be loaded from that file at a time when that file won't yet be visible. Even copying the modified CONFIG.SYS file to the host volume will not solve this problem. The device driver mentioned in the new line must also be copied to the corresponding directory on the host volume. Most application installation programs are not able to do this for you, and many people find doing these things confusing and difficult.

4. If you accidentally trash your CONFIG.SYS file, or even merely alter it so that it no longer correctly points to the file compression device driver, then that driver will not load, and poof!—your entire virtual drive setup disappears. All you are left with is whatever you have in the host volume, plus the compressed volume files. Since those CVFs are hidden, it will appear that you have lost all the files on your C drive.

The new DoubleSpace strategy solves all four problems at once. There are no subdirectories on the host volume, nor any device drivers. You have only one CONFIG.SYS file, so there is nothing to get mismatched. Application installation programs work exactly as they always have. And finally, since

DBLSPACE.BIN is loaded by IO.SYS automatically, even deleting your CONFIG.SYS file will not prevent you from accessing all the files inside your CVFs.

If you look in the CONFIG.SYS file of a DoubleSpaced disk, you may wonder about some of these claims. You will notice a line that reads

```
DEVICE=C:\DOS\DBLSPACE.SYS /MOVE
```

No doubt you're recalling that DoubleSpace didn't load from a DEVICE line in the CONFIG.SYS file. So, what is going on here? The answer is that this line is not loading the compression engine. It line merely controls where in memory that compression engine will finally end up. The details of this process are discussed later in this chapter in the section "DoubleSpace and Memory Use Considerations."

A related and surprising fringe benefit to using DoubleSpace is that a compressed drive appears to be faster as well as larger. You might have thought that doing a file compression or decompression on-the-fly would add time to the process; after all, there is more computing being done. That is true, and on a slow PC you will notice this. But on a PC with a fast CPU (anything using at least a 16MHz 386SX chip), the time it takes to do this extra computation is dwarfed by the time saved in not shuttling as many bytes out to the physical disk drive and back again.

DOUBLESPACE PITFALLS

Removing DoubleSpace Once you have installed DoubleSpace, you cannot easily return to a previous version of DOS because the earlier version would not be able to make sense of the CVFs, and currently, there is no graceful means of extracting all the files from within a CVF.

If you do decide to remove DoubleSpace from your system, first you must realize that you won't be able to store as many files on your system once you do—that was, after all, its purpose, to make it possible to store a greater number of files. If you decide to remove DoubleSpace soon after you install it—that is, before you added a lot of new files—then it should not be a problem. Everything in your CVF will probably fit on the physical hard disk volume once you eliminate the big CVF files.

The DoubleSpace installation process moves files inside the CVF and enlarges the CVF incrementally. Unfortunately, there is no easy way to reduce it as you remove files. Therefore, the most practical approach is to back up all your files from within the CVF, deleting it and rebooting, then restoring all your files from the backup copies.

Once you delete the CVF files, DBLSPACE.BIN, and DBLSPACE.INI from the host volume(s) and reboot, you will find that DBLSPACE is gone. You

> **Warning:** Backups and backup processes have been known to fail. Before you trust all your files to your backup, test that backup to be very, very sure you can restore all of your files perfectly. You may have to make more than one backup set on disks or tapes. But remember, if the problem is in the process, all of them may be equally flawed.

now have your original drive configuration back, with all the old, familiar volume letter designations. Finally, you must restore the software configuration from the backups.

Modifying the DBLSPACE.INI File Perhaps the easiest way to corrupt your system, once DoubleSpace is installed, is to modify the DBLSPACE.INI file without being fully aware of what you are doing. Every other Microsoft product with INI files allows, and even encourages its users to edit those INI files. Furthermore, the DBLSPACE.INI file, like all those other editable INI files, is a plain ASCII text file that looks like it ought to be easy to edit.But remember, the DBLSPACE.INI file is a hidden system, read-only file, which makes it more difficult to modify.

The entire contents of a DBLSPACE.INI file is shown in Figure 9-7. Although it's not very complicated, its syntax is not documented and tiny, inappropriate changes in this file can totally defeat DoubleSpace.

> **Warning:** The next several sections detail what is known about the DBLSPACE.INI file, its syntax, and its functions.If you decide to alter or experiment with this file, be very sure to have total and perfect backups of all your hard disk volumes before you start!

DBLSPACE.INI SYNTAX

Normally, you will not need to edit the DBLSPACE.INI file. Whenever DoubleSpace perceives a need to change an entry in the INI file, it will do so without informing you. You can influence what those changes are, to a degree, through some of the options presented when you run the DBLSPACE.EXE program in its full-screen, interactive mode. This is a safe way to change the INI file, as DBLSPACE.EXE will make sure that all its changes conform to the required syntax.

There are some changes, however, that DBLSPACE.INI is not built to let you make. It is these changes—should you decide to make them—that you

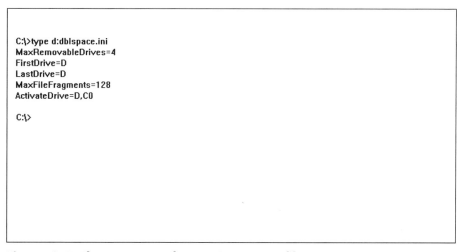

```
C:\>type d:dblspace.ini
MaxRemovableDrives=4
FirstDrive=D
LastDrive=D
MaxFileFragments=128
ActivateDrive=D,C0

C:\>
```

Figure 9-7 The contents of a DBLSPACE.INI file

must take great care with, as you really are on your own here. As already stated, Microsoft has not documented this file, which means reparation support, should you require it, will be limited.

Before you can edit DBLSPACE.INI you will have to remove the hidden system and read-only attributes with the ATTRIB command.There are five kinds of lines in a DBLSPACE.INI file. The first four occur once; the last one may occur any number of times. The first four lines read

```
MaxRemovableDrives=n
FirstDrive=D1
LastDrive=D2
MaxFileFragments=nn
```

where *n* is a number, typically 2; *D1* and *D2* are each a single letter; and *nn* is another number.

If you have only two drives in which you can place a removable disk, leave *n* at its default value of 2. If you have more removable disk drives and want to be able to mount DoubleSpace volumes in each of them simultaneously, you may increase *n* to the maximum number of removable DoubleSpaced disks.

`FirstDrive` specifies the drive letter that DoubleSpace will assign to the first virtual drive it creates from a CVF. `LastDrive` specifies the last drive letter DoubleSpace will use for a host volume. (You will understand these entries better after you study the `ActivateDrive` lines, discussed below.)

`MaxFileFragments` isn't documented, but we suspect it may tell DoubleSpace how to decide when it must defragment its internal structure. We recommend that you don't change this line. If DoubleSpace perceives a need to change it, it will make the change.

The final line in a DBLSPACE.INI file reads

```
ActivateDrive=D1, D2n
```

where *D1* and *D2* are each a single letter, and *n* is a number, typically a single-digit number. There will be as many of these lines as there are CVFs that you want DBLSPACE.BIN to mount when you boot your PC.

In an `ActivateDrive` line, the second drive letter, *D2*, specifies the original host volume drive designation on which the CVF may be found. The number following *D2* indicates to which CVF on that drive it is referring.

The first drive letter in an `ActivateDrive` line, *D1*, can have one of two meanings. If the number after *D2* is a 0, *D1* is the drive letter that this host volume will assume, and the DBLSPACE.000 CVF on that host volume will assume the original host volume drive designation. If the number after *D2* is anything other than a 0, then *D1* is the drive letter assigned to the virtual drive created from this CVF. (The host volume's letter for this drive is determined by the line referring to the DBLSPACE.000 CVF on that drive, if there is one. If there is no DBLSPACE.000 file on that host drive, then it will retain its original drive letter.)

Refer back to the example shown in Figure 9-5. In this case, the first `ActivateDrive` line specifies that the DBLSPACE.000 compressed volume file will become the C drive, and the original C drive, which is the host of that CVF, will become G. The next `ActivateDrive` line specifies that the DBLSPACE.001 CVF, which is also located on the original C drive, will become the logical D drive. In this instance, logical drives E and F are not used. They could be used for a RAM disk, for example, or for a fictitious drive defined by the SUBST command.

A more complex example of a DBLSPACE.INI file's contents reads as follows:

```
MaxRemovableDrives=2
FirstDrive=D
LastDrive=M
MaxFileFragments=125
ActivateDrive=H,C0
ActivateDrive=D,C1
ActivateDrive=E,C2
ActivateDrive=F,C3
ActivateDrive=G,C4
ActivateDrive=L,M0
```

In this system, there is one physical hard disk volume, originally referred to as the C drive. It has five compressed volume files (CVFs) named DBLSPACE.000 through DBLSPACE.004. These CVFs are referred to in the INI file as C0 through C4.

When this system was first set up, the last `ActivateDrive` line shown above was not in the INI file. At that time, the CVF files were given drive letters C, D, E, F, and G; the host volume became H. Later, a line was added to the CONFIG.SYS file to create a RAM disk which appeared as drive M. The system was DoubleSpaced, at which time the last `ActivateDrive` line shown above appeared in the INI file. This line specifies that the DBLSPACE.000 CVF on the RAM disk will assume the drive designation M, and the host volume (the RAM disk itself) will become the L drive. The `LastDrive` line was altered by DoubleSpace at the same time to properly reflect the highest drive letter involved in any of the `ActivateDrive` lines.

INSTALLING DOUBLESPACE

The MS-DOS 6 SETUP program does not install DoubleSpace. If you want to use on-the-fly file compression, you will have to explicitly install DoubleSpace as a separate installation step, which can be very easy. Just type `DBLSPACE` at the DOS prompt and press the Enter key.

Warning: Be sure to get to a "raw" DOS prompt before installing DoubleSpace. Exit from any programs you may be running, including the DOSSHELL, Windows, DESQview, WordPerfect Office, Xtree, or any similar shell program. It is not safe to run DBLESPACE.EXE at a DOS prompt from one of those products. Fortunately, at least in a DOS window in Windows, DoubleSpace will notice that it is not in a safe place and will refuse to run.

Don't boot from a bare DOS floppy disk. If your PC is normally connected to a network, be sure to have your network software loaded so that DBLSPACE.EXE will see all your drives, both local and network, before it assigns drive letters to the new logical drives it is going to create.

Express Setup The easiest way to install DoubleSpace is to select Express Setup. DoubleSpace will compress all the files it can on your C drive and put them into a DBLSPACE.000 file on that drive. The next time you reboot, that CVF will appear as your C drive and it will appear to be about twice the size of the original C drive.

In addition to the four hidden files DoubleSpace must leave on the host volume in order for your PC to be able to boot properly (IO.SYS, MSDOS.SYS, DBLSPACE.BIN, and DBLSPACE.INI), it also will leave any other hidden files, such as your Windows permanent swap file. You must not move the Windows permanent swap file inside any compressed volume file, whether it has been created and is being managed by DoubleSpace or by Stacker or SuperStor. Also on this host volume, of course, is the hidden compressed volume file DBLSPACE.000.

Custom Setup To initially compress a drive other than C, create a CVF without any files in it (which will be a DBLSPACE.00n volume with *n* not equal to 0) and give it a drive letter other than C. To exercise some control over the way that DoubleSpace sets up the DBLSPACE.000 file, you must choose DoubleSpace's Custom Setup option.

Your first decision when you enter Custom Setup is whether to compress an existing drive or create a new drive. "Compressing an existing drive" means creating a DBLSPACE.000 CVF on that drive and putting most of the files on that drive in that CVF. When DoubleSpace is finished, the files still will be accessible on what appears to be the same drive letter as the original host. Remember: The host drive will have been assigned a new drive letter. "Creating a new drive" is quite different. This process takes some free space on a specified host volume and uses it to create a DBLSPACE.00n CVF with no files in it. When DoubleSpace finishes this task, the host volume will remain with the drive letter it had and the newly created drive will be given a letter that was not in use before. The host volume's free space will have decreased by the size of the newly created CVF, and the new logical volume will be approximately twice the size of that CVF (unless you chose a different compression ratio while you were creating it).

Compressing an existing drive can take a long time, especially if it is a large volume with many files. Creating a new drive takes almost no time at all. Whichever type of compression you chose, DoubleSpace will display a list of the drives it can compress. Select one. DoubleSpace always defaults to assuming that the files you place on a DoubleSpaced drive will compress, on average, to about half their original size, a 2:1 compression ratio. If you know you are going to store compressible graphics files, you probably should choose a larger ratio, which will make the newly created drive seem much larger. This will allow you to store more files, but only if those files actually do compress by the amount you chose as your compression ratio. Each time you reboot, DoubleSpace reassesses the actual compression of the files in each CVF. It then readjusts the number it reports as space available on each logical drive created to match its estimate of how many new files can be compressed onto that drive.

> ***Note:*** You may change the compression ratio or CVF at any time, so it is not a problem if you choose a ration that is incorrect.

COMPRESSING A DRIVE WITH FILES

You may compress any uncompressed DOS logical disk volume at any time—well, almost any. You cannot compress a network drive, for example, but contrary to what Microsoft says, you can compress a RAM disk. (Compressing RAM disks will be discussed more later in this chapter.)

If the drive you choose to compress has files on it, probably you'll want to compress them, which is what happens to your C drive if you choose the Express Setup option during the initial installation of DoubleSpace. A DBLSPACE.000 volume gets created on the drive you designated. The virtual drive created from that CVF acquires the drive letter of the host volume and the host volume gets a new drive letter. DoubleSpace will choose that drive letter for you, trying to avoid any letter that is already in use by a physical or virtual disk volume, including any RAM disks or network drives you can access. If necessary, DoubleSpace will even alter some of its existing drive designations to eliminate drive letter conflicts.

If you compress a removable drive, the DoubleSpace information in the DOS Help file and in the *User's Guide* says that you will end up hiding the original host volume. Actually, it will be given a new host drive letter, just as is the case with hard disk volumes or RAM disks. You won't, however, be able to control how much of that host volume remains uncompressed—that is, you cannot do this at the time you compress the drive. Later, you can adjust the size of the CVF file and, therefore, the free space on the host, just as you can on any DoubleSpace compressed drive.

COMPRESSING AN EMPTY DRIVE

You also can create any number of new virtual drives. To do so, first make some space on one or more of your existing physical drive volumes. You may have to reduce the size of a CVF that DoubleSpace created there, which is possible as long as you don't attempt to reduce its size to the point that the compressed files already in that CVF would no longer fit.

Each time you create a new CVF with `DBLSPACE /CREATE`, you are creating a new, empty virtual drive. You only need to tell DoubleSpace which uncompressed drive to use to create a new CVF. DoubleSpace will assign the new drive a previously unused drive letter and edit the DBLSPACE.INI file on the boot host volume to include any new drives it creates.

It is your decision how much of the free space DoubleSpace will use to create a new drive. You exercise that choice either by telling DoubleSpace how large a drive to create (with the /SIZE option) or how much of the host's free space not to use (with the /RESERVE option). (These two options are mutually exclusive.) You cannot ask DoubleSpace to use all the remaining space on the host volume; DoubleSpace will insist on leaving at least 100KB or so as uncompressed space.

COMPRESSING REMOVABLE DRIVES

Removable drives may be compressed, but you cannot directly create an empty compressed volume from a portion of the space on a removable disk. (Actually, we'll show you a somewhat roundabout way to accomplish this anyway.)

To compress a removable disk, choose `Compress existing drive` from the `Compress` menu within DBLSPACE, or use the command line

```
DBLSPACE B: /CREATE
```

if you have the removable disk in your B drive.

You won't be offered a choice about how much free space to leave, and the new logical volume will necessarily have the same drive letter as the original physical disk drive. The host volume will appear as some other drive letter chosen by DoubleSpace.

> **Warning:** If you want to have the virtual drive appear as the new drive letter and continue to see your physical B drive as B, you can accomplish this, but only by doing some potentially dangerous direct editing of the DBLSPACE.INI file we warned you about. In short, you first must rename the CVF on B to DBLSPACE.001. Then go into the DBLSPACE.INI file and change B0 wherever it appears to B1.

COMPRESSING RAM DISKS

To repeat: RAM disk compression *can* be done—but it might be more trouble than it's worth. For starters, you cannot compress any very small drives. The overhead for DoubleSpace, plus its restrictions of how much free space to leave just won't permit this. If, however, your RAM disk is 1MB or larger, you can compress it. Do so by running DBLSPACE in its interactive mode; don't attempt to do it from the command line. (If you have a huge RAM disk, you may be able to get away with using the command line, but approximately 1MB of the host volume will remain uncompressed.)

When you choose the `Compress an existing drive` menu option, you will see the RAM disk. Select it. Be sure to adjust the free space DoubleSpace proposes to leave. If you don't, it will leave almost all of the RAM disk uncompressed and create a very small CVF.

When it compresses the RAM disk, DoubleSpace will also alter the DBLSPACE.INI file to reflect the new number of DoubleSpace-managed drive letters. It increases the `LastDrive` letter by one and adds one new `ActivateDrive` line, which is appropriate to the DoubleSpace setup. Unfortunately, it also is the seed of a problem that will flower the next time you reboot and try to compress that RAM disk.

During the boot process, DBLSPACE.BIN reads the DBLSPACE.INI file. It mounts the drives it is told to activate if it can, and it reserves the other drive letters through the specified `LastDrive` value. Later in the boot process, when RAMDRIVE.SYS or any other RAM disk device driver loads, it will receive the next available drive letter. If you now DoubleSpace this new RAM disk at that new drive letter, DoubleSpace will again adjust the DBLSPACE.INI file and the `LastDrive` value will again advance by one. If you continue this, soon you will be out of drive letters, which may be the reason Microsoft discourages the compression of RAM disks.

Tip: There is a workaround you can use to avoid running out of drive letters. After you have created and mounted your RAM disk, invoke DBLSPACE in its interactive mode. Go to Tools/Options and decrease the `LastDrive` letter by one.

In summary, RAM disks can be compressed successfully. But continually re-creating them does not. While it may not seem worth the effort after all, consider some significant potential benefits if you do create a compressed RAM disk. A compressed RAM disk gives you roughly twice as much ultra-fast disk space for temporary files as in an uncompressed RAM disk for the same commitment of your physical RAM chips. So, if you think you can afford perhaps 5MB of RAM disk without compression and still have enough RAM left over for Windows and your Windows applications, then you effectively could have a 10MB RAM disk and still have enough left over RAM for those other uses. This could make the difference between a RAM disk that was large enough for your CorelDRAW! temporary files and one that was not. And that could be the difference between a system that frequently crashed and one that worked trouble-free.

In the end, only you can decide if this is a viable option or merely one to think about wistfully while waiting for the next version of DoubleSpace. (Alternatively, you may decide to use Stacker instead of DoubleSpace, for this among other reasons.)

MOUNTING AND UNMOUNTING CVFS

Whenever you create a compressed volume file, DoubleSpace will mount it for you. It also will alter the DBLSPACE.INI file so that the new volume will be mounted every time you reboot your PC. There are two exceptions: DoubleSpace doesn't automatically remount compressed removable disks, and DoubleSpace can't automatically mount a RAM disk, since the CVF for that host volume disappears each time you reboot.

You can add a command to your AUTOEXEC.BAT file to mount a compressed floppy. Type

```
DBLSPACE B: /MOUNT
```

if the compressed floppy is in your B drive. The floppy must already have the needed CVF file there for DoubleSpace to mount. (You might also be able to create and mount RAM disks in a similar manner, but you could run into some difficulties, as mentioned in the previous section.)

In addition to mounting and unmounting compressed volumes at the command line, you can do these tasks by running DBLSPACE.EXE in its full-screen interactive mode and selecting the appropriate options from its menus.

OTHER DBLSPACE.EXE OPTIONS

Figure 9-8(a) shows the initial screen presented by running DBLSPACE.EXE with no command line parameters. There are four menus from which you may select the various things DoubleSpace can do. Figures 9-8(b) through 9-8(e) show these menus. Figure 9-8(f) shows the dialog box that appears if you choose `Options` from the `Tools` menu.

The assistance you access from the Help menu inside DBLSPACE is a completely different set of screens from those resulting by using the DOS HELP command. Like the regular Help program, these screens have hypertext links. You will want to explore this Help system to learn the topics it incorporates. (DoubleSpace is only one of a dozen programs in MS-DOS 6 that have separate help files. Look in your DOS directory for all the files with extension HLP to see which external commands they are.)

A basic option for DoubleSpace is its INFO screen. To access information on any of the compressed drives in your system, either choose an Info menu selection or issue the command

```
DBLSPACE d: /INFO
```

where *d:* is the logical volume you wish to learn about.

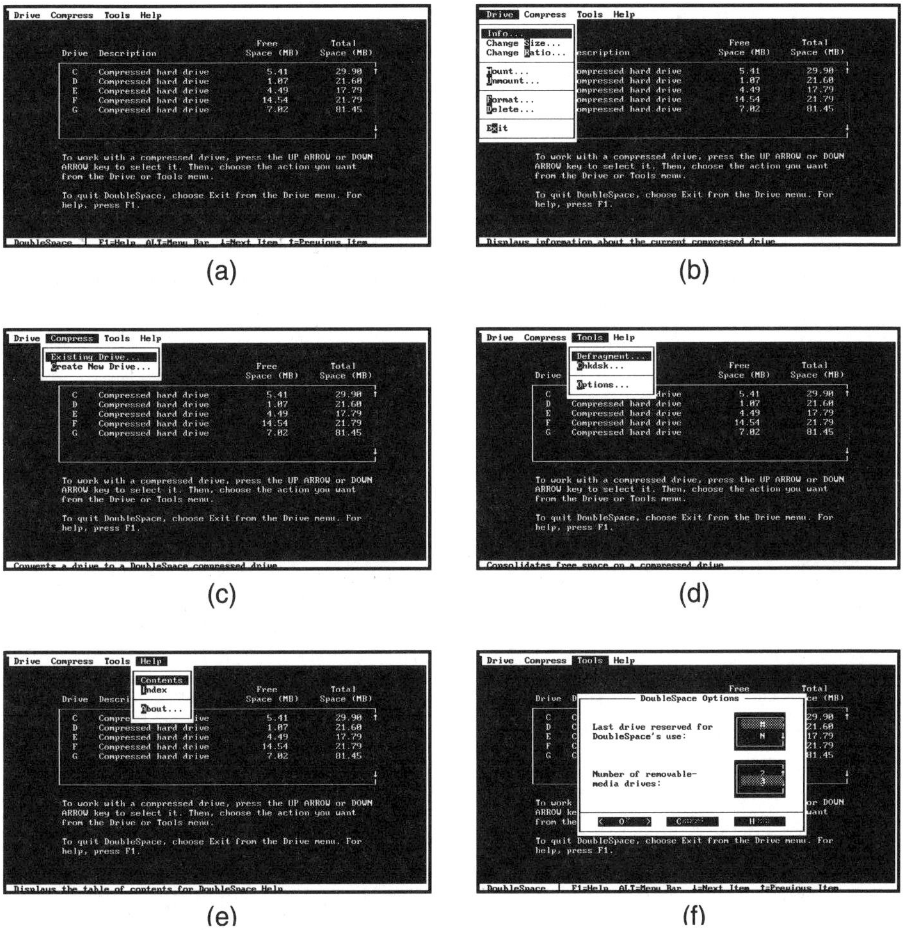

Figure 9-8 DBLSPACE.EXE in interactive mode

One of the most important entries is on the `Tools` menu. It is called `Defragment`. DoubleSpace seems to be much more sensitive to fragmentation inside CVFs than DOS is to fragmentation on uncompressed disk volumes. Defragment your compressed volumes frequently. Invoking DEFRAG at the DOS prompt and specifying a compressed volume is another way to do this. Also, be sure to run DEFRAG on a host volume before you attempt to compress the files it contains or create a new compressed drive using some of the free space on that volume.

The functions performed by most of the remaining options are pretty obvious, although the `Options` entry on the `Tools` menu is less so. It provides the safe way to set the DBLSPACE.INI entries for `LastDrive` and `MaxRemovableDrives`.

DOUBLESPACE AND MEMORY USE CONSIDERATIONS

The DBLSPACE.BIN block device takes up some RAM, but just which patch of RAM it uses can change from one point in the boot process to another. You can exercise some control over where it goes through the DEVICE=C:\DOS\DBLSPACE.SYS line in your CONFIG.SYS file.

When DBLSPACE.BIN is loading into RAM, the CONFIG.SYS file has not yet been opened. Clearly, HIMEM.SYS and EMM386.EXE have not been loaded, so there is no such thing as XMS or EMS memory or any upper memory blocks (UMBs) into which a program could be loaded. DBLSPACE.BIN will work if it is loaded into upper memory, but that cannot happen until some memory management program or programs have been loaded.

If DBLSPACE.BIN were to be loaded near the bottom of RAM, just on top of IO.SYS, it would prevent the placement of other device drivers there. If you later moved DBLSPACE.BIN to upper memory, you'd leave a hole in lower RAM, and it might be hard to make efficient use of that space.

Actually, this is not so different from the situation when you specify DOS=HIGH when, in effect, you are instructing IO.SYS to put as much of itself as possible into the HMA. But until HIMEM.SYS or some other XMM is loaded, there is no HMA. DOS solves this by scanning your CONFIG.SYS file looking for the line DOS=HIGH as its very first task. If it finds that line, IO.SYS will put a portion of its kernel code somewhere fairly high in RAM (but below 640KB) until after HIMEM.SYS or some other XMM is loaded. Then DOS will ask the XMM for the HMA. Since DOS can slip that request in before any other program gets a chance to do so, it will get the HMA. At that point, it can move its kernel code and the DOS disk buffers into their final position in the HMA.

DBLSPACE.BIN is treated in a similar fashion. Initially, it is loaded high in RAM. After the XMM and the upper memory provider are loaded (and thus, upper memory can exist), DOS will ask the XMM to allocate to it all of the available upper memory (if DOS=UMB was specified). Now it can load device drivers and TSR programs into upper memory whenever they ask to be loaded high.

Some programs ask on their own. INTERLNK and POWER, for example, will load their program code into upper memory if they can, unless you explicitly tell them not to do so with a /LOW switch. For most programs, you have to tell DOS what to do by using either a DEVICEHIGH line to load a device driver into upper memory or a LOADHIGH command to load a TSR there.

Because DBLSPACE.BIN was loaded into memory automatically by IO.SYS, you had no opportunity to tell it to load high, nor was there any upper memory into which it could be loaded at the time. But, by including the line DEVICEHIGH=C:\DOS\DBLSPACE.SYS in your CONFIG.SYS file, you can get DOS to put DBLSPACE.BIN into upper memory just before it completes the processing of the CONFIG.SYS file. If you don't tell it this, DBLSPACE.BIN will be moved down in RAM from its initial location to just on top of the last device drivers and TSRs installed via DEVICE and INSTALL lines in CONFIG.SYS. Figure 9-9 shows these steps graphically.

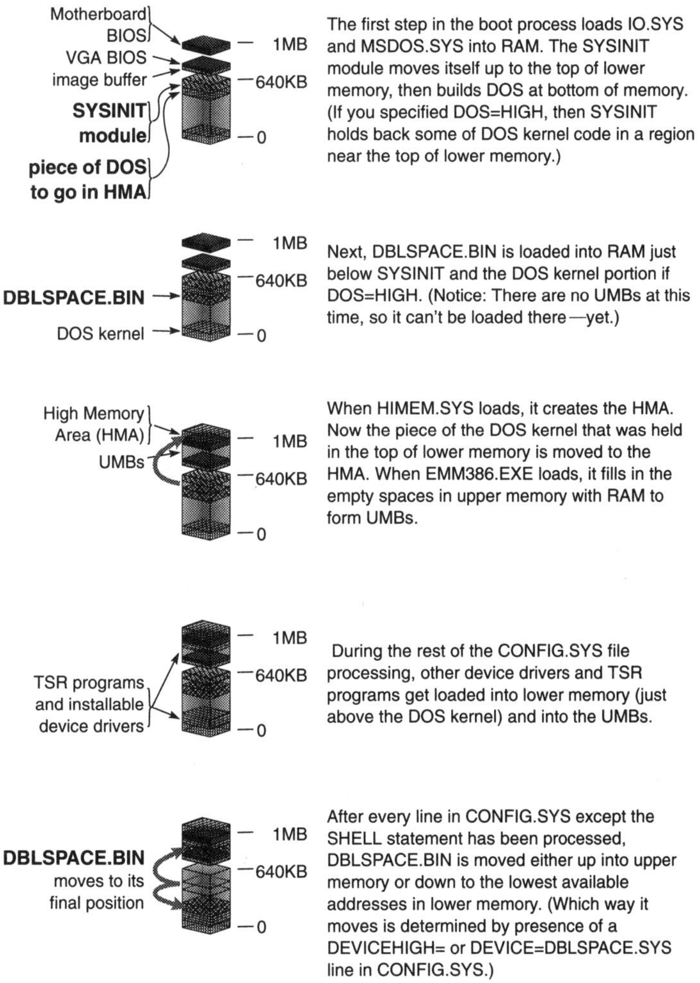

Figure 9-9 Location of DBLSPACE.BIN in memory at various stages of the boot process

Third-Party File Compression Programs

There are times when you don't need to compress an entire disk, but still want some of the benefits of file compression. For example, when you're sending files by modem, the smaller you can make a given file, the quicker you can upload or download it. Or you may wish to cram as many files on a disk as possible, but not have to depend on the recipient having DoubleSpace on their system. Situations like this call for third-party programs like LHA or PKZIP.

Figure 9-10 shows schematically what LHA and its kin do. They work on files that are on your disk and deposit the results on your disk. Further, they can take a collection of uncompressed files and create from them a single compressed file, or they can reverse the process. Contrast this with Figure 9-3. In Figure 9-3, each file is handled separately and the uncompressed version of that file never appears anywhere on the disk, while the compressed version never appears anywhere off the disk.

A copy of LHA is included on the DOS Power Tools diskette. The PTOOLS program, also on that diskette, will explain how to use LHA and help you construct valid command lines for it. One additional outstanding feature of LHA is that its author has declared this program a copyright-protected free-use program. This is unlike almost all the other PC compression programs, most of which are either commercial software you buy in a store or by mail-order, or shareware programs.

General file compression programs like LHA and PKZIP all are intended for use on any files you have. Some types of files will compress more than others. The compression algorithms used in these programs have been chosen to give the best overall compression ratio on a "typical" mixture of PC files.

If you know in advance what kinds of files you will be compressing, it is possible to build an even better file compressor just for them. This has been done by several authors who have introduced special purpose file compression programs. Primarily, these programs are optimized for use on other executable programs.

An early example of such a special purpose file compressor is the program Space Maker (SM.EXE) from Realia. It was created explicitly to allow a software manufacturer to cram more and larger programs on fewer diskettes for distribution.

Space Maker introduced another idea. The files it creates are self-expanding and executable. From a SOMETHNG.COM file you create another SOMETHNG.COM file that is smaller than the original. When DOS loads the new SOMETHNG.COM into memory and lets it run, the first thing that happens is that a small portion of the program relocates itself high in RAM (but below 640KB, normally). That small portion then works on the rest of the file to

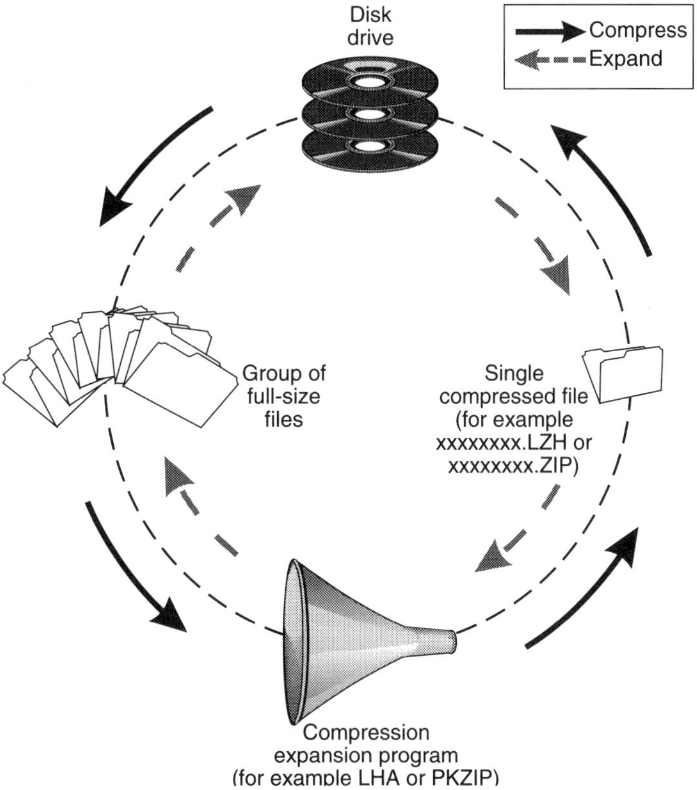

Figure 9-10 Modern compression programs put multiple files into one compressed file and take them back out again.

create in memory a reconstruction of the original uncompressed file. Then it transfers control to that original file.

Space Maker can do this with either COM or EXE files. Be aware though, once you have compressed a file using Space Maker, you will not be able to uncompress it. So keep a copy of the original uncompressed file elsewhere or under a different name. Not every executable file can be successfully compressed by this strategy. Generally, the exceptions are programs like DEBUG that ordinarily load themselves near the top of available RAM.

Microsoft offers an option with most of its language products called EXEPACK. This option tells the language compiler to create a compressed version of the file it is compiling. The result is very much like taking the normal compiler output and running Space Maker on it.

Most of the general purpose file compression programs such as LHA and PKZIP now offer an option to create a self-exploding file out of any archive file they create. The difference between this and what EXEPACK or Space Maker does is that these self-exploding files will simply reconstruct some or all of the compressed files contained in that archive, without executing any of them.

Finally, this discussion would be incomplete without pointing out that Microsoft ships almost all its products with each file compressed. This is indicated by the replacement of the last character in the file type with an underscore. Each of its products also includes at least a couple of uncompressed files; typically, they are called SETUP.EXE and EXPAND.EXE. SETUP manages the installation of the product; EXPAND is used by SETUP to decompress all the other files.

EXPAND differs from the other programs discussed in this section in several ways. It is a one-way program. It reconstructs the original file from a compressed version; it cannot be used to create compressed files. Also, EXPAND expects to find only one file to be reconstructed for each compressed file; the others all deal with multifile archives. Finally, EXPAND does not rename the file it extracts automatically; all the other programs store the uncompressed file name inside the archive and re-create it in the same step that reconstructs that file's contents.

C H A P T E R

10

◆ ◆ ◆ ◆ ◆

Printing

PC users spend most of their work time in front of a monitor looking at screen images, but the information that is transferred to hard copy is often used as the measure of their productivity.

Conventional printing has a long and rich tradition in comparison to computer printing. Until recently, computer printouts were ugly, dull affairs. If you weren't interested in the information the printout contained, you were not likely to spend any time looking at it. Now we have the capability to create beautiful, visually stimulating documents on a PC. This chapter explores printing and PCs from a nuts and bolts point of view. We won't teach you how to format documents or deal with fonts, but we will explain how to configure DOS to make your printer accept data from your PC and print it. Along the way you will learn about some of the many variations possible in printer connections, print spooling, and related issues.

The earliest PC printers were line, daisywheel, and dot-matrix printers. All three designs are considered impact printers, which means they form images on paper by pressing a physical representation of a character against an inked ribbon, forming an impression on the page. Line printers traditionally have been used only in large computer installations where their considerable speed and ruggedness make them worth their rather high price. Daisywheel printers were slow, inflexible (a fixed fond), noisy, and prone to failure. They have disappeared from the PC printer marketplace altogether.

Currently, the printers favored by many are laser printers. These high-resolution, nonimpact printers mimic the process used in photocopiers. The printer's controller receives instructions from a computer and, for each page, constructs a bit map of every dot on the page. The controller then ensures that the printer engine's laser sends an exact replica of the bit map to a photostatically sensitive drum or belt. The beam moves across the drum, repeatedly turning on and off; as the beam moves, the drum charges the areas exposed to the beam, which attract toner (ink) when the drum moves past the toner cartridge.

Sending Information to a Printer

There are many ways that information can be sent to a printer, and some printers recognize only one or two of these formats while others can recognize and properly print most of them. If you ever have trouble printing files, a logical place to begin looking for the bottleneck is the format. This section will define the most common formats, explain how to recognize them on screen or on a printed page, and what to do when your printer cannot handle the format of a file you wish to print.

Popular Print Stream Formats

Text mode printers divide the page into character cells, each of which can have one character printed in it; and all the characters must be from some particular set of symbols, called a character set. Graphics mode printers view the contents of a printed page as an image made up of a huge number of dots. Whereas a typical computer graphics screen will have no more than about 75 dots per inch in either the horizontal or vertical direction, typical graphic printer resolutions range from a few hundred to approximately one thousand dots per inch. Each dot is then printed—in black and white on most PC printers. These dots are called *pixels* (or *pels*), an abbreviation for picture element; a pixel is the smallest element that a device can display on the screen and from which the displayed image is constructed.

The nature of the information sent to a printer depends on what type it is and the form the output is to take. Before printing, therefore, it is necessary to determine if the data you are sending to the printer matches its capabilities. To help you recognize the different kinds of printer data, the following section discusses, roughly in descending order of popularity, the most popular kinds.

ASCII TEXT

The original PC printers were modeled after teletypewriters. They could accept only a stream of text characters plus some control characters. The text characters got printed; the control characters directed the teletypewriter when to start a new line, return to the left margin, move to a tab stop, eject the page, or perform certain other simple operations.

A stream of text and simple control characters is termed *printable ASCII text.* Often the only acceptable control characters are these:

ASCII Value	*Abbreviation*	*Function*
13	CR	carriage return
10	LF	line feed
12	FF	form feed (new page)

Some printers add:

9	HT	horizontal tab
8	BS	backspace

The contents of a typical file of printable ASCII text consists of letters, numbers, punctuation symbols, space characters, CR-LF pairs of control characters to mark the ends of lines, and FF characters at the start of each new page. If you see a file with format, it can be printed on any PC text mode printer.

A sample of a printable ASCII text is shown near the top of Figure 10-1. The control characters are enclosed in a small rounded rectangle. A file containing printable ASCII text usually has one of four extensions: TXT, DOC, ASC, or PRN; it might, however, have a different extension, and not all files with those extensions are printable ASCII text files.

BIT-MAPPED GRAPHIC IMAGES

If you want to invoke a dot-matrix printer to print a graphics image you must do two things. First, you have to tell the printer that it is not to interpret the incoming stream of data as text symbols, but instead to use those data to define the color (perhaps only black or white) of each dot on the page. One common way to specify the content of a graphic image is simply as a raster scan (bit-map pattern), which is exactly the same way that images get drawn on a computer monitor. For simplicity we will describe how this works only for a black-and-white printer. Color printers require several times as much information, but it is coded in a very similar manner.

Printer file format	Sample of a typical file's contents (CR) = Carriage Return (ASCII 13) (LF) = Line Feed (ASCII 10) (ESC) = Escape (ASCII 27)
printable ASCII text	Printable ASCII text consists of lines(CR)(LF) of characters, each one terminated by(CR)(LF) a CR-LF pair of characters.(CR)(LF) (CR)(LF) Paragraphs are separated by two pairs(CR)(LF) of CR-LF characters.(CR)(LF)
uncompressed bit-mapped graphic image	00000000 00000000 00011111 11000000 00000000 00000000 00011101 11111111 10000000 00000000 00000011 11000000 00001100 00000000 00111100 00000111 11111111 11111111 11111000 00000000 00000000 00000111 11000000 11000000 00000001
run-length encoded bit-mapped graphic image	00010011 00000111 00011001 00000011 00000001 00001010 00010101 00000100 00001010 00000010 00001100 00000100 00000111 00011000 00011000 00000101 00000110 00001101 ...
Hewlett-Packard PCL	(ESC)E(ESC)&10L(ESC)&11H(ESC)&12a4d1e42F (ESC)&10o1E(ESC)*t300R(ESC)*p265Y(ESC)*p315X (ESC)*c16385D(ESC))s64W
PostScript	%!PS-Adobe-2.0 EPSF-2.0 %%BoundingBox: 2 192 334 312 %%Creator: CorelDRAW! %%Title: 14COMIRQ.EPS %%CreationDate: Sun Jan 31 21:54:04 1993
Hewlett-Packard HP-GL	IN; IP0 0 4673 7416; SP1; SC-2297 2297 -3650 3650; SP1; PU-258 825; PD-227 924;

Figure 10-1 Examples of common print stream formats

Uncompressed Bit-Mapped Graphics The printer—once it is told to go into an uncompressed, bit-mapped graphics mode—treats each byte it receives as a description of the color (black or white) that it is to print at each of eight adjacent dot positions; usually a 0 bit indicates to leave it white and a 1 bit indicates to print black. The first byte describes the leftmost 8 dots on the top line; the next byte describes the 8 dots to the right of those, and so on. The second sample in Figure 10-1 shows the details for a very small portion of an image produced in this format, where each byte is shown as 8 bits, each a 0 or a 1. Only the first 200 pixels of the image are shown. This represents an image as it might be stored in a file with the TIF extension. There are many other graphic file formats with other file names and internal structures, but most of them are not printable by most PC printers.

Compressed Bit-Mapped Graphics Most printed pages actually are large areas of white space interrupted by small regions of black. Of the nearly 8 million bits sent to the printer to describe a page, the majority will be zeros, i.e., white; and, where there is black on the page, typically many dots per row will be black.

An easy way to quickly send bit-mapped graphic images to this kind of printer is to compress the image information, that is, reduce it to just its essential content. Then the number of bytes of data you need to send is drastically reduced. Once at the printer, though, the reduced byte stream is reexpanded to the original bit-mapped image before being printed.

There are many possible ways to achieve this compression. The easiest one to describe, and the one most commonly used in printers, is called run-length encoding, where each byte in the compressed data stream is a number. The first number specifies how many white dots to draw (from 0 to 255); the next number specifies how many black dots to draw, then another byte for white dots, and so on. Every other byte is for white, with the rest for black.

The third sample in Figure 10-1 shows how the second sample would look if encoded in this fashion. The first byte in the third sample is the binary translation of 19; it represents the 19 zeros at the beginning of the second sample. The next byte in the compressed file has the value 7, representing the seven ones following the 19 zeros. Check the rest of the bytes in this sample to verify your understanding of how they were generated.

The sample in Figure 10-1 shows that the original 25 bytes were reduced to 18. Normally, of course, the compression is much greater, as a typical page has longer runs of single color bits. Using the scheme described, two bytes are required to specify each pair of white and black runs of dots, or two bytes for every 255 dots of the same color. (You can code a long run of white dots, for example, by saying that they are many repetitions of a pattern of 255 white dots followed by zero black dots.) In the most extreme case—a totally white page—this would result in a file with just under 59,300 bytes, which is little greater than one-sixteenth the size of the uncompressed image.

This, obviously, is not the ultimate in compression routines. In fact, it is just about the simplest and least effective. Still, it can reduce a bit-mapped image of a typical page of text to a fraction of its original size.

Until very recently, the only compression routines used for sending data to a printer were *lossless*, which means that it was always possible to reconstruct the original image from the compressed version of the data. (The preceding example of run-length encoding is lossless compression.)

Because acceptable readability of a printed page does not require that every pixel on the screen be exactly reproduced on paper—text and pictures need only to be clear to the reader—there has been an increase in the achievable compression rations for bit-mapped graphic image data streams. As a user, then, you must choose between fidelity and compression. If you want your image data reduced to a mere 1 percent of its original size, certainly you may have that, but you must accept the concomitant degradation of the final output. Conversely, you may reduce an image to a twentieth of its original size, in which case you will see little degradation.

HEWLETT-PACKARD'S PCL

When Hewlett-Packard introduced their LaserJet printer, they also introduced a new way to communicate with a printer—its Printer Control Language, commonly abbreviated as HPPCL or just PCL. Initially, PCL was a minor enhancement to simple printable ASCII text files. In addition to the printable characters and control characters, a PCL file included some escape sequences that each set some feature, such as line spacing or font.

HP was not the first to use this strategy. In fact, almost all dot-matrix printers, both impact and nonimpact, support some set of escape sequence controls. The original IBM graphics printer made by Epson used a variation of the escape sequences that Epson had been using on its own printers for several years. What was new about PCL was the extent to which it attempted to control the printer. Over the years, as printer technology improved and pressure to compete with PostScript (see next section) increased, HP upgraded the PCL specification several times. In its current form (version 5), PCL includes many of the features of PostScript. A PCL print job starts with an extensive header that sets up many aspects of how the printer will deal with the upcoming print job. (PostScript uses the same strategy, and carries it even farther.)

The fourth sample file in Figure 10-1 shows the beginning of a PCL file. Any time you see an ASCII text file with embedded escape codes and you know the file was meant to be sent to a printer (and if you have no reason to believe it was constructed for some other dot-matrix printer), you can be fairly sure it is an HPPCL print file. If it is using a modern version of PCL, it may also have a significant number of nonprintable characters, which are bytes of binary data.

> **Note:** PCL printers also can print plain vanilla ASCII text, just like any inexpensive dot-matrix printer. Special codes are necessary only when you want to enhance the printed image over what can be achieved from a simple text file.

POSTSCRIPT

There is one basic problem with any bit-mapped graphic image format. The creator of the image must know exactly what the resolution is for the output device. Creating an image for a 10-inch screen with 75 dots per inch is a very different task than creating that same image for a printer capable of 300 dots per inch on an 8-inch page. Re-creating the image so that it will take full advantage of an imagesetter with 2470 dots-per-inch resolution is something else again.

Ideally, it would be possible to compose a page without having to pay attention to that level of detail. To do so requires a *device-independent page description language*. PostScript is such a language. Actually, PostScript is more than just a page description language; it also is a programming language. PostScript printers are full-fledged computers in their own right. (Often a PostScript printer is a more powerful computer than the PC to which it is attached.)

Programs that send images to a PostScript printer are actually sending computer programs that instruct the printer how to craft and print the pages. The capabilities of the PostScript language allow for a very flexible definition of a page's contents and especially for defining the appearance of type.

If you look at the byte stream that gets sent to a PostScript printer, it resembles ASCII text. (Some PostScript files have what is called a *binary header*, which is a small bit-mapped image that approximates what the page will look like. Some programs can display that image so you can see which PostScript file you are working on.) If you try to print a PostScript printer file on either a text printer or a PCL printer, the output will be pages of seemingly meaningless text. Actually, it is the PostScript program that an interpreter inside the printer should have used to create the pages. Conversely, if you try to print a regular printable ASCII text file on a PostScript printer, you won't see anything. Without the proper PostScript program, the printer doesn't know what to do, so it just discards the incoming text.

The fifth sample file in Figure 10-1 shows the beginning of a typical PostScript file. This file was created by CorelDRAW! and illustrates only a few of the header remarks that typically are inserted at the beginning of an EPS file (*Encapsulated PostScript file*—PostScript page description language used to write instructions for storing graphic images).

HEWLETT-PACKARD'S HPGL

Another type of output device is the pen plotter, a machine used for making precise drawings. A pen plotter literally takes a pen, puts it somewhere on the page and moves it to draw. It can lift and lower the pen and position it anywhere on the page. Some plotters also are able to select different pens containing various colors of ink or draw lines of varying widths.

Hewlett-Packard makes some of the most popular plotters on the market. They also have defined a special language—Hewlett-Packard's Graphics Language (HPGL)—now in version 2. Nearly all plotter manufacturers have adopted this language, and it now is regarded as an industry standard and is usually recognizable by its PLT extension. The last sample in Figure 10-1 shows a segment of an HPGL file comprised of all printable ASCII; each line is a separate command to the plotter. After a few lines of setup (for example, SP1 means "select pen #1," and the IP0 lines specify the initial pen position), the file continues with many lines of PU ("pen up") and PD ("pen down") commands, each of which also includes numbers that indicate X and Y movements.

Although HPGL was designed specifically for commanding pen plotters, the development of high-resolution, nonimpact page printers (especially those that can handle large pages or print in color) has motivated many users of plotters to switch to using a printer instead. Most printers designed to replace plotters usually are built to understand HPGL, and they can produce equally precise drawings and in much less time than plotters. (Other printers can output images described in HPGL, but only if the images are first loaded into a suitable graphics program such as CorelDRAW!, which can then output the files in PostScript, PCL, or some other format that the printer understands.

Other Formats

Most brands of impact dot-matrix printers have their own language of escape sequences, which direct the printer to go in or out of graphics mode, change line or character spacing, change type size, and sometimes, fonts. The capabilities of these other formats usually are a small subset of what PCL supported in its first version, but they still allow for significant enhancement of printed output.

Certain specialized printers are designed to work with other special purpose languages. For example, Printronix made a number of *line matrix printers* that print entire rows of dots at one time, but must print several rows to form a set of characters. They are, therefore, a cross between line printers and dot-matrix printers.

DOS Formats

DOS is primarily a character-based operating system; thus, it puts messages on the screen or directs it to a printer as ASCII text files. If you do a *screen dump* by using the Shift-PrtScrn key combination (or use the Print Screen key) and if you have previously loaded the GRAPHICS external DOS command, your PC will send an uncompressed bit-mapped image of the screen to the printer. DOS never creates output in any other printer data stream formats.

Many application and utility programs that run on DOS-based PCs can create output in one or more of the alternative printer file formats. Word processors often support HPPCL and PostScript output in addition to printable ASCII text, which make it possible to print richly formatted pages, rather than just text in 12-point Courier.

Most paint programs can direct output to a printer as an uncompressed bit map. Drawing programs usually send output as a PCL or PostScript job, although they sometimes are able to send output in an uncompressed bit-map format or as an HPGL file.

Printing to a Device or File

Depending on whether you decide to direct your output to the printer, another file, to the screen, or to a fax card, there are many different strategies you can use.

Standard Output Devices

Many DOS programs send output to the screen by writing to a *standard output* device (*stdout*). Anything a program sends to stdout can be redirected to a file or to another device by using the standard output redirection symbols (> and >>). For example, the command

```
CHKDSK C: > PRN
```

will print a CHKDSK report on your C drive on paper. The command

```
MEM /D > MEM-USES.TXT
```

will direct a report on all the programs you have resident in memory to a text file. (The latter approach also enables you to edit the information. You might, for example, want to add some comments regarding changes you made to your setup before you ran the report.)

If you output to a file, you can later print that file simply by copying it to the printer. Suppose that you have now annotated your MEM /D report file and wish to put in on paper for further study. Issuing the command

```
COPY MEM-USES.TXT PRN
```

will do the trick, assuming your printer accepts printable ASCII text files. You can accomplish the same thing by using this command:

```
TYPE MEM-USES.TXT > PRN
```

Saving a work in progress to a file can be done in two ways. One is simply to use the `Save` (or `Save As...`) command in the application that created the document. This is appropriate if the work is going to continue in the same application, either on your PC or on someone else's. The other way is to `Export` the document or use your application's `Print to a file` option, if it has one. This makes it possible to save your work in some other form than the one native to the application that created it. (Several of the file format samples in Figure 10-1 were created this way.)

Preparing a file for a graphics service bureau to output usually is done by selecting a PostScript printer as the designated printer for your application, then printing the output to a file. You can compress the resulting file with LHA or PKZIP and then either take it to the service bureau on a diskette or send it there over a phone line.

Many PCs now sport fax cards. Some of them come with Windows printer drivers that add a `Print to fax` menu option to every Windows application. Other fax boards require you to print your output to a file, exit your application, and at the DOS prompt invoke their special program to convert your output file to facsimile format and send it.

Some applications don't provide the option of printing to a file. It is still possible, however, to capture the output this program sends to your printer, provided the program uses the normal DOS or BIOS services to direct its output to the printer port. To do this, load a TSR program that will intercept all the messages going to your printer port and send them to a file instead. One such program available for free noncommercial use is LPTX by Mark DiVechio.

Screen Dumps

Text Mode Screen Dumps

A *screen dump* is simply a printout of the current screen display. When you initiate a Print Screen operation, you are actually invoking a special interrupt service routine (ISR). The standard ISR for this purpose simply copies the contents of every other character in video memory to the printer. (In Chapter 5 we explained how information is stored in video memory. In text mode the characters to be printed alternate with attribute bytes describing the foreground and background colors of the character and other qualities.) This works if you have a standard video card, are running in text mode, and your printer understands and properly prints the IBM extended ASCII character set. If it doesn't, any boxes displayed on screen probably will be replaced by rows or columns of letters or other characters.

If you use an HP LaserJet, it will print the IBM graphics characters correctly when you choose the PC-8 character set either from the printer's front panel or send the printer the following five-character escape sequence:

```
ESC (10U
```

where ***ESC*** stands for the escape character (ASCII value 27).

An easy way to send this sort of command is from a batch file. Then you have to type it only once. HPPCL commands must be typed with particular care, because that language is case-sensitve; it is responsive to upper- and lowercase letter designations. (Chapter 14 describes how to create batch files and includes examples relating to working with LaserJet printers.)

Some PCs will not let you use the screen dump feature until the CONFIG.SYS file is done processing, which is unfortunate, since many people want to be able to see all the messages that appear on screen during that process; usually, however, it goes by too quickly.

Tip: Your PC will execute its CONFIG.SYS file just one line at a time in DOS 6 if you press F8 briefly during the message `Starting MS-DOS`. IO.SYS will ask you for permission before it acts on each line. At that point you may be able to do a screen dump. If not, at least you can write down the messages. Press Y to let IO.SYS process the next line.

Graphics Mode Screen Dumps

If you have one of the popular Hewlett-Packard or IBM printers or one that can emulate them, the simple way to print images in graphics mode is to load the GRAPHICS program. It is a TSR that inserts itself in front of the interrupt call to do screen dumps.

The syntax of the GRAPHICS command is

```
GRAPHICS [type] [[drive:][path]filename] [switches]
```

where *type* is the model of printer you are using (or emulating) and the file specification

```
[[drive:][path]filename]
```

points to the GRAPHICS.PRO or another "profile" file. If you don't specify a type of printer, GRAPHICS assumes an IBM Graphics printer. If you don't specify a profile file, GRAPHICS will look for GRAPHICS.PRO in the current directory or in the directory from which GRAPHICS.COM was loaded. The valid types are `COLOR1`, `COLOR4`, `COLOR8`, `HPDEFAULT`, `DESKJET`, `GRAPHICS`, `GRAPHICSWIDE`, `LASERJET`, `LASERJETII`, `PAINTJET`, `QUIETJET`, `QUIETJETPLUS`, `RUGGEDWRITER`, `RUGGEDWRITERWIDE`, `THERMAL`, or `THINKJET`. All those with JET suffixes are HP printers. `GRAPHICS` indicates the original IBM Graphics printer, the IBM Proprinter, or the IBM Quietwriter. The `COLORn` types are all IBM color printers with various ribbons (1=black, 4=red, green, blue, black, and 8=cyan, magenta, yellow, black). The valid switches are `/R`, `/B`, `/LCD`, and `/PRINTBOX:`*shape* where *shape* is either `STD` or `LCD`.

The `/R` switch stands for reverse, that is, to print white letters on a black background if the screen was black letters on white, the usual default. The `/B` switch indicates that you have a COLOR4 or COLOR8 printer and you want the background printed in color. The `/LCD` switch or `/PRINTBOX:LCD` indicates that you want to use an aspect ratio for letters that is appropriate to an LCD screen. You should use whichever shape (LCD or STD) is specified in your GRAPHICS.PRO file.

Tip: Look in the DOS directory. Use the LIST program from the DOS Power Tools disk to examine the contents of the file GRAPHICS.PRO. Use the \ key to initiate a case-insensitive search. Type PRINTBOX and press Enter. List will highlight the first occurrence of this word. It will either be followed by STD or LCD, whichever is the appropriate shape for your PC. This file also contains a lot of information on all the printers that GRAPHICS supports, complete with the IBM model numbers for the IBM printers.

For COLOR or GRAPHICS printers, if you are in a color medium-resolution graphics mode with 320 by 200 pixels, GRAPHICS will print screen dumps in portrait orientation (the longest measurement oriented vertically) in color or in four shades of grey. If the screen resolution is 640 by 200, GRAPHICS will print screen dumps to the same printers in landscape orientation (text and/or graphics are printed horizontally across the longer axis of the page). For other printers and other screen modes you will have to experiment to find out what GRAPHICS will do.

Common Problems and Solutions

This section explores a couple of problems regarding screen dumps that have plagued many a PC user. If you have found yourself frustrated in either of these situations, the solutions detailed here should help with any future

> **Warning:** There is no way to do a screen dump if your printer understands only PostScript. Neither the BIOS nor the GRAPHICS program knows how to wrap the appropriate PostScript program around the graphics data representing the screen image contents. If, however, you have a PostScript printer that can be put into a PCL emulation mode, do that and it will be able to print screen dumps. The command
>
> ```
> GRAPHICS LASERJET II
> ```
>
> will work with most PCL printers. Even without loading GRAPHICS, most PCL printers will handle text mode screen dumps as if they were standard IBM Graphics printers.

occurrences. If you've been lucky enough to avoid both of these pitfalls, read on anyway, because chances are, your day will come.

YOU ACCIDENTALLY PRINT SCREEN

Let's assume you're working along and accidentally trip the Print Screen key (or press Shift-PrtScrn) and your printer is off-line. This causes your PC to freeze in its tracks. You don't want to print the screen image and you don't want to reboot. What can you do?

First of all, your PC is not really hung; it is only waiting until the printer has acknowledged receipt of the screen dump. If you can reach the back of your PC or the back of your printer, you could unplug the printer data cable briefly. That will signal to DOS that the printer is ready to receive data, and it will immediately output the screen dump information.

> **Warning:** If you are using a workstation on a Novell network and your local printer is off-line, be very careful before plugging in the printer data cable. It may cause your PC to really freeze. This will be the case if you are running NetWare 2.x and you have not redirected your local printer. It also might happen with other versions or situations, so before you try this the first time, be very careful to save all your work!

If you cannot unplug the printer data cable, you may have to put your printer back on-line and accept output of the screen dump—this time. Then, insert the number 1 into memory location 500h. This tells DOS that it is already doing a screen dump, and DOS will not respond to the Print Screen key in the future. If later you want to reenable screen dumps, just insert a 0 in this location. (Chapter 15 includes instructions for creating a small program that will turn off screen dumps and another one to enable them again. You can put the screen dump disabler in your AUTOEXEC.BAT and never have to worry about this problem again.)

YOU HAVE A POSTSCRIPT PRINTER AND WANT TO PRINT STDOUT TEXT

If you have a printer that only knows how to print from PostScript programs, and you want to print a simple ASCII text file, you have several options:

1. You can use the DOS Power Tools program POST to send the file to the printer. This program will wrap the text in a suitable PostScript program. You have many options for controlling how POST does its work. See Chapter 18, "Command Reference," for the details.
2. You can purchase PCPANEL from LaserTools. (This program is also bundled with many PostScript printers.) This is a TSR program that intercepts print jobs to determine which are PostScript, PCL, or ASCII jobs. Once it has made the determination, PCPANEL either wraps suitable PostScript code around the PCL or ASCII print jobs, or it sends the necessary command to the printer to switch on its PCL emulation, if it has such a mode.
3. When redirecting stdout you don't have to send it to PRN; send it to a file instead. Then fire up your word processor and load the resulting text file. Print it from within the word processor.

Printer Echoing

Normally, output from a DOS program goes to only one place at a time—the screen, a printer, or a device. There is an interesting exception to this rule. If you hold down the Ctrl key and press the Print Screen key, you will turn on *printer echoing.* Doing the same thing again turns printer echoing off. (On many PCs, Ctrl-P will do the same thing, a holdover from CP/M computers.)

Whenever printer echoing is in force, each character that DOS sends to the screen is also sent to the printer. This lets you capture a hard copy of everything that comes across your screen. (As noted earlier, if you have a character printer, turning on printer echoing also lets you use your PC as if it were a typewriter.)

Note: Printer echoing works only on printers able to output simple ASCII text (this includes all but pure PostScript printers), and then only for programs that simply output characters on the screen in an unformatted display. (That is to say, it works for programs that treat the display subsystem more or less like a typewriter or teletypewriter.)

Tip: A page printer doesn't print anything until it has a full page composed in its memory and has received a command directing it either to eject the page or force it to write on the next page. If you echo only a few lines to such a printer, you may be frustrated by not being able to see what it received. One solution is to get up, go to the printer, take it off-line, and push the Form Feed button on the front panel. A much more convenient solution, if you are at the DOS prompt, is to type

```
ECHO ^L
```

where `^L` indicates holding down the Ctrl key while tapping the L key. If printer echo is on, this will send the Ctrl-L character (which is the Form Feed character) to the screen and the printer. You will see `^L` on the next line and the page will be printed.

When printer echoing is turned off and you want to eject a page, type the command

```
ECHO ^L > PRN
```

and press Enter. This time you won't see the `^L` on your screen, but the page will print.

Printer Echoing Pitfalls

Convenient as it may be at times, printer echoing can cause difficulties. Perhaps the worst situation is when you have told DOS to wait for a specified amount of time for a response when it tries to output anything to the printer, and your printer is either on- or off-line. If, at this point, you inadvertently turn on printer echoing, the next character that goes to the screen seemingly will cause the PC to hang.

Tip: Use the MODE command to tell DOS how long to wait for your printer to respond. For a parallel printer, type

```
MODE LPTn: ,,r
```

or

```
MODE LPTn: RETRY=r
```

where *n* is 1, 2, or 3 to indicate which parallel port is being configured, and *r* is either B, E, N, P, or R. The default for MODE is N, which means do no retries. If you specify P, you are telling DOS to try forever, which is useful if your printer is not always able to respond before DOS gives up waiting. Don't use it, though, if you are using the MODE command over a network.

Actually, DOS is not hung, it is merely waiting as instructed for the printer to tell it that it has received its copy of that character. Because the printer is not paying any attention to the PC, it won't give that acknowledgment and DOS will patiently wait and wait and wait.... This problem is especially insidious because it will crop up when you are not thinking at all about your printer. If you were intending to print documents, your printer would be turned on and on-line. As it is, though, your mind is elsewhere, then this happens, and your PC is stuck.

The solution, once you realize what has happened, is to reenable your printer and immediately turn printer echoing off (assuming you don't really want a hard copy record of whatever is sent to the screen). Your printer will receive that first character and perhaps a few more. (To avoid wasting a page, you could try the trick mentioned earlier, but remember also to take heed of the warning there.)

To avoid this problem in the future, instruct DOS never to retry when the printer port indicates the printer is not ready. If you have a MODE LPT1:,,P command in your AUTOEXEC.BAT file, remove it, unless, of course, you know your printer won't work without it. That command takes up a segment of RAM for a resident part of MODE, and not issuing it will, therefore, save some memory as well as prevent the problem just discussed.

Printer Port Connection Issues

Hooking up a printer to a PC is very simple. Usually it's just a matter of plugging the printer's data cable into the port marked "Printer." There are, however, other circumstances that may complicate the PC-printer hookup.

For example, your PC may have more than one port labelled "Printer"; or, you may have more than one printer but don't have multiple printer ports. Another possibility is that you might have a printer that needs to be connected to a serial port instead of a parallel port. (Connecting a PC to a serial printer is the only hookup situation that can cause a problem, and that problem can be easily solved, as is explained later in this section.)

When preparing to attach your PC to a printer, the first thing to do is conduct an inventory of the ports on your PC and determine what devices you have that need to use them. Almost all PCs come with one parallel and one serial port; many have more, although it is unusual to find more than four serial ports on a PC or more than three parallel ports.

Most devices that attach to these ports can be plugged into only one or the other kind (serial or parallel). Printers that have both serial and parallel connections are exceptions.

Port Names and Addresses

Chances are, your printer probably can connect only to a parallel port. Even if you have a choice of serial or parallel, usually for reasons of speed and simplicity of setup, you should choose to use a parallel port. If you have only one, it is called LPT1; if you have two, they are LPT1 and LPT2; if you have all three, their names are (of course) LPT1, LPT2, and LPT3. Although it may seem superfluous to explain the parallel port designations, it is important for purposes of comparison: This arrangement is not used for serial ports, which may have a COM3 and COM4 ports, but no COM1 or COM2. (We will return to this point in a moment.)

Each parallel port is actually more than one port. That is, the hardware needed to communicate with a printer (or other peripheral device connected to a parallel port) requires the use of registers at several I/O port addresses. Reference sources commonly designate the standard PC parallel ports addresses to be I/O 3BCh, 378h, and 278h. These are the *base addresses.*

A standard PC parallel port takes up three addresses. When IBM brought out the PS/2 line, it upgraded the capabilities of the parallel port by adding the capability to transfer data in as well as out of the PC. Still, each parallel port used the same three port addresses per parallel port. Beginning with PS/2 models 57, 90, and 95, IBM introduced what it calls Type 3 parallel ports. These ports use only the standard three I/O addresses when they are in communication with an ordinary printer, but they also have an advanced DMA mode which enables them to be used to transfer data in or out very rapidly. In the DMA mode, a type 3 parallel port uses as many as six port addresses. When Intel introduced the 386SL chip set, it improved on the

Parallel Port Addresses

Standard port assignments	LPT1	LPT1-alt	LPT2	LPT3	LPT4
Printer data register	3BCh		378h	278h	
Printer status register	3BDh		379h	279h	
Printer control register	3BEh		37Ah	27Ah	
IBM type 3 parallel port					
Printer data register	3BCh	1278h	378h	278h	1378h
Printer status register	3BDh	1279h	379h	279h	1379h
Printer control register	3BEh	127Ah	37Ah	27Ah	137Ah
Interface control register		127Bh	37Bh	27Bh	137Bh
Interface status register		127Ch	37Ch	27Ch	137Ch
Reserved		127Dh	37Dh	27Dh	137Dh
Intel 386SL Fast Mode parallel port					
Printer data register			378h	278h	
Printer status register			379h	279h	
Printer control register			37Ah	27Ah	
Auto-address strobe			37Bh	27Bh	
Auto-data strobe registers			37Ch	27Ch	
			37Dh	27Dh	
			37Eh	27Eh	
			37Fh	27Fh	

Figure 10-2 I/O port addresses for parallel ports

standard parallel port in a different way. Intel's development, called Fast Mode, uses up to eight port addresses. Figure 10-2 shows all these possibilities.

The original PC parallel port came in two forms. One was a stand-alone plug-in card that carried only the one parallel port. The other was a parallel port included on a monochrome display adapter (MDA). The two forms made it possible to equip either a PC with just an MDA card and get both a display and a printer port, or a CGA display card (which had no room on the card for a printer port), plus a parallel port card if you needed color or graphic images.

The MDA parallel printer port has a base address of 3BCh. The original (stand-alone) parallel port card could be set to either of two base addresses: 378h or 278h. The use of different addresses on the two kinds of card meant that it was possible to install both cards and operate them without conflict. In fact, you can have one MDA card and two stand-alone parallel port cards in a PC without conflict, if you remember to set the port cards to different addresses. Advances in circuit design and manufacturing have made it possible to put many ports and other functions on a single plug-in card.

During the *power on self-test* (*POST*) that precedes booting in all PCs, a survey is done of the hardware devices attached to the PC. It stores a record of what it finds in the BIOS data area. At address 400h it puts the base

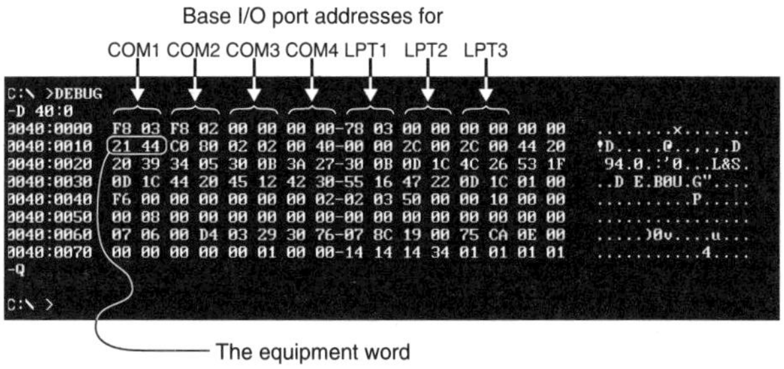

Figure 10-3 Using DEBUG to see what ports you have

addresses of the serial and parallel ports it finds. At address 410h it puts a word (called the *equipment word*) whose 16 bits encode a variety of things. The most significant 2 bits report the number of parallel ports (from 0 to 3); bits 9 through 11 report the number of serial ports (from 0 to 7).

You can look at these memory locations by using DEBUG. Figure 10-3 shows how this is done. After you enter DEBUG, type `D 40:0` at its hyphen prompt and press Enter. Next, type Q and press Enter to leave DEBUG (before you alter anything you shouldn't).

Remember that DEBUG displays bytes in a rather peculiar order. The first byte on a line is the least significant part of a word, but its nibbles are shown with the more significant one on the left. Thus, at addresses 400h and 401h is the 2-byte number 03F8h. This is the base address of the first serial port. At addresses 408h and 409h you will see the 2-byte number 0378h, which is the base address of the first parallel port on this computer. In this machine the POST found two serial ports and one parallel one, indicated by the number of base address values that are not 0. You also can verify that DOS has stored this in the equipment word at the start of the second line of the DEBUG display.

HOW DOS ASSIGNS PORT NUMBERS

Parallel Port Numbers The POST searches for parallel port adapters in this order: 3BCh, 378h, and 278h. At the first place it finds one, it puts the address of that port hardware into the first "slot" at address 408h. The next one it finds goes into the slot at 40Ah. If it finds a third one, it goes into the slot at 40Ch. So far, so good—nothing strange about this.

Serial Port Numbers The POST also searches for serial ports at addresses 3F8h and 2F8. (Most BIOS makers do not have their POST code search for more than two serial ports, even though there is a more or less standardized set of addresses for COM3 and COM4.) The addresses of the serial ports get stored in memory starting at address 400h.

Cause for Confusion When DOS comes on the scene, it assigns letters to drives and numbers to parallel and serial ports. Its naming strategy is inconsistent, however. Drives and logical volumes are assigned letters in the order that DOS finds them (except that C is always the first hard disk volume). Parallel ports are numbered from 1 to 3, according to the location of their base addresses in the table at 408h. Serial ports are different. The are numbered by DOS according to the base address they access, and according to the location of that address on the table at 400h.

When you view the DOS naming strategy as described above, at first it may seem that the serial ports cause the confusion. Actually, the parallel port names cause at least as many problems. If you have only an MDA card, you have only an LPT1, and it is at address 3BCh. If you have only a parallel port on a card other than an MDA, you still have LPT1, but its address is at 378h or 278h, depending on how you set the jumper on that card.

If you have more than one printer port, you must set them all to different base addresses. You can't choose those addresses with a monochrome card; on most plug-in port cards you usually can choose between 378h and 278h. (Rarely will you have the option to set a parallel port on a plug-in port card to 3BCh. And in very few circumstances will a parallel port on a video card—other than an IBM MDA card—be at 378h instead of 3BCh.)

These naming conventions can have some strange results. For example, suppose you have a VGA video card and just one parallel port, and it is at 378h. Then you add an MDA video card so you can have both a high-resolution color image from a CAD program on the VGA display, plus that program's menu of command choices on a monochrome text display. What you may find is that you can no longer print anything, because you now have two parallel ports. They are not conflicting—they are at different port addresses. The problem is with their names.

Most software comes preconfigured to print to LPT1, which is also what you use when you send something to the PRN device. Once you have an MDA card, its parallel port hardware is found before the port card's parallel port. Therefore, the printer port on the MDA card is now LPT1, which is where the data is going from your programs. But, unless you considered this in advance, you would not think to move the printer's data cable from the place it always worked before: connected to the port card whose parallel port is now LPT2 to DOS.

The solution could be to move the cable, but perhaps an easier solution is to move the names around. Since DOS associates the names of the devices with the port addresses it finds in the slots at 408h, 40Ah, and 40Ch, you can change the LPTn names of your parallel ports simply by shuffling around the entries in these three RAM locations. You can do that with DEBUG, or you can do it much more easily (and safely) by using the SWAP_LPT program from the DOS Power Tools disk. That program also shows you what arrangement you currently have; in addition, it can easily return things to the default arrangement without you having to remember what that is.

Preparing a Serial Port for Printing

Unlike parallel ports that are always ready to work, serial ports have to be prepared. A serial port changes each byte that it is sent into a stream of bits surrounded by some framing bits. (See Chapter 16 for a detailed discussion of what these framing bits are.) The speed at which the bits are sent, and the number of data, parity, and other framing bits, are called the *communications parameters* for that port. Configuring a serial port so that its communications parameters agree with those in the printer is necessary before you can work with a serial printer successfully.

Setting a serial port's communication parameters is another job for the MODE command. The syntax for this situation is

```
MODE COMn[:] [b[,p[,d[,s[,r]]]]]
```

or

```
MODE COMn[:] BAUD=b, PARITY=p, DATA=d, STOP=s, RETRY=r
```

where *n* is 1, 2, 3, or 4 to specify which serial port you are configuring. The baud rate, *b*, can be set to a number of different two-digit values each of which implies a speed, in bits per second, as shown in the following table:

Value for b	*Bits per second*
11	110
15	150
30	300
60	600
12	1200
24	2400
48	4800
96	9600
19	19,200

Not all PCs will support communication at 19,200 bits per second. The PARITY setting *p* can be M, S, E, O, or N. These stand for Mark, Space, Even, Odd, and None. The default for parity is Even, but most printers want it to be set to None, especially if you are sending 8 data bits per character. The number of data bits *d* tells how many actual bits of data will be sent in one character frame. If you want to send all possible byte values, this should be set to 8; its default value is 7. Normally, the number of stop bits should be set to 1, normally, which is its default. The retry setting is the same as that for the MODE command used to configure a parallel port. To protect yourself against getting hung if you accidentally invoke printer echoing when the printer is turned off or off-line, leave this parameter off; its default value is None, which is what you want.

After you have properly configured the serial port so it can exchange bytes with the printer successfully, you have to direct the PC to send its output there. Some application programs give you the option of printing to COMn; most do not. If you want all printed output from every application or utility program to go to a printer on a serial port, use yet another of the MODE command's many functions. The syntax for this is

```
MODE LPTn[:]=COMx[:]
```

where *x* specifies the serial port to which you wish to send printed output for LPTx.

Combining the two previous steps into one example for a printer connected to COM1, and with that printer configured to receive data at 9600 bits per second, with 8 data bits per character and no parity, you would issue these commands:

```
MODE COM1,96,N,8,1
MODE LPT1=COM2
```

If you find that your printer frequently doesn't respond quickly enough (you keep getting the `Write fault error writing device LPT1`), you may have to add `,B` to the end of the first MODE command. (The retry value `B` is the same as `P`, but Microsoft seems to want us to stop using `P`.) Figure 10-4 shows what this looks like on screen.

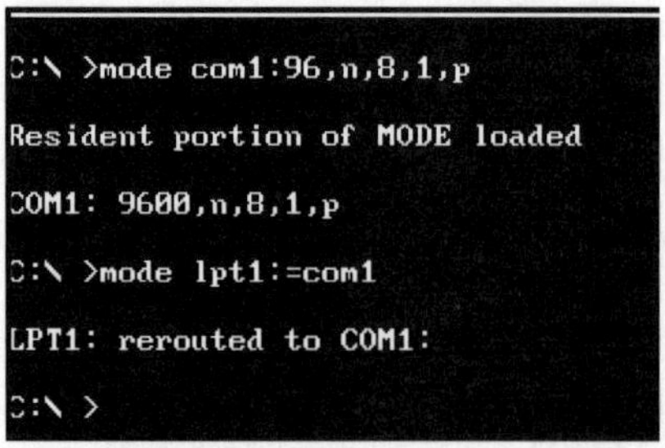
C:\ >mode com1:96,n,8,1,p
Resident portion of MODE loaded
COM1: 9600,n,8,1,p
C:\ >mode lpt1:=com1
LPT1: rerouted to COM1:
C:\ >

Figure 10-4 Redirecting a printer device to a serial port

To stop printer redirection, issue the command

```
MODE LPT1
```

which, in this case, assumes that you want to stop data headed for LPT1 from being redirected.

> ***Note:*** The use of the term redirection in this section is different from that defined with greater than and less than symbols (> and <) or the pipe operator (|) discussed earlier in this chapter and in Chapter 8. This section describes redirection that refers to sending data nominally destined for one device to a different device. The earlier use described the process that sends output normally headed for the screen to a different device or to a file, and is the result of a single DOS command. The printer to serial port redirection continues as long as you do not turn it or reboot your PC.

Cable Issues

Printers can't work without a data cable to bring them bytes of information to print. Parallel cables for PC printers are fairly well standardized; serial cables are not. Figure 10-5 shows the wiring of a cable from a standard PC parallel port to a standard printer Centronics connector.

All the ground pins on Centronics connector (pins 19-31 and 33-36) shown on the right side of this figure should be connected together and to ground. When you buy a commercial cable for this purpose, many of them will not be connected to anything. Depending on the printer, that may not matter, or it may prevent the printer from working properly.

Officially, parallel cables are not supposed to be any longer than about 15 meters (roughly 50 feet). If you use shielded cables and ground them carefully, you may get away with cables that are several times this long. (If, as you should, you have both the printer and the PC cases grounded to the same electrical ground, then don't connect the shield on the cable to the printer's case, but to the PC's case, instead.) Usually, though, you will have difficulty getting printers to work properly over any parallel cables that are more than about 20 feet long. Good shielding and grounding helps, but it can't overcome a poorly designed printer interface at either end of the cable.

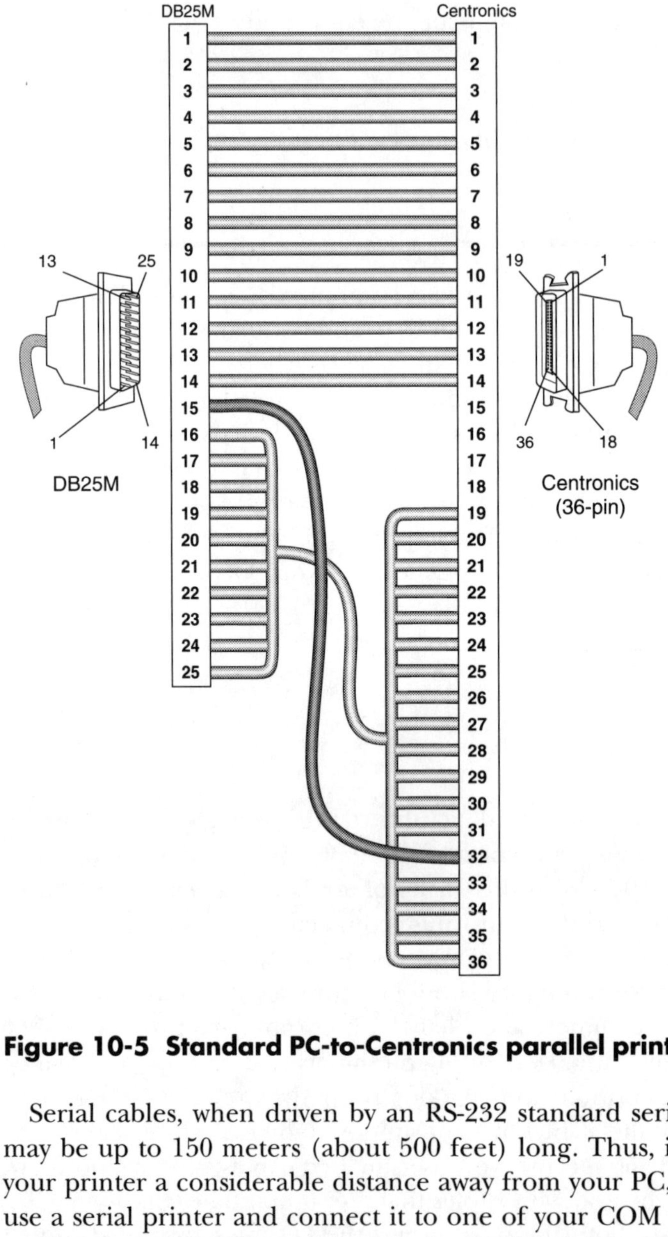

Figure 10-5 Standard PC-to-Centronics parallel printer cable

Serial cables, when driven by an RS-232 standard serial port, supposedly may be up to 150 meters (about 500 feet) long. Thus, if you have to place your printer a considerable distance away from your PC, you may choose to use a serial printer and connect it to one of your COM ports. Alternatively, you can buy a pair of long line drivers, which are devices that receive parallel data on one side, turn it into serial data and pump it at high speed across a very long cable, then reconvert it to a parallel signal at the other end. These devices let you take advantage of the simple parallel connection without suffering either the short cable limitation or the speed limitations mentioned above.

Speed Issues

Printer speeds vary widely. Daisywheel printers reach their maximum speed over a serial link operating at 300 baud. Most laser printers are limited by the speed at which you deliver data to them. Impact dot-matrix printers typically fall somewhere in between.

Parallel port connections usually output data much faster than serial connections partly because parallel ports use eight wires to carry data in parallel, in contrast to serial ports, which send the data one bit at a time and wrap each 8 bits in a frame with at least a couple of other bits.

If you want to use a long cable to connect your printer to your PC, it stands to reason that you will be more successful if you don't ask too much of the electronics at either end. Reducing the speed of transmission is one way to make it easy on those circuits. Generally, to operate a serial printer at 19,200 baud, it is best to keep the cable as short as you can. But, if you are willing to tolerate slower print times, you can reduce the baud rate and use much longer cables, up to the 150-meter limit.

PRINTING GRAPHICS

Graphics printing is more time-consuming because it takes longer to send the 8 million or so bytes of data for a full-page graphic image to the printer. Over a serial link, with no data compression, and at the maximum serial port speed of 19,200 bps, that could take over an hour! Therefore, if you have a printer that outputs pages as large bit maps, you definitely will want to use a parallel port connection, a short cable, and a good print spooler. (More on print spoolers in a moment.)

Some printers may be slow to output a complex page of graphics, not because it takes so long to send them the information, but because they must do a lot of calculating with that information before they are ready to print the page. PostScript printers are notorious for this. Therefore, if you often print complex PostScript graphics, you can get away with a relatively slow serial connection and the rate at which pages are printed will not be affected.

Print Spooling

If you print large documents or complex graphics you may find that you often must wait a long time for your PC to send the job to the printer. This may not be something you just have to grin and bear. There are some things you can do to speed up this process, and the key is a good print spooling strategy.

Print spooling is a process that accumulates files to be printed in a print queue, and then doles out those files one at a time to the printer. And while the spooler is regulating the information to the printer, you can be working on your next project at the same time.

Variations on a Theme

There are three methods of print spooling. Figure 10-6(a) shows these methods preceded by the process of data flowing directly from the application to the printer in the absence of spooling. Figure 10-6(b) illustrates the data flowing from the application to a region of extended memory, typical of a good in-RAM print spooler. In (c) the data flows from the application to the hard disk, then later on flows on to the printer. In (d) the data flows out of the PC just as in (a), but it then is stored temporarily in an external print spooling box before it goes on to the printer.

Each of these methods has its advantages and drawbacks. Spooling output to a buffer in RAM works very well, but it can require the commitment of a lot of RAM to this purpose. One of the best programs for creating an in-RAM print spooler is PC-Kwik's Print Spooler, which comes in the PCKwik Power Pak. The advantage this spooler has over most others is that it will use only RAM for print spooling when it needs to. When you are not printing or don't have a lot of output waiting to go to the printer, the SuperPCKwik disk cache program can use that RAM to speed up accesses to your disk. But when you need the cache for a large print job, SuperPCKwik lends the Print Spooler program as much RAM as it needs.

Spooling print jobs to disk takes a little longer than sending them to a RAM buffer, but because a disk can receive data so much faster than even the fastest printers, spooling print jobs to the disk is very effective. A good example of this genre is the Print Cache (PCACHE) program from LaserTools. You can set up PCACHE so that its buffer space is in extended memory (refer to the diagram in Figure 10-5(b)), expanded memory (a good idea only if you have a hardware EMS card plugged into your PC), or to disk. You must set aside the amount of cache space you want PCACHE to use. Most people have more disk space than RAM can spare, therefore it is recommended that if you choose PCACHE, put its cache on your disk drive.

Also, there are external print cache boxes, which require an extra expenditure, and the RAM they contain cannot be used for any other purpose than spooling print jobs. One real advantage to an external print spooler is that if your PC hangs, an external print spooler will keep on going; either of the internal schemes would fail at that point. Also, you don't have to load yet another TSR program and take up more of that precious first megabyte of memory for the print spooler's program code.

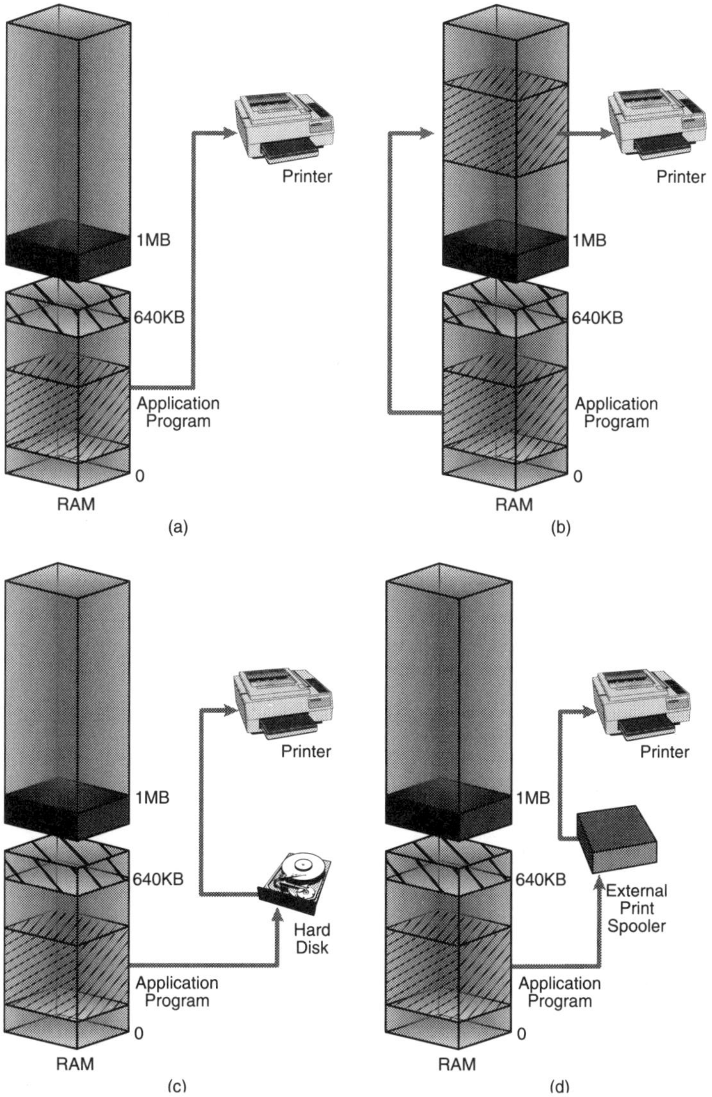

Figure 10-6 Print spooling options

DOS and Windows Print Spoolers

DOS comes with a print spooler of its own. The PRINT command is a TSR program that will manage background printing of files from the disk to the printer. All you have to do is type `PRINT` *`filename`* and DOS will send that file's contents to the printer a little at a time, at which point you may continue with other work on your PC.

The full syntax of the PRINT command is:

```
PRINT [options] [files] [flags]
```

If you specify one or more file names, PRINT will print those files one after another. By specifying the options, you can control how PRINT works and the device to which it will send its output. The flags let you add or remove files from the queue. You direct PRINT where to send its output with the `/D:device` option. Valid names for the device are LPT1, LPT2, LPT3, COM1, COM2, COM3, or COM4. (PRN is a synonym for LPT1.)

The performance options work only the first time you issue the PRINT command. Thereafter, since PRINT is already resident (and has its performance characteristics set), it will ignore any of these options. To change how PRINT does its job, you must unload and reload it. There is no option to unload PRINT from its own command line, so you must either reboot your PC or else use the DOS Power Tools programs MARK and RELEASE (or some equivalent TSR management program).

The four parameters under your control are the buffer size, the maximum time PRINT will wait for the printer to become available, the number of eighteenths of a second PRINT is given to send each character to the printer, the number of eighteenths of a second PRINT is allowed to have control of the PC before it must give it back to the foreground program, and the maximum number of files that can be in the print queue at one time.

The buffer size is set with a `/B:size` command line parameter; the default is 512 bytes (which is the legal minimum value); the maximum size is 16KB. The times are all specified in *clock ticks* which, in a PC, means the interval between events that occur about 18.3 times per second. The maximum time to wait for the printer to be available is set by the `/U:ticks1` parameter; the default value for `ticks1` is 1. The time allowed for printing one character is set by `/M:ticks2`, and the default value is 2. The amount of time given to the PRINT command is set by `/S:ticks3`, which defaults to 8. All of these tick values must be in the range from 1 to 255. You can specify a maximum queue size, `/Q:qsize`, as anything from 4 to 32 files; the default is 10.

The flags with which you manage the queue are `/T`, `/C`, and `/P`. The `/T` switch deletes all files in the queue. You can delete just one or a few files from the queue by specifying their file names and the `/C` switch. Put the switch either before the names of all the files you wish to delete or after the first of them. To add files to the queue, use the `/P` switch. Like the `/C` switch, this acts on the file named just before it and all those named after it, up to the one preceding the next switch of the opposite kind.

Invoking PRINT all by itself (no parameters on the command line) makes it become resident with its default options set, or, if it already is resident, report on which files are in the queue.

Warning: As you know, legal DOS file specifications may be 78 characters long: two characters for a drive letter and the colon, 64 for a path, plus 12 for the file name, extension, and the period that goes between them. The maximum length of a file specification to the PRINT command, however, is only 64 characters. Therefore, don't try to PRINT files from very deep subdirectories. Or, if you must, change to that directory first. Then you can simply give the file name without the path for each file you wish to print.

To use the PRINT program as a print spooler, you must first print your application's output as a file to the disk, then at the DOS prompt type

```
PRINT filename
```

If this is the first time you have invoked the PRINT command since you rebooted, this will make its resident portion load with the default settings for all the options. To use a different set all the time, insert a line to your AUTOEXEC.BAT file that loads PRINT with those values and that does not specify a file name. Then, when you issue the PRINT command later, you will get the performance you want. For example, to insert a command to AUTOEXEC.BAT that allots space for 25 file names in the print queue, type

```
PRINT /Q:25
```

The Windows Print Manager is another Microsoft print spooler. It takes output from Windows applications and from DOS programs running in a DOS window within Windows. It puts the data into RAM, which Windows may then temporarily swap to the disk if it needs the RAM for something else. Print Manager allows you more control over the queue than is possible with PRINT, including the ability to reorder files that are waiting to begin printing.

The major drawback to the Windows Print Manager is that you have to wait until the entire print job has been received by Print Manager before it will begin to send anything to the printer. Most commercial alternatives (including PCACHE) will begin printing as soon as the cache begins to receive data. For large print jobs that require extensive calculations to generate, the difference can be quite significant.

Recommendations

Using PCACHE to spool print jobs to a disk file provides the ideal balance between speed and resource utilization. If you are short of disk space, but have a lot of RAM to spare, we recommend that you install the PCKwik Power Pak and use its print spooler.

Printer Sharing Devices and Strategies

Some people have more printers than printer ports and need a way to share a port among two or more printers. Still others have several PCs, but not enough printers and want a way to share a printer among several ports. Both of these situations can be handled in a number of ways.

Simple Switches

The simplest solution, and one that is altogether appropriate if you don't need to do this very often, is to disconnect the data cables between printers and PCs and plug them in again in a different setup. This same procedure can be accomplished electrically through the use of a mechanically operated switch. Small A-B switch boxes are commonly used to alternate between two printers attached to a single PC. More complex switch boxes can be used to switch one printer among several PCs.

> **Warning:** Although these switches work, they can cause serious problems. Some printer interface circuits are vulnerable to transient electrical signals of just the sort that are generated when you move one of these switches from one position to another. If you are going to use a mechanical switch, try to avoid switching when data is being sent from your PC. This will not protect your printer totally, but it helps.

Electronic Switches

A better approach, at a somewhat higher cost, is an electronic switch box. A box of this kind will have the same connectors as a simpler mechanical switch box, but internally it will be built quite differently. The path followed by the data through such a switch is controlled by transistors, much as is the case for data flowing through various paths within the many integrated circuit chips in your PC.

Since the switching happens at a microcircuit level, the transients can be limited to a safe value. Thus the first benefit of an electronic switch is safety for the printers and PCs attached to it. (To be sure you get that safety, you must insure that all the PCs and printers connected to the switch box share a common ground connection. Don't depend on grounding them through the switch box; use three-wire plugs on the power cords and be sure they are plugged into three-wire outlets. Also, use good surge protection on your electrical line.)

A second benefit of some electronic switches is their ability to be switched remotely. You may be able to run a program in one of the attached PCs that will let you send signals to the switch and force it to the switch setting you desire.

Others are automatic switches. These scan the several inputs looking for data. Once some data comes in one input they will lock onto it and send only data from that source through to the output. This continues until that source of data is idle more than some preset time. At that moment the switch will resume scanning.

A fancier version of this is an auto-switching print buffer box. This box has RAM in it and can hold several complete large print jobs inside itself. Any data coming in from any of the inputs will be stored inside. The first input to begin sending will have its data routed out the far side to the printer beginning immediately. Any data that arrive faster than the printer can accept them get put into the internal RAM in the switch box. Any time data arrives on another input while the first one's job is still being printed, those data are put into RAM and marked for later printing.

With either of these automatic switches, you no longer have to go turn a switch or send a command to the switch. All print jobs will eventually get printed, and none gets its output mixed in with part of another print job. The only functional difference between the two switches is that in the one case, if you try to send data while the printer is busy with some other PC's print job, your PC will be told the printer is unavailable. You will be able to send data any time by using an automatic printer switch and buffer. The box will hold it all until the printer is ready to receive it.

Warning: If you use one of these switches and you are printing from an application that issues output in spurts, you may be in for a nasty surprise. The first time your job starts printing, then pauses while your PC continues computing the output, if another PC attached to the switch starts sending data, your job will be declared over, the page ejected, and the second PC's job printed. The only way to prevent this from happening with this sort of automatic switch is to print your output to a file on your disk. Then send it all as a unit to the printer.

Network Connection Modules

Some network printers are attached to one of the workstations that is on the network. Other network printers are attached to the network directly. A directly attached network printer must have a network interface card within it and enough "smarts" to be able to notice not only which packets of data are addressed to it, but also where each one came from. Functionally, they act just like the automatic electronic switch boxes, only they have a single input—from the network. Indeed, from the network's perspective, the interface box is a workstation—it just doesn't have any keyboard, monitor, or disk drives.

DOS Commands Relating to Printing

The principal DOS commands that are useful in printing are PRINT, MODE, and GRAPHICS. We have discussed each of them extensively in this chapter. We also discussed one use for DEBUG. Refer to Chapter 15 for more on that program, and to the Command Reference for more details on all the DOS 6 commands.

DOS Power Tools Programs Relating to Printing

Dot matrix printer owners should check out IMAGPRNT (IT.EXE), LQCHAR, and PRTPLUS (P64.EXE). A variety of useful tools for HP LaserJets and compatibles can be found in FONTLODR, JetPilot (JP.COM), LJLAND, and LM. PostScript printer owners will find POST a real boon to getting DOS documents to print on a PostScript-compatible output device.

PART Two

Advanced Techniques and Cautions

C H A P T E R

11

◆ ◆ ◆ ◆ ◆

Flexible Configurations

The optimum configuration for each of the various tasks you perform on your PC may be different. In this chapter you will learn how to create flexible configurations several different ways. You'll also learn how to recover when you try something that doesn't work.

Optional Actions at Boot Time

Sometimes all you need is a way to interact with your PC as it boots up: suppressing the loading of a device driver or choosing which of several optional paths to follow through your AUTOEXEC.BAT file, for example. In previous versions of DOS this was not easy to accomplish. DOS 6, fortunately, includes three different tools each of which help to expedite this procedure.

Clean Booting with the F8 key

A major advance in DOS 6 is the Clean Boot concept. Now you can indicate to IO.SYS at the outset that you want to have a say before it does anything with any line in CONFIG.SYS and before COMMAND.COM runs the AUTOEXEC.BAT file.

DOS 6 has a new message when you first boot up: `Starting MS-DOS...` It will linger on your screen for several seconds before anything happens. As soon as you see this message, press F8. Another message will appear:

```
MS-DOS will prompt you to confirm each CONFIG.SYS command
```

followed immediately by your first choice about how it will deal with your CONFIG.SYS file.

If you specified DOS=HIGH and/or DOS=UMB anywhere in your CONFIG.SYS file, IO.SYS will first ask you whether or not it is to follow those directives. Like all the questions that follow, this must be answered either with a press of the `Y` or `N` key. All other responses are ignored, including Ctrl-Break.

IO.SYS will then go through your CONFIG.SYS file asking you about each line as it encounters it. If the line specifies the loading of a device driver and you press the `Y` key, you will see the messages from that driver as it loads. The processing of any INSTALL statements and the SHELL statement, if you have one, are deferred until after all other lines in your CONFIG.SYS file have been processed.

Next comes the SHELL statement, and then any INSTALL statements. Finally, you choose whether the command interpreter is to process your AUTOEXEC.BAT file. You may only choose to do it all or none of it at this point. (Of course, you can break out of any batch file by pressing Ctrl-Break at the right moment. You also could have built in user interactions at critical points by using the new CHOICE command, as we will explain in a moment.)

This process can be a marvelous device for troubleshooting a newly modified CONFIG.SYS file. We will discuss how to use it for that purpose in the section "Diagnosing Bootup Problems" later in this chapter. This new use of the F8 key applies only during the processing of the CONFIG.SYS file (and the start of processing the AUTOEXEC.BAT file). Thereafter, you may redefine it or use it in another way.

User Options in CONFIG.SYS

If you know your CONFIG.SYS file consists of lines you want executed every time, except for one or two that you would sometimes like to skip, DOS 6 enables you to set this up. All of the lines in a CONFIG.SYS file are of the form

```
ACTION=DETAILS
```

where ACTION can be BREAK, BUFFERS, COUNTRY, DEVICE, DEVICEHIGH, DOS, DRIVPARM, FILES, FCBS, INSTALL, LASTDRIVE, SHELL, STACKS, or SWITCHES. (These are almost all the active lines. The only other one is SET, which follows a slightly different syntax—the same one used in batch files and at the DOS prompt. You also can have remark lines starting with REM, and a space, followed by any text you like.)

You can direct IO.SYS to prompt you for a response before it acts on any of the `ACTION=DETAILS` lines simply by preceding the equal sign with a question mark. Unfortunately, using this feature also implies relinquishing another feature of CONFIG.SYS files that many users never knew existed—the capability to improve the "format" of these files.

You can enhance substantially the readability of CONFIG.SYS files by inserting "white space." Normally, IO.SYS ignores any spaces you add before or after the equal sign. Thus, you can have your CONFIG.SYS file read like this:

```
FILES=80
BUFFERS=30
BREAK=ON
STACKS= 9,256
LASTDRIVE=Z
DOS=HIGH,UMB
DEVICE=c:\dos\HIMEM.SYS
DEVICE=c:\dos\EMM386.EXE RAM 3072 FRAME=D400 I=E400-F7FF
X=A000-D1FF
DEVICEHIGH=c:\setup\STACKER.COM /NB /EMS @ @ @ @
DEVICEHIGH=c:\setup\drivers\ASPI2DOS.SYS /Z /Y- /P140
DEVICEHIGH=c:\setup\drivers\CUNI_ASP.SYS /ID:4 /N:1 /D:MSCD001
DEVICEHIGH=c:\uv\ANSI-UV.SYS
DEVICE=c:\setup\drivers\MVSOUND.SYS D:3 Q:10 T:1 V:65
DEVICE=c:\wfwg\PROTMAN.DOS /I:c:\wfwg
DEVICE=c:\wfwg\WORKGRP.SYS
DEVICE=c:\wfwg\EXP16.DOS
INSTALL=c:\dos\SHARE.EXE /f:4096
INSTALL=c:\mouse\ballpnt\MOUSE.COM
SHELL=c:\dos\COMMAND.COM c:\dos /p /e:624
```

or like this:

```
FILES       =    80
BUFFERS     =    30
BREAK       =    ON
STACKS      = 9,256
LASTDRIVE   =     Z
DOS         = HIGH,UMB
DEVICE      = c:\dos\HIMEM.SYS
DEVICE      = c:\dos\EMM386.EXE RAM 3072 FRAME=D400 I=E400-F7FF
X=A000-D1FF
DEVICEHIGH = c:\setup\STACKER.COM /NB /EMS @ @ @ @
```

```
DEVICEHIGH = c:\setup\drivers\ASPI2DOS.SYS /Z /Y- /P140
DEVICEHIGH = c:\setup\drivers\CUNI_ASP.SYS /ID:4 /N:1 /D:MSCD001
DEVICEHIGH = c:\uv\ANSI-UV.SYS
DEVICE      = c:\setup\drivers\MVSOUND.SYS D:3 Q:10 T:1 V:65
DEVICE      = c:\wfwg\PROTMAN.DOS /I:c:\wfwg
DEVICE      = c:\wfwg\WORKGRP.SYS
DEVICE      = c:\wfwg\EXP16.DOS
INSTALL     = c:\dos\SHARE.EXE /f:4096
INSTALL     = c:\mouse\ballpnt\MOUSE.COM
SHELL       = c:\dos\COMMAND.COM c:\dos /p /e:624
```

You also can add blank lines or indent some of the lines if you have a block of actions that you want to stand out visually. Any CONFIG.SYS file is, essentially, a program, and ideas about formatting a program listing to make it easy to read are both common sense and good programming practice.

MS-DOS 6, however, makes you choose between choosing the look of a CONFIG.SYS file and the new feature that enables you to make some lines optional at boot time. As stated, any of the lines in your CONFIG.SYS file can be made optional by preceding the equal sign with a question mark. Unfortunately, you must not have any spaces between the question mark and the end of the ACTION name. If you follow these directions in some, but not all, of the lines in your CONFIG.SYS file, when you next boot your PC, you will be prompted whether to execute each of the lines with question marks, but not any of the others. This is done without your having to press any special key (like the F8 key) at a special moment (during the `Starting MS-DOS...` message) first.

You also cannot use the question mark if you are using the DEVICEHIGH statement with its optional parameters between the word DEVICEHIGH and the equal sign. Other than that limitation, though, you can make any line prompt the user at boot time whether or not it is to be executed. (Note that you may have white space *after* the equal sign, but not up to that point on the line.)

The SET command is another special case. The syntax of this command is a bit different from the rest of the active lines in a CONFIG.SYS file. It is

```
SET name=definition
```

where the name will be treated as if it is all uppercase letters, but the definition will not. This command is special in two respects, both having to do with spaces. Unlike all the other CONFIG.SYS commands, the SET command does not ignore spaces on either side of the equal sign. The lines

```
SET ADAM=EVE
```

and

```
SET ADAM = eve
```

are treated as totally separate definitions. The four-character name "ADAM" is equated to "EVE", and the five-character name "ADAM " is equated to " eve"—both spaces and case matter to the right of the equal sign.

The reason you cannot use the ?= with a SET command is the same as the reason it won't work with DEVICEHIGH with its optional parameters. In both cases there must be a space after the ACTION word, and the ?= special action cannot deal with that space.

Normally, you will use the ?= construction when you are adding some new line to your CONFIG.SYS file and you are not sure you got its syntax just right. If you answer `Y` and all goes well, you probably did just fine. Remove the question mark (and add any white space you wish) and the line will be a permanent part of your CONFIG.SYS file.

If your PC bombs when you attempt to boot with that line being executed, just reboot and say `N` when you are prompted. That will let you boot without that one line, but with all the rest. Now you can edit that line or do anything else you were able to do before. There is no need to use a special DOS boot floppy diskette to avoid having your PC crash, and no need, therefore, to have that boot diskette load all that might be necessary to access a network or whatever else you are used to doing.

Multiple PC Personalities

You don't have to use these new features in DOS 6 to give a PC multiple personalities. In this section we will explain several popular power user schemes.

Multiple Matched Sets of Startup Files

The simplest way to change your PC's personality is to alter its startup files, CONFIG.SYS and AUTOEXEC.BAT. The lowest-tech route is to have a number of alternate boot floppies, each with a specific pair of matched CONFIG.SYS and AUTOEXEC.BAT files. A better approach, though, is to create a number of alternate forms of each and store them under evocative names in a subdirectory called, perhaps, C:\CONFIGUR. You might have files called CF-BARE and AE-BARE that are bare bones CONFIG.SYS and AUTOEXEC.BAT files, respectively. CF-WIN and AE-WIN could be the pair to use when you plan to run Windows. CF-NET and AE-NET might be for logging onto your network, but not running Windows. CF-MAX and AE-MAX might be for logging onto the network, running Windows, and also supporting a CD-ROM drive and a sound card.

The next step is to create several batch files and call them SET-BARE.BAT, SET-WIN.BAT, SET-NET.BAT, and SET-MAX.BAT. Each of them would look similar. For example, here is what the first pair might look like:

```
C:
CD \
COPY CONFIGUR\CF-BARE CONFIG.SYS
COPY CONFIGUR\AE-BARE AUTOEXEC.BAT
CFG Warmboot
```

The first line makes sure the C drive is your DOS default drive. The next line puts you in the root directory. The next two lines copy the designated matched pair of startup files to the root directory and gives them their proper names. The last line invokes one of the DOS Power Tool programs with a command line parameter that causes it to do, essentially, "the three finger salute" (pressing Ctrl-Alt-Del).

A variation on this scheme is to build a batch file to invoke a program that is a memory hog, like Ventura Publisher for the GEM interface, but instead of directing the batch file to actually invoke the program, it will save the current startup files, load a new set, and reboot. The new set of startup files will run the memory-hungry application in an environment that has been stripped of all possible device drivers, TSR programs, and other memory users that can be dispensed with for the duration. Once you exit the application, the AUTOEXEC.BAT file will go on to restore the original set of startup files and reboot your PC again. Figure 11-1 shows how such a set of files might look.

Third-Party DOS Boot Managers

For many years there have been a variety of third-party "DOS boot manager" programs available both as shareware and as shrink-wrapped commercial software. Some of these do nothing more than automate the process just described. Others instruct you to build one monster pair of CONFIG.SYS and AUTOEXEC.BAT files and then select which subset you wish to use at boot time.

The DOS Power Tools program CFG is a bit different. It allows you to add a variety of functions to your CONFIG.SYS and AUTOEXEC.BAT files, some of which duplicate features added to DOS 6; much of it does not. (See Chapter 18 for details on the CFG program.)

VP.BAT

```
@echo off
echo.
echo               VP.BAT  --  Setup and run Ventura Publisher
echo.
echo        First we will save the old CONFIG.SYS and AUTOEXEC.BAT files,
echo        then copy new ones from C:\CONFIGUR directory and reboot.
echo.
c:
cd \
if exist cf.old ECHO *** Warning:  CF.OLD is about to be deleted. ****
if exist cf.old PAUSE
if exist cf.old DEL cf.old
if exist cf.sav REN cf.sav cf.old
REN config.sys cf.sav
COPY c:\configur\cf-vp config.sys
if exist ae.old ECHO *** Warning:  AE.OLD is about to be deleted. ****
if exist ae.old PAUSE
if exist ae.old DEL ae.old
if exist ae.sav REN ae.sav ae.old
REN autoexec.bat ae.sav
COPY  c:\configur\ae-vp autoexec.bat
reboot
```

CF-VP

```
FILES     = 20
BUFFERS   = 16
BREAK     = ON
```

AE-VP

```
@echo off
echo           AE-VP  --  Special AUTOEXEC.BAT file for Ventura Publisher
echo.
echo                                Invoking programs
echo.
PATH C:\DOS;C:\UT\MAIN;C:\SETUP
PROMPT $P $G
c:\mouse\MOUSE
D:
CD \VENTURA
DRVRMRGR VP %1 /S=SDFAST86.VGA /M=32 /X=D: /A=10
echo.
c:\ut\nor\beep /F440 /D2 /R3
echo              You have 5 seconds to decide:
c:\ut\main\TIMER-VP L 5
if errorlevel 50 goto stayhere
if errorlevel 25 goto goback
if errorlevel 10 goto goback
:goback
c:\setup\GOBACK
:stayhere
```

Figure 11-1 Altering CONFIG.SYS and AUTOEXEC.BAT

Third-Party Managers vs. the DOS 6 Approach

In most of the third-party multiple configuration products, the essential strategy is very similar to the batch file setup described in the previous section. You select a configuration, the appropriate set of CONFIG.SYS and AUTOEXEC.BAT commands are put in place, and your system reboots.

A few of them use a different approach. One in particular merits some attention. BOOT.SYS by Hans Salvisberg takes control of your PC through a DEVICE line. It then processes a series of menus you have written and put in your CONFIG.SYS file just after the DEVICE line that loads BOOT.SYS. These menus are presented on screen and your inputs are recorded. Eventually, BOOT.SYS finishes processing its menus and lets IO.SYS resume processing the CONFIG.SYS file, including the portion that it has edited to conform to your menu choices.

BOOT.SYS is the most like the new DOS 6 CONFIG.SYS menu approach, but it misses out on one point. Starting with DOS 5 the DOS command was included for CONFIG.SYS files. (The line `DOS=HIGH,UMB` is a typical example of this command.) This line gets processed by IO.SYS before any of the DEVICE lines, which means that BOOT.SYS cannot control what that line says.

Boot Commander, from V Communications, attempted to deal with the fact that DOS 5 and later read and act on the DOS line before any other in the CONFIG.SYS file. It was perhaps the nicest and safest way to develop multiple configurations prior to DOS 6 (and if you want something more than the multiple matched set of batch files approach described above).

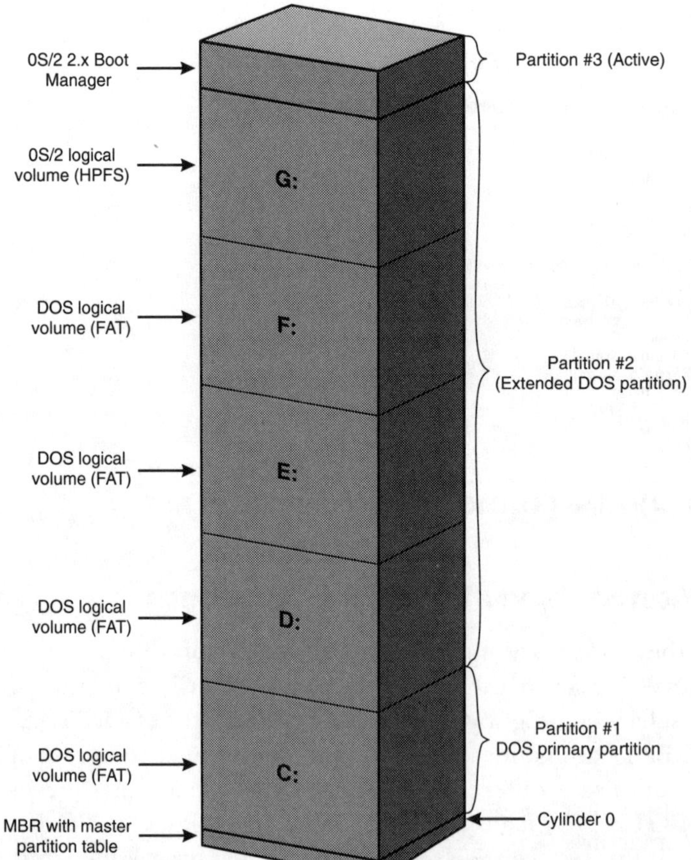

Figure 11-2 The OS/2 Boot Manager divides a hard disk for OS/2 and DOS.

If you have OS/2 installed on your computer in addition to DOS, you probably installed either the *dual boot* or *boot manager* mechanism for switching between the two operating systems.

The OS/2 dual boot closely mimics the matched startup files approach to varying a DOS configuration. The difference is that the OS/2 dual boot approach replaces not only the startup files, but also the hidden system files and boot record. Each time you boot you will get whichever operating system you had the last time. A DOS batch file and an OS/2 CMD file carry you from one operating system to the other and back again.

The OS/2 boot manager approach is really different. To use this strategy you must repartition your disk and designate a 1MB partition for the boot manager's exclusive use with the OS/2 FDISK program.

The OS/2 boot manager's partition becomes the active one and it maintains a record of which other partitions are "startable." As far as FDISK is concerned, those other partitions are not active; the OS/2 boot manager knows better. When you boot a computer with the OS/2 boot manager installed, you get a menu like the CONFIG.SYS menus available in DOS 6. After a time limit (if you have defined one), it will default to booting from one of your startable partitions; or you can choose one, and it will boot from that.

The OS/2 boot manager also makes it possible to load the OS/2 operating system files in any logical volume. Unlike the DOS restriction to the A or C drives, OS/2 can be installed wherever you indicate, and once installed there, it will boot from that location. Figure 11-2 shows the logical volumes on one system, which has both OS/2 and DOS plus OS/2's boot manager.

More Multiple Personalities

Boot managers are not the only way to develop multiple personalities for your PC. Prior to DOS 6, menus in the AUTOEXEC.BAT file were used extensively. They range from simple, home-brew concoctions to high-powered shareware programs like CONED. DOS 6 provides the option to easily build menus in the CONFIG.SYS file using nothing more than what comes with DOS.

Menus in AUTOEXEC.BAT

Many power users have created batch file menus in the AUTOEXEC.BAT files on their machines and those of their friends. The simplest of these merely combine a simple text file and several small batch files. To see how simple this can be, consider the following example: Suppose you create a text file called MENU.TXT that contains these lines:

```
           MY MENU
Enter your choice from among the following:
    1. Run BASIC interpreter
    2. Run checkbook program
    3. Run word processor
```

and you also create three batch files called 1.BAT, 2.BAT, and 3.BAT. Each of these batch files does one of the things specified on the menu, and each one ends by returning you to the MENU directory, clearing the screen, and redisplaying the MENU.TXT file. Here is how that might be done for 1.BAT:

```
@ECHO OFF
REM     This is 1.BAT
D:
CD \BASIC
QBASIC
C:
CD \MENU
CLS
TYPE MENU.TXT
```

This assumes that you have a directory called BASIC on your D drive and that you want to run QBASIC from within that directory. The other two batch files would be similar, differing only in the details of how they invoke the corresponding applications.

To start the whole process, the AUTOEXEC.BAT file on this PC should end with the lines:

```
C:
CD \MENU
CLS
TYPE MENU.TXT
```

This sort of menu approach works, but it is not very sophisticated. It offers no security at all, since the user is actually typing at a DOS prompt when he or she chooses a menu option and could just as easily type any other DOS command. Still, for many situations this is good enough.

Menus in CONFIG.SYS

The real news in DOS 6 regarding flexible configurations is its support for menuing commands. Now, at last, we can have CONFIG.SYS files that are menu-driven, work in color, and can control the building of your PC's configuration from the ground up each time you boot.

The only limitation to the DOS 6 menu approach (and one that cannot be circumvented by any third-party boot manager), is that IO.SYS loads

DBLSPACE.BIN before it starts processing the CONFIG.SYS file. As a result, you can choose to load DBLSPACE.BIN in some configurations, but not in others. This is one case where the old-fashioned floppy-based approach still works (you may have to delete DBLSPACE.BIN from the boot floppy if you used SYS to add the system files), but be very careful not to do anything that might damage or delete your CVFs while you're working without DBLSPACE active.

SETTING UP CONFIG.SYS MENUS

It is very easy to set up menus in your CONFIG.SYS file. The structure required is very similar to an INI file for most of Microsoft's application programs or to a WIN.INI file for Windows. The syntax is a simple repetition of blocks, each one preceded by its name enclosed in square brackets:

```
[block_name]
items for block
...
[next_block]
...
```

The first, or top-level, menu must always be called `[MENU]`, must be enclosed in square brackets, and must be the first entry on that line. (You can type it `[menu]`, `[Menu]`, etc.; it is case-insensitive.) The only other reserved menu name is `[COMMON]`, which is discussed later.

Between each block name entry you may have either a group of CONFIG.SYS commands and directives (a *configuration block*) or more menu commands (a *menu block*), but every block must be either a menu block or a configuration block, and the top-level `[menu]` block must be a menu block. Note that you cannot mix menu commands and other kinds of CONFIG.SYS commands or directives in one block.

There are only five menuing commands: MENUITEM, SUBMENU, MENUDEFAULT, MENUCOLOR, and INCLUDE (all of them are case-insensitive), and they are valid only within a block. Since a block extends from one block name entry to the next, including the mandatory first block name entry—`[menu]`—is sufficient to make these commands legal.

> **Note:** Microsoft says that NUMLOCK is another of the menuing commands, and they may have intended that you use it only in a configuration block, but in fact it works just fine in a CONFIG.SYS file with no block labels and none of the menuing commands listed here.

The syntax of these menuing command lines is:

```
MENUITEM=configuration_block_name[,Text]
SUBMENU=menu_block_name[,Text]
MENUDEFAULT=block_name[,time]
MENUCOLOR=forecolor,backcolor
INCLUDE=configuration_block_name
```

where `configuration_block_name` and `menu_block_name` are the names of other blocks you want to branch to; `block_name` is the name of one of the blocks mentioned in either a `menuitem` or `submenu` in this menu. The `text` item may be anything you like, up to 70 characters long. (Actually, it may be longer, but only the first 70 characters will be displayed.) `Time` is a number of seconds after which you want the CONFIG.SYS file to continue as if the item `block_name` had been selected. `Forecolor` and `backcolor` are numbers representing the color scheme in which you want this menu presented. This color scheme will apply until it is reset by a device driver you are installing, by another `menucolor` command in a later block, or by a clear screen command (CLS) at the DOS prompt.

The valid color numbers follow the convention used in QBASIC color commands (which is different from the ANSI convention). `Forecolor` values may be from 0 to 15; `backcolor` may be only from 0 to 7.

0	black	8	dark grey
1	blue	9	bright blue
2	green	10	bright green
3	cyan	11	bright cyan
4	red	12	bright red
5	magenta	13	bright magenta
6	brown	14	bright yellow
7	dim white	15	bright white

The MENUITEM, SUBMENU, MENUCOLOR, and MENUDEFAULT commands are valid only in a menu block. All MENUITEM lines must point to a configuration block; all SUBMENU lines must point to a menu block.

The INCLUDE lines may be placed only within a configuration block. They cause IO.SYS to act as if all of the statements in the block whose names follow the equal sign had been copied to the current block.

The following minimal menu

```
[menu]
menuitem=onward, Welcome to CONFIG.SYS menus!
menucolor=10,0
menudefault=onward,1
[onward]
...
```

is actually very useful. It gives you only one choice: go onward; after one second it will go onward by itself. That doesn't sound too useful so far. The utility in this menu is that it lets you display a line of text (`Welcome to CONFIG.SYS menus!` in this case) and set the color scheme for what follows. You might think you could set the time-out value to 0 and thus have the menucolor take effect without anything appearing on the screen. Instead, none of the lines in this block get executed at all (except the time-out, which is instantly true), no matter what the order of those lines within the block.

Figure 11-3 shows a more complex CONFIG.SYS menu with one top-level menu that has three MENUITEMs and one SUBMENU. The submenu has two more menuitems. In all, there are nine blocks. The last block shown, `[COMMON]`, plays a special role. It is the name of a block consisting of commands that will always be executed no matter which menu choices are made. It also is a very useful block to put at the end of your CONFIG.SYS file, as we will explain shortly.

The remarks at the end of this CONFIG.SYS file are important. They document all the final menus through which it is possible to pass. The name of the last menu traversed on a given startup is stored in an environment variable named CONFIG. The ability to access this information from within the AUTOEXEC.BAT file means that the effect of menu choices may be extended easily through the processing of that file, as well as controlling what happens in CONFIG.SYS.

When you boot a PC with the CONFIG.SYS menu shown in Figure 11-3, the first thing you will see is displayed in Figure 11-4.

AUTOEXEC.BAT Files that Use CONFIG.SYS Menus

Usually, only a portion of the steps necessary to set up a configuration will take place inside the CONFIG.SYS file. Additional steps are often required in the AUTOEXEC.BAT file. In order to complete the configuration that you began in the CONFIG.SYS file, your AUTOEXEC.BAT file can be forced to use the CONFIG environment variable value to control its actions.

There are two basic strategies you can use. One is to set up your AUTOEXEC.BAT file to consist of blocks of lines (similar in concept to the configuration blocks in the CONFIG.SYS file), with each block completing the setup of one configuration. Then, at the start of the batch file, you can insert a `GOTO %CONFIG%` statement to direct the flow through the desired block. At the end of each block, you can insert another GOTO statement causing the batch file processor to jump to the end of the file. The other strategy is to include `IF "%CONFIG%"=="`*`name`*`" ...` statements throughout the batch file. Each of these statements will allow only the associated action (indicated by the ellipsis) to be completed if the value of the CONFIG variable is equal to *`name`*. Examples of both of these techniques can be found in Chapter 14.

```
rem  Here you can put some reminder to yourself of what version menu this is.
rem  ======================================================================

[MENU]
MENUITEM              = CLEAN, Real minimalist configuration
SUBMENU               = MAIN, Usual configuration alternatives
MENUITEM              = BERNOULI, Load Bernoulli support
MENUITEM              = TEST, Test modifications to system
MENUCOLOR             = 14,1
MENUDEFAULT           = MAIN, 60

[CLEAN]
rem         Here is the truly minimalist configuration!
STACKS                = 0,0

[MAIN]
rem         Offer a choice between loading the network drivers
rem         or simply using the system without network access
MENUCOLOR             = 10,0
MENUITEM              = USUAL, Normal setup with network drivers
MENUITEM              = OFTEN, No Network connection
MENUDEFAULT           = USUAL, 60

[BERNOULI]
INCLUDE USUAL
DEVICE                = c:\setup\drivers\rcd.sys

[TEST]
rem         Put here anything you want to test, but don't want
rem         to use other than when you are doing those tests.
INCLUDE USUAL

[USUAL]
DOS                   =  umb
FILES                 =   80
FCBS                  = 16,0
BUFFERS               = 30,0
LASTDRIVE             =    z
DEVICE                = c:\dos\HIMEM.SYS
DEVICE                = c:\dos\EMM386.EXE noems highscan
DEVICEHIGH            = C:\DOS\DBLSPACE.SYS /MOVE
DEVICE                = C:\DOS\RAMDRIVE.SYS 1024 512 128 /e
INCLUDE OFTEN
INCLUDE NetStuff

[OFTEN]
DOS                   =  high
DEVICEHIGH /L:1,12048 = c:\dos\SETVER.EXE
BREAK                 =    on
STACKS                = 9,256
INSTALL               = c:\dos\SHARE.EXE /f:4096
DEVICE                = c:\dos\SMARTDRV.EXE /double_buffer

[NetStuff]
DEVICE                = c:\workgrp6\PROTMAN.DOS /i:C:\workgrp6
DEVICEHIGH /L:1,7280  = c:\workgrp6\WORKGRP.SYS
DEVICEHIGH /L:1,11168 = c:\workgrp6\EXP16.DOS

[COMMON]
SHELL                 = c:\dos\COMMAND.COM c:\dos\ /e:624 /p

rem  At this point the possibilities for the CONFIG environment variable are:
rem      CLEAN, USUAL, OFTEN, BERNOULI, and TEST
```

Figure 11-3 A CONFIG.SYS menu of moderate complexity

```
MS-DOS 6 Startup Menu
=====================

   1. Real minimalist configuration
   2. Usual configuration alternatives
   3. Load Bernoulli support
   4. Test modifications to system

Enter a choice: 2        Time remaining: 59
```

Figure 11-4 An MS-DOS 6 CONFIG.SYS menu

Warnings and Suggestions

This section includes several tips, warnings, and other ideas to keep in mind when experimenting with your PC's configuration.

Make a Safety Boot Diskette

A safety boot diskette used to be just about the most essential tool in your kit. Now, with the Clean Boot strategy supported by DOS 6, it is a lot less important. It is *not*, however, irrelevant. Your hard disk still could develop a trouble spot in the middle of one of the key system files, or the boot record could get munged, or your PC's CMOS configuration memory might get corrupted.

In any of these situations, you will be totally unable to boot your system from the hard disk. In the first two situations, once you boot from a floppy diskette with the right version of DOS on it (and any necessary other files), you will be able to retrieve all the files on your hard disk without any problem. You would also then be in a position to fix what went wrong. In the second case, once you restored the CMOS configuration memory's contents, you could again boot from the hard disk, and all of the damage would be fixed by that time. It should be clear that a safety boot diskette is still a good idea, if not a necessity.

What Is a Safety Boot Diskette?

A safety boot diskette is a bootable disk that has the same version of DOS on it that you have on your hard disk, and it has any other files you need to access your hard disk. The whole purpose of a safety boot diskette is to assure you that, as long as your hard disk keeps turning and the electronics are working, you can access your data from even the most corrupt of hard disks.

Making the Safety Boot Diskette

First, FORMAT the diskette in your A drive. Next, use the DOS command SYS to transfer the system files from C to A. The exact commands are:

```
FORMAT A:
SYS C: A:
```

(Including both source and destination drive letters in the SYS command prevents problems that occur if you issue the SYS command when the DOS default drive is not a bootable one.)

> **Note:** If you are wondering why in the previous commands we didn't just add the /S switch after the FORMAT command to do both jobs in one step, it is because in DOS 6, FORMAT /S will put the two most essential hidden system files (IO.SYS and MSDOS.SYS) on the floppy. It will not, however, put the new, third hidden system file (DBLSPACE.BIN) there. This is not always a problem, though, because when you boot from a floppy, if IO.SYS cannot find DBLSPACE.BIN on the floppy, it looks at the hard drive to see if it can find a copy there. If it does, then IO.SYS will load that copy and start it up. If DBLSPACE.BIN finds DBLSPACE.INI on the hard disk, it will follow the directions contained in that file to mount any DBLSPACE volumes you may have. Therefore, you might be able to get by with a bootable floppy diskette that doesn't have DBLSPACE.BIN on it, even though you have some DoubleSpaced volumes on your hard drive. Don't count on that approach, though, as you will be relying on the integrity of that one copy of DBLSPACE.BIN. It is safer to arrange to have a spare copy on the diskette, which is why we suggest creating the bootable DOS diskette in two steps.

Now you have a diskette from which you can boot. If you use any device drivers (other than DBLSPACE.BIN) that are necessary to access your hard disk, such as Disk Manager (DMDRVR.BIN), you will have to copy them to the floppy diskette and create a CONFIG.SYS file so they load when you boot from this diskette.

You don't, however, want to load any unnecessary device drivers or TSR programs from your safety boot diskette. Do include the following:

- memory managers such as HIMEM.SYS and EMM386.EXE
- the usual default parameters for your sytem
- an AUTOEXEC.BAT file
- a CONFIG.SYS file
- the usual number of FILES, BUFFERS, and STACKS
- LASTDRIVE
- the usual PROMPT and PATH

Arrange it so using your PC when it is booted from this diskette will feel as natural as possible, yet don't depend on any file on the hard disk being readable. (Insert any directories you have on the safety boot floppy at the front of the PATH, so the files in those directories are loaded in preference to the ones on the hard disk. You may have to wait a bit longer to run a program, but at least you will have a copy you can count on.)

There are some secondary elements to consider including on your safety floppy, such as certain key DOS external commands. Copy at least FDISK, FORMAT, SYS, CHKDSK to a DOS directory on the floppy diskette. Perhaps include the DOS Power Tools program MH-RESTR and its data file (see Chapter 18). The data file should contain at least the CMOS and extended CMOS contents, plus the Master Boot Record and the DOS boot record for your C drive. (Don't try to keep a data file with all the things that MH-RESTR's companion program, MH-SAVE, can store; that would get out of date too quickly.) The other item you may want to keep on the boot floppy is the latest version of a computer virus scanning program. The new DOS 6 program MSAV is one good choice.

Testing Your Safety Boot Diskette

Once you have made what you think is a good safety boot diskette, you *must* test it. Remember, this is your safety net. The test is very simple: Determine that you can boot from the disk and still access your hard disk. Then, if you are sufficiently comfortable working inside your PC's system unit, there is a second test you can perform, which can reveal a weakness in your safety boot diskette that you were not aware of. The second test may be broken down into several numbered steps:

1. Turn off power to your PC. Disconnect the system unit from ground by all possible paths. This means more than just unplugging the power cord. It also means disconnecting the data cable from your PC to each peripheral device that is connected to ground (such as your monitor and your printer).

2. Open up the case. *Touch the power supply first!* (Do this *every* time you reach inside the box, before you touch anything else.) Find the cable(s) that runs from the power supply to the hard disk(s). These are four-wire cables with a plastic housing on the end that plug into the disk drive. Disconnect them from the hard drive(s). This may take a rather firm tug. Be careful to pull the plug straight out of its housing without bending it to one side. (Caution: If you pull on the wires, they may come out of the plug, instead of the plug coming out of its socket!) Don't worry about pulling too hard, as long as you pull straight.

3. Now you can reconnect the power and data cables to your PC system unit. Leave the box open for now; just be careful not to drop anything

inside and don't reach inside until after you have disconnected all those cables once more.

4. Repeat the original test of the safety boot diskette. This time you will find that your PC reports a bad hard drive. And it *is* bad—you made it that way (temporarily) by disconnecting it from the power supply. Ignore those messages and look for any that indicate that the system had trouble finding a file while it was booting. If that happens, your safety boot diskette was not made correctly.
5. If you saw such a message, it means that your startup files (CONFIG.SYS and AUTOEXEC.BAT) on the safety boot diskette are trying to access that file. Check them over carefully to be sure that all the device drivers mentioned are on the floppy diskette and that the lines in the startup files that mention those programs point to the copy on the A drive.
6. Once you have successfully completed this test, you can again unplug the power and data cables from the system unit, reconnect the power cables to your hard drive(s), close up the case, and then plug things in again. Don't do this, though, until you have fixed any problems that you found with your safety boot diskette and have successfully completed this test.

Once you have a fully tested safety boot diskette, write-protect it, make a DISKCOPY of it, and write-protect that copy. Then store one copy next to the PC (or some place that is very handy). Keep the other copy in another place entirely.

Note: You must make a safety boot diskette for each PC you have, if you are to achieve full protection. In particular, the MH-SAVE/MH-RESTR data file must be created on each machine that you want to have protection. Also, remember to update that data file each time you change the hardware configuration of the PC.

The Clean Boot Safety Net

One problem common to many power users is to make a mistake when changing the CONFIG.SYS or AUTOEXEC.BAT files. This used to be one of the situations in which you would reach for your safety boot diskette. You still can do that, but DOS 6 provides an even easier alternative.

There are two ways to recover, involving three different keypress sequences. In all cases, you must act when the message `Starting MS-DOS...` appears on your screen. The simplest way to avoid any problems caused by a defective CONFIG.SYS or AUTOEXEC.BAT file is to press the F5 key (or either Shift key) at this moment. The message

```
MS-DOS is bypassing your CONFIG.SYS and AUTOEXEC.BAT files.
```

will appear, followed immediately by the usual DOS version announcement and the DOS default prompt. (Note: This prompt is something like `C:\>` rather than the past default prompt which was simply `C>`. The change is made automatically by DOS, putting a minimal prompt definition, `PROMPT=$P$G`, in the DOS environment.)

This method of recovery is fine if you want to avoid processing all those files. If, however, you want to use some of them, then you must avoid processing only those lines that may contain errors. In this case, press F8 instead of F5. You will see (briefly, if you are using a CONFIG.SYS menu) the line

```
MS-DOS will prompt you to confirm each CONFIG.SYS command.
```

after which you will see the first menu if you have one. At the bottom of the screen will be two options:

```
F5=Bypass startup files
F8=Confirm each CONFIG.SYS line [Y]
```

At this point, if you press F5, you will again bypass the entire CONFIG.SYS and AUTOEXEC.BAT file processing. Pressing F8 toggles the letter in square brackets between `Y` and `N`. As long as you leave it at `Y`, you will be prompted for each command. The command is displayed followed by a space and `[Y,N]?` Enter `Y` and the command is executed; press `N` and just that one line is bypassed.

This process is repeated for each line that is executable in your CONFIG.SYS file. (REM statements and blank lines are not shown.) Finally, you will see the message

```
Process AUTOEXEC.BAT [Y,N]?
```

At this point a `Y` will cause normal processing of the AUTOEXEC.BAT file; an `N` will bypass it entirely.

If you want to execute only some of the AUTOEXEC.BAT file lines, you have two choices: One is to bypass it on the first bootup, then edit out the lines you don't want to execute, then reboot; the second is to watch closely and press Ctrl-Break at just the right moment. This will interrupt processing of the AUTOEXEC.BAT file part way through. You cannot gracefully pick up after the next line, for example, but often that is not necessary.

Diagnosing Bootup Problems

Armed with these tools you usually can sort out bootup problems caused by mistakes in CONFIG.SYS or AUTOEXEC.BAT. The first task is to find out which file(s) contains the mistake(s).

First, verify that you can boot without either startup file. Do this by pressing either F5 or a Shift key when you see the now familiar startup message from DOS. Next, see if you can boot successfully when you allow all the error-free lines of the CONFIG.SYS file to execute, but suppress those you suspect of causing problems and bypass the AUTOEXEC.BAT file. If you can boot successfully this way, add one more line that will run each time you reboot until the problem surfaces. If it doesn't appear when CONFIG.SYS is processed, you know you have a problem in the AUTOEXEC.BAT file.

Often, you can find out in which file the problem is simply by watching the messages on the screen during boot up. If they go by too fast, use F8 to force the PC to stop after each line of CONFIG.SYS. Add PAUSE statements to your AUTOEXEC.BAT file at intervals to do the same there. (The PAUSE statement is described in more detail in Chapter 14.)

It is possible that the problem precedes the lines you *thought* had an error. If you didn't have a problem when you bypassed the startup files, then you simply need to exclude one more line each time you reboot until the problem goes away.

Once you have narrowed your focus to the problem line, usually you will see the error immediately. Use an editor to fix it. If nothing else is available, use the DOS editor EDIT, which probably is in your DOS directory. At the DOS prompt in the root directory of C, enter the command

```
C:\DOS\EDIT CONFIG.SYS
```

or

```
C:\DOS\EDIT AUTOEXEC.BAT
```

and you will be back on track in no time.

[COMMON] Sense

Microsoft suggests that you include a `[COMMON]` configuration block at the end of the file if you choose to use CONFIG.SYS menus. You don't have to insert any configuration commands in this block, though you may if you want. A `[COMMON]` configuration block will circumvent the problem caused by programs that will try to add lines to your CONFIG.SYS file without your knowledge or consent. Usually those programs add their lines at the end. Therefore, if you have a `[COMMON]` block at the end, those lines will be executed for all configurations (no matter how you answer the menu prompts as you are booting).

After the application has been installed, you can edit the CONFIG.SYS file to move those added lines to a more appropriate place. For example, you may want to have these lines active only if you have chosen a specific configuration in which to run that application.

A similar problem may occur in your AUTOEXEC.BAT. The equivalent of a `[COMMON]` configuration block for AUTOEXEC.BAT is a label, `:COMMON`, on a line by itself near the end of the AUTOEXEC.BAT file. Any section of that file that ends with a branch to a label at the end of the file will use this label. As a result, any lines that are added to the end of your AUTOEXEC.BAT file will execute no matter which configuration you are using.

Catching Changes to the Startup File

Catching all the changes to your startup files requires a more systematic approach. As a true power user, you should be aware of when those files get altered, as well as which program altered them. Then, perhaps, you can also figure out why they were altered in the way that they were.

The simple way to accomplish this is to create a subdirectory in which to keep copies of all versions of your startup files. Include comments to help you remember why you built this assortment of commands.

Each time you are going to install a new program (or any other time you suspect that your startup files may be altered without your knowledge and permission), copy the current set of CONFIG.SYS and AUTOEXEC.BAT to some unique file names in the CONFIGUR directory. Do whatever backups you deem prudent, and then reset the archive attribute bits for all the files in at least the root directory. (See Chapter 8 for a discussion of file attributes.)

Now you can install your new program, or do whatever else you were about to do. When you finish, compare the startup files with the copies made just before this episode. Then you can be sure that any changes are recent. Also determine which files have their archive bit turned on (set). Include all the files that have changed since you reset those bits. (It is possible that some files will have their archive bits set even though they did not get changed. It is also possible, but much less likely, that some files will get changed without that bit being set, or that it will get reset before you notice it.)

This approach lets application programs and their installation routines complete their procedure on your startup files, and it lets you know exactly what happened and when. Armed with that knowledge, you can incorporate the changes you approve of and delete those you don't. When you finish, we suggest that you make a copy of the new startup files under other unique names in CONFIGUR so you will be ready to detect the next unexpected change in them.

The /K and [TRASH] Alternatives

To keep programs from altering your startup files in the first place is not always easy to do, but there are some possibilities worth considering. The strategy discussed in this section was not possible before DOS 6. But before explaining the strategy, a few words are necessary regarding the way IO.SYS processes the SHELL statement in your CONFIG.SYS file.

The main purpose of the SHELL statement in your CONFIG.SYS file is to specify which file to use as the command interpreter. If you don't have a SHELL statement, IO.SYS will act as if you have one reading:

```
SHELL=C:\COMMAND.COM /P /E:256
```

This line tells IO.SYS to look for COMMAND.COM in the root directory of your C drive and load it as the command interpreter. Once it is loaded, COMMAND.COM will notice the `/P` and `/E:256` switches, which make it the permanent command interpreter and cause it to set aside 256 bytes for the Master DOS environment. (These concepts are explained more fully in Chapter 13.)

The SHELL statement can be used to load an alternative command interpreter, such as NDOS or 4DOS. Even if you use it to load the default command interpreter, COMMAND.COM, you can use the SHELL statement to tell IO.SYS to look in a different place for the command interpreter. The SHELL statement also can be used to give the command interpreter a different set of directions, once it is loaded.

Perhaps the most popular alternative SHELL statement is

```
SHELL=C:\DOS\COMMAND.COM C:\DOS /P /E:624
```

(possibly with another number after the `/E:`). This line tells IO.SYS to look in the DOS directory for COMMAND.COM, and tells COMMAND.COM that it came from the DOS directory. Then it informs COMMAND.COM that it is going to be the permanent command interpreter. Finally, this line directs COMMAND.COM to set aside some larger amount of environment space than its normal default size (in this case 624 bytes).

The `/P` switch means two things to COMMAND.COM:

1. Ignore the command EXIT.
2. Look for a file C:\AUTOEXEC.BAT and process it, or else prompt the user for the date and time.

In DOS 6, COMMAND.COM has a new switch, `/K` *`filename`*, which is used to tell COMMAND.COM not to process the AUTOEXEC.BAT file, even though it is the permanent command interpreter; instead, it is directed to process *`filename`* as if it were AUTOEXEC.BAT.

Actually, this new switch turns out to be very similar to the /C switch. Both cause COMMAND.COM to execute whatever DOS command follows them on the command line. The difference is that a copy of COMMAND.COM followed by the /C switch exits after it finishes its specified command. A COMMAND.COM followed by /K presents a DOS prompt at that point. This similarity means that you can execute any program or batch file if you give the program's file name (or its path and file name if it is not in C:\); you can let COMMAND search for any such file with extension COM, EXE, or BAT. If the specified file doesn't exist, you will get the familiar `Bad command or filename` message.

Microsoft doesn't recommend that you use /K in the SHELL statement; essentially it wants its applications able to find and interfere with your AUTOEXEC.BAT file! Microsoft uses this line to tell COMMAND when it is loaded in a DOS window of Windows to execute some batch file and then give you a DOS prompt.

If you don't agree with Microsoft's point of view, use /K (along with /P and /E:nnn) in your SHELL statement to specify your choice of an alternate initial command to execute. Then, when that application program is installed, probably it will look for your CONFIG.SYS and AUTOEXEC.BAT files to modify. Although you can't do much about CONFIG.SYS, by using the /K switch you will have totally frustrated the application's search for your AUTOEXEC.BAT file. The installation program probably will create a brand new AUTOEXEC.BAT file.

You can look at that file and decide which portions to copy to your real startup batch file and which to avoid. Of course, if the installation program at some point reboots your computer, expecting that its changes in CONFIG.SYS and AUTOEXEC.BAT will take effect, it (and you) may be in for a bit of a surprise. The CONFIG.SYS changes will happen only if you had a `[COMMON]` block at the end. The AUTOEXEC.BAT changes won't happen at all.

This brings us to the second strategy for protecting startup files. If you don't want programs to interfere with your startup files, put a [TRASH] menu block at the end of the CONFIG.SYS file and never mention that submenu in any of your menus. This prevents any lines that get appended to your CONFIG.SYS file from being executed.

MemMaker and CONFIG.SYS Menus

As noted in Chapter 6, MemMaker has some problems dealing with menus in CONFIG.SYS, which is unfortunate, as MemMaker and CONFIG.SYS menus are two of the highlights of DOS 6. The problem is not a trivial one. For now, Microsoft recommends not to mix menus and MemMaker. Fortunately, there is a way to apply that advice and still be able to get full benefit from these exciting new DOS 6 features. Any menu structure you build in CONFIG.SYS can be reduced to a series of actions leading to a particular number of possible paths through the file. Along each path IO.SYS will execute a particular set of commands. Often many of those paths will share a number of commands, so Microsoft has included the option to have configuration blocks that are shared by several of the paths. The mechanism that implements this is the INCLUDE command and the COMMON block.

Start by making a copy of your CONFIG.SYS file with all its menus and commands. Keep the original in your CONFIGUR directory. If your menus use any INCLUDE commands or if you have any commands in a COMMON block, you will have to do some editing to clarify which commands are invoked along each path through your CONFIG.SYS file. Simply replace each INCLUDE statement with a copy of all of the commands from the block to which the INCLUDE command pointed. Once you have done this for all the blocks, you will find that you have some blocks that are never mentioned. Delete them. Now you should have a menu structure implemented in menu blocks, plus some number of configuration blocks, one per path through the menu tree.

Copy each of these configuration blocks to a separate file with a unique file name. Throw away the intermediate file you have been editing. You now have the original master CONFIG.SYS file and several separate would-be CONFIG.SYS files for the many configurations your original CONFIG.SYS file supported.

Do the same thing for your AUTOEXEC.BAT file. Copy it, then edit it until you have its commands separated into distinct portions, so that each portion is executed for one configuration only (one route through the menu tree). Now create separate files, one from each of those distinct portions. Again, toss the edited copy of the master AUTOEXEC.BAT file.

Now you should have a matched pair of files, one CONFIG.SYS and one AUTOEXEC.BAT file (with, of course, unique names) for each configuration you plan to support. None of these files has any menu commands or any branching statements that depend on the value of the CONFIG variable in the DOS environment.

Put all these files in a subdirectory. Copy one set only to the root of your C drive, and give those copies the names CONFIG.SYS and AUTOEXEC.BAT. Now you are ready to run MemMaker.

Refer to Chapter 6 to recall how to use MemMaker to determine which regions of upper memory to use for UMBs, which programs to load into which regions, and in what order. Repeat this process for all configurations, each time optimizing a different pair of startup files. When you are finished, you are ready to recombine them into one big CONFIG.SYS file and one big AUTOEXEC.BAT file.

If you value convenience over elegance, simply let each path through the menus in CONFIG.SYS lead to a single configuration block with all the appropriate commands in it. In the AUTOEXEC.BAT file use GOTO statements at the top to direct execution to a totally separate section of the AUTOEXEC.BAT file—the one that contains the commands appropriate to that configuration. At the end of each of those sections use another GOTO to branch to the label at the end of the AUTOEXEC.BAT file.

If, on the other hand, you value elegance over convenience, you must decide how many of the commands are common to which configurations in each of the startup files. Then use the full flexibility of the AUTOEXEC.BAT file batch language and all of the power of the INCLUDE and COMMON statements in CONFIG.SYS to reduce each of the final startup files to its minimum length. This is not a simple task.

DOS Commands for Flexible Configurations

There are many DOS internal and external commands that are of use in creating flexibly configured PCs. All of the CONFIG.SYS commands and directives may get used as you build your menued CONFIG.SYS file. You also will use many of the batch file commands in your AUTOEXEC.BAT file. This section lists most of the relevant commands. If any of them are unfamiliar to you, turn to the Command Reference for a brief explanation.

CONFIG.SYS Directives

There are twelve directives you can use in a CONFIG.SYS file, plus five commands. In addition, you can use any of seven keywords in constructing menus in that file and as many REMarks as you like.

The twelve directives are: BREAK, BUFFERS, COUNTRY, DOS, DRIVPARM, FILES, FCBS, LASTDRIVE, NUMLOCK, SWITCHES, and VERIFY. Each of these is used to set some parameter inside DOS or define the size of a DOS internal data structure.

The five commands are: DEVICE, DEVICEHIGH, INSTALL, SET, and SHELL. Each of these causes some program to be loaded (or, in the case of SET, a string to be defined in the DOS environment).

DOS Loadable Device Drivers

The DEVICE and DEVICEHIGH commands are used to load installable device drivers. The programs bundled with DOS for which you use the DEVICE command include: ANSI.SYS, DISPLAY.SYS, DBLSPACE.SYS,

EGA.SYS, EMM386.EXE, HIMEM.SYS, INTERLNK.EXE, POWER.EXE, RAMDRIVE.SYS, SETVER.EXE, and SMARTDRV.EXE. The files with extension EXE are also executable files that can be run from the DOS prompt. (Most of them won't do much when run from the DOS prompt, however, unless they also have been loaded via a DEVICE line in your CONFIG.SYS file.)

CONFIG.SYS Menuing Commands

There are five CONFIG.SYS menuing commands, plus two reserved words used only as block names. The commands are INCLUDE, MENUCOLOR, MENUDEFAULT, MENUITEM, and SUBMMENU. The reserved words are [MENU] and [COMMON]. Any other name within square brackets (if it is first on a line) is considered a block name.

AUTOEXEC.BAT Configuration Commands

Several internal and a few external DOS commands are useful in setting up flexible configurations. The most prominent are: CHOICE, GOTO (especially GOTO %CONFIG%), IF "%CONFIG%"=="name", IF "othervar"=="definition", LOADHIGH (or LH), and batch file labels (lines beginning with a colon and a name). Others that may come into play include: BREAK, ECHO, FOR...IN...DO, GOTO name, IF ERRORLEVEL..., IF [NOT] EXIST..., PATH, PROMPT, REM, SET, and VERIFY.

Power Tools Commands for Flexible Configurations

The CFG program has a number of interesting options for use in CONFIG.SYS files, including some port masking capbilities that will get you past some driver conflicts, along with some very useful screen-setting and sound capabilities that you can use along with timed and key pauses to rev up your configuration menus. You may also find the DMM package's LDEVICE command will let you get around some driver-loading conflicts without recourse to explicitly distinct configurations.

CHAPTER

12

◆ ◆ ◆ ◆ ◆

Device Drivers

Device drivers manage the sources and destinations of data, including printers, disk drives, serial and parallel I/O ports, and programs. *Installable device drivers* are those that can be added to control a new device or to manage an existing device differently.

The most commonly installed device driver is probably MOUSE.SYS, which recognizes input from a mouse. Disk caches, such as the SMARTDRV.EXE program included in MS-DOS 6.0, and on-the-fly file compression device drivers such as DoubleSpace and Stacker, are examples of device drivers that modify the way DOS handles existing devices.

Installable device drivers have made it possible for DOS to keep up with hardware developments. They aren't a luxury; they are a necessity. Unfortunately, they also are often a nuisance, requiring you to get "down and dirty" with your CONFIG.SYS file (adding and perhaps tweaking some DEVICE lines), and often with the hardware add-ins and add-ons as well (changing jumpers or DIP switch settings).

How Device Drivers Work

Device drivers serve as extensions of the operating system. Each driver manages communication between the CPU and a specific hardware device. The collection of device drivers in your PC provides all the channels of communication between the CPU and the devices from which it reads or to which it writes data.

A device driver program must include the information needed to initialize the device it serves, plus information on how to exchange information between it and the CPU. There are two classes of device drivers: *block* and *character*. Character device drivers handle data one character at a time to control printers, keyboards, screens, and mice; block device drivers move data to and from disks and other storage devices in blocks that contain some fixed number of characters (usually 512 bytes) at one time.

The Chain Gang

All device drivers are "chained together." DOS sends requests to device drivers by sending them to the first device in the chain. Whenever DOS needs a device to do something, it sends two messages down the chain. The first message asks a particular device driver to declare its presence and readiness to work. The second message tells the driver what to do.

When a request is passing down the chain, each device driver examines the message in turn. Either it will act on the request, or it will pass the request along to the next driver in the chain. This continues until some driver acts on the request, or the request is simply passed off the end of the chain and lost. (If the message falls off the end of the chain, DOS won't get the "I'm here and ready to do your work" response it is looking for. Usually, DOS will then send a message about an unavailable device.)

The first driver in the chain is always named NUL. It does not actually have an associated device to control. Nevertheless, it is a very useful object. You can use the NUL device as a receptacle for unwanted messages (which it will immediately discard). In this role it is referred to as the "bit bucket." A common example of this use is when a program would normally print messages on the screen, but output redirection sends that message to the NUL device instead. It is also possible to seek input from the NUL device. In that role its job is simply to say "I'm done!" every time it is asked for anything, so that way DOS gets an end-of-message signal without any associated message content.

NUL's other job is as the starting point anchor for the device chain. As long as DOS knows where the NUL device is, and as long as the device chain has been built correctly, DOS can simply send messages to the NUL device and trust that they will get handed down the chain to the correct driver. (What the device driver chain looks like and how it gets built is covered in a later section in this chapter.)

The Bad Old Days

In MS-DOS 1.0, all the device drivers were incorporated into the operating system code. There was no way to add new devices or change the way the CPU handled inputs and outputs. Because the earliest PCs could handle only single-sided floppy disks with a maximum capacity of 160K, Microsoft had to completely re-create DOS (version 1.1) when IBM introduced the double-sided 360K diskette drive. It was not a very graceful way for Microsoft to manage the inevitable upgrades to DOS needed to support the inevitable upgrades to PC hardware.

DOS 2.0 Improvements

Beginning with DOS 2.0, it became possible to install separate drivers to control additional devices without replacing the entire operating system. Now you could upgrade DOS to support new hardware merely by adding a new driver to the existing device driver chain. Even the default drivers were no longer "hard-wired" into DOS; they too were built into the device driver chain.

DOS Default Device Drivers

There are thirteen default device drivers inside the hidden system file IO.SYS. These default drivers provide the minimum set of devices that DOS needs to support a "plain vanilla" PC. The default devices include: one null device, one block device driver (to support both floppy and "ordinary" hard disks), and eleven character devices. Five of the character devices support four serial ports. (One port can be accessed via either of two device drivers.) Four of them support three parallel ports. (One of these ports can be accessed two ways also.) One more supports the clock, and the last one supports

NUL	a waste basket for data in and no data out, ever
CON	the keyboard and screen
AUX	another name for COM1
PRN	another name for LPT1
CLOCK$	the clock device
Block: 3 units	the driver for floppy disks and "normal" hard disks
COM1	first serial port
LPT1	first parallel port
LPT2	second parallel port
LPT3	third parallel port
COM2	second serial port
COM3	third serial port
COM4	fourth serial port

Figure 12-1 Table of default drivers

Name	Type	Description
ANSI.SYS	Character	Pre-empts the CON driver to control the keyboard and screen
DBLSPACE.BIN	Block	Pre-empts the block device driver to compress data before it's written to a disk, and uncompress data after DOS reads it from a disk
DBLSPACE.SYS	Character	Controls final location of DBLSPACE.BIN in memory
DISPLAY.SYS	Character	Pre-empts the CON driver to permit switching between character sets
DRIVER.SYS	Character	An added block device driver that creates a phantom additional logical drive from a physical floppy drive
EGA.SYS	Character	Stores state of EGA registers to facilitate task swapping
EMM386.EXE	Character	Creates simulated expanded memory and upper memory from XMS memory; also enables or disables a Weitek coprocessor
HIMEM.SYS	Character	Manages XMS, upper, and high memory; creates XMS memory from extended memory
POWER.EXE	Character	Activates built-in power consumption controls on a PC that conforms to the Advanced Power Management (APM) specification.
RAMDRIVE.SYS	Character	An added block driver that creates a simulated disk drive from some RAM
SETVER.EXE	Character	Lying program; reports phony version of DOS to programs it knows need that lie before they will run
SMARTDRV.EXE	Character	Disk cache program; buffers flow of data to and from disk drive

Figure 12-2 Installable DOS device drivers

the console. Figure 12-1 lists the names of these default drivers in MS-DOS 6 in the order they are linked into the device chain, and gives a brief description of each.

Installable DOS Device Drivers

In addition to the default drivers in IO.SYS, the MS-DOS 6.0 package includes twelve installable device drivers. Figure 12-2 is a list of these programs, with a brief description of each.

Other Installable Device Drivers

If the installation instructions (for a mouse or any other new hardware device) tell you to add a DEVICE line to your CONFIG.SYS file, or if a setup program for that hardware adds such a line automatically, then you know that the hardware device uses an installable device driver. Not all hardware peripherals use device drivers in CONFIG.SYS, however. Another popular option is to load a TSR program from your AUTOEXEC.BAT file (or, since DOS 4, use the INSTALL option to load it from within the CONFIG.SYS file).

Some hardware add-ons must be activated even before DOS reads your CONFIG.SYS file. Most notably, this includes any device that alters the way your PC accesses its screen or disk drives. All EGA and VGA cards carry option ROMs on them, which allows their special program code to be bonded into the operating system early in the boot process. In fact, they do so before the first messages show up on your screen.

Similarly, any nonstandard bootable hard or floppy disk drive must be supported by a plug-in card with an option ROM. After all, until you can read the disk, there is no way to load a device driver from that disk.

Apart from these two categories of devices, most of the rest use installable device driver or TSR program files on the disk to add new operating system support.

Links in the Device Driver Chain

The device driver chain is, properly, a "linked list" where each element contains a link field that tells it where to contact the next device driver in the chain. Because of this structure, DOS doesn't need to know where any specific device driver is located in memory (other than the NUL device). Neither does it need to know the total number of device drivers to be loaded.

Character devices have names; block devices know which drive letters they support. The DOS service requests are tagged either by the name of the device that is to service them, or the letter of the drive for which they are destined.

Whenever DOS sends an instruction to a device driver, it sends a request for service to the NUL device. Most of the time, the NUL device will not fulfill the request. The part of DOS that passes the message from device to device along the chain inspects each device to see what its name is (or which drive letters it supports). As soon as it notices that the request is not for that device, it looks at the first 4 bytes of the device driver. At that location it finds the address of the next driver in the chain. It then inspects that driver to see if it is the right one to provide the requested service.

In the default chain, the second driver is the CON (console) driver, which controls the keyboard and screen. To add a new character driver to the chain, copy the existing pointer to the CON device to the new driver, and place a pointer to the new driver into the NUL driver. This process inserts the new driver into the chain immediately after NUL and ahead of the default drivers.

Since DOS always starts searching for drivers at NUL driver, DOS finds most of the new drivers added through DEVICE lines in the CONFIG.SYS file before it reaches the built-in default drivers. Messages to character devices are delivered by device driver name; therefore, if an installed device driver has the same device name as a previously installed driver, the new device driver will grab all the messages that DOS thinks it is sending that default driver. When this happens, the installed device driver performs the action requested by DOS, using the instructions and structures contained in that driver, instead of the ones in the default driver. For example, ANSI.SYS preempts DOS instructions to and from the CON driver in order to provide enhanced keyboard and screen services.

DOS usually places installable character device drivers at the beginning of the chain, just after the NUL driver, whereas it places most block drivers after the existing block drivers, and assigns the next available drive letters to them. There are some exceptions, including the DBLSPACE.BIN driver that must place itself ahead of the driver that controls disks so that it can compress and decompress the data before information flows to or from the disk drive.

Because each driver contains a pointer to the next one, it is not necessary for adjacent drivers in the chain to be located in adjacent parts of memory. Figure 12-3 lists the device drivers in the order they occur in the device chain for one somewhat heavily loaded PC. The first column in this figure shows the starting address of the device driver. At each of the listed addresses you would find the next address in this list. The last address has an offset value of FFFFh. This is the signal that you have reached the end of the device driver chain.

Notice that each driver is either one of the default drivers contained in IO.SYS, or it can be associated with a file that was loaded through a DEVICE line in the CONFIG.SYS file. The last column on the right shows those file names. A MEM /D command was used to determine the correct names to associate with the drivers.

Figure 12-4 shows a different representation of the information in Figure 12-3. All the device driver files are listed in the right column in order of their locations in memory. To the left is a column listing all the same memory addresses as those shown in Figure 12-3. The bottom group of default drivers are all contained in the file IO.SYS on the diskette, and get loaded below the start of the memory control block chain on which MEM /D reports. The looping lines show the rather convoluted sequence in which the various entry points are connected in the device chain.

Notice that some of the device driver programs have several entry addresses. In effect, they contain several independent device drivers. A single character device driver program may have several names and a block device may have more than one unit. It even is possible for one device driver

Segment:offset memory address	Type of Device	Device Name	Removable Media?	File Name
0142:0048	Character	NUL	No	
07CC:0000	Character	EXP16$	Yes	EXP16.DOS
06BB:0000	Character	NETHLP	No	WORKGRP.SYS
06B3:0000	Character	PROTMAN$	No	PROTMAN.DOS
0477:0000	Character	MVPROAS	No	MVSOUND.SYS
F018:0000	Character	CON	No	ANSI-UV.SYS
EB83:0000	Character	MSCD001	Yes	CUNI_ASP.SYS
E99E:0000	Character	SCSIMGR$	No	ASPI2DOS.SYS
E403:0000	Block 1 device		Yes	STACKER.COM
03CD:0000	Block 1 device		Yes	PCKRAMD.SYS
039E:0000	Character	SMARTAAR	No	PCKWIN.SYS
02D3:0000	Character	EMMXXXX0	No	EMM386.EXE
028F:0000	Character	XMSXXXX0	No	HIMEM.SYS
0070:0023	Character	CON	No	default DOS device
0070:0035	Character	AUX	No	default DOS device
2460:094E	Character	PRN	Yes	PCPANEL.COM
2221:01E4	Character	PRN	Yes	PCACHE.COM
0070:0059	Character	CLOCK$	No	default DOS device
0070:006B	Block 10 devices		Yes	default DOS device
0070:007B	Character	COM1	No	default DOS device
2460:096C	Character	LPT1	Yes	PCPANEL.COM
2221:01AE	Character	LPT1	Yes	PCACHE.COM
2221:01C0	Character	~LTOOLS	Yes	PCACHE.COM
2460:0A02	Character	~PCACHE	Yes	PCPANEL.COM
2221:01D2	Character	~PCACHE	Yes	PCACHE.COM
2460:098A	Character	LPT2	No	PCPANEL.COM
0070:009F	Character	LPT2	No	default DOS device
2460:09A8	Character	LPT3	No	PCPANEL.COM
0070:00B8	Character	LPT3	No	default DOS device
0070:00CA	Character	COM2	No	default DOS device
0070:00DC	Character	COM3	No	default DOS device
0070:00EE	Character	COM4	No	default DOS device
2460:09C6	Block 76 devices		No	PCPANEL.COM
0070:FFFF	No more device drivers			

Figure 12-3 A sample full device driver chain

program, loaded through a single line in your CONFIG.SYS file, to have both character and block device units within it (although this is rare).

The purpose of the device driver program PCPANEL.COM is to catch information on its way to a printer (which could be on any of the parallel or serial ports) and convert the format of that information. (This program, from Laser Tools, manages on-the-fly emulation switching for a PostScript printer so it can print screen dumps, HPPCL print jobs, and ASCII text—all things a PostScript printer cannot do on its own.)

To accomplish its task in all situations, PCPANEL must precede each of the character devices to which printer output might be sent. In each of those places an address within PCPANEL appears in the device chain with a device name that is the same as that of the default device driver it is attempting to preempt. (For some reason, PCPANEL also shows up as a block device supporting a huge number of drives at the very end of the list.)

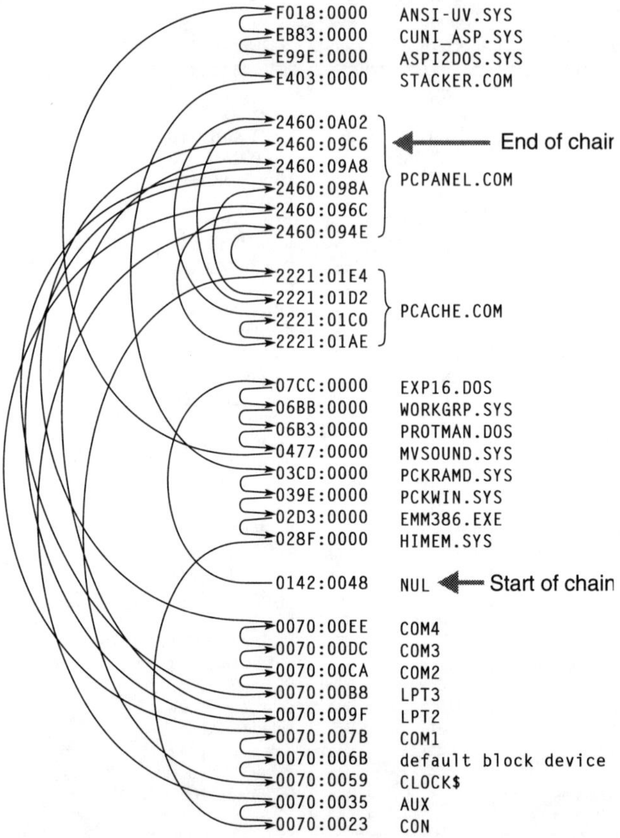

Figure 12-4 Memory locations of drivers listed in Figure 12-4 and how the chain links them

PCACHE.COM, the print spooling program introduced earlier in this book, also needs to catch all output that is destined for a printer. To do this it inserts itself before each default device to which printer output might be directed. PCACHE was inserted in the chain after the PCPANEL program, an order dictated by the sequence in which the lines invoking those two programs appeared in the AUTOEXEC.BAT file in this particular PC. (Both PCPANEL and PCACHE are device drivers that get loaded as TSR programs rather than through a DEVICE line in the CONFIG.SYS file.)

Device Drivers that Aren't

Not all programs that seem to be device drivers are linked into the device chain. For example, MSCDEX is a program used to access CD-ROM drives, and although it sounds like a device driver, it doesn't appear anywhere in the device chain. It does its work by hooking some interrupts; it never needs to see any of the requests DOS passes down the device chain.

Interlnk is a DOS program, new in DOS 6, that lets you connect two PCs. One of them (the client) is able to access the drives and printers on the other PC (the server). Again, this sounds like a block device driver, or perhaps both a block and a character device (to handle both disk drives and printers). But, technically, it is not an installable device driver; it is a TSR program that hooks some interrupts to accomplish its task. Like MSCDEX, INTERLNK will not show up anywhere in the device chain.

DOS-Provided Installable Device Drivers

ANSI.SYS

ANSI.SYS is a character driver that changes the way DOS handles screen displays, the keyboard, and the on-screen cursor. ANSI.SYS lets you display messages on the screen in color, move the cursor around the screen, and assign characters or strings of characters to individual keys or to a combination of an individual key plus the Ctrl, Shift, or Alt key.

LOADING ANSI.SYS

Assuming that the ANSI.SYS file is located in the C:\DOS subdirectory, you can load it by adding this line to your CONFIG.SYS file:

```
DEVICE=C:\DOS\ANSI.SYS
```

The next time you boot your PC, this device driver will load and handle the keyboard and screen. If you don't want ANSI.SYS to take up any lower memory, you can use DEVICEHIGH in place of DEVICE in that command. (If ANSI.SYS is located in a different directory, change the path to identify the correct location of the program.)

USING ANSI.SYS

When the ANSI.SYS device driver is active, it intercepts every string of characters that DOS or any other program sends to the screen by way of the DOS interrupts for writing to the screen. (Notice that it does not recognize any characters that get sent to the screen around DOS. Many programs directly call the BIOS routines to put characters on the screen, because they generally work much faster than the DOS routines. Those programs will not benefit at all from loading ANSI.SYS.)

ANSI.SYS recognizes the ESC character (ASCII 27, hex 1B) followed by a left bracket as the start of an ANSI command. Those commands are interpreted and acted upon by ANSI.SYS, and they are not allowed to pass to the screen. (The ASCII 27 character is a left-pointing arrow (←) in the IBM graphics definition of screen characters.)

All ANSI commands begin with these two characters, and because the first one is the ESC character, these commands are called *escape sequences*. (The Command Reference contains a complete list of ANSI commands.) ESC is used to indicate the Escape character, but you should use the ASCII 27 character when you create escape sequences.

When you press the Esc key at the DOS prompt, DOS regards it as an instruction to cancel the current command. It displays a backslash (\) and moves the cursor to the start of the next line so it is ready to receive a new command. This makes it impossible to enter a command that includes an ANSI escape sequence directly from the DOS prompt.

To circumvent this limitation, temporarily redefine your PROMPT string to whatever you normally want, plus the escape sequence you'd like to send to the ANSI.SYS driver. This works because of a special *metacharacter*, $E, that the PROMPT command processor in COMMAND.COM understands as representing the escape character.

For example, if you use the popular PG as your normal prompt and you want to send the ANSI command to clear the screen, you could type

```
PROMPT $E[2J $P$G
```

and press Enter. When COMMAND.COM issues the next DOS prompt it will clear the screen first, then issue the prompt. Note, though, if you don't change the prompt back to PG again, the screen will be cleared before each command.

A better approach is to create a batch file that contains some ECHO commands that will send the ANSI escape sequences to the screen (and thus, to the ANSI.SYS driver). The tricky part about this approach is to figure out how to enter the escape characters required to start each ANSI command.

One way is to use the DOS EDIT program to create the batch files and enter the ESC characters by this subterfuge: First hold down the Ctrl key and press the P key followed by the left square bracket key. You will see a left-pointing arrow on screen, showing that you have successfully entered an ESC character. To start an ANSI command, you must follow this action by releasing the Ctrl key and then pressing the left square bracket key again.

ANSI.SYS executes commands that begin with escape sequences whenever DOS displays the commands on your screen. You can use a PROMPT com-

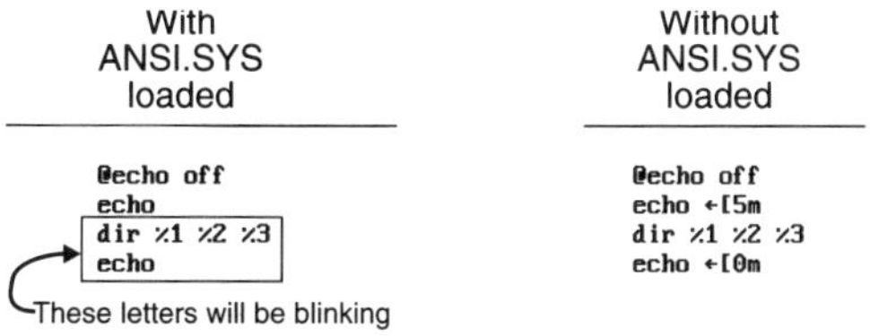

Figure 12-5 BLINK.BAT with and without the ANSI.SYS device driver loaded

mand that includes an ANSI command, use TYPE or MORE to display the contents of a text file, or place the commands in ECHO commands within a batch file and run the batch file.

For example, you might create a batch file called BLINK.BAT with the following contents:

```
@ECHO OFF
ECHO ESC[5m
DIR %1 %2 %3
ECHO ESC[0m
```

When you enter BLINK at the DOS prompt, this batch file will cause DOS to display the current directory's contents in blinking letters, but thereafter turn off blinking. (The `ESC[5m` is the ANSI command to turn on blinking attributes for all characters written after that point; `ESC[0m` cancels that request.) The %1, %2, and %3 in this batch file are called replaceable parameters. They let you use this batch file to display a directory listing of other directories or of only some of the files in the current directory.

If, instead, you use the DOS command TYPE to display the contents of BLINK.BAT you will see one of two things (Figure 12-5). With ANSI.SYS loaded, the line that contains the word DIR and the one after both will blink, and the ANSI commands won't appear. If you don't have ANSI.SYS loaded, all the characters in the file will be typed to the screen, and none of them will blink. Whenever you see strings of "garbage" symbols on your screen, and they all are preceded with the left-pointing arrow and left square bracket, you know you are seeing ANSI escape sequences.

Unlike most other DOS commands, ANSI escape sequences are case-sensitive. In DOS you may type `dir`, `DIR`, or `dIr`, for that matter. But if you enter `ESC[p5M` instead of `ESC[P5m`, ANSI won't understand or do what you expect.

THE DARK SIDE OF ANSI.SYS

Let's suppose you receive a new disk from a friend, or perhaps download a file from a bulletin board. You decide not to run this program until it's been checked for virus contamination. Still, you want to know what it does, so you might choose to TYPE these files to see what they contain. If you had ANSI.SYS loaded at the time and the file contained some infected ANSI commands, you would have sent them to screen and thus to the ANSI.SYS driver. You wouldn't see the commands, but they would be free to corrupt your system.

To see just how bad this could be, consider this command:

```
ESC[0;61;"@ECHO Y ¦ FORMAT C: /U > NUL"p
```

which tells ANSI.SYS to redefine your F3 key. The next time you press F3 at the DOS prompt—intending to repeat your last DOS command—you discover that you have just ordered a reformatting of your C drive, complete with answering yes to the question "Are you sure?" You won't even see the question or any progress messages!

There are several ways to protect yourself from this kind of mischief. One is to not use ANSI.SYS—or at least to use it only when you really need it. Another is to use an alternative to ANSI.SYS that specifically disables key redefinition. There is a freeware program called MCROANSI.SYS, (created by David Nugent and Unique Computing Pty Ltd) that does exactly that. A third way is to use the LIST program from the DOS Power Tools disk to examine those interesting (and potentially harmful) batch files and README.DOC files. LIST doesn't send its output to the screen through DOS, so you will see the ANSI escape sequences and they won't take effect.

DBLSPACE.BIN

DoubleSpace is a new utility in MS-DOS 6 that compresses data on-the-fly on its way to or from a disk drive. This creates the illusion that the disk has increased its capacity. (See Chapter 9 for a detailed discussion of what it is, how it works, and how to use it.)

DISPLAY.SYS

The DISPLAY.SYS device driver makes it possible to switch the screen display among multiple character sets. (See Chapter 4 for details.)

DRIVER.SYS

DRIVER.SYS creates a phantom logical disk drive that is really just another way of accessing an existing physical disk drive. This device driver makes it possible for your PC to support drives that normally it would not recognize. You also can make it regard one physical drive as if it were two different drives.

To make an exact duplicate of a floppy diskette, the command to use is

```
DISKCOPY A: A:
```

DOS will prompt you to change the diskette in the A drive from the source to the target (destination) diskette, as appropriate. If you try to COPY or XCOPY files from A to A, instead, DOS will indicate you can't do that. If you have only one diskette drive of the right capacity, you may have a hard time copying the files from one diskette to another.

If you have space to spare on your hard disk, you could copy the files from the source diskette to a subdirectory on the hard disk, then copy them back to the destination diskette. This requires two DOS commands, but less disk swapping.

If you only have one diskette drive and want to copy files directly, there is an easy solution. DOS will treat the single physical diskette drive as if it were two drives, A and B. You can COPY or XCOPY from A to B and DOS not only will permit this, it will supervise the process and prompt you to change diskettes appropriately, just as it does with DISKCOPY. This trick works only if you have just one physical floppy diskette, and then only between the A and B drives. DRIVER.SYS lets you do this with any disk drive and imposes no limit on how many physical drives you can have. DRIVER.SYS also can direct DOS to view a floppy disk drive as if it had a different capacity than it actually does.

INSTALLING DRIVER.SYS

To use DRIVER.SYS, place this line in CONFIG.SYS:

```
DEVICE=[path]DRIVER.SYS /D:number [/C] [/F:factor]
[/H:heads] [/S:sectors] [/T:tracks]
```

To place the device driver in high memory, use DEVICEHIGH or run MemMaker or another memory manager's optimization program and let it decide which drivers and TSR programs to load high.

The `/D:number` switch identifies the physical drive to which you want to assign the logical drive. To assign another logical drive letter (in addition to A) to the first physical drive, use `/D:0`. To assign another logical drive letter to the second floppy drive (drive B in a two-floppy-drive system), or to an external drive with only one internal diskette drive, use `/D:1`. For a third diskette drive (ordinarily an external drive), use `/D:2`.

DOS always treats the first diskette drive as the A drive. If there's a second internal floppy, it's always drive B. After that, it assigns letters in the order that it finds drives. On most PCs DOS will look for a hard drive next and call it C. It will continue to assign letters to any physical drives it finds, which could be a mixture of internal or external hard or floppy drives. Then, the initial DOS startup process stops assigning drive letters.

During the CONFIG.SYS file processing, more letters may be assigned to RAM disks and other devices including tape drives, CD-ROM drives, network drives, and any other block device driver supported devices you may have, including the phantom drives that DRIVER.SYS creates. Those letters also are assigned in the order that the devices are encountered by DOS during the installation of those block device drivers.

Consequently, if you want to control the letter that DRIVER.SYS assigns to the phantom drive it creates out of the actual drive, you must be careful where in your CONFIG.SYS file you put the DEVICE command that loads DRIVER.SYS relative to any other DEVICE commands that also load block device drivers.

If you don't specify a drive type, DRIVER.SYS assumes a default of a 720 KB, 3.5-inch two-sided drive, with 80 tracks per side, 9 sectors per track, 2 heads, and no change-line support. If you're working with a different kind of diskette drive, add an /F switch. The available /F switch options are:

0	360KB (or a 160KB, 180KB, or 320KB), 5-1/4" floppy
1	1.2MB, 5-1/4" floppy
2	720KB, 3-1/2" floppy
7	1.44MB, 3-1//2" floppy
9	2.88MB, 3-1/2" floppy

Unless you're using an obscure disk drive, there will be an appropriate /F switch to set the proper number of heads, sectors, and tracks for each type of diskette. To override one of those settings, use the /H switch to set the number of heads, the /S switch to specify the number of sectors, and /T to set the number of tracks.

Some disk drives can inform the computer when the door to the drive has been opened or closed, a procedure called *change-line support.* This support ensures that DOS will read the disk before making any assumptions about its contents. To turn on change-line support, add /C to the device driver command in CONFIG.SYS.

HOW TO USE DRIVER.SYS

After you've loaded DRIVER.SYS into memory, you can refer to the physical drive indicated by the /D parameter by using either of two different drive letters. For example, assume your B drive is a 1.44MB 3.5-inch drive and that you have only one hard disk volume, which is your C drive. If you put this line in your CONFIG.SYS file

```
DEVICE (or DEVICEHIGH)=C:\DOS\DRIVER.SYS /D:1 /F:7
```

and reboot your PC, you will find that you now have drives A, B, C, and D. The drives A, B, and C remain as before. D is a newly created, logical phantom copy of B.

With this setup you can easily copy all the files from one diskette to another of the same size, using only the B physical drive by issuing the command

```
COPY B:*.* D:
```

switching disks in the B drive when prompted.

Another use for DRIVER.SYS is to make a high-density floppy diskette drive appear as both a high-density diskette drive (using the original drive letter) and a low-density one (using the new, phantom drive letter). When you type FORMAT B:, the FORMAT program assumes you want to format a disk at the maximum capacity of that drive. If you have defined the alternate drive letter (D in the example above) as a low-density drive, you can format low-density diskettes in the same physical drive by issuing the command FORMAT D: and not bother with the /F:720 switch or the /N:9 /T:80 switches for a 720KB diskette (or the corresponding switches for a 360KB diskette).

If all you want to do is alter the characteristics of a diskette drive for all accesses to it, the preferred technique is to use the DRIVPARM directive in your CONFIG.SYS file, which is covered later in this chapter.

EGA.SYS

EGA.SYS is a device driver that supports use of an EGA monitor with task swapping programs such as the Task Swapper in the DOSSHELL or Windows. (See Chapter 5 for details.)

EMM386.EXE

EMM386.EXE does two things: It can provide the upper memory for device drivers and TSR programs. EMM386 also can be used to create simulated expanded memory. In both cases EMM386 requires some XMS memory, which can be provided by loading HIMEM.SYS first, assuming you have some extended memory that HIMEM can convert to XMS memory. Chapter 6 explains extended memory and expanded memory in more detail. EMM386.EXE works only on PCs with a 386 or 486 CPU chip.

Unlike most other device drivers, this one has an EXE instead of a SYS file type, signaling the fact that, in addition to loading this device driver with a DEVICE line in your CONFIG.SYS file, you can execute it from the DOS prompt. EMM386 has different purposes, depending on how it is executed, and its syntax reflects those differences. The Command Reference details the syntax for both.

INSTALLING EMM386.EXE

To load the EMM386.EXE device driver, add this line to CONFIG.SYS:

```
DEVICE=[path]EMM386.EXE [parameters]
```

The command parameters control the way that EMM386.EXE manages expanded memory. The Command Reference explains all the EMM386.EXE parameters in detail.

> **Note:** HIMEM.SYS must be loaded before you load EMM386, or it will not have any XMS memory to work with. (See the discussion of HIMEM.SYS later in this chapter for details.) In addition, because EMM386 creates the upper memory from which UMBs are allocated, EMM386 itself cannot be loaded into upper memory.

You can choose the parameters to go on the DEVICE=EMM386 line in your CONFIG.SYS file yourself, or you can use MemMaker to help you. See Chapter 6 for more information on optimizing your system's use of memory and the use of HIMEM and EMM386 to accomplish that goal.

When run at the DOS prompt, EMM386 is used to turn on or off expanded memory support or a Weitek math coprocessor. You also can use it to report whether or not expanded memory support has been turned off.

HIMEM.SYS

HIMEM.SYS is the DOS-included extended memory manager (XMM), which implies that it manages the High Memory Area (HMA) and upper memory. Like any memory manager, HIMEM allocates and deallocates memory blocks at the request of other programs. Any extended memory managed by HIMEM is XMS memory, referring to the Extended Memory Specification (XMS) that describes how HIMEM or any other XMM does its job.

The blocks of memory HIMEM can allocate are extended memory blocks (EMBs), upper memory blocks (UMBs), and the High Memory Area (HMA). Only one program at a time is allowed to use any given block in any of these three areas, though several programs may share the use of the same blocks of memory sequentially. Any program that needs to use these three kinds of memory must be loaded after HIMEM. Also, HIMEM cannot itself be loaded into upper memory.

INSTALLING HIMEM.SYS

To load the HIMEM.SYS device driver, place this line at the beginning of CONFIG.SYS:

```
DEVICE=[path]HIMEM.SYS [switches]
```

There are nine switches that you can use to configure HIMEM.SYS and the Command Reference contains a complete explanation of all of them. The explanations that follow detail only one switch at a time, but you may create a command that includes as many switches as you need.

Controlling the A20 Command Line The A20 memory address line (the 21st line) controls access to the region of memory just beyond 1MB. In real mode, much of the time the A20 line is held at its zero state to prevent programs from accessing any memory past 1MB. Accessing memory beyond that point, according to the XMS standard, must be regulated by your XMM program.

HIMEM.SYS is built to regulate the A20 line in most PCs. Some PCs, however, use very special methods that HIMEM cannot always detect. To accommodate these PCs, HIMEM has a special `/MACHINE:`*`nn`* switch, where *`nn`* is the number of the machine type appropriate for that PC. Check the Command Reference for the valid numbers and what they usually mean. If your PC still won't work (HIMEM will send a message when it loads indicating that it cannot control the A20 line or that the HMA is not available), you may have to try each number in turn until you stumble on the one that will work for your PC.

Occasionally you may run a program that manages the A20 line itself. In that case, simply invoke HIMEM with the switch `/A20CONTROL:OFF` on the command line, and it will not attempt to manage A20.

Setting Minimum HMA Program Size HIMEM.SYS permits only one program to use the HMA at a time. Normally, it allocates the HMA to the first program that requests HMA access. But if you know that another program loading later will be able to use the HMA more efficiently, you can direct HIMEM not to let any program use the HMA unless it says it needs more than some minimum amount of that space. You do so by adding the switch `/HMAMIN=`*`min`*, where *`min`* is replaced on the actual command line by the minimum number of kilobytes you want to require a program to use before it can get the HMA.

Keeping the CPU Clock Up to Speed Some computers have trouble accessing memory past 1MB in real mode at full speed. HIMEM enables those computers to reduce their clock speed at what it perceives to be the right times. To invoke HIMEM in this way, use the command line switch `/CPUCLOCK:ON` or `/CPUCLOCK:OFF`. Turning this option ON will fix problems in some PCs, but at the expense of some operating speed; its default is off.

Using HIMEM with an EISA Computer If your EISA (Extended Industry Standard Architecture) computer has more than 16MB of memory and you want it to convert all your extended memory into XMS memory (or any of the memory past the 16MB address), invoke HIMEM.SYS with the switch `/EISA`. Without this switch on in EISA machines, HIMEM is unable to see any memory past 16MB.

Using EMB Handles A few programs require more than the default 32 extended memory block (EMB) handles open at one time. If a program tells you to reduce or increase the maximum number, use the switch `/NUMHANDLES=`*n*, with *n* replaced by the maximum number of handles you want HIMEM to provide.

Reserving Space for an Interrupt 15h Interface There are still a number of popular programs extant that use the Interrupt 15h method of allocating extended memory, rather than asking an XMM for EMBs. To reserve some of your extended memory for those programs, add the switch `/INT15=`*xxxx* to the HIMEM.SYS line in your CONFIG.SYS, where *xxxx* is the number of kilobytes of extended memory you wish to reserve. The value of *xxxx* should be 64KB greater than the total amount those older applications require (to allow for the HMA plus what the applications want).

Controlling Shadow RAM Many PCs have something called shadow RAM, random access memory that is used to store copies of the contents of the PC's main ROM chips. Using shadow RAM often enables you to access information stored there more quickly than from ROM.

Some PCs allow you to enable or disable shadowing of ROMs. And sometimes, if you disable ROM shadowing, the PC will make that unused memory appear as additional extended memory. If your PC uses RAM for ROM shadowing and you disable it, and it then creates additional extended memory, you may want HIMEM to give your PC that command. The command line switch is `/SHADOWRAM:OFF`. To attempt to force ROM shadowing, use `/SHADOWRAM:ON`. If you have less than 2MB of total RAM, HIMEM will default to trying to turn ROM shadowing off in an attempt to access more XMS memory for your programs to use.

Again, not all PCs respond to this switch, and even those that do may not move unused shadow RAM into extended memory. You may have to conduct some experiments to learn what your PC is capable of doing.

POWER.EXE

The POWER.EXE device driver monitors applications and devices and reduces power consumption when they are idle. This can extend by as much as 20 percent the life of a battery in a laptop computer that conforms to the Advanced Power Management (APM) specification.

If your computer doesn't include APM compatibility, POWER.EXE can reduce power consumption by as much as 5 percent, but it also reduces performance of some applications so the saving might be insignificant. If your battery is close to the end of its life, it might be worth using POWER.EXE to save your files before the computer completely dies.

To load POWER.EXE into memory, add this line to CONFIG.SYS:

```
DEVICE=[path]POWER.EXE [/LOW] [/ADV[:MAX¦REG¦MIN]¦STD¦OFF]
```

DOS normally loads POWER.EXE into high memory if it is available. To force it into conventional memory, use the command line switch `/LOW`.

POWER has three modes: advanced, standard, and off. You can set the mode when you install the device driver or change it with a DOS command. (Like EMM386, POWER is both a device driver and a program you can run from the DOS prompt.) Advanced mode conserves power whenever applications and hardware devices are idle, but it can affect performance of an active application. Use the MAX setting for maximum power conservation, REG for a balance between power conservation and performance, and MIN for a minimum level of power conservation.

To change the advanced setting after POWER.EXE has been loaded, use this command at the DOS prompt:

```
POWER ADV:MAX¦REG¦MIN
```

POWER's standard mode uses the APM specification built into many newer laptop computers. On PCs that don't support the APM specification, standard mode turns off power management. To load POWER into memory in standard mode, use this command in CONFIG.SYS:

```
DEVICE=[path]POWER.EXE STD
```

To change to standard mode after POWER.EXE has been loaded, use this command at the DOS prompt:

```
POWER STD
```

It's also possible to load POWER.EXE into memory, but instruct it not to perform any power management functions until you direct it to do so. Use this line in CONFIG.SYS:

```
DEVICE=[path]POWER.EXE OFF
```

To turn off power management after POWER.EXE has been loaded, use this command at the DOS prompt:

```
POWER OFF
```

RAMDRIVE.SYS

RAMDRIVE.SYS creates a virtual disk drive (called a RAMdisk) in your PC's memory. Because the CPU can exchange information with memory locations more quickly than it can with a mechanical disk drive, operations on a RAMdisk are much faster than the corresponding operations on a "real" disk drive.

> ***Note:*** IBM called this driver VDISK.SYS in earlier versions of PC-DOS; starting with PC DOS 5.02 they adopted the Microsoft name RAMDRIVE.SYS. (Versions of VDISK prior to PC-DOS 4 used a different and generally inferior strategy for accessing extended memory, which gave VDISK a bad name. Changing to RAMDRIVE.SYS was, therefore, probably a good decision on IBM's part.)

DOS treats a RAMdisk like a physical disk drive, but since it stores files on memory chips instead of magnetic media, everything stored on a RAMdisk is lost the instant you turn off the computer or restart it with a reset switch or the Ctrl-Alt-Del keys.

You could use conventional memory for a RAMdisk, but that limits the amount of memory available to applications and other device drivers, and is almost always a bad thing to do. A better idea is to create all your RAMdisks using memory that is somewhere (anywhere) outside out of the first megabyte of system memory. Normally, this involves putting the RAMdisk in either extended or expanded memory. Notice that the RAMDRIVE.SYS program itself must be somewhere inside the first megabyte (as must any real-mode program that is going to run), but it can store all the data on its simulated disk drive in that other exterior region.

The smallest possible RAMdisk is 4KB; the largest is 32MB, or whatever amount of free memory you have in which to create the RAMdisk. Given the choice, the preferred memory to use is extended. Don't use simulated expanded memory. (Hardware expanded memory on a plug-in expanded memory card is okay, but in a 386 or 486 computer a RAMdisk created in extended memory will work appreciably faster.)

DOS assigns the next available drive letter to a RAMdisk. If you have one hard disk, and you're not using DoubleSpace, your RAM drive will be D; whereas, if you do use DoubleSpace, the RAMdisk will be assigned a letter past the last drive letter reserved for DoubleSpace host volumes.

Tip: It is possible to use an on-the-fly file compression program, such as DoubleSpace or Stacker on a RAMdisk. Doing so will result in an apparently larger RAMdisk, which will run somewhat slower than the real, underlying RAMdisk, but it will still be vastly faster than a mechanical disk drive. The real benefit in using this tip is that you can have a much larger RAMdisk at less cost in terms of free XMS memory for other uses.

INSTALLING RAMDRIVE.SYS

To create a RAMdisk in conventional memory, add this line to CONFIG.SYS:

```
DEVICE=[path]RAMDRIVE.SYS [disksize sectorsize [entries]]
```

To place the RAMdisk in extended memory, add a `/E` on the end of the command line. To place the RAMdisk in expanded memory, add a `/A` on the end of the command line.

For *disksize*, specify the size of the RAMdisk, in kilobytes, up to the maximum available in your PC's memory. If you don't specify a larger size, RAMDRIVE creates a 64KB RAMdisk. For *sectorsize*, set the size of the disk sectors. DOS uses 512 bytes for physical drives, and you should use the same value for your RAMdisk.

The *entries* variable limits the number of files and directories on the RAMdisk's root directory. The maximum setting is 1024 entries. The default is 64 entries in the root directory.

USING A RAMDISK

What good is a disk that loses everything stored on it when you turn off the computer? As a fast-access temporary storage location, it can have several uses. Many programs use the TEMP environment variable to store temporary files while they're working on them. If you set TEMP to a directory on the RAMdisk, your application will read and write to those files more efficiently, and it won't use up space on your hard drive. Nor will you find your drive littered with temporary files that some "untidy" application program forgot to delete.

If your RAMdisk is your D drive, place these lines in your CONFIG.SYS or AUTOEXEC.BAT file:

```
MD D:\TEMP
SET TEMP=D:\TEMP
```

Then create a TEMP directory on the RAMdisk and point your TEMP variable at that location each time you reboot your PC. (The advantage to using a subdirectory is that you may have an unlimited number of files in a subdirectory, unlike the root directory. This guarantees that you won't run out of room on the RAMdisk until all of its storage capacity actually has been used.)

Microsoft has long recommended that Windows users not use any (or at least not very much) of their RAM for a RAMdisk, explaining that Windows will make better use of any extended memory (or XMS memory, actually) than a RAMdisk could. That is not always true, especially if you are able to compress your RAM disk and thus make it appear to be larger than it really is. Also, many Windows applications do not let Windows take full advantage of all the RAM you have, but they will use the disk space you have quite effectively. For example, if you use CorelDRAW!, you will notice a remarkable speedup if you simply copy your drawing files to a RAMdisk before you open them. But after you save them to the RAMdisk, remember to copy them back to the hard disk before you power down. And realize that if your PC gets hung in the middle of a work session, you will lose whatever was on the RAMdisk at the time.

Another use for a RAM disk comes into play if you are going to work on a file located on a remote machine. Suppose your local PC is diskless (or has insufficient free space on its disks). If your only connection to that remote machine is an Interlnk, or some other serial or parallel port "zero-slot" connection, the time to transfer large files becomes significant. Copy the file across the link once to your RAMdisk. Work on it there, then copy it back across the link to the disk drive where it will be stored for the longer term. This saves the time that would otherwise be spent copying temporary copies of that file back and forth across the link. Again, remember the vulnerability of a RAMdisk: It's a good idea to save your work more often to the real disk at the opposite end of the link than if your local storage were on a real disk drive.

SETVER.EXE

Many programs have been written to determine what version of DOS is resident to ensure that the DOS service required is available on that version.

Ideally, a program finds out for itself if the version is the one it needs to run properly. DOS reports that it is *greater than or equal* to some number. In most cases, it's not productive to have DOS report *exactly* the version you expect, unless the program in question is an external command program, which may have been written with special knowledge of how a specific version of DOS did some undocumented procedures.

Fortunately, most of the recent versions of DOS provide all the services included in earlier versions and usually it is safe to run older programs with a more recent DOS—if you can force them to accept the later version.

SETVER is Microsoft's workaround for forcing those finicky programs to run. It hooks the appropriate interrupt and, whenever a program asks DOS what version it is, SETVER intercepts the question. First SETVER checks to see which program asked the question and then consults an internal table it keeps. If it finds the requesting program, it also will find the DOS version that program needs. SETVER reports to the program that it is running on a machine booted with that version.

Naturally, since this is a form of computer deceit, relying on this strategy can sometimes get you into trouble. But most of the time it works, and it is the only way to get some programs to perform.

If you type SETVER at the DOS prompt, it first will output its entire internal table, which is just a list of program names and, for each one, a DOS version number. (It's a long list, so you may want to pipe SETVER's output through the MORE filter to display the list one screenful at a time.) When it finishes displaying the table, and if you have not loaded SETVER through a DEVICE line in your CONFIG.SYS file, SETVER will report

```
NOTE: SETVER device not loaded. To activate SETVER version reporting
      you must load the SETVER device in your CONFIG.SYS.
```

Do this by adding this line to your CONFIG.SYS file:

```
DEVICE=[path]SETVER.EXE
```

The Microsoft SETUP program that installs DOS 6 will put that line in your CONFIG.SYS file automatically. If you don't wish to use SETVER, you will have to remove the line manually.

As supplied, the version table includes a list of many of the programs that demand a special version of DOS. It includes all of the DOS 5 external commands that were removed from MS-DOS 6, but are available on the DOS

Supplemental disk. The list is not comprehensive, and you may want to add some programs to it. If you need space, remove some of the programs that are shipped on the SETVER table.

To add an item to the version table, enter this command at the DOS prompt

```
SETVER program ver.no
```

where *program* is the file name of the program you want to add, including its extension. For *ver.no*, use the DOS version number that the program expects. (Some programs will report when refusing to run that they are doing so because you aren't running DOS version x.xx, which makes it obvious which version to insert to SETVER's table. Other programs are not so forthcoming. For them you will have to look in the documentation that came with the program—or make some shrewd guesses.)

Warning: The programs listed in SETVER have been tested and are known to run once they are deceived in the prescribed fashion. This won't be true for all programs, so test carefully any program you induce into running in this fashion.

Removing entries from the SETVER table is almost as easy as adding them. The command is

```
SETVER program ver.no /DELETE
```

To clear the entire table in one step, first invoke SETVER at the DOS prompt, but redirect its output to a file. Next, edit that file, adding `SETVER` and a space before each line, and a space plus `/DELETE` at the end of each line. Edit out the closing message and remove the lines for any programs you'd like to leave in the SETVER table. Save your work. This file is now a batch file. Run it, and it will cause each of the listed programs to be removed from the SETVER table.

Note: After you've finished changing the SETVER version table, you must restart your PC before the changes will take effect.

SETVER takes up 784 bytes of memory. You can load it into upper memory to keep it from reducing your free lower memory, but you will have to give up a corresponding amount of upper memory. In PC-DOS 6, SETVER will load into the HMA (if you use `DOS=HIGH` to put the DOS kernel there). For that DOS brand and version, you can freely load SETVER without any worries about RAM usage.

SMARTDRV.EXE

SmartDrive is the disk cache supplied with MS-DOS. It increases your PC's speed by copying data sent to or retrieved from the hard drive into RAM. When DOS sends an instruction to read that same data again, the disk cache reads the copy in RAM instead of having to wait to access the disk drive again. This takes much less time. Similarly, when data is written to the disk, keeping a copy in RAM prevents the cache program from repeatedly writing the same information to the same place on the disk. In applications that read and write to disk a lot, the improvement in performance can be dramatic.

Previously, SmartDrive was a mediocre disk cache program. Starting with version 4.0, which Microsoft shipped with Windows 3.1, SmartDrive began to improve. Now, with version 4.1 in MS-DOS 6, SmartDrive is the equal of most third-party disk cache programs.

LOADING SMARTDRIVE

If your computer has enough extended or expanded memory so that you can afford to dedicate a substantial amount of it to SmartDrive's disk cache, and if you have space in a UMB to load the SmartDrive program, you can give yourself the gift of much faster apparent disk speed without using any of your PC's lower memory. The DOS SETUP program automatically adds SMARTDRV.EXE to the AUTOEXEC.BAT file on any PC that can use it.

If you used SmartDrive with an earlier version of DOS, you may recall that you used a DEVICE line to load SMARTDRV.SYS. You may be surprised to learn that Microsoft has changed the file name and the loading strategy with DOS 6. (Actually, they made the change with Windows 3.1, but DOS 6 is the first MS-DOS version to have the new file name.)

Tip: The DOS 6 SETUP program does not erase any files that it is not replacing directly. This means it could end up leaving the old SMARTDRV.SYS file in your DOS directory along with the new SMARTDRV.EXE, which won't cause a problem if you always remember the correct syntax for invoking the new program. It is safer, however, to simply delete the earlier SMARTDRV.SYS file.

With the new SMARTDRV.EXE you don't use a DEVICE line to load the disk cache device driver. It is loaded from a line in your AUTOEXEC.BAT file. Nevertheless, you may need a DEVICE line mentioning SMARTDRV.EXE, not to load the cache program, but to set up "double buffering" in order to make the program work safer in certain situations. We will explain when and how to do this in the section "Double Buffering" later in this chapter.

The Command Reference contains detailed information about SMARTDRV syntax. This section presents only the features of the program.

CONFIGURING THE CACHE

The amount of space in the cache determines the amount of data it can hold. When the cache is large, applications don't have to read from the disk as often, and the computer's performance improves. Beyond a certain point, however, which varies for different applications, larger caches provide only marginally better performance.

Microsoft suggests that the best thing you can do for Windows is to supply it with substantial memory, and Windows will use that memory better than any other program in your PC. SmartDrive was written to notice if Windows loads, and if it does, to relinquish some of the memory that SmartDrive was using for disk caching so that Windows can use it instead. (Many third-party caching programs have adopted this strategy as well. Super PC-Kwik is one example. PC-Kwik also can "lend" its cache memory to other programs that can ask for it the same way that Windows does.)

When you invoke SmartDrive, you tell it how much memory to use for its cache and the minimum amount to hold and not lend to Windows.

Element Size SmartDrive moves data into memory in segments called *elements,* 1024, 2048, 4096 or 8192 bytes at a time. The primary size considerations of the element are: A large element size allows SmartDrive to work a bit faster, but it also uses more lower memory since it must accumulate at least one element's worth of data before it can send it to extended memory. A large element size also means it takes longer for SmartDrive to move the data to extended memory, during which you might lose some interrupts if you are communicating over a high-speed modem.

Buffer Size One reason SmartDrive 4.1 is faster than earlier versions is thanks to its read-ahead strategy. If you ask for data from one location on the disk, SmartDrive reads that *and* the next several sectors as well. If your files are not fragmented, usually you will want that subsequent information soon thereafter. The information will already be in the cache memory, an effective time-saver. The down side to this strategy is that the larger the buffer, the more lower memory SmartDrive will use.

Note: The buffer size must be a multiple of the element size. In other words, if the element size is set to 4096 bytes, the buffer size must be 4KB or a multiple of 4KB.

DOUBLE BUFFERING

When you put a 386 or 486 processor into its most advanced operating mode (386 protected mode), it is possible to direct the processor to remap its memory address space. This is how EMM386 can move extended memory into the upper memory region, either to create simulated EMS memory or UMBs.

Once this memory paging is active, there is no way to determine which logical addresses have been assigned to a given segment of physical memory. Most of the time, this causes no problems, but one situation is exceptional. If you have a hard disk controller that wants to put its disk buffers into upper memory, it will put them into physical addresses that it assumes are located in the CPU's upper memory space. The CPU may, however, unbeknownst to the disk controller, swap some memory addresses around. At that point, the disk controller may be reading or writing to the wrong place. Serious corruption of the data on your hard disk is the immediate and inevitable result.

Not all hard disk controllers have this vulnerability. Those to watch out for are called "bus mastering controllers." These frequently are high-performance SCSI (Small Computer System Interface), ESDI (Enhanced Small Device Interface), and MCA (Micro Channel Architecture) drive controllers.

Some high-performance disk controllers avoid this issue by using "programmed I/O" to transfer data to the disk drive. They send data from the CPU to an I/O port instead of to a memory address, and the controller retrieves the data from that port instead of from memory. Port addresses never get remapped, so there is no problem in this case.

If this is something you face, Microsoft has the solution. To the line in your AUTOEXEC.BAT file that loads SMARTDRV, simply add a line to your CONFIG.SYS file that reads

```
DEVICE=C:\DOS\SMARTDRV.EXE /DOUBLE_BUFFER
```

This uses about 2KB of lower memory. (You cannot use DEVICEHIGH on this driver, even though you can load the main disk cache program into

UMBs. As a matter of fact, you don't have to tell DOS to load SmartDrive high—it will do so automatically if it can, unless you tell it not to.)

Tip: If you aren't sure you need double buffering, load SMARTDRV in both places (in CONFIG.SYS for double buffering, in AUTOEXEC.BAT to install the cache). Then pay attention to the messages when it loads. If the messages go by too quickly, type SMARTDRV at the DOS prompt to repeat the report. The report tells you all the drives it is aware of, and indicates for which it is doing read or write caching. The report also includes a column called `Buffering`. If any item in this column says `yes`, you need double buffering; if all the entries read `no`, you can remove the SMARTDRV command from CONFIG.SYS. If any of the lines have a hyphen in them instead of a `yes` or a `no`, SmartDrive was unable to tell if you need buffering for that drive or not. In that case, consult the manufacturer of the drive or controller to find out whether it is safe to remove the double buffering line in your CONFIG.SYS file. When in doubt, play it safe and leave that line in place.

ANOTHER WAY TO IMPROVE SMARTDRIVE PERFORMANCE

Defragmenting your disk helps speed access to your files. It is especially important if you use SmartDrive to read ahead a lot. Run DEFRAG, or the third-party disk defragmenter of your choice from time to time. If it reports more than a small amount of fragmentation, let it defragment the disk.

Changing a DOS Default Driver

The default block device driver controls the way DOS exchanges data with disk drives and other storage devices. It expects each block device to be a particular type, with specific characteristics. For example, a high-density 5.25-inch diskette drive normally has a 1.2MB capacity.

Circumstances may dictate that you need to change DOS's view of a device's characteristics, perhaps to install a 3.5-inch disk drive in a PC whose BIOS doesn't recognize that such things exist, or to change the track and sector configuration of a tape drive. You might also want to downgrade a high-density drive to only accept double-density diskettes. The DRIVPARM directive in CONFIG.SYS provides a way to modify the default device driver without replacing it.

DRIVPARM is not a device driver; it is a CONFIG.SYS directive, like FILES, FCBS, STACKS, BUFFERS, and LASTDRIVE. It tells DOS how to do something it is already going to do—in this case, how to access a particular drive that it already knows you have.

To redefine the block device parameters for a drive, place this line in your CONFIG.SYS file:

```
DRIVPARM=/D:nn /F:type
```

Use the `/D` switch to specify the physical drive number: Use 0 for the A drive, 1 for the B drive, and so forth. You can specify a hard disk by using physical drive numbers over 127; the number is 128, the second is 129. (This is not the same as the D drive necessarily. You could have more than one hard drive volume on a single physical drive, for example.)

Use the `/F` switch to specify the type of drive. Choose the appropriate type number from this list:

0 160–360K 5.25-inch diskette
1 1.2MB 5.25-inch diskette
2 720K 3.5-inch diskette
5 Hard disk
6 Tape drive
7 1.44MB 3.5-inch diskette
8 Read/write optical disk
9 2.88MB 3.5-inch diskette

There are several other switches you can use. The Command Reference contains a complete explanation of the syntax for DRIVPARM.

DRIVPARM vs. DRIVER.SYS

DRIVPARM and DRIVER.SYS do similar things, but in different ways and with different results. DRIVPARM modifies the parameters of an existing physical drive; DRIVER.SYS creates a logical drive that points to a physical drive. DRIVER.SYS is restricted to working with floppy diskette drives; DRIVPARM can also be used on hard disks, tape drives, and read/write optical disk drives. Finally, DRIVER.SYS is an installable device driver, and as such it uses up some of your RAM. DRIVPARM, since it is only a directive, is acted upon, but does not result in any extra code residing in memory.

DOS Power Tools and Device Drivers

For drivers you'll only use infrequently, try LDEVICE along with NOTE and FREENOTE as a way of loading and unloading the drivers on the fly.

C H A P T E R

13

The DOS Environment

Among its services, DOS maintains the equivalent of "public bulletin boards" on which any program—or DOS power user—can place short messages, or from which they can retrieve messages left by others. This *DOS environment,* as it is called, is also used by DOS to keep track of some information it needs, and that others also are free to use.

In this chapter, how and when one or more DOS environments may be created in your PC will be explained, as well as how to use and modify the information stored there.

Introduction to the DOS Environment

If you carefully examined the output of the MEM /D command (for an example, see Figure 6-5), you will see that some of the lines in the right-hand column are labelled `Environment` and the column heading says it gives the `Type` for each entry. In the previous column (the one labelled `Name`) is the name of a program. Not every program has a corresponding line labelled `Environment`, but many do.

Before explaining what an environment is and when it gets created, you need to know more about how programs load into memory.

Loading Programs into Memory

Once the boot sector has loaded the hidden system files, DOS is resident in memory and it takes control of memory allocation. When IO.SYS reads the CONFIG.SYS file, it loads the device driver specified in each DEVICE statement and allows that program to initialize itself. Before loading a program, the IO.SYS portion that processes the CONFIG.SYS file must invoke the DOS memory manager for an allocation of memory. Each time a program is loaded, it is given as much memory as it needs (in the EXE header, if it is an EXE-style program) or all the free memory there is (if it is a COM-style, *memory image* program). When a device driver completes its initialization process, it returns to DOS all the RAM it hasn't used. Similarly, when IO.SYS finishes building the DOS disk buffers, system file table, and any other data structures it builds at this time, it must return to DOS any RAM that it didn't use.

In DOS 6, the CONFIG.SYS processor may now do something new before executing the INSTALL statements and SHELL statement. If you have created some environment definitions with SET statements in your CONFIG.SYS file, the CONFIG.SYS processor will ask DOS for a region of memory that becomes the *DOS environment* for the program it is about to load. It will copy into that block all of the definitions then in force. The SHELL statement specifies the program to use as the command interpreter. (The default is COMMAND.COM, the DOS command interpreter.) When the command interpreter begins execution, it creates its own environment and copies all the data from the environment it was given to this new *master DOS environment.* The output of `MEM /D` will identify the original environment for COMMAND.COM as `Data` belonging to COMMAND.COM. If, however, there were no definitions created by SET statements, then no environment blocks will have been created prior to the creation of the master DOS environment. After the command interpreter is loaded, most programs get loaded by it. Each time it loads a new program, it also creates an environment for that program, complete with a copy of all the environment definitions then in the master environment.

Most programs run, finish their business, and terminate, at which point COMMAND.COM takes back the resources they have been using and recycles them for use by other programs. The resources will include the memory used by that program for its instructions and the data it was working with, the memory for its copy of the environment, and any *file handles* that the program had "open." (The open file handles are numbers by which the program tells DOS which device or file it wishes to access.) TSR programs, however, don't terminate in the usual way. After completing their work, they tell the program that loaded them to resume control of the PC, but *not* any resources that the "terminating" program has at that time. Thus, these programs retain control of any files they have open and as much memory as they had been allocated, less any that they had previously returned to DOS.

Structure of the DOS Environment

To be exact, an environment is a region of memory that holds many definitions. Just as in a dictionary, an environment definition has two parts: the name of the item being defined and its definition. Each definition is stored as an ASCII text string, plus a *null byte* (a byte whose value is a binary 0). The strings are all of the form

```
NAME=DEFINITION
```

The name is always all in uppercase letters, but the definition may be a mixture of cases. (There is one exception to this rule: Microsoft Windows bypasses DOS and puts a special definition in the environment, a variable named is `windir`—all lowercase letters—whose definition is the path to the Windows directory.)

After the end of the last definition, there is an extra null byte to indicate that there are no more definitions stored here. You might reasonably think that this marked the end of the environment space. Not true. In every environment space *except the master environment,* the definitions are followed by a 2-byte binary number indicating how many more items follow (this number is always 1, or `01 00` when displayed by DEBUG). The only item after this is the *fully qualified file specification*—the drive letter, colon, path, and full file name with extension—of the program for which this environment block has been created. This information is followed by another null byte which ends the active information in the environment. The environment block may be longer than is necessary to hold this much information. Most of the environment blocks will be slightly larger—their size is rounded up to the next multiple of sixteen. The master environment may be larger still; this will be elaborated on later.

How DOS Uses the Environment

COMMAND.COM creates environment blocks because it needs the information kept there. In this section are described the four items whose definitions COMMAND.COM will use. COMMAND.COM will define three of them for you, but you can redefine them if you choose.

COMSPEC

The most important item defined in the environment is COMSPEC, the fully qualified file specification for the command interpreter. In DOS 6, the default definition for this item is `C:\DOS\COMMAND.COM`. (Earlier versions defaulted to `C:\COMMAND.COM`.) COMSPEC's value is always initially set by the SHELL statement in the CONFIG.SYS file. If you are using the DOS command interpreter, COMMAND.COM, that will be the program that is named on the SHELL line and in the COMSPEC definition. If you used an alternative such as 4DOS.COM or NDOS.COM, that alternative program will be mentioned in both places. For the rest of this chapter, it will be assumed that you are using the DOS COMMAND.COM.

COMMAND.COM splits itself into two parts. One part is simply the front end of the file. It resides low in memory where it was initially loaded and is called the permanent part. The rest of the file relocates to the top of lower memory and is called the transient part. COMMAND.COM uses the definition of COMSPEC every time it reloads the transient portion of itself. The permanent part occupies a *memory area* (a region described by a memory control block), just like every other program; the transient part is in a region that DOS considers free memory.

If, when it is loaded, an application program needs all the available lower memory or just the upper portion of that memory, it will overwrite the transient part of COMMAND.COM. This is perfectly acceptable. When the program terminates, and COMMAND.COM regains control of your PC, it determines if the transient part of itself was overwritten by adding up all the bytes in that memory region and comparing the sum to the amount it received when the transient part was first loaded there. If the checksum tells COMMAND.COM's permanent part that the transient part was not overwritten, COMMAND.COM usually proceeds and presents you with another DOS prompt. If the transient portion of COMMAND.COM was overwritten, the permanent part looks in the master environment for the COMSPEC definition. It loads the upper portion of its image on the disk (in the file at the location indicated by COMSPEC) into the top of lower memory—exactly where that same portion was previously loaded—and again checks that what is now in the upper end of lower memory is the same as what was there previously. If it is, all is well, and COMMAND.COM procedes to its next task. If, however, the new copy of itself is different from the original version, COMMAND.COM will print the message `Unable to load COMMAND.COM, system halted`. Then it shuts down completely and you must reboot to regain control of your PC. Since this variable is so important to DOS, it will put the proper path and file name into the environment as it is booting. As long as you don't change its definition, that works fine.

Many people never change the COMSPEC definition; power users sometimes do, and for good reasons. For example, if you have a RAM disk, you can speed up your PC a bit by copying COMMAND.COM to the RAM disk and using the SET command to direct COMSPEC to that copy. From then on, any time COMMAND.COM reloads its transient portion, it will quickly get it from the RAM disk. The commands to put in your AUTOEXEC.BAT file are

```
COPY C:\DOS\COMMAND.COM J:\
SET COMSPEC=J:\COMMAND.COM
```

(assuming that your RAM disk is drive J and that COMSPEC starts out pointing to a copy of COMMAND.COM in your C:\DOS directory). The potential for disaster is very high if you have dissimilar copies of COMMAND.COM on your hard disk. Your system will hang if COMSPEC points to a copy of COMMAND.COM that is different from the one that was loaded into memory during the boot process and tries to reload its transient part. Avoid this problem; delete any duplicate copies of COMMAND.COM.

PATH

The second most important definition in the environment is the DOS PATH. This is a list of directories that COMMAND.COM searches when directed to run an external DOS command or an application or utility program.

COMMAND.COM EXECUTES COMMANDS

When you type a command at the DOS prompt, or when COMMAND.COM reads a line of a batch file, it has to determine what you want it to do and then do it—if it can. DOS commands are divided into two categories: internal and external. Internal commands are actions that are performed by code within the command interpreter. External commands are programs that the command interpreter finds and runs.

Before COMMAND.COM can execute a command, it interprets what you have told it to do by "parsing" (analyzing) the command line. The first "word" (anything on the line up to the first space, tab, slash character, plus sign, or other character that is invalid in a file name) it takes to be the verb—the action to be performed. COMMAND.COM regards the verb as the command; the rest of the command line is called the *command tail*. COMMAND.COM deals with the verb in two different ways, depending on whether or not the verb has an explicit path in it. If you have included a drive letter, colon, and/or any path with a backslash character, COMMAND assumes this verb is an external command. Otherwise, it tries to determine if the verb is an internal command.

> **Note:** If you have loaded DOSKEY, the sequence of events is somewhat altered. Before looking for the verb as an internal command, COMMAND.COM will look for it as a DOSKEY alias. See Chapter 14 for details.

Once COMMAND.COM decides the verb is an internal command, it trims the verb. First, it discards any leading spaces and lops off the end of the verb starting at the first period (if any). It considers what is left as the name of an internal command and checks that name against a list within the COMMAND.COM file, which, for DOS 6, includes the following thirty-six internal command names:

BREAK	CALL	CD	CHCP
CHDIR	CLS	COPY	CTTY
DATE	DEL	DIR	ECHO
ERASE	EXIT	FOR	GOTO
IF	LH	LOADHIGH	MD
MKDIR	PATH	PAUSE	PROMPT
RD	REM	REN	RENAME
RMDIR	SET	TIME	TRUENAME
TYPE	VER	VERIFY	VOL

All of these are documented commands except TRUENAME, which first appeared in COMMAND.COM in DOS 4. Any of them except GOTO can be used at the DOS prompt; all of them can be used in batch files.

The first two forms of the TRUENAME command work fine. Use them if you are unsure of the real address for some drive or directory. Unfortunately, the full path with file name form doesn't do what you probably expect it would. In this form, the command shows you the full path to the present directory and then the file name you specified, no matter where that file may be. (The named file doesn't even have to exist!) This is less useful than what Microsoft probably intended, and may account for this intriguing command's undocumented status.

> **Note:** TRUENAME may be undocumented because it doesn't work properly—or at least the way it works may confuse you. The intent of the command is to resolve any ambiguity in a path or

file specification. In particular, if you are using the SUBST, ASSIGN, or JOIN command to make some drive letters or directories masquerade as others, TRUENAME will see past that ruse. Issue the command

```
TRUENAME
TRUENAME drive:
```

or

```
TRUENAME filename
```

and you will get back the current drive and directory, the current DOS directory on the specified drive, or a fully qualified pathname for the specified file. The last of these is given in the usual manner (drive letter, colon, path, file name, and file type).

In addition to the thirty-six internal commands just listed, COMMAND.COM recognizes a number of other words, including the following:

ERRORLEVEL, EXIST, and NOT (all used with the IF command)
ON and OFF (used with BREAK and VERIFY)

If COMMAND.COM finds the verb on its list of thirty-six internal commands, it immediately branches to that command's code which is somewhere inside of COMMAND.COM. That code is given the command tail, from which it determines what to do. (The commands CLS, EXIT, VER, and VOL don't accept any additional parameters, so they don't need to see the command tail; all the other internal commands can accept some input and so must examine the command tail.)

If COMMAND.COM cannot find the verb among the thirty-six internal commands, it assumes that you have specified an external command—a DOS external command (one of the programs shipped with DOS) or any other executable program on your disk. COMMAND.COM searches for external commands in a strictly defined way. If you have specified an explicit path to the command, then it looks *only* in the place you indicated. Otherwise, it looks for the program first in the current directory, then in each directory specified on the DOS PATH. If COMMAND.COM is unable to find the file, it issues the familiar complaint: `Bad command or filename`.

Tip: Until DOS 5, COMMAND.COM looked for a file whose file name portion (without the file type) was the same as the verb's root file name plus one of three designated extensions. (The root file name does not include a drive letter, a path preceding it, or a file type [file extension] following it.) No matter what extension you typed, or if you did not type any extension, COMMAND.COM would look first for a COM file, then for an EXE file, and last for a BAT file. COMMAND.COM now (in DOS versions 5 and later) regards the extension, if you type one. It will search in the specified directory (if any) or in the current directory and each directory on the path, but in each place it will look only for the specified file name with the specified extension. This allows you to force COMMAND.COM to run DYNAMO.EXE or DYNAMO.BAT even if there is a DYNAMO.COM in the same directory. The only extensions that COMMAND.COM will accept for an executable file are still COM, EXE, and BAT. You now can explicitly enter the extension, but this merely lets you force the execution of commands without regard to the usual COM, then EXE, then BAT file search order. Be careful, however. If you specify an extension, COMMAND.COM responds to it and ignores any other files with the same name and any other extension. If you are unsure of a program file's extension, play it safe and don't specify one.

STRUCTURE OF THE DOS PATH

When COMMAND.COM searches for executable files, it looks to the DOS PATH to specify a number of directories. The DOS PATH is an environment variable named PATH, and its definition is merely several directory specifications strung together and connected by semicolons. (Never put any spaces in the PATH, and be careful to distinguish between the colons that follow a drive letter and the semicolons that separate PATH elements.) In DOS 6, when COMMAND.COM creates the master environment, it automatically puts into it a PATH definition that points to the directory holding your DOS files. Usually, that is a line that reads

```
PATH=C:\DOS
```

but it could be different if you told SETUP to put your DOS files in some other directory.

Most people reset the PATH from a line in their AUTOEXEC.BAT file. (Using the SET command in the CONFIG.SYS file lets you set the PATH before COMMAND.COM creates the master environment. If you do so, even if you did not include C:\DOS within that PATH, COMMAND.COM will simply copy your definition into the master environment without change.) Be very careful when you type your PATH statement. It is strongly recommended that each element of the PATH include the full specification of that directory location, complete with drive letter, colon, and the path from the root directory of that drive. Thus, while this is a legal PATH statement

```
PATH=..;\TEMP;E:
```

it's far better to use

```
PATH=C:\DOS;D:\TEMP;E:\
```

because each element in the second PATH statement has a fixed meaning regardless of the current drive or directory. That is not true for a PATH with some elements that specify only a drive letter, that don't include the drive letter, or that use relative path notation, as in the first (counter) example.

Note: There is one exception worth noting. In a special situation, it may be desirable to have one particular relative path element (specifically, the element ..) included in the PATH. For example, suppose you use several different application programs and you put each one in a separate directory. Under each of those program directories you put one or more data subdirectories (see Figure 13-1). None of these directories are listed in the DOS PATH definition. By default, each of these application programs creates its data files in the current DOS directory.

If you change the current DOS directory to be one of the data directories, and if you use the PATH definition shown in Figure 13-1, you will be able to invoke the program in the parent directory of the current subdirectory and have it act on a file in that subdirectory in one easy command. For example, if you have put Microsoft Word for DOS in your D:\WORD55 directory and the current directory is D:\WORD55\LETTERS.92, then you can edit a letter to Ms. Jones (in the file JONES.DOC) by issuing the command

```
WORD JONES
```

Later, when the current DOS directory is E:\QP4\BUDGETS, you can work on your FALLFEST.WQ1 spreadsheet with the simple command

```
Q FALLFEST
```

Notice that this is a rather special situation, and the only relative path entry in the PATH definition is the double dot that refers to the immediate parent of the current DOS directory.

A portion of the directory tree

```
D:\
├──SUPERCLC
│  ├──BUDGETS
│  ├──FORECAST
│  └──EXPENSES
├──RAPID
│  ├──PRODUCTS
│  ├──WIDGETS
│  └──WHATSITS
├──WORD55
.  ├──LETTERS.91
.  ├──LETTERS.92
.  ├──LETTERS.93
   ├──RESUMES
   └──PROPOSAL
```

The PATH definition

```
PATH=..;C:\DOS;C:\UTILS;C:\BAT
```

Figure 13-1 One common way to organize program and data directories, and a useful PATH definition for this situation

SAVING YOUR PATH IN A FILE

You can use the PATH command to do two things. One is to set a new value for the PATH, as just discussed. The other is to report your current PATH definition. If you enter the command

```
PATH
```

at the DOS prompt with nothing after it, you will see your current PATH definition displayed. If you type the command

```
PATH > C:\SETUP\U-PATH.BAT
```

you will have created a batch file in the C:\SETUP directory called U-PATH.BAT. (You must already have a C:\SETUP directory or this will not work.) Once you have done this, you can recover from any inadvertent change to your PATH by simply typing the command

```
C:\SETUP\U-PATH
```

or, if C:\SETUP is one of the directories on your PATH at the time, simply type

```
U-PATH
```

It is recommended that you create just such a batch file and keep it in some directory that is likely to be always on the path (or that you can easily remember and type). If you make a mistake or a program does something unexpected and your PATH definition gets wiped out, simply invoking the U-PATH batch file is easier than having to reboot to restore your normal PATH definition.

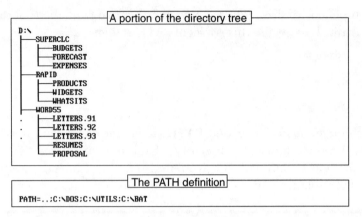

There is another use that some people make of this file. Instead of a PATH definition in their AUTOEXEC.BAT file, they have a line that reads

```
CALL C:\SETUP\U-PATH
```

which will cause COMMAND.COM to briefly interrupt its processing of the AUTOEXEC.BAT file. It will execute U-PATH, after which it will resume processing the rest of AUTOEXEC.BAT. There are at least three reasons why they might be useful.

1. You can more easily edit this simple, one-line batch file than your AUTOEXEC.BAT file, if all you wish to do is update your PATH definition. If you use only this one batch file as a means of setting your normal PATH, then you are sure that your latest edits to your PATH have been put there. Therefore, when you need to restore order to your PATH, you can be sure you will be restoring it to whatever you most recently decided was the best PATH definition to use.
2. Users who keep multiple alternative pairs of CONFIG.SYS and AUTOEXEC.BAT files so they can load different pairs to get different configurations may find it onerous to edit all of those AUTOEXEC.BAT files every time they decide to change their PATH definition. If each of the individual AUTOEXEC.BAT files CALLs the same U-PATH.BAT file, editing that one U-PATH.BAT file changes the PATH for all the AUTOEXEC.BAT files at once.
3. This strategy can give you a measure of protection against applications with aggressive installation programs. Most of these programs examine your AUTOEXEC.BAT file and if they don't find a PATH statement there, they will insert one that points wherever they want it to. If they find a PATH statement already there, they may add their program's directory at the head of the PATH. Either way, they are not necessarily doing something you would choose. But if your real PATH definition is in the U-PATH.BAT file, unless the installation is very clever, it will not find that definition. After the installation is complete, you simply get back to the DOS prompt and type in `C:\SETUP\U-PATH` to restore your choice of the best PATH definition. Then edit your AUTOEXEC.BAT file to remove their version (simply delete any line that starts with `PATH`).

HOW LONG CAN A PATH BE?

Although the DOS PATH is stored in the environment, it has a length limit that is independent of the size of your environment. If you don't have room in your environment for all of the PATH you have defined at the time you define it, however, the excess will be omitted.

Note: DOS 6 has an odd quirk in this connection. If you have specified a smaller environment size in the SHELL statement than is needed to store all the definitions you have made in your CONFIG.SYS and AUTOEXEC.BAT files, and if (but only if) you have defined some environment variables in your CONFIG.SYS file, then COMMAND.COM will expand the master environment to fit all of the definitions from both CONFIG.SYS and AUTOEXEC.BAT (and any more it chooses to put there) plus enough additional bytes to round out the size to a multiple of 16. That means that even one SET statement in CONFIG.SYS can be enough to guarantee that you won't see the `Out of environment space` message during the processing of the CONFIG.SYS and AUTOEXEC.BAT files. Don't rely on this odd fact. Not only is it undocumented and subject to change without notice when DOS is upgraded, it can create a situation that may frustrate you. If you let COMMAND.COM stretch the master environment just enough to barely fit the existing definitions, you will find that you have so little room left in the environment that the next time you enter a new definition you will get the `Out of environment space` message. Since it is often useful to create definitions of temporary environment variables in batch files, this can be a nuisance. The right way to deal with this is described in the section "Expanding the Environment's Size" later in this chapter.

The length limit to the PATH is the length limit to any single DOS command. The entire line must be able to fit into a 128 byte buffer, complete with a length byte. Therefore, the PATH definition itself cannot exceed 122 characters (allowing five characters for PATH= plus the length byte).

Some people have been confused about the effect of multiple PATH statements. They thought that they could get the combined effect of many PATH statements in a very long PATH simply by having many PATH statements in their AUTOEXEC.BAT file. Others thought that there might be some special "continuation character" available that would tell DOS that a command such as PATH was to be continued on the next line, thereby avoiding the line length limitation. Neither of these ideas works. When you issue a second

> **Warning:** You can get longer PATH definitions into the environment space with some environment editors or by using DEBUG or another tool to force the relevant characters into the memory locations. Don't do this. Many programs have been built "knowing" that the DOS PATH would never be longer than 128 characters. They allocate a buffer that is only that long, then read from the environment the entire PATH definition, no matter how long it is, and overwrite a portion of their own code, thus destroying themselves.

PATH definition it simply replaces the first. (This is true for all definitions in the environment.)

Tip: If you want the effect of a long path statement with many directory elements, there is a way you may be able to do it. Use the SUBST command to replace some of the longer elements with phantom drive letters by specifying a LASTDRIVE value that is higher than all the drive letters DOS has already assigned to physical drives, RAM disks, optical drives, DoubleSpace volumes, or any other use. (Some networks also will need to fit the drive letters for remote drives in before the LASTDRIVE letter you have specified in your CONFIG.SYS file; others must put them after that letter.)

Here is what those commands might look like on a typical PC. The CONFIG.SYS file would include this line

```
LASTDRIVE=Z
```

and the AUTOEXEC.BAT file would include these lines

```
SUBST M: D:\WINDOWS\SHAREWAR\MONSTER
SUBST N: C:\SYMANTEC\NORTON
SUBST Q: E:\QUICKEN
PATH=C:\DOS;C:\UTILS;M:\;N:\;Q:\
```

which together create a path that includes the DOS and UTILS directories on the C drive, plus the three special directories named in the SUBST commands, all in a PATH definition that is only 27 characters long. Without the SUBST commands the equivalent PATH definition would read:

```
PATH=C:\DOS;C:\UTILS;D:\WINDOWS\SHAREWAR\MONSTER;C:\SYMANTEC
\NORTON;E:\QUICKEN
```

in which the definition portion is 73 characters long.

There are some good arguments for not having very long PATH statements, which will be recounted shortly. If, however, you decide you want to have a super-long PATH, this may be the only way you can safely accomplish it.

MANIPULATING THE PATH

You can create a PATH definition in two ways. One is by using the PATH command; the other is by using the SET command. Thus,

```
PATH=C:\DOS
SET PATH=C:\DOS
```

and

```
PATH C:\DOS
```

are equivalent, because if you use the PATH command (but not the SET PATH command) COMMAND.COM will insert the equal sign for you. However, if you wish to set up a PATH through a line in your CONFIG.SYS file, you must use the form with SET as the first word, since SET is a valid command in a CONFIG.SYS file while PATH is not.

> **Note:** There is one minor difference, besides the equal sign, between using PATH and SET PATH. If you use the PATH command, COMMAND.COM will uppercase every letter you enter. If you use SET PATH, it will not. Since, when it is using the PATH definition, COMMAND.COM will treat all the letters in that definition as capital letters, this may not matter to you. If, however, you are particular about the way your PATH is displayed, you may prefer one or the other way to define the PATH. Of course, if you always type directory names in uppercase letters, the two methods really will be the same.

The section "Batch Files and the Environment" later in this chapter will explain how you can read your current PATH definition in a batch file and add an element at the front or back end. Chapter 14 will elaborate on that batch file to make it even more useful. Using these same techniques, you can save the present path in another environment variable or in a file. Then you can redefine it for some special purpose and later restore the original PATH definition.

You have already learned how to save your PATH definition in a file, U-PATH.BAT. To save the current PATH definition in another environment variable, use the command

```
SET OLDPATH=%PATH%
```

(Remember, this will work only if this line is in a batch file.) To restore the PATH from this saved copy (and clear out the extra copy) use the command:

```
IF NOT %OLDPATH%.==. SET PATH=%OLDPATH%
IF NOT %OLDPATH%.==. SET OLDPATH=
```

(The IF NOT construction and the use of the double equal signs will be explained in Chapter 14.)

MORE PATH TRICKS AND TIPS

When you consider that DOS must search for every external command in the current directory and all the directories on the PATH (until it finds the file you specified), you can see that it might not always be prudent to make the PATH as long as possible. This is especially true if you are prone to mistyping commands and your computer is slow. Even though you may realize almost as soon as you have pressed the Enter key that CLR is the wrong way to clear the screen, DOS will immediately search for CLR.COM, CLR.EXE, or CLR.BAT in all the places you told it to look. Only after it has finished that search will it tell you `Bad command or filename`, and only then may you retype the correct command, CLS.

One popular strategy is to create a batch file for almost every program you normally use. Each batch file will change to the appropriate directory, or it will set up the appropriate PATH and also may put some variable in the environment that the application program expects to find, then it runs the application. When you exit the application, the batch file will reset the PATH to its original definition and clear out the other environment variables it created. Creating batch files that do these things is discussed further in Chapter 14, in the section "Where to Keep Your Batch Files." An example of such a batch file also is shown in the next section of this chapter. If you follow this strategy, and if you put all those batch files into a C:\BAT directory, your normal PATH definition might be only

```
PATH=C:\DOS;C:\BAT
```

PROMPT

The third thing that COMMAND.COM puts in the environment and looks for there is the PROMPT string. Prior to DOS 6, it did not put this string there, but it would use it if you put one there. Now, COMMAND.COM will put

```
PROMPT=$P$G
```

in the environment, unless it finds that you have already defined it as some other string. This string tells COMMAND.COM how you want to have it prompt you each time it is ready to receive another command from the keyboard. If you like the folksy approach, you might use this prompt string:

```
PROMPT=Okay, good buddy. I'm ready. What are we gonna do
next? $G
```

or

```
PROMPT=Hello, Mary. What shall I do for you now? $G
```

(though these may be better in a book than on your screen if you see one of them many times each day).

Entire magazine feature articles have been written on fancy prompt strings. Someday, David Letterman may have a featured spot on his show for "stupid PC PROMPT tricks." However, once the euphoria over being able to "make your computer say to you" anything you like has died down, most people want a fairly simple prompt that gives useful information in a straightforward way. Without any PROMPT definition in the environment, COMMAND.COM used to show you the infamous `A>` or `C>` prompt. That is, it showed you just the drive letter that is the current DOS default drive, plus a greater than sign. Finally, with DOS 6, COMMAND.COM has been changed to put the most popular PROMPT string of all, PG, into the environment as the new default. (See Chapter 5 for an explanation of all the different metacharacters that are valid in a prompt string.) You can change the prompt string any time you like. Most users set it through a line in their AUTOEXEC.BAT file. As is the case with the PATH command, there are two ways this can be done. Both `PROMPT=`*`string`* or `SET PROMPT=`*`string`* work equally well.

SAVING YOUR PROMPT DEFINITION IN A FILE

Just as you can save your normal PATH definition in a file called U-PATH.BAT, you can save your usual PROMPT definition in a file called U-PROMPT.BAT. Before you leap to the keyboard to create this batch file, you must know that there is a significant difference between the PATH and PROMPT commands. Both have similar syntax for setting the corresponding environment definition (`PATH=`*`definition`* or `PROMPT=`*`definition`*). But, whereas PATH by itself will report on the current PATH, PROMPT by itself removes the PROMPT definition from the environment. This forces

COMMAND.COM to use the old default DOS prompt, which is C> for *any* directory on the C drive. The safe way to capture your current PROMPT definition to a file is to issue the command

```
SET > C:\SETUP\U-PROMPT.BAT
```

and then edit the resulting file, deleting all the lines except the one that starts out PROMPT=.

ONE GOOD TIME TO REDEFINE YOUR PROMPT

One useful change in the PROMPT string is in a batch file that you use to launch an application. If that application allows you to "Shell to DOS" or "Run a DOS command," it may be offering to run a copy of COMMAND.COM and then let you tell that copy whatever DOS command you would like to run. If you simply let it execute COMMAND.COM, you will get a new DOS prompt. Often, the application will put a message on the screen reminding you to type EXIT to return from this secondary DOS prompt to the application, but that message soon scrolls off your screen. Unless you have changed your PROMPT string, this secondary DOS prompt will look just like the original one. If you do more than a tiny bit of work at this new prompt, it is very easy to forget that you are "shelled out" from your application program. An example of one easy way to help keep aware of where you are is shown in the following batch file:

```
@ECHO OFF
PROMPT Type EXIT to return to WORD. $P $G
SET OLDPATH=%PATH%
PATH=D:\WORD55
WORD %1 %2 %3
PATH=%OLDPATH%
OLDPATH=
U-PROMPT
```

Only the second and last lines in this batch file are relevant to our present discussion. The definition in line 2 means that while you are in the application your prompt is set to the new value, but the last line resets it to the usual value. So the only time you will ever see the PROMPT set in line 2 is when you are shelled out to DOS from the application program. The rest of the file shows some of the ideas presented in the last section.

DIRCMD

The last item that COMMAND.COM looks for in the environment is a variable named DIRCMD. COMMAND.COM will not put any definition for it there, but if you have given DIRCMD a definition in the environment, COMMAND.COM will use it to direct how it will display DIR listing. Suppose, for example, that you almost never want DIR to display the names of subdirectories. You just want to see the files you have in a given subdirectory. You can determine that DIR's default behavior in your AUTOEXEC.BAT file by including the definition

```
SET DIRCMD=/A:-D
```

Thus, you are not prevented from having DIR show you directory names, but to get it to do so you must put a `/A:+D` on the command line each time you do want to see directory names. You may SET the definition of DIRCMD to be any valid combination of command line switches for the DIR command. As is true for any environment variable, you can completely remove the DIRCMD definition from the environment by typing the command

```
SET DIRCMD=
```

Other Programs Use the DOS Environment

Clearly, COMMAND.COM makes good use of the DOS environment, but its four variables, COMSPEC, PATH, PROMPT, and DIRCMD, are hardly the only useful ones that can be put there. Batch files can put information into the environment and later retrieve it from there. One example of this was shown in the batch file in the preceding section. Application programs also can access the environment to either read or change environment definitions.

Batch Files and the Environment

Batch files are ASCII text files. For the most part, they just contain a collection of DOS commands, entered one command per line. (There are some special DOS commands that are valid only in a batch file. All of them are discussed in detail in Chapter 14; here will be discussed only the DOS commands that deal with environment variables, whether they work only inside batch files or not.)

THE SET COMMAND

You can see all of the definitions that are currently in effect in the environment by issuing the command

```
SET
```

```
C:\>set
COMSPEC=C:\DOS\COMMAND.COM
PROMPT=$P$G
PATH=C:\DOS;D:\WINDOWS;C:\BAT;C:\UTILS;E:\NORTON;D:\WORD55
NU=E:\NORTON
LIB=D:\BAC
TEMP=J:\TEMP
TMP=J:\TEMP
DIRCMD=/A:-D
CATDISK=/F?
windir=D:\WINDOWS

C:\>
```

Figure 13-2 The environment definitions in a PC are displayed by the SET command.

with no command line parameters at all. This will generate a list of definitions, one per line, of all the things now in the DOS environment. Figure 13-2 shows the result of issuing this command on one PC.

The SET command is also the normal way to put definitions into the DOS environment. (The only other options you have, without going outside the standard DOS commands, are using the PATH and PROMPT commands; they essentially do the same things as SET PATH and SET PROMPT, respectively.) The syntax for the SET command is simple:

SET NAME=*definition*

When you want to change the definition for a given name that is stored in the environment, just issue another SET command using the same name and the new definition. It will replace the old one.

Tip: Trivia buffs may enjoy knowing that the definitions go into the environment in the order that they are made. When you redefine a name, its earlier definition is removed from the list, the space it occupied is closed, and the new definition is put at the end of the list. The real significance of this is that if your new definition causes the total size of all the definitions to exceed the size of the environment, the new definition will get truncated. An easy way to check that you have not exceeded the size of the environment is to issue the SET command with no parameters. If your latest definition appears in its entirety in the output SET generates, you can be sure it made it safely to the environment.

To remove a definition from the list simply enter

SET NAME=

with no definition to the right of the equal sign. (If you put even a single space after the equal sign, you will be defining NAME as that space character. If you then issue the command SET with no parameters, you will see that new definition at the end of the list. If you don't see NAME at the start of any line of SET's output, you can be sure you eliminated its definition in the environment.

ACCESSING ENVIRONMENT DEFINITIONS FROM BATCH FILES

Any batch file can put definitions into the environment by using the SET command, but how does a batch file read a definition from the environment, and what can it do with what it reads? COMMAND.COM treats the percent (%) character in a special way. At the DOS prompt, a % character followed by a letter can be used as a replaceable parameter in the FOR...IN...DO. In a batch file, however, a % character followed by a number is considered a *replaceable batch file parameter.* COMMAND.COM replaces it by one of the parameters on the command line that invoked the batch file. Both of these uses of the percent sign are described in detail in Chapter 14.

In a batch file, COMMAND.COM will treat %NAME% as a reference to the definition of NAME in the DOS environment. When it executes that line of the batch file, it will first replace %NAME% with the definition of NAME that it finds in the environment at that time. (If you have %JUNK% on a line in a batch file and there is no environment variable JUNK, COMMAND.COM will replace %JUNK% with one percent sign, which it then will discard when it processes the command.) Here is a simple example of how this might be used. Suppose you want to add a new directory, C:\NEW, to your present PATH definition. You can use the single line batch file

```
PATH=C:\NEW;%PATH%
```

if you want the new directory at the front of the search path, or

```
PATH=%PATH%;C:\NEW
```

if you want it at the end. In either case, when COMMAND.COM executes this batch file, %PATH% will be replaced with the present definition of the PATH. COMMAND.COM will attach that definition and C:\NEW with a semicolon in between and put the result back into the environment. (See Chapter 14 for another version of this batch file that lets you enter the name of the directory to be added to the PATH definition as a command line parameter, as well as a second parameter to specify if the new directory is to be added at the head or tail of the present PATH definition.)

Application and Utility Programs and the Environment

Any program can access the DOS environment, and a great many do. There are four common uses that application and utility programs make of environment definitions:

1. Programs use the environment definitions to find out where the subsidiary files are that this application or utility program needs to function. Most often, they will look for a variable whose name either matches their own or is some designated abbreviation of it. The definition of that name is the path to the directory where those files are stored.
2. A program may make use of the environment to find out how you want it to function. Remember that the purpose of your CONFIG.SYS and AUTOEXEC.BAT files is to customize your PC. These programs allow you to customize them in the process by giving your customization instructions to them as a definition of some special name in the environment.
3. Many programs use the same one or two environment names to find out where to put temporary files. Specifying a temporary files directory can help limit clutter on your disk and make it obvious when a program has left some temporary files lying around after it finishes its work. (If that happens, and it often does, you can clean up your disk and create more room by deleting all of those unnecessary temporary files.)
4. Some programs use the environment to find the current definition of COMSPEC, which they use to execute a new copy of COMMAND.COM in order to give you a DOS prompt or execute some DOS command.

Look again at Figure 13-2. There are ten items defined in the DOS environment in that PC. The first two (COMSPEC and PROMPT) were put there by COMMAND.COM. The third one (PATH) had been more simply defined by COMMAND.COM, but that definition was later modified by the user (probably through a line in AUTOEXEC.BAT). The rest of the items were inserted by the user (except for the last one—`windir`—which was put there by Windows). The line `NU=E:\NORTON` is used by the Norton Utilities programs to find others of those programs, plus their Help and INI files. Having this definition in the environment and the E:\NORTON directory on the PATH means that all of the Norton Utilities can be used from any directory on any disk volume in this system.

The lines defining the TEMP and TMP variables are referenced by many programs. Older programs look for TMP; the modern standard is to use the name TEMP. In either case, this definition tells any application that looks for it in the environment which directory to use for temporary files. In this case, that value has been set to J:\TEMP, a subdirectory on a RAM disk. It is not set to the root directory of that disk, since RAM disks often have a small number of files that they can store in the root directory. By pointing TEMP to a subdirectory, you can prevent the possibility of seeming to run out of space on this disk when actually you have run out only of spaces for file names in the root directory. The definition for TMP is, of course, set to the same place. If you set your TEMP and TMP variables to point to a directory that has no other use, should you later find some files left in there you may safely delete them— but be sure you have exited from all your applications first. Also, exit Windows, DESQview, or any other task-swapping or multitasking operating environment first. (Don't just get to DOS prompt; be sure you choose the command that shuts down the multitasker altogether. For Windows and the DOSSHELL the hot key is Alt-F4. For DESQview, you have to choose `Quit DESQview` from the main popup menu.) Being sure that the multitasker or task swapper has been stopped assures that you won't be deleting the working copy of something you were doing in an application in another window.

The DIRCMD variable is used by COMMAND.COM to set the default behavior of the DIR command. Many programs do something similar; in this case, CATDISK is using the definition given to its name as an instruction on how to find and open the catalog files it manipulates. In both these cases, and generally with programs that look in the environment for directions telling how they are to do their jobs, you can override the directions in the environment with other, contrary directions given on the command line or within the application's interactive screens.

The last entry in the environment, `windir`, cannot be put there by any normal DOS command. There is one giveaway to this fact: Normally, COMMAND.COM will uppercase the name of any environment variable you define. Windows put this line there for its own use, and it will clear that line when you exit Windows. (It doesn't want you to modify this line, which is why it put it there in lowercase letters.) You can use that information also, and it is a good way to check if you really have quit Windows and are back to the DOS prompt or merely are at a DOS prompt within a window in Windows. Issue the command SET and if you see a definition for `windir` you know you are in a DOS window inside Windows.

Tip: An even easier and safer way to find out if you are in a DOS window is to put the line

```
SET WINPMT=[WINDOWS]$P$G
```

in your AUTOEXEC.BAT, which will put the text string [WINDOWS] before the normal PG path information in your DOS prompt whenever you're running DOS under Windows.

You might think you could use the value of `windir` in a batch file so it could find the Windows subdirectory or some subdirectory below it on the directory tree. This is not as easy to do as you might imagine, because the %NAME% trick only works on names that are all uppercase, no matter what case you use when you type the line in your batch file. That restriction comes about because when COMMAND.COM reads the line before it and executes it, it will uppercase whatever you have typed. As with almost all of the DOS command manipulations, COMMAND.COM accepts commands and environment variable names in any case, but acts as if they had been typed all in capital letters. If you are writing a program in something more powerful than the COMMAND.COM batch language, you will be able to retrieve the definition for `windir` and make whatever use of it you like. For example, the following QBASIC program fragment reads the current definition of the `windir` variable in the environment, separates the drive and path portions, and then switches the current DOS drive and directory to the place pointed to by `windir`:

```
A$=ENVIRON$("windir")      ' Get the Windows directory
IF LEN(A$)=0 THEN PRINT "Not in Windows": STOP
D$=LEFT$(A$,2)             '  Get the drive identifier
P$=MID$(A$,3)              '    and path to directory
SHELL D$+":"               '  Change current DOS drive
SHELL "CD "+P$             '    and directory
```

So far you have seen how DOS uses environment variables, how you can use them in batch files, and some of the ways that programs use them. But can you use environment variables at the DOS prompt? Unfortunately, the answer is no. COMMAND.COM only evaluates %NAME% as the definition of NAME in the environment for commands that are a part of a batch file. Try the command

```
ECHO %PATH%
```

and all you will get is the string `%PATH%`.

DOS Master Environment and Its Children

Now that CONFIG.SYS supports SET statements, the notion of which environment is the master one has become muddied. The environment created by COMMAND.COM is different, but the explanation gets subtle at some points and is sometimes not what you expect. Almost every program that is loaded into memory in a PC is given a memory block called its environment. Some programs execute, finish, and then disappear. Their memory and other resources are returned to the pool of available resources to be allocated to other programs later on. This cycle of receive, use, and relinquish applies to all the resources the program gets—and that includes the environment memory block as well as the memory blocks containing the program's instructions and data. Other programs linger. Their work done for the moment, they nonetheless stay in memory (and may hold onto other resources) waiting for the moment when they will be needed again. These are called TSR (terminate and stay resident) programs.

A typical PC has many layers of programs in its memory. At any given moment, all but one of these layers are dormant. If the active layer has an environment, it is—at that moment—the *active environment.* In the good old days—a few months before there was a DOS 6—the first environment block created in a freshly booted PC was the one that COMMAND.COM created for itself, termed the *master environment.* Thereafter, as it launched programs, COMMAND.COM created a copy of its environment for each one of them. Those programs are called *child processes,* with COMMAND.COM as their *parent process.* As soon as each *child environment* is created, it is filled with copies of all the definitions in effect in its parent's environment at that moment.

You could complicate things a bit by loading a secondary command processor. One way is simply by typing the command COMMAND at the DOS prompt. Once it loads, this secondary copy of COMMAND.COM will create for itself a new environment, which you could call a secondary master environment. As long as that secondary copy of COMMAND.COM is in memory, it launches any other programs that get started, and as it does so it creates their environments (complete with copies of all the definitions then in the secondary master environment). Those processes are children of the secondary COMMAND.COM and their environments are children of its secondary master environment. When you are through with this secondary command interpreter you can remove it by typing EXIT at the DOS prompt. It's removal returns to DOS all of the resources it was using, including all of the memory blocks it inhabited (its environment space).

With this hierarchy in mind, it is easy to see why the original environment created by the original and permanent command interpreter was called the master environment. Now let's look at what has changed with DOS 6 and why this is no longer such a simple story. DOS 6 lets you use SET statements in your CONFIG.SYS file, which allow you to communicate easily between the CONFIG.SYS and AUTOEXEC.BAT files. If you use menus in your CONFIG.SYS file, DOS will put a variable named CONFIG in the environment for just this purpose. Each time you traverse a menu block in CONFIG.SYS, the definition of CONFIG is updated to be the name of that menu block. Another way you can use this new capability is to SET some environment variable that will be needed by a program you plan to INSTALL. Prior to DOS 6, if you wanted to run any such program, you would have to wait until sometime in your AUTOEXEC.BAT file or later, so you would have had the opportunity to SET the needed environment definition first.

Naturally, these changes mean that there are some environment memory blocks allocated and definitions put in them before COMMAND.COM is first loaded into memory. So when COMMAND.COM finally gets around to creating its master environment it is not the first one. In this situation, one might wonder at the appropriateness of the name "master" for that environment. Every environment block created before COMMAND.COM loads is a copy of the first one. Each contains the definition of CONFIG, if you had any menus in your CONFIG.SYS file, plus any other definitions you created with SET commands. (If you neither had any menus nor used any SET commands, there would be no environment blocks created before COMMAND.COM loads.) These environment blocks are created for each program that is installed and for the command interpreter. Since each of these environment blocks is made only large enough to hold the elements that are initially put in them, the programs that get installed may only read those definitions, or change them in a way that doesn't lengthen them. Only when COMMAND.COM loads and creates the master environment can you control the size of the environment. With a bit more difficulty, you also can create some free space in all the child environments.

There are two ways in which a master environment (primary or secondary) differs from all the other environments. One is that since it is created by the (primary or secondary) command interpreter, and since it often is larger than any previously created environment, the master environment is normally located at a higher memory address than the command interpreter whose environment it is. (All other environments are created before their programs are loaded and, thus, the environment blocks always fall at an address lower than the program.) The other difference is that, unlike all the other environments, master environments don't have the fully qualified path name of their controlling program stored just after the end of the last definition.

Programs with and without Their Own Environments

Device drivers loaded by IO.SYS are always written to assume that there is no environment at the time they are loaded, and so it would serve no purpose to provide them with an environment memory block. Before every other program is loaded, an environment memory block is allocated for it. The only exception is that if your CONFIG.SYS file has no menus and no SET statements, there are no environment variables to put in an environment when TSR programs get loaded by INSTALL statements or when the permanent command interpreter is loaded. In those cases, IO.SYS will not create environment blocks for those programs. *Every* program that gets loaded by COMMAND.COM has an environment block created for it before it is loaded.

There are no exceptions. Even secondary command processors are given an environment block (the primary one is if menus or SET statements were used in the CONFIG.SYS file). Command interpreters are different in that they receive their environment from the program that loaded them, then create a new one for themselves. After that, they ignore the original one they were given. (Strangely, it seems that COMMAND.COM does not give back to DOS the memory used for the initial environment block it received, even though it no longer needs that memory.)

Size of Each Environment

The environments created before COMMAND.COM loads are created exactly large enough to hold the definitions established by the SET commands and the definition of the CONFIG variable (plus a few bytes to round up their size to a multiple of 16 bytes). You cannot INSTALL a program that will create new environment definitions, however, unless you can get that program first to remove from its environment some of the existing definitions to make room for the new ones. The master environment created by COMMAND.COM will be exactly 256 bytes long, unless one of three conditions forces it to be longer. One condition that will force the creation of a larger master environment is that you have specified a size for it in a SHELL statement in your CONFIG.SYS file. Almost all power users do this. You can do it by appending `/E:`*nnn* where *nnn* is the size in bytes that you want the master environment to be. The full command line is

```
SHELL=C:\DOS\COMMAND.COM C:\DOS /P /E:nnn
```

The other way the master environment may be forced to be larger than its default size, or even larger than you have specified in your SHELL statement, is if you define enough things by use of menus and SET commands in CONFIG.SYS and SET, PROMPT, and PATH statements in AUTOEXEC.BAT. Notice carefully: The master environment will not be expanded to hold all your definitions unless you have given at least one of them in your CONFIG.SYS file.

Finally, there is one atypical case in which the environment may be as large as you like, up to 32KB. If you have no AUTOEXEC.BAT file, then you may enter SET commands at the DOS prompt quite awhile before you run out of environment space. (It is hard to see *why* anyone would want to do this, but that is the way things work.) If you later load another copy of COMMAND.COM, that secondary command processor also can be told to create a large environment. Again, you do this by adding a `/E:`*nnn* switch on the command line when you load that copy of COMMAND.COM.

Each time COMMAND.COM creates a child environment it makes it just large enough to hold all the definitions that are at that moment in its master environment, plus the fully qualified path name of the program it is loading. As is the case with programs loaded by INSTALL statements, this means that these child processes are sharply limited in what new definitions they can create. If they try to make one that won't fit, the portion that does fit will be inserted and an error message generated. If you are not sure how much space your present environment definitions take up, there is an easy way to find out. Just issue the commands

```
SET > XXXX
DIR XXXX
LIST XXXX
```

where XXXX is simply a name that is different from that of any existing file. The first line copies all current environment definitions into the file XXXX, and the second line lets you see how big that file is. This is roughly, but not exactly, the amount of space taken up in the current environment by those definitions. The third line uses a DOS Power Tools program, LIST, to display the file's contents. LIST also can show you on the top line of the screen the number of lines in the file if you simply press the END key. You will see a fraction on the top line; the first number is the line of the file at the top of the display and the second number is the number of lines in the file. (The numbers displayed here refer only to the current page, but the file XXXX will not have any form feed characters in it, so it appears to LIST like a single page, no matter how long it is.)

Now, let's compute the amount of space taken up by your environment definitions: The file size for XXXX counts all the characters in all the definitions, plus two for the end of each line (for a carriage return and a line feed character). In the environment each definition except the last one is followed only by a single separator byte (the one with a binary value of 0). So, subtract from the file size shown by DIR the number of lines shown by LIST and add one. The result is exactly the number of bytes of environment space used by all the definitions currently stored there.

AVOID WASTING MEMORY ON CHILD ENVIRONMENTS

Since each program you INSTALL and each TSR you load through your AUTOEXEC.BAT file will receive an environment, you could end up wasting quite a lot of space on them. By keeping them all as small as possible you may be able to recover as much as several kilobytes of lower memory for other programs to use. Now that you know how the size of each environment is determined, you can see exactly what you need to do in order to keep them small. First, don't define any environment variables until you really need them. For example, don't define a PATH or PROMPT near the beginning of your AUTOEXEC.BAT file. Each time you wish to invoke a program from a line in your AUTOEXEC.BAT file, use the full file specification for the program, complete with drive designator, path, and file name. Not only does this save on memory allocated to that program's environment, it also allows COMMAND.COM to load the program more quickly than if it had to search for it in all the directories along your PATH. If, as is usual, you turn ECHO OFF at the start of your AUTOEXEC.BAT file, the PROMPT definition won't be used until your COMMAND.COM is finished processing that file and is ready to show you another DOS prompt. Thus, there is no need to define it until just before you reach the end of that batch file. And each time a TSR loads before you define your prompt, it won't receive a larger environment in which to store that prompt string. Of course, if your prompt is simply PG, that will only save you 12 bytes in each child environment. If, on the other hand, you choose to have an elaborate prompt, you could save more than 100 bytes per child environment.

Some programs you launch from within your AUTOEXEC.BAT file must have some environment variable defined before they will run properly. If that is the case, and if you find that you are loading a lot of TSR programs after the program that needs the environment definition, you can save memory by putting a SET statement before the program is invoked to create the definition and another SET statement right afterwards to remove that definition. These lines might be:

```
SET BLABBER=LOUD,LONG,RAUCOUS
NOISEMAK
SET BLABBER=
```

where NOISEMAK.EXE is a program that makes noises and needs an environment variable BLABBER defined to tell it what kinds of noises to make.

RESERVING SPACE IN CHILD ENVIRONMENTS

Sometimes, you have the opposite problem. You run a batch file that puts something into the environment and it doesn't work right. Instead, you get the `Out of environment space` message and some different effect than intended. Consider, for example, the batch file shown earlier in this chapter to set a special prompt and then run an application. The objective is to make a prompt that will remind you, if you are shelled out of the application, to type EXIT to return. If you run this batch file at the primary DOS prompt, it works just fine. But, if after you have shelled out of one application you run a similar batch file to invoke a second application from which you might also shell to DOS, you will find that it won't work right. Here is what happens, and why. You run the first batch file, shell to DOS from the application, and run the second batch file. All of a sudden, you have no prompt or your prompt is somehow corrupted. You also will get an `Out of environment space` message, but that may not be nearly as dramatic as what happens to your screen image because of the altered prompt. This occurs because you have invoked the second batch file while you were within the application program launched by the first program. Often, these applications give you a DOS prompt by launching a second command interpreter. And when they do so, they usually won't specify how large its secondary master environment is to be. This means that the newly created secondary master environment might be full of definitions copied from the application's environment. Consequently, your batch file fails because it cannot create the OLDPRMPT variable, or at least not all of it.

There is a way around this. You can intentionally define a space-holding environment variable near the end of your AUTOEXEC.BAT file. Use a command like

```
SET SPACEHOLDER=12345678901234567890
```

which creates a 33-character entry (including the terminating null byte) in the primary master environment. Now, in any batch file that you anticipate might run out of room you can put

```
IF %SPACEHOLDER%.==12345678901234567890. SET SPACEHOLDER=
```

followed by whatever new definition you wish to create. (Notice that there is a period after the `%SPACEHOLDER%` and again at the end of the string of numbers. These are an essential part of the comparison process invoked by the double equal signs. See Chapter 14 for more on this.)

Programs that Release Their Environment

As noted several times earlier, almost every program that is loaded gets an environment space. However, if you look carefully at Figure 6-5, you will notice that there are not nearly as many lines of type `Environment` as there are lines of type `Program` (3 versus 6 in that figure). There are two possible explanations for this. One is that some of those programs might have been loaded by INSTALL statements without SET statements of menu blocks in the CONFIG.SYS file. (In fact, in this PC there weren't.) But there is another way that this could occur and, in this case, it also applies. Many TSR programs have been written to reduce themselves once they have finished their initialization so as to occupy as little memory as possible. One way they can do this is by giving back to DOS the memory block that holds their child environment. In fact, many modern TSR programs do this. Those that do completely release their environment space may remove all the definitions from their child environment, and then ask DOS to reduce that memory block to the minimum size needed to hold just the full file specification for that TSR program. (Doing this allows other programs to find out what the name is for the program that owns the environment block. Sometimes, TSR programs need to identify which of their sibling TSR programs are currently loaded in memory.)

Scope of Environmental Definitions

You may wonder if all this information about primary and secondary master environments and child environments will be useful to you. The answer is yes. You may think you can do some things with environment variables, but when you try them out they don't work. Understanding the many different environments is the first step to understanding why the things you tried did not work, and that is the beginning of finding a way that will work. Perhaps the most important aspect of all these environments to get clearly in mind is the scope of the definitions stored there. You now know that the environment that belongs to the currently active process (if it has an environment) is the active environment from which definitions will be retrieved and into which new ones will be put. You also know that each newly created environment starts out with the same definitions existing at that moment in the environment belonging to their parent process. Therefore, each new process inherits a flock of definitions, and the new process can repeatedly change those definitions. Once it terminates (if it is not a TSR program), its environment space and all the definitions that process created will disappear. This is by design so that child processes may function without corrupting their parent's environment.

Where this may be a disadvantage is when you nest batch files. Chapter 14 will explain how to do that by using COMMAND /C and CALL. One of the differences between the two is how they are affected by the scope of environment definitions. See the section in Chapter 14 titled "Loops, Layers, and Other Complexities" for the details.

Note: Another term sometimes used to describe how the parent's environment definitions get put into the environment of the child process is to say that the child "inherits" the parent's definitions. Inheritance in this sense is the rage in programming circles these days. In the cases of both environment variables and "programming objects," the inherited copies may be modified without affecting the source of those copies. This scheme provides an efficient means of setup (it takes no effort on the child's part to get a full copy of the originals), while protecting the originals from unwanted alteration. The problem in the case of environment variable definitions comes when the child's alterations are just what you do want back at the level of the parent. Achieving such a "reverse inheritance" resembles the notion suggested by a popular bumper sticker that says, "Insanity—we inherit it from our children."

Environment-Related DOS Commands

The most fundamental DOS commands that affect the environment are COMMAND, with its `/E:`*`nnn`* command line option to set the size of a master environment, plus SET, PATH, and PROMPT to define items to be stored there. `MEM /D` is useful for seeing how much memory is tied up in the various environment memory blocks. The `MEM /D` display also tells you the module names you need to use with `MEM /M:`*`modulename`* to see all of the blocks of memory that belong to any given program. Finally, from the `MEM /D` display you can get the segment addresses of the environment blocks. Then using DEBUG and its `D` (dump) capability, you can look directly at the contents of those blocks.

Environment-Related DOS Power Tools Programs

The utility programs CHGENV and PATHINC will help you manage your environment and PATH interactively. LIST also is helpful for browsing and changing the files that create your environment variable, especially CONFIG.SYS and AUTOEXEC.BAT.

C H A P T E R

14

◆ ◆ ◆ ◆ ◆

Batch Files and DOSKEY Macros

DOS Power users often don't think of themselves as programmers. Yet, some of the most common and powerful ways to customize your PC and make it work better and faster for you involve creating batch files—which is a kind of programming. This chapter explains the ins and outs of batch file programming and how DOSKEY macros both resemble and differ from batch files.

Batch File Programming

Batch files essentially are collections of DOS commands which could be typed at the DOS prompt. The good news is that once you have some commands in a batch file, you no longer have to type them each time you want that action to take place. Anything you can do at the DOS prompt, you can do in a batch file. There even are some things you can do in a batch file that you cannot do directly from the DOS prompt. On the other hand, after you work with them for awhile, you'll learn how to make batch files flexible enough to be able to alter what they do as circumstances change. A major advantage of a batch file is that, if you type the commands correctly when you create it, it never mistypes or misspells a command. All you have to do is type the commands right once (as you create the batch file). And even if you make an error, you can edit your batch files to correct them.

As will be explained shortly, DOSKEY macros are similar to batch files. They also can be used to reduce the number of keystrokes to execute multiple commands from a single, short command, and accept replaceable parameters. DOSKEY macros are different from batch files in some important ways, which will be explained as well.

Simple Batch Files

The simplest batch files are only one line long, a DOS command captured in a file. They can be very useful, but before showing you some examples, it would be helpful to review some of the ways you can create a batch file.

CREATING BATCH FILES

You can create such a file in many ways. For example, the

```
COPY CON filename
```

command described in Chapter 8 always works, and it doesn't depend on your using an editor of any kind. The main drawback is that you must type the file perfectly. You may correct errors on each line until you press the Enter key, after which that line goes into the file and you cannot recall it for further editing. When you finish, hold down the Ctrl key and tap Z, then release the Ctrl key and press Enter. A better way is to use the DOS external command EDIT. This is a good full-screen ASCII text file editor that uses the QBASIC.EXE program as its engine, so you can only use EDIT if you have QBASIC.EXE installed as well. (See Chapter 8 for a detailed description of how to use EDIT.)

You also may use any editor you like, as long as you can (and remember to) save your work as a pure ASCII text file. The best check is to use the DOS command TYPE on the finished result. If you don't see anything unexpected on your screen, you probably did it right. If you see what you typed plus a lot of "garbage" characters either mixed in or at the end, you probably forgot to save the file as ASCII text. Those extra characters are the editor's formatting instructions.

BATCH FILE BASICS

Almost every line in a batch file is a command that you could have typed at the DOS prompt; conversely, anything you can type at the DOS prompt without triggering an error message is a valid line for a batch file. An easy way to try out many lines proposed for batch files is to type them at the DOS prompt. For example, type this at the DOS prompt and press Enter:

```
REM      This is a remark
```

You saw each character as you typed it, but when you pressed Enter you merely got another DOS prompt. You saw no error message and apparently nothing was done with what you typed. That is the essence of the REMark command. For something different, type this command and press Enter:

```
ECHO     This is an echo command
```

COMMAND.COM treats this line differently from the REM line. Again, you saw each character as you typed it, but this time after you pressed Enter the whole line, minus the first five characters, was echoed back to you, followed by the DOS prompt. A slight, but important variation on that last example is this one. Type ECHO immediately followed by a period and press Enter. You will get back the DOS prompt, but first you will get a blank line. Any time you want a blank line in the batch file output, use `ECHO.` on a line by itself.

Here is something less conventional to try. Type the following lines, pressing Enter after each one. (Disregard what you may or may not see on the screen—just continue until you finish.)

```
ECHO OFF
REM     Whatever you like here
ECHO    Something or other
ECHO ON
```

The first line, ECHO OFF, tells COMMAND.COM to stop prompting you for commands, which is why you did not get a prompt for any of the other lines. The REM command let you see what you typed, then it was discarded. The ECHO command showed you what you were typing, then again showed you everything except the word ECHO and the space just after it. The last line, ECHO ON, restored the normal DOS prompt. There is one caution in connection with the REM command, which the next exercise shows. First, check that you don't have a file in your current directory called PRUDENT by typing

```
DIR PRUDENT
```

If you get a `File not found` message, type the two lines shown below at the DOS prompt and see what happens. (If you have a file named PRUDENT in the current directory, you can change the last word in the second line to some name that you don't have.)

```
REM It is not a good idea to use input redirection < from a remark
REM Neither is output redirection > prudent.
```

This time, you do get an error message on the first line but not on the second. Now, repeat your check for the file PRUDENT by reissuing the command

```
DIR PRUDENT
```

and you'll find that you now have a 0-length file named PRUDENT, because COMMAND.COM parses each line it is about to execute to see what is being requested and checks for redirection symbols (<, >, >>, and |) before it actually "reads" the words on the line. If it sees the *input redirection* symbol (<), it assumes that you wish to perform some command that takes input from stdin and to have that input come from a file you have named just after the input redirection symbol. Therefore, COMMAND.COM tries to open a file with the name it sees just after the < symbol. In our case, unless you happen to have a file named `FROM`, this open file request to DOS will fail, causing the error message you probably saw. If COMMAND.COM sees either of the *output redirection* symbols, it assumes that the command you are about to execute will send something to stdout and that you wish to have that output deposited in a file whose name will be the word immediately following the output redirection symbol. If you used the > symbol, COMMAND.COM first will erase any file by that name already in the current directory or whatever directory specified after the > symbol. In our case, the output file will be one named `PRUDENT`. (If you had used the >> symbol and the named output file already existed, COMMAND.COM would merely open the file and add data at the end of it.) Since the REM command does not generate any output, no data gets put in the file `PRUDENT`. It is not often that you want to create a 0-length file, but this is one technique you can use. With just these two commands, you can create some powerful and useful batch files, which will be shown in the next section.

SOME ONE-LINE ZINGERS

It's pointless to create a batch file to do something for which you could easily type the command at the DOS prompt. For example, if you created a batch file called DW.BAT and its one line read

```
DIR /W
```

you would have a one-line batch file, but not an important or useful one. Indeed, with DOS 5 or later versions, you can achieve the effect of this batch file by defining the DIRCMD environment variable as `/W`. This batch file doesn't save you many keystrokes, however, nor does it perform a specific task. If you expand this batch file, adding replaceable parameters such as echo lines, etc., you might develop something useful. Examples of how to do each of those things will be shown later, but here are some really useful one-line batch files.

One good example is a batch file that runs a program that resides in a directory that is not on your path. (Sometimes, it takes a multiline batch file to do that; other times it can be the simple, single-line batch file shown here.) If the program doesn't need any command line input, just type its fully qualified path name. For example, suppose you have a program BABABOOM.EXE in a subdirectory deep in your directory tree. Type the one-line batch file

```
G:\GAMES\CHILDREN\SOUNDFX\CURIOUS\BABABOOM.EXE
```

and name it BABA.BAT. If you put BABA.BAT in a directory that is named on the PATH, you can run BABABOOM from any directory on any drive simply by typing BABA. That is just four keystrokes instead of forty-two (plus the Enter). Many users have several batch files created to launch application programs. They keep all of these batch files in a special directory included on the PATH, so they can run these applications from any directory on any disk volume. The pros and cons of this approach will be discussed in the section "Where to Keep Your Batch Files" near the end of this chapter.

Chapter 10 pointed out that you can control a PCL printer (such as the Hewlett-Packard LaserJet series) by sending some arcane escape sequences. You cannot type these commands at the DOS prompt, nor would you want to. The first problem is that COMMAND.COM will not let you type an escape character (ASCII 27) as part of a command line; it reserves that character for your use to "start this command over." The second problem is that the sequences you need are difficult to remember and must be typed perfectly each time. Each of these characteristics makes these commands ideal candidates for one-line batch files. On the other hand, once you create a batch file, it's to your advantage to add another line or two with remarks to remind you of its purpose. Figure 14-1 shows several short batch files for sending various useful PCL commands to a printer. They each have only one active line; the others are included to document that one active line or make the screen display neater.

You can type copies of these batch files using the EDIT program. To enter the escape characters, hold down the Ctrl key and tap the `P` and `[` keys once each in succession. You will see a left-pointing arrow on the screen, which is the way the escape character looks on an IBM graphics display. All the other characters are just what they appear to be; type them carefully and check that what you see on your screen matches what you see in the figure. These batch files could easily be made more complex. For example, you could add a replaceable parameter to tell each batch file which printer port your PCL printer is attached to. For now, though, these are some good examples of the

ESC means enter an Escape character (ASCII 27)

```
@echo off
echo      Set printer to PC-8 IBM line draw character set,
echo                 Courier 12, 10 CPI font
echo.
echo ESC (10U ESC (sp12v10hsb3T                          > LPT1:
```

```
@echo off
echo      Set printer to PC-8 IBM line draw character set,
echo                 Courier 10, 12 CPI font
echo.
echo ESC (10U ESC (sp10v12hsb3T                          > LPT1:
```

```
@echo off
echo      Set printer to PC-8 IBM line draw character set,
echo            Lineprinter 8.5, 16.6 CPI font
echo.
echo ESC (10U ESC (sp8.5v16.66hsbT                       > LPT1:
```

```
@echo off
echo      Set page orientation to landscape (wider than tall),
echo            Lineprinter 8.5, 16.6 CPI font
echo.
echo ESC &l1O ESC &k2S ESC &l8D                          > LPT1:
```

```
@echo off
echo      Set page orientation to portrait (taller than wide),
echo                 Courier 12, 10 CPI font
echo.
echo ESC &l0O ESC &k0S ESC &l6D                          > LPT1:
```

Figure 14-1 Some useful PCL printer control batch files with only one active line

power of a single- (active-) line batch file. The batch file presented in Chapter 13 (to add an element to your current PATH definition) was another useful one-liner. Later in this chapter, you will see a much more elaborate and useful version of that file. Just realize that many of the more complex things you will be reading about later can be applied to the one-line batch file.

Medium Complexity Batch Files

This section will cover some sample batch files that can do more than one-line batch files. More complex ones are discussed later in the chapter.

CLEANING UP THE SCREEN

Beginning batch file programmers are often advised to leave ECHO turned on, but they eventually will want to turn it off. When ECHO is ON (the default state), COMMAND.COM shows each line of a batch file before executing. If you are unsure what each line will do and a particular line does something totally unexpected, looking carefully at the line COMMAND.COM thought it was to execute may help you figure out what went wrong. For example, COMMAND.COM may have interpreted some replaceable parameter differently than you had imagined or, when it made the indicated replacements, the resulting long line got truncated before being executed. Both of these situations show up clearly when you see the line before COMMAND.COM tries to execute it, but neither of them will be obvious to you unless you know how the line looks to COMMAND.COM. After a while, though, seeing all the lines echoed on-screen before they are executed can become tedious, even confusing. The echoed lines can make finding the "real" information in the display—the output generated by the executed lines—very difficult.

It is recommended that as soon as you understand what a batch file is doing, you insert an ECHO OFF statement at the beginning. If one section puzzles you, insert an ECHO ON statement before that section and an ECHO OFF just after it. To keep an ECHO OFF line from being echoed, add an @ sign on the front of the word ECHO. All of the batch files in Figure 14-1 start out this way. If you are still using a version of DOS prior to 3.3, however, this won't work. In that case, you can omit the @ and the ECHO OFF statement will continue to be echoed to the screen. Or, if you don't mind clearing everything that was previously on the screen, put ECHO OFF as the first line and CLS as the second. Thus, as soon as the ECHO OFF is printed on the screen it (and everything else) will be erased, leaving a clean screen for the rest of your batch file to print whatever you like. Prefacing a command with an @ suppresses the echoing of that one line. That can be useful, but it also can lead to a problem if you have a file name beginning with an @ symbol. Not many people run programs whose names start with an @ symbol, but if you do and you want to invoke one of them in a batch file, just add an extra @ on the front of the command name. (This will suppress the echoing of that line, but it also will allow the command to execute properly.)

WAITING AWHILE

The DOS command PAUSE is very useful in batch files. It puts on the screen the message:

```
Press any key to continue . . .
```

and then waits until you press a key. This command interrupts the flow of this batch file long enough to see what is on the screen before additional output causes it to scroll off; it also serves as a troubleshooting tool. When you use PAUSE in the first of these roles, you may wish to add information to indicate whether or not to press a key to continue. Consider the example:

```
ECHO Copy down these numbers, then
PAUSE
```

which shows on-screen as

```
Copy down these numbers, then
Press any key to continue . . .
```

That will tell you what you want, but it has an incorrect capital P at the start of the second line. To correct the capital P or alter the wording, redirect the output from PAUSE to the NUL device (the "bit bucket") and use ECHO statements before it to say whatever you like, such as:

```
ECHO  Press the space bar to go on, or Ctrl-Break to Exit.
PAUSE > NUL
```

PAUSE in a batch file also can help you isolate a problem and track down the line that is causing it: Put a pair of lines at a number of key points in your batch file. The first line ECHOes some statement about what you expect to be doing next or what you have just finished; the second line is the PAUSE that lets you read the message put on-screen by the ECHO command. Later, when you have that section of the batch file working perfectly, you can "REMark out" those lines. That is, add the characters R, E, M, and a space at the start of both lines, which will deactivate them. Leaving them in place allows you to reactivate them later. When you finally have finished troubleshooting the whole batch file, you can delete the ECHO/PAUSE line pairs.

Remember that any file takes up a minimum amount of disk space, which is one cluster (ordinarily 2KB). Not many users write batch files larger than 2KB. If yours are smaller than this limit, you could retain your ECHO and PAUSE lines. COMMAND.COM must read them, however, in order to know not to do anything with them. Therefore, you will want to remove them from batch files you frequently run, but it is not worth removing them from ones you run only occasionally.

BATCH ANSI ESCAPE COMMANDS

Chapter 4 described the ANSI.SYS escape sequences that you can use to redefine the meanings of keys. Chapter 5 described how other ANSI escape sequences can be used to alter the colors of text, move the cursor, clear the screen, etc. In those chapters you learned the individual commands you need. Here, you will learn how to create a batch file to automate the issuing of a group of those commands. All you need are the batch file commands you have learned, plus the ANSI escape sequences discussed in Chapters 4 and 5. Figure 14-2 shows two simple batch files: One redefines several keys; the other sets those keys back to their normal meanings.

Run DEFKEY. At the DOS prompt type ECHO, followed by some text using the altered keys. End the command line with `> PRN` and press Enter. Notice

```
@echo off
echo                DEFKEYS.BAT
echo.

rem  Using CFG program to test for presence of ANSI.SYS
CFG ANSI
if errorlevel 1 goto doit
   echo  This batch file only works if ANSI.SYS is loaded
   goto alldone

:doit
echo Redefining keys as follows:
echo.
echo    ALT+ 2 = superscript 2                     ←[0;121;253p
echo    ALT+ 4 = fraction form of one-quarter      ←[0;123;172p
echo    ALT+ 5 = fraction form of one-half         ←[0;124;171p
echo    ALT+ 6 = cent sign                         ←[0;125;155p
echo    ALT+ 0 = radical sign                      ←[0;129;251p
echo.
echo    And one fun redefinition:
echo ←[0;38;"The hypotenuse = ";251;"((side1)";253;"+(side2)";253;")"p
echo    Press Alt+ L   to see the law of Pythagorus.
echo.
:alldone
```

```
@echo off
echo                UNDEFKEYS.BAT
echo.

rem  Using CFG program to test for presence of ANSI.SYS
CFG ANSI
if errorlevel 1 goto doit
   echo  This batch file only works if ANSI.SYS is loaded
   goto alldone

:doit
echo Restoring keys to usual meanings as follows:
echo.
echo    ALT+ 2 restored  ←[0;121;0;121p
echo    ALT+ 4 restored  ←[0;123;0;123p
echo    ALT+ 5 restored  ←[0;124;0;124p
echo    ALT+ 6 restored  ←[0;125;0;125p
echo    ALT+ 0 restored  ←[0;129;0;129p
echo    Alt+ L restored  ←[0;38;0;38p
echo.
:alldone
```

Figure 14-2 Batch files make it easy to redefine your keys and to reset their meanings.

what you see on your screen display and printer. If your printer supports the same character set as your display card, both will look the same; otherwise, the printed output may not match the on-screen display. Run UNDEFKEY and you will find that your keys have been returned to their normal meanings.

The example with Alt-L shows that you can make one keystroke act as if it were many. Don't plan to use this capability to store a large volume of macro text, though. The ANSI.SYS driver reserves only a few hundred bytes for all the key redefinitions in effect at any one time. Leaving room for new definitions is one good reason to run UNDEFKEY as soon as you no longer need the special definitions set by DEFKEY. Another reason is to avoid a nonstandard response from a key you redefined and then forgot. Figure 14-2 shows what these files look like when viewed on-screen without ANSI.SYS loaded, or with a program (like DOS Power Tools LIST) that puts the characters into the video buffer directly, bypassing the ANSI.SYS driver. In particular, each escape character shows as a left-pointing arrow.

When you type a copy of each of these batch files and try them out, remember to enter an escape character in place of the left-pointing arrows. (As explained previously, if you use the DOS program EDIT to create the files, you will have to hold down Ctrl and press the `P` and `[` keys successivley to insert an escape character into the text. EDIT shows that character on-screen as the left-pointing arrow, as shown in Figure 14-2.)

A SIMPLE MENU SYSTEM

One popular use of batch files is to create a menu system for a PC. You can buy commercial menuing systems, which may include some features that would be difficult to implement solely with DOS batch commands. But nearly all of those features can be done in batch files. Perhaps the easiest way to make a batch file menu system is to start by making a subdirectory called C:\MENU, and adding these lines at the end of your AUTOEXEC.BAT file:

```
C:
CD \MENU
MAIN
```

The first of these lines assures that C is the current DOS default drive; the second line moves you into the MENU subdirectory; the third line runs a batch file, MAIN.BAT, the contents of which are shown in Figure 14-3. When MAIN.BAT runs, it clears the screen, prints a menu, then exits. That means that COMMAND.COM will give you another DOS prompt. At that point, if you type one of the letters shown on the menu and press Enter, and if you have suitable batch files called L.BAT, N.BAT, S.BAT, and W.BAT in that directory, the selected batch file will run. Also shown in Figure 14-3 are possible contents for those small batch files. Notice that each one ends by returning you to the C:\MENU subdirectory and then runs MAIN.BAT once again.

The batch files for 1-2-3 change the current DOS directory to that of the program before the program is invoked. The batch files for Norton Utilities, Windows, and WordStar don't do this. The reason for this is that 1-2-3 is best run from its home directory, while the others may be run from anywhere, as long as they have been properly installed. (In this case, proper installation means putting the directories of those programs on the path and defining an NU environment variable to point to the directory with the Norton Utilities files.) As long as you respond to the menu only by typing a selection and pressing Enter, this all works well. It also has the feature that you are always

MAIN.BAT

```
@echo off
rem        This is MAIN.BAT -- version 1 of menuing system
cls
echo.
echo.
echo.
echo.
echo                                   MAIN MENU
echo.
echo                 Enter a choice:
echo.
echo                      L   to run       Lotus 1-2-3
echo.
echo                      N   to run       Norton Utilties
echo.
echo                      S   to run       WordStar
echo.
echo                      W   to run       Microsoft Windows
echo.
echo.
```

L.BAT

```
@echo off
F:
CD\123
123
C:
CD\MENU
MAIN
```

S.BAT

```
@echo off
E:
CD\WS5
WS
C:
CD\MENU
MAIN
```

N.BAT

```
@echo off
NORTON
C:
CD\MENU
MAIN
```

W.BAT

```
@echo off
WIN
C:
CD\MENU
MAIN
```

Figure 14-3 The linked batch files of a simple menuing system

working at the real DOS prompt. Any valid DOS command will be acceptable there. For a power user, that may well be an advantage; for an inexperienced user, it could lead to confusion or worse. If, for example, you type DIR and press Enter, the menu will scroll off the screen. If you don't recall the letters you were to choose from and you don't know to type MAIN and press Enter, you may have to press the Reset button at that point.

A VARIATION ON THE SAME THEME

Some users prefer to do their menus differently by giving MAIN.BAT only the lines

```
@ECHO OFF
CLS
TYPE MENU.TXT
```

to store the menu in MENU.TXT. One advantage of this approach is that you can easily format the menu to add color enhancements using ANSI escape sequences without having to add ECHO and a space at the start of every text line and ECHO. at the start of every blank line.

A BETTER MENU SYSTEM

A dramatic improvement you can make in this system is to restrict user input to only the valid choices and to just one keypress, eliminating the need to press Enter. Before DOS 6, there was no way to do these things without going outside of the DOS tools. Now, we have the new CHOICE command whose syntax is

```
CHOICE [/C[:]keys] [/N] [/S] [/T[:]c,nn [text]
```

where *keys* is a list of letters, numbers, or other symbols you choose, such as *c*, *nn*(number of seconds to wait for user input), and *text* (a prompt string). If you use the /N switch, CHOICE will display the specified text string and wait for input. Without the /N, it will add the acceptable input keys, enclosed in square brackets and separated by commas, and with a question mark after the brackets. Thus, the command

```
CHOICE /C:ABC Which letter from this list do you choose
```

produces the prompt

```
Which letter from this list do you choose [A,B,C]?
```

after which the batch file will be paused until you press one of these three letters (or Ctrl-Break). Adding the /S switch forces you to enter the letter in the proper case (lowercase or capital letters); without it, the prompt shows all capital letters, no matter how you typed them after the /C:.

Once you have typed an input letter that is acceptable to CHOICE, it will let the batch file proceed. It reports which key it received through something called the ERRORLEVEL or the *exit code*. Every program can, as it relinquishes control of the PC, issue an exit code. By default, the exit code will be 0, but anything from 0 through 255 is possible. Some programs do this to signal if they encountered some problem doing their task; others use the exit code to send information about what they discovered during their operation.

Note: In addition to CHOICE, thirteen other MS-DOS 6 commands issue exit codes that can be tested with the IF ERRORLEVEL command. They are: CHKDSK, DEFRAG, DELTREE, DISKCOMP, DISKCOPY, FIND, FORMAT, MOVE, MSAV, REPLACE, RESTORE, SETVER, and XCOPY. This is a welcome improvement in these programs. Many functions that used to require convoluted batch file techniques now can be done with a simple IF ERRORLEVEL command, or a small group of them. The DOS 6 HELP program gives details on what exit code values each of these programs can issue, and the circumstances under which they do so.

A batch file can access the exit code issued by the last program to run through the use of the IF ERRORLEVEL or IF NOT ERRORLEVEL batch file commands. To see how this works, try the following experiment. At the DOS prompt type:

```
CHOICE /C:ABC
```

and when it prompts you with `[A,B,C]?` tap the C key (don't press Enter). You will get another DOS prompt. This time type

```
IF ERRORLEVEL 3 ECHO ^G You typed C!
```

and press Enter. (For the `^G` you need to hold down the Ctrl key and tap the G key; you will see `^G` on your screen, but you really have entered only the character with ASCII value 7.) If all went well with your experiment, you should have heard a beep from your speaker (Ctrl-G is the "bell code" symbol) and seen the message `You typed C!` on the next line.

Note: The next few steps will be easier to do if you have DOSKEY installed (or some alternative program that lets you recall, edit, and reissue commands easily). You can do all the experiments without the aid of any such program, but that will require that you type a lot more and that you make no mistakes in your typing.

Repeat the CHOICE command, exactly as you typed it before. This time, tap the B key. Now repeat the IF ERRORLEVEL command, also exactly as before. This time, nothing will happen. You will get the DOS prompt back, but there will be no sound and the message will not appear on your screen. Try this yet again, but tapping the A key in response to CHOICE. First, though, try tapping any other key; none will be accepted. (CHOICE will beep and not go on until you enter an acceptable keystroke.) Experiment with various letter answers to CHOICE and various numbers (among 1, 2, and 3) in the IF ERRORLEVEL command. If you love to solve mysteries, don't read the next several paragraphs until you have completed your experiments and formed your own ideas about how CHOICE and IF ERRORLEVEL work.

The IF ERRORLEVEL command is just one specific case of the IF command. It is almost always used in a batch file, although as you have just seen, it can be used at the DOS prompt. The syntax of the IF command is

```
IF [NOT] ERRORLEVEL target command
```

or

```
IF [NOT] EXIST target command
```

or

```
IF [NOT] string1==string2 target command
```

where `target` can be either a number (for the ERRORLEVEL test) or a file specification (for the EXIST test). If the test is true, then the specified *command* gets executed. (Often in a batch file, *command* will be a GOTO statement. Using the IF command that way will be explained in the section "Loops, Layers, and Other Complexities," later in this chapter.)

If you use the IF command in its string comparison mode, there is a subtlety you need to watch out for. You can compare any two strings, and one or both of them can be replaceable parameters or the values of environment variables. You may not use, however, a null string (a string with no characters—that is, a string of 0 length). If you make the mistake of comparing something to nothing, the test will fail, but if you compare nothing to nothing, COMMAND.COM will complain of a syntax error and stop processing your batch file. Since replaceable parameters often are not present in the command line and environment variables might not be defined at the time, you have to protect yourself by adding something identical to both `string1` and `string2`, such as quotation marks ("), an exclamation point (!), or a period (.) after each string. Thus the line

```
IF %1==%EnvVar%
```

is legal only if both the first command line parameter (the value that will be given to `%1`) and the ENVVAR environmental variable are actual strings with at least one character in them. (Even though the batch file line says `%EnvVar%`, the actual definition in the environment will have the variable's name in all capital letters, ENVVAR. This difference will cause no problems when the batch file executes.) On the other hand, the line

```
IF %1!==%EnvVar%!
```

or

```
IF %1.==%EnvVar%.
```

or

```
IF "%1"=="%EnvVar%"
```

are all legal and safe. It would be a mistake to use

```
IF %1!==!%EnvVar%
```

which generally will not work. It won't produce a syntax error or perform as you expect. When both `%1` and `%EnvVar%` are null strings, the comparison will succeed—if they are both actual strings longer than 0 characters (or even equal). The test will fail, however, unless both strings contain an exclamation point. Check that the added characters are put on the same side of both strings.

The most obscure fact about the IF ERRORLEVEL command is that it will act as if the test is true, if the exit code being tested is greater than or equal to the number following the word ERRORLEVEL. Thus, the test IF ERRORLEVEL 0 will always be true (since exit codes are numbers between 0 and 255). IF ERRORLEVEL 255 will be true only for one exit code value (255); IF ERRORLEVEL 10 will be true for all exit codes between 10 and 255, inclusive. To understand the results of your experiments, it is important to know that CHOICE returns an exit code equal to the position of the symbol it accepted in the string you gave it after the `/C:` command line switch. So, with `/C:ABC` and a press of C, the exit code will be set to 3. If you press B, the exit code will be set to 2; for A, it is set to 1. All other keystrokes cause a beep and CHOICE does not exit; instead, it waits for you to press A, B, or C.

Tip: There are two other possible ways the CHOICE command can exit: If it detects an error condition, CHOICE will exit with an exit code of 255; if you press Ctrl-Break or Ctrl-C, CHOICE will exit with an error code of 0. Always test first for an errorlevel value that is one higher than your highest valid choice to detect a value outside of the allowable range or any other error), and then for an errorlevel of 0 (to see if you want to abort the operation). How you choose to handle these possibilities is your decision, but don't ignore them.

Armed with this information, you may see how to modify MAIN.BAT to provide the menu and respond to your input, restricting you to only the valid options. Actually, you need to know about one more concept and command before you can do so: The concept is *labels* in a batch file and the command is GOTO, which uses those labels. A label is any batch file line that starts with a colon followed immediately by one or more words. You may make the label line say anything, but only the first 8 characters or only those up to the first space, tab, semicolon, or other character that is not acceptable in a file name will be used by the GOTO command. As with remarks, avoid putting any redirection symbols on a label line. The syntax of the GOTO command is

```
GOTO label
```

which causes COMMAND.COM to read through the batch file, starting at the beginning, until it finds a line that starts

```
:label
```

at which point COMMAND.COM reads the next line and executes it. Notice that GOTO always forces COMMAND.COM to start over, reading the batch file from the beginning, no matter where it was in the batch file when it encountered the GOTO. Therefore, if you have two or more identical labels, any GOTO anywhere in the batch file will always go to the first of them. This branching option is an important part of the power of the batch file programming language. (COMMAND.COM will insist that the value of `label` that is typed after the GOTO match the value of `label` that is after the colon up to the eighth character or to the end of the first word. If the two words are different lengths and one is less than 8 characters long, COMMAND.COM will consider it not a match, even if the two match as far as the end of the shorter word. If you point a GOTO at a label that doesn't occur in the batch file, COMMAND.COM will issue the message `Label not found` and exit from the batch file.

Now, you have all the pieces to put together to make a new version of the menuing system. Try it on your own, or look at Figure 14-4 for our solution.

We have included two lines that you probably did not anticipate: `NOBREAK ON` and `NOBREAK OFF`, which involve the one non-DOS part of our solution. NOBREAK is a small TSR program we have written that hooks the hardware keyboard interrupt (INT9) and can turn on or off your PC's ability to respond to Ctrl-Break. As used here, it turns it off. The NOBREAK.COM program is further described in Chapter 18, and you will find it among the DOS Power Tools on the disks that come with this book. You might also have wondered about the lines IF ERRORLEVEL 5 and IF ERRORLEVEL 0. It is good programming practice to "cover all the bases." If CHOICE were to encounter some error or thought it had received a Ctrl-Break or Ctrl-C interruption (NOBREAK ON won't let it), it would exit with exit code 255 or 0. The two "extra" IF ERRORLEVEL tests are there in case one of these unanticipated events occurs.

The menu program shown in Figure 14-4 will work without NOBREAK, but with one important vulnerability. If you hold down the Ctrl key and press repeatedly on the Break key (in front of the Pause key on some keyboards

MENU.TXT

```
                    MAIN MENU

        Enter a choice:

          L    to run       Lotus 1-2-3

          N    to run       Norton Utilties

          S    to run       WordStar

          W    to run       Microsoft Windows
```

MAIN.BAT

```
@echo off
rem         This is MAIN2.BAT -- version 2 of menuing system
:start
NOBREAK ON
C:
CD\MENU
cls
type MENU2.TXT

CHOICE /C:LNSW /N > NUL
IF ERRORLEVEL 5 GOTO start
IF ERRORLEVEL 4 GOTO Lotus
IF ERRORLEVEL 3 GOTO Norton
IF ERRORLEVEL 2 GOTO WordStar
IF ERRORLEVEL 1 GOTO Windows
IF ERRORLEVEL 0 GOTO start

:Lotus
F:
CD\123
NOBREAK OFF
123
goto start

:Norton
NOBREAK OFF
NORTON
goto start

:WordStar
E:
CD\WS5
NOBREAK OFF
WS
goto start

:Windows
NOBREAK OFF
WIN
goto start
```

Figure 14-4 A better version of the batch file menuing system using CHOICE to restrict user input

and the Scroll Lock key on others), COMMAND.COM soon will interrupt the execution of the batch file and present the message

```
Terminate batch job (Y/N)?
```

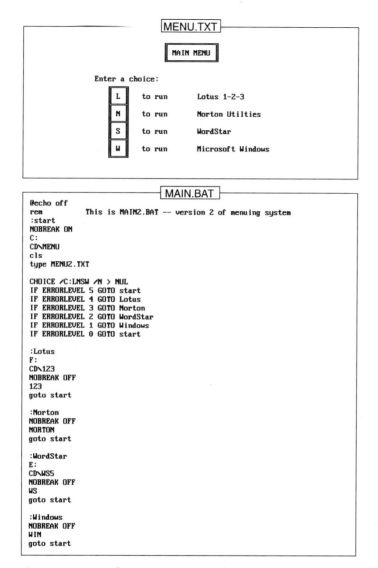

Responding with a `Y` will end the batch file and COMMAND.COM will display a DOS prompt. By including NOBREAK, it is almost impossible for you to break out of this batch file. By putting NOBREAK OFF in each of the subroutines that invoke other programs, it is possible for those programs to operate normally, responding to Ctrl-Break the way they always did. If you wish to make it even harder to avoid or break out of the menu, you can put in your CONFIG.SYS file the lines

```
SWITCHES /N
INSTALL C:\SETUP\NOBREAK.COM ON
```

where you probably have chosen to keep NOBREAK.COM in your C:\SETUP directory. The NOBREAK command prevents exiting a batch file by using the Ctrl-Break or Ctrl-C key combinations. The `SWITCHES /N` directive tells IO.SYS not to respond to the Shift, F5, or F8 keys during bootup. (Those are the keystrokes that normally allow you to bypass the processing of both the CONFIG.SYS and AUTOEXEC.BAT files, or to selectively bypass individual lines in CONFIG.SYS and, optionally, bypass the AUTOEXEC.BAT file.) The only way to interrupt the execution of the CONFIG.SYS, AUTOEXEC.BAT, and MAIN.BAT files will be by using Ctrl-Alt-Del, pressing the reset button, or turning off the PC's power.

Note: Unfortunately, the DOS directive BREAK cannot be used to handle this problem. When BREAK is turned off DOS checks only for a pending Ctrl-Break combination keystroke in the input buffer when it is about to read from that buffer or write something to the screen. When you turn BREAK ON, you are asking DOS to also check for a pending Ctrl-Break before each time it is about to access a disk drive. The NOBREAK program (or something like it) is the only way to turn off the Ctrl-Break program interruption mechanism.

CLOSING THE LAST CHINKS IN THE ARMOR

While you may boot your PC from a floppy disk and, once in an application, may "shell to DOS" or open a DOS window to do just about anything, it is advisable to use a menu and enter one of the allowed options.

If you are an inexperienced user and want to avoid inadvertently damaging something or getting confused and lost, use the menu and choose an option listed there.

Another advantage in creating a menuing system is to keep unauthorized users out of your PC. If that is your goal, modify your PC so it cannot boot from the A drive. There are some PCs now being sold with a version of the

AMI BIOS on the motherboard that allows you to choose this option from within their ROM BIOS setup program and to set a password that must be entered before the setup screens can be reentered. With those two features enabled, it's nearly impossible to boot the PC from a floppy diskette. Another way to accomplish this is to make the PC into a diskless workstation.

So far, you have seen some ways to avoid trouble booting from a floppy. To provide near total security, you must add password protection to the batch menuing system, which can be done with the tools DOS provides (assuming our NOBREAK program has been activated before the following example batch file begins).

Figure 14-5 shows a batch file fragment that will force you to enter a password before it lets the batch file execution proceed. In this version, the needed password is "hard coded" into the batch file. You can devise several variations that would allow the password to be changed easily and quickly, by using either secondary batch files that establish an environment variable and then erase it after you log in or the CHGENV program from the Power Tools utilities.

PASSWORD.BAT

```
@echo off
REM     This batch file fragment forces the user to enter a
REM     pre-specified password before it will allow execution
REM     of the batch file to proceed. In this example, the
REM     password is 6X9A, and is case-insensitive.
echo.
:start
echo.
echo            Please enter your password
echo.
CHOICE /c:1234567890abcdefghijklmnopqrstuvwxyz /n > nul
if errorlevel 6 if not errorlevel 7 goto 2s
goto 2f
:2s
CHOICE /c:1234567890abcdefghijklmnopqrstuvwxyz /n > nul
if errorlevel 34 if not errorlevel 35 goto 3s
goto 3f
:3s
CHOICE /c:1234567890abcdefghijklmnopqrstuvwxyz /n > nul
if errorlevel 9 if not errorlevel 10 goto 4s
goto 4f
:4s
CHOICE /c:1234567890abcdefghijklmnopqrstuvwxyz /n > nul
if errorlevel 11 if not errorlevel 12 goto success
goto failure
:2f
CHOICE /c:1234567890abcdefghijklmnopqrstuvwxyz /n > nul
:3f
CHOICE /c:1234567890abcdefghijklmnopqrstuvwxyz /n > nul
:4f
CHOICE /c:1234567890abcdefghijklmnopqrstuvwxyz /n > nul
:failure
echo.
echo    Sorry, wrong password
CHOICE /c:° /t°,5 /n > nul
goto start
:success
echo.
TYPE MENU.TXT
```

Figure 14-5 A password batch file using CHOICE

> **Note:** Another subtlety is incorporated in the batch file in Figure 14-5. The fifth line from the bottom is a CHOICE line, but there are no IF ERRORLEVEL lines after it. This line will function as a delay, unless you know the odd single character it will accept to let you past. (The degree symbol is ASCII 248, which you can get by holding down the Alt key and tapping out 248 on the numeric keypad. But if you do, you merely will have succeeded in speeding up the return to the original "Please enter your password" prompt.) The reason this is only a delay is that, after the time indicated in the /T option has passed, CHOICE will act as if the default character (which is also the only acceptable character) had been typed. This delay is useful if you are trying to build a secure system and want to prevent someone from trying many passwords. Enforcing a delay after an unsuccessful attempt is one of the easier ways of enhancing security. In fact, you should increase the delay time from the 5 seconds shown here to at least 30 seconds.

Additionally, you could use one password routine to keep all but authorized users out of the main menu program. Then, you could have one item on that menu that required entering yet another password, which would allow certain authorized users access to the full DOS prompt, while other authorized users would be limited to running the application programs listed on the menu.

Finally, it is not possible to accomplish this using the CONFIG.SYS menu. There is no equivalent to CHOICE among the menuing commands that are valid in CONFIG.SYS, and all the menu choices must be made before the first configuration block is entered, thus, before the first chance to run any DOS programs. You also can make your menus visually attractive by loading ANSI.SYS and using the ideas presented in Chapter 5, and you can create multilevel menus in ways already shown. Other ways you can interact with your batch files are discussed in the following section.

Loop, Layers, and Other Complexities

The most useful batch files can do different things at different times; one-line batch files that always do a directory listing in exactly the same way are not very useful. In this section we will explain how to add flexibility to a batch file to make it do any one of a number of possible actions each time it is invoked.

THE REPLACEABLE PARAMETERS %0 THROUGH %9

Chapter 13 described how in a batch file the expression `%NAME%` is replaced by COMMAND.COM with the current definition of NAME stored in the DOS environment before the line is executed. That is one kind of replaceable parameter that you can use in a batch file; there is another kind: `%n`, where *n* is a numeral from 0 to 9 inclusive. When you use these parameters in a batch file you are telling COMMAND.COM to replace that symbol with one of the "words" on the command line that invoked this batch file. (For this purpose, the entire command line is broken down into words, where each word is a group of characters, all of which could be used in a file name, and the words are separated by groups of characters, all of which cannot legally be used in a file name.)

The first word on any command line is the verb—the name of the action you want performed; the rest of the line is often called the *command tail.* In the case of a batch file invocation, the verb is the name of the batch file and gets plugged in by COMMAND.COM in place of %0. The next word is what is used in place of %1. The word after that replaces %2, and so on until you run out of words in the command line or of `%n` values to replace. (You will see in a moment how to handle a batch file with more than nine words in its command tail.)

Chapter 13 also showed you two simple, single-line batch files that let you add a new directory to the current PATH definition. The examples were hard coded to add C:\NEW to either the beginning or end of the PATH, which required use of the %NAME% kind of replaceable parameter. Now you will see how to make a more flexible version of this, a batch file that allows you to add any path element (a fully qualified or relative path to a particular directory) to either the front or back of the present PATH definition (see Figure 14-6).

Several of the lines in this batch program demonstrate important points about batch file programming. First, notice the inclusion of the name of the file in the first ECHO statement, which lets you see on-screen that you are running the batch program you intended. Next, notice line four, which compares the `%1.` and `.` strings. The periods are essential in this command, as pointed out in the discussion of the IF command in the section "A Better Menu System" earlier in this chapter. If you invoke this batch file without anything on the command tail, then %1 will be replaced by a null string, the string comparison will test as true, and the batch file processing will jump to the line after the label `:explain`. This causes the batch file to print syntax information and usage tips on the screen. This batch file has been written to show what it is doing as it does it. You could add CHOICE commands to get confirmation that what is about to be done is in fact what you want. There are

ADD2PATH.BAT

```
@echo off
echo          ADD2PATH.BAT
echo.
if %1.==. goto explain
echo Your current path is:
echo.
PATH
echo.
echo You asked to add  %1  to that PATH.
if %2.==H. goto athead
if %2.==h. goto athead
echo.
PATH=%PATH%;%1
goto report
:athead
PATH=%1;%PATH%
:report
echo Your PATH now is:
echo.
PATH
echo.
goto alldone

:explain
echo  Usage:  ADD2PATH path_element [place]
echo.
echo          Adds path_element to the current DOS PATH.
echo.
echo          (You may specify that path_element be,added at the head
echo           or tail of the existing PATH by appending an H or a T
echo           on the command line. Default is to put it at the tail.)
echo.
:alldone
```

Figure 14-6 The ADD2PATH batch file

two tests (at lines 10 and 11) for the %2 parameter, which cause you to type in the letter signaling where to add the new path element in either upper- or lowercase.

MODIFYING ACTIONS BASED ON RESULTS

You have already been introduced to the IF command in the form IF ERRORLEVEL and learned that it also can be used as

```
IF EXIST filename
```

or

```
IF string_comparison
```

Each of these forms frequently gets used in sophisticated batch file programs. Also, remember that you can put in the NOT modifier after IF to reverse the sense of the test. A command of the form

```
IF test command
```

will execute `command` if `test` evaluates as true. The line

```
IF NOT test command
```

will only execute `command` if `test` turns out false. The form of the IF command that tests for a file's existence can be used to be sure you are copying files to the right destination. Application installation batch programs often use it to be sure you have inserted the right diskette before they attempt to copy or expand some source files.

Another use of this command, and one whose value may not be obvious, is to test for the existence of a device in a certain subdirectory. DOS will always find all devices in all subdirectories, but it will find the device only if the subdirectory exists. So, testing for the existence of a device that you know exists (such as the NUL device) can be used indirectly as a test of the existence of a subdirectory. This batch file fragment shows the essential idea:

```
IF EXIST C:\TARGET\NUL GOTO okay
ECHO Directory C:\TARGET does not exist. Shall we create it?
CHOICE /C:YN
IF ERRORLEVEL 2 MD C:\TARGET
:okay
```

This technique is not foolproof—if you give the IF EXIST test a relative path name such as C:FRED, it will find C:FRED\NUL, whether or not FRED exists, and it won't balk if you give it a path like C:\WAYTOOLONG\NUL. But if you're sure you'll be working with well-formed path names, it's less clumsy than writing a test file to the directory and then running an IF EXIST test on the file. This doesn't work with DR DOS, but that is not a problem since DR DOS includes a specific IF subcommand DIREXIST for that purpose.

BATCH FILES THAT CALL OTHER BATCH FILES

Sometimes it is not possible, or may be awkward, to accomplish some task in a single batch file. Often, that same task is easy to do if you split the work between two batch files. Here are a couple of examples, and in the process, an introduction to the SHIFT command.

Suppose you want a batch file that will manipulate some environment definitions and you know the names of the items you are interested in, but you don't know their current definitions. The challenge is to write a batch file that will accept as a command line parameter the name of the environment variable, and will work with the environment definition of that name when it executes some of its internal commands. For simplicity, the batch file will just echo the definition string to the screen. If you are interested only in handling the definition of a single environment variable, you could write a special purpose batch file to do this. For example, a single-line batch file that says

```
ECHO %TEMP%
```

will display your current definition for the environment variable TEMP. A harder challenge is to write a batch file that will show you the current definition of whatever variable you want, without having to hard code that variable's name in the batch file. Try

```
ECHO %%%1%%
```

The reason for using that many percent signs is that a pair of percent signs is converted to a single percent sign, and one percent sign followed by a number is converted to the corresponding word on the command line that invoked this batch file. If you call this batch file SHOWENV.BAT, and type

```
SHOWENV TEMP
```

all you get as output is `%TEMP%`—not the current value of the TEMP environment variable—because the %1 is replaced as you wanted by TEMP; %TEMP% is not replaced further. COMMAND.COM just won't nest replacements like that. The solution is simple: Make the batch file create and run another batch file. The one you write, SHOWENV.BAT reads

```
IF EXIST SHOWENV1.BAT GOTO OOPS
@ECHO %%%1%% > SHOWENV1.BAT
SHOWENV1.BAT
IF EXIST SHOWENV1.BAT DEL SHOWENV1.BAT
GOTO DONE
:OOPS
ECHO    Processing stopped to avoid overwriting
SHOWENV1.BAT
:DONE
```

When you run this batch file with the command

```
SHOWENV TEMP
```

you will see

```
J:\TEMP
```

(or whatever your TEMP variable is defined as) on the screen. The reason this works is that, while the first batch file is being processed, all those percent signs and the 1 get converted to %TEMP%, as you saw when you ran the first version of this batch file. That is what gets echoed to the second batch file. When the second batch file is run, COMMAND.COM has only one replacement job to do, substituting the definition of TEMP for %TEMP%, and it does that.

The SHOWENV.BAT file also demonstrates another point about good batch file programming: Test your assumptions and guard against errors. In this case, we first test to be sure there already isn't a SHOWENV1.BAT file and if there is, we make SHOWENV decline to overwrite that other batch file and announce why it stopped. Add some remarks and perhaps a section like that following the `:explain` label in ADD2PATH.BAT and you will have a good utility batch program.

HANDLING LOTS OF COMMAND LINE PARAMETERS WITH SHIFT

This section deals with batch file invoking command lines that have more than ten words in them. There are only the ten replaceable parameters %0 through %9, but they can be made to work overtime with the help of the SHIFT command. A line in a batch file that says SHIFT tells COMMAND.COM to move all the replacement words over by one. Thus, what was going to replace %1 will replace %0, what was going to replace %3 will replace %2, etc. The word that used to replace %0 (originally, this is the name of the batch file itself) is lost in this process. What is gained is that the %9 is now replaced by the tenth word on the command tail (the eleventh word on the command line). You can use SHIFT any number of times. With the help of SHIFT, the ten replaceable parameters become a ten-word wide window on the command line.

Eventually, COMMAND.COM will run out of words to shift. There is no reverse SHIFT command, so be prepared to do whatever you need to do with each word while it is in the window of accessibility provided by %0 through %9. A simple experiment will clarify this, but since COMMAND.COM only replaces `%n` with something if it receives the line from a batch file, you can't do this experiment by typing at the DOS prompt. Create the following batch file called SHIFTEST.BAT:

```
@echo off
echo %0 %1 %2 %3 %4 %5 %6 %7 %8 %9
echo.
shift
:loop
echo %0 %1 %2 %3 %4 %5 %6 %7 %8 %9
shift
if %0.==. goto outahere
goto loop
:outahere
```

Now, type the command

```
SHIFTEST A simple test of batch file replaceable
parameters shifting
```

When you press Enter you will see on your screen

```
SHIFTEST A simple test of batch file replaceable
parameters shifting

A simple test of batch file replaceable parameters shifting
simple test of batch file replaceable parameters shifting
test of batch file replaceable parameters shifting
of batch file replaceable parameters shifting
batch file replaceable parameters shifting
file replaceable parameters shifting
replaceable parameters shifting
parameters shifting
shifting
```

Figure 14-7 shows a pair of batch files that produce an amusing output; type and run them to see what we mean. The solid black bars are characters with ASCII value 219, which you can type into most editors by holding down the Alt key and tapping out 2, 1, 9 on the numeric keypad. (First, though, try to predict what you will see. Don't be surprised if you miss on a few features; you have to think like a computer to get them all just right.)

Did you correctly anticipate the shape of the image at the bottom? Remember that an ECHO command outputs every space as a space. COMMAND.COM replaces each replaceable parameter as a null byte, if there is nothing on the command line to use for the replacement. Finally, a null byte takes up no space on the screen. Thus, %3, for example, takes up two spaces in the batch file, but one or no spaces on the output line. If you are impatient for answers or may not be reading this next to your computers, Figure 14-8 shows the output generated by CRAYON.BAT.

CRAYON.BAT

```
@echo off
echo      CRAYON.BAT
echo.
echo      Display a "crayon"
echo.
echo      Press a key when you are ready
pause  > nul
call fly n o y a r c - █ █ █ █ █ █ █ █ █ █  - n o y a r c - █ █ █ █ █ █ █ █ █ █
echo.
```

FLY.BAT

```
@echo off
rem       FLY.BAT - Scroll a message across a seventeen column window
echo.
:loop
shift
if %0.==. goto outahere
echo                          %9 %8 %7 %6 %5 %4 %3 %2 %1 %0
goto loop
:outahere
```

Figure 14-7 A pair of linked batch files uses replaceable parameters and the SHIFT subcommand to form an interesting image.

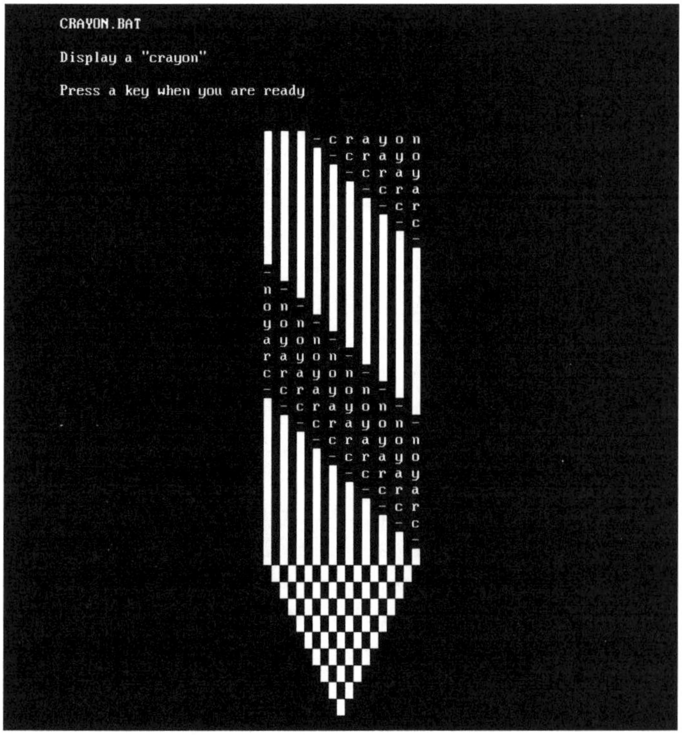

Figure 14-8 Output generated by CRAYON.BAT

NESTING BATCH FILES—CALL VERSUS COMMAND /C

The batch file examples in the preceding section, in which one batch file called another, all had the calling batch file finish its work, then activate the other one. Sometimes, you will want to stop one batch file momentarily, run another batch file, and then return to the first one. This has always been possible; with DOS 3.3 it became easy by including in the first batch file a line that reads

COMMAND /C *second_batch_file_name [parameters]*

When COMMAND.COM comes to this line, it loads a secondary command processor and gives it the command line

second_batch_file_name *[parameters]*

That, of course, runs the second batch file. (The optional parameters represent any additional words you need to give the second batch file. The secondary command processor will then substitute those words for the replaceable parameters %1 through %9 inside the second batch file.) When the second batch file completes its work, the secondary command processor is finished executing the command specified to it after the /C switch, so that when the specified command is finished the secondary command processor ends its own execution. At that point, the original copy of COMMAND.COM regains control and resumes processing the original batch file.

This scheme works, but it has some side effects. First, you must devote between 3KB and 4KB of RAM to the secondary command processor. That might keep you from running some RAM-hungry application from the second batch file. Second, the new command processor creates its own master environment and all the definitions in the original master environment will be copied into it. However, any changes you make in the environment definitions from within the second batch file will be lost when that batch file ends, the secondary command processor exits (and in the process gives up its environment space), and the first batch file resumes. Starting with version 3.3, DOS has offered another way to accomplish much the same thing: The batch language now has a CALL command. When you CALL one batch file from within another, the first COMMAND.COM stops what it was doing in the first file and it (the first command interpreter) runs the second batch file. This costs no extra RAM and it lets the second batch file modify the definitions in the original master environment. Chapter 13 pointed out the advantages of putting a CALL to a U-PATH.BAT file into your AUTOEXEC.BAT file. Unless you want to defer defining your PATH to the last line of your AUTOEXEC.BAT file, you will have to use CALL or COMMAND /C to invoke U-PATH. Otherwise, the rest of your AUTOEXEC.BAT file will never get executed.

Super-Simple "Batch" Commands

Sometimes, you want the repetitive actions typical of a batch file, but you don't want to stop and write one. Often, you can get away with typing a single "batch" command at the DOS prompt. The FOR...IN...DO command is particularly useful in this connection. The syntax of the FOR command is

```
FOR var IN (set) DO command
```

where *var* is yet another kind of replaceable parameter, which is indicated by a percent sign followed by anything other than a numeral, commonly a single letter. Unlike almost anything else in DOS, this variable name is case sensitive. Thus `%a` and `%A` are completely different objects to the FOR command's perception.

> **Note:** If you use a FOR command in a batch file you must add an additional percent sign at the front of *var*, so instead of `%A` you need to use `%%A`.

The `(set)` in the FOR command can be specified in several ways. A wildcard file specification, like `(*.*)`, `(*.TXT)`, or `(C:\MARY\*.DOC)`, is one common form. An explicit list of possibilities, such as `(1 2 3 4 5)` is another. You can even mix the two forms as in `(ALEXANDR.RAG *.TXT D:\RAPID\BUDGET\OCT*.RPT)`. In this last case the variable will take on in turn the values

ALEXANDR.RAG
the name of each file in the current directory of type TXT
the name of each file in D:\RAPID\BUDGET\ starting with OCT and of type RPT.

The description of the `set` must be contained within parentheses. The items of the `set`, if there are several explicitly listed, must be separated by something that COMMAND.COM recognizes as a name separator. That can include a space, tab, semicolon, or several other special characters. The *command* that comes at the end of a FOR line may (but doesn't have to) include the *var* that is taking on the several values indicated by *set*. If the FOR command is contained within a batch file, the *command* may also include some of the other kinds of replaceable parameters (%*NAME*% and %*n*). Here are some examples to clarify this. First, try one you can type at the DOS prompt. Enter the command

```
FOR %a in (*.TXT) DO TYPE %a
```

and you will see the contents of each TXT file in the current directory scroll across your screen. Add `> PRN` on the end and you will get them all printed on paper. Add `>>` *filename* on the end and the contents of all those files will end up all in one file. (This last operation could more simply be done by the command

```
COPY *.TXT filename
```

so the FOR is not really needed in that case.) Now, for a more complex example, create a batch file with one line that reads

```
FOR %%a in (*.BAT) DO CALL SHOWX %%a
```

and another one called SHOWX.BAT that reads

```
@ECHO OFF
TYPE %1 ¦ FIND "X"
```

When you run the first batch file you will see displayed on your screen every line in every batch file in the current directory that has an X somewhere on the line. Another example is to show the use of nested FOR commands. Create one batch file called MATRIX that reads

```
@echo off
for %%a in (1 2 3) do call M %%a
```

and another, M.BAT, that reads

```
@echo off
for %%a in (4,5,6) do echo %1 %%a
```

Here you see that you can put the FOR command itself in either upper- or lowercase. Only the variable name (`%a` in this case) is case sensitive. Also, you see here the use of the double percent signs and that the `%%a` in the first batch file is completely independent of the `%%a` in the second batch file. These are called *local variables.* When you issue the command MATRIX, you will see on your screen the nine lines

```
1 4
1 5
1 6
2 4
2 5
2 6
3 4
3 5
3 6
```

as the `%%a` variable in the first file takes on the values 1, 2, and 3 in succession, and for each of them the `%%a` in the second file is 4, then 5, and then 6. The `@ECHO OFF` commands in both batch files ensure that we see only the output we want to see, with no superfluous DOS prompts intervening.

There is one important point about batch files and the batch command FOR: They produce no output of their own; the only output that happens comes from the commands they run. Therefore, never try to redirect or pipe output from a FOR command or from a batch file. Always put the redirection symbols on the lines within the batch file that generate the actual output. With a FOR command, use a GOTO and put the output-producing command on the line after the target label. If you forget this, you will wonder why you keep getting output on your screen and 0-length files on your disk.

Tip: When you use a CALL command, you are telling COMMAND.COM to interrupt its processing of the first batch command or file in order to process a second one. As a side effect of how it manages this process, you may sometimes be able to execute FOR commands that simply won't work without it. Thus the command

```
FOR %a in (1 2 3) DO MYPROG
```

should run MYPROG three times. (This is an example of a FOR command that doesn't use the variable's values in the command; it simply executes the command as many times as there are members in the set.) Sometimes, MYPROG will run three times. Other times, especially if MYPROG is a compiled BASIC program, it will run only once. A way to get around this is to modify the command to read

```
FOR %a in (1 2 3) DO CALL MYPROG
```

which will run MYPROG three times, just as you would expect. Apparently, what happens is that a compiled BASIC program will overwrite the transient part of the command interpreter and, in the process, wipe out its record of where it was in the FOR command. By preparing itself to run a second batch file, COMMAND.COM protects the information it needs to continue the first batch file or command. In this way the CALL command neatly avoids the difficulty of using the FOR command with programs that use all of lower memory when they run.

Where to Keep Your Batch Files

The issue of where to keep one's batch files is divided into two schools of thought. One group argues that the best way to run programs is from a batch file, and the best PATH definition is a very short one. Typically, members of this group will run DOS external commands and some other utility programs directly, but they have made batch files to run all their other application programs. These users keep all their batch files (or all those used to launch applications) in a special batch file directory. If that directory is C:\BAT, and assuming they keep most of their utility programs in a C:\UTILS directory, their usual PATH definition might be

```
PATH=C:\DOS;C:\UTILS;C:\BAT
```

If you mistype a command name, DOS won't take long to discover that fact and give you an opportunity to retype it (after the `Bad command or filename` message).

Users in the other school tend to have many application and utility programs scattered across a large number of directories, and they have a different set of arguments. They are likely to covet every extra cluster of disk space, have a pretty fast machine, and be a good typist, so the issue of waiting for DOS to find a mistyped command until after it has searched through a dozen or more directories is a nonissue. These users are likely to have PATH definitions that push the 122 character limit, and may even be using the SUBST command to shorten the PATH definition to push the limit further.

One of the authors of this book falls into this latter camp. His main PC has over 750 directories on seven logical volumes, probably a few hundred application programs, plus a like number of utility programs. His path statement spans thirteen directories. Each time he mistypes a command, COMMAND.COM must examine over 1200 file names in fourteen directories (current one, plus thirteen on the PATH) before it knows it will not find an executable file with the specified name. However, this takes less than a second. (Achieving this speed mainly depends on having a good, large disk cache which, after the first search down the PATH, will have all those directories saved in the cache.) With several hundred executable files on this PC, making a batch file to launch each one would be an un pleasant task. Storing them would use about a megabyte of disk space (at 2KB per batch file). For both of these reasons, this PC power user has chosen to let DOS do most of the work. His usual PATH definition is 118 characters long (exclusive of the 5 characters for "PATH="). There are also several hundred batch files on this hard disk and several dozen of them get used frequently; some are used to launch applications. A mere thirteen directories and 118 characters in the PATH definition would be insufficient if the home directory for all the applications had to be included.

BATCH FILE COMPILERS

Batch files are simple, human-readable ASCII text files that are easy to create and modify. That can be wonderful, but if you spend hours or days developing some clever batch file, you don't want anyone to come along and ruin it. You can write-protect your batch files and keep copies in a safe place. But neither of these strategies will stop a determined user from tinkering with a batch file. Further, you might have some information coded in your batch file that you'd rather not have anyone see, such as the password in the file in Figure 14-5. Fortunately, there is a solution for both the privacy and the integrity issues: You can compile your batch files into COM or EXE files.

There are commercial batch file compilers such as Builder by Hyperkinetix, and there are shareware and freeware programs such as BAT2EXEC and BAT2COM. None of them is perfect; there are some legal batch file and nested batch file constructions that will not get compiled correctly. However, for most batch files these programs are wonderful. As a side effect, a compiled batch program will usually execute more quickly. The reason for this is clear, once you understand that COMMAND.COM processes an ordinary, uncompiled batch file by opening the file, reading one line, storing some information in a small memory block (including the file name and where in the file it was reading), closing the file, and executing that one line. Only after that execution is complete will COMMAND.COM reopen the batch file and read the next line. In contrast, a compiled batch file is loaded into memory as a whole and then executed like any other program. Once it has started the process, COMMAND.COM has no further role to play. All the file opening and closing needed to execute a long batch file can take time, especially if you have lots of IF...GOTO constructions. An alternative to using a batch file compiler is to copy your batch file to a RAM disk and execute it from there. Instead of the command

```
MYBAT
```

use the commands

```
COPY MYBAT J:\
J:\MYBAT
```

and your formerly slow batch files will fly.

DOSKEY Macros

Chapter 4 described one aspect of the DOSKEY program. This DOS external command was introduced in DOS 5 and has two purposes: One is to remember your old commands and help you recall, edit, and reissue them; the other is to implement a scheme for creating and using keyboard macros. Keyboard macros are just another name for the concept discussed (in Chapter 4 in the section "ANSI Macros") and demonstrated earlier in this chapter (in the section "Batch ANSI Commands"): Make a single key do the work of many. DOSKEY macros differ from simple key redefinitions in one important respect. They substitute (presumably shorter or more mnemonic) strings of characters for other strings of characters. You are not limited to redefining just single keystrokes, possibly in combination with some of the shift keys.

The DOSKEY Command Syntax

DOSKEY is a TSR program you can load in lower memory with an INSTALL statement in your CONFIG.SYS file, or in upper memory with a LOADHIGH command in your AUTOEXEC.BAT file. The syntax is straightforward:

```
DOSKEY [switch(es)] [macro=[text]]
```

where the switches can be some combination of `REINSTALL`, `BUFSIZE=`*`size`*, `MACROS`, `HISTORY`, `INSERT`, and `OVERSTRIKE`. The last two control the behavior of DOSKEY as a command line editor; the others are used to control aspects of its role as a keyboard macro program. The details of what each of these switches does are given in the Command Reference.

DOSKEY Macros Are Like Batch Files

In many ways, a DOSKEY macro is like a batch file; in some ways, they are different. By first looking at the similarities, and then the differences, you clearly will see what macros and batch files are and when to use them. Here are the principal ways in which DOSKEY macros are like batch files:

1. A DOSKEY macro replaces a short string of characters with many more characters. This makes it easy to issue and reissue complex commands, and helps avoid typographic errors in your commands.
2. A single DOSKEY macro can include multiple DOS commands.
3. DOSKEY macros provide support for replaceable parameters. Instead of using %1 through %9, a DOSKEY macro uses $1 through $9. One way in which the DOSKEY macro replaceable parameter strategy improves on the batch file one is that it provides a $* wildcard replaceable parameter that stands for "the entire command tail."
4. A DOSKEY macro can include a CALL to a batch file. (Just invoking the batch file's name is enough; you don't have to use a CALL keyword.) Also note that, while either a batch file or a DOSKEY macro may CALL another batch file, a batch file may not invoke a DOSKEY macro command, nor can a macro invoke another macro.

DOSKEY Macros Are Unlike Batch Files

There are ways in which DOSKEY macros lack some of the capabilities of batch files. Here are the three most prominent ones:

1. DOSKEY macros work only when they have been loaded into RAM. While this means that they run blazingly fast, there is a limit to how much RAM in your first megabyte you wish to commit to this use. It also means that you must recreate or reload your macros each work session. (You will see how this may automatically be done later in this section.)
2. Branching and looping are not supported. This is an important and powerful capability in the batch language.

3. Error trapping and input validation are very difficult in a DOSKEY macro. (Actually, we don't know how to do this at all. If you do, please write and tell us.)
4. Any individual DOSKEY macro is limited by the legal limit on a command line's length. (This applies after the substitution of the replaceable parameters by the words you type on the invoking command line.)

Creating DOSKEY Macros

Creating DOSKEY macros is a lot like defining environment variables. The command form is the same

```
DOSKEY macro_name=macro_definition
```

with DOSKEY replacing SET as the verb. However, where an environment variable's definition may literally be anything you like, a DOSKEY macro must consist of valid DOS commands, plus a few enhancements supported specifically for DOSKEY macros, which are all implemented through metacharacters. These resemble the metacharacters used in the PROMPT command, though their functions differ. The DOSKEY metacharacters fall into four groups:

1. The replaceable parameters. When you use a DOSKEY macro, you may just name it or you can add after the name some words you want the macro to use as input. When you define the macro, you refer to these words to come by the stand-in names $1 through $9, which will be replaced by the first through the ninth word on the command tail, or by $*, which stands for the entire command tail.
2. The redirection symbols. If you wish to include redirection of stdin and/or stdout in a DOSKEY macro, instead of using the <, >, >>, and ¦ symbols you must use $L, $G, $GG, and $B, respectively. (You may also use $l, $g, $gg, or $b—letter case doesn't matter.)
3. The command line separator. If you want to define a DOSKEY macro as multiple DOS commands, separate each DOS command with a $T (or $t) metacharacter.
4. Miscellaneous. If you wish to include a $ in a DOSKEY macro definition, use the metacharacter $$ in its place. This is like the rule that in a batch file % must be replaced by %%. (You can use percent signs in DOSKEY macros just as you would use them at the DOS prompt, and not doubled as you would use them in a batch file.)

You create DOSKEY macros by invoking the DOSKEY command with the macro definition on its command tail, and you must repeat this for each macro you define. You can undefine a macro just as you would undo an environment definition, by issuing the command

```
DOSKEY macro_name=
```

with nothing to the right of the equal sign. The DOSKEY lines that create macro definitions may be typed at the command prompt or included in batch files.

Saving DOSKEY Macros

Once you have defined several macros, it is a good idea to save your work. This can be done easily: The DOSKEY switch /MACROS (or /M) causes DOSKEY to list all the macro definitions it currently is holding to stdout, one per line. Just redirect this output to a file and you have captured all your macro definitions. For example,

```
DOSKEY /M > MACROS.LST
```

captures all the macros in the file MACROS.LST.

Reloading Saved Macros

Once you have your macro definitions in a file (whether you put them there by using output redirection on the DOSKEY /M command, as just suggested, or by directly creating that file in an editor), you can use it to easily reload those same macros. Open the file in an editor (EDIT will do just fine), add at the start of every line the seven characters "DOSKEY ", and save the result as a batch file. If you have done this to MACROS.LST and, in the process, created MACROS.BAT, the command to reload those macros is simply

```
MACROS
```

which could be one line in your AUTOEXEC.BAT file. If you have an option in a CONFIG.SYS menu that lets you choose at boot whether or not to load DOSKEY, you could use the value of the environment variable CONFIG in a command

```
IF [NOT] %CONFIG%.==menuname. DO MACROS
```

to run the MACROS batch file only if DOSKEY is loaded into memory. Naturally, you also could have one batch file that would present a whole menu of batch files, each created to load a different set of DOSKEY macros. Pick one off the list, and the menu batch file would CALL the specified macro-setting batch file.

Modifying a DOS Command

In Chapter 13, the section "How COMMAND.COM Executes Commands" explained that COMMAND.COM normally checks any command verb that is not preceded by a path or drive specification to see if it is an internal command—before it checks if it is the name of an executable file—and that loading DOSKEY changes this slightly. With DOSKEY loaded, COMMAND.COM will first look to see if the verb is the name of one of the currently defined DOSKEY macros. If it is, COMMAND.COM executes that macro. This makes it possible to create a DOSKEY macro that replaces any of the DOS internal commands (as well as any external command program in the current directory or in any directory on the PATH).

Try the following experiment to see how this works: First, be sure that DOSKEY is loaded into memory in your PC by looking at the output of the MEM /C command. If it is not, simply issue the command DOSKEY. Next, enter the command

```
DOSKEY ver=echo This replaces the normal VER command.
```

and press Enter. To see that your definition was accepted, issue the command

```
DOSKEY /M
```

which will display

```
ver=echo This replaces the normal VER command.
```

and any other macros that are currently defined. Now type `VER` and press Enter. You will see

```
echo This replaces the normal VER command.
This replaces the normal VER command.
```

on your screen. You see the command that DOSKEY issues to replace `VER` plus the results of that command. Next, press the space bar once, then type `VER` and press Enter. This time you will see

```
MS-DOS Version 6.00
```

or whatever is correct for your PC's operating system.

The difference between the two commands shows one subtlety about DOSKEY macros: When COMMAND.COM is matching a command verb against its list of internal commands, it first strips off leading and trailing spaces. When it is looking for a match to a DOSKEY macro, it trims off trailing spaces but not leading spaces. This gives you a way to redefine the DOS internal commands and still be able to access the original meanings.

> ***Warning:*** There is one way in which using a DOSKEY macro to redefine another DOS command can become a "gotcha." Suppose you want to protect yourself against accidentally deleting files by defining a DOSKEY macro with the name `DEL` and giving as its definition `DEL $* /P`. Now, each time you issue a delete command you will be prompted before it deletes each file. Then, one day you accidentally press the space bar once before you issue some command like DEL A*.*, expecting to be asked whether or not to delete each file in the current directory whose name begins with A. Wham! All those files just got deleted and you weren't asked anything—just typing an extra space. DOSKEY macros are no substitute for an alert awareness of what you are

A couple of other subtleties involve the ECHO command and the @ symbol. If the DOSKEY macro issues an ECHO command, you will see the command plus the text it echoes. You might think that you could suppress the first of these two lines by adding the @ symbol in front of the word ECHO, as you would in a batch file. But COMMAND.COM doesn't support that meaning for the @ symbol at a DOS prompt, so trying this will only result in seeing the modified command

```
@echo This replaces the normal VER command.
```

plus the message

```
Bad command or filename.
```

Alternatively, you might have thought that issuing an ECHO OFF command would work. That will keep COMMAND.COM from showing you any more DOS prompts until you issue an ECHO ON command, but it will still show you each character you type, each character in any DOSKEY macro you invoke, plus the output those commands generate.

Alternative Command Processors

All of the discussion in this chapter has been about the batch file programming language and the DOSKEY macro provisions in standard MS-DOS and PC DOS, Version 6. If you use an alternative command processor, like 4DOS or NDOS, you will have access to a substantially enhanced batch file language. Refer to the manuals that came with your alternative command processor for the details.

The DOS Batch File Commands

Which DOS commands are useful in batch files? All of them. There is only one DOS command (GOTO) that *must* be used only in a batch file, and all the rest *may* be used there. If you are unclear on the details of how to invoke a particular DOS command, what options it offers, or what it does, see the Command Reference or look it up in the index and read the indicated pages.

The DOS Power Tools Batch File Programs

There are a number of useful utilities that you can use to enhance your batch files: ANSCOLOR can provide a variety of colors within a single file (but you have to install ANSI.SYS to use it.) DOSVER lets you test to see what version of DOS is running on a given machine from within a batch file. MB and SECHO provide a variety of on-screen effects, including boxes, beeps, character fills, and cursor control.

CHAPTER

15

Using DEBUG

DEBUG is a powerful program originally written by and for programmers, but that has many uses for non-programmers, as well, including viewing a region of memory to see what numbers are stored there and creating small COM programs from scripts such as those that appear in computer magazine articles. We'll show you how to use such scripts, and give you some insight into how they interact with DEBUG. DEBUG also will help you become more facile with assembly-language programs—which all DEBUG scripts are—and enable you to run through a program one instruction at a time to get a better understanding of what the program does.

No chapter of this length can provide in-depth coverage of all the benefits and uses of DEBUG, but this chapter lays the foundation. Additional details on all the DEBUG commands are given in the Command Reference. The end of this chapter lists the DEBUG commands, along with descriptions of their best use.

Starting DEBUG

DEBUG is an interactive program. When you type DEBUG at the DOS prompt, DOS loads it into memory. DEBUG, like DOS, has a special command prompt: a single minus sign (-).

DEBUG Commands

Probably the most important DEBUG command is Q (short for Quit), which allows you to get out of DEBUG and return to DOS. To exit DEBUG, type Q at DEBUG's hyphen prompt and press Enter. Most DEBUG commands are a single letter, possibly followed by one or more parameters. The following sections illustrate how to use a number of them. Whenever you're running DEBUG, you can use the ? command to view a short list like the one below of all DEBUG commands.

```
-?

assemble      A [address]
compare       C range address
dump          D [range]
enter         E address [list]
fill          F range list
go            G [=address] [addresses]
hex           H value1 value2
input         I port
load          L [address] [drive] [firstsector] [number]
move          M range address
name          N [pathname] [arglist]
output        O port byte
proceed       P [=address] [number]
quit          Q
register      R [register]
search        S range list
trace         T [=address] [value]
unassemble    U [range]
write         W [address] [drive] [firstsector] [number]
allocate expanded memory        XA [#pages]
deallocate expanded memory      XD [handle]
map expanded memory pages       XM [Lpage] [Ppage] [handle]
display expanded memory status  XS
-
```

Creating and Running Programs in DEBUG

This is where the fun begins—creating small, useful programs using DEBUG. Even if you don't know assembly language, you'll learn how to create a couple of simple, but useful programs to run on your computer.

The key to writing programs in DEBUG is the A (Assemble) command. This command turns (relatively) human-readable instructions, such as MOV AH, AL into two hexadecimal numbers, 88 C4, so that they are comprehensible to an 80x86 microprocessor.

The first example we'll develop is a very short program called BEEP.COM. This program will sound a short tone from your computer's speaker every time you run it, and this is a nice addition to batch files when you want to get someone's (including your own) attention.

Creating the BEEP Program

First you'll create this program by hand. Then, in the next section you'll develop a *script* to build the program automatically, which is how you'll create a couple of other programs after that. Start DEBUG and at the prompt, type

```
A 100
```

and press Enter. This command tells DEBUG to start its built-in assembler. DEBUG will assemble any "commands" you type until you press Enter on a new line. You should see something like the following on your screen.

```
-a 100
1D76:0100 _
```

At this point, type in your program, which is listed next. If you make any mistakes, type `A 100` and press Enter to start all over again. After you type the last line and press Enter, press Enter again to return to the hyphen prompt. Here are the lines to type. Note that DEBUG will respond as you do this.

```
mov ah,2
mov al,7
int 21
int 20
```

The above is actually a complete program that you can run. In fact, you can run this program entirely within DEBUG, which you'll do next. But first, make sure you typed everything correctly. To do so, either check what you typed to make sure it agrees with the listing above, or use DEBUG's `U` command to list the program in memory. Here is the output you should see, with a few caveats we'll mention shortly, if you use `U 100` to list this program:

```
-u 100
1D76:0100 B402          MOV     AH,02
1D76:0102 B207          MOV     DL,07
1D76:0104 CD21          INT     21
1D76:0106 CD20          INT     20
1D76:0108 E790          OUT     90,AX
1D76:010A 007405        ADD     [SI+05],DH
1D76:010D F6C702        TEST    BH,02
1D76:0110 7548          JNZ     015A
1D76:0112 893EAB90      MOV     [90AB],DI
1D76:0116 FF06AB90      INC     WORD PTR [90AB]
1D76:011A C606340065    MOV     BYTE PTR [0034],65
1D76:011F 1D06AE        SBB     AX,AE06
-
```

Figure 15-1 shows this process as it appears on screen. In actual practice, the first four lines (`MOV AH, 02` through `INT 20`) should be the same. But after these lines, you'll probably see something different because you're looking at the leftovers of some other program. These additional lines are data that was in memory from other programs you ran before you started DEBUG. Just ignore them.

If your U listing doesn't exactly match the first four lines, type `A 100`, then retype the first lines again. It's very important that you have these lines correct before you try to run the program; your computer might crash if these lines aren't correct. Assembly language programming is very powerful, but it's also very susceptible to mistakes that can cause it to crash,and require you to make that three-fingered salute (Ctrl-Alt-Del).

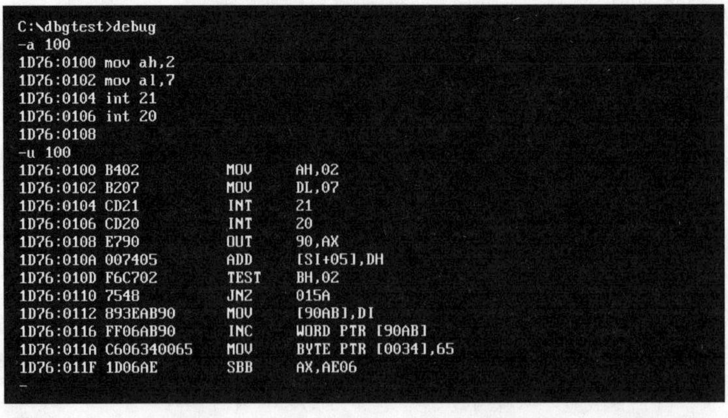

Figure 15-1 Entry and listing of BEEP.COM using DEBUG

Using DEBUG to Run BEEP

When you know your program is typed in correctly, type

```
G 100
```

This command will run your program at line 100h and you'll hear a beep from your computer.

Now, to see exactly what this program was doing, we'll start BEEP over again, but this time run it one instruction at a time. But first, you'll need to make sure DEBUG will start your program at the beginning. In case you're wondering why your program starts at 100h, every COM program always starts with something known as the PSP (Program Segment Prefix) that contains information that DOS uses to run your program. This area, which is 256 (or 100h) bytes long, includes, among other things, the command line that you typed when you started your program. DOS requires that every COM program start at address 100h within a segment (the rules for EXE programs are different, and we'll not cover them here).

Stepping through BEEP

Direct DEBUG where to start your program by setting the Instruction Pointer (IP) register to 100h. The IP register tells the 80x86 microprocessor where to find the next instruction. The full address is actually in the pair of registers CS:IP, but you don't really need to worry about the CS part to create simple programs. Type the following two commands, pressing Enter after each one, to set IP to 100h so it points to the first instruction in BEEP:

```
R IP
100
```

Confirm that this worked by typing `R` followed by Enter, which should display a register listing similar to that in Figure 15-2.

Look at the following lines in that figure:

```
-r
AX=0000  BX=0000  CX=0000  DX=0000  SP=FFEE  BP=0000  SI=0000  DI=0000
DS=1D76  ES=1D76  SS=1D76  CS=1D76  IP=0100   NV UP EI PL NZ NA PO NC
1D76:0100 B402          MOV     AH,02
-
```

Two parts of these lines are important. First, in the middle of the second line you'll see `IP=0100`, which confirms that you've set IP to 100. The third line shows the instruction to which IP is currently pointing—the instruction that DEBUG will run. Also notice that the AX register (at the start of the first line) is currently holding a 0.

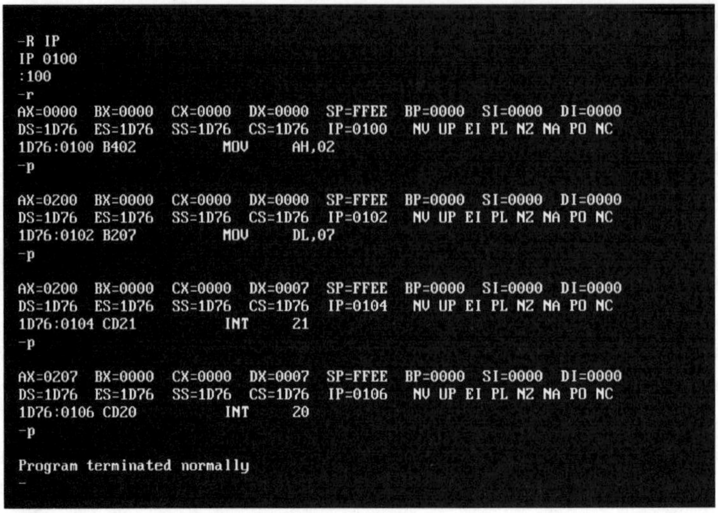

```
-R IP
IP 0100
:100
-r
AX=0000  BX=0000  CX=0000  DX=0000  SP=FFEE  BP=0000  SI=0000  DI=0000
DS=1D76  ES=1D76  SS=1D76  CS=1D76  IP=0100   NV UP EI PL NZ NA PO NC
1D76:0100 B402          MOV     AH,02
-p

AX=0200  BX=0000  CX=0000  DX=0000  SP=FFEE  BP=0000  SI=0000  DI=0000
DS=1D76  ES=1D76  SS=1D76  CS=1D76  IP=0102   NV UP EI PL NZ NA PO NC
1D76:0102 B207          MOV     DL,07
-p

AX=0200  BX=0000  CX=0000  DX=0007  SP=FFEE  BP=0000  SI=0000  DI=0000
DS=1D76  ES=1D76  SS=1D76  CS=1D76  IP=0104   NV UP EI PL NZ NA PO NC
1D76:0104 CD21          INT     21
-p

AX=0207  BX=0000  CX=0000  DX=0007  SP=FFEE  BP=0000  SI=0000  DI=0000
DS=1D76  ES=1D76  SS=1D76  CS=1D76  IP=0106   NV UP EI PL NZ NA PO NC
1D76:0106 CD20          INT     20
-p

Program terminated normally
-
```

Figure 15-2 Step-by-step register dumps of BEEP.COM as displayed by DEBUG

The MOV instruction, logically, moves data from one place to another, and from the right side to the left side of the comma. Therefore the MOV AH,02 instruction moves the number 02 into the upper (high) half of the AH register. The next step we took was to run a single instruction. To do that we typed P (for Proceed) and pressed Enter. This produced the following display:

```
-p

AX=0200  BX=0000  CX=0000  DX=0000  SP=FFEE  BP=0000  SI=0000  DI=0000
DS=1D76  ES=1D76  SS=1D76  CS=1D76  IP=0102   NV UP EI PL NZ NA PO NC
1D76:0102 B207          MOV     DL,07
-
```

Notice that AX has a value of 0200, which means that AH is now 02, as a result of the first MOV instruction. If you look at the second line of the display, you'll notice IP=0102, which is the address of the second instruction in BEEP (this second instruction appears again in the last line). It will move the value 07 into the DL register (the lower half of the DX register). Type P again to run this second MOV instruction and you'll see that DL has changed.

```
-p

AX=0200  BX=0000  CX=0000  DX=0007  SP=FFEE  BP=0000  SI=0000  DI=0000
DS=1D76  ES=1D76  SS=1D76  CS=1D76  IP=0104   NV UP EI PL NZ NA PO NC
1D76:0104 CD21          INT     21
-
```

This brings us to the INT 21 instruction, which is the reason we set AH to 2 and DL to 7. INT 21h is a special instruction that asks DOS to do some work for us. Loading 02 into the AH register tells DOS that we want it to *print* a character onto the screen. DOS uses the number in the DL register to determine which character to print. Setting DL to 7 instructed DOS to sound the bell (7 is the ASCII code for BELL). Use the P command to run this instruction, and you'll hear a beep and then see the following:

```
-p

AX=0207  BX=0000  CX=0000  DX=0007  SP=FFEE  BP=0000  SI=0000  DI=0000
DS=1D76  ES=1D76  SS=1D76  CS=1D76  IP=0106   NV UP EI PL NZ NA PO NC
1D76:0106 CD20          INT     20
-
```

This final instruction, in effect, is DOS's way of indicating that it's done, and you can take over again. When you create the BEEP.COM program in the next section, this instruction will exit your program and return control to DOS. Here it simply displays a message indicating that the program just finished running:

```
-p

Program terminated normally
-
```

Saving BEEP.COM

Once you have a program built inside DEBUG, you can save it to disk as a COM program (you can't use DEBUG to create EXE programs for rather technical reasons). First you must give DEBUG the name of your program and its size. You name a program using the N command. We'll call this program BEEP.COM, so at the hyphen prompt type:

```
N BEEP.COM
```

The N command assigns a name to the program; it doesn't create the program. In the case of BEEP, DEBUG won't use this name until you use the W command to write DEBUG.COM to the disk, but before you can do that, you need to tell DEBUG how large your program is.

There's a very easy way to find out how large your program is. Use the U command to list your program, and the first address after your program will tell you how large it is. Unassembling BEEP produces this output:

```
1D76:0100 B402          MOV     AH,02
1D76:0102 B207          MOV     DL,07
```

```
1D76:0104 CD21          INT     21
1D76:0106 CD20          INT     20
1D76:0108 E790          OUT     90,AX
```

The first line following your program (which ends with INT 20) starts with the numbers 1D76:0108. The first number, 1D76, will almost certainly be different on your computer since it depends on where your program is loaded in memory. The 108 means that your program occupies addresses 100h through 107h. To find the size of your program, simply subtract 100h (the first instruction address) from 108h (the first address after the last instruction); thus, BEEP is 8 bytes long.

To tell DEBUG how large your program is, type:

```
R CX
8
```

The W command expects to find the size of your program in two registers: BX and CX. Using two registers allows you to write files larger than 64K, but all the files we'll create will be less than 64K, which means you can leave BX at 0 and set CX to the size of your program. You can use the R command to make sure you set these two registers correctly. Finally, use the W command, followed by Enter to write BEEP.COM to the disk. DEBUG will report what it did, after which you can tell it you are ready to quit.

```
-w
Writing 00008 bytes
```

This process is pictured in Figure 15-3. You now have a short program, 8 bytes long, that sounds a beep whenever you run it. This is one of the shortest programs you'll find anywhere.

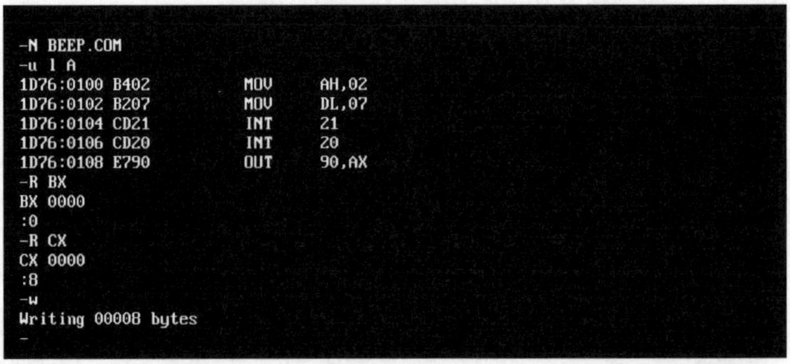

Figure 15-3 Process of saving BEEP.COM using DEBUG

Using DEBUG and Script Files

DEBUG script files are those that contain all the commands necessary to build a small COM program. It's amazing how many small, useful programs you can create with script files. Computer magazines often publish small programs as DEBUG script files because anyone who has DOS can create programs using such files. (This applies only if you have MS-DOS or PC-DOS; if you use DR DOS it comes with its own debugger, but unfortunately that program, SID, won't accept DEBUG scripts.) This section explains how to use script files to create programs and provides several programs written as script files.

Script files are simple text files that contain lines. Each line is a single DEBUG command, and the last line is always the Q command to exit DEBUG and return to DOS. Let's say you have a script file called BEEP.SCR, which you created using the DOS EDIT command. You would then run this script file using the following command:

```
DEBUG < BEEP.SCR
```

This command uses redirection to send the contents of a file to DEBUG as input, rather than as characters from the keyboard. Here is the script file for the BEEP.COM program:

```
A
MOV AH, 2                    ; Ask to print a character
MOV DL, 7                    ; Print the BELL character
INT 21                       ; Ask DOS to print this character
INT 20                       ; Exit and return to DOS

R CX
8
N BEEP.COM
W
Q
```

Note: There are two things you must have in this, or any other script file: One is a blank line between the last program instruction (INT 20 here) and the R CX command. This blank line tells DEBUG that you've finished entering the program and want to exit Assembly mode. Second, you must press Enter after the Q at the end of the file. If you don't, you won't be able to exit DEBUG.

This script has some comments that explain how the code works. DEBUG completely ignores these comments so you don't need to type them in—they're optional, but they do make the program script easier to read.

A Disable Print Screen Script

The disable print screen program is actually very simple and requires only a few lines of code. But we'll give you a slightly longer version that allows you to enable and disable the Print Screen key, to give you more control over this key.

Using the E Command to Disable Print Screen

Before we present the first program, we'll show you how to use DEBUG directly to disable the Print Screen key. The Print Screen key is handled by the ROM BIOS in your computer. Whenever you press it, the ROM BIOS runs some code that copies the contents of your screen to a printer. If, however, your computer is currently printing the screen and you press this key again, you wouldn't want your computer to start printing the screen again.

The ROM BIOS uses a single byte in low memory to keep track of whether it is currently printing the screen or not. If this byte is set to 1, your computer thinks it is currently printing your screen; therefore, it will ignore the Print Screen key. It sets this byte back to 0 as soon as it finishes printing the screen. Thus, by setting this byte to 1, the ROM BIOS will ignore the Print Screen key even if it is not actually printing the screen.

The all important byte is located at the absolute address 500, which must be written as 0:500 to tell DEBUG that we want the byte at 500h in the first segment of memory (segment number 0). To determine how this byte is currently set, use the D command:

```
-d 0:500 l 1
0000:0500  00
-
```

In this case, we've asked DEBUG to dump the byte at location 0:500 and display just one byte (L 1 means use a length of 1). This byte is currently 00, which tells your computer that it can respond to the Print Screen key.

To disable the Print Screen key, use the E command to modify this byte in memory:

```
-e 0:500
0000:0500  00.1
-
```

Type E 0:500, at which point DEBUG responds with the current value of this byte (00), followed by a period. Then type 1 and press Enter, which changes this value to 01. Now the Print Screen key won't work. To enable the Print Screen key again, change the byte at 0:500 back to 00 using the E command.

Building the NOPRTSCR Program

Now that you know how to disable the Print Screen key, we'll present a simple script that disables the Print Screen key by setting the byte at 0:500 to 01. Once you run this program, you won't be able to use Print Screen until you reboot DOS, or until you use the more advanced version presented in the next section. Here is the simple version:

```
A
MOV AX, 0                   ; Clear AX
MOV DS, AX                  ; Set DS to low memory
MOV Byte Ptr [500], 1       ; Disable Print Screen
INT 20                      ; Exit back to DOS

R CX
C
N NOPRTSCR.COM
W
Q
```

> ***Note:*** When you build and run this program, the Print Screen key won't work until you reboot your computer.

Like the BEEP program, this one is only four lines long. But instead of using 8 bytes, this program is 0Ch bytes long (12 bytes). The reason this program is larger even though it has the same number of lines is that assembly language instructions come in a number of different sizes, from 1 byte up to several bytes. The long MOV instruction on the third line is actually 5 bytes long, and there are other instructions even longer (up to 7 bytes long). Fortunately, the 80x86 microprocessor knows exactly what to do with all the numbers and, normally, it's not necessary to know how long instructions are.

> ***Note:*** Microsoft Windows changes the way the Print Screen key works, and it completely ignores the byte at 0:500. This means that you won't need the NOPRTSCR program, nor will it do anything useful as long as Windows is running. NOPRTSCR affects your computer only while DOS is running without Windows.

Enhancing NOPRTSCR

The long version of NOPRTSCR is 26 bytes, which in the scheme of programs really isn't very long. Some of the assembly language programs written for the disk, such as NOBREAK, are several hundred bytes long. In part this is because NOBREAK does more work. But NOBREAK is also larger than it might need to be in order to make it more robust, which we'll explain next.

The advanced version of NOPRTSCR allows you to supply either a + or a - on the command line to turn NOPRTSCR on or off. If you want to allow the Print Screen key to work again, you would type:

```
NOPRTSCR -
```

This command disables the NOPRTSCR program, which is the same as allowing the Print Screen key to work again. Typing

```
NOPRTSCR +
```

disables the Print Screen key (because of the NO at the start of NOPRTSCR). The nonrobust part of this program is that you must have one, and only one, space between the NOPRTSCR and the + or –. This limitation exists because we chose to make the NOPRTSCR program as simple as possible. That said, here's the script that creates the program NOPRTSCR.COM:

```
A
XOR AX, AX                  ; 100:  Set AL=0 for enable & DS=0
MOV ES, AX                  ; 102:  Point ES to low memory
CMP Byte Ptr [80], 2        ; 104:  Is there a char?
JB  112                     ; 109:  No, disable Print Screen
CMP Byte Ptr [82], 2D       ; 10B:  Is this a -?
JE  114                     ; 110:  Yes, enable Print Screen
INC AL                      ; 112:  No, set AL=1 for disable
ES:                         ; 114:  Set 0:500 using ES=0
MOV [500], AL               ; 115:  Enable/Disable Print
Screen
INT 20                      ; 118:  Exit back to DOS

R CX
1A
N NOPRTSCR.COM
W
Q
```

There are a number of new instructions in this program. First we used the XOR instruction to set the AX register to 0 instead of using MOV AX,0 as before. The XOR AX, AX instruction is a trick programmers often use to clear a register, since it takes only 2 bytes for the instruction versus 3 bytes for MOV AX, 0.

Next we set the ES register to 0, which is used in the final MOV instruction to set the byte in low memory. The ES: instruction before this final MOV instruction tells the 80x86 to use the ES register to find the data rather than the DS register, which is the default for any memory read or write.

The CMP instruction compares two numbers. The command line is stored in memory starting at 80h, and the first byte is the total of how many characters there are in the rest of the command line. So, the first CMP instruction checks to see if you have at least two characters (a space and a + or a -). If you don't, the next instruction, JB (Jump if Below, which means less than) skips to the instruction at 112, which increments the AL register (INC AL) so it will become 1 (we started with AL set to 0).

If the command line contains at least two characters, the next CMP instruction checks to see if the second character is a minus sign. If it is, the JE instruction (Jump if Equal) skips to address 114, which is the start of the MOV instruction that sets the byte to 0:500 (to 0 in this case, which allows Print Screen to work). If the second character on the command line is *not* a minus sign, this program adds 1 to AL (INC AL) so it will be 1; and then it sets the byte at 0:500 to 1, which disables the Print Screen key. The final instruction is the INT 20 instruction that exits back to DOS.

Tip: Most programmers who write DEBUG scripts start with a program written using the Microsoft Macro Assembler, which is the best way to create large assembly language programs. MASM, as it's known, allows programmers to build programs without knowing the address to use in jump instructions. Instead, symbolic names for lines of code may be used, and MASM will automatically supply the correct address when you assemble the program.

Some short programs, however, may be written directly as DEBUG scripts. To create the NOPRTSCR script in this section, we first wrote the DEBUG script with comments. For the addresses in the JB and JE instructions, we used the number 100 because we didn't know what the correct address would be. We also used size 10 for CX since we didn't know how large the program would be. Next we ran the script through DEBUG, which displays each line as it is assembled. From this listing we were able to add the addresses for each instruction to the comments on the right side, and we also accessed the correct size for the program. Using these addresses we were able to edit the DEBUG script to use the correct addresses for both the JB and JE instructions.

Testing for a Task Swapper

The following script tests to see if Microsoft Windows, the DOS Task Swapper, or some other task-swapping environment, is running (it may not catch all non-Microsoft environments), and if so, returns an ERRORLEVEL of 1; otherwise it returns an ERRORLEVEL of 0. You can use the IF command in a batch file to change how it runs if you use it while a task swapper is running.

Here is the complete DEBUG script, along with comments on how it works. (The documentation on this program is hard to find.)

```
A
mov ax, 1600          ; 100:  Ask for Windows check
int 2F                ; 103:  See if in Windows
or  al, al            ; 105:  Is enhanced mode Windows?
jz  113               ; 107:  Don't know, do another test
cmp al, 80            ; 109:  Is enhanced mode Windows?
je  113               ; 10B:  Don't know, do another test
mov al, 1             ; 10D:  Yes, return ERRORLEVEL 1
mov ah, 4C            ; 10F:  DOS return function
int 21                ; 111:  Exit to DOS
mov ax, 4680          ; 113:  Test for real/standard mode
int 2F                ; 116:  See if we're in windows
or  ax, ax            ; 118:  Is this Windows?
jz  10D               ; 11A:  Yes, return ERRORLEVEL 1
mov al, 0             ; 11C:  No, return ERRORLEVEL 0
jmp 10F               ; 11E:  Jump to exit code

R CX
20
N INWINDOW.COM
W
Q
```

Using DEBUG to Run a Program in ROM

We showed you how to run the BEEP program using the G command. There is another use for that command that is at least as important.

Many option cards for PCs come with an option ROM on them. These read-only memory chips hold programs for activating the rest of the pieces on that option card. Generally, these program fragments are treated by the system as extensions to the motherboard Basic Input/Output System (BIOS) programs, so we call the option ROM a BIOS extension. And for the most part it's not necessary to know the details of what is where in that ROM.

During the Power On Self Test (POST), an intialization program in that ROM is given a chance to execute. After it has finished, various pointers have been changed and, functionally, the programs in the ROM are as much a part of your PC as those in the motherboard BIOS ROM.

When you need to run a special-purpose program that resides in one of those option ROMs, you will discover the second important use of the G command in DEBUG. The Always Technologies IN-2000 SCSI host adapter is a fine example of this circumstance. This high-performance SCSI host adapter is often used to connect several hard drives and other SCSI peripherals to a PC.

In the option ROM on the IN-2000 there is a small program that can be used to do diagnostic tests on the card and on the SCSI bus attached to the card. To run this program, you must be able to get the PC's CPU to load its instructions and execute them. The easiest way to do this is by first running DEBUG, then using the G command to run the program in the option ROM. Suppose you have set the switches on the card to put the option ROM into the CPU's memory address space starting at address C8000h. You can also write that address in segment:offset form as C800:0.

To run the program in the option ROM, you have to know exactly where it starts. Once you know, it is very simple to make CS:IP point at that address. Instead of loading the Code Segment register with C800h and loading IP with 5 (which is the magic number you need to find in the IN-2000's manual), you can simply issue the command

```
G=C800:5
```

and away you go. The next thing you will see is the menu for the IN-2000's diagnostic program. (This program is also needed if you must redo the low-level format on a SCSI hard drive that is attached to this card's SCSI bus.)

When you enter a number in the G= command, you are telling the CPU to go to the indicated place and execute whatever instructions it finds there. It has no way of validating your instruction, so it will simply follow it, no matter what happens next. If you enter the wrong number after G=, usually your computer will "hang" and you will have to reboot it or possibly shut it off or press the reset button (if your PC has one).

This use of DEBUG, while common, is not something you will ever need to do unless the documents that come with an option card instructions tell you to do so. Those instructions will also tell you the right offset number to use. For the segment portion of the address you will use whatever segment address you set for the option ROM on that board by the use of some jumpers, switches, or software commands.

Using DEBUG to Patch a Program on the Disk

This section explains how to use DEBUG to change other programs. The most common reason to modify another program is to change a default setting. For example, the DOS EDIT program always assumes you want to open TXT files whenever you select Open... from the File menu. But if instead you usually work with BAT files instead of TXT files you can change this setting in EDIT, and DEBUG is just the tool you need.

Before you can use DEBUG, though, there are a number of steps to follow, along with a few warnings. Although DEBUG is a very powerful and versatile program, it is also potentially dangerous. Before you modify any program, therefore, make an exact copy of it in case your changes don't take effect and you can't change your program back again. Here, then, are the steps:

1. Make a copy of your file under a new name, and work with the copy. If you plan to modify an EXE program, you'll also need to rename the program so it will have a different extension, such as BIN. DEBUG's W command will not write a file with the EXE extension.
2. Make the changes to your program.
3. Use the W command to write your program back to the disk.
4. If your program was an EXE program, rename it to have the EXE extension again.
5. Run your program. If it doesn't run properly, try again, or restore your original, unmodified copy.

Loading EDIT into DEBUG

As an example, we'll show you how to change EDIT's open dialog box to display .BAT files instead of .TXT files by default. The EDIT program is nothing more than a small program that runs QBASIC with a few switches, so you'll make the actual changes to QBASIC.EXE rather than EDIT.COM.

First, make a copy of QBASIC.EXE. We suggest you use a different extension for your backup copy, such as .ORG, for original:

```
COPY QBASIC.EXE QBASIC.ORG
```

Next, rename QBASIC.EXE so it has the .BIN (or any other) extension:

```
RENAME QBASIC.EXE QBASIC.BIN
```

This will allow you to load QBASIC.BIN into DEBUG and, more importantly, enable you to write it back to the disk. Now load QBASIC.BIN into DEBUG using this command:

```
DEBUG QBASIC.BIN
```

Next comes the tricky part. DEBUG has a command, S, that scans memory looking for a character or a string of characters, which is exactly what we want; we want to look for the string *.TXT. The problem, however, is that the S command can scan only 64K of memory at a time; QBASIC.BIN is nearly 200K. How do you find *.TXT when you can only search 64K? The answer is that you have to search 64K at a time, until you've searched all of QBASIC.BIN. To do this, you need a couple of pieces of information, which you can obtain from the register display. Type R and press Enter, and you should see a display similar to the following:

```
AX=0000  BX=0002  CX=F705  DX=0000  SP=FFEE  BP=0000  SI=0000  DI=0000

DS=2CDE  ES=2CDE  SS=2CDE  CS=2CDE  IP=0100   NV UP EI PL NZ NA PO NC

2CDE:0100 4C            DEC     BP
```

The important pieces of information are the numbers for BX, CX, and DS. The number in DS tells you where the image of QBASIC.BIN starts in memory; the BX and CX registers tell you how long QBASIC.BIN is, in hexadecimal.

Write down the number in DS, which in this case is 2CDE. You'll use this number to start the search. Also, read the number in BX (0002 in this example) and add 1 to it (to get 3 in this example). This last number is how many 64K chunks of memory you'll need to search.

Now comes the fun. Start by searching the first 64K block of memory. Use the following command (substitute your own value of DS for our 2CDE):

```
S 2CDE:0 FFFF "*.TXT"
```

It's important here that you type *.TXT in all uppercase letters. If DEBUG returns just the hyphen prompt, it means that DEBUG didn't find your string. In that case, use the H command to add FFF to the first number (2CDE in our example) to find the starting address for the next search:

```
-H 2CDE FFF
3CDD  1CDF
-
```

Then use the first number (3CDD here) as the starting address for the next search:

```
S 3CDD:0 FFFF "*.TXT"
```

If DEBUG still remains silent, you'll have to add another FFF to the starting address and try the search with this new address. Keep doing this until you've searched for the string the same number of times as the other number you wrote down (3 in this case):

```
-S 4CDC:0 FFFF "*.TXT"
4CDE:DD70
-
```

The only information returned from a successful search is a list of addresses where DEBUG found a match. In this case DEBUG found the string *.TXT at address 4CDE:DD70.

The next step is to change this string. You'll use the E command along with the exact address that DEBUG returned from your search (don't use these numbers because no doubt they're different from your own). Type E *address* and press Enter. Then press the Spacebar twice to keep the *. the same. Finally, type 42, press space, type 41, and press Enter. You have now changed the *.TXT to *.BAT. To confirm this, use the D command with the same address:

```
-E 4CDE:DD70
4CDE:DD70  2A.      2E.      54.42   58.41
-D 4CDE:DD70
4CDE:DD70  2A 2E 42 41 54 00 F1 E2-5C 85 9C 89 A5 79 7B 6D
*.BAT...\....y{m
```

On the right side of the last line the *.BAT shows you that you've correctly changed *.TXT to *.BAT.

At this point you can write your new version back to the disk using the W command:

```
-W
Writing 2F705 bytes
-
```

Now rename QBASIC.BIN to QBASIC.EXE and run EDIT. When you select Open... from the File menu, you should see *.BAT filled in as the default name.

The DEBUG Commands

DEBUG has 22 different commands it understands, not all of which you will use. Therefore, as you read through the following brief synopsis of those commands, note those you will need or want to explore.

Q The most important DEBUG command. Use it to **Q**uit—exit out of DEBUG and back to the DOS prompt.

D Use **D** or the **D**ump command to tell DEBUG to display the contents of a patch of memory. It shows both the hexadecimal byte values and their ASCII symbols, if those symbols are printable. Use this command to explore your PC from the interrupt vector table in low memory to the motherboard BIOS ROM at the top.

R Use the **R**egister command to display the contents of one or all of the registers, or to modify any of those values.

X This is the prefix for a group of four commands dealing with expanded memory. Normally, the only one you will have any use for is **XS**, which gives the e**X**panded memory **S**tatus display for your PC at that moment.

G Use the **G**o command to run programs you have written or programs that are in a ROM. Either way, you have to direct it to a valid entry point for a program or you will crash your PC.

I Use **I**nput to access a byte of information directly from a specified input port.

O Use **O**utput to send data to the external world one byte at a time.

H is a **h**exadecimal arithmetic command. Give it two hexadecimal numbers (no larger than FFFFh, please) and it will return their sum and their difference.

N Use the **N**ame command to give a name to a file you are going to save or to tell DEBUG the name of a file you wish to load. (For the serious programmer, use **N** to set up a command line for the program being debugged.)

L **L**oads a file into memory from the disk. Alternatively, use the **L** command to load a sector from the disk by its absolute address.

S Tells DEBUG that you want it to **S**earch for a data pattern in some region of memory. If you want to search through a file, load it into memory first with the **L** command, then use **S** to perform the search.

E Allows you to **E**nter values into memory locations. Use it to put a number in a particular place or to display what is there and, optionally, alter that value.

C Allows you to **C**ompare the contents of two regions of memory.

F Use **F** to **F**ill a region of memory with specified data.

M Use **M** to **M**ove a block of data from one location to another.

A Tells DEBUG that you are about to give it some assembly language instructions that you want **A**ssembled into machine language instructions.

U Reverses the Assemble process. This command tells DEBUG to read the bytes of memory, interpret them as instructions, and show the results in assembly language form. This is called **U**nassembling a program.

W Is the most dangerous DEBUG command of all. It tells DEBUG to **W**rite some information to a specified file or disk location. Use extreme caution before issuing this command. (The N command must be used first to tell DEBUG where the information is to go. If you fail to use the N command, DEBUG may use random information to make this determination.)

P Tells DEBUG to **P**roceed with execution of the currently loaded program. Use this to single-step your way through a program to understand what is occurring.

T Lets you **T**race a program. The program runs until it comes to a specified address (a breakpoint), at which time DEBUG will stop the program and let you display or alter the CPU register contents or the contents of memory. This is used to facilitate debugging of larger programs.

The only way to learn to use DEBUG is to use DEBUG, and once you have done so, you will have achieved mastery over your PC.

CHAPTER

16

Communications

This chapter contains information about techniques for connecting your computer to the rest of the world—to exchange data with another computer, for example. When you connect your PC to another computer, you add the power of the second computer to your own. (That other computer may be located underneath your desk, on the other side of the world, or anyplace in between.) You can move files from one computer to the other, display characters on your screen that were typed on the other computer's keyboard, and run programs stored on the other computer. With the right programs, you can use your computer as a remote terminal for a PC or mainframe in a distant city or observe a distant computer's operation for training or diagnostic purposes.

To add communication to your collection of power tools, you need to understand how the computer communicates, and how to take advantage of different kinds of communication. How PCs send and receive data will be explained in general terms, and you'll learn how to apply these principles to use your PC as a communications device.

Serial and Parallel Ports

Chapter 6 described the I/O ports inside the CPU. The sockets into which various cables can be plugged also are called *ports*, and are the interfaces between the computer and other devices. Some ports are designed for very specific purposes, including the keyboard connector, video output, and maybe a dedicated mouse port. Most PCs also have at least two general-purpose ports that you can use to move data to and from a variety of devices, including printers, mice, remote terminals, and other computers. Since these general purpose ports receive data from the outside world to the computer and transmit data from the computer to the rest of the world, they're known as "input/output" ports, usually abbreviated to "I/O." There are two kinds of I/O ports; parallel and serial. Virtually every PC has at least one of each.

The computer's CPU processes data in 8-bit bytes; depending on the type of CPU, it may process more than 1 byte at a time. As shown in Figure 16-1, those 8 bits can enter and leave the computer through 8 separate wires, as "parallel data," or they can move through a single wire, 1 bit at a time, as "serial data." The parallel I/O port is a connector with a separate pin for each CPU data bit, and an additional "strobe" bit that notifies the receiver that all 8 bits are ready for sampling. Because the parallel approach moves 8 bits at the same time, it's faster than serial transmission. This is fine for short distances, but as the distance increases, it becomes more complicated. At distances greater than a few hundred feet, all 8 signals require separate but synchronized line drivers and receivers, which can get expensive. For short-distance data transfer, the added cost of all that extra wire isn't a problem, so the standard printer connection is parallel.

A serial port reduces the cost of building a transmission link by reducing the cost of wire and ancillary hardware needed to transmit the same data. Outbound data from the CPU passes through a serializer that arranges all 8 bits into a single bit stream, which it transmits through a single pin on the serial port connector. The port connector receives an incoming stream of serial data on a different pin, which is wired to a deserializer that assembles each group of 8 successive bits into a byte to send to the CPU. The serializer and deserializer are located on an integrated circuit called a UART (*Universal Asynchronous Receiver Transmitter*). This strategy allows you to use only one wire to send your data, which can save a significant amount of money if the wire has to go a long distance; it also will take at least 8 times as long to get the data sent. Data transmission through a PC's serial port is not synchronized with a common clock signal. Therefore, it's known as *asynchronous* transmission. In order to separate the end of one byte from the beginning of the next, an asynchronous serial channel adds markers to the sequence at the beginning and end of every character.

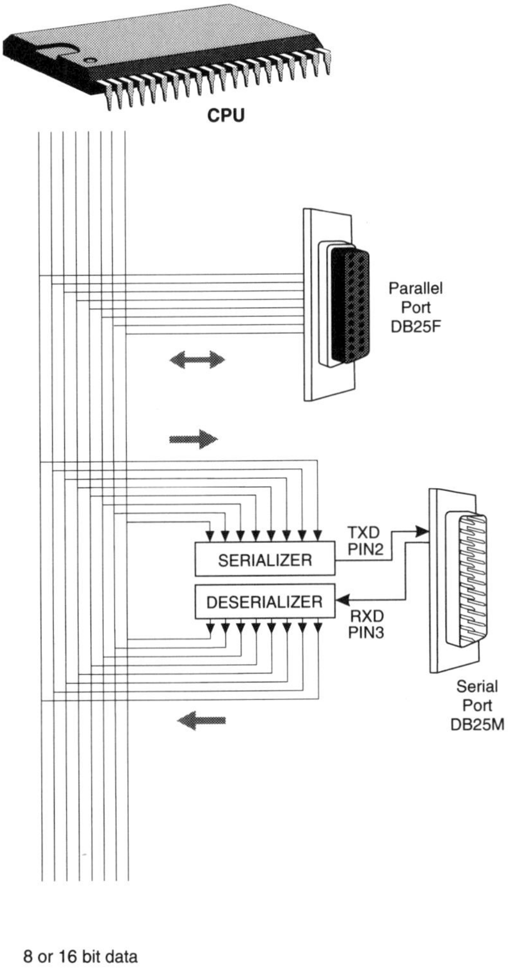

Figure 16-1 Serial and parallel data I/O

The form and terminology of serial data transmission goes back to the days of Morse Code and mechanical teleprinters. The signal lead can either have current flowing (the 1 state or "Mark" condition) or no current (the 0 state or "Space" condition). When there's no data on the line, the line stands "idle" with current flowing in the 1 state (it is "marking time," waiting for the next byte to send). Before the transmission begins, the operators of the transmitter and receiver agree on the transmission speed, the number of data bits in each byte, the type of parity if any, and the duration of the stop bit. Most applications that use a serial port have a function for setting data bits, stop bit, and parity, or you can use the MODE COM command in DOS. If the two ends of a serial link are not configured the same, the receiver won't

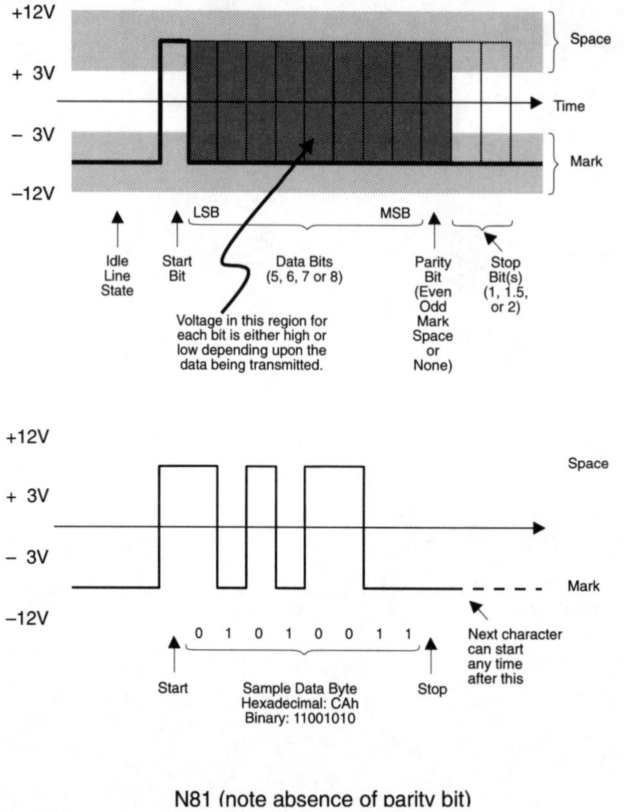

Figure 16-2 Asynchronous data character format

understand the transmitted data. Figure 16-2 shows the structure of an asynchronous serial data character. Each byte begins with a *start bit,* which is always a 0; each data bit holds the line at either the 1 or 0 state. At the end of the byte, the serializer may add a *parity bit,* for which there are four possible uses. The most common is to set it in each byte to either a 0 or a 1, whichever makes the number of 1 bits in that byte even (if *even parity* has been selected) or odd (if *odd parity* was chosen). The other options are to always set the parity bit to a 1 (*mark* parity) or to a 0 (*space* parity). The *stop bit* is always a 1 state, which provides a guaranteed transition to the 0 state that indicates the start bit of the next character. The duration of the stop bit is sometimes set equal to that of a data bit (called 1-stop bit), 50% longer (1.5-stop bits), or twice as long (2-stop bits). This variation in the standard is permitted to accommodate some mechanical teleprinters that require longer amounts of time than others to return to the idle condition.

In practice, the choice between serial and parallel communication has probably been made for you by the designers of the equipment you want to connect to your PC. When a modem requires a serial connection, that's how you'll attach it to the computer; a printer with a parallel input will connect to a parallel port on the computer. When you're connecting two computers together directly, the choice may be dictated by practical rather than technical considerations; for example, the only parallel port on one computer may already be connected to a printer. Rather than installing another I/O port, you might just as well use a serial link between the two computers (unless you need the fastest possible data transfer rate).

Connectors and Cables

If all you want to do is move bits from Computer A to Computer B in a continuous stream, you could use a serial connection with just one wire (plus a ground connection to complete the electrical circuit). Usually, however, you want to establish a two-way communications channel, so each computer can communicate with the other. The standard PC serial port uses two separate wires to send and receive information, so a minimal bidirectional serial link between two PCs will have three wires (send, receive, and ground). More commonly, there will be several more wires in the link used to send control signals from one PC to the other, indicating when each is ready to send or receive data. Each wire is identified by a *pin number*, which corresponds to a specific pin on the I/O port connector, and by a name describing the logical function of the signals on that pin. The customary names of these hardware handshake signals generally are self-explanatory. They are: *transmit data* (TXD), *receive data* (RXD), *data set ready* (DSR), *data terminal ready* (DTR), *ready to send* (RTS), *clear to send* (CTS), *carrier detect* (CD), and *ring detect* (RD). The last two of these signals are often not supported by a PC's serial port. When using that port, a device such as a modem must send to the PC the information that could have gone over the CD or RD wires as messages on the received data line. There are at least two standard (and many non-standard) ways to wire a serial cable. Almost all parallel cables are wired in one of two ways. Some of those wiring patterns, and when to use each, will be explained later in this chapter.

The standard *parallel port* on a PC uses a 25-pin female connector called a DB25F. Your computer may identify the parallel port as a "printer port." The name of the DOS device driver that supports that circuitry is `LPTn`, where *n* is a 1, 2, or 3. This name stands for Line Printer, but you can also use it for parallel communication. On the original IBM PC and the PC/XT, the *serial port* was a similar 25-pin male connector, a DB25M. When IBM introduced the AT, it introduced a serial port with a 9-pin male connector called a DB9M. As in many other design issues, the clone makers followed IBM's lead and the 9-pin serial port is the new standard. However, many other data communications devices and PC I/O expansion boards still use DB25 connectors, so the marketplace is full of cables and adapters to interconnect devices bearing DB9 and DB25 connectors. The name of the DOS device driver to support a serial port is `AUX:` or `COMn:`, where *n* = 1, 2, 3, or 4. Many PCs have labels at the port connectors, with the parallel ports called "printer" and the serial ones called "COM"—designations which match the DOS device names LPTn and COMn. If all the built-in serial or parallel ports in your PC are already in use, you can install more on a plug-in expansion card.

> ***Note:*** The usual maximum number of parallel ports is three; the usual maximum number of serial ports is four. You can have more in a PC, but it is difficult to find enough IRQ values (interrupt request levels) for all of them. Often, the best solution is to get a coprocessor board with many ports (serial and/or parallel) on it, and let the coprocessor on that board *multiplex* them into a single port. Suitable software running in your PC can separate those messages as they come in from that multiplexed port card.

Straight-Through versus Cross-Over Cables

The simplest type of communications cable connects each pin on the plug at one end to the same pin on the plug at the other end. Pin 1 goes to pin 1, pin 2 to pin 2, and so forth. This is called a *straight-through* cable; but there's a complication. The computer uses separate pins to send and receive serial data, so the device connected to the other end of the cable has to receive on the pins that your end uses to transmit data, and transmit on the pins where your end receives data. The computer transmits data on pin 2 of a DB25M connector, so the device at the other end of the cable has to receive data on pin 2. The same applies to most of the other pins; they're either transmitters or receivers, but not both. In order to distinguish the transmitters from the receivers, the industry uses two names to describe ways to wire a serial port: *Data Terminal Equipment* (DTE) and *Data Communications Equipment* (DCE). Your computer is a DTE; a modem or serial printer is a DCE. The complication arises when you want to connect two computers or other DTE devices together. Figure 16-3 shows the wiring for PC serial communications cables (three styles of cable are shown).

The first cable in this figure is the normal straight-through connection between two DB9 connectors. This cable connects all 9 pins in one connector (male) to the corresponding pinholes in the connector (female) at the other end of the cable. The next cable in the figure shows the normal straight-

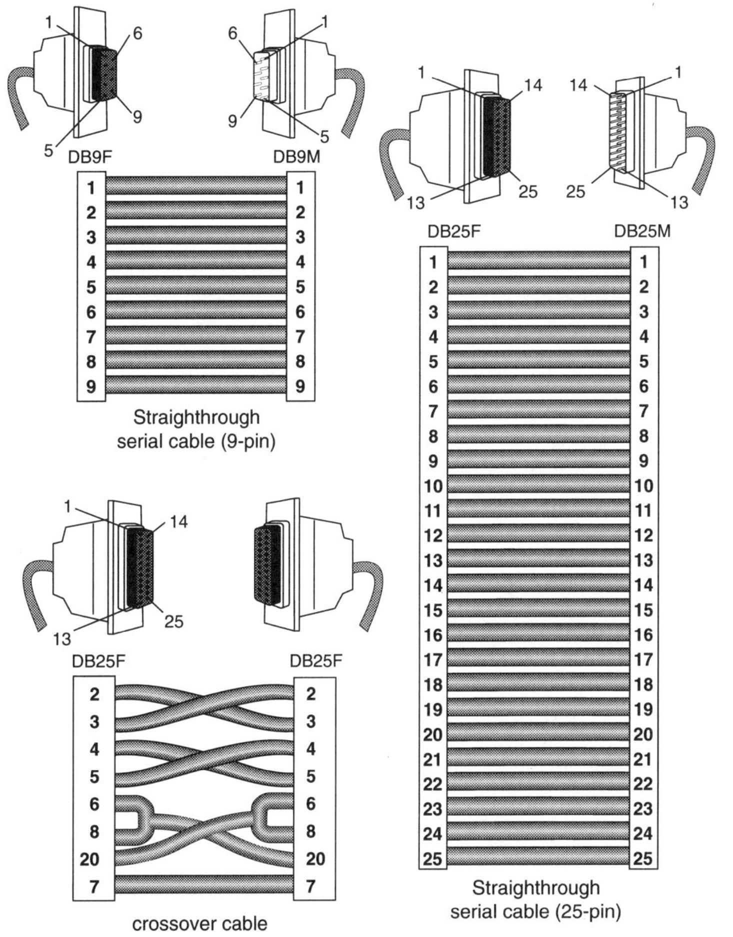

Figure 16-3 Serial cables: direct and "null-modem" connections

through connection of all 25 pins of two DB25 connectors. Again, notice that the two ends of the cable have male/female connectors. Those first two cables will work in all normal computer-to-modem (or more correctly DTE-to-DCE) connections. The only other variations needed are cables with a 9-pin connector on one end and a 25-pin connector on the other. (To see how such a cable must be wired, look at Figure 16-5 later in this chapter.)

A different sort of cable is needed to connect two PCs to each other via their serial ports, because each computer will transmit serial data on pin 2 and expect to receive data on pin 3. If you attempt to use a straight-through cable, you will be connecting pin 2 to pin 2 and pin 3 to pin 3. In this case, neither computer will ever receive anything (and they will compete for the voltage on the wire connected to their pins numbered 2, which is not good).

The solution is to use a specially wired cable to connect pin 2 of each plug to pin 3 of the other plug. There are other transmit and receive control signals that also need to be rerouted, but pins 2 and 3 are the most important.

The third cable shown in Figure 16-3 is sometimes called a *null-modem* cable, but is more precisely referred to as a *crossover* cable. This is the cable you need to connect two DTE devices together, and has a DB25F (female) connector at each end. It also has the wires crossed over so that the transmit data pin on each side is connected to the receive data pin on the other (and corresponding cross-connections for the various hardware handshaking signals). There is no standard way to make a crossover or null-modem cable; Figure 16-3 shows one of the more common ways. (If you need a DB9 connector at either end, you can figure out which pins to connect to which by reference to both Figures 16-3 and 16-5.)

There is one other wiring pattern that is sometimes used for serial cables: a minimalist, three-wire connection that only allows data transfer without any *hardware handshaking* signals to control the flow of the data. (It is just like the crossover cable shown in Figure 16-3, except that only pins 2, 3, and 7 are connected at each side.) If you use a three-wire cable, the software at each end of the link must be able to accept data as fast as it is sent, or else to tell the sender to pause until the receiver is ready for more. This is called *software handshaking*. The most common protocol for doing software handshaking is called *X-ON/X-OFF*.

Warning: If you own both straight-through and crossover cables, be careful not to get them confused. Unless you trace the wires, they all look the same. Whenever you build or buy a crossover cable, boldly mark both connectors "CROSSOVER." Using a crossover cable instead of a straight-through cable, or a straight-through cable where you need a crossover cable, is the source of a large number of data communication problems.

MS-DOS 6.0 includes a utility called Interlnk, which makes it possible to connect one computer to a second computer and use the files and printers from the first on the second computer. The special cables required for Interlnk connections will be discussed later in this chapter.

Data Transmission Speed

As mentioned earlier, users at the two ends of a communications link must agree in advance on the speed at which they will exchange data. Transmission speed is calculated in terms of data elements transmitted or received over a period of time. You will see data speed expressed as either baud or bits per second (bps). DOS supports data transmission speeds ranging from 110 baud to 19,200 baud. (A "Baud" is one signalling unit per second, a unit for expressing data transmission speed named after the nineteenth-century French telegrapher Emile Baudot, who invented an early transmission code.)

Note: Many people use the terms "baud" and "bits per second" interchangeably, but there is a technical difference between the two terms. Baud rate represents the number of discreet signalling elements transmitted in one second. Modern high-speed modems sometimes pack as many as 4 bits into one tone signal, thereby effectively sending more than 1 bit at a time. The PC-to-modem connection always operates at a baud rate equal to the bits-per-second rate. A modem-to-modem link may operate with a bits-per-second rate that is a multiple of its baud rate. For example, what is commonly referred to as 9600 baud is only 2400 baud between modems, but it is 9600 bits-per-second communication. Likewise, "2400 baud" modems actually exchange information between themselves at 600 baud, but communicate with the PCs to which they are attached at 2400 baud. Most PC programs tell you the connection speed and call it baud or bps interchangeably, which is proper, since the PC-to-modem link operates at equal baud and bps rates.

Obviously, there's an advantage to moving data as fast as possible, but there's a trade-off between convenience and reliability. Faster links are more susceptible to corruption than slow ones. As a general rule, it's good practice to set up the link at the highest speed that both ends can handle. If the link won't support that speed, try a lower speed. Most communications programs include a method for setting the baud rate that the program uses to send and receive data, and you can also change it from the DOS prompt. To set the transmission speed for serial port COM1, type `MODE COM1: BAUD=`*`nn`*, using the first two digits of the baud rate in place of *nn*. The MODE command will accept settings of 110, 150, 300, 600, 1200, 2400, 4800, 9600, and 19,200 baud, but many older PCs don't support the highest speed.

Direct Connection Between Two Computers

The least complicated communications link between two computers is a direct cable connection from one to the other. Since both ends of the link are

DTE devices, the serial interconnection must be made using a crossover cable. The two computers could be a laptop and a desktop PC, two desktop units, or any other combination. When two PCs are linked together, either computer can transfer files to the other, and the operators of the two computers can conduct an on-line conversation by typing messages back and forth. It's also possible to use the distant computer as a remote terminal in place of the local keyboard and screen. Since there's no modem, telephone line, or other obstacle limiting transmission speed, the two computers should support very high speed data transfer—at least 9600 baud, and perhaps 19,200 baud. Some communications programs use data compression techniques to further increase the transmission speed, to 115,000 baud in some cases. Because transmission is subject to degradation due to resistance of the wires, electrical interference and other evils, the practical limit for direct connection is about 500 feet. If you reduce the speed at which the data travels, you can increase the distance, but as a rule of thumb, use a pair of modems or line drivers for data exchange over greater distances.

Modem Links

Modem is constructed from the words "modulator" and "demodulator." A modem changes digital information coming from the PC into analog tone signals that it will send out over the phone line; that is its modulator function. It also receives analog tone signals from the telephone line and converts them to digital data signals to send to the PC. The modem-to-modem connection is often over a standard telephone connection, but also could be over a dedicated point-to-point telephone circuit, a packet data network, or a radio data network. The distant computer can be anything from another PC to a mainframe.

As far as the PC is concerned, connection to another computer through a pair of modems and a telephone line is identical to connection through a direct cable. Asynchronous data enters and leaves the computer through a serial port, including start and stop bits, parity bits, and control signals. The modulation and demodulation between the two computers changes the signal to something the telephone system or other network can handle, and changes it back at the other end.

Some Reasons for Using a Modem

A modem enables a PC to go anywhere the telephone network goes—and that's almost everywhere. When you connect your computer to the telephone network through a modem, you can communicate with any other modem-equipped computer. Once the connection between the two computers is established, you can use your PC as either a "dumb terminal" or "host" to the distant computer and transfer files, electronic mail, and facsimile messages in both directions.

Remote control programs add several other interesting possibilities to this list of things you can do with a modem. (Some of the commercial remote control programs are pcANYWHERE from Symantec, Commute from Central Point Software, Carbon Copy from Microcom, and Norton-Lambert's Close-Up.) These programs allow you to take over the remote PC, making your PC's keyboard and screen effectively become the remote PC's console. Usually, they also allow a remote PC user to see what you see, and permit that other person to use that PC's keyboard in parallel with your use of yours. Once you have connected in this fashion with a remote computer, you can work on files stored in that remote computer as if they were on your own PC. In fact, that remote computer might be your own desktop computer that you are accessing from a hotel somewhere using your laptop PC.

Other uses for remote control programs include training a user of the remote PC or doing diagnostics on that PC's hardware, all without having to travel to the site of the remote PC. This is an increasingly common practice at some of the major mail-order PC manufacturers. (This works best if the only screen images one needs to send across the link are text screens. If you thought Windows was slow, try using it with a remote control program—it will be unbearable. On the other hand, this will make screen redraws so slow you can actually see each step in the process!) Access to an electronic mail (usually called *e-mail*) network is becoming a business essential; the number of e-mail users is growing every year. If you're not already tied to a network through a LAN, you will need a modem to call into an e-mail service. Commercial services including Compuserve, The Well, and MCI Mail offer worldwide message exchange. These networks and many others, including those maintained by businesses, government, and educational institutions, are all tied together in a worldwide "network of networks" called the Internet. From a computer connected to the Internet, you can exchange files and messages with thousands of other computers and terminals.

Power users typically want the fastest modem they can afford. Fast modems minimize long-distance and connect-time charges, along with the amount of time your phone line is unavailable for either voice or fax data. There's one exception to the "fastest is best" rule. Compuserve and other commercial on-line services calculate charges based on connect time, with higher rates for connection through high-speed modem links, and lower rates for slower speed. When you're downloading files from one of these services, you will save money by connecting to them at the highest possible speed. If, on the other hand, you are browsing on the system or participating in a real-time "chat" service (reading messages on the screen as other people type them and typing your own replies), you can minimize your cost by connecting at a slower speed. Even at 300 bps, you'll have no trouble keeping up with the conversation. Any faster than that and the information channels from your eyes to your mind and from your mind to your fingers become the limiting factor. No sense in paying for a higher speed link to the remote service when you won't be using its full capacity.

Compressed files take less time to transfer. An off-line file compression utility, such as the DOS Power Tool LHA or the equally popular PKZIP, will let you reduce files to the minimum possible size before you send them. Alternatively, you can use a modem with built-in hardware compression. If the modem at the other end of the connection has similar hardware, the two modems may do the equivalent of a DoubleSpace compression and decompression on-the-fly. In that case, precompressing your files with LHA or PKZIP won't do much good.

Modem Commands

The standard PC modem command set was created by the makers of Hayes modems, so modems that use them are known as "Hayes compatible." Most of these commands begin with the letters "AT," which is an attention signal to the modem. You should not consider installing a modem that doesn't support AT commands, because every modern modem control program uses them.

Internal versus External Modems

PC modems come in a variety of forms: Some plug into I/O slots inside your PC's system unit; some connect to a serial port connector on the back panel; some are on PCMCIA (credit card size) modules that plug into a special PCMCIA slot. Internal modems and those on PCMCIA cards include the serial port circuitry. This type of modem uses one of the possible COM port designations in your PC; external modems connect to a serial port already installed in your PC. If you add an internal modem or one on a PCMCIA card, be careful not to allow it to conflict with another serial port already in that PC.

An external modem doesn't use an expansion slot, and it usually will have status lights that show the progress of a call. It's easy to disconnect an external modem to move it to another computer; you can share a handful of modems among a larger number of PCs simply by moving the modems from PC to PC. On the other hand, external modems are more expensive than equivalent internal modems, because they need a separate power supply and other hardware. They also require additional space on the desktop, access to an AC power outlet, and a cable from the PC's serial port, and the PC must have an available serial port installed in it.

An internal modem has some advantages, however: It is located inside the PC case, so there's less danger that it will be borrowed or stolen. It doesn't tie up an I/O connector, but still requires a vacant expansion slot and an available IRQ and port address. It's not possible to see status lights with an internal modem, but for most users, that's not a serious inconvenience. (If you really want to see the lights, you can load a TSR program like BRKBOX that will simulate the most important of them as on or off blocks in a corner of your PC's screen.) In terms of performance, there's not much difference between an internal and external modem. If you have expansion slots to spare but no extra serial ports, choose an internal unit. If the computer has an unused serial connector, an external modem will do the job. If your laptop PC has a PCMCIA slot, a modem card is a good choice.

The UART used in the serial port circuitry in many PCs imposes a limit to how fast that serial port can send or receive data. Internal modems come with their own UART (as a portion of the serial port circuitry they must contain) and, naturally, the manufacturers of those modems make sure that the UART they use can handle the speed of their modem. If you add an external modem using an existing serial port, you may have problems using that modem at its highest speeds. To find out if this is a problem on your PC, enter `MSD` to start the Microsoft Diagnostic program (another external command that is new in DOS 6) and select the `COM Ports` option. At the bottom of the display, MSD reports "UART Chip Used." If the display shows either "8250" or "16450," your serial ports won't handle data faster than 9600 bps. If your existing COM ports use one of these UART chips, you may wish to get an internal modem because it will exchange data with the CPU through the expansion bus and, therefore, won't be speed limited by the UART.

Port Addresses and Interrupts

Interrupts and memory addresses were discussed in earlier chapters of this book. Getting hardware consistently installed with nonconflicting IRQ settings, port addresses, memory addresses, and DMA channel selections is critical to making your PC function properly. If you're using an external modem, this won't be a problem, because it doesn't connect to the expansion bus. The existing serial ports are, presumably, already set in a manner that doesn't conflict with anything else in your PC. When you install an internal modem, be careful to avoid conflicts with other devices.

The *Port Address* is the location in the computer's memory that controls communication to and from one of the serial COM ports or parallel LPT ports. (Actually, most devices use a range of several port addresses. Serial

Communication Port Adresses and IRQs

DOS Device Name	Port Address	Usual IRQ
COM1	3F8	IRQ4
COM2	2F8	IRQ3
COM3	3E8	IRQ4
COM4	2E8	IRQ3

Figure 16-4 Usual communication port addresses and IRQ values

ports use eight addresses; parallel ports use either four or eight.) An internal modem card may be able to be configured for any of the four COM ports, or it may restrict you to COM1 or COM2. Choosing a COM port number implies a choice of port addresses; and you must choose one that isn't already in use in your PC. If you have serial ports built into your PC, especially if they are on the motherboard, you may disable them or move them to different addresses by use of your PC's setup software or by some jumpers or dip switches on the motherboard.

Figure 16-4 lists the port address and the traditional IRQ settings for each of the four DOS COM devices. Note that COM1 and COM3 share the same IRQ, as do COM2 and COM4. This sharing of IRQ settings is a source of many problems. Essentially, you normally cannot get interrupt services for more than one device on a given IRQ line. Sometimes you are using a serial port for some purpose that doesn't need interrupt support, or you may simply have the serial port and not be using it for anything. That doesn't present any problems. Port address conflicts, however, must be avoided, or neither of the conflicting devices will work at all. There are switches or jumpers for setting IRQ value and port address range on many plug-in cards, including many internal modems and network interface cards. Other boards allow you to configure them using a software program. Either way, be sure to choose nonconflicting port addresses, and—if you can—nonconflicting IRQ settings.

Data Modems versus Fax Modems

In addition to data, many modems also can exchange facsimile images with a stand-alone fax machine or another fax modem. Fax communications software converts text and images to Group III fax protocols, rather than using the communication protocols that are customarily used for data transfer. When shopping for a combined fax and data modem, note that some modems may send facsimile at 9600 baud or more because they recognize Group

III fax protocols at that speed, but their maximum data transfer speed may be considerably slower. While fast-fax, slower-data modems cost less than modems with high-speed data capability, a power user will most likely choose to send and receive data at the highest possible speed, especially when the call is long-distance.

Serial Data Communication Application Programs

Now that your PC can talk to another computer, it's possible to control the transfer of data by using DOS commands to send and receive files through a serial port and display incoming text on your screen—but that is generally not recommended. For any serious data transfer, you'll need a communications program, which most modem suppliers include with their hardware. Purchased separately, Datastorm's ProComm Plus, Crosstalk Communications' Crosstalk, and QMODEM from the Forbin Project are among the most popular PC communications programs. Both Procomm and QMODEM also exist in shareware versions. Several popular remote control communications programs (pcANYWHERE, Commute, Carbon Copy, and Close-Up) were mentioned previously. You can use any of these to do remote diagnostics or training, or to use the remote PC's computing power with your local PC as its console device (an alternative that doesn't require you to buy any extra program).

Using DOS Commands for Simple Remote Control Connections

There is one exception to the general recommendation that you shouldn't rely on the DOS communications tools for remote PC use: when you are able to dedicate a PC to remote use by another PC and are not concerned with access security or other special features. In that case, you can set up a serial port on your PC using the MODE command, then use the command `CTTY COMn` to tell the local PC to use that serial port as if it were the console device (which means the keyboard and screen). That serial port can be connected directly to another PC, using a crossover cable, or to a telephone using a modem. In the latter case, be sure to send the appropriate command to your modem to put it in *auto-answer mode* before you issue the CTTY command.

The remote PC can run any standard communications program that provides a terminal emulation. Now, whenever the remote PC calls this PC's phone number (assuming a modem connection) or establishes a local connection (if it is directly wired), the remote PC will become the console of this

PC. To end the connection, either reboot the local PC or, from the remote PC, enter the command

```
CTTY CON
```

which will restore the usual console connection for this PC with its own keyboard and screen. This strategy is a bare-bones approach to remote control. You get none of the convenient functions, such as simultaneous use of both keyboards, duplicate images on both screens, file transfer capabilities, or password protected access, but for a quick and simple setup, it will suffice.

Local Area Networks

Another popular way to connect computers is via *Local Area Networks* (LANs), which connect groups of computers, printers, and other equipment together for exchange of messages and files. A LAN adds an *installable file system* (IFS) to DOS, which is a block device driver that augments the DOS default block device driver. When a PC is connected to a LAN, it has access to devices over the network (via the IFS) as well as its local devices (by using the default block device driver). A LAN may include just a handful of computers in a small office or several hundred computers in a large building or on a campus. *Metropolitan Area Networks* (MANs) and *Wide Area Networks* (WANs) can connect computers that are more widely separated.

Many LANs are built around a model called client-server computing. They have one or more computers with large, fast hard disks that serve the other computers on the network as librarians—retrieving and saving files on demand. These computers are called *servers*; the other computers on LANs are where users are located, and are called *workstations*. Another model motivates the design of other LANs; it is called peer-to-peer networking. In these LANs, every computer is (at least potentially) the equal of all the others. Any of the computers can be used as a workstation, and each one also can "publish" some or all of its disk directories, printers, or other resources for use by other workstations. Some PC LANs run as extensions of DOS; Microsoft's Windows for Workgroups is a good example. Others use their own operating system instead of DOS on the server, and use DOS on the workstation; Novell's NetWare is the most popular of these.

The world of LANs is large and often mysterious, and this book provides only a necessarily abbreviated overview. One way to describe a network is based on the physical connections between the computers. These include coaxial cable (similar to what cable TV uses), unshielded twisted pair (similar to telephone wiring), and shielded twisted pair (simply telephone-style wiring encased in a conducting metal shield). Also in this group are the terms bus, star, and ring, which describe the topology of the network links. In a bus network, each PC is directly connected to every other PC on a common set of wires. A star connects each PC to a hub which shares messages between those PCs. A ring connects each PC to exactly two other PCs, with the whole array of connected PCs forming a ring.

Other names for networks describe a manner of managing the flow of messages among the connected stations. Arcnet divides time into fixed size slices and allocates each to a different station until all stations have received one time slice; then it repeats the process over and over again. Ethernet allows each station to send a message any time it wishes; it must, therefore, deal with collisions (when two stations send at the same time). Ethernet does this by a scheme called *Carrier Sense Multiple Access with Collision Detection*, or CSMA/CD. Token ring networks constantly circulate a special data packet called a token. Stations are allowed to transmit data only after they have received the token and before they send the token on to the next station. Ethernet may be implemented on a bus-wired network using either of two sizes of coaxial cable. (Such a system is called either Thicknet or Thinnet, depending on the size and rigidity of the cable used. Other names for these two wiring schemes are 10Base5 and 10Base2, respectively.) Alternatively, Ethernet may be implemented with star wiring using unshielded twisted pairs; this is called a 10BaseT network. Arcnet also uses a star network configuration, while Token Ring uses a ring, which can be comprised of either individual workstations or a mix of workstations and *Multistation Access Units* (MAUs) with several workstations attached to each.

Wireless networks also exist. They use infrared light, radio waves, or a building's power wiring to connect the stations. These networks are called broadcast networks, and work just like a bus-connected network. Usually, they will use Ethernet as the protocol for managing data flow in the network. Most PCs are attached to a network by installing a *network interface card* (NIC) in one of the PC's I/O expansion bus slots. Alternate methods include special adapters that plug into the parallel or serial port.

Avoiding Access Conflicts with SHARE

Any time two people on a LAN work on the same file at the same time, there is a possibility that they could corrupt that file's contents. Data will be lost if each of them makes changes to the file simultaneously. In this context, simultaneous changes means that both users read the file, then work on a copy of that file in their PC's memory. They make some changes, after which they write those changes back to the disk. If the second person to write changes reads the file before the first person wrote any changes, the first person's changes will be overwritten and data loss will occur. The only way to prevent this is to prevent two users from having simultaneous access to a file with both users having permission to edit in its contents. (While any number of people can be allowed to read the file; only one at a time may be authorized to make changes.)

DOS was designed as a single-tasking, single-user operating system, so it doesn't enforce this sort of discipline. As soon as PCs became connected into networks, people saw the possibility of data loss. Microsoft and IBM responded to this vulnerability by introducing SHARE with version 3.0 of DOS (although DOS's network support wasn't enabled until version 3.1). DOS permits files to be opened by programs for read-only purposes, or for read-write purposes. If a program requests read-only access, DOS will not permit it to write to that file. But any program that requests and receives read-write access can modify the file at will. SHARE protects you by "locking" any file that has been opened by one program for read-write access. Thereafter, until that program closes its access to that file, and thereby causes SHARE to release the lock, no other program can get read-write access to the same file. (But any program can get read-only access at any time.)

The syntax for SHARE is simple. You may either use INSTALL to load it from your CONFIG.SYS file, put the invocation command in your AUTOEXEC.BAT file, or type that command at the DOS prompt. The command line will read

```
SHARE /F:space /L:locks
```

where `space` is the amount of memory you are allowing SHARE to use to store the names of files it is locking and `locks` is the maximum number of files SHARE will be able to keep track of at one time. Both the `/F` and `/L` directives are optional. The space allocation defaults to 2KB and the number of locks to 20. Some network software goes further, by allowing multiple programs to access large data files simultaneously, with each of them having write access to only a portion of the file. This is called record locking, and is a level of sophistication in data access protection that is not provided by SHARE. Still, the simple SHARE protection is sufficient to prevent data corruption. Its only drawback is that it may force programs to wait longer for access to files that are already being used by another program.

This section began with a description of the vulnerability that exists if you are working on a LAN-connected PC. Actually, you need to use SHARE even to access files from more than one process (program) in your PC at the same time. Anytime you "drop to DOS" or switch from one task to another in a multitasking system, let alone when you have multiple programs running simultaneously (in different windows of Windows or DESQview, for example), you are vulnerable to file damage if you don't have SHARE loaded.

Other Ways to Communicate between Computers

All the information in this chapter about modems, LANs and data transfer can obscure the ultimate objective—moving information from one computer to another. Sometimes, you can use primitive, low-tech methods to efficiently accomplish that objective—but don't forget *sneakernet*, which is a common term for the process of physically carrying a diskette or tape from one computer to another. Sneakernet offers several benefits: It's easy, doesn't require special equipment, and works on almost any PC (except workstations with no disk drives, but they're already connected to a LAN). Sometimes, it's quicker to walk upstairs or drive across town than to transfer a large file through a modem link—especially if the computer on the other end has a modem with a top speed of 1200 baud. A station wagon full of floppy disks has a huge bandwidth. On the other hand, its data transfer time may be longer than the transmission time over a network or modem connection that runs at nearly the speed of light.

There are other limitations to sneakernet: Both machines must have compatible disk drives. Carrying a 3.5-inch diskette to a PC with a 5.25-inch drive doesn't accomplish anything useful, nor does trying to read a 1.2-megabyte diskette in a 360-kilobyte drive. You must have physical access to the receiving machine. One or both machines with poorly aligned diskette drives also can frustrate a sneakernet "connection." You can circumvent the need for physical proximity by mailing diskettes or using overnight express, but the cost in time is substantial. Still, when economy is more important than instantaneous delivery, the best way to transfer files often is to mail it or ship it via an express courier service.

Interlnk

Interlnk (Microsoft spells it that way to fit the 8-character limit on DOS file names) is the newest way to connect two PCs. Introduced with PC DOS 5.02, Interlnk is now a part of MS-DOS 6 and is similar to Traveling Software's LapLink and Rupp's FastLynx, in that it allows one computer to read and write files or run programs on a second computer, but it has fewer features. Drives and printers on the *server*—the PC running INTERSVR—become additional drives and printers on the *client*—the PC running INTERLNK. The server's drives appear on the client as some new drive letters; the server's printers appear as extra printers.

Almost any DOS program will see the Interlnk server's drives and printers exactly as it does the drives and printers physically attached to the client. So far, it sounds a lot like a LAN connection, but there is one very important difference: When you use Interlnk, the server is totally dedicated to that use and cannot be used for any other purpose for the duration. This is less flexible than connecting two computers through a LAN, but it has its uses. For example, to transfer files between a laptop PC and a desktop unit, or to print directly from the laptop to an office laser printer. You also can gather field information on your portable and use Interlnk to transfer it to an office machine, move sales or technical data from a desktop computer to the laptop for field use, or share files and printers between two computers in an office.

Connecting your laptop directly to a LAN or other network is a better technique than connecting through Interlnk. It gives the client the same kind of access to the server, but it doesn't tie up the server. Remember, when Interlnk is active, you can't enter commands on the server's keyboard or display files on its screen. To run Interlnk between two PCs, at least one of them must be running MS-DOS 6; the second computer can use any version later than DOS 3.0.

INTERLNK CABLING

You can connect two PCs together by using either a serial port on each or a parallel port on each. Serial ports can be connected by using a 3- or 7-wire crossover cable. Parallel ports are connected by using a special bidirectional parallel cable. To transfer the Interlnk programs through the cable, you must use the 7-wire (serial) crossover cable. Figure 16-5 shows the required wiring for each of these options.

The top two cables in Figure 16-5 are sometimes called *hydra cables*; they have both 9- and 25-pin connectors at each end. A cable of this sort will allow you to connect to either style of serial port at each end.

Note: Incidentally, this kind of four-headed cable also can be used as a straight-through serial cable from either of its two connectors on one end to the other connector on that same end. To use the cable in this way, you also will need a *gender bender* of the right size, which is a double-ended connector with all its pins wired straight through. (Both ends are the same gender—male or female. Gender benders come in both 9- and 25-pin sizes; you will need a male gender bender, but you may need either size, depending on what devices you hope to connect. Using a four-headed cable this way often is not feasible, as the two connectors at one end tend to be close together. At a minimum, though, Figure 16-5 includes the correct wiring for a straight-through, 9-pin to 25-pin serial adapter. Just use the far left end of the top row as a guide. You will have to use a male connector on one end or the other—depending on which device (DTE or DCE) has the 25-pin connector. (Rather than tell you the rule for which type of device uses which gender of connector, simply look carefully at the two boxes you need to connect. Then buy or build the requisite cable, making sure it is wired as shown in the upper-left corner of Figure 16-5.)

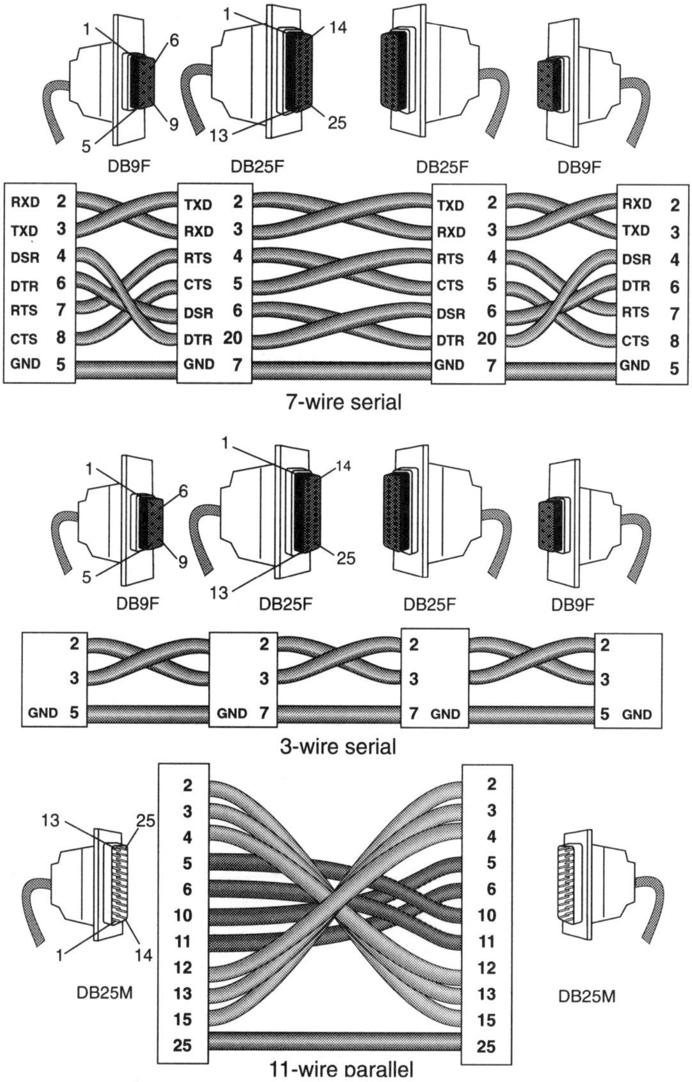

Figure 16-5 Interlnk cables

The lower cable in Figure 16-5 shows the proper way to wire an Interlnk bidirectional parallel cable, which is the same as the wiring used by other popular file transfer programs, such as FastLynx and LapLink.

Warning: An Interlnk parallel cable can look a lot like a crossover cable. Both may use DB25 connectors (of opposite genders), but the internal wiring is very different. Clearly label all your serial and parallel cables as STRAIGHT-THROUGH, SERIAL CROSSOVER, or BIDIRECTIONAL PARALLEL. Any straight-through, 25-pin cable can be used for either serial or parallel connections, but watch out: Some of these cables have been wired for only one of those uses, in which case many of the wires may have been omitted. The best solution may be to avoid buying those cables. Also, remember that most PC printers use a different style of connector (a Centronics connector), for which you need a standard PC-to-Centronics parallel cable, as is shown in Figure 10-5.

LOADING INTERLNK

The MS-DOS 6 SETUP routine loads the Interlnk files into the DOS directory. If only one computer has DOS 6 installed, connect the two machines together using a 7-wire serial crossover cable. Enter `INTERSVR /RCOPY` on the machine running DOS 6 to transfer the Interlnk programs to the other computer. The PC will ask you which of the other PC's COM ports you plan to use. (It finds the cable to that other computer by scanning the serial and parallel ports in the local computer.) Once you tell it, INTERSRV will display a MODE command and a CTTY command that you are to type on the remote computer. After you have done so, INTERSRV will copy the necessary files to the remote PC.

Warning: If you are going to use any port other than COM1 on the PC that will receive the Interlnk programs, make sure SHARE is not loaded on that PC. Change its AUTOEXEC.BAT or CONFIG.SYS file by adding `REM` at the start of the line that loads SHARE, then restart that computer.

Both machines will display the current status as they copy the files. When the transfer is complete, if you had disabled SHARE, remember to reenable it.

When the Interlnk files are present on both computers, you need to decide which will be the client and which the server. The issues are these: The client machine will require a special device driver loaded to access the server, which takes up some RAM. (You will see in a minute how to avoid this penalty, except when you wish to use the Interlnk connection.) The client machine is the one whose keyboard you will be typing on, and whose screen you will be watching. The server machine will do nothing else as long as it is running the Interlnk server software; but when it is not running that software, it need not have any Interlnk device driver loaded in its RAM. On the machine you have decided will be the client, add this line to CONFIG.SYS:

```
DEVICE=C:\DOS\INTERLNK.EXE
```

If you have loaded support for upper memory blocks, you may be able to save some of your lower memory by changing this line to a DEVICEHIGH line. Running MemMaker can help you decide if that is so in your PC.

If you expect to use Interlnk connections only occasionally, you could use the new CONFIG.SYS menu capabilities to make loading the INTERLNK.EXE device driver optional each time you reboot. Here's the relevant fragment from a typical CONFIG.SYS menu:

```
[I-link stuff]
menuitem=Interlink,Interlink Active
menuitem=No_Interlink,Interlink Not Active
menudefault=No_Interlink, 8

[Interlink]
DEVICE=C:\DOS\INTERLNK.EXE

[No_Interlink]
```

This menu fragment says not to load the Interlnk client device driver if no entry is made for eight seconds after the I-link stuff menu is presented. (For details on CONFIG.SYS menus, including restriction on how menu blocks may be named, see the discussion in Chapter 11.) Once you have completed your modification of CONFIG.SYS, either to add Interlnk to a menu or with a simple DEVICE line, you will have to restart the PC before it will load the device driver. Then, you are ready to communicate using Interlnk.

RUNNING INTERLNK

To start Interlnk on the server, enter this command at the DOS prompt on that PC:

```
INTERSVR
```

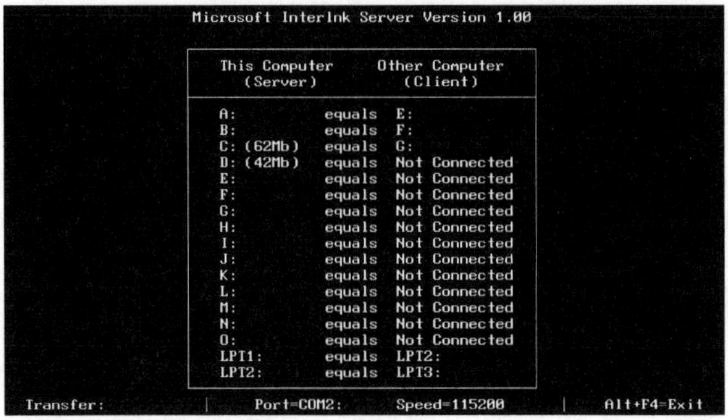

Figure 16-6 The Interlnk server screen

The server will display the Interlnk Server screen, with the `Other Computer` column blank. Figure 16-6 shows the server screen.

You may wonder at all the drive letters listed. In this computer, LASTDRIVE had been set to O. The `Port` shown is the serial or parallel port that the server is using to communicate with the client; the listed `Speed` is the transmission rate at which the two PCs will exchange data, expressed in bits per second (bps).

With the INTERLNK.EXE device driver active on the client, enter the command:

```
INTERLNK
```

If the server is not running INTERSVR, the client will display a `Connection NOT established` message; if the server is running INTERSVR, the client displays an Interlnk status message similar to Figure 16-7.

The `Port` is the serial or parallel port on the client computer that's connected to the server. The `This Computer` column shows the drive letters and printer device numbers that the client uses to access the drives and printers on the server. The `Other Computer` column shows the server's actual drive letters and printer numbers on the same line as the designation used for that device by the client. If a drive has a label, Interlnk includes it in

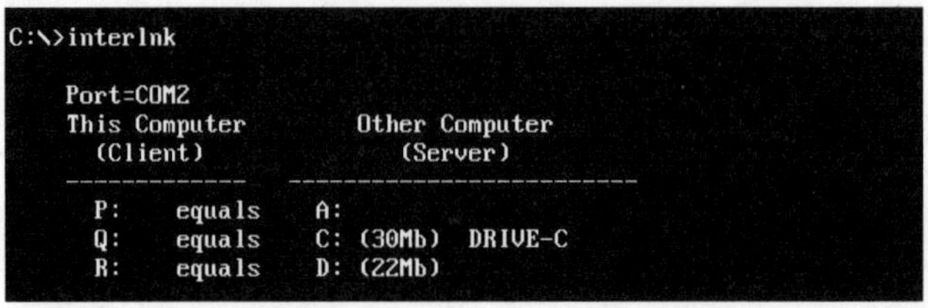

Figure 16-7 The Interlnk client screen

the display. Interlnk does not recognize network drives, CD-ROM drives, or other devices that use the DOS redirection interface.

With Interlnk running, it appears that the client has some additional drives. To run a program resident on the server, use the new drive letter in the command path. Any program loaded on either machine can read or load any data file on either machine. Applications with a file menu, such as a word processor or data base, now show the contents of the server's disks as well as those on the client.

Note: You should be aware that if you run a program you see on one of the server's drives, you will be loading it across the Interlnk cable into the client PC's RAM and running it there. This is in contrast to what you do with remote control software, with which you enable yourself to run software on a remote machine using your local PC only as its console. Transferring whole files takes some time. (Even the fastest, parallel Interlnk connection cannot transfer data nearly as fast as most LANs.) Once a program is in the client machine, though, it will run as fast as if it had been loaded from one of the client's own disk drives, at least until that program asks for a program overlay file or a data file from the disk on the remote PC. Thus, if you have an application on both the client and server PCs, no matter which machine holds the data file with which you wish to work, use the local copy of the application program. On the other hand, if you wish to exploit the speed and processing power of the remote PC, you will need to get remote control software instead of using Interlnk.

To transfer a file from the client to the server or vice versa, simply use the DOS COPY command. For example, you might type

```
COPY Q:\SALES\CLIENTS.LST C:\SALES
```

Use DOS wildcards to transfer multiple files, just as you normally would. For example:

```
COPY Q:\SALES\*.LST C:\SALES\
```

To use a printer connected to the server, use PRINT, specifying the printer port number for that printer as shown by Interlnk. You can use any printer to print files located on either machine.

> **Note:** Slow printers may be used without concern about whether they are local or remote. Fast laser printers can be noticeably slowed if they must receive their data across an Interlnk connection.

The DOS Commands Relating to Communications

The principal DOS commands that affect communications are MODE, CTTY, and SHARE, along with the commands related to the Interlnk program, INTERLNK and INTERSVR. This chapter explained how to use MODE COM to configure a serial port; the other MODE commands are in the chapters that describe printers (Chapter 10), keyboards (Chapter 4), and screens (Chapter 5). Also described were two simple ways to use the CTTY command. (One is to set up a bare-bones remote control connection; the other is to let Interlnk transfer its files across a 7-wire serial cable to another PC.)

The DOS Power Tools Relating to Communications

You'll find several useful programs to aid in your communcications tasks on the accompanying Power Tools disks. ADDCOMM, BRKBOX, MDR, and PORTTEST will help you troubleshoot and configure your COM ports. IL (Invisible Link) will let you initiate and maintain serial communications in background, without the need to go to a task-swapping environment such as DOSSHELL or Windows.

C H A P T E R

17

◆ ◆ ◆ ◆ ◆

Warnings and Hints

This chapter contains information, some of which is common knowledge; other points are more controversial. All of it, however, is vital to DOS 6 power users, and the viewpoints expressed here are backed by experience.

SHARE

The SHARE program originally was designed to permit multiple users or tasks a safe way to access files without risking data damage. This is a vital function when you're task swapping, multitasking, or networking. SHARE's major role is to prevent multiple tasks from attempting to modify a file simultaneously. When one task opens a file for both reading and writing, SHARE locks that file so that other tasks can open it for reading only. No other task can open the file for writing until the original task releases it. Without SHARE, two or more tasks could open a file for reading and writing simultaneously. Each task would make its updates in the original version of the file, unaware of the updates being made by the other tasks. Whenever a task saves the file to disk, it saves the original version with its updates only, overlaying any updates already saved by other tasks. In the meantime, more tasks may be accessing the file for reading and writing, each one possibly accessing a different version, updating that version, and writing it back to disk, again overlaying updates made by other tasks. SHARE is designed to prevent this particular form of chaos.

With DOS 4, SHARE was assigned a second job: making it safe to run programs that used the older file control block (FCB) strategy for file access on disk volumes larger than 32MB. Many users of DOS 4 were puzzled by the message indicating that they needed to load SHARE for "large media." Unfortunately, if you didn't load SHARE and you used the wrong sort of program on your large disk volume, you could lose massive amounts of data. With DOS 5, Microsoft and IBM moved the code for FCB access into the operating system core code, where it belonged. Many users who never quite understood the mysterious message about loading SHARE for large media concluded that they had no need for it. They weren't using their PC on a network, so why worry about sharing files?

When You Need SHARE

Whenever the possibility exists of two or more tasks attempting to modify a file simultaneously, you should load SHARE to protect your files. You need SHARE if you do any of the following things:

- Run DOSSHELL and use its task swapping feature.
- Run Windows.
- Connect to any network.
- Use a DOS command prompt from within an application or shell program, such as that provided by WordPerfect's "Shell to DOS" command or the DOSSHELL "Run" command.

Loading SHARE

Most of the time, you can load SHARE using all its default settings by entering the command:

```
SHARE
```

This sets aside a 2K buffer for file sharing information and space to lock as many as 20 files simultaneously. You can add `/F:`*`bytes`* to change the size of the buffer or `/L:`*`number`* to specify the maximum number of locked files. The following command installs SHARE with a 3K buffer and the ability to lock as many as 50 files at once:

```
SHARE /F:3072 /L:50
```

SHARE can be installed from CONFIG.SYS using the INSTALL command, or from a DOS prompt or batch file. We recommend you load it early in the boot process, using the INSTALL command. If, however, you want to load it into upper memory, you will have to wait until the beginning of your AUTOEXEC.BAT file where you can use the LOADHIGH command. More information on SHARE can be found in the Command Reference.

Using MSBACKUP

The most important data protection tool in DOS 6 is the MSBACKUP program (or its Windows counterpart, MWBACKUP). If you're familiar with earlier versions of DOS, you know that the old BACKUP program had more than its share of faults. DOS 6's backup system is completely new; that is, it is new to DOS. MSBACKUP is essentially a version of the well-respected Norton Backup.

This is considered the *most important* DOS data protection tool because if you have a complete, up-to-date set of backups, plus a collection of older backups in a safe location, you usually will be able to recover your data.

Installing MSBACKUP

To use MSBACKUP, first install it and let it configure itself. It will do some hardware tests to see which tricks it can safely employ and those it ought to avoid. It generally completes this task efficiently and with minimal user interaction required or permitted. Watch out, though; if you change your configuration in any way that might affect the backup process, let MSBACKUP repeat its compatibility and configuration tests to be sure it still knows what it can safely do.

Backup Setups

Not everyone wants to do a backup in exactly the same way, and there are different kinds of backup for different purposes. Circumstances may call for a full backup, an incremental one, or a differential backup. (We will explain these terms in a moment.) You also may want to include or exclude certain groups of files on occasion. Fortunately, MSBACKUP has the flexibility to support all these options. In fact, it lets you store your choices in a file and later recall those choices simply by selecting and loading that file.

The first time you prepare a backup, you select all the options you want to use, the drives and files you want to back up, the drive to which you want to back up, and so on. All this information is recorded in a *setup file*, so that the next time you want to make the same backup, all you have to do is open the setup file and press the Start button.

> **Note:** All the backup parameters, except the file selections, are recorded in a file with the name *setup*.SET. Your file selections are recorded in a separate file named *setup*.SLT. If you decide to redo your file selections, you can eliminate the existing ones by deleting *setup*.SLT.

Most people need only one backup setup, but you can establish multiple setups if that suits your style. And of course, if you share your computer with others, they can create their own setup files. Setup files can also be transferred to other DOS 6 computers so that you can standardize backup procedures within a workgroup.

Backup Cycles

Backups are only as valuable as they are complete and up-to-date. MSBACKUP is designed to help you establish and maintain good backup habits and accommodate your personal choices. It lets you choose from three types of backups: full, incremental, and differential.

A full backup stores a copy of the information in all the files that you have selected, regardless of their archive attribute setting. Whenever a file is opened by a program, if that program is given access with permission to change the file, DOS will automatically turn on (set) the archive bit for that file—no matter whether the file actually was changed or not. A full backup will also turn off (reset) the archive attribute bit for each file it copies. This serves to indicate that the current versions of these files have been backed up. A full backup performed in this manner establishes the baseline for a backup cycle.

Incremental and differential backups copy only those files whose archive attribute bit is set; in other words, only those files that may have been changed since the last backup. The difference between the two types lies in how they treat the archive attribute. An incremental backup turns the archive attribute off; the differential backup leaves it on. If you use incremental backups on a regular basis, each one archives only those files that have been modified since the last incremental backup. You have to save all your incremental backups to maintain a complete set of files that were modified since the last full backup. A differential backup, on the other hand, archives all the files that have been modified since the last time the archive attributes were turned off, which should be the last full backup. Since each differential backup will contain all the files that have been modified since the last full backup, theoretically you have to save only the most recent differential backup (and the last full backup). However, we recommend that you keep all of your backup disks for a lengthier period of time so that you can retrieve deleted files and earlier versions of files.

How do you decide whether to use differential or incremental backups? And how often should you make full and partial backups? Everyone does it a little differently. Some people start a new cycle every Friday evening or every Monday morning and make partial backups once a day. Others make backups when the mood strikes them or when they have finished an important new file. Some people never make a second full backup. After the first one, they just continue to stack up incremental or differential disks forever. You have to decide for yourself which approach makes you feel secure that you can get back to the files you need when necessary.

One consideration often drives people to use differential backups when they really prefer incremental ones: large files. If you have one or more very large files that you change in only a small percentage of its bytes, it seems unacceptably time-consuming and media-consuming to make an incremental backup with any frequency, but unless you do so, you are at risk. Therefore, a set of differential backups may seem to be a good alternative. After all, you need only enough backup diskettes to hold two copies of all your files (the full set and the most recent differential set). And that's true, but only if nothing ever goes wrong.

But life isn't like that, and you will want more security. Doing incremental backups can provide that increased security since you have copies of your critical files at every intermediate stage. But how can you do that and include those really large files? Normally, you can't. Luckily, there are some products we can suggest that can remove this obstacle to doing incremental backups.

One is RT-Backup or Deltafile. These programs, from Pocket Soft and Hyperkinetix, respectively, take two versions of a large file and create a small file that contains essentially only the changes in the large file, plus enough information to let those products insert the changes where they belong.

Selecting Backup Files

It's unlikely that you ever will want to back up every file on your hard drive every time. In fact, you may never want to back up some of them, assuming you have the original disks for all your programs. Furthermore, most of them won't change, so one accurate and secure backup may be enough. Certainly, you don't need to keep all your BAK and temporary files. And you really don't need data files with no lasting significance, such as internal memos, "to do" lists from last month, and the like.

MSBACKUP lets you create include/exclude statements to set up a general pattern of files to be included in and excluded from the backup setup. For example, you might want to include all *.DOC files but exclude all MEMO*.DOC files. It also displays a directory tree and file list so that you can select specific directories and files to be included or excluded, which override those set up by the more general include/exclude statements. In addition, you can specify some exclusion parameters based on date/time stamps and attributes.

Once you've identified all the files to be included in the setup, a full backup will copy all of the specified files, whereas an incremental or differential backup will make copies of only those files whose archive attribute has been turned on.

Backup Options

MSBACKUP offers a number of options to control exactly how the backup is done. Two of these must be considered carefully before you decide how to tell MSBACKUP to make backups for you. These two options are:

1. Whether or not to have MSBACKUP reread what it writes and verify the accuracy of the copy.
2. Whether or not to have MSBACKUP store error correction codes (ECC) with the backed up file data.

In both cases, the trade-off is the same: time to do the backup (and space in which to store it) versus reliability. We strongly favor choosing reliability over everything else, but if you are both so time and budget restricted that the extra diskettes will cost so much that you simply won't get them, then by all means use the quicker, less-reliable method in preference to forgoing backups altogether.

Another backup option with an important consequence is whether or not you want MSBACKUP to use compression as it creates your backups. Compression removes all redundancy from the stored data, which saves space, and, since fewer bytes have to be written to the diskette, time as well. It also means that every byte counts (since the normal amount of redundancy is gone). Consequently, saving ECC information along with the backed-up data is even more important.

The compression algorithm used by MSBACKUP is similar to that used by DoubleSpace. Like that program, it probably will compress your average files to between half and two-thirds their original size.

Backup Catalogs

MSBACKUP automatically creates a catalog for each backup it makes. The catalog records the entire directory structure of the drive being backed up and lists every file that was backed up. MSBACKUP uses these catalogs when you want to compare and restore functions. It stores the catalog on the hard drive as well as on the backup disks. It deletes outdated backup catalogs from the hard drive so that the catalogs on the hard drive represent only the current backup cycle. A backup catalog's name gives some important information about the catalog. It takes the form *ccymmddx.typ*, where *cc* identifies the first and last drives that were backed up; *ymmdd* identifies the date of the backup, *x* is simply a letter that makes the name unique, and *type* is FUL, INC, or DIF. If you want to compare or restore files from a backup, open the catalog (from within MSBACKUP), select files from it, and press `Start Compare` or `Start Restore`. MSBACKUP asks for disks by the catalog name, so be sure to write it on each disk.

MSBACKUP also creates a master catalog for each backup setup on your system. The master catalog shows the names of the individual catalogs belonging to that setup. This is an ASCII file that you can read (and even maintain yourself, if need be, although MSBACKUP maintains it for you). If you open a master catalog when you want to restore or compare files, you have access to all the files in all the backup catalogs that appear in the master catalog. Only the most recent version of each file is displayed in the file list, but you can ask to see all available versions of a file if you're trying to restore an older version.

Comparing and Restoring Files

Clearly, comparing and restoring files is a simple task with MSBACKUP. All you have to do is open the desired catalog, select the files you want, and press Start. If you have stored error correction code, MSBACKUP automatically corrects any errors it identifies on the backup disks. You can compare and restore files to their original locations or to different locations, so you could, for example, use MSBACKUP to transfer files to another computer or to compare files between two computers.

> **Note:** There are other ways to transfer files between computers, of course. If they are physically close to one another and if you have a suitable cable and free ports on the two machines, the new DOS program INTERLNK works nicely. You also could simply copy files to a stack of diskettes and carry them to the other machine; a process often called "sneakernet."

What, if any, are the advantages of using MSBACKUP for the large-scale transfer of files between machines? If the machines are physically remote from one another, it is infeasible to connect them by cable, and it may be too expensive to use a dial-up phone connection for the time it will take to move a lot of files. Sneakernet will work, but using MSBACKUP offers a couple of distinct advantages, and one additional possible advantage, over the usual sneakernet approach.

Normal sneakernet just carries DOS files copied one by one to the diskettes. This means that you can use it only for files that fit entirely on a single diskette. Also, normal sneakernet doesn't compress the files. If you use DoubleSpace to compress your floppy diskettes, however, you can get the benefits of file compression and save on the number of diskettes you need, plus get larger individual files onto those diskettes. One clear advantage to MSBACKUP is gained if you use its ECC strategy. It will help you get files to their destinations intact even if they are mistreated along the way.

Staying Out of Trouble

The makers of MS-DOS and PC-DOS have done a credible job overall, but there still are some risky elements to these products. This section points out those to avoid using at all costs and those to use in carefully circumscribed ways. Figure 17-1 lists these troublemakers, and the following sections explain the reasons each has qualified for a place on this list.

Programs *Never* to Be Used

RECOVER was designed to rescue as much data as possible from a cluster that has developed bad spots and can no longer be accessed in the normal way. But used incorrectly—which is altogether too easy to do—RECOVER will trash your entire directory structure. Microsoft *finally* eliminated the RECOVER program in DOS 6, but if you upgraded from an earlier version, the DOS 6 SETUP program will not have deleted the RECOVER.EXE file from your DOS directory. We urge you never, never to use this program. Delete RECOVER.EXE from your DOS directory immediately.

NEVER USE!	DON'T USE		
	in a UMB	in Windows	
RECOVER FASTOPEN	EMM386 HIMEM SMARTDRV /Double_Buffer	APPEND CHKDSK /F DBLSPACE DEFRAG EMM386 FASTOPEN JOIN MEMMAKER MSCDEX NLSFUNC SMARTDRV SUBST VSAFE	APPEND JOIN SUBST

Figure 17-1 Some programs to avoid using or treat with great caution

If ever you cannot access a file because it has developed a bad sector and you can't restore the file from its backup, buy a third-party utility package such as PC Tools or our personal favorites, SpinRite and the Norton Utilities. These packages include safe programs that will extract as much data as possible from a damaged area of your disk, and they will block that area from further use.

FASTOPEN is supposed to speed disk access, and thus improve your entire system performance, by caching file location information in memory so that DOS doesn't have to access the FAT and directory structure on disk every time it reopens a file. But FASTOPEN doesn't work correctly. There is plenty of anecdotal evidence to indicate that you will lose files when FASTOPEN is installed. This is another program that you should never use. Remove it from CONFIG.SYS or AUTOEXEC.BAT and delete the FASTOPEN.EXE file from your DOS directory. Every power user should have some good disk caching program, such as SMARTDRV, installed. With a good disk cache active, you simply don't need FASTOPEN. Any good disk cache does everything that FASTOPEN does and a lot more.

Programs You Can't (or Shouldn't) Load High

DOS 6 includes two programs that can't be loaded into upper memory blocks and one program that shouldn't be. Neither HIMEM.SYS nor EMM386.EXE can be loaded into upper memory for the simple reason that UMB support doesn't exist until after these two programs are loaded. The same is true for third-party memory managers that you're using in place of these two DOS drivers such as QEMM, 386MAX, or their competitors.

The one DOS program that shouldn't be loaded into upper memory is SMARTDrive's double-buffering facility. Not every hard disk controller (or SCSI host adapter) needs this program loaded, but those that do really need it. (If you are unsure, load it, then ask SMARTDRV.EXE to show you if you needed the double-buffering or not.)

If you have the type of drive controller that requires double-buffering, you must load that portion of SMARTDRV.EXE through your CONFIG.SYS file by using this command:

```
DEVICE=C:\DOS\SMARTDRV.EXE /DOUBLE_BUFFER
```

The entire point of double-buffering is to allow your disk controller to have a buffer in lower memory where it can be sure to find it no matter what fancy memory remapping your CPU may be doing. SMARTDRV /DOUBLE_BUFFER provides just that.

If you were to move the double-buffering program into upper memory, you would be undoing the good that loading this program accomplished. For this reason, MemMaker won't change this particular DEVICE command into DEVICEHIGH, and you shouldn't either.

Tip: You might also need to load the remainder of SMARTDrive in conventional memory if you use double-buffering. If you notice a general system slowdown after loading double-buffering, try out the /L switch on your SMARTDRV command in AUTOEXEC.BAT (not on the DEVICE command for double-buffering) to see if that helps speed things up.

Programs Never to Be Used from within Windows

Some programs are safe to use (at least with some special precautions) as long as you are operating at the DOS prompt, but they are positively dangerous to use in a DOS window in Windows.

APPEND

APPEND lets you append one or more directories to the current directory so that applications interpret it that all the files are in the current directory. The only reason for using APPEND is if you have certain old-fashioned applications and want to run them from somewhere other than their home directory. These are applications that need data files or program overlay files but that don't know how to find those files except if they are in the current directory.

Although APPEND accomplishes this purpose admirably—letting those old applications read the files they want to read—it can cause a problem when the application prepares to write something. Because APPEND has done such a good job of fooling the application, it cannot tell the difference between the current directory and the APPENDed one. We recommend that you avoid this program if you can, and in particular, don't use it from within Windows.

If you do choose to use APPEND, take these precautions:

1. Load APPEND *with no specified path* in your AUTOEXEC.BAT file (but only if you know you will need to use it).
2. Create a batch file to run each application that needs APPEND's support. In that batch file issue the command

   ```
   APPEND path
   ```

   where `path` is the path to the directory (or directories) that particular application must be able to access. Follow that line with the commands you need to load and run your application program. Then insert this command

   ```
   APPEND ;
   ```

   which will remove the APPEND path, thus turning off its effects.
3. Never run this batch file from within Windows. (To ensure this, add a line that checks to see if Windows is running. See Chapter 15 for a DEBUG script file you can use to create a program that will display an exit code if Windows is running. See Chapter 14 for the batch file techniques for using IF ERRORLEVEL to detect this exit code and use it to protect yourself.)

JOIN AND SUBST

JOIN and SUBST also play around with the true directory structure. JOIN makes an entire drive look like a branch in another drive's directory tree. SUBST lets you refer to a directory by a drive name. If you are going to use them, do so *before* you start up Windows—never run one of these programs from within Windows.

Note: Earlier versions of DOS also included the ASSIGN command, which substituted one drive name for another. If you upgraded to DOS 6, you might still have ASSIGN in your DOS directory. Microsoft is withdrawing support from ASSIGN, and you should convert any of your batch programs or DOSKEY macros that use it to use SUBST instead.

CHKDSK /F AND DEFRAG

In any multitasking or task swapping environment, many different processes may be accessing different places on the disk at virtually the same time. If the environment is working correctly, it will keep disaster at bay quite well. (Do remember to load SHARE, of course.)

What almost certainly will disrupt things is if you run a program that goes out to the hardware and changes things without checking with the multitasker first. Although it is perfectly safe to look at anything you like, it is never safe to make any changes without the permission and participation of the environment manager program. Consequently, when you are in Windows, DESQview, DOSSHELL, or any other situation where multiple programs can be accessing the disk and several of them may have files open, don't run DEFRAG or CHKDSK with its /F parameter specified. (CHKDSK without the /F is perfectly safe; it is only reading information, not making any changes.)

DISK AND MEMORY MANAGEMENT PROGRAMS

When Windows starts, it seizes control of the memory management functions normally handled by HIMEM.SYS and EMM386.EXE, as well as disk caching functions managed by SMARTDrive. All three of these drivers are loaded long before Windows starts, but in the case of EMM386 and SMARTDrive, you can enter commands at the command prompt to alter their functions. The EMM386 command (as opposed to the device driver) can be used to enable and disable the EMM386 functions, and the SMARTDRV command lets you rework the caching setup for your drives. Neither of these commands should be used under Windows since they attempt to access functions that Windows insists on controlling by itself. Neither should you use MemMaker, FASTOPEN, or DBLSPACE.

NLSFUNC

Microsoft also recommends that you don't load NLSFUNC under Windows. We are not sure why, but since both NLSFUNC and Windows are their programs, we'll take Microsoft's word on this one.

VSAFE

MSAV and VSAFE are the DOS 6 antivirus products for use at the DOS prompt. Use them only at the DOS prompt. Also bundled with DOS 6 are the corresponding Windows programs, MSWAV and MWAVTSR. Use them from within Windows. (We discuss computer viruses in some detail later in this chapter.)

Some Caveats about Disk Compression and Disk Caches

Many people have run into trouble attempting to use on-the-fly disk compression programs such as Stacker and SuperStor with a disk caching program such as SMARTDrive. It can be done, and done safely, but you have to take a few precautions to avoid confusing the caching system about which drives are where.

If you don't understand how disk cache programs interact with on-the-fly file compression programs, you could lose virtually all of the data on your hard disk. This happens only in a few circumstances, but when it does, it is catastrophic. Avoiding these circumstances is difficult if you don't know what they are.

First, you need to understand an important distinction between two classes of disk cache programs. Most of the early programs operated at the "physical level"; that is, they took over INT13h and cached all requests for disk access after they had been translated by DOS down to the BIOS level where disk locations are specified by head number, cylinder number, and physical sector number. One of the early cache programs, and still one of the most popular, is Super PC-Kwik from the PC-Kwik Corporation (formerly Multisoft). It has always used an INT13h physical approach to disk caching.

The other class of disk cache program operates at a much higher level of abstraction from the hardware, the "logical level." This class intercepts disk access requests at a place in DOS where disk locations are specified by logical volume letter and logical sector number within the volume. (This is the same level as INT25h and INT26h, but these programs cannot simply hook those interrupts. They must, instead, link themselves into DOS more intimately, which means using "secret" information about how DOS really works at that level.)

SmartDrive and the Norton Cache program are examples of these logical level disk cache programs. Once quite rare, they are becoming more and more popular, which in some ways is unfortunate, as only the logical level disk cache programs are able to cause the very serious data damage we are about to describe.

On-the-fly file compression programs like DoubleSpace and Stacker or SuperStor also work at the logical level. They must work at this level, as the essence of what they do is to intercept all disk access requests that are directed at the virtual disk volumes they maintain. Then they convert those requests into ones to the real, host disk volumes and deliver them to the BIOS via INT13h. The file compression or expansion occurs as data passes through these programs going from the logical to the physical level or vice versa. (See Chapter 9 for explanations of disk compression and virtual versus host drives; see Chapter 12 for a discussion of disk caching.)

Working at the logical level gives these programs the opportunity to swap the logical volume letter designations around. DoubleSpace and SuperStor do this only for virtual volumes they manage and the host volumes holding the actual data for those virtual volumes. Stacker lets you swap letters for any disk volumes in your system arbitrarily.

If you use an on-the-fly file compression program and a disk cache, and if the two programs you choose work at different levels, there is no problem with data integrity. Since all of the on-the-fly file compression products must work at the logical level, there is no danger if you use Super PC-Kwik or any other disk cache program that operates exclusively at the physical level.

If, on the other hand, you choose to use SmartDrive, the Norton Cache, or one of the other programs that operate at the logical level, you could receive DOS's scariest error message. You won't, however, if you always load the disk cache program last, after the on-the-fly file compression program, and after it has done any drive letter swapping it is going to do.

With DoubleSpace you can't go wrong. It gets loaded and all the drive letters get swapped before your CONFIG.SYS file is read and before you could possibly have loaded your disk cache program. You can't go wrong with SuperStor and SmartDrive either, as SuperStor loads as a device driver from CONFIG.SYS, and SmartDrive is loaded as a TSR from the AUTOEXEC.BAT file or through an INSTALL statement in CONFIG.SYS. SuperStor also normally does its drive letter swapping right after being installed.

Stacker gives you more flexibility, and along the way it also gives you some opportunities to make some very bad decisions. You install Stacker as a device driver in CONFIG.SYS, but you can do the drive letter swapping at any time. Heed this warning: *Don't* do it after loading SmartDrive, Norton Cache, or any other logical-level disk caching program. Swapping drive letters after the logical-level cache program has taken its first look at the system leads to mass confusion and data misrouting.

There is another issue relating to the mixture of on-the-fly file compression programs and disk caching programs—the issue of which disk volumes get cached. Ideally you would like to be able to control which volumes get cached and which do not. The logical-level cache programs typically allow you to specify this. Some of them will (imprudently) allow you to specify caching for any drive letters you choose.

The right way to do disk caching in the presence of compression is to cache only the compressed data on its way on or off the host disk drive. (The reason you should not cache virtual volumes is that you would then be caching the same data twice, once as it is written to or read from the virtual drive and again at the lower level when it goes on or off the physical, host volume.) This would be a drastic waste of cache space, and it also would slow things down, relative to caching only once, and then only the compressed version of the data.

Physical-level cache programs and disk cache hardware that is a part of the disk controller have no possibility of doing anything else. All logical-level disk cache programs, on the other hand, are doing their work at a level that could mean they will be dealing with your data following decompression after it is read from the disk or before it gets compressed in preparation for a disk write.

One of the features of SmartDrive is that it is coded to recognize compressed (virtual) disk volumes and automatically not cache them. Many other popular logical-level disk caching programs do this as well. But check the features on the one you choose to use, and be sure you know whether or not you will have to tell it not to cache virtual volumes.

These warnings might lead you to conclude that we recommend that you avoid all logical-level disk cache programs. Not so. We do think highly of Super PC-Kwik, and SmartDrive and the Norton Cache are also fine programs—provided they are used correctly.

The one serious drawback to Super PC-Kwik, at least so far, is that you cannot choose to cache only some of the physical partitions on a disk drive. If you have two physical drives, you can cache one and not the other. But, if you have only one physical drive, even though it is partitioned at a very low hardware level into a primary DOS partition and an extended partition with several logical volumes within it, Super PC-Kwik can only cache the whole shebang or none of it. (You can tell Super PC-Kwik to cache your C drive and not your D drive; what you might not realize is that the program will look at those two instructions then choose to ignore the first and honor the second, thus not caching anything on that physical drive.) None of the logical-level disk cache programs have this drawback.

Another cache and compression related issue is which logical volumes should be cached. The answer is, cache only host volumes. SMARTdrive and most other disk cache programs are now, in their latest releases, able to detect compressed virtual drive volumes and refuse to cache them. If you have an older cache program, though, it might not be able to help you in that way. In that case, be vigilant and don't let it cache the compressed volumes. The issue is mainly one of performance, not data safety, though there is some potential for data damage. Try to avoid caching the same information twice—once in its uncompressed form and once in its compressed form. By caching only the latter, you will have fewer bytes to cache and thus make your cache RAM go farther and perform more quickly.

Getting Out of Trouble

No one can avoid trouble with DOS 100 percent of the time. When you encounter problems and face the chance of losing data, there's one way to recover without losing even one byte. If you have followed our advice in this chapter, you will be able to restore any damaged or missing files from their backups, no matter what happened to the files. You can restore the most recent versions or, if those are corrupted, go back to earlier, uncorrupted versions. You might lose some information if you have to use older backups.

Other DOS recovery tools are discussed in this section, but don't count on them. They're unreliable and you could end up "recovering" incorrect data or no data at all. If you're thinking of skipping frequent backups because UNDELETE and UNFORMAT might be able to fill in the gaps, reconsider. We'd rather see you eliminate both UNDELETE and UNFORMAT from your system and keep your backups up to date.

UNDELETE

The UNDELETE program is designed to help you recover files deleted in the not too distant past. There are two major aspects to UNDELETE: deletion protection and recovery. Deletion protection actually preserves information about deleted files for awhile to facilitate the recovery process.

LIMITATIONS TO UNDELTE'S SAFETY NET

If you use UNDELETE with its Delete Tracker option, your protection is severely limited. The dangers associated with UNDELETE, and in particular Delete Tracker, include:

1. Programs that move clusters around, such as DOS 6's DEFRAG or the Norton Utilities' SpeedDisk, invalidate the entries in PCTRACKR.DEL,

and you must be careful to delete the tracking file when you use such programs.

2. The big problem with Delete Tracker is that it doesn't guarantee that you can recover a file. It tells UNDELETE where the file used to be, but DOS might have stored another file in those clusters in the meantime. So, when you try to recover a file, UNDELETE may tell you that the file can't be recovered or that only part of it can be recovered. Recovering part of text file may help if you're desperate, but recovering part of a binary file is next to useless.
3. If DOS stored another file in the deleted file's clusters and then deleted the second file, UNDELETE sees the clusters as available and tells you that the original file can be completely recovered. But when you undelete the file, it contains the wrong data. At this point, there's no way to recover the data through UNDELETE.
4. Suppose you move or copy some files from one directory to another. If any files already existing in the destination directory have the same names as the new files, the existing files will be replaced without warning. DOS replaces the directory entries for those files, but it intentionally doesn't overlay their clusters so that you have the chance to recover the data from those clusters. But DOS doesn't give you any means to recover the data. UNDELETE doesn't see this type of file replacement as a deletion, so neither Delete Sentry nor Delete Tracker preserves the files. They can't be undeleted by the DOS directory method since the directory entries were replaced. Here again, your backups are your best means of recovering deleted data.

Note: A more sophisticated undeletion program, such as The Norton Utilities' UnErase, may be able to recover a replaced file by searching the free space for the missing data. But if you lose a binary file, how will you recognize the missing data when you see it?

UNFORMAT

No doubt you'll probably end up reformatting the wrong disk some day. If you keep your backups up to date, this will be a minor irritation at most. All you need to do is restore the destroyed directories and files from their backups. But if you accidentally reformat a floppy disk that contains data that you haven't yet backed up, the UNFORMAT program may be your only recourse. UNFORMAT is designed to recover data from a disk that you reformatted by accident. And it actually will succeed under these conditions:

1. The formatting program must not have done a low-level format. A low-level format lays out new sectors on the disk and tests the entire surface for defects. In the process, any previous data is destroyed and no recovery is possible. DOS's FORMAT program does a low-level format when you specify (or let it default to) an Unconditional format.
2. The formatting program must have saved an image file on the disk before reformatting it. An image file is a snapshot of the root directory and FAT. DOS's FORMAT program automatically stores the image file if there's room on the disk—if you're not doing a low-level format, and if you don't specify the /U switch. With other formatting programs, the image file might be optional.

> ***Note:*** DOS 5 let you capture an image file at any time with the MIRROR command, but this tended to create images that quickly became obsolete as directories and files were added, updated, and deleted. Unformatting a disk with obsolete image data can create havoc, so Microsoft wisely dropped MIRROR from DOS 6. If you still have it in your DOS directory, you should delete it. The only appropriate time to capture an image file is when you are reformatting a disk.

3. You must not have added any data to the disk since reformatting it. Even if you just used the /S switch to make the disk bootable (which adds at least MSDOS.SYS, IO.SYS, and COMMAND.COM, if not DBLSPACE.BIN), unformatting the disk will restore directory entries for files whose data has been destroyed.

If all of these conditions are met, you can safely unformat the disk with UNFORMAT. All UNFORMAT does is restore the root directory and FAT from the image file. This should make the entire directory structure and all its files available once more.

If the image file is missing or obsolete, UNFORMAT will still try to recover some data, but frankly it does a lousy job. You're much better off restoring the directories and files from their backups. If you can't do that and you really need to recover the former data from the disk, reach for a more sophisticated unformatting program, such as the one included in The Norton Utilities.

Computer Viruses

Everyone talks about computer viruses. Many people know someone who knows someone whose hard disk was wiped out by one. With a little effort on your part, you can protect your data from *most* virus attacks. We wish we could tell you how to prevent all virus attacks, but that's not possible unless you shut down your system altogether, which falls in the category of throwing the baby out with the bath water. Since you can't provide 100 percent protection for your system, your best defense against viruses, as with all other possibilities of data loss, is to keep your backups up to date.

What is a Computer Virus?

A computer virus is a program that, much like a biological virus, infects a host and replicates and spreads itself at will. In the case of a computer virus, the host is usually some other program that in itself is at least harmless and often very useful—perhaps one that you've been using for quite some time. The computer virus spreads to other programs in your system and, given the opportunity, to other systems, so that eventually it could become worldwide. Many viruses don't announce their presence for a long time; they're busy replicating themselves in your system. They might be present in your system for months, or even longer, before you even become aware of their presence.

The majority of viruses were designed to do very little harm. Some of them simply announce their presence with a message or a graphic; others may do nothing overt at all. Still others were intended to be "helpful" by seeking out and destroying harmful viruses. (Most researchers in the anti-virus field agree that this is a *very bad* idea.) The goal for virus programmers seems to be to infect as many systems as possible, not to destroy them. Nevertheless, there are so many variations of hardware and software in the PC world, a virus that has no adverse effects on nine systems may destroy the tenth. Even if a virus doesn't damage the files or directory structure of a disk, it might irretrievably damage the program files that it infects.

Note: You may have heard the terms *worm* and *Trojan horse.* These aren't the same as viruses. A Trojan horse is a separate program that neither invades a host nor replicates itself. It tempts you into installing and running it by pretending to be something else. Once you know that you have a Trojan horse on your system, you can eliminate it completely by deleting its file. A worm is also a separate program, but it's capable of replicating and spreading itself over a network. Here again, you can stomp it out by deleting all copies of its program file. A virus is much harder to identify and to completely remove from your system, since it may have infected many of your program files before you discover it, and you won't necessarily know which files to remove.

How Common Are They?

If you believe rumors and news stories, computer viruses are running rampant in today's PC world. But how many people do you know who have actually encountered a virus? Probably not very many, if any at all. You can't completely ignore the possibility of a virus invading your system, but you don't have to stay up nights worrying about it. If you follow our recommendations in this chapter, you can be reasonably assured that you'll detect a virus early and keep it from doing any harm in your system. You're much more likely to lose data due to poorly debugged software, power outages, unexpected sources of magnetism, malfunctioning hardware, and bad work habits than you are from a virus.

How PCs Get Infected

There are a lot of misconceptions around regarding how PCs get infected with viruses in the first place. You're probably less likely to download one from a bulletin board system than you are to install one from a shrink-wrapped software package. Perhaps the most common culprit is the shared floppy disk. Many viruses are programmed to infect the boot sectors of floppy disks; they travel on floppies from system to system. Viruses also frequently travel over networks, especially public access networks where one user doesn't really care what happens to the other computers on the network.

Many people are afraid to put a modem on their computer. Or, if they have a modem, they are afraid to call a bulletin board system. A computer virus can't operate until you load it into memory by starting up its host program. If it has infected an application such as your word processor, it stays dormant until you load the word processor. Then it can begin replicating and spreading itself as well as performing whatever overt actions it is designed to do. A virus that infects a boot sector or partition table is loaded when you boot from that disk; if you don't boot from the disk, it can't function.

You significantly reduce the chances of infecting your PC when downloading software from a bulletin board if you always check it for viruses *before* running it for the first time. The same is true for any floppy disks that you insert in your system; if you check them first, you'll catch most viruses before they have a chance to spread. But you can't expect miracles from your anti-virus program. If you haven't added the latest virus information to it, or if you encounter a virus that's so new that it hasn't been identified yet, then a virus could get past your virus scanner and infect your system.

A Simple, But Not Too Helpful, Precaution

One relatively easy step to take that can help protect your program files from amateurish viruses is to set the read-only attribute on all your program files. This won't do you much good, however, when faced with expert viruses because they know how to override a file's attributes. In fact, they know enough to reset the original attributes after infecting the file so that you won't notice any change in the file's directory entry. The read-only attribute also won't make any difference to viruses that infect partition tables and boot sectors, which don't have attributes. But go ahead and set them anyway because they will prevent *you* from accidentally modifying or deleting an important program file.

One thing you're likely to discover as soon as you set the read-only attributes is that you have a program that regularly modifies its own program file. Of course, you'll need to remove the read-only setting for this file so the program can function. But you'll have discovered a valuable piece of information for the virus scanning process. Many virus scanning programs look for two different kinds of evidence of viral damage: one is a *viral signature* (a sequence of bytes known to be in a particular computer virus); the other is simply any change in a program file. If you are told that a program has changed, you have to decide whether this is likely to be a benign or a malign change. If you know that the program changes it own file, you'll know that it's (usually) safe to ignore the "file has changed, so it could be virally infected" warning.

Techniques to Detect and Stop Computer Viruses

The best time to check a program for virus infection is *before* you install it. Scan all of its program files, whether they're on installation diskettes or downloaded from a BBS. If you're absolutely diligent in scanning all new software and in keeping your anti-virus program up to date, you'll prevent most viruses from entering your system.

Of course, you also must keep other people away from your system unless they agree to follow your anti-virus methods. Remember that a virus scanner can detect only the viruses it knows about when examining new software. Read on for a technique that helps to identify and block unknown viruses.

You can locate any type of virus by looking for changes in program files. This works only if you know that a program was virus-free the first time it was scanned, because that initial scan establishes the baseline from which to determine future changes. A good virus scanner of this type records information about a program file during the initial scan and uses that information in future scans to identify any changes to the file. The recorded data includes the file's date/time stamp, its attributes, its size, and a value called a CRC (Cyclic Redundancy Check) that is calculated from the contents of the file. (Some people call the CRC a "checksum," but it's more than a simple summation of the file's contents. It's calculated from an algorithm that is virtually guaranteed to produce a unique value from the contents of the file.) If even one byte of the file is modified, the CRC value changes and the scanner warns you of a possible virus. This system has the potential of locating *all* viruses that enter your system, known or unknown, as long as you manage it properly.

We've already mentioned a couple of the factors involved in proper management. You have to make sure that each program is virus-free before recording its CRC data. And, of course, you can't do that if you don't keep your anti-virus program up to the minute with the latest virus information.

Today's viruses are, of course, perfectly aware that many anti-virus programs use these stored values, and if they can find them, they will change the stored values in such a way that you will not notice that they have infected your files. You can best protect your system by storing your CRC data on a write-protected floppy diskette where viruses can't get at it. This takes some extra effort because you'll have to copy the CRC data to the floppy, write-protect the floppy, then copy it back to the hard disk when you want to scan for program file changes.

Scanning for program changes can result in some virus alerts that actually are perfectly innocent situations. We've already mentioned programs that modify their own program files. You'll also see many such messages just after you upgrade an application. In the case of a self-modifying program, you should be able to ignore the changed file and continue the scan. In cases where you have just upgraded an application, you should be able to ask the scanner to update its CRC data. And, of course, in cases where you suspect that a virus has, in fact, infected a file, you should be able to ask the scanner to delete the file for you.

You don't need to scan all your program files on a daily basis. Checking each program for both known and unknown viruses as you load it would prevent almost any new virus (except the sneakiest ones) from being loaded and given the opportunity to execute. Generally, a virus monitor has the capability to scan every program being loaded for known viruses and to check its CRC data for any changes. A good anti-virus system should include a TSR that will check programs as they're loaded.

Note: Some newer software programs check themselves for viruses whenever they're loaded, but since this practice isn't yet universal, you'll still need to set up your system to scan all programs as they're loaded.

You should, of course, scan your entire system for viruses on a regular basis. When you're ready to do that, we recommend that you first boot your system from a write-protected diskette that's known to be virus-free. (This can be the same diskette that contains your CRC data.) Booting from a virus-free diskette prevents a virus that's located in your hard disk's partition table from being loaded during booting and taking actions to prevent the scanner from identifying it, which many viruses are capable of doing. Remember to write-protect the diskette to keep a virus from infecting it during the scan. If you belong to a network, sign off from it before doing the scan. Or, if you do stay on the network, scan all the stations in the network from a single location so that a virus can't evade the scan by moving itself around.

Virus scanning suffers from two weaknesses that can render it useless if you're not careful. First, you must continually update the scanner with the latest information about known viruses. Known viruses are detected by their signatures—a series of bytes contained in the virus program that serve to identify it. New viruses are among the most likely to be spreading, so it's vitally important that you keep your signature file as up to date as possible. Second, a certain class of viruses (usually called "stealth" viruses) are capable of evading detection by masking their signatures using such techniques as encrypting themselves or changing themselves on a regular basis. Such viruses can't be caught by their signatures, but they can be caught by CRC checking if you're careful to protect your CRC data from being modified by them.

Another technique to prevent viruses from taking up residence or damaging your system is to monitor all system activity for suspicious behavior such as reformatting the hard disk or changing the partition table. Virus monitoring can provide an important supplement to scanning when you aren't sure that your system was virus-free to start with.

You can limit virus monitoring to just the most suspect actions, such as the two already mentioned, or you can extend it to include almost any behavior that a virus might exhibit, such as writing to the hard disk. At the upper extreme, you might find yourself dealing with a lot of "false positives"; that is, the virus monitor will be warning you about activities that are perfectly normal. In fact, if you monitor all disk writes, you can tie up your system so completely that you won't be able to get any work done and the overall effect will be worse than a virus attack. At the lower extreme, you may suffer from too many "false negatives"; virus actions that weren't caught because you weren't monitoring for them.

Finally, the best way to protect yourself still is to keep those "perfect" backups, which includes both up to the minute copies of all significant work, and older copies as well, in case your newer files are flawed, damaged, or infected.

Which Anti-Virus Protection Should You Use?

You probably don't want to take all possible steps to protect yourself from viruses; they take too much time and energy. But which ones do you absolutely need? If you're on a network, you can benefit from a resident load-time virus detector and/or one that watches all programs as they execute to see and prevent any specified suspicious behaviors.

The same holds true if you share your computer with others (unless you *really* trust them to observe good anti-virus practices when installing or downloading software, borrowing floppy disks, and so on). If you install new software frequently, you also should be checking programs as you load them and monitor for suspect actions. If you rarely install new software, you might be able to get away with just scanning the software when it's installed, supplemented by an occasional system-wide scan.

If your system is already clogged with TSRs and device drivers, you probably want to avoid any anti-virus techniques that involve TSRs, such as checking programs as they're loaded and monitoring for suspect activities. If your system is one that would otherwise be a good candidate for a resident anti-virus technique, you might need to substitute more frequent scanning instead.

The DOS Anti-Virus Programs

DOS 6 includes several anti-virus programs, grouped under the name Microsoft Anti-Virus. MSAV is an anti-virus scanner that runs from the DOS command prompt. MWAV is the Windows equivalent of this scanner. VSAFE is an anti-virus monitor that runs under both DOS and Windows, with MWAVTSR as a necessary Windows component to let VSAFE deliver its messages to you while you are in Windows.

MSAV and MWAV scan memory and selected drives for both known and unknown viruses. If you want, they will record CRC values and other anti-virus data in files named CHKLIST.MS stored in every directory on a scanned drive. Subsequent scans can then identify changes in program files. You can save time by turning off CRC checking and scanning only for virus signatures, but you're increasing your chances of missing a virus that has infected your system. MSAV and MWAV both offer to clean known viruses out of the infected host file when that's possible. We recommend that you don't take this option. It's much better to delete the infected file and restore it from its backup. (You may have to go back a few backups to find an uninfected version of the file.)

You can set up a virus scanner to run automatically, building a report of how many viruses were found without reporting each virus at the time of discovery. It runs a lot faster this way; if the report shows that a virus was detected—which shouldn't happen very often, if at all—you can rerun the scan in a more interactive mode and deal with the virus when it's reported.

Microsoft maintains a bulletin board that lets you download the latest virus signatures. It also gives you instructions on how to add them to your anti-virus software. You should download new virus signatures frequently, so check the bulletin board often to see if new signatures have become available. The instructions for accessing the bulletin board are included at the back of your DOS User's Guide. You'll also see instructions for how to obtain upgrades to your Microsoft anti-virus programs. That's not nearly as important as keeping your signature files up to date. Upgrading the programs lets you clean the latest viruses as well as detect them, and in our opinion, you ought to be deleting and restoring infected files instead of cleaning them.

VSAFE is a TSR that, once loaded, constantly monitors for virus-like activity. You can choose up to eight monitoring options, ranging from preventing modifications to the hard drive partition table to intercepting and reporting all disk writes. VSAFE includes options to check all programs for both known and unknown viruses as they're loaded and to intercept and report any attempt to change a program file. Whenever VSAFE detects a suspicious behavior, it displays an alert box so that you can decide what to do next. In general, your choices are to prohibit or permit the activity.

Don't Panic

If your system suddenly starts behaving oddly or not behaving at all, don't panic! It's probably not as bad as you think. Take a deep breath and apply some rational thought to what's happening. In all likelihood, the change in your system is the result of some change that you made. Even the most inconsequential changes, such as moving a line in AUTOEXEC.BAT, can produce what appear to be drastic results.

Make sure that what you see is what you see. Is your system really dead, or did the cleaning staff accidentally turn down the brightness control on your video monitor? Have you really lost all the data on your hard drive, or is

DOSSHELL using a file name filter that you forgot about? Before you go any further, check to see if you can repeat the problem and that you're not simply confused.

If you still haven't located the source of the problem, try returning to where you were when everything was okay. If you can get back to that stage, you should be able to identify what it was that caused the problem. Try sneaking up on it one step at a time. Make one small change and see if that creates trouble. If not, make the next change. Eventually, you'll replicate the problem and you'll know which step caused it.

If you're still in trouble, try doing a clean boot from a floppy disk that loads only those drivers that are essential to your system. Then, step by step, add features to your system until you locate the one that caused the problem. If that fails, it's time to get help.

Getting Help

It's okay to ask for help. People do it all the time, as evidenced by the long waits when you call a Technical Support hotline. If you work for a fairly large company, you should be able to get some expert help in-house. If you're on your own, you probably need to build a personal support system. Friends with similar computer systems can be the biggest help, as they often have run into the same problems. The people in a user's group expect to be asked for help; in a sense, that's the purpose of the group. Bulletin board forums can put you in touch with system experts who are more than willing to answer your questions and solve your problems; you might have to wait a couple of days for the answer, however. And don't forget those technical support hotlines and direct response facsimile numbers. Hardware and software manufacturers usually have the largest database of known problems with their products, and they can guide you through the solutions or even send you an immediate fix.

CHAPTER

18

◆ ◆ ◆ ◆ ◆

Command Reference Guide

This chapter is a complete reference guide to all the commands in MS-DOS, version 6. Included in this alphabetical listing are all the internal and external commands, as well as the directives for use in CONFIG.SYS and AUTOEXEC.BAT files.

Tables 18-1 and 18-2 contain the same list in tabular form, showing which commands are internal, which are external, which are of use in CONFIG.SYS files, which in AUTOEXEC.BAT files. It also shows what files are associated with these commands (besides the main program file for each external command). The items in Table 18-2 are ones that only get installed for special hardware configurations, or to support Windows, or they are programs used by the MS-DOS 6 SETUP program.

Syntax Notes

The command reference uses many industry-standard notation conventions. To be sure you understand our usage, here is a recap of some of the more significant points.

Command or Directive (ASSOCIATED FILES)	Internal Command	External Command	Device Driver	DOS 5.0 file removed from DOS 6.0	Use in CONFIG.SYS	Use in Batch Files	International Language Support
ANSI.SYS			✓				
APPEND.EXE		✓					
ASSIGN.COM				✓			
ATTRIB.EXE		✓					
BACKUP.EXE				✓			
Break	✓				✓	✓	
Buffers					✓		
Call	✓					✓	
Chcp	✓						✓
Chdir [Cd]	✓						
CHKDSK.EXE		✓					
CHOICE.COM		✓				✓	
Cls	✓						
COMMAND.COM		✓					
COMP.EXE				✓			
Copy	✓						
Country					✓		✓
COUNTRY.SYS							
Ctty	✓						
CV.COM				✓			
Date	✓						
DBLSPACE.EXE		✓					
DBLSPACE.BIN	DBLSPACE.BIN is an installable block device loaded by IO.SYS before CONFIG.SYS processsing						
DBLSPACE.HLP							
DBLSPACE.INF							
DBLSPACE.INI							
DBLSPACE.SYS			*				
DEBUG.EXE		✓					
DEFRAG.EXE		✓					
DEFRAG.HLP							
Del	✓						
DELOLDOS.EXE		✓					
DELTREE.EXE		✓					
Device					✓		
Devicehigh					✓		
Dir	✓						
DISKCOMP.COM		✓					
DISKCOPY.COM		✓					
DISPLAY.SYS			✓				✓
Dos					✓		
DOSKEY.COM		✓					
DOSSHELL.COM		✓					
DOSSHELL.EXE							
DOSSHELL.GRB							
DOSSHELL.HLP							
DOSSHELL.INI							
DOSSHELL.VID							
DOSSWAP.EXE							
EGA.SYS							
DRIVER.SYS			✓				

* - Specified by a DEVICE line in CONFIG.SYS but not inserted into the DOS device chain.

Figure 18-1 MS-DOS 6 Commands

Command or Directive (ASSOCIATED FILES)	Internal Command	External Command	Device Driver	DOS 5.0 file removed from DOS 6.0	Use in CONFIG.SYS	Use in Batch Files	International Language Support
Drivparm					✓		
Echo	✓					✓	
EDIT.COM		✓					
EDIT.HLP							
QBASIC.EXE							
EDLIN.EXE				✓			
EGA.SYS			✓				
EMM386.EXE		✓	✓				
EXE2BIN.EXE				✓			
EXPAND.EXE		✓					
Erase	✓						
Errorlevel	✓					✓	
Exist	✓					✓	
Exit	✓						
FASTHELP.EXE		✓					
DOSHELP.HLP							
FASTOPEN.EXE		✓					
FC.EXE		✓					
Fcbs					✓		
FDISK.EXE		✓					
Files					✓		
FIND.EXE		✓					
For	✓					✓	
FORMAT.COM		✓					
Goto	✓					✓	
GRAFTABL.COM				✓			
GRAPHICS.COM		✓					
GRAPHICS.PRO							
HELP.COM		✓					
HELP.HLP							
QBASIC.EXE							
HIMEM.SYS			✓				
If	✓					✓	
Include					✓		
Install					✓		
INTERLNK.EXE			*				
INTERSVR.EXE		✓					
JOIN.EXE				✓			
KEYB.COM							✓
LABEL.EXE		✓					
Lastdrive					✓		
LOADFIX.COM		✓					
Loadhigh [Lh]	✓						
MEM.EXE		✓					
MEMMAKER.EXE		✓					
CHKSTATE.SYS							
MEMMAKER.HLP							
MEMMAKER.INF							
SIZER.EXE							
MenuColor					✓		

* - Specified by a DEVICE line in CONFIG.SYS but not inserted into the DOS device chain.

Figure 18-2 MS-DOS 6 Commands *(continued)*

Command or Directive (ASSOCIATED FILES)	Internal Command	External Command	Device Driver	DOS 5.0 file removed from DOS 6.0	Use in CONFIG.SYS	Use in Batch Files	International Language Support
MenuDefault					✓		
MenuItem					✓		
MIRROR.COM				✓			
Mkdir [Md]	✓						
MODE.COM		✓					✓
EGA.CPI							
LCD.CPI				✓			
MORE.COM		✓					
MOVE.EXE		✓					
MSAV.EXE		✓					
MSAV.HLP							
MSAV.INI							
MSAVHLP.OVL							
MSAVIRUS.LST							
MSBACKUP.EXE		✓					
MSBACKDB.OVL							
MSBACKDR.OVL							
MSBACKFB.OVL							
MSBACKFR.OVL							
MSBACKUP.HLP							
MSBACKUP.INI							
MSBACKUP.OVL							
MSBCONFG.HLP							
MSBCONFG.OVL							
*.SET							
MSCDEX.EXE		✓	*				
MSD.EXE		✓					
MSHERC.COM				✓			✓
NLSFUNC.EXE		✓					
Numlock					✓		
Path	✓						
Pause	✓					✓	
POWER.EXE		✓	✓				
PRINT.EXE		✓					
PRINTFIX.COM				✓			
PRINTER.SYS				✓			✓
4201.CPI				✓			
4208.CPI				✓			
5202.CPI				✓			
Prompt	✓						
QBASIC.EXE		✓					
QBASIC.HLP							
QBASIC.INI							
RAMDRIVE.SYS			✓				
RECOVER				✓			
Rem	✓				✓	✓	
Rename [Ren]	✓						
REPLACE.EXE		✓					
RESTORE.EXE		✓					
Rmdir [Rd]	✓						

* - Specified by a DEVICE line in CONFIG.SYS but not inserted into the DOS device chain.

Figure 18-3 MS-DOS 6 Commands *(continued)*

Command or Directive (ASSOCIATED FILES)	Internal Command	External Command	Device Driver	DOS 5.0 file removed from DOS 6.0	Use in CONFIG.SYS	Use in Batch Files	International Language Support
Sample Basic Programs (*.BAS)				✓			
Set	✓				✓	✓	
SETVER.EXE			✓				
SHARE.EXE		✓					
Shell					✓		
Shift	✓					✓	
SMARTDRV.EXE		✓	✓				
SORT.EXE		✓					
Stacks					✓		
Submenu					✓		
SUBST.EXE		✓					
Switches					✓		
SYS.COM		✓					
Time	✓						
TREE.COM		✓					
Truename (Undocumented)	✓						
Type	✓						
UNDELETE.EXE		✓					
UNDELETE.INI							
UNFORMAT.COM		✓					
Ver	✓						
Verify	✓				✓		
Vol	✓						
VSAFE.COM		✓					
XCOPY.EXE		✓					

Figure 18-4 MS-DOS 6 Commands *(continued)*

Anything that appears on your monitor will generally be shown in `monospaced screen font`. That font, lower-case, and italic is used for *`things that you have to specify`*. Things that you must type exactly as they are shown, are here displayed in all `UPPER-CASE MONOSPACED SCREEN FONT`.

Optional parts of a command line are enclosed in square brackets `[ ]` and alternatives are separated by a vertical bar `¦`. When you type a command that has these options in its syntax description, don't type the brackets or the vertical bar.

ANSI.SYS Commands

The ANSI.SYS device driver accepts commands to change on-screen graphics, move the cursor, and reassign keys on the computer's keyboard. Before using

Command or File name (ASSOCIATED FILES)	On Installation Diskettes Only	Installed only for Certain Configurations of Hardware or Software	DOS 6.0 Windows 3.x Support Tools
MOUSE.COM		✓	
MOUSE.INI			
MWAV.EXE		✓	✓
MWAV.HLP		✓	✓
MWAV.INI		✓	✓
MWAVABSI.DLL		✓	✓
MWAVDLG.DLL		✓	✓
MWAVDOSL.DLL		✓	✓
MWAVDRVL.DLL		✓	✓
MWAVMGR.DLL		✓	✓
MWAVSCAN.DLL		✓	✓
MWAVSOS.DLL		✓	✓
MWAVTREE.DLL		✓	✓
MWAVTSR.EXE		✓	✓
MWGRAFIC.DLL		✓	✓
MWBACKUP.EXE		✓	✓
MWBACKF.DLL		✓	✓
MWBACKR.DLL		✓	✓
MWBACKUP.HLP		✓	✓
MWBACKUP.INI		✓	✓
VFINTD.386			✓
MWUNDEL.EXE		✓	✓
MWUNDEL.HLP		✓	✓
MWUNDEL.INI		✓	✓
MWGRAFIC.DLL		✓	✓
SETUP.EXE	✓		
BUSETUP.EXE	✓		
SETUP.MSG	✓		
DOSSETUP.INI	✓		
SMARTMON.EXE			✓
SMARTMON.HLP			✓
(Special configuration support files)			
DBLWIN.HLP			✓
WINA20.386		✓	
MSTOOLS.DLL			✓
WINTOOLS.GRP		✓	
DMDRVR.BIN		✓	
XBIOS.OVL			
SSTOR.SYS		✓	
MONOUMB.386			✓
(Installation support)			
CONFIG.SYS	✓		
AUTOEXEC.BAT	✓		
PACKING.LST	✓		
NETWORKS.TXT			
OS2.TXT		✓	
README.TXT			

Figure 18-5 Additional MS-DOS 6 Commands and Installation files

any of these commands, the ANSI.SYS device driver must have been loaded into memory by a DEVICE line in the CONFIG.SYS file.

All ANSI.SYS commands begin with an escape character (ASCII 27, hex 1Bh) followed by a left angle bracket ([). The escape character appears in this list as ESC, but don't attempt to enter it by typing the letters E, S, and C.

Moving the Cursor

`ESC[x;yH or ESC[x;yf`

Move the cursor to the position on the screen specified by the coordinates *x* and *y*. For *x*, use the number of the line; for *y*, use the number of the column. Line 0, column 0 is at the upper-left corner of the screen.

`ESC[nA`

Move the cursor up *n* lines.

`ESC[nB`

Move the cursor down *n* lines.

`ESC[nC`

Move the cursor to the right *n* spaces or columns.

`ESC[nD`

Move the cursor to the left *n* spaces or columns.

`ESC[s`

Save the current position of the cursor. Use `ESC[u` to restore the cursor to this position.

`ESC[u`

Restore the cursor to the position saved with `ESC[s`.

Erasing the Display

`ESC[2J`

Clear the screen and move the cursor to the upper left corner.

`ESC[K`

Clear everything on the current line, from the cursor position to the end of the line (to the right).

Graphics Mode

`ESC[`*`code;...;code`*`m`

Set attributes, using the numbers in the following list in place of code. Note that the final letter in this command must be a lower-case m.

TEXT ATTRIBUTES

0	All attributes off (reset the screen to normal white on black)
1	Bold on
4	Underscore (on monochrome display adapter only)
5	Blink on
7	Reverse video on
8	concealed on

FOREGROUND COLORS

30	Black
31	Red
32	Green
33	Yellow
34	Blue
35	Magenta
36	Cyan
37	White

BACKGROUND COLORS

40	Black
41	Red
42	Green
43	Yellow
44	Blue
45	Magenta
46	Cyan
47	White

For example, use `ESC[0m` to reset the screen to white letters on black. Use `ESC[31,44m` to display red characters on a blue background. Enter `ESC[5m` to make the character or string of characters that follow, blink on and off.

Screen Mode

`ESC[=`*`code`*`h`

Set the screen mode, using a number from the following list in place of code.

`ESC[=`*`code`*`l`

Reset the screen mode, using a number from the following list in place of code. Note that "l" is a lowercase L, and not a number 1.

0	40 x 25 monochrome (text)
1	40 x 25 color (text)
2	80 x 25 monochrome (text)
3	80 x 25 color (text)
4	320 x 200 4-color (graphics)
5	320 x 200 monochrome (graphics)
6	640 x 200 monochrome (graphics)
13	320 x 200 color (graphics)
14	640 x 200 color (16-color graphics)
15	640 x 350 monochrome (2-color graphics)
16	640 x 350 color (16-color graphics)
17	640 x 480 monochrome (2-color graphics)
18	640 x 480 color (16-color graphics)
19	320 x 200 color (256-color graphics)

`ESC[=7h`

Turn on line wrapping. When data extends beyond the extreme right end of a line, the next character appears on the left end of the next line.

`ESC[=7l`

Turn off line wrapping. Data that extends beyond the right end of the screen overtypes the extreme right character. Note that `l` is a lowercase L and not a number 1.

Keyboard Control

`ESC[`*`code;stringp`*

Assign a single character or string of characters to a key. Use the code in the following list to specify a key, or a combination of Shift, Ctrl, or Alt plus a key. For a string, either specify the ASCII code of a single character, or a string of characters within quotation marks. Notice that the final letter in this command must be a lower-case p.

For example, to assign the letter A to the F6 key, either enter `ESC[0;64;65p` or `ESC[0;64;"A"p`. To assign the word "Tuesday" to the up arrow key, enter `ESC[224;72;"Tuesday"p`.

Key	*Code*	*SHIFT +code*	*CTRL +code*	*ALT +code*
F1	0;59	0;84	0;94	0;104
F2	0;60	0;85	0;95	0;105
F3	0;61	0;86	0;96	0;106
F4	0;62	0;87	0;97	0;107
F5	0;63	0;88	0;98	0;108
F6	0;64	0;89	0;99	0;109
F7	0;65	0;90	0;100	0;110
F8	0;66	0;91	0;101	0;111
F9	0;67	0;92	0;102	0;112
F10	0;68	0;93	0;103	0;113
F11	0;133	0;135	0;137	0;139
F12	0;134	0;136	0;138	0;140
Home	0;71	55	0;119	—
Up Arrow	0;72	56	(0;141)	—
Page Up	0;73	57	0;132	—
Left Arrow	0;75	52	0;115	—
Right Arrow	0;77	54	0;116	—
End	0;79	49	0;117	—
Down Arrow	0;80	50	(0;145)	—
Page Down	0;81	51	0;118	—
Insert	0;82	48	(0;146)	—
Delete	0;83	46	(0;147)	—
Home (gray key)	(224;71)	(224;71)	(224;119)	(224;151)
Up Arrow (gray key)	(224;72)	(224;72)	(224;141)	(224;152)
Page Up (gray key)	(224;73)	(224;73)	(224;132)	(224;153)
Left Arrow (gray key)	(224;75)	(224;75)	(224;115)	(224;155)
Right Arrow (gray key)	(224;77)	(224;77)	(224;116)	(224;157)

Key	*Code*	*SHIFT +code*	*CTRL +code*	*ALT +code*
End (gray key)	(224;79)	(224;79)	(224;117)	(224;159)
Down Arrow (gray key)	(224;80)	(224;80)	(224;145)	(224;154)
Page Down (gray key)	(224;81)	(224;81)	(224;118)	(224;161)
Insert(gray key)	(224;82)	(224;82)	(224;146)	(224;162)
Delete (gray key)	(224;83)	(224;83)	(224;147)	(224;163)
Print Screen	—	—	0;114	—
Pause/Break	—	—	0;0	—
Backspace	8	8	127	(0)
Enter1	3	—	10	(0)
TAB	9	0;15	(0;148)	(0;165)
NULL	0;3	—	—	—
A	97	65	1	0;30
B	98	66	2	0;48
C	99	66	3	0;46
D	100	68	4	0;32
E	101	69	5	0;18
F	102	70	6	0;33
G	103	71	7	0;34
H	104	72	8	0;35
I	105	73	9	0;23
J	106	74	10	0;36
K	107	75	11	0;37
L	108	76	12	0;38
M	109	77	13	0;50
N	110	78	14	0;49
O	111	79	15	0;24
P	112	80	16	0;25
Q	113	81	17	0;16
R	114	82	18	0;19
S	115	83	19	0;31
T	116	84	20	0;20
U	117	85	21	0;22
V	118	86	22	0;47

Key	*Code*	*SHIFT +code*	*CTRL +code*	*ALT +code*
W	119	87	23	0;17
X	120	88	24	0;45
Y	121	89	5	0;21
Z	122	90	26	0;44
1	49	33	—	0;120
2	50	64	0	0;121
3	51	35	—	0;122
4	52	36	—	0;123
5	53	37	—	0;124
6	54	94	30	0;125
7	55	38	—	0;126
8	56	42	—	0;126
9	57	40	—	0;127
0	48	41	—	0;129
-	45	95	31	0;130
=	61	43	—	0;131
[	91	123	27	0;26
]	93	125	29	0;27
	92	124	28	0;43
;	59	58	—	0;39
’	39	34	—	0;40
,	44	60	—	0;51
.	46	62	—	0;52
/	47	63	—	0;53
‘	96	126	—	(0;41)
Enter (keypad)	13	—	10	(0;166)
/ (keypad)	47	47	(0;142)	(0;74)
* (keypad)	42	(0;144)	(0;78)	—
- (keypad)	45	45	(0;149)	(0;164)
+ (keypad)	43	43	(0;150)	(0;55)
5 (keypad)	(0;76)	53	(0;143)	—

The codes in parentheses are not available on all keyboards, and some of the characters in this list may not work on every computer. To specify one of these codes on such a keyboard, the DEVICE=ANSI.SYS command in CONFIG.SYS must include the /X switch.

APPEND

Type: External command

Purpose: Search for files in specified directories as if they were in the current directory.

Syntax: `APPEND path[;...]`
`[/X¦/X:ON¦/X:OFF][/PATH:ON¦PATH:OFF][/E]`

`path`

The name of the directory where Append will search for files. To append more than one path, list all the paths you want to append, separated by semicolons.

`/X or /X:ON`

Append executable files (.COM, .EXE and .BAT) as well as data files

`/X:OFF`

Do not append executable files. /X:OFF is the default

`/PATH:ON`

Search for appended directories as well as any directories included in an application command.

`/PATH:OFF`

Search only in the directories specified in the command line.

`/E`

Store the append path or paths in an environment called APPEND. You may only use the /E switch the first time you enter APPEND after turning on the computer. After you enter `APPEND /E`, you can use the SET command to display or change the APPEND path.

`APPEND;`

Cancel the current list of appended directories.

```
APPEND
```

Displays the current list of appended directories.

Notes: APPEND performs a similar function to PATH, but it can include both data files and executable files. Do not try to use APPEND with Windows or the Windows Setup program.

ATTRIB

Type: External command

Purpose: Change or display attributes of a file or group of files, or of a directory.

Syntax: `ATTRIB [+A¦-A] [+R¦-R] [+S¦-S] [+H¦-H][path][filename] [/S]`

Enter ATTRIB by itself to display all of the attributes of all files in the current directory.

`[path]filename`

The name of the file or files whose attributes the command will change. Use the * or ? wildcards to change the attributes of a group of files at the same time (ATTRIB won't recognize wildcards for a directory name).

+	Turn on the specified attribute
-	Turn off the specified attribute
A	Turn on or off the archive file attribute
R	Turn on or off the read-only file attribute
S	Turn on or off the system file attribute
H	Turn on or off the hidden file attribute
/S	Search the current directory and all of its subdirectories for the specified file or files

Notes: Use the /S switch to search for a file from a disk's root directory. Enter:

```
ATTRIB filename /S
```

If RMDIR refuses to delete an apparently empty subdirectory, use ATTRIB with the H switch to display the names of any hidden files and also use SUBST by itself to see if that directory or one lower down in the directory tree is involved in a drive substitution.

BREAK

Type: CONFIG.SYS directive, can also be used at DOS prompt

Purpose: Turn extended checking for Ctrl-C on or off, or display the current status.

When BREAK is off, DOS checks for CTRL-C only when it is reading from the keyboard or writing to the screen or a printer. When BREAK is on, DOS also checks for CTRL-C at other times, including disk read and write operations.

Syntax: In CONFIG.SYS

```
BREAK=ON¦OFF
```

At the DOS prompt

```
BREAK [ON¦OFF]
```

BREAK alone displays the current status.

`On` Turn on extended checking for Ctrl-C.
`Off` Turn off extended checking for Ctrl-C.

The default is OFF.

Notes: To turn on the BREAK function every time you use the computer, place BREAK=ON in the CONFIG.SYS file.

Even if BREAK is set OFF, a user can press Ctrl-C to stop a program or a DOS activity (such as file sorting) that reads from the keyboard or writes to the screen. When BREAK is set ON, Ctrl-C also extends to reading to or writing from a disk.

Be aware that many programs turn BREAK OFF, and most of them do not have the courtesy to turn it back on again when they are through, even if it was on before. So you may have to reassert BREAK ON many times in a work session if you want to keep it on most of the time.

BUFFERS

Type: CONFIG.SYS directive

Purpose: Allocate memory for disk buffers. DOS uses buffers to hold data during read and write operations.

This command may only appear in CONFIG.SYS.

Syntax:

```
BUFFERS=B[,S]
```

`B`

Create the specified number of buffers. Acceptable values are within the range from 1 to 99

`S`

Create the specified number of buffers in the secondary buffer cache, within the range from 0 to 8

If you don't include the BUFFERS command in CONFIG.SYS, DOS will allocate the default, which depends on the amount of RAM in your system:

RAM	*Buffers*
<128K (360K disk)	2
<128K (>360K disk)	3
128K to 255K	5
256K to 511K	10
512K to 640K	15

Notes: DOS holds data in the memory allocated as buffers as it reads and writes information to block devices. Each buffer takes up about 532 bytes of memory. If you use a disk cache, such as SMARTDRV, you need not allocate so many disk buffers, and allocating fewer will save significant amounts of conventional memory. On the other hand, if you specify DOS=HIGH and have an HMA, then both the DOS kernel and the DOS disk buffers will be put there, provided you don't specify more than about 35 or 40 buffers. Otherwise all of the buffers will be placed in conventional (lower) memory.

Use the command `MEM /D /P` to display the amount of memory DOS is using for buffers.

CALL

Type: Batch file command

Purpose: Call one batch file from inside another batch file.

Syntax: `CALL [path]filename [parameters as required]`

The filename must be a .BAT file or you will get a `Bad command or file name` error messsage (even if you explicitly tell the CALL command the actual file name with extension).

Notes: If your batch file has a CALL to itself, include an exit command to prevent an endless loop. Similarly, if two batch files each have a call to the other batch file, they will loop forever, unless you give them a way to stop.

Use CALL to start a batch program from inside another batch file. For example, AUTOEXEC.BAT can contain calls to other batch files that run routine diagnostics or open the DOS shell or some other file manager.

When the called batch file has run its course, the parent batch file resumes with the next command in the file.

CD

Same as CHDIR

CHCP

Type: Internal command

Purpose: Change or display the current code page (character set). NLSFUNC must be running before you can use CHCP.

Syntax: `CHCP [code page number]`

`[code page number]`

437 United States
850 Multilingual (Latin I)

852	Slavic (Latin II)
860	Portuguese
863	Canadian-French
865	Nordic

To display the current code page, enter CHCP with no code page number.

Notes: CHCP is the command to change code pages, which changes the character set. In order to use this command, CONFIG.SYS must contain a COUNTRY= command to specify the location of the COUNTRY.SYS file, and NLSFUNC must have been loaded to memory.

CHDIR (CD)

Type: Internal command

Purpose: Move to a new directory or display the current directory.

Syntax: `CHDIR [drive:]path`

or

`CD [drive:]path`

`[drive:]path`

The new directory which will become the current directory.

To move to the parent of the current directory (one level up), use

`CHDIR ..` or `CD ..`

To move to the root directory, use

`CHDIR \` or `CD \`

To move to a subdirectory one level down from the root directory, use

`CHDIR \path` or `CD \path`

To display the current directory, enter CHDIR or CD without a path name.

Notes: CHDIR, or more often CD, is the standard command for moving around the file structure of a drive with many subdirectories.

CHKDSK

Type: External command

Purpose: Run a status test on a disk, test a file or group of files for fragmentation, create a status report, or repair disk errors.

Syntax: `CHKDSK [drive:][[path]filename] [/F] [/V]`

`[drive:]`

The drive that CHKDSK will test.

`[path]filename`

The file or group of files that CHKDSK will test. Use the * and ? wildcard characters to specify groups of files.

`/F`

Fix disk errors as they are identified.

`/V`

Display the path and name of each file on the disk as CHKDSK checks it.

To test the current drive, enter CHKDSK with no filename. For a file fragmentation report for all files, enter:

```
CHKDSK *.*
```

If CHKDSK finds fragmented files, run the DOS DEFRAG command.

To send the CHKDSK report to a file, enter:

```
CHKDSK > filename
```

Notes: CHKDSK is a basic tool for testing the condition of a disk. When `CHKDSK /F` finds errors it may display any of several messages. If the only message it displays is this one:

```
xx lost allocation units found in y chains.
Convert lost chains to files?
```

then you may safely accept its findings. Otherwise it is safer to get a second opinion from another diagnostic utility program.

If CHKDSK finds lost chains, press Y for yes to let CHKDSK save those chains as files. CHKDSK will create a file in the root directory called FILEnnnn.CHK. Use TYPE, EDIT, or some other utility to examine the contents of these files. If they contain data that you want to save, edit the data to the proper format, and rename the files.

Answering N for no to "Convert lost chains...?" tells DOS to discard the chains. You get back the disk space that was being used, but you have no easy way of knowing what data was stored there.

CHKDSK sometimes reports "*filename* is cross linked on allocation unit *n*" for several different files. There will always be at least two of these messages for each allocation unit (cluster) that is cross-linked. At least one of those cross-linked files has been corrupted. The safest solution to this problem is to delete all the files involved and restore them from backups. If that solution is difficult or impossible, reboot your computer, and then check with some other program to be sure CHKDSK was not simply mistaken.

CHOICE

Type: Batch file command

Purpose: Allow the user to select one of two or more options in a batch program.

Syntax: `CHOICE [/C[:]keys] [/N] [/S] [/T[:]c,nn [text]`

`/C[:]keys`

Accept the specified keys as options. The letters will appear inside brackets as a prompt, separated by commas, followed by a question mark. The colon is optional. For example, /C:ABC will produce [A,B,C]?

`/N`

Do not display the prompt. CHOICE still displays the text, and waits for one of the keys specified with /C:keys.

`/S`

Accept options only if they are the same case specified in the command. If /S is not included in the command, CHOICE will accept either upper- or lowercase characters

`/T[:]c,nn`

Wait *nn* seconds and then default to the c character. C must be one of the characters included in the /C[:]keys switch.

`text`

Display the specified text before the prompt. CHOICE adds a question mark at the end of the text. For example, CHOICE /C:ABC Which Option will produce:

```
Which Option [A,B,C]?
```

Notes: A CHOICE command should be followed by a series of IF ERRORLEVEL commands with each one testing for a different one of the options.

CLS

Type: Internal command

Purpose: Clear the screen.

Syntax: `CLS`

CLS removes all data from the screen and displays the command prompt and cursor.

COMMAND

Type: External command

Purpose: Start a new instance of the command interpreter COMMAND.COM (start a child process), or—in CONFIG.SYS—specify COMMAND.COM as the permanent command interpreter.

Syntax: `COMMAND [path] [device] [/C string] [E/:size] [/K:filename] [[/P] [/MSG]]`

When you launch a child process, you must type `EXIT` to return to the parent process, unless you use the /C switch.

CONFIG.SYS

Syntax: `SHELL=[path]COMMAND.COM [path] [device] [/E:size] [/P[ /MSG]]`

path

The location of the COMMAND.COM file.

device

A device other than COMMAND.COM for command input and output.

`/C` *string*

Perform the command *string* and then exit.

`E/:`*size*

Set the master DOS environment to *size*, in bytes.

`/K:`*filename*

Run the *filename* program and then display a DOS prompt.

`/P`

Make the new command interpreter permanent.

`/MSG`

Store all error messages in memory instead of on disk. This switch is only useful if you're running DOS from diskettes. If you use /MSG, you must also use /P.

Notes: COMMAND.COM is the program that normally displays a prompt and recognizes DOS commands. There are also third-party command interpreters that replace COMMAND.COM, including NDOS (part of The Norton Utilities) and 4DOS (widely distributed as shareware).

Many application programs use COMMAND to permit a user to "shell to DOS" in order to issue DOS commands without closing the application. To return to the application, use the EXIT command.

If you enter COMMAND from the DOS prompt, DOS starts a new command environment that is identical to the old one. If you make changes to the environment (such as a different prompt), the original environment will not change.

Each "nested" process uses up an amount of memory equal to the size of the permanent part of COMMAND.COM plus the size of the current environment, rounded up to the next 16 bytes.

Always use the /P switch when you invoke COMMAND.COM as your permanent command interpreter (through a SHELL statement). If you don't, then if you ever type EXIT, COMMAND.COM will vanish, and you will be left unable to communicate with your computer. On the other hand, don't ever use /P when invoking COMMAND.COM to create a child process. If you do, you will be unable to terminate that process and return to the parent process.

The /K parameter can be used to make COMMAND.COM run a batch file or program and then give a DOS prompt. (The /C parameter is used if you only want to run a program and then exit from the child process.)

COPY

Type: Internal command

Purpose: Copy files to a specified location.

Syntax: `COPY [/A¦/B] [`*`path`*`]`*`source`*` [/A¦/B] [+ `*`source`*` [/A¦/B] [+...]][`*`destination`*` [/A¦/B]] [/V]`

`[`*`path`*`]`*`source`*

The current location and name of the files.

`destination`

The new location of the copied file. If you want the copy to have a different file name from the source file, include the new file name in destination.

`/A`

Treat the file as an ASCII text file. (Treat Ctrl-Z as an end-of-file indicator.)

`/B`

Treat the file as a binary file; copy all characters to the end of the file as defined by length in directory entry.

If there's a /A in a COPY command, COPY will treat all files as ASCII text files until it encounters a /B later in the command. If there's a /B, COPY will treat all files as binary files until it encounters a /A. The default is /B. If you don't include /A or /B, COPY will copy the entire file or files.

`+source`

Combine two or more source files into a single destination file

`/V`

Verify that new files are correct

Notes: It's possible to COPY to or from a device name instead of a file. For example, COPY filename.txt LPT1 will instruct the computer to print filename.txt on the printer connected to parallel port LPT1.

COPY CON filename.txt creates (or overwrites) a file and writes data typed into the keyboard in that file. This is less flexible than using an editor, but it is always possible. As an internal command, it is always available, even if all the DOS external command programs are not. At the end of the text, press either Ctrl-Z or F6 followed by the Enter key to tell COPY that you are through.

A copy of a read-only file created with COPY will not be read-only. COPY will not copy files of zero length. This latter fact can be used by a batch file to test whether a given file has zero length.

`COPY *.*` *`newpath`* will create copies of all files in the current directory in the directory named *`newpath`*, but it won't copy subdirectories. To copy both files and subdirectories (including the files in the subdirectories), use XCOPY instead.

COUNTRY

Type: CONFIG.SYS command

Purpose: Configure MS-DOS for a specific country; use the time and date formats, currency symbol, case conversions and decimal separator conventions used in the specified country.

Syntax: `COUNTRY=`*`code`*`[,[`*`codepage`*`][,[`*`path`*`]COUNTRY.SYS]`

code

The country code

codepage

The character set (code page) for the country. If you do not specify a character set but you include [path]COUNTRY.SYS, you must include the extra comma that would have separated the country code from the codepage. For example, `COUNTRY=061,,\DOS\COUNTRY.SYS`.

path

The location of the COUNTRY.SYS file, which contains country information.

Each country code is limited to certain character sets. For, example, you can use only character set 437 or 850 with country code 003. The first character set listed for each country or language is the default character set.

Country or language	*Country code*	*Character sets*
Belgium	032	850, 437
Brazil	055	850, 437
Canadian-French	002	863, 850
Czechoslovakia	042	852, 850
Denmark	045	850, 865
Finland	358	850, 437
France	033	850, 437
Germany	049	850, 437
Hungary	036	852, 850
International English	061	437, 850
Italy	039	850, 437
Latin America	003	850, 437
Netherlands	031	850, 437
Norway	047	850, 865
Poland	048	852, 850
Portugal	351	850, 860
Spain	034	850, 437
Sweden	046	850, 437
Switzerland	041	850, 437
United Kingdom	044	437, 850

Country or language	*Country code*	*Character sets*
United States	001	437, 850
Yugoslavia	038	852, 850

Notes: COUNTRY is part of the somewhat complicated procedure for customizing a computer for a language other than American English. The others are KEYB, MODE, and NLSFUNC.

CTTY

Type: Internal command

Purpose: Change control of your computer to a different terminal device. For example, use a remote terminal connected to COM1 instead of the keyboard and monitor.

Syntax: `CTTY device`

`device`

Assign control of the computer to a terminal device plugged into this port.

Use one of these device names:

`AUX` or `COM1`
`COM2`
`COM3`
`COM4`
`PRN` or `LPT1`
`LPT2`
`LPT3`
`CON`

`CON`

specifies the computer console. Use CTTY CON (from the current terminal device) to restore control to the keyboard and monitor.

Notes: Before assigning a serial port as the terminal device port, use MODE to set baud rate, parity, number of data bits, and stop bits for that serial port.

The CTTY command goes back to the days when a computer used a teletypewriter (TTY) rather than a video display and keyboard as a terminal device. If two TTYs were connected to two ports on the computer, CTTY would instruct the computer to Change to the TTY plugged into a different port. As far as the computer is concerned, there's not much difference (except the speed of response and some mechanical considerations) between the CON ports (video display and separate keyboard) and one of the parallel or serial ports.

To specify a different port as the standard terminal device, use this command in CONFIG.SYS: (See listing for COMMAND.)

```
SHELL=COMMAND.COM device
```

DATE

Type: Internal command

Purpose: Display or change the date.

Syntax: `DATE [mm-dd-yy]`

or

`[mm.dd.yy]`

or

`[mm/dd/yy]`

mm-dd-yy	Set the date to the specified month, day and year.
mm	the month (1–12)
dd	the day (1–31)
yy	the year (80–99 or 1980–2099)

DATE accepts periods, hyphens, or slash marks to separate the month, day and year. The date format is different for different COUNTRY settings. Use the COUNTRY command to change the date format.

Notes: In MS-DOS 6, DATE accepts years up to 2099.

DBLSPACE

Type: External command

Purpose: Start the DoubleSpace program to compress one or more disk drives, or configure drives compressed with DoubleSpace.

Syntax: `DBLSPACE`

Enter DBLSPACE by itself to display the DoubleSpace menu, which includes all of the options that are available from the DOS prompt.

DBLSPACE /CHKDSK

Purpose: Run a status check on a compressed drive.

Syntax: `DBLSPACE /CHKDSK [/F] [`*`drive`*`:]`

or

`DBLSPACE /CHK [/F] [`*`drive`*`:]`

`/F`

Fix errors on the compressed drive.

`drive``:`

The drive letter of the disk where the status check will run.

DBLSPACE /COMPRESS

Purpose: Compress a disk.

Syntax: `DBLSPACE /COMPRESS `*`drive1`*`: [/NEWDRIVE=`*`drive2`*`:] [/RESERVE=`*`size`*`]`

or

`DBLSPACE /COM `*`drive1`*`: [/NEWDRIVE` (or NEW) `=`*`drive2`*`:] [/RESERVE` (or RES) `=`*`size`*`]`

`drive1``:`

Compress the drive with this drive letter.

`/NEWDRIVE=`*`drive2`*`:` or `/NEW=`*`drive2`*`:`

Assign this drive letter to the uncompressed drive. The default is the next available drive letter.

`/RESERVE=`*`size`* or `/RES=`*`size`*

Leave the specified number of megabytes uncompressed.

DBLSPACE /CONVSTAC

Purpose: Convert a Stacker volume to DoubleSpace format.

Syntax: `CONVSTAC` (or CONVST) `=`*`stacvol drive1`*`:[/NEWDRIVE` (or NEW) `=`*`drive2`*`:][/CVF=`*`sss`*`]`

`drive1``:`

Convert the Stacker volume on the hard disk with this drive letter.

`/CONVSTAC=`*`stacvol`* or `/CONVST=`*`stacvol`*

Convert to the specified Stacker volume.

`/NEWDRIVE=`*`drive2`*`:` or `/NEW=`*`drive2`*`:`

The drive letter of the converted drive. The default is the next available drive letter.

`/CVF=`*`sss`*

The file extension of the new compressed volume file. Use a number in the range from 000 to 254.

DBLSPACE /CREATE

Purpose: Create a new compressed drive using free space on an uncompressed drive.

Syntax: `DBLSPACE /CREATE` (or CR) *`drive1`*`:[/NEWDRIVE` (or N) `=`*`drive2`*`:[/SIZE` (or /SI) `=`*`size`*`][/RESERVE` (or RE) `=`*`size`*`]`

`drive1``:`

The uncompressed drive.

`/NEWDRIVE` (or /N) `=`*`drive2`*`:`

Assign the specified drive letter to the new compressed drive. The default is the next available drive letter.

`/RESERVE` (or /RE) `=`*`size`*

Leave the specified number of megabytes uncompressed on drive1.

`/SIZE` (or /SI) `=`*`size`*

Use the specified number of megabytes on the uncompressed drive to create the compressed drive.

Do not use both /RESERVE and /SIZE in the same command line. If neither switch appears on the command line, DoubleSpace will reserve 1 megabyte of free space.

DBLSPACE /DEFRAGMENT

Purpose: Defragment a compressed drive.

Syntax: `DBLSPACE /DEFRAGMENT [`*`drive`*`:]`

or

`DBLSPACE /DEF [`*`drive`*`:]`

`drive``:`

The drive letter to defragment.

DBLSPACE /DELETE

Purpose: Delete a compressed drive.

Syntax: `DBLSPACE /DELETE` *`drive`*`:`

or

`DBLSPACE /DEL` *`drive`*`:`

`drive``:`

The drive letter of the drive that the command will delete.

DBLSPACE /DELETE erases a file on the uncompressed drive that contains the compressed information, called a compressed volume file. If you delete a drive, you also delete all files stored on that drive.

If you delete a drive by mistake, immediately use the UNDELETE command to restore the compressed volume file. The file name is DBLSPACE.nnn (where nnn is some three-digit number).

DBLSPACE /FORMAT

Purpose: Format a compressed drive.

Syntax: `DBLSPACE /FORMAT` *`drive`*`:`

or

`DBLSPACE /F` *`drive`*`:`

`drive``:`

The drive letter of the drive that the command will format.

Formatting a compressed drive deletes all files stored on that drive. It is not possible to unformat a formatted compressed drive.

DBLSPACE /INFO

Purpose: Display information about a compressed drive.

Syntax: `DBLSPACE /INFO` *`drive`*`:`

or

`DBLSPACE` *`drive`*`:`

`drive``:`

The drive letter of the drive about which the command will display information.

DBLSPACE /LIST

Purpose: List all of the computer's drives, showing which are DoubleSpace volumes and which are physical volumes.

Syntax: `DBLSPACE /LIST`

DBLSPACE /MOUNT

Purpose: Assign a drive letter to a compressed volume file.

DoubleSpace normally mounts compressed volume files automatically, but it may be necessary to use the /MOUNT command to re-mount a file that has been unmounted, or a file on a diskette.

Syntax: `DBLSPACE /MOUNT` (or /MO) `[=`*`nnn`*`]` *`drive1`*`:[/NEWDRIVE` (or /NEW) `=`*`drive2`*`:]`

`/MOUNT` (or MO) `=`*`nnn`*

Mount the compressed volume file with this file extension. The default is 000, which will mount DBLSPACE.000.

`/NEWDRIVE` (or NEW) `=`*`drive2`*`:`

Assign this drive letter to the newly mounted drive. The default is the next available drive letter.

DBLSPACE /RATIO

Purpose: Change the compression ratio of a compressed drive.

Syntax: `DBLSPACE /RATIO` (or RA) `[=`*`r.r`*`]` `[`*`drive`*`:]`

or

`DBLSPACE /RATIO` (or RA) `[=`*`r.r`*`]` `[ALL]`

`/RATIO` (or RA) `=`*`r.r`*

Change the compression ratio to this number. The valid range is from 1.0 to 16.0. The default is the average actual compression ration for all files on the drive.

`drive``:`

The drive letter of the drive where the command will change the compression ratio.

`/ALL`

Change the compression ratio of all compressed drives.

It is not possible to use both *`drive`*`:` and `/ALL` in the same command line.

DBLSPACE /SIZE

Purpose: Change the size of a compressed drive.

Syntax: `DBLSPACE /SIZE` (or SI) `[=`*`size1`*`]` *`drive`*`:`

or

`DBLSPACE /SIZE` (or SI) `[/RESERVE` (or RES) `=`*`size2`*`]` *`drive`*`:`

`/SIZE` (or SI) *`=size1`*

Change the size of the specified drive to the specified number of megabytes of space on the uncompressed drive.

`/RESERVE` (or RES) *`=size2`*

Leave the specified number of megabytes of uncompressed space on the uncompressed drive.

It is not possible to use both a *size1* specification and `/RESERVE` on the same command line.

The default, when neither *`size1`* nor `/RESERVE` appears on the command line, is to make the drive as small as possible.

DBLSPACE /UNMOUNT

Purpose: Remove the assignment of a drive letter to a compressed volume file. Data on an unmounted drive is not accessible until it has been mounted again.

Syntax: `DBLSPACE /UNMOUNT [`*`drive`*`:]`

`drive``:`

Unmount the drive with this drive letter. The default is the current drive. It is not possible to unmount drive C.

Notes: DBLSPACE is a new command in MS-DOS 6.0. It's effect on apparent disk size is similar to that of Stacker or SuperStor, but it avoids some of their drawbacks.

DEBUG

Purpose: Start the Debug program to test an executable file, execute a script file, or use any of its interactive commands.

Syntax: To test a program

`DEBUG [`*`path`*`]`*`file`* `[`*`parameters`*`]`

`[`*`path`*`]`*`file`*

The file that DEBUG will test.

`parameters`

Any parameters required by the file.

To run a DEBUG script file:

```
DEBUG < [path]scriptfile
```

`[path]scriptfile`

The file that DEBUG will test.

To enter Debug commands:

```
DEBUG
```

When debug is running, it displays a hyphen as a prompt. At that prompt you can enter any of a large number of commands. To see what all of those commands are, you can simply enter the command ? and press Enter.

Parameters to use in DEBUG commands:

Spaces don't count to DEBUG. Adding spaces in your DEBUG commands can make them more readable, though, so we encourage you to follow our examples and add spaces. (The one exception is in a quoted string of characters, where each space will be interpreted by DEBUG as an ASCII 20h symbol.)

`address`

You can specify an address to DEBUG as a segment:offset pair of hexadecimal numbers, or as a single hexadecimal number. If you use only the single number, DEBUG will assume you wish to use the current value in one of its segment registers.

When executing an A, G, L, T, U, or W command, DEBUG will use the Code Segment (CS) register contents if no segment value is specified. In all other commands, DEBUG uses the value in its Data Segment (DS) register.

All four of DEBUG's registers (CS, DS, SS, and ES) have the same value initially. They can get changed either by using the R command or by running a program.

`range`

A range (of addresses) can also be specified two ways. One is to give the starting and ending addresses. Or, you can put the letter L after the starting address and then follow it with a single hexadecimal number specifying the length (in bytes) of the range. In either method you can give the starting address either as a segment:offset pair of hexadecimal numbers, or as a single hexadecimal number. If you specify an ending address you may only specify its offset portion; the segment is assumed to be the same as the starting address.

`numbers`

DEBUG assumes all numbers you enter in its commands are expressed in hexadecimal notation. You don't need any suffix or prefix to indicate this, and you can't force DEBUG to treat entered numbers as decimal values.

`list or string`

Some commands accept either a string of numbers or a string of characters. The string of numbers are assumed to be two-symbol hexadecimal values for successive bytes. The character string, which must be enclosed in a pair of single (') or double (") quotation marks, is interpreted a character at a time, with each character being replaced by the ASCII code value for that character. Thus the string

```
"A string"
'A string'
```

and

```
41 73 74 72 69 6E 67
```

are treated by DEBUG exactly the same.

DEBUG accepts the following commands:

?

Purpose: Display a list of Debug commands

A (Assemble)

Purpose: Accept assembler instructions (mnemonic equivalents to machine code instructions) and place the corresponding machine code bytes into memory. Each time you press Enter a new instruction is assembled and loaded into memory at the next address above the previous one. To stop the A command you must press Enter on an empty line.

Syntax: `A [address]`

address

The starting location where Debug will place the code. The default is the location where A last stopped.

DEBUG uses the standard Intel x86 assembler mnemonics. Segment overrides are specified as CS: DS: ES: or SS: A far return is RETF. String manipulations require explicit string size designations (e.g., MOVSW and MOVSB to move a string of words or bytes, respectively). The contents of a register or memory location is indicated by enclosing the register name or address in square brackets.

C (compare)

Purpose: Compare the content of two segments of memory.

Syntax: `C` *`first second`*

first

The first region of memory, specified as either a starting and an ending address, or a starting address and length. Here are three ways to express the same region:

```
45A9:0100 010F
```

explicit segment:offset and ending offset value

```
100 10F
```

implicit segment, explicit starting and ending offset values

```
100 L 10
```

using the length form of specification.

second

The starting address for the second region of memory.

D (Dump)

Purpose: Display the contents of a region of memory.

Syntax: `D [`*`range`*`]`

range

The range that Debug will display, expressed either as a starting and ending address, or as the starting address and length. The default is the 128 bytes that immediately follow the range shown by the last D command.

E (Enter)

Purpose: Enter data into memory.

Syntax: `E` *`address [data]`*

address

The address where Debug will begin to write the specified data.

data

The data that Debug will write at the specified location. Debug will accept data either as hexadecimal byte values or as a string of characters. Separate values with a space, comma or tab. Enclose character strings between single or double quotation marks.

If the command does not include data, Debug will display the address and its current contents and repeat the address on the next line. At that point your options are:

Replace the current data by typing new hexadecimal data.
Advance to the next byte by pressing the space bar.
Return to the preceding byte by pressing the hyphen key.
Stop the E command by pressing Enter.

F (Fill)

Purpose: Fill a segment of memory with data.

Syntax: `F` *`range list`*

range

The range that Debug will fill, expressed either as a starting and ending address, or as the starting address and length.

list

The data DEBUG is to use. If *list* is shorter than the range to be filled, DEBUG uses *list* over and over again until the region is filled. If *list* is longer than the region, any excess bytes in *list* are ignored.

G (Go)

Purpose: Execute a program in memory.

Syntax: `G[=address] [pause-address]`

address

The address of the program that Debug will run. The default is the current address in the CS:IP registers.

pause-address

The address of a break point in the program. A G command may include up to ten break points. At each break point, Debug stops, displays the contents of all registers, the status of all flags, and the last instruction executed.

To restart the execution of the program after a breakpoint, enter G again, this time with no parameters.

H (Hex Arithmetic)

Purpose: Perform hexadecimal arithmetic on a pair of numbers. Debug adds the two numbers together and subtracts the second number from the first. Both results appear on one line. The first number in the result line is the sum; the second number is the difference.

Syntax: `H value1 value2`

values

Any hexadecimal numbers in the range 0 through FFFFh.

I (Input)

Purpose: Read or display one byte from a specified port.

Syntax: `I` *`port`*

`port`

The address of the port from which Debug will read.

L (Load)

Purpose: Load data from a disk into memory.

Syntax: `L [`*`address`*`]`

or

`L` *`address drive start number`*

`address`

The location in memory where Debug will write the data.

`drive`

The disk drive that contains the data, expressed as a number (drive A = 0, B = 1, C = 2, etc.).

`start`

The hexadecimal value of the first sector that Debug will read from the disk.

`number`

The hexadecimal number of sectors that Debug will load.

M (Move)

Purpose: Copy data from one block of memory to a second block of memory.

Syntax: `M` *`source destination`*

`source`

The starting and ending addresses, or the starting address and length of the block of memory that Debug will read.

`destination`

The starting address of the block of memory where Debug will write the data.

The M command overwrites any data that is already in the `destination` locations.

N (Name)

Purpose: Name a file for loading or writing.

Syntax: `N [path]filename`

[path]filename

The name of the file to load or write.

To clear DEBUG's memory of a previously entered file name, use N without a filename.

O (Output)

Purpose: Send a byte to an output.

Syntax: `O port data`

port

The address of the output port.

data

The data, expressed as a byte value, that the program will send to the specified port.

P (Proceed)

Purpose: Execute one or more instructions.

Syntax: `P[=address][number]`

address

The location of the first instruction that Debug will execute. The default address is the current address in the CS:IP registers.

number

The number of instructions that Debug will execute. The default is one instruction.

Q (Quit)

Purpose: Quit Debug without saving the current file.

Syntax: `Q`

R (Register)

Purpose: Display or change one or more CPU register.

Syntax: To display all registers

```
R
```

To display or change specific registers

```
R register
```

To display a flag

```
RF
```

register

The name of the register that Debug will display. Valid register names are AX, BX, CX, DX, SP, BP, SI, DI, DS, ES, SS, CS, IP, PC. F ins

`F`

Display the current setting of each flag as a two-letter code:

Flag name	*Set*	*Clear*
Overflow	OV	NV
Direction	DN (decrement)	UP (increment)
Interrupt	EI (enabled)	DI (disabled)
Sign	NG (negative)	PL (positive)
Zero	ZR	NZ
Auxiliary Carry	AC	NA
Parity	PE (even)	PO (odd)
Carry	CY	NC

At the end of the list of codes, Debug displays a prompt. To change a flag or flags, type the new two-letter codes at the prompt, or press Enter to return to the Debug prompt.

S (Search)

Purpose: Search for a specified set of characters.

Syntax: `S range pattern`

range

The starting and ending addresses within which Debug will search.

pattern

The pattern of byte values or the string of characters that Debug will search for. To search for more than one byte value, separate them with spaces or commas. To search for a character string, enclose the string within quotation marks.

T (Trace)

Purpose: Execute an instruction and show the contents of registers and the status of flags.

Syntax: `T[=address] [number]`

address

The address where Debug will start tracing instructions. The default is the address specified in the program's CS:IP registers.

number

The number of instructions that Debug will trace, expressed as a hexadecimal number. The default value is 1.

U (Unassemble)

Purpose: Examine a segment of machine code and display it as a series of source statements. The Unassembled code resembles a listing of assembly language.

Syntax: `U [range]`

range

The starting and ending addresses of the code that Debug will disassemble. The default is the 20h bytes at the first address after the address displayed in the last U command.

W (Write)

Purpose: Write data to disk.

Syntax: `W [`*address*`]`

or

`W` *address drive start number*

address

The beginning address in memory of the file that Debug will write to the disk. The default value is CS:100.

drive

The disk drive where debug will write the file.

start

The hexadecimal number of the first sector where Debug will write the file.

number

The number of sectors where Debug will write.

> **Warning:** Using the W address drive start number command format bypasses the MS-DOS file handler. Unless you are certain you are using the correct values, don't use that form of this command. Your data, and even your ability to access your disk, is at risk otherwise.

XA (Allocate Expanded Memory)

Purpose: Allocate some expanded memory. DEBUG will return a handle number by which this memory is to be referred in future (until it is deallocated).

Syntax: `XA [`*pages*`]`

pages

The number of 16-kilobyte pages that Debug will allocate.

XD (Deallocate Expanded Memory)

Purpose: Deallocate the expanded memory corresponding to a particular handle number.

Syntax: `XD` *`handle`*

handle

The handle that Debug will deallocate.

XM (Map Expanded Memory)

Purpose: Map a logical page of expanded memory to a physical page of expanded memory.

Syntax: `XM [`*`logical page`*`] [`*`physical page`*`] [`*`handle`*`]`

logical page

The number of the logical page of expanded memory.

physical page

The number of the physical page.

handle

The handle that controls the specified logical page.

XS (Expanded Memory Status)

Purpose: Display the current status of expanded memory.

Syntax: `XS`

The display shows the number of pages allocated to each handle, and the frame segment numbers of each physical page.

DEFRAG

Type: External command

Purpose: Reorganize storage of files on a disk to eliminate fragmented files.

Syntax:

```
DEFRAG [drive:]
[F/][/S[:]ordercode][/V][/B][/SKIPHIGH][/LCD¦/BW][/G0]
```

or

```
DEFRAG [drive:][/U][/V][/B][/SKIPHIGH][/LCD¦/BW¦/G0]
```

DEFRAG with no switches or variables starts the DEFRAG program in the default configuration.

drive

The drive letter of the disk that the program will defragment. The default is the current drive.

/F

Do not leave any empty spaces between files

/U

Leave empty space between files

/S

Specify the order in which DEFRAG will sort files within directories. If you do not specify an order, DEFRAG will use the existing order on the disk. The colon is optional. You can use any combination of ordercodes. If you specify more than one ordercode, do not use spaces to separate them.

ordercode

valid ordercodes are:

N	Alphabetical order by name
N-	Reverse alphabetical order by name
E	Alphabetical order by file extension
E-	Reverse alphabetical order by file extension
D	Date and time, earliest first
D-	Date and time, most recent first
S	Size, smallest first
S-	Size, largest first

/B

Restart ("boot") the computer when defragmenting is complete.

/V

Verify that the new copies of files are written correctly. Note that this slows down the DEFRAG process.

/SKIPHIGH

Load DEFRAG into conventional memory. If you don't specify /SKIPHIGH, DEFRAG will load into upper memory if space is available.

/LCD

Use a color scheme optimized for a liquid crystal display.

/BW

Use a black and white color scheme.

/G0

Disable the graphic mouse and graphic character set.

Notes: DEFRAG is new in MS-DOS 6. It's a licensed version of the Speed Disk defragmenter that is a part of Symantec's Norton Utilities.

When DOS starts writing files on a clean disk, it places the data in adjacent sectors. Over time, as DOS deletes files and stores new files in whatever empty space is available, the files become fragmented (stored in non-contiguous locations). The time required to read data increases. Defragmentation reorganizes the data on a disk, so that every file is written to adjacent allocation units, thus reducing the time DOS requires to read files. If you have been operating your computer for several months or more without defragmenting the hard drive, the improvement in speed after running DEFRAG the first time will probably be impressive. After that, it's a good idea to defragment on a regular basis.

After running DEFRAG, it is not possible to use the standard level of UNDELETE to restore erased files.

DEL (ERASE)

Type: Internal command

Purpose: Delete a specified file or group of files.

Syntax: `DEL [path]filename [/P]`

or

`ERASE [path]filename [/P]`

[path]filename

The location and name of the file(s) the command will delete.

/P

Prompt for confirmation before deleting the file(s). DOS will ask you to confirm that you want to delete the specified file(s) with the message

`filename, Delete (YN)?`

To confirm the deletion, type Y for yes. To cancel the deletion, type N for no.

Notes: To delete a group of files at one time, use the * or ? wildcard characters. It's a good idea to use the /P prompt with wildcard file specifications.

If you enter a global wildcard (DEL *.*), DOS will warn you and ask you for confirmation with the message

All files in directory will be deleted! Are you sure (Y/N)?

If you delete a file or files by mistake, try using the UNDELETE command to retrieve it. If you haven't written over the file, or if you're using Delete Sentry, you will probably be able to recover deleted files. If you realize that you've deleted something by mistake, try running undelete as soon as possible.

DELTREE

Type: External command

Purpose: Delete a directory and all files and subdirectories within the directory.

Syntax: `DELTREE [/Y] path`

/Y

Do not ask for confirmation before deleting the directory.

`path`

The location of the directory that DELTREE will delete.

Notes: DELTREE is a faster way to delete an entire directory than DEL. Unlike DEL, DELTREE deletes all files in a directory, including those with hidden, system and read-only attributes, and all files in all subdirectories under the specified one.

Unlike RMDIR, which only works on empty directories, DELTREE deletes a directory and its files and subdirectories at the same time. DELTREE will not delete the current subdirectory, nor any parent of the current subdirectory. **However**, it **will** delete the files in those subdirectories!

DEVICE

Type: CONFIG.SYS command

Purpose: Load a device driver into memory.

DEVICE loads device drivers into conventional memory. Use DEVICEHIGH to load drivers into upper memory.

Syntax: `DEVICE=[path]filename [parameters]`

`[path]filename`

The location and name of the device driver that DEVICE will load.

`parameters`

The parameters needed by the device driver.

Notes: DEVICE loads device drivers into lower memory. MS-DOS includes about a dozen device drivers, including ANSI.SYS, DISPLAY.SYS, DRIVER.SYS, DBLSPACE.SYS, EGA.SYS, EMM386.EXE, HIMEM.SYS, INTERLNK.EXE, POWER.EXE, RAMDRIVE.SYS, SETVER.EXE, and SMARTDRV.EXE.

Many applications, hardware peripherals such as scanners and mice, and third-party utilities also include device drivers. They often have an "Install" program that adds these drivers to your CONFIG.SYS file. If it is necessary to add them manually, use the standard DEVICE or DEVICEHIGH syntax.

Certain device drivers must be loaded in a specific order. For example, EMM386.EXE will not work unless HIMEM.SYS has already been loaded.

Despite their names, COUNTRY.SYS and KEYBOARD.SYS are not device drivers. Do not try to use the DEVICE command to load these files.

If you use MEMMAKER to configure the computer's memory, run it again after you add device drivers to an existing CONFIG.SYS file. This will attempt to reconfigure memory for most efficient usage.

DEVICEHIGH

Type: CONFIG.SYS command

Purpose: Load a device driver into upper memory. If no upper memory blocks are available, DEVICEHIGH acts exactly like DEVICE, loading the specified device driver into lower memory.

In order to use DEVICEHIGH, your computer must have extended memory. Further, you must use HIMEM.SYS and EMM386.EXE, or a third party memory manager, such as QEMM or 386MAX to convert your extended memory into XMS memory, and then convert some of that into upper memory blocks. Finally, your CONFIG.SYS file must include the directive DOS=UMB. Unless all of these conditions are met, and enough free upper memory is available to load the specified device, DEVICEHIGH will load the device driver into lower memory.

Syntax: To load a device driver into high memory

```
DEVICEHIGH [path]filename [parameters]
```

To load a device driver into a specific region of high memory

```
DEVICEHIGH=[[/L:region1[,minsize1][;region2
[,minsize2] [/S]] [path]filename
```

filename

The name of the device driver that DEVICEHIGH will load into high memory.

parameters

The parameters needed by the device driver.

/L:region1, region2...

The region or regions of upper memory where DEVICEHIGH will load the device driver. For example, to load the driver to the largest free block in region 2, use /L:2. To load the device driver to two or more regions of memory, separate the region numbers with semicolons. For example, /L:2;4.

minsize

Some device drivers require more memory when they run than when they are loaded into memory. In that case, you must use the minsize parameter to specify the minimum size needed to run the driver. If that minimum size is not available in an upper memory block (UMB), DEVICEHIGH will load the driver into conventional memory.

/S

Shrink the UMB to the minimum size while loading the device driver. /S is used by the MEMMAKER program.

Notes: To load programs into upper memory, use the LOADHIGH command. To learn which regions are free, use MEM /F at the DOS prompt.

DIR

Type: Internal command

Purpose: Display or print a list of files and subdirectories in a directory. Normally, DIR displays one directory or file per line, including the file extension, the size of the file in bytes, and the date and time the file was created or most recently changed.

Syntax: `DIR [switch(es)]`

DIR with no path or filename displays the current directory.

`DIR path`

DIR followed by a path displays the directory at the location described by that path.

`DIR [path] filename`

DIR with a filename displays information about that file. If you use the ? and * wildcard characters, it will display all files that fit the specification. For example, if you enter DIR S*, it will display all files in the current directory that begin with S. If you enter DIR *.EXE, it will display all files that have the .EXE file extension.

Switches:

`/P`

Pause after each screen is full. Press a key to display the next screen

`/W`

Display the directory in wide format, with up to five files or directories on each line. When you use the /W switch, DIR does not display information about each file.

`/A`

Display all files, including hidden and system files.

`/A[:] code`

Display only the directories and files with specific attributes. The colon is optional. If you include more than one code, do not separate the code with spaces.

Codes:

H	Hidden files
-H	Files except hidden files
S	System files
-S	Files except system files
D	Directories
-D	Files only
A	Files ready for archive (backup)
-A	Files that have not changed since the last backup
R	Read-only files
-R	Files except read-only files

`/O`

Display directories in alphabetical order, followed by files in alphabetical order

`/O[:] code`

Display directories and files in the order specified by the code or codes. The colon is optional. If you specify more than one code, do not separate the codes with spaces.

Codes:

N	Alphabetical order by name
-N	Reverse alphabetical order by name
E	Alphabetical order by file extension
-E	Reverse alphabetical order by file extension
D	By date and time, oldest first
-D	By date and time, most recent first
S	By size, smallest first
-S	By size, largest first
G	Group directories before files
-G	Group files before directories
C	By compression ratio, lowest ratio first
-C	By compression ratio, highest ratio first

`/S`

Include all subdirectories of the specified directory

`/B`

Display brief listings. Show directory names and file names with file extensions only.

`/L`

Display directory names and file names in lower case characters.

`/C`

Display the compression ratio of files compressed with Doublespace.

It's possible to set DOS to your own standard set of DIR switches by placing a SET DIRCMD command in your AUTOEXEC.BAT. For example, if you want to turn on the "pause" switch every time you request a directory, add this line to your AUTOEXEC.BAT file:

```
SET DIRCMD=/P
```

Notes: If a directory has more than one screen full of files and subdirectories, the names will scroll up too quickly to read. Use either the /P (pause) or /W (wide) switch to make the display more useful.

DIR/O:C arranges directory names and file names in order of compression ratio, but it won't display the compression ratio unless you include the /C switch.

At the end of the list of directories and files, DIR shows the total number of files in the directory (including the current directory and the parent directory, which it lists as "." and "..") or the number of files in the number of files that meet the command specification, along with the number of bytes in the directory, and the amount of free space remaining on the disk. (DIR does not display the free space if it finds no files that match `[path] filename`.)

DISKCOMP

Type: External command

Purpose: Compare the contents of two diskettes.

DISKCOMP does not work with hard drives, or with disks having different capacities.

Syntax: `DISKCOMP [drive1: [drive2:]] [/1] [/8]`

`drive1: [drive2:]`

The drives that contain the diskettes that DISKCOMP will compare.

`/1` Compare only the first sides of the disks.
`/8` Compare only the first eight sectors per track.

Notes: If you do not specify any drives, DISKCOMP will use the current drive for both diskettes. If you specify only one drive, DISKCOMP will use the current drive for the second drive. If `drive1:` is the same as `drive2:` (either by your explicit specification or after DISKCOMP makes its assumptions), DISKCOMP will prompt you to insert the first and second diskettes to be compared alternately until it is finished.

Starting with Version 4.0 of DOS, DISKCOMP ignores the serial numbers of the disks it's comparing. So it will report two otherwise identical diskettes with different serial numbers as identical.

If DISKCOMP finds differences between the two disks, it gives error messages resembling

```
Compare error on
side n1, track n2
```

To compare individual files on the two disks, use the FC command.

DISKCOPY

Type: External command

Purpose: Copy everything on a diskette to another diskette. Format the target diskette if necessary.

DISKCOPY does not work with hard drives.

Syntax: `DISKCOPY [source: [destination:]] [/1] [/V]`

source

The drive letter of the source diskette

destination

The drive letter of the destination diskette.

/1

Copy the first side of the diskette only.

/V

Verify that the copy is accurate.

Notes: If you do not specify any drives, DISKCOPY will use the current drive for both diskettes. If you specify only one drive, DISKCOPY will use the current drive for the second drive. If you specify only one drive, DISKCOPY will use the current drive for the second drive. If *drive1*: is the same as *drive2*: (either by your explicit specification or after DISKCOPY makes its assumptions), DISKCOPY will prompt you to insert the first and second diskettes to be compared alternately until it is finished.

DISKCOPY overwrites the current contents of the destination disk as it copies data from the source disk. It will format an unformatted disk before copying data to it.

DISKCOPY puts a unique serial number on the destination disk. This serial number is the one exception to the rule that DISK-

COPY makes an exact copy of the source diskette, including fragmentation. This happens because DISKCOPY copies entire tracks from the source to the destination.

It's possible to run DEFRAG on the source diskette first or on the copy after it has been made. However, using the command

```
XCOPY source: destination: /S /E
```

is generally an easier way to get an undefragmented copy of a fragmented original, because XCOPY copies each file on the disk one file at a time. However, XCOPY won't copy hidden files or system files.

DISPLAY.SYS

Type: Device driver

Purpose: Support multiple character sets for the keyboard and video display.

Syntax:

```
DEVICE=[path]DISPLAY.SYS CON[:]=type[,codepage][,n][,m]
```

or

```
DEVICEHIGH=[path]DISPLAY.SYS CON[:]=type[,icodepage][,in][,im]
```

path

The location of DISPLAY.SYS

type

The type of video adapter. Valid types are EGA and LCD. EGA supports both EGA and VGA adapters.

codepage

The character set code page number. Valid types are:

437 United States
850 Multilingual (Latin I)
852 Slavic (Latin II)
860 Portugese
863 Canadian French
865 Nordic

n

The number of additional character sets the computer will support. Use the CHCP command to change code pages. The valid range is from 0 to 6 for EGA adapters, or 0 to 1 for LCD adapters.

m

The number of subfonts supported for each code page.

DOS

Type: (CONFIG.SYS directive)

Purpose: Loads MS-DOS into the high memory area, and/or directs DOS to manage the use of upper memory blocks (UMBs).

Syntax: `DOS=[HIGH¦LOW][,][UMB¦NOUMB]`

`HIGH`

Try to load part of DOS into the high memory area.

`LOW`

Load all of DOS in conventional memory.

`UMB`

Manage upper memory blocks.

`NOUMB`

Do not manage upper memory blocks.

The defaults are DOS=LOW and DOS=NOUMB.

You may combine the two functions in one line (DOS=HIGH,UMB) or put them in two separate lines (DOS=HIGH in one and DOS=UMB in the other).

HIMEM.SYS or another extended memory manager such as QEMM or 386MAX must be installed or the directives DOS=UMB or DOS=HIGH will have no effect. DOS=UMB also requires EMM386.EXE or some other UMB provider.

Notes: DOS=HIGH instructs DOS to load part of itself into the high memory area. This leaves more lower memory for programs.

DOS=UMB instructs DOS to manage upper memory blocks, which means that it can load programs and device drivers into upper memory, using DEVICEHIGH and LOADHIGH. If resident programs and device drivers are placed in upper memory, there will be more space left in lower memory for application programs.

DOSKEY

Type: External command

Purpose: Hold recent DOS commands in memory. When DOSKEY is running, you can recall earlier commands and edit the current command line.

Syntax: `DOSKEY [switch(es)] [macro=[text]]`

Switches:

`/REINSTALL`

Install a new copy of DOSKEY. If DOSKEY is already running, /REINSTALL clears the buffer.

`/BUFSIZE=size`

Set the buffer to the specified size, in bytes. The minimum size is 256 bytes. The default is 512 bytes.

`/MACROS`

Display a list of all DOSKEY macros.

`/HISTORY`

Display all commands stored in the buffer.

`/INSERT`

Insert new text into existing text.

`/OVERSTRIKE`

Replace existing text with new text.
You may specify /INSERT or /OVERSTRIKE, but not both. The default is /OVERSTRIKE.

`macro=[text]`

Create a macro to run one or more DOS commands. `Text` is the list of instructions to include in that macro.

When it is loaded into memory, DOSKEY will accept the following commands:

Up arrow	Recalling a command
Down Arrow	Recall the command immediately before the one displayed.
Page Up	Recall the command immediately after the one displayed.
Page Down	Recall the oldest command in the buffer.
Editing the current command line	Recall the most recent command in the buffer.
Left Arrow	Move back one character.
Right Arrow	Move forward one character.
Ctrl-Left Arrow	Move back one word.
Ctrl-Right Arrow	Move forward one word.
Home	Move to the beginning of the line.
End	Move to the end of the line.
Esc	Clear the command from the display.
F1	Copy one character from the last command typed.
F2[character]	Search forward in the last command typed for character, and insert the text up to but not including that character.
F3	Copy that portion of the most recent command to the left of the cursor.
F4[character]	Delete characters, from the cursor to the character to the right of character.
F5	Store the current command and clear the command line.
F6	Place a Ctrl-Z end-of-file character at the current position on the command line.
F7	Display all commands in the buffer, with a number for each.
Alt F7	Delete all commands from the buffer.
F8[string]	Search for a command. String may be the first character, or the first few characters of the command.

F9	Request a command by number. Use F7 to display command numbers.
Alt F10	Delete all macro definitions.

`Insert`

Turn Insert Mode on or off. When Insert Mode is active, characters typed into the middle of a command will push existing characters to the right instead of overwriting them. DOSKEY does not remain in Insert Mode from one command to the next; you must press the Insert key again to return to Insert Mode on the next command. When Insert Mode is active, the cursor is a square instead of the normal underline. To keep Insert Mode active all the time, use the /INSERT switch as part of the original DOSKEY command.

Notes: DOSKEY is a memory-resident program that holds commands in a memory buffer and allows a user to copy an earlier command at the current prompt. This can be a great convenience when typing repetitive commands and commands that change only slightly from one to the next.

DOSKEY uses about 3 kilobytes of memory, but it can be memory well spent if you often type commands at the DOS prompt. DOSKEY is an excellent candidate for your AUTOEXEC.BAT file.

DOSSHELL

Type: External command

Purpose: Run the DOS Shell program.

Syntax: `DOSSHELL [/T[:`*res*`[`*n*`]]] [/B]`

or

`DOSSHELL [/G[:`*res*`[`*n*`]]] [/B]`

`/T`

Start the shell in text mode.

`/G`

Start the shell in graphics mode.

`/B`

Start the shell in black and white.

`res[n]`

Set the screen resolution. For *`res`*, use L for low, M for medium, or H for high. For *n*, use a number to choose among resolutions available for your display adapter in the general range selected by *`res`*. Use the `Options` menu, `Display...` entry to learn what the possibilities are for your PC.

The following choices are typical for a VGA display:

`/G:L`	25 lines	`/T:L`	25 lines
`/G:M1`	30 lines	`/T:H1`	43 lines
`/G:M2`	34 lines	`/T:H2`	50 lines
`/G:H1`	43 lines		
`/G:H2`	60 lines		

Notes: DOSSHELL provides a graphical user interface without the overhead of Windows. DOSSHELL allows task swapping as well as point and shoot file manipulation.

DRIVPARM

Type: (CONFIG.SYS command)

Purpose: Designate the parameters DOS shall use in referencing the specified drive.

Syntax: `DRIVPARM=/D:`*`number`* `[`*`switch(es)`*`]`

`/D:`*`number`*

The physical drive number. For number, use 0 for drive A, 1 for drive B, 2 for drive C and so forth.

Switches

`/C`

Specifies that the drive and controller provide change line support to inform DOS when a disk in the drive has been changed.

`/F:factor`

The drive type. For *factor*, select one of the following numbers:

0 160K/180K or 320K/360K (5.25-inch diskette)
1 1.2 megabyte (5.25-inch diskette)
2 720k (3.5-inch diskette)
5 Hard drive
6 Tape drive
7 1.44 megabyte (3.5-inch diskette)
8 read/write optical disk
9 2.88 megabyte (3.5-inch diskette)

`/H:heads`

The maximum number of heads. For *heads*, use a value between 1 and 99

`/I`

Use a 3.5-inch diskette drive. Use /I if your ROM BIOS does not support 3.5-inch diskette drives.

`/N`

Specifies a non-removable block device

`/S:sectors`

Specifies the number of sectors per track. For *sectors*, use a value between 1 and 99

`/T:tracks`

Specifies the number of tracks per side

Notes: DRIVPARM changes how a drive or other storage device appears to your PC. In most cases, the installation software or documentation of a storage device will include specific DRIVPARM settings.

Installing the DRIVER.SYS device driver can accomplish much the same thing as using DRIVPARM, but DRIVER.SYS will create a phantom extra drive, using a new drive letter (and the original, physical drive will still be accessible under its original drive letter). DRIVPARM, in contrast, merely modifies the characteristics of the existing drive and does not add a new drive letter. DRIVPARM also does not use up any RAM, as a loadable device driver like DRIVER.SYS does.

ECHO

Type: Internal batch file command

Purpose: Turn command echoing on or off. In a batch file, display a message.

Syntax: `ECHO ON`

Turns command echoing on until the next ECHO OFF statement.

`ECHO OFF`

Turns command echoing off until next ECHO ON statement.

`@COMMAND`

Suppresses echoing of a particular line in a batch file.

`ECHO` *`message`*

Displays a message when the batch file runs.

`message`

The text of the message that will appear when the batch file runs.

Notes: In a batch file, DOS normally displays commands. Use @ECHO OFF as the first line of a batch file to suppress echoing of that and all subsequent lines.

To echo a blank line, enter ECHO followed by a period, with no space in between.

EDIT

Type: External command

Purpose: Run the DOS Editor full screen ASCII text editor.

Syntax: `EDIT [[`*`path`*`]`*`filename`*`] [/B] [/G] [/H] [/NOHI]`

`[`*`path`*`]`*`filename`*

The location and name of an ASCII text file. If the file already exists, EDIT opens it. If it does not exist, EDIT creates a new file with this name. If you do not specify a file, EDIT starts with no file loaded.

`/B`

Display in black and white.

`/G`

Use fastest screen updating for CGA.

`/H`

Display the highest possible number of lines of text.

`/NOHI`

Assume monitor can only display eight colors.

Notes: In order to run EDIT, the file QBASIC.EXE must be in the current directory, in the search path, or in the same directory as EDIT.COM.

If your monitor does not display shortcut keys, try using the /B switch with a CGA monitor, or the /NOHI switch on a system that does not support boldface characters.

Edit is a simple text editor that is frequently faster and easier to use than a full-fledged word processor. It does no formatting, saving text as a pure ASCII text file.

In addition to text editing, EDIT is a more flexible substitute for TYPE as a method of viewing the contents of text files.

EGA.SYS

Type: Device driver

Purpose: Save and restore the display on an EGA monitor, when the DOSSHELL or another task swapper is used.

Syntax: `DEVICE=[path]EGA.SYS`

path

The location of EGA.SYS.

Notes: Use this device driver only if you are using an EGA monitor and a task swapping program such as DOSSHELL or Windows.

Putting this device driver before your mouse driver saves some memory.

EMM386

Type: External command

Purpose: Enable or disable EMM386 expanded memory support; enable or disable Weitek coprocessor support.

CONFIG.SYS must include the EMM386.EXE device driver for this command to work.

Syntax: At DOS prompt or in batch file

```
EMM386 [ON¦OFF¦AUTO] [W=ON¦OFF]]
```

`ON`

Make the EMM386.EXE device driver active (this is the default).

`OFF`

Disable the EMM386.EXE device driver.

`AUTO`

Make expanded memory support active when a program calls for it.

`W=ON`

Make Weitek coprocessor support active

`W=OFF`

Disable Weitek coprocessor support (this is the default)

Enter EMM386 with no switches to display the current status of the EMM386 device driver.

Syntax: CONFIG.SYS

```
DEVICE=[path]EMM386.EXE [switch] [memory]
[MIN=size] [W=ON¦OFF] [variables] [NOEMS]
[NOVCPI] [NOHIGHSCAN] [/VERBOSE or /V] [NOHI]
```

Switch values

`ON`

Activate the EMM386.EXE device driver (this is the default).

`OFF`

Disable the EMM386.EXE device driver.

`AUTO`

Activate expanded memory support and upper memory support when a program calls for it.

`memory`

The maximum amount of expanded (EMS/VCPI) memory, in kilobytes.

`MIN=size`

The minimum amount of expanded (EMS/VCPI) memory, in kilobytes. EMM386.EXE reserves this amount of extended memory.
The minimum size value is 0. The maximum value is equal to memory. Default value is 256. If the value of size is greater than the value of memory, EMM386.EXE will use the value specified by size.

`W=ON`

Make Weitek coprocessor support active.

`W=OFF`

Disable Weitek coprocessor support (this is the default).

Variables

`Mx¦FRAME=address¦/Paddress`

Three different ways to specify the address of the page frame.

`Mx`

x may be one of the following hexadecimal addresses:

1 => C000h	2 => C400h
3 => C800h	4 => CC00h
5 => D000h	6 => D400h
7 => D800h	8 => DC00h
9 => E000h	10 => 8000h
11 => 8400h	12 => 8800h
13 => 8C00h	14 => 9000h

Use values from 10 to 14 only on computers with at least 512k of memory.

`FRAME=address`

Specify the page frame address directly. Use one of the hexadecimal values listed under Mx, or use FRAME=NONE to disable the page frame. FRAME=NONE may cause programs that require expanded memory to work improperly.

`/Paddress`

Specify the page frame address directly. Use one of the hexadecimal values listed under Mx.

`Pn=address`

Specify the starting segment address of page *n*, using one of the hexadecimal values listed above under Mx.

`X=mmmm-nnnn`

Exclude a range of memory segment addresses from use by an EMS page or UMBs.

mmmm start of the range
nnnn end of the range

`I=mmmm-nnnn`

Include a range of memory segment addresses for use by an EMS page or UMBs.

mmmm start of the range
nnnn end of the range

`B=address`

Set the lowest address for EMS swapping of 16-kilobyte pages into conventional memory ("banking").

`L=minXMS`

Set the minimum amount of extended memory available after you load EMM386.EXE, in kilobytes.

`A=altregsets`

Set the number of high-speed alternate register sets to allocate to EMM386.EXE (for multitasking). Minimum value is 0, maximum value is 254. The default value is 7. Each alternate register set takes up an additional 200 bytes of memory.

`H=handles`

Set the number of handles EMM386.EXE can use. Minimum is 2; maximum is 255. The default is 64.

`D=dma`

Set the amount of memory to be reserved for buffered direct memory access (DMA), in kilobytes. The value of DMA should be big enough for the largest DMA transfer that will take place while EMM386.EXE is active. The minimum value is 16, maximum value is 256. The default is 16 kilobytes.

`RAM=mmmm-nnnn`

Use this range of hexadecimal segment addresses for upper memory blocks (UMBs). If no range is specified, EMS386.EXE will use any available extended memory.

mmmm	start of the range
nnnn	end of the range

`WIN=mmmm-nnnn`

Reserve this range of memory segment addresses for Microsoft Windows instead of EMM386.EXE. If the range of X=mmmm-nnnn overlaps this range, the X switch takes precedence.
mmmmstart of the range
nnnnend of the range

`ROM=mmmm-nnnn`

Use this range of memory segment addresses for shadow RAM as read-only memory (ROM). This can speed up your system operation if it does not already use shadow RAM

mmmm	start of the range
nnnn	end of the range

`NOEMS`

Provide access to upper memory (UMB), but not to expanded memory.

`NOVCPI`

Do not support VCPI (Virtual Control Program Interface) applications. You must include both NOEMS and NOVCPI to disable VCPI support. These two switches will cause EMM386.EXE to ignore the memory and MIN parameters.

`NOHIGHSCAN`

Do not scan the upper memory area for available memory. Use this switch only when you have difficulty using EMM386.EXE.

`/VERBOSE or /V`

Display status and error messages while loading EMM386.EXE.

`NOHI`

Do not load EMM386.EXE into the upper memory area.

Notes: EMM386 creates upper memory blocks (UMBs), which DOS=UMB manages to allow programs and device drivers to load into upper memory, using DEVICEHIGH and LOADHIGH. This leaves more space in conventional memory for application programs.

Never use EMM386 and a third party memory manager like 386MAX or QEMM at the same time.

`ERASE`

This command is identical to DEL.

EXIT

Type: Internal command

Purpose: Quit COMMAND.COM and return to the program or command interpreter that started COMMAND.COM.

If you started COMMAND.COM with the /P switch, EXIT does nothing.

Syntax: `EXIT`

Notes: If you "drop to DOS" from an application, use EXIT to return to the application.

EXPAND

Type: External command

Purpose: Expand a compressed file.

Syntax: `EXPAND [path]filename [...] destination`

`[path]filename [...]`

The file or files that EXPAND will uncompress.

`destination`

Write the expanded file or files to this location. If destination includes a file name, use that file name for the expanded file. If you specify more than one filename, you must only specify a destination location, but no destination filenames. In that case, EXPAND will create filenames for you.

Notes: Use this command to expand the files on the Setup disks supplied with MS-DOS 6.0. These compressed files have file extensions that end with an underscore character (_). EXPAND is especially useful for transferring files from the Setup disks to a hard drive without running the whole DOS installation routine again. You will have to give the destination file names, or else rename the files once they have been expanded, as EXPAND does not replace the final underscore with the appropriate letter.

FASTHELP

Type: External command

Purpose: Gives a minimal amount of help on DOS commands

Syntax: `FASTHELP commandname`

or

`FASTHELP`

Notes: See HELP for more information on the DOS help facilities.

FASTOPEN

Type: External command

Purpose: Hold the names and locations of files in a memory buffer to reduce the time needed to open frequently used files.

Syntax: `FASTOPEN` *`drive`*`:[[=]`*`n`*`] [`*`drive`*`:[[=]`*`n`*`]][...] [/X]`

`drive`

Track files from this disk drive. You may specify more than one drive.

`n`

The number of files to track at one time. The minimum value is 10; maximum is 999. The default value is 8.

`/X`

Hold the file information in expanded memory instead of conventional memory.

Notes: FASTOPEN stores the name and location of each file in a name cache as it is opened. Since DOS is able to find files in the name cache more quickly than in a large directory, it reduces the time needed to find and open a file.

FASTOPEN does not work over a network or on diskettes. Do not use FASTOPEN with the DOS Shell. The combination can lock up your computer.

Better still, don't use FASTOPEN at all; use a good disk cache—SMARTDRV or a third party alternative—instead. (FASTOPEN is known to cause file corruption in some not-well-understood situations.)

FC

Type: External command

Purpose: Compare two files and display the differences between them.

Syntax: For an ASCII comparison

`FC [`*`switch(es)`*`] [/`*`lines`*`] [`*`path`*`]`*`file1`*` [`*`path`*`]`*`file2`*

For a binary comparison

`FC /B [`*`path`*`]`*`file1`*` [`*`path`*`]`*`file2`*

Switches

`/A`

Abbreviate the output of the comparison. Rather than displaying every line that is different, display only the first and last line of each set of differences.

`/C`

Ignore upper and lower case.

`/L`

Compare files in ASCII mode.

`/LB`*`n`*

Compare up to *n* lines. If there are more than *n* consecutive lines that have differences, FC will cancel the comparison.

`/N`

Display line numbers during an ASCII comparison.

`/T`

Do not expand tabs to spaces. If this switch is not present, FC will treat tabs as spaces, with tab stops every eight character positions.

`/W`

Compress white space. Treat consecutive tabs and spaces as a single space during the comparison. Ignore white space at the beginning and end of a line.

`/`*`lines`*

The number of lines that must match before FC treats the files as resynchronized. If a smaller number of lines match, FC will display the matching lines as differences. Default is 2 lines.

`/B`

Compare in binary mode, byte by byte. Do not try to resynchronize after finding a mismatch.

`[`*`path`*`]`*`file1`*

The first of the two files to compare

`[`*`path`*`]`*`file2`*

The second of the two files to compare

Binary comparison is the default for files with a file extension of .EXE, .COM, .SYS, .OBJ, .LIB, and .BIN. FC performs an ASCII comparison for all other file extensions unless the /B switch is included on the command line.

You can use the * wildcard character to compare more than one pair of files with a single command. For example, to compare all of the batch files in two directories, enter:

```
FC path1\*.BAT path2\*.BAT
```

To compare a single batch file to all other batch files in a directory, enter:

```
FC *.BAT NEWFILE.BAT
```

Notes: For ASCII files, FC displays the sections of the two files that are not identical, starting with the last identical line, and ending with the first line where the two files are again identical.

If the two file are different for more than about fifty lines, FC will stop and report that the files are "too different."

For binary files, FC shows the hexadecimal address of each non-identical pair of bytes, measured from the beginning of the files, and the hexadecimal values of the two bytes.

FCBS

Type: CONFIG.SYS directive

Purpose: Specify the number of File Control Blocks (FCBs) that can be open at the same time.

Syntax: `FCBS=`*`blocks`*

blocks

The number of FCBs that may be open at one time. Minimum value is 1, maximum is 255. The default value is 4.

Notes: If a program that uses file control blocks tries to open more files than FCBS allows, DOS will close programs that were already open.

You can save a small amount of lower memory if you are not going to run any programs that need FCBs by setting FCBS=0.

FDISK

Type: External command

Purpose: Configure hard disk partitions.

Syntax:

```
FDISK
```

or

```
FDISK /STATUS
```

or

```
FDISK /MBR  {Undocumented}
```

The FDISK command without the switch starts the hard disk partitioning program. The program can create partitions, make a partition active, delete a partition, and display partition data.

`/STATUS`

Display partition information about the computer's hard disk without starting the FDISK program.

`/MBR`

Rebuild master boot record program without changing data stored in the master partition table in that sector.

FDISK does not work on a drive created with the SUBST command, or on a network or Interlnk drive. If DoubleSpace is running, FDISK displays the uncompressed size of the drives rather than the compressed size.

Notes: Use FDISK to reconfigure a hard disk, by changing the number or size of partitions and DOS logical drives. Maximum partition size is 2 gigabytes.

Before running FDISK, back up the data on that drive. An accidental deletion of a drive or partition will wipe out access to all the data that had been in that drive or partition.

The /STATUS switch is newly documented in DOS, but has been supported since version 4. Its original purpose was to enable the SELECT program (a predecessor to SETUP) to read the partition table easily.

The /MBR switch is still undocumented. Use the /MBR switch to remove a computer virus that is a partition table infector. This can work when no other method of virus removal will, and it will salvage all of the data on your hard disk—plus it only takes a few seconds.

FILES

Type: CONFIG.SYS directive

Purpose: Specify the number of files that DOS can access at one time.

Syntax: `FILES=x`

x

The number of files that DOS can access at the same time. Minimum value is 8, maximum value is 255. The default value is 8.

Notes: FILES sets the maximum number of files that DOS can have open at one time. DOS uses at least three files before any application runs.

Individual programs are limited to using 20 files (unless they have been specially coded to support more). The primary use for setting FILES to a larger number is if you use multitasking or task swapping.

Each additional file handle after the first eight ties up 48 bytes of low DOS memory. Therefore, there's a slight memory consumption by using a very high FILES setting.

FIND

Type: External command (filter)

Purpose: Locate and display a specific string of characters in a file or files.

Syntax: `FIND [/V] [/C] [/N] [/I] "string" [[path]filename[...]]`

/V

Display all lines that do not contain the string.

`/C`

Display only a count of lines that contain the string.

`/N`

Display the line number preceding each line that contains the string.

`/I`

Ignore upper and lower case.

`"string"`

Locate and display this group of characters. string must be enclosed in quotation marks.

`filename`

Search for string in this file.

Notes: FIND doesn't recognize the * and ? wildcard characters. To accomplish the effect of a wildcard file specification, use the FOR...IN...DO construct (either in a batch file or at the DOS prompt).

The /C and /V switches together instruct FIND to display a count of lines that do not contain the string. In a command line with both /C and /N, FIND will ignore /N.

If you don't use the /I switch, FIND will treat upper and lower case versions of the same letters as different characters.

FOR

Type: Batch file command

Purpose: Run a specified command for each file in a set of files.

Syntax: From the command prompt

```
FOR %variable IN (file set) DO command [parameters]
```

In a batch file

```
FOR %%variable IN (file set) DO command [parameters]
```

`variable`

Any arbitrary character except the numerals 0 through 9. FOR will replace *`%variable`* or *`%%variable`* with every file or text string in file set, and run command.

(file set)

One or more file names or text strings. The file name or text string must be surrounded by parentheses.

command[*parameters*]

The command to perform on file set.

For example, to expand all files that end with the file extension .EX_ and place the expanded files in the subdirectory C:\DOS, use this command at the DOS prompt:

```
FOR %R IN (*.EX_) DO EXPAND %R C:\DOS
```

In a batch file, use this command line:

```
FOR %%R IN (*.EX_) DO EXPAND %%R C:\DOS
```

Notes: A FOR command must include both an IN clause and a DO clause.

FORMAT

Type: External command

Purpose: Format a diskette or hard drive.

Syntax:

```
FORMAT drive: [/V[:label]] [/Q] [/U] [/F:size] [/B¦/S]

FORMAT drive: [/V[:label]] [/Q] [/U]
[/T:tracks /N:sectors] [/B¦/S]

FORMAT drive: [/V[:label]] [/Q] [/U] [/1] [/4] [/B¦/S]

FORMAT drive: [/Q] [/U] [/1] [/4] [/8] [/B¦/S]
```

drive

Format the disk in the drive with this drive letter.

/V:*label*

Place this volume label on the disk.

/Q

Perform a quick format. Zero out the FAT and the root directory, but do not scan for bad sectors. Use /Q only to reformat a disk that has been previously formatted.

`/U`

Perform an unconditional format. Destroy all existing data on the disk. A disk formatted with the /U switch cannot be unformatted.

`/F:`*`size`*

The size of the floppy disk, in kilobytes or megabytes. For size, use one of the following:

160	160k	160kb			
180	180k	180kb			
320	320k	320kb			
360	360k	360kb			
720	720k	720kb			
1200	1200k	1200kb	1.2	1.2m	1.2mb
1440	1440k	1440kb	1.44	1.44m	1.44mb
2880	2880k	2880kb	2.88	2.88m	2.88mb

`/B`

Reserve space for the hidden system files IO.SYS and MSDOS.SYS. In earlier versions of MS-DOS, the /B switch was required before using the SYS command. It is no longer required in MS-DOS 6.0.

`/S`

Copy the system files (IO.SYS. MSDOS.SYS and COMMAND.COM from the startup drive to the newly formatted disk.

`/T:`*`tracks`*

Create this number of tracks on the disk. If possible, use the /F switch instead of /T and /N.

`/N:`*`sectors`*

Create this number of sectors per track. If possible, use the /F switch instead of /T and /N.

`/1`

Format one side of a floppy disk

`/4`

Format a 5.25-inch, 360kb double density floppy disk in a 1.2mb disk drive

/8

Format a 5.25-inch disk with 8 sectors per track. If your diskette must be compatible with MS-DOS versions earlier than 2.0, use this switch.

Notes: The /F switch for diskettes is easier to use than the /T and /N, but the older switches are still supported and they allow you to specify a non-standard format should you ever have a need to do so.

By including the /U switch, you direct FORMAT to save a copy of the disk's FAT and root directory information. This allows you to reverse FORMAT's effect by using UNFORMAT. You can only do this if FORMAT found room on the disk to store that safety information (it will tell you if it cannot), and if you use UNFORMAT before you have overwritten anything you value on that disk.

Use the /U switch to format a new disk for the first time. This reduces the formatting time, and there's no risk of lost data on a new disk.

GOTO

Type: Batch file command

Purpose: Jump to a specified line in a batch program. GOTO is usually used with IF or IF NOT.

Syntax: `GOTO label`

label

Jump to the specified line. Label lines in batch file programs begin with a colon. DOS treats these lines as labels and does not process them as commands.

For example, in the following batch file fragment, DOS jumps over several lines when it reaches the GOTO command (so you would only see the last ECHO line's output if you ran a batch file including this code):

```
...
GOTO BLAZES
ECHO Nothing happens on this line.
ECHO Nor on this one, since it is never executed.
```

```
ECHO Still nothing happening here.
:BLAZES
ECHO Something happens here.
...
```

Notes: GOTO is frequently used in an IF command, to instruct the batch file processing to jump to the labeled line when a specified condition is met.

Label names may be of any length, but DOS will only use the first eight characters.

GRAPHICS

Type: External command

Purpose: Load a program to print the graphic information on your screen when you press Shift-PrtSc (or Print Screen on some keyboards).

Syntax: `GRAPHICS [`*type*`] [[`*path*`]`*profile*`] [/R] [/B] [/LCD] [/PB` or `/PRINTBOX:[STD¦LCD]`

type

The type of printer. The following values are valid:

COLOR1	IBM Personal Computer Color Printer with black ribbon
COLOR4	IBM Personal Computer Color Printer with RGB (red, green, blue, and black) ribbon
COLOR8	IBM Personal Computer Color Printer with CMY (cyan, magenta, yellow, and black) ribbon
HPDEFAULT	Any Hewlett-Packard PCL printer
DESKJET	Hewlett-Packard DeskJet printer
GRAPHICS	IBM Personal Graphics Printer, IBM ProPrinter, or IBM QuietWriter printer
GRAPHICSWIDE	

	IBM Personal Graphics Printer with an 11-inch-wide carriage
`LASERJET`	Hewlett-Packard LaserJet printer
`LASERJETII`	Hewlett-Packard LaserJet II printer
`PAINTJET`	Hewlett-Packard PaintJet printer
`QUIETJET`	Hewlett-Packard QuietJet printer
`QUIETJETPLUS`	Hewlett-Packard QuietJet Plus printer
`RUGGEDWRITER`	Hewlett-Packard RuggedWriter printer
`RUGGEDWRITERWIDE`	Hewlett-Packard RuggedWriterwide printer
`THERMAL`	IBM PC-convertible Thermal Printer
`THINKJET`	Hewlett-Packard ThinkJet printer

`[`*`path`*`]`*`profile`*

The printer profile file that contains information about all supported printers. If this parameter is omitted, MS-DOS will look for a file called GRAPHICS.PRO in the current directory and in the directory that contains GRAPHICS.COM.

`/R`

Print the image as it appears on the screen (white characters on a black background) rather than reversed (black characters on a white background). Black on white is the default.

`/B`

Print the background in color. This switch is valid for COLOR4 and COLOR8 printers.

`/LCD`

Print an image with liquid crystal display (LCD) aspect ratio instead of the CGA aspect ratio. The effect of this switch is the same as /PRINTBOX:LCD.

`/PB` or `/PRINTBOX:[STD¦LCD]`

Select print-box size. The PRINTBOX statement in the GRAPHICS.PRO file specifies the correct value.

Notes: Loading GRAPHICS will allow you to print a faithful copy of a graphics screen on your printer. To print a screen, press Shift-Print Screen (or just Print Screen). When GRAPHICS is not active, Shift-Print Screen will only cause the text on the screen to be printed on the printer.

There is no GRAPHICS option for printing to a Postscript printer.

HELP

Type: External command

Purpose: Display detailed information about a DOS command

Syntax: `HELP [/B] [/G] [/H] [/NOHI] [`*`topic`*`]`

`/B`

Use a monochrome monitor with a color graphics card.

`/G`

Update a CGA screen as fast as possible.

`/H`

Display the maximum number of lines that the hardware will permit.

`/NOHI`

Use a monitor without high intensity support.

`topic`

The name of the command about which HELP will display information.

Notes: MS-DOS 6.0 contains two levels of online help. FASTHELP resembles the MS-DOS 5 HELP system. Invoked with no command line parameter, it just gives a scrolling list of all the DOS commands and a "one-liner" on each one. Invoking any DOS command as *`command`* `/?` or issuing the command `FASTHELP` *`command`* displays a brief description of each command. The DOS command HELP displays a great deal more information, including syntax details, examples, and general advice about commands and device drivers.

If you enter HELP without a topic, DOS will display an index of HELP topics. To select a help topic from the index, use the tab key and the up and down arrow keys to highlight the topic and press Enter, or click on the topic with your mouse.

Much of the information in HELP appeared in the printed manuals for earlier versions of MS-DOS, but there are significant changes you will only find in the HELP screens.

HIMEM.SYS

Type: Device driver

Syntax:

```
DEVICE=[path]HIMEM.SYS [/A20CONTROL:ON¦OFF]
[/CPUCLOCK:ON¦OFF] [/EISA] [/HMAMIN=m]
[/INT15=xxxx] [NUMHANDLES=n] [/MACHINE:xxxx]
[SHADOWRAM:ON¦OFF] [/VERBOSE or /V]
```

`/A20CONTROL:ON`

Instruct HIMEM to take control of the A20 line, even if A20 was active when HIMEM was loaded. This is the default.

`/A20CONTROL:OFF`

Instruct HIMEM to take control of the A20 line only in A20 was off when HIMEM was loaded.

`/CPUCLOCK:ON`

Correct a clock speed problem that may occur when HIMEM is installed.

`/CPUCLOCK:OFF`

Do not try to correct clock speed. This is the default.

`/EISA`

Allocate all available extended memory on an EISA computer with more than 16 megabytes of memory. This is automatic on other types of computers.

`/HMAMIN=m`

Set the minimum number of kilobytes of memory a program must require before HIMEM grants use of the high memory area. If this option is not specified, HIMEM will allocate the high memory area to the first application that requests it, regardless of the amount of memory required.

```
INT15=xxxx
```

Allocate this amount of extended memory, in kilobytes that DOS will reserve for the Interrupt 15h interface. The default value is 0.

```
NUMHANDLES=n
```

Set the number of extended memory block handles that HIMEM can use at the same time. The valid range is from 1 to 128. The default value is 32.

```
/MACHINE:xxxx
```

Identify the type of computer in use. HIMEM can detect most types automatically, but there are a few exceptions. The value of xxxx may be either a code or a number:

Computer	*Type Code*	*Number*
IBM AT or compatible	AT	1
IBM PS/2	PS2	2
Phoenix Cascade BIOS	PTLCASCADE	3
HP Vectra (A & A+)	HPVECTRA	4
AT&T 6300 Plus	ATT6300PLUS	5
Acer 1100	ACER1100	6
Toshiba 1600 & 1200XE	TOSHIBA	7
Wyse 12.5 Mhz 286	WYSE	8
Tulip SX	TULIP	9
Zenith ZBIOS	ZENITH	10
IBM PC/AT (alternative delay)	AT1	11
IBM PC/AT (alternative delay)	AT2	12
CSS Labs	CSS	12
IBM PC/AT (alternative delay)	AT3	13
Philips	PHILIPS	13
HP Vectra	FASTHP	14
IBM 7552 Industrial	IBMM7552	15
Bull Micral 60	BULLMICRAL	16
Dell XBIOS	DELL	17

`SHADOWRAM:ON`

Leave ROM code running from RAM.

`SHADOWRAM:OFF`

Disable shadow RAM.

`/VERBOSE` or `/V`

Display status and error message while HIMEM loads.

Notes: The default HIMEM values are all that you need for most computers. Major exceptions are the Acer 1100, the Wyse 12.5 286, and the IBM 7552 Industrial Computer, which require special /MACHINE:xxxx settings. If you are unsure which machine number to use, and if HIMEM reports when it loads that it cannot control the A20 line, you will simply have to try all the possible machine numbers. In that case, try them in this order:

Don't try to load HIMEM.SYS and a third party memory manager like QEMM or 386MAx at the same time.

IF

Type: Batch file command

Purpose: Perform a command if a specified condition is true.

Syntax: `IF [NOT] ERRORLEVEL` *`number command`*

or

`IF [NOT]` *`string1==string2 command`*

or

`IF [NOT] EXIST` *`filename command`*

`NOT`

Perform *command* only if the condition is false

`ERRORLEVEL` *`number`*

Perform *command* if a previous program returned an exit code equal to or greater than *number*.

command

Perform *command* when the condition is true (or if NOT is present, when it is false).

string1==string2

Perform *command* only if *string1* and *string2* are identical. The two equals signs are required. *String1* and *string2* may be strings of characters or arbitrary variables.

EXIST *filename*

Perform *command* only if *filename* exists.

Notes: To test for a specific errorlevel you can use the syntax

IF ERRORLEVEL *n* IF NOT ERRORLEVEL *n+1* GOTO *label*

INCLUDE

Type: CONFIG.SYS menu command

Purpose: Incorporate by reference the contents of one configuration block in another configuration block. This can save lines in defining multiple configurations that share many of the same lines. It can also badly confuse MemMaker.

Syntax: INCLUDE=*block*

block

The name of the configuration block that INCLUE will incorporate into the current block.

For example, the following menu in CONFIG.SYS uses the INCLUDE command to incorporate all of the No_Interlink commands into the Interlink option:

```
[Menu]
menuitem=Interlink,Interlink Active
menuitem=No_Interlink,Interlink Not Active

[No_Interlink]
dos=high
device=c:\dos\himem.sys
```

```
[Interlink]
include=No_Interlink
device=interlink.sys
```

Notes: Include and the other CONFIG.SYS menu commands are new in MS-DOS 6. See Chapter 11 for more details on their use.

INSTALL

Type: CONFIG.SYS command

Purpose: Load a memory-resident program (a TSR) from CONFIG.SYS instead of AUTOEXEC.BAT.

Syntax: `INSTALL=[`*`path`*`]`*`filename`*` [`*`parameters`*`]`

[*path*] *filename*

The location and name of the program to load.

parameters

Switches and variables that apply to filename.

Notes: All INSTALL directives are processed after all DEVICE directives and before the SHELL statement, no matter where they may be in your CONFIG.SYS file. The only importance location has is the relative order of several INSTALL directives (they get processed in the order they are read), or as a menu structure that may affect which INSTALL statements are read.

Since INSTALL loads programs before the command interpreter, the programs you can INSTALL are limited to those that don't insist on having a DOS environment (which is created by the command interpreter) or on using DOS interrupts that require the command interpreter's support.

Since INSTALLing a TSR does not create a copy of the DOS environment for it, that TSR may end up using slightly less memory than it would if it had been loaded from the AUTOEXEC.BAT file or at the DOS prompt. (Some TSRs will ask COMMAND.COM to deallocate their environment space. Loading those progams with an INSTALL statement will not save any RAM.)

INTERLNK

Type: External command

Purpose: Display the current Interlnk status or redirect requests for drives on the Interlnk client to the Interlnk server.

The INTERLNK.EXE device driver must have been loaded through a line in your CONFIG.SYS file (see next entry).

Syntax: For use at DOS prompt or in a batch file:

```
INTERLNK [client[:]=[server][:]]
```

Enter INTERLNK with no parameters to display the current Interlnk status. `INTERLNK client:=server:` redirects a drive connected to your computer through an Interlnk connection.

client

Assign this drive letter on this computer to a drive on the other computer.

server

The drive letter that the other computer uses to identify the drive that client identifies on this computer.

If you do not specify a server, Interlnk will cancel redirection of the client drive.

Notes: To run Interlnk, the INTERLNK.EXE device driver must be loaded, and the distant computer must be running INTERSVR. The Interlnk connection is in place whenever the device driver is loaded and the server is running INTERSVR; it's not necessary to enter a special command on the client.

To display the drive letters and port numbers that the client recognizes, enter INTERLNK with no parameters. You my treat those drives and ports just like the drives and ports on the local computer.

The local computer running INTERLNK is the client; the distant computer running INTERSVR is the server. Interlnk connection ties up the server and makes it unavailable for any other use until the Interlnk connection is terminated.

INTERLNK.EXE

Type: CONFIG.SYS device driver

Purpose: Connect to another computer through a parallel or serial port and share the other computer's disks and printer ports.

Syntax:

```
DEVICE or DEVICEHIGH=[path]INTERLNK.EXE [/DRIVES:n]
[/NOPRINTER] [/COM[:][n¦address]]
[/LPT[:][¦address]][/AUTO] [/NOSCAN] [/LOW]
[/BAUD:rate] [/V]
```

`[path]`

The location of INTERLNK.EXE.

`/DRIVES:n`

Redirect this number of drives. The default is 3. When Drives:0, Interlnk only redirects printers.

`/NOPRINTER`

Do not redirect printers. The default is redirection of all printer ports.

`/COM[:]n`

Transfer data between the server and the client through serial port COM*n*.

`/COM[:]address`

Transfer data between the server and the client through the serial port with this address.

If the /COM switch is present with no port or address specified, the client will search for a serial connection to the server. If no /COM or /LPT switch is present, the client will search for either a serial or parallel connection.

`LPT[:]n`

Transfer data through parallel port LPTn.

`LPT[:]address`

Transfer data through the parallel port with this address.

If the /LPT switch is present with no port or address specified, the client will search for a prallel connection to the server. If no /COM or /LPT switch is present, the client will search for either a serial or parallel connection.

`/AUTO`

Load INTERLNK.EXE into memory only if connection to a server is available at startup. The default will load INTERLNK.EXE regardless of whether a server connection is possible at startup.

`/NOSCAN`

Install INTERLNK.EXE in memory, but do not try to establish a connection at setup.

`/LOW`

Load INTERLNK.EXE into conventional memory. The default loads it into upper memory if it is available.

/BAUD:*rate*

Set the maximum baud rate for serial connection. Valid baud rates are 9600, 19200, 38400, 57600 and 115200. The default is 115200.

`/V`

Avoid conflicts with the computer's timer. Use /V if one of the two computers stops when you try to access a drive or port through an Interlnk connection.

INTERSVR

Type: Start the Interlnk server.

Purpose: Redirect the drives and printer ports on this computer to appear as additional drives and ports on a client computer connected to this computer through a parallel or serial port.

Syntax: To copy Interlnk files from one computer to another through a serial port connection

```
INTERSVR /RCOPY
```

To start the Interlnk server

INTERSVR [*drive*:] [/X=*drive*:] [/LPT:*n*¦*address*] [/COM:[*n*¦*address*] [/BAUD:*rate*] [/B] [/V]

`drive`

Redirect the drive with this drive letter to the other computer. The default is to redirect all drives.

`/X=drive`

Exclude specified drive from redirection.

`LPT:[n|address]`

Use parallel port LPT:n or the parallel port at this address to move data to the other computer. If you do not specify a port, Interlnk will use the first port it finds connected to a client.

`COM:[n|address]`

Use serial port COM:n or the serial port at this address to move data to the other computer.

`/BAUD:rate`

Specify the maximum serial baud rate. Valid values are 9600, 19200, 38400, 57600 and 115200. The default is 115200.

`/B`

Display the Interlnk server screen in black and white.

`/V`

Prevent a conflict with a computer's timer. If one of the computers stops running when you try to access a drive or printer port through a serial connection, add this switch to the command.

Notes: `INTERSVR /RCOPY` requires a connection between serial ports and the use of a 7-wire crossover cable.

Run Intersvr on the computer that you want to control from another computer; the computer that reads and writes files or uses the server's printer(s) must have the INTERLNK.EXE device driver loaded.

To quit INTERSVR and return control to the server, press Alt-F4 on the server.

INTERSVR disables task switching or multitasking environments. To restore these functions, quit the server.

KEYB

Type: External command

Purpose: Configure a keyboard for a specified language.

Syntax: `KEYB [code[,[charset][,[path]filename]]] [/E] [/ID:keyb]`

Syntax: CONFIG.SYS

`INSTALL=[path]KEYB.COM [code[,[charset][,[path]filename]]] [/E] [/ID:keyb]`

code

The two-letter country code that identifies a keyboard layout.

charset

The three-digit code of a character set.

[*path*]*filename*

The location and name of the keyboard definition file. The default is KEYBOARD.SYS.

/E

Use an enhanced keyboard with an 8086 computer.

/ID:*keyb*

Use the keyboard with this keyboard ID number. This switch is only valid for countries where more than one keyboard layout is used—France, Italy and the United Kingdom.

Country or language	*Keyboard layout*	*Character set (charset value) (code value)*	*Keyboard identification (ID:keyb value)*
Belgium	be	850, 437	
Brazil	br	850, 437	
Canadian-French	cf	850, 863	
Czech Republic	cz	852, 850	
Denmark	dk	850, 865	
Finland	su	850, 437	

Country or language	*Keyboard layout*	*Character set (charset value) (code value)*	*Keyboard identification (ID:keyb value)*
France	fr	850, 437	120, 189
Germany	gr	850, 437	
Hungary	hu	852, 850	
Italy	it	850, 437	141, 142
Latin America	la	850, 437	
Netherlands	nl	850, 437	
Norway	no	850, 865	
Poland	pl	852, 850	
Portugal	po	850, 860	
Slovakia	sl	852, 850	
Spain	sp	850, 437	
Sweden	sv	850, 437	
Switzerland	sf	850, 437 (French)	
Switzerland	sg	850, 437 (German)	
United Kingdom	uk	850, 437	166, 168
United States	us	850, 437	
Yugoslavia	yu	852, 850	

Notes: To start the computer with a keyboard other than the United States keyboard layout, include an INSTALL=KEYB.COM command in CONFIG.SYS, or a KEYB command in AUTOEXEC.BAT. To change keyboards after startup, use a KEYB command at the command prompt.

LABEL

Type: External command

Purpose: Create, change or delete the volume label on a disk.

Syntax: `LABEL [drive:] [label]`

Use the LABEL command with no parameters to display the current volume label and serial number.

drive:

The drive letter of the disk where LABEL will create or change the label.

label

The text of the new drive label. label may have up to 11 characters. Do not use the following characters in a label:

```
* ? / \ ¦ . , ; : + = [ ] ( ) & ^ < > "
```

Notes: This sets the volume label that is stored as an entry in the root directory with the directory attribute turned on. This name will be displayed on all CHKDSK, DIR, and VOL output for this disk. (There is another volume label stored in the DOS boot record for each volume, but so far no DOS utilities set or use that value.)

LABEL converts lower case letters to capitals. It's not possible to assign a label to a drive created with SUBST or ASSIGN.

LASTDRIVE

Type: CONFIG.SYS directive

Purpose: Define the maximum number of accessible drives.

Syntax: LASTDRIVE=*x*

x

The drive letter of the last accessible drive. The default is the letter that follows the last one in use. For example, if your computer has an A: drive and a C: drive, the default is D.

Notes: The LASTDRIVE setting can be used to allow for fictitious drives created by DRIVER.SYS or SUBST command, network drives and Interlnk drives as well as physical drives. DOS maintains a current directory structure data table in memory, and this directive tells it how large to make that table.

Some network software demands that LASTDRIVE not be set too large, as those programs wish to map network drives to letters beyond LASTDRIVE. Other network software insists on having all mapped drives less than LASTDRIVE.

LOADFIX

Type: External command

Purpose: Load a program above the first 64K of conventional memory and run the program. Use this command if a "Packed file corrupt" message appears.

Syntax: `LOADFIX [path]program[parameters]`

`[path]program`

Load this program.

`[parameters]`

Any parameters required by program.

Notes: LOADFIX consumes any free memory up to address 10000h (64KB) and then loads the specified program above that point. This is a clumsy and wasteful approach to the problem of access to the first 64k of lower memory. Rather than waste the first 64k with LOADFIX, force some other device driver or TSR to load low before loading the program that produces the `Packed file corrupt` message.

LOADHIGH (LH)

Type: Internal command

Purpose: Load a program into the upper memory area.

An XMS memory manager (such as HIMEM.SYS) and an upper memory block provider (such as EMM386.EXE) must be loaded before LOADHIGH can be used. You must also include the directive DOS=UMB in your CONFIG.SYS file.

Syntax: To load a program to upper memory

```
LOADHIGH [path]program [parameters]
```

To load a program to a specific region of upper memory

`LOADHIGH` (or LH)
`[/L:`*`region1`*`[,`*`minsize1`*`][;`*`region2`*`[`*`minsize2`*`]...`
`[/S]]  [`*`path`*`]`*`program`* `[`*`parameters`*`]`

`/L:`*`region1`*`[,`*`minsize1`*`][;`*`region2`*`[,`*`minsize2`*`]...`

The region or regions of upper memory where LOADHIGH will load the program. For example, to load the program to the largest free block in region 2, use /L:2. To load the program to two or more regions of memory, separate the region numbers with semicolons. For example, /L:2;4. To learn which regions are free, use the MEM/F at the DOS prompt.

`minsize`

Some programs require more memory when they run than when they are loaded into memory. In that case, you must use the minsize parameter to specify the minimum size needed to run the program. If that minimum size is not available in an upper memory block (UMB), LOADHIGH will load the program into conventional memory.

`/S`

Shrink the UMB to the minimum size while loading the program. /S is used by the MEMMAKER program.

`[`*`path`*`]`*`program`* `[`*`parameters`*`]`

The program that LOADHIGH is to load, with any parameters required by that program

Notes: In order to use LOADHIGH, an XMS manager and UMB provider must be loaded. The DOS programs are HIMEM.SYS and EMM386.EXE. You can use a third-party alternative such as QEMM or 386MAX that do both jobs in one program. It used to be true that the third party memory managers could only load programs high using their own loaders. Now, most of them will allow DOS to load programs into UMBs they have created.

Loading TSRs into upper memory leaves more space in conventional memory for applications. Use MEM/C to confirm that LOADHIGH was able to load the program into high memory.

To load device drivers into upper memory, use the DEVICEHIGH command.

MD

This command is identical to MKDIR.

MEM

Type: External command

Purpose: Display information about memory usage.

Syntax: `MEM [switch] [/PAGE or /P]`

MEM with no switch displays the current amounts of used and free memory.

switch values (use only one switch per command):

`/CLASSIFY or /C`

List the programs currently loaded into memory and summarize overall memory use.

`/DEBUG or /D`

List the programs and internal drivers currently loaded into memory and show the size, segment address, and type for each module.

`/FREE or /F`

List the free areas of conventional and upper memory, show the segment address and size of each free area of conventional memory, and the largest free UMB in each region of upper memory.

`/MODULE program or /M program`

List the areas of memory that the specified program currently uses, and show the address and size of each area.

`/PAGE or /P`

Pause after each screen of output.

Notes: Use MEM commands to learn how much space is available in conventional and high memory, how memory management tools such as MEMMAKER or QEMM have configured your computer's memory, and which programs and device drivers are resident in memory.

If the computer reports, `Out of memory` when you enter a command, use `MEM /C` to display a list of active programs and device drivers. It may identify programs that are still resident but no longer doing anything useful. Try removing them, either temporarily or permanently, and run the application again.

MEM displays are frequently longer than one full screen. Use the /P switch to pause when the screen is full.

Sometimes it's useful to print a MEM display before making a change to CONFIG.SYS, starting a resident program, or running MEMMAKER. This can be done by using a redirection command, such as `MEM /C > PRN`.

MEMMAKER

Type: External command

Purpose: Optimize the computer's memory usage by moving device drivers and memory resident programs (TSRs) into upper memory.

MEMMAKER only works on a PC with an 80386 or 80486 CPU chip and extended memory.

Syntax:

`MEMMAKER [/B] [/BATCH] [/SESSION] [/SWAP:`*`drive`*`] [/T] [/UNDO] [/W:`*`size1,size2`*`]`

`/B`

Display MEMMAKER screens in black and white.

`/BATCH`

Run in unattended (batch) mode, and take the default action at all prompts. Store status messages in the file MEMMAKER.STS.

`/SESSION`

MEMMAKER uses this switch during optimization; do not specify it when you start the program.

`/SWAP:`*`drive`*

The current drive letter used by the original startup disk drive. Use this switch only if a disk-compression program has performed disk swapping. /SWAP is not required with DoubleSpace or Stacker.

`/T`

Disable detection of IBM Token Ring networks

`/UNDO`

Restore the computer to its configuration before the most recent set of MEMMAKER changes.

`/W:size1,size2`

Reserve two amounts of upper memory space for Windows translation buffers. The default values for both regions are 12. If you do not use Windows, specify `/W:0,0` to keep MEMMAKER from reserving any upper memory for Windows.

Notes: MEMMAKER can make memory management with the DOS memory management programs HIMEM and EMM386 much easier than doing all the work yourself.

Don't use MEMMAKER if you are using a third-party memory manager such as QEMM or 386MAX.

MENUCOLOR

Type: CONFIG.SYS menu command

Purpose: Specify the text and background colors for the startup menu.

Syntax: `MENUCOLOR=x[,y]`

x

Display the menu text in the specified color value.

y

Display the screen background in the specified color value.

Use different colors for foreground and background; otherwise it won't be possible to read the text.

Color values:

0	Black	8	Gray
1	Blue	9	Bright blue
2	Green	10	Bright green

3	Cyan	11	Bright cyan
4	Red	12	Bright red
5	Magenta	13	Bright magenta
6	Brown	14	Yellow
7	White	15	Bright white

Notes: MENUCOLOR is purely cosmetic; it only affects the appearance of a startup menu. If you want to call attention to the menu, select a background color that is a strong contrast to the screen's background color. Bright red or bright magenta can be especially effective.

The color scheme from the last menu you go through in your CONFIG.SYS file during a given bootup will be the color scheme in effect when AUTOEXEC.BAT starts to be processed. To change colors after that you can use ANSI.SYS commands, provided you have that device driver (or a third-party alternative) loaded.

MENUDEFAULT

Type: CONFIG.SYS menu command

Purpose: Specify the default item on a startup menu, and specify a timeout duration.

If no MENUDEFAULT has been specified, the default will be Item No. 1 on the menu.

Syntax: `MENUDEFAULT=`*`blockname`*`[,`*`timeout`*`]`

`blockname`

The default menu item, as defined by a MENUITEM command.

`timeout`

The number of seconds that DOS will wait before it starts the default configuration. If you do not specify a timeout, the computer will wait until you select an option and press the Enter key. The minimum value is 0; the maximum is 90 seconds. A timeout value of 0 selects the default automatically, which has the same effect as no menu at all.

For example, the following set of menu commands is a possible starting for a menu with two items, "Interlink Active" and "Interlink Not Active." The default specified here is "Interlink

Not Active," with a timeout of eight seconds.

The menu in CONFIG.SYS:

```
[Menu]
menuitem=Interlink,Interlink Active
menuitem=No_Interlink,Interlink Not Active
menudefault=No_Interlink, 8
...
```

This menu would produce the following on your screen when you reboot your computer:

```
MS-DOS 6.0 Startup Menu

  1. Interlink Active
  2. Interlink Not Active

Enter a choice: 1
```

MENUITEM

Type: CONFIG.SYS menu command

Purpose: Define an item on a startup menu. A startup menu may have a maximum of 9 menu items.

Syntax: `MENUITEM=`*`blockname`*`[,`*`text`*`]`

blockname

The name of the configuration block that will be selected when a user selects this menu item. When a configuration block is selected, the command lines in that configuration block become active. The specified blockname may contain up to 70 characters, using any printable characters except spaces, backslashes (\), forward slashes (/), commas, semicolons (;), equals signs (=), or square brackets ([and]).

text

The text of the description of this menu item that will appear in the menu. If no text is specified, the menu will display blockname as the menu text. The specified text may contain up to 70 characters.

For example, the following menu in CONFIG.SYS:

```
[Menu]
menuitem=Interlink,Interlink Active
menuitem=No_Interlink,Interlink Not Active
menudefault=No_Interlink, 8

[Interlink]
...
[No_Interlink]
...
```

produces the following menu on your screen when you turn on the computer:

```
MS-DOS 6.0 Startup Menu

  1. Interlink Active
  2. Interlink Not Active

Enter a choice: 1
```

MIKDIR (MD)

Type: Internal command

Purpose: Create a subdirectory.

Syntax: MKDIR [*drive*:]*path*

or

MD [*drive*:]*path*

[*drive*:]*path*

The name and location of the new directory.

The maximum length of the new path is 63 characters, including backslashes.

To create a new subdirectory under the current directory, enter the new subdirectory's name without any other path information.

For example, if you are in the root directory of drive C:, and you want to create a new subdirectory called SUB (C:\SUB\), enter:

```
MKDIR SUB
```

To create a new subdirectory under the root directory, place a backslash ahead of the new directory's name. For example, to create that same SUB subdirectory under the root directory, while you are in some other subdirectory, enter:

```
MD \SUB
```

Notes: MKDIR (or MD) is a fundamental tool for organizing a disk. It's a lot easier (for both you and the computer) to find programs and data files on a hard disk when they're arranged in subdirectories rather than all lumped together in the root directory.

MODE

Type: External command

Purpose: Configure system devices. There are seven different tasks performed by the MODE command, each with a different command syntax:

1. Configure the printer.
2. Configure a serial port.
3. Display status of a device or of all devices.
4. Redirect printing from a parallel port to a serial port.
5. Set Device Code Pages.
6. Specify and configure the active display adapter.
7. Set the keyboard's typematic rate.

Frequently, the most convenient way to use MODE commands is to place them in the AUTOEXEC.BAT file, so that the new configuration is automatically set every time you start the computer.

1. MODE (Configure the printer)

Purpose: Configure a printer connected to a parallel port.

Syntax: `MODE LPTn[:] [COLS=c] [LINES=l] [RETRY=r]`

or

`MODE LPTn[:] [c][,[l][,r]]`

If you do not include one or more parameters, the commas that would have separated them must still be in place.

`LPTn[:]`

The parallel port attached to the printer. Valid options are LPT1, LPT2, LPT3 or PRN. LPT1 and PRN are interchangeable. The colon is optional.

`COLS=c or c`

The number of characters or columns per line. The only valid values for c are 80 and 132. The default value is 80.

`LINES=l or l`

Vertical spacing, expressed as the number of lines per inch. The only valid values are 6 and 8. The default value is 6.

`RETRY=r or r`

The retry action that MODE will take when a time-out error occurs. The valid values of r are:

E Return an error from a status check of a busy port.
B Return "busy" from a status check of a busy port.
P Continue to retry until the printer accepts the output.
R Return "ready" from a status check of a busy port.
N or NONE Take no retry action.

To break out of a time-out loop, press CTRL-BREAK.

If you omit a parameter, MODE will use the most recent setting for that item while adjusting other parameters to those specified in the current command.

2. Configure a serial port

Purpose: Set the parameters for a serial communication port.

Syntax: `MODE COMm[:] [BAUD=b] [PARITY=p] [DATA=d] [STOP=s] [RETRY=r]`

or

`MODE COMm[:] [b[,p[,d[,s[,r]]]]]`

`COMm`

The number of the serial port. Valid values are COM1, COM2, COM3 and COM4.

`Baud=b or b`

The first two digits of the transmission rate, in bits per seconds. Valid values are as follows:

11	110 baud
15	150 baud
30	300 baud
60	600 baud
12	1200 baud
24	2400 baud
48	4800 baud
96	9600 baud
19	19,200 baud

Some computers do not support 19,200 baud. Look in your hardware manual for specific information about your machine.

`PARITY=p or p`

The parity value for transmission through the specified serial port. Valid values are as follows:

N	No parity
E	Even
O	Odd
M	Mark
S	Space

The default is E.

`DATA=d or d`

The number of data bits in a character. Valid values are 5, 6, 7, and 8. The default value is 7.

`STOP=s or s`

The number of stop bits that define the end of a character. Valid values are 1, 1.5 and 2. The default value at 110 baud is 2. The default value for all other values is 1.

`RETRY=r or r`

The retry action that MODE will take when a time-out error occurs. The valid values for r are:

E	Return an error from a status check of a busy port
B	Return "busy" from a status check of a busy port
P	Continue to retry until the printer accepts the output

R   Return "ready" from a status check of a busy port
N or NONE   Take no retry action

To break out of a time-out loop, press CTRL-BREAK. If you omit a parameter, MODE will use the most recent setting for that parameter.

3. Display status of a device or of all devices

Purpose: Display the current status of devices installed on the computer.

Syntax: `MODE [device] [/STATUS or /STA]`

To display the status of all devices installed on the system, enter:

`MODE`

`device`

The name of the device whose status will be displayed.

`/STATUS or /STA`

Display the status of redirected parallel printers. If this switch is not present, MODE will display the status of all devices except redirected parallel printers.

4. Redirect printing

Purpose: Redirect printing from a parallel port to a serial port.

Syntax: `MODE LPTn[:]=COMm[:]`

`LPTn`

The parallel port. Valid values are LPT1, LPT2 and LPT3.

`COMm`

The serial port. Valid values are COM1 through COM4.

5. Set Device Code Pages

Purpose: Specify a character set for display and printing.

Syntax: `MODE device CODEPAGE PREPARE=((yyy [...]) [drive:][path]filename)`

or

```
MODE device CP PREP=((yyy [...])
[drive:][path]filename)
```

or

```
MODE device CODEPAGE SELECT=yyy (or CP SEL=yyy)
```

or

```
MODE device CODEPAGE REFRESH (or CP REF)
```

or

`MODE device CODEPAGE [/STATUS]` (or CP /STA)

device

The device that will use the character set. Valid device names are CON, LPT1, LPT2 and LPT3.

`CODEPAGE PREPARE` or `CP PREP`

Prepare character sets for the specified device.

yyy

The number of the code page that contains a specific set of characters. For codepage, use one of these three-digit numbers:

437	United States (default)
850	Multilingual (Latin I)
852	Slavic (Latin II)
860	Portugal
863	Canada (French)
865	Norway/Denmark

`[path]`*filename*

The location and name of the .CPI code page information file for the specified drive. MS-DOS include five .CPI files:

EGA.CPI	EGA adapter or IBM PS/2
4201.CPI	IBM Proprinters II and III Models 4201 and 4202
4208.CPI	IBM Proprinter X24E Model 4207 and XL24E Model 4208
5202.CPI	IBM Quietwriter III printer
LCD.CPI	IBM PC Convertible liquid crystal display

`CODEPAGE SELECT` or `CP SEL`

Use the specified code page with the specified device. You must enter the CODEPAGE PREPARE command before using CODEPAGE SELECT to select a code page.

`CODEPAGE REFRESH` or `CP REF`

Restore the prepared character sets if they have been lost due to a hardware problem.

`CODEPAGE` or `CP`

Display the current character sets for the specified device

`CODEPAGE /STATUS` or `CP /STA`

Display the current character sets for the specified device. Yes, this is exactly the same as entering CODEPAGE without the STATUS switch.

6. Set the Display Mode

Purpose: Specify or configure the active display adapter and its display mode.

Syntax: `MODE [`*`mode`*`][,`*`shift`*`[,T]]`

or

`MODE [`*`mode`*`][,`*`n`*`]`

or

`MODE CON[:] COLS=`*`c`*` [LINES=`*`n`*`]`

`mode`

The active video mode. Valid mode values are:

40 or 80	Characters per line.
BW40 or BW80	CGA adapter with color disabled.
CO40 or CO80	CGA adapter with color enabled.
MONO	Monochrome display adapter with 80 characters per line.

`shift`

Shift the CGA screen to the left or right. To shift left, use L for shift. To shift right, use R.

`T`

Display a test pattern for alignment of the screen.

`MODE CON[:]`

Set screen length and width

`COLS=40` or `COLS=80`

The number of characters or columns per line.

`LINES=n`

The number of lines that can appear on the screen. Valid values are 25, 43 and 50. To set the number of lines, the ANSI.SYS device driver must be active.

7. Set the keyboard's typematic rate

Purpose: Set the repeat rate when you hold down a key. Some keyboards may not recognize this command.

Syntax: `MODE CON: [RATE=`*r* `DELAY=`*d*`]`

`RATE=`*r*

The repeat rate, on a scale of 1 through 32, equal to approximately 2 to 30 characters per second. The default for AT-compatible keyboards is 20. The default for PS/2-compatible keyboards is 21.

r Value	*Repetitions per second*
1	2.0
2	2.1
3	2.3
4	2.5
5	2.7
6	3.0
7	3.3
8	3.7
9	4.0
10	4.3
11	4.6
12	5.0
13	5.5
14	6.0

15	6.7
16	7.5
17	8.0
18	8.6
19	9.2
20	10.0
21	10.9
22	12.0
23	13.3
24	15.0
25	16.0
26	17.1
27	18.5
28	20.0
29	21.8
30	24.0
31	26.7
32	30.0

`DELAY=`*`d`*

The delay before the character starts to repeat. This is the amount of time that a key must be held down before the first repetition. Valid values are:

1	.25 second
2	.50 second
3	.75 second
4	1 second

The default value is 2.

MORE

Type: External command (filter)

Purpose: Receive input from stdin (standard input, normally the keyboard) and send it to stdout (standard output, normally the screen), but after every 23 lines of output issue an extra line —`More`—and pause until a key is pressed.

More can have its input and output redirected (which is how it normally gets used).

Syntax:

`MORE < [path]filename`

or

`command ¦ MORE`

[path]filename

A file to be displayed one screen at a time.

command

A command whose output (to stdout) is to be displayed one screen at a time.

Notes: MORE is useful with any program which, like the DOS command TYPE, spews output unceasingly for more than 24 lines.

MOVE

Type: External command

Purpose: Move a file or files from one location to another. Rename a directory.

Syntax:

MOVE *[path]filename [...] destination*

MOVE *[path]olddirname [path]newdirname*

[path]filename

The location and name of the file that MOVE will move.

destination

The new location of the file or the new name of the directory. If you are moving one filename, destination can be a new filename. If the new filename already exists, MOVE will overwrite it.

olddirname

The name of the existing directory that MOVE will rename.

newdirname

The new name of the directory.

MOVE can change a directory name, but it can't move the directory to a new location in the directory tree.

Notes: The difference between MOVE and COPY is that COPY creates a second copy of a file or files; MOVE only writes a new directory entry for the file (and deletes the original directory entry) if it can. When moving a file from one disk to another MOVE does exactly the same thing as COPY followed by DEL.

UNDELETE cannot restore a file to its original directory after the file has been moved (within the same drive). Use COPY or MOVE if you wish to return the file to its original location.

MSAV

Type: External command

Purpose: Run the antivirus program to scan the computer for viruses.

Syntax: `MSAV [drive:] [switches] [vidswitch]`

drive:

The drive that MSAV will scan. The default is the current drive.

Switches

`/S`

Scan the specified drive, but do not remove viruses.

`/C`

Scan the specified drive and remove viruses.

`/A`

Scan all drives except drive A and drive B.

`/L`

Scan all local drives except network drives.

`/R`

Create a report file, MSAV.RPT, in the root directory. The default is no report.

`/N`

Display a command line interface instead of the default graphic interface. Do not display results of the scan on the screen, but save them in MSAV.RPT.

`/P`

Display a command line interface instead of the default graphic screen.

`/F`

Do not display the names of files that have been scanned. This switch requires either the /N or the /P switch.

`/VIDEO`

Display a list of display configuration switches.

`vidswitch`

`/25`	Set screen display to 25 lines. This is the default.
`/28`	Set screen display to 28 lines. Use only with a VGA adapter.
`/43`	Set screen display to 43 lines. Use only with a EGA or VGA adapter.
`/50`	Set screen display to 50 lines. Use only with a VGA adapter.
`/60`	Set screen display to 60 lines. Use only with a Video 7 adapter.
`/IN`	Use a color display scheme, even if there is no color display adapter.
`/BW`	Use a black and white display scheme.
`/MONO`	Use a monochrome display scheme.
`/LCD`	Use an LCD display scheme.
`/FF`	Use the fastest screen updating for a CGA adapter. This may produce lower video quality.
`/BF`	Use the computer's BIOS to display video.
`/NF`	Do not use alternate fonts.
`/BT`	Allow use of a graphics mouse in Windows.
`/NGM`	Use the default mouse character instead of a graphics character.
`/LE`	Swap the left and right mouse buttons.
`/IM`	Disable the mouse.
`/PS2`	Reset the mouse if the cursor disappears or locks up.

Notes: MSAV is a licensed version of Central Point Anti-Virus. It scans files, boot sectors, and memory for known viruses, and it looks for clues that unknown viruses may be present.

Enter the MSAV command without any switches to start the program and display a menu screen that will include all of the switch options.

As it scans for viruses, Anti-Virus places a CHKLST.MS file in every directory. This file contains checksums for each executable file in the directory. The next time Anti-Virus runs, it re-calculates the checksums and compares them to the old values. If there is a difference, the program calls attention to the fact, since that might indicate an infected file.

MSBACKUP

Type: External command

Purpose: Run the backup program to back up or restore one or more files to another disk.

MSBACKUP can back up all files, or only those files that have changed since the last backup.

Syntax: `MSBACKUP [setupfile] [switch]`

`setupfile`

The setup file that identifies the files that MSBACKUP will back up, and the type of backup that MSBACKUP will perform. The file extension must be .SET. The default is DEFAULT.SET.

`Switches`

`/BW` Start the program with a black and white display.
`/LCD` Start the program with an LCD-compatible display.
`/MDA` Start the program with a monochrome display.

The MSBACKUP program files must be located on a hard disk. MSBACKUP will not run from a floppy disk.

Notes: MSBACKUP replaces the old BACKUP program and offers a lot more flexibility. To restore files backed up with MSBACKUP, select `Restore` from the main Backup screen.

MSD

Type: External command

Purpose: Run the Microsoft Diagnostics program, which displays detailed technical information about the computer.

Syntax: To run the program and display technical information

```
MSD [/B] [/I]
```

To create a report

```
MSD [/I] [report switch]
```

`/B`

Run the program in black and white instead of color

`/I`

Do not initially detect hardware. Use this switch if MSD will not run otherwise.

Report switch

`/F[path]filename`

Prompt for name, address and telephone number, and then write a complete report to the specified file.

`/P[path]filename`

Write a complete report to the specified file.

`/S`

Display a summary report

`/S[path]filename`

Write a summary report to the specified file

Notes: MSD displays a menu screen with thirteen button options and several more in the menu bar across the top of the screen. Use the arrow and tab keys to select an option and then press Enter, or click on the option with your mouse.

When you call a hardware or software vendor for technical support, the information in MSD can be very helpful if the tech support representative needs to know your computer's configuration. It could also be useful to compare MSD reports before and after service to see what work was actually performed.

NLSFUNC

Type: External command.

Purpose: Load country-specific information for national language support (NLS).

> **Warning:** Do not enter this command from within Windows.

Syntax: From the DOS prompt or in AUTOEXEC.BAT

`NLSFUNC [[path] filename]`

Or it can be INSTALLed in your CONFIG.SYS file.

[path] filename

The file that contains country-specific information. The default is the file specified by the COUNTRY command in your CONFIG.SYS file. If there is no COUNTRY command in CONFIG.SYS, the second default is COUNTRY.SYS in the root directory of the startup drive.

NUMLOCK

Type: CONFIG.SYS directive

Purpose: Set the numeric keyboard Num Lock function on or off at startup.

Syntax: `NUMLOCK=[ON¦OFF]`

`NUMLOCK=ON`

Set Num Lock on at startup.

`NUMLOCK=OFF`

Set Num Lock off at startup.

NUMLOCK is a special command used in CONFIG.SYS startup menu blocks.

Notes: NUMLOCK defines the condition of Num Lock at startup. Although it has nothing to do with startup menus, it can only appear in a CONFIG.SYS menu block.

PATH

Type: Internal command

Purpose: Set the DOS search path for executable programs (.COM, .EXE and .BAT files).

Syntax: `PATH` *path1*`[;`*path2*`[;...]]`

To remove the path definition, enter

```
PATH;
```

To display the current search path, enter

```
PATH
```

path1, path2, ...

A drive and directory that COMMAND.COM is to search when looking for an executable file. If the total search path contains more than one path entry, separate each entry from the next with a semicolon.

Notes: When you give COMMAND.COM a command with a file name not preceeded by an explicit path, COMMAND.COM first checks to see if you have specified a DOSKEY macro, then if you have specified an internal command, and if neither is true, it looks for an executable file by that name to load and run. COMMAND.COM first searches in the current directory. After that it searches in each path specified in the most recent PATH command.

If the command you issued had an explicit path in it, COMMAND.COM will not use the PATH definition, even if it cannot find the specified program in the specified location.

PAUSE

Type: Batch file command

Purpose: Suspend processing a batch program and wait for the user to press a key.

Syntax:

```
PAUSE
```

When PAUSE appears in a batch file, DOS displays this message:

```
Press any key to continue...
```

It will not restart the batch program until a user presses a key on the keyboard.

Notes: Use PAUSE in a batch program when you want a user to do something before the program continues, such as replacing a diskette or pressing Ctrl-C to terminate the program. In most cases, an ECHO command that explains what program expects the user to do should be on the line immediately before the PAUSE command.

You can redirect the output of PAUSE to the NUL device if you wish to have only the output of an immediately previous ECHO command displayed.

POWER

Type: External command and device driver

Purpose: Reduce the computer's power consumption when no applications or devices are active.

The POWER.EXE device driver must have been loaded by CONFIG.SYS before you can run the POWER program at the DOS prompt.

In CONFIG.SYS

DEVICE=[*path*]POWER.EXE ADV:*setting*¦STD¦OFF [/LOW]

At the DOS prompt

POWER ADV:*setting*¦STD¦OFF

`ADV:[setting]`

Conserve power when the computer is idle at the level specified by the setting option.

Options for *setting*

`MAX`

Use maximum power conservation.

`REG`

Balance power conservation with performance.
This is the default setting.

`MIN`

Use minimum power conservation.

`STD`

If the computer supports the Advanced Power Management (APM) specification, use the computer's power management features to conserve power. If the computer does not support APM, turn off power management.

`OFF`

Turn off power management.

`/LOW`

Load the device driver into conventional memory, even if upper memory is available. If the /LOW switch is not present, DOS loads POWER.EXE into upper memory if it is available.

Notes: POWER conserves battery usage on a laptop or other portable computer.

PRINT

Type: External command

Purpose: Print a text file. PRINT can work in background while you use other DOS commands.

Syntax:

```
PRINT [/D:device] [/B:size] [/U:ticks1] [/M:ticks2]
[/S:ticks3] [/Q:qsize] [/T] [[path]filename[...]]
[/C] [/P]
```

Enter PRINT with no parameters to install PRINT with the default parameters, or to display the contents of the print queue.

`[path] filename[...]`

Print the specified file or group of files.

`/D:device`

Print the file on this device. A device may be a parallel port (PRN, LPT1, LPT2 or LPT3) or a serial port (COM1 through COM4). The default is LPT1, which is the same as PRN. If the command includes a filename, it must also include the /D switch.

`/B:size`

Set a print buffer of this size, in bytes. The minimum and default size is 512. The maximum size is 16384. Increasing size may speed printing, but it will take memory away from other applications.

`/U:ticks1`

Wait up to this number of clock ticks (at approximately 18 clock ticks per second) for the printer. If the printer is not available within `ticks1`, the job will not print. The minimum and default value is 1. The maximum is 255.

`/M:ticks2`

Wait up to this number of ticks for the printer to print a character. The minimum value is 1. The maximum is 255. The default value is 2. If the interval between characters is greater than ticks2, DOS will display an error message.

`/S:ticks3`

Instruct the DOS scheduler to allocate this number of clock ticks to background printing. The minimum value is 1. The maximum is 255. The default value is 8. Increasing `ticks3` can speed printing, but it will slow other programs running at the same time.

`/Q:qsize`

Allow this number of files in the print queue. The minimum value is 4. The maximum value is 32. The default is 10.

`/T`

Remove all files from the print queue.

`/C`

Remove the specified files from the print queue.

`/P`

Add the preceding files in the command to the print queue, or add the files that follow /P until a /C or the end of the command line.

The /D, /B, /U, /M, /S and /Q switches are only functional if the computer has received no PRINT commands since it was turned on. To change one of these switch settings, restart your computer.

Use a MODE command to configure a printer connected to a serial or parallel port.

Notes: Print does not spool print jobs. It merely maintains a table of queued files to print and the position in the current file. Each time the printer is ready for more data, PRINT will snatch some from the current file and send it to the printer, then return control to your foreground application.

Use PRINT to print ASCII text files from the DOS command line. PRINT is not a replacement for the print commands in applications, which can perform formatting specific to each application.

After each job in the print queue, PRINT adds a form feed command, which will start each file at the top of a new page.

Print expands tabs in text by adding spaces to the next tab position (next multiple of eight columns).

PROMPT

Type: Internal command

Purpose: Define the DOS prompt.

Syntax: `PROMPT [`*`string`*`]`

`string`

Define the DOS prompt as the *`string`* of characters and metacharacters. *`String`* may contain any characters in combination with any of the special PROMPT metacharacters.

The special PROMPT metacharacters all start with a dollar sign ($) character:

$B	¦ (pipe character)
$D	The current date
$E	Escape character (ASCII code 27)
$G	> (greater-than character)
$H	Backspace (erase the previous character)
$L	< (less-than character)
$N	The current drive
$P	The current directory
$Q	= (equals sign)
$T	The current time
$V	The DOS version number
$$	$ (dollar sign)
$	CR/LF (move down to the next line on the screen)

In the absence of any prompt definition, COMMAND.COM uses the drive letter and a greater than sign. (This is equivalent to having the PROMPT string be NG. If SETUP doesn't find a PROMPT statement in the AUTOEXEC.BAT file in the root directory of the boot drive it puts PROMPT=PG there.

To change the DOS command prompt for a DOS window in Windows 3.1, set the WINPMT environment variable.

If the ANSI.SYS device driver is active, you can use ANSI.SYS escape sequences in your prompt to change to foreground and background colors of the prompt, and make the prompt bold, blinking, or in reverse video.

QBASIC

Type: External command

Purpose: Load the Microsoft QBASIC interpreter. QBASIC is a BASIC programming evironment.

Syntax: `QBASIC [`*`switch`*`] [/EDITOR] [/RUN] [`*`path`*`]`*`filename`*

`/B`

Display QBasic in black and white on a color monitor.

`/G`

Display with fastest CGA monitor update.

`/H`

Display in high resolution, using the maximum possible number of display lines that your monitor will allow.

`/MBF`

Make the following function conversions:

MKS$	MKSMBF$
MKD$	MKDMBF$
CVS	CVSMBF
CVD	CVDMBF

`/NOHI`

Tells QBASIC that your monitor does not support high-intensity video. Do not use this switch with Compaq laptops.

`/EDITOR`

Start the DOS editor.

`/RUN`

Run the specified program before displaying it.

Notes: The DOS program EDIT essentially just starts QBASIC with the /EDITOR switch. MS-DOS 6 HELP also uses the QBASIC engine. These programs won't run if you delete QBASIC.EXE.

RAMDRIVE.SYS

Type: CONFIG.SYS device driver

Purpose: Create a drive in RAM memory that simulates a hard drive.

Syntax:

```
DEVICE=[path]RAMDRIVE.SYS
[disksize sectorsize [entries]][/E¦/A]
```

or

```
DEVICEHIGH=[path]RAMDRIVE.SYS
[disksize sectorsize [entries]][/E ¦ /A]
```

`path`

The location of RAMDRIVE.SYS.

`disksize`

The size of the RAM drive, in kilobytes. The valid range is from 4 to 32767, up to the amount of memory available on the computer. The default is 64K.

`sectorsize`

The disk sector size, in bytes. Valid values are 128, 256 or 512 bytes. The default is 512.

`entries`

The maximum number of files and directories on the RAM drive's root directory. Valid values are in the range from 2 to 1024. The default is 64.

`/E`

Create the RAM drive in extended memory.

`/A`

Create the RAM drive in expanded memory.

If neither the /E nor /A switch is present, DOS creates the RAMDRIVE out of conventional memory, which reduces the amount of memory available for applications.

Notes: DOS can read and write to a RAM drive much more quickly than to a hard drive, because there's no mechanical delay involved.

The trade-off for increased speed is that data stored on a RAM drive will be lost when you turn off the computer. Remember to transfer anything you want to save to a "real" drive.

RD

Identical to RMDIR

REM

Type: CONFIG.SYS and batch file command

Purpose: The batch file processor in COMMAND.COM and the CONFIG.SYS processor in IO/SYS will ignore any line that begins with REM.

Syntax: `REM [text]`

or (but only use this second form in a CONFIG.SYS file)

`; [text]`

`[text]`

Any text you want to see when you edit or examine this batch or CONFIG.SYS file, but which you want not to have acted on.

Notes: There are two basic reasons to use REM (or, in a CONFIG.SYS file, a semicolon). One is to add clarifying remarks to remind yourself what you did and why when you wrote this file. The other is to temporarily remove a command line. This latter use is often very helpful in troubleshooting. It will be much less necessary now in CONFIG.SYS files with the new Clean Boot support, but it still has a place in the DOS power user's arsenal of tricks.

RENAME (REN)

Type: Internal command

Purpose: Change the name of a file or group of files.

Syntax: `REN [path]oldfile newfile`

or

`REN [path]oldfile newfile`

`[path]oldfile`

The name of the file that RENAME will change.

newfile

The new name that RENAME will assign to the file.

If you use the ? or * wildcard characters, RENAME can change the names of multiple files with a single command. For example, to change all of the .TXT files in the current directory to .DOC files, enter:

```
REN *.TXT *.DOC
```

REPLACE

Type: External command

Purpose: Remove files from the destination directory and replace them with files from the source directory with the same name.

Syntax: `REPLACE [path]filename [path2] [switches]`

`[path]filename`

The source file.

`path2`

The destination directory or target directory.

switches

`/A`

Add new files to the target directory.

`/P`

Prompt before replacing the file.

`/R`

Replace read-only files along with other specified files.

`/S`

Search all subdirectories and replace matching files.

`/W`

Wait for a new diskette before searching for source files.

`/U`

Update only those files in the target directory that are older than the same files in the source directory.

A REPLACE command that includes the /A switch may not also include the /S or /U switch.

Use the ? and * wildcards to replace multiple files with one command. REPLACE will replace each target file with the file with the same name from the source directory.

RESTORE

Type: External command

Purpose: Restore files that were backed up with an earlier version of DOS. To restore files that were backed up with MSBACKUP, use MSBACKUP.

Syntax: `RESTORE` *`drive1`*`:` *`drive2`*`:[`*`path[filename]`*`]` *`[switches]`*

`drive1``:`

The drive that contains the backed-up files.

`drive2``:`

The destination drive for the restored files.

`path`

The destination directory.

`filename`

The file or files that RESTORE will restore.

`switches`

`/S`

Restore all subdirectories.

`/P`

Prompt before restoring read-only files and files that have changed since the last backup.

`/B:date`

Restore files that have changed on or before date.

`/A:date`

Restore files that have changed on or after date.

`/E:time`

Restore files that have changed at or earlier than time.

`/L:time`

Restore files that have changed at or later than time.

`/M`

Restore files that have been changed or deleted since the last backup.

`/N`

Restore files that are no longer on the destination drive or directory.

`/D`

Display a list of files on the backup disk that match filename, but do not restore any files.

RESTORE is a carry-over from DOS 5 and earlier releases. Use it to restore old backups created with BACKUP. You don't need RESTORE if you're making backups with MSBACKUP.

RMDR (RD)

Type: Internal command

Purpose: Remove a directory.

The specified directory must be empty. If it contains any files or subdirectories, RMDIR does not work.

Syntax: `RMDIR [drive:]path`

or

`RD [`*`drive`*`:]`*`path`*

`[`*`drive`*`:]`*`path`*

The name and location of the directory that RMDIR will remove.

It is not possible to delete the current directory.

Notes: RMDIR only works on directories that contain no files or subdirectories. If a directory appears to be empty, but DOS won't let you remove it, use DIR /A to look for hidden and system files. If a hidden file is part of an application's copy-protection scheme, use the application to uninstall it. For all other hidden programs, use ATTRIB to change their file attributes and then use DEL to delete them.

To delete a directory that contains files and subdirectories, use DELTREE.

SET

Type: Internal command

Purpose: Display or change an environment variable. Variables include CONFIG, COMSPEC, PATH, PROMPT and TEMP. Use SET to make a one-time change. To make a permanent change, use the CONFIG.SYS file.

Syntax: To display all environment variables.

```
SET
```

To clear the specified environment variable.

```
SET [name=]
```

To define the specified variable.

```
SET [name[=value]]
```

name

The variable that SET will define or clear.

value

The value that SET will assign to the variable.

Notes: Many programs look for environment variables. SET assigns a string, which could be a character string, a path, or a file, to a variable. For example, SET TEMP=C:\TEMP assigns the C:\TEMP directory to the TEMP variable. When a program uses the TEMP variable to store temporary files, it will place them in C:\TEMP.

SETVER

Type: External command and CONFIG.SYS device driver

Purpose: Report a specified DOS version number to a program or device driver.

Some programs may have been designed to run with a specific earlier version of DOS. A version table lists these programs, and the version number that they expect to find. Use SETVER to add program names to the version table.

SETVER requires that the SETVER.EXE device driver must be loaded into memory. DEVICE=[path]SETVER.EXE must be present in CONFIG.SYS.

Syntax: To report the specified version number to the specified program

```
SETVER [path]filename n.nn
```

To delete the specified program from the version table.

```
SETVER [path] filename [/DELETE [/QUIET] or [/D
[/QUIET]
```

To display the version table.

```
SETVER [path]
```

`[path]`

The location of the SETVER.EXE file.

`filename`

The name of the file that SERVER will add to the version table.

`n.nn`

Report the specified DOS version number for filename.

`/QUIET`

Do not display a message after deleting the item from the table.

The version table loads into memory during startup. To load the new table, restart the computer.

Notes: SETVER.EXE is a list of programs that require earlier versions of MS-DOS. If you get a "Wrong DOS Version" message, consult the program's documentation and try adding the program to SETVER.EXE.

If you don't use any of the programs listed in SETVER.EXE, you can save about 800 bytes of memory by placing REM in front of the DEVICE=SETVER line in CONFIG.SYS.

SHARE

Type: External command

Purpose: Allow file sharing to permit more than one program to use the same file at the same time. This is most often used in networking or multitasking environments, but it's useful any time you need to do task swapping or return to the DOS prompt from within an application.

Syntax: From the DOS command line

```
SHARE [/F:space] [/L:locks]
```

In CONFIG.SYS

```
INSTALL=[path]SHARE.EXE [/F:space] [/L:locks]
```

path

The location of the SHARE.EXE file. For best performance, place SHARE.EXE in the root directory, or in a directory in the PATH search path.

/F:*space*

Allocate the specified number of bytes to record information about file sharing. Each open file uses enough space for the full path and file name. The average file uses 20 bytes. The default value is 2048 bytes.

/L:*locks*

Set the maximum number of files that can be locked at one time.

Notes: SHARE loads code that validates read and write requests from programs. If two computers on a network, or two programs on the same computer are trying to read or write to a file at the same time,

SHARE manages access to the program, in order to prevent conflicts.

The locking function sets the number of files that cannot be used by more than one program or process at a time.

SHARE also monitors diskette drives, and knows when drive doors have been opened and closed. It can issue a warning if you've switched disks in the middle of a disk write.

SHELL

Type: CONFIG.SYS parameter

Purpose: Use a specified file as the DOS command interpreter. The command interpreter supplied with MS-DOS is COMMAND.COM. To use a different command interpreter, specify the new interpreter in CONFIG.SYS.

Syntax: `SHELL=[`*`path`*`]`*`filename`* `[`*`parameters`*`]`

`[`*`path`*`]`*`filename`*

Use the specified file as command interpreter. The default is COMMAND.COM in the root directory.

`parameters`

Apply these parameters to the command interpreter. Consult the documentation for the command interpreter for information about specific parameters.

Notes: If COMMAND.COM is not located in the root directory, you must use a SHELL command to specify its location. If you want to use a command interpreter other than COMMAND.COM, use a SHELL command to identify it to DOS.

In addition to COMMAND.COM, there are several other widely available command interpreters for DOS, including 4DOS and NDOS.

SHIFT

Type: Batch file command

Purpose: Change the value of a replaceable parameter, or use more than ten parameters in the same batch file.

SHIFT changes the value of each parameter to the previous value. For example, SHIFT copies %4 to %3 and %5 to %4. If the batch file has more than ten parameters, SHIFT copies the values of the ones that appear after %9 into %9, one at a time.

Syntax:

```
SHIFT
```

Notes: SHIFT can save a lot of repetition in a batch file that carries out the same operation on many parameters.

SMARTDRV

Type: CONFIG.SYS device driver

Purpose: Start or configure the SMARTdrive disk cache utility.

Syntax: To start SMARTDrive from the DOS command line or from AUTOEXEC.BAT

```
[path]SMARTDRV [[drive[+¦-]]...] [/E:elementsize]
[initcachesize][wincachesize]] [/B:<buffersize>]
[/C] [/R] [/L] [/Q] [/S]
```

Once SMARTDrive is running

```
SMARTDRV [[drive[+¦-]]...]] [/C] [/R]
```

`[path]SMARTDRV`

The location of SMARTDRV.EXE

drive

Enable read caching and disable write caching for the specified drive

drive+

Enable read and write caching for the specified drive

`drive-`

Disable read and write caching for the specified drive.

If no drive is specified, SMARTDRV will enable read caching and disable write caching for floppy drives and drives created by Interlnk; it will enable both read and write caching for hard drives, and ignore CD-ROM, network and compressed drives, and Microsoft Flash memory card drives.

`/E:`*`elementsize`*

Move this number of bytes at one time. Valid values are 1024, 2048, 4096 and 8192. The default is 8192.

`initcachesize`

Create a cache of this number of kilobytes when SMARTDrive starts and Windows is not running.

`wincachesize`

Reduce the cache by this number of kilobytes for Windows.

`/B:`*`buffersize`*

Use this number of bytes as the read-ahead buffer. Valid values are any multiple of elementsize.

`/C`

Write all cached information from memory to the hard disk.

`/R`

Clear the existing cache and restart SMARTDrive.

`/L`

Load SMARTDrive into conventional memory, even if upper memory blocks (UMBs) are available.

`/Q`

Do not display error and status messages at startup.

`/S`

Display additional status information.

Notes: SmartDrive is the extended memory disk chache supplied with MS-DOS. A disk cache increases the speed of disk operations by copying data to extended memory, where the CPU can find and read it more quickly than from the disk.

Do not use SmartDrive and another disk cache, such as NCACHE or PC-KWIK, at the same time.

SMARTDRV—Double Buffering

Type: CONFIG.SYS command

Purpose: Use SMARTDrive with EMM386.EXE or Windows enhanced mode.

Syntax: `DEVICE=[path]SMARTDRV.EXE /DOUBLE_BUFFER`

path

The location of SMARTDRV.EXE.

Notes: Double buffering makes hard drive controllers, including SCSI and some ESDI and MCA controllers, compatible with memory provided by EMM386.EXE or Windows in 386 enhanced mode.

To find out if your system requires double buffering, add the SMARTDRV/DOUBLE_BUFFER device driver to CONFIG.SYS, and SMARTDRV to AUTOEXEC.BAT. Then restart the computer and run MemMaker. When that routine is done, enter MEM/C/P to confirm that the computer is using upper memory. Assuming it is running, enter:

```
SMARTDRV
```

The computer will display an information screen. If any line in the "Buffering" column says "yes," the system requires double buffering.

SORT

Type: External command (filter)

Purpose: Read data from a file or the output of a command, sort the data, and display or write the result.

Syntax: `SORT [/R] [/+n] [<] [path]file1 [>[path]file2]`

or

```
[command ¦]SORT[/R] [/+n] [>[path]file2]
```

`/R`

Sort in reverse order (from Z to A, then 9 to 0).

`/+n`

Sort the file based on the character in the specified column. The default is column 1.

`[path]file1`

Sort data from this source file.

`>[path]file2`

Write the sorted data to this destination file.

Sort treats upper case and lower case letters as identical letters. Sort treats accented characters from the extended character set as if they are unaccented.

For example, to sort the items in the file LIST.TXT and display the result on the monitor, use the command:

```
SORT LIST.TXT
```

To use the FIND command to identify all entries in LIST.TXT that contain the word "Orange," sort them in alphabetical order and display the result, use the command:

```
FIND "ORANGE" LIST.TXT ¦ sort
```

The maximum SORT file size is 64K.

Notes: Use the ¦MORE command to display SORT output one screen at a time.

STACKS

Type: CONFIG.SYS directive

Purpose: Allocate data stacks for hardware interrupts.

Syntax: `STACKS=n,s`

n

Allocate this number of stacks. Valid values are 0 and 8 through 64.

s

Allocate stacks of this size, in bytes. Valid values are 0 and 32 through 512.

Default values are 0,0 for the IBM PC, PC/XT and PC-Portable. Default values are 9,128 for all other computers.

Notes: Stacks are memory areas that DOS uses to store transient information. Every time it receives a hardware interrupt, DOS allocates one stack.

Most computers do not require any STACKS allocation. By setting STACKS=0,0, you can save about a kilobyte of low memory for use by applications. If the computer becomes unstable, go back to the default values of STACKS=9, 128.

SUBMENU

Type: CONFIG.SYS menu command

Purpose: Display a startup menu item that allows another set of choices.

Syntax: `SUBMENU=`*`block`*`[,`*`text`*`]`

block

Create a submenu with this name, which must be defined in the CONFIG.SYS file.

text

Display this text in the main startup menu.

For example, the following set of menu commands creates a menu with two items, an "Interlink Active" submenu, and "Interlink Not Active."

```
[Menu]
submenu=Interlink,Interlink Active
menuitem=No_Interlink,Interlink Not Active
```

```
[Interlink]
menuitem=Option_A, Use Parallel Link
menuitem=Option_B, Use Serial Link
```

produces the following menu on your screen when you turn on the computer:

```
MS-DOS 6.0 Startup Menu
  1. Interlink Active
  2. Interlink Not Active
Enter a choice: 1
```

If you select Item 1, the computer will display the following submenu:

```
MS-DOS Startup Menu
  1. Use Parallel Link
  2. Use Serial Link
```

SUBST

Type: External command

Purpose: Substitute a drive letter for a path.

SUBST assigns a virtual drive letter to a path, which can be useful when a frequently used subdirectory has a long path name.

Syntax: To define a virtual drive

```
SUBST newdrive: [drive:]path
```

To delete a virtual drive

```
SUBST newdrive: /D
```

To display all currently defined virtual drives

```
SUBST
```

newdrive:

The letter that SUBST will assign to the new virtual drive. The newdrive letter must be within the range defined by LASTDRIVE in CONFIG.SYS.

[*drive*:]*path*

The directory to which SUBST will assign the virtual drive letter.

/D

Delete the specified virtual drive

Do not use the SUBST command from within Windows.

Do not use any of these commands on a virtual drive created with SUBST:

ASSIGN	DISKCOMP	MIRROR
BACKUP	DISKCOPY	RESTORE
CHKDSK	FDISK	RECOVER
DATAMON	FORMAT	SYS
DEFRAG	LABEL	

Notes: SUBST can replace a long drive path that has several layers of subdirectories with a drive letter. This can save a lot of keystrokes, and it can extend a PATH or APPEND command beyond the normal character limit.

SWITCHES

Type: CONFIG.SYS command

Purpose: Set certain special configuration options.

Syntax: `SWITCHES=[/W] [/K] [/N] [/F]`

/W

Search for WINA20.386 in a directory other than the root directory. Windows 3.0 enhanced mode normally looks for WINA20.386 in the root directory. If WINA20.386 is in a subdirectory, SWITCHES=/W must be in CONFIG.SYS, and a DEVICE command that specifies the location of WINA20.386 must be under the [386Enh] heading of SYSTEM.INI. Note that this switch is only useful with Windows 3.0. Do not use it with other versions of Windows.

/K

Use an enhanced keyboard as if it were a conventional keyboard. If the ANSI.SYS device driver is active, the /K switch must also be in the DEVICE=ANSI.SYS command line of CONFIG.SYS.

`/N`

Do not permit use of the F5 or F8 key to bypass startup commands.

`/F`

Skip the two-second delay during startup, after the "Starting MS-DOS..." message.

Notes: SWITCHES has become a catch-all command in MS-DOS 6.0. In MS-DOS 5, it only included the /K switch.

The /W switch can be helpful in keeping your root directory clean, but remember to add the DEVICE command to SYSTEM.INI. Use /K if a program doesn't correctly interpret keyboard entry from an enhanced keyboard. /N and /F seem to be solutions for which there was no apparent problem.

SYS

Type: External command

Purpose: Copy the hidden DOS system files (IO.SYS and MSDOS.SYS), COMMAND.COM and DBLSPACE.BIN to a disk.

In earlier versions of DOS, SYS didn't copy COMMAND.COM. The MS-DOS 6.0 version copies all four files. If COMMAND.COM is not in the root directory, SYS does not copy it.

Syntax: `SYS [`*`path`*`] `*`targetdrive`*`:`

[*path*]

The location of the system files. The default is the root directory of the current drive.

targetdrive:

The drive where the new copy of the system files will be written. SYS will copy the files to the root directory of the new drive.

Notes: Use SYS to copy DOS to a formatted diskette. Use FORMAT/S to copy DOS to a diskette while you format it.

TIME

Type: Internal command

Purpose: Display or set the time on the computer's internal clock.

Syntax: To display the current time

```
TIME
```

To set the time

```
TIME [hours[:minutes[:seconds[.hundredths]]][A ¦ P]
```

hours[:*minutes*[:*seconds*[.*hundredths*]]]

Set the internal clock to the specified time.

A

Set the clock to AM (this is the default).

P

Set the clock to PM.

Use A or P to set the clock using 12-hour time format. If you set the clock using 24-hour format, DOS will convert it to 12-hour format. If you set the time as 17:34 and then enter TIME again, the computer will display the time as 5:34 pm.

If you set the time to 12-hour time format, place the A or P immediately after the time setting. Do not leave a space between the time and the letter. It's important to specify AM or PM because the date changes following 11:59:59 pm every day.

The TIME command with no parameters displays the current time, and asks for changes. To keep the current time settings, press ENTER.

TREE

Type: External command

Purpose: Display a diagram that shows the directory structure of a disk.

Syntax:

```
TREE [drive:][path] [/F] [/A]
```

drive:

The drive letter of the disk whose structure TREE will display. The default is the current directory.

path

The directory whose structure TREE will display.

/F

Display all file names.

/A

Use text characters instead of graphic characters to display thc structure. Use this switch to print the structure on a printer that does not use graphic characters.

To display the entire structure of the current disk, starting with the root directory, use a backslash (TREE \).

Notes: Use ¦MORE to display Tree structure one screen at a time. TREE is helpful when you're trying to understand the structure of a complex hard drive, and for finding subdirectories and files that can be deleted to create more free space on a disk.

TYPE

Type: Internal command

Purpose: Display the contents of a file.

Syntax: TYPE [*path*] *filename*

[*path*] *filename*

The name and location of the file that TYPE will display.

Notes: Use TYPE to display the contents of a text file, or to redirect the contents of a file to another file or a printer.

Type wraps text to the next line after 80 characters. It stops at Ctrl-Z (end of file) characters.

If a file is longer than one screen full of text, it will scroll across the screen too fast to read. Use the MORE command to read the file one screen full at a time.

UNDELETE

Type: External command

Purpose: Restore files previously deleted with the DEL or ERASE command.

Syntax: `UNDELETE [path] filename [/DT¦/DS¦/DOS]`

`UNDELETE [/LIST¦/ALL¦/PURGE[:drive]¦ /STATUS¦/LOAD¦/U_¦/S[:drive] ¦/Tdrive [-entries]]`

`[path]filename`

The file that UNDELETE will restore. If no file is specified, UNDELETE will restore all files in the current directory.

`/DT`

Restore only the files listed in the deletion-tracking file.

`/DS`

Restore only the files listed in the SENTRY directory.

`/DOS`

Restore only the files internally listed as deleted.

`/LIST`

List deleted files, but do not restore them.

`/ALL`

Restore all deleted files without prompting for confirmation. If UNDELETE is using the Delete Sentry, it will restore the first character. Otherwise, it will use the number sign (#) as the first character. If a duplicate filename exists, it will substitute another character.

`/PURGE[:drive]`

Delete the contents of the SENTRY directory.

`/STATUS`

Display the active type of delete protection for each drive.

`/LOAD`

Load the UNDELETE program into memory, using the configuration specified in UNDELETE.INI. If UNDELETE.INI does not exist, use the default configuration.

`/U`

Unload the UNDELETE program from memory.

`/S[:`*`drive`*`]`

Turn on Delete Sentry for this drive, and load UNDELETE into memory, using the configuration specified in UNDELETE.INI. If UNDELETE.INI does not exist, use the default configuration. If no drive is specified, turn on Delete Sentry on the current drive.

`/T[:`*`drive`*`]`

Turn on Delete Tracker for this drive, and load UNDELETE into memory, using the configuration specified in UNDELETE.INI. If UNDELETE.INI does not exist, use the default configuration. If no drive is specified, turn on Delete Tracker for the current drive.

`-entries`

Hold a maximum of this number of items in the deletion-tracking file PCTRACKER.DEL. The default depends on the size of the disk.

Notes: The version of UNDELETE in MS-DOS 6.0 has more features than the one in DOS 5. There are three levels of Undelete protection—standard, Delete Tracker, and Delete Sentry.

Standard protection makes it possible to restore files only if they have not been overwritten by other files. Standard is the lowest and least secure level of protection. It does not require any memory or disk space.

Delete Tracker records the location of deleted files in a hidden file called PCTRACKR.DEL. It is the intermediate level of protection. Delete Tracker can restore a file if DOS has not placed another file in the same location as the deleted file. It requires 13.5K of memory and enough space on the disk for PCTRACKR.DEL.

Delete Sentry is the most secure level. It moves deleted files to a hidden SENTRY directory, but leaves information about a file's location in the File Allocation Table. Undeleting a file moves that file back to its original location. Delete Sentry uses up to 7% of the hard disk space and 13.5K of memory.

UNFORMAT

Type: External command

Purpose: Restore the directories and files that were erased by the FORMAT command.

Syntax: `UNFORMAT` *`drive`*`: [/L] [/TEST] [/P]`

`drive``:`

The drive letter of the disk that UNFORMAT will restore. The default is the current drive.

`/L`

List every file and subdirectory found by UNFORMAT. If this switch is not present, UNFORMAT lists only subdirectories and fragmented files. To suspend scrolling, press Ctrl-S. To restart, press any key.

`/TEST`

Display the way UNFORMAT would restore the disk, but do not perform the recovery. Use this switch to find out if UNFORMAT can actually restore a formatted disk.

`/P`

Send output messages to the LPT1 printer.

Notes: UNFORMAT cannot restore data from disks formatted with the FORMAT/U switch.

When UNFORMAT finds a fragmented file, it may only recover part of the file. If it doesn't recognize a fragmented file, it may try to recover it, but only succeed in recovering part of the file. Truncated program files probably won't run properly; truncated data files won't include all the information originally in the file, or won't be readable using the program that created it. Utilities like Norton's Disk Editor can help salvage what's left of a truncated data file. That's why you keep backup copies, isn't it?

VER

Type: Internal command

Purpose: Display the DOS version number.

Syntax: `VER`

VERIFY

Type: CONFIG.SYS directive, also can be used at the DOS prompt

Purpose: Sets a flag to force DOS to read every disk sector that it writes.

Syntax: `VERIFY [ON¦OFF]`

`ON`

Turn on the VERIFY function.

`OFF`

Turn off the VERIFY function.

Enter VERIFY without the switch to display the current status.

Notes: VERIFY only confirms the readability of the destination sectors. It *does not* compare the data there with anything.

When VERIFY is active, disk write operations are slower, but only by a small amount, and it will trap some errors writing to disks.

COPY /V and XCOPY /V simply direct COPY or XCOPY to act as if VERIFY were turned on.

VOL

Type: Internal command

Purpose: Display the volume number and serial number of a disk.

Syntax: `VOL [drive:]`

drive:

The drive letter of the disk whose volume number the command will display. The default is the current drive.

VSAFE

Type: External command

Purpose: Load a memory-resident program that continuously monitors the computer for viruses.

Do not start VSAFE from within Windows.

Syntax:

```
VSAFE [/option[+ | -]...] [/NE] [/NX] [/Ax | /Cx]
[/N] [/D] [/U]
```

`option`

`1`

Warn when formatting can completely erase the hard disk. The default is "on."

`2`

Warn when a program tries to remain in memory. The default is "off."

`3`

Do not permit programs to write to disk. The default is "off."

`4`

Check .EXE, .COM and .BAT files as they are opened. The default is "on."

`5`

Check all disks for boot sector viruses. The default is "on."

`6`

Warn when an attempt to write to the boot sector or partition table of the hard disk occurs. The default is "on."

`7`

Warn when an attempt to write to the boot sector of a floppy disk occurs. The default is "off."

`8`

Warn when an attempt to modify a .COM, .EXE or .BAT file occurs. The default is "on."

`+`

Turn the specified option on.

`-`

Turn the specified option off.

`/NE`

Do not load VSafe into expanded memory.

`/NX`

Do not load VSafe into extended memory.

`/Ax`

Make the hot key Alt plus the specified key.

`/Cx`

Make the hot key Ctrl plus the specified key.

`/N`

Monitor network drives for viruses.

`/D`

Turn off checksumming.

`/U`

Unload VSAFE from memory.

Notes: VSAFE monitors the computer for viruses as the computer operates. It uses 22K of memory. The VSAFE command should be in AUTOEXEC.BAT.

When VSAFE detects a possible virus, it displays a warning message. Run MSAV to remove the virus and repair your files and memory.

Remove VSAFE from memory when you install Windows. To use VSAFE with Windows and display VSAFE messages, place this line in WIN.INI:

```
LOAD=MWAVTSR.EXE
```

XCOPY

Type: External command

Purpose: Copy files and directories, including subdirectories.

Syntax: `XCOPY` *`source`* `[`*`destination`*`] [`*`switches`*`]`

`source`

The path and directory of the files that XCOPY will copy.

`destination`

The path of the directory where XCOPY will place the copied files or directories.

`Switches`

`/A`

Copy files with the archive bit set.

`/M`

Copy files with the archive bit set and reset the archive bit.

`/D:date`

Copy only files created or changed on or after the specified date.

`/P`

Prompt for confirmation before copying each file.

`/S`

Copy the specified directory and all of its subdirectories, except for empty subdirectories.

`/E`

Copy all subdirectories, including empty subdirectories. Use this switch with the /S switch.

`/V`

Verify that each copied file is identical to the original.

`/W`

Display a prompt and wait for a response before starting to copy files.

Notes: XCOPY is a faster method of copying lots of files at one time. Unlike COPY, XCOPY can copy subdirectories as well as files. Where COPY copies files one at a time, XCOPY fills conventional memory with files before writing them to the new location on the disk.

In MS-DOS 6, XCOPY does not copy hidden files or system files.

To copy a lot of files to diskettes, use the /S and /M switch. When XCOPY fills the first diskette, replace it and enter the same command again (use the F3 key or, if you're using DOSKEY, the up arrow). XCOPY will use the archive bit of the original file to pick up wherc it left off.

XCOPY is often a better way to copy a diskette to another identical diskette than DISKCOPY, because DISKCOPY makes fragmented copies of fragmented originals. Still, DISKCOPY is the only way to copy a diskette complete with any files it may contain that have their hidden and system attributes turned on; thus you must use DISKCOPY to make bootable copies of bootable DOS diskettes.

CHAPTER

19

DOS Power Tools Utilities

New to this edition are more than 100 utilities, culled from the best freeware and shareware programs available. We've tried to select programs that offer functionality out of the ordinary, and that complement, rather than duplicate, the utilities from the previous editions of this book.

The freeware programs, as the name implies, may be freely used and distributed without obligation. Please note that there is a distinction between a program being considered freeware and a programs specifically put into the public domain. The copyright for freeware generally resides with the author, and thus commercial use or distribution requires permission, whereas material specifically put into the public domain can be used for any purpose without restriction.

Shareware is an interesting approach to distributing intellectual property that has no real counterpart in many other fields of human endeavor. It's hard to imagine a restaurant operating on the proposition that if you like a meal, you'll pay whatever you felt it was worth—at least, not any restaurant since Alice's.

What is Shareware

Shareware distribution gives users a chance to try software before buying it. If you try a shareware program and continue using it, you are expected to register. Individual programs differ on details—some request registration while others require it, some specify a maximum trial period. With registration, you get anything from the simple right to continue using the software to an updated program with printed manual. Copyright laws apply to both shareware and commercial software, and the copyright holder retains all rights, with a few specific exceptions as stated below. Shareware authors are accomplished programmers, just like commercial authors, and the programs are of comparable quality. (In both cases, there are good programs and bad ones!) The main difference is in the method of distribution. The author specifically grants the right to copy and distribute the software, either to all and sundry or to a specific group. For example, some authors require written permission before a commercial disk vendor may copy their shareware.

Shareware is a distribution method, not a type of software. You should find software that suits your needs and pocketbook, whether it's commercial or shareware. The shareware system makes fitting your needs easier, because you can try before you buy. And because the overhead is low, prices are low also. Shareware has the ultimate money-back guarantee—if you don't use the product, you don't pay for it.

We can't police your conscience in this matter, but we've tried to reduce the hassle of locating the author of a specific piece of shareware and registering the software, should you decide that you want to use it regularly. We think you'll be surprised, pleasantly, at the quality of the software, and urge you to support those authors whose work you find worthwhile.

Summary of Programs

PTOOL.EXE	Launches programs, displays file contents
!.EXE	Enhances and improves DOS commands such as CHKDSK, DIR, TREE, and allows you to apply filters or specify criteria for these operations.
ADDCOMM.EXE	Allows you to define the address of your COM ports in the DOS lower-memory segment.
ALARM.EXE ALARMSET.EXE	Provides a memory-resident on-screen alarm clock and alarm.
ANSCOLOR.EXE	Changes screen colors.

ANSICTRL.DOC	Provides a convenient method for controlling screen colors and screen modes.
BL.COM	Highlights the line on which the onscreen cursor appears.
BLANKS.EXE	Blanks the screen after a selectable time interval.
BRKBOX.COM	Displays the status of a COM port.
CBEEP.COM DBEEP.COM CHGINT.COM	Replaces the standard beep sound.
CFG.COM	Provides many useful CONFIG.SYS and batch file commands.
CHGENV.EXE	Interactively changes the DOS environment.
CHK_VL.EXE	Checks volume labels.
CMOS.EXE	Reads and displays battery backup system information.
CMOSALAR.EXE	Checks PC's COMS battery for valid functionality.
CPYDSK.EXE	Copies entire diskettes without extra swapping.
DEGRAPH.EXE	Strips text files containing line-drawing characters from the IBM Extended Character Set (ECS).
DMM.EXE FREENOTE.EXE LDEVICE.EXE NOTE.EXE	Displays memory usage, loads and unloads device drivers and TSRs.
DOSVER.EXE	Determines the current version of DOS.
FD.EXE	Searches and locates duplicate files on specified drives.
FONTHT.EXE	Changes the font height.
FONTLODR.EXE	Loads soft fonts to LaserJet printers.
FORK.EXE	Split the output of a DOS pipe command.
FSN.EXE	Finds lost files on disk.
ICK!.COM SETUPICK.EXE	Retrieves cursor and screen colors.
IL.COM	A general purpose asynchronous communications

INFOBAR.COM	Displays X and Y coordinates of the onscreen cursor.
IP.EXE	Prints ASCII files and enhances the print quality of IBM, Epson, or compatible dot-matrix printers.
JP.COM	A stand-alone or memory-resident manager for LaserJet printers.
KBSYNC.EXE	Sets keyboard lights to agree with shift states stored in lower memory.
KBTEST.EXE	Makes a binary counter of keyboard shift lights to test functioning.
KEYS.EXE	Maintains up to 4 sets of character strings for the KEYSINT.EXE function keys F1 through F12.
KEYSCOPE	Reads and displays the scan codes generated by keystrokes.
LASTBYTE.SYS	The Last Byte Memory Manager is a collection of advanced memory management utilities including CHIPSET.EXE, CLOCK.EXE, HIGHDRVR.SYS, HIGHMEM.EXE, HIGHTSR.EXE, and HIGHMUMM.SYS.
LHA.EXE	High-performance file-compression and archiver program.
LIST.COM	Locates and views files.
LJLAND.EXE	Prints text files in landscape orientation on any HP LaserJet or 100% compatible printer.
LM.EXE	Conserves paper by printing multiple-page LaserJet images on single sheets.
LOOK4.EXE	Finds and, optionally, brings any selected file to the current directory.
LPTX701.COM	Intercepts data sent to a printer port and writes it to a disk file.
LQCHAR.COM	Utility for designing downloadable character fonts for Epson 24-pin or compatible dot-matrix printers.
MAKE.EXE	Makes it possible to create an empty text file of a specified length.
MAM.COM	Maps and manages memory allocation.

MB.EXE	Provides a variety of useful functions from either the DOS prompt or within a batch file.
MCBS.EXE	Lists the memory control block chains in both high and low memory.
MDR.EXE	Runs tests on modem and COM ports.
MH-ESDI.EXE	Reports ESDI drive information.
MH-IDE.EXE	Reports IDE drive information.
MH-RESTR.EXE	Restores all or parts of a backup of system information created with a companion utility, MH-SAVE.EXE.
MH-SAVE.EXE	Saves vital information about a hard drive.
MH-SYS.EXE	An improvement on the DOS SYS command, companion to MH-RESTR.EXE and MH-SAVE.EXE
MKD.COM	Creates and moves to a new directory
MRFILTER.EXE	An easy-to-use text file cleaning/sweeping utility.
NAME.COM	Renames directories/subdirectories.
NEW.COM	Two utilities to list files created since a specified date.
NOBREAK.COM	Turns off the ability to interrupt an operation via Ctrl-C or Ctrl-Break.
NUM.EXE	Converts a user-specified number into hexadecimal or decimal notation.
OPTICOPY.EXE OPTIMOVE.EXE	An optimizing file copier/mover.
PAGES.EXE	Counts the number of pages in a disk file.
PARK.COM	Parks the read/write heads on a hard drive to prepare the computer for moving.
PATHINC.EXE PATHINC.COM	Adds or drops (PATH INCludes) directory names from the path environment variable.
PCL2ENG.EXE	Interprets PCL 4 commands in files, displays each command and an English description of its function.
PLIST.EXE	Prints ASCII files.
PORTTEST.EXE	A comprehensive diagnostic program for I/O ports.
POST.EXE	Prints DOS files to PostScript printers.

PPPD.EXE	Saves/ restores current drive:\directory.
P64.EXE	Provides an interactive print control utility.
QUADRIVE.SYS	A device driver that supports the 720Kb format on high-capacity (1.2Mb) 5 1/4" disk drives.
REFORMAT.EXE	Changes the line length of ASCII (text) files.
SECHO.EXE	Replaces the DOS ECHO command; supports many formatting, color, and variable commands.
SEPARATE.COM	Separates the file name from the extension in a filespec.
SHO.EXE SIZE.EXE	Displays used and available disk space graphically.
SNR.EXE	A multistring search-and-replace filter.
STF.EXE	Compares two ASCII text files side by side.
SUBCOPY.EXE	Copies all files in the current subdirectory to one or more floppy disks.
SWAP_LPT.EXE	Swaps parallel port assignments and displays status.
TESTHEAD.EXE	A diagnostic tool for dot-matrix print heads.
TIMEPARK.COM	Parks drive heads in given number of minutes.
TOUCH.EXE	Stamps file with the current system date and time.
TPP.COM	A menu-driven DOS print utility.
VORCOMP.EXE	Compares two files or two complete directories for differences.
ZIP.COM ZIPCFG.COM ZIPDUP.COM	Transfers files between two IBM PC compatible computers using a serial (null modem) cable.

PTOOLS.EXE Chesire Group Freeware

Purpose: The PTOOLS program launches programs in three ways:

- By double clicking on the program name in the file list or by pulling down the File menu and selecting Execute
- By using Build Command to compose a command line, which is then executed.
- By building a menu file for the program, then pulling down the File menu and selecting Menu

Syntax: Load the PTOOLS.EXE program by entering the following command at the DOS prompt:

```
PTOOLS
```

Once the program is loaded, the PTOOLS display consists of a file list on the left side of the screen and a description box/browser on the right.

Program files (.EXE, .COM, and .BAT) and binary files (.DLL, .OVL, .OBJ, and .TUN) are linked to .DOC files with the same name. Otherwise the contents of the selected file are displayed.

File menu presents commands for executing programs, building command lines, invoking menu files, and changing the current directory (top left) using the mouse or hotkeys (Alt + highlighted letter).

To Build a Menu File

The PTOOLS program lets you use simple menu files to build command lines for execution. Menu files are ASCII files, each line of which represents a menu selection. You can create checkboxes to create lists of user-selectable options. And you can create text boxes for entering command-line specifications like filenames, file specifications, or search targets.

Menu items are executed in the order they appear in the menu file. Use the same order you would when building a command line for execution at the DOS prompt.

Use the following syntax to create menu items:

```
$[C or T], "label", value, [,ON]
```

The quotation marks and commas must be included in the ASCII file; and the following descriptions apply:

`C or T`

designates either a checkbox (C) or text box (T)

`"label"`

is the menu text, and appears next to checkboxes and text boxes

`value`

is the command-line entry that is executed when the menu item is invoked

`[,ON]`

is used for checkboxes only, it enables (checks) the menu item by default.

Example: Suppose you want to create a menu file for the NEW.COM program. NEW.COM lists files created since a specified date. So you want to create a list of checkboxes for one day, three days, and seven days; and you want the "3 DAYS" box checked by default. You also want to create a text box (FILE SPEC) for entering file specifications. When the text box is displayed, you want the *.* specification to appear, because this is the specification you most often use. You know you can change the text in the text box when it appears.

The ASCII file must be named NEW.MNU and would contain these lines:

```
$C,"1 DAY"
$C,"3 DAYS",ON
$C,"7 DAYS"
$T,"FILE SPEC",*.*
```

Remarks: You are limited to 19 menu items per program, using only checkboxes and text boxes, and to creating menus that do no exceed the screen size. If your menu scrolls off the screen, an error message is generated and no menu is created.

!.EXE — William J. Claff — Shareware

Purpose: The ! (pronounced "Bang") program enhances and improves on DOS commands such as CHKDSK, DIR, TREE, and provides additional, useful commands for managing directories and files. The ! program also allows you to apply filters or specify criteria for these operations. You can: search across multiple disk drives, select files according to specified criteria, sort files, format output displays, verify operations before execution, and generate information about network drives.

Syntax:

[d:][path]! *Subcommand* [*Search specification*] [*Select specification*] [*Sort specification*] [*Format specification*] [*Options*]

All parameters (such as a *SEARCH specification*) are optional. The specification parameters and options can be entered in any order. Keep in mind that the specifications listed may be "phrases," or combinations of symbols and values.

Subcommands:

`CHKDSK`

Similar to the DOS CHKDSK utility; provides information about disk usage.

`DIR`

Similar to DOS DIR; lists files according to specified parameters.Won't work with multiple drives, but will accept several search specifications in the same path.

`DUP`

Lists only duplicate filenames.

`DUPCMD`

Lists only program files that occur more than once in directories specified by the PATH statement in your AUTOEXEC.BAT file.

`FREE`

An abbreviated CHKDSK that lists total and free (available) disk space.

`LABEL`

Lists volume label(s) for specified drive(s).

LS

Similar to DIR; lists filenames in alphabetical order.

TREE

Similar to the DOS TREE command; lists all directories and subdirectories on specified drive(s).

UNIQUE

Lists only filenames that occur once (the opposite of DUP). Requires two search specifications

WHERE

Locates specified file(s).

If no subcommand is specified, the default is DIR.

Search specifications:

The Search specification limits the files to which a ! command is applied. Only files meeting the specified search criteria are affected.

The syntax for a Search specification is

d:*path**filename*

You can specify multiple drives for commands other than DIR and LS simply by separating them with a colon. The entry C:D: applies an operation to files on drives C: and D:. You can also use the following wildcards to specify drives:

C:	The C drive
C:D:	The C and D drives
*:	All hard disk drives
?:	All network drives
\\\\name	A network drive (name)

You can control the target directory or directories using these wildcards:

\\	indicates starting at the root directory.
.	indicates starting at the current directory.
..	indicates starting at the parent directory.

Use the DOS wildcards (* and ?) to specify search targets for filenames.Multiple search specifications are allowed.

When any portion of the Search specification is missing, the following default values are used:

CHKDSK	current drive
DIR	current drive and directory, *.*
DUP	all hard disks, root directory, *.*
DUPCMD	does not apply
FREE	current drive
LABEL	current drive
LS	current drive and directory, *.*
TREE	current drive, root directory
UNIQUE	current drive, root directory, *.*
WHERE	all hard disks, root directory, *.*

DUPCMD only searches directories listed in the PATH statement of your AUTOEXEC.BAT file.

Search specifications for DIR and LS must all be from the same path; if you want to search multiple paths or drives, use WHERE instead.

UNIQUE requires both specifications.

Examples: The Search specification:

```
C:\DOC\RESUME.TXT
```

applies the operation to the file, RESUME.TXT, provided it is located in the \DOC directory of drive C:.

Or, another example:

```
\\SERVER\WORK\DOC\RESUME.TXT
```

applies the operation to the file, RESUME.TXT, provided it is located on the \\SERVER\WORK network drive in the \DOC directory.

Select Specifications:

A Select specification filters files according to file attributes (such as size or time of creation). Only one Select expression is allowed per ! command line.

The syntax for Select expressions is: *(Attribute.Qualifier.Value)*. The parentheses are required!

Use the following symbols to specify *attributes* for the Select operation.

$U	Drive letter or Unit
$N	Filename (no extension)
$E	File extension (no name)
$F	Filename (name and extension)

$S	File size in bytes
$D	Date of last modification
$T	Time of last modification
$A	Attribute (R, H, S, A)

Use the following symbols to specify *Qualifier* actions for the SELECT operation.

EQ	EQual
GE	Greater than or Equal
GT	Greater Than
LE	Less than or Equal
LT	Less Than
NE	Not Equal
IS	Has all of the attributes (used only with $A)
ISNT	Does not have all of the attributes (used only with $A)

Values for select operations depend on the select field. Use the following guidelines:

1. $U, $N, $E and $F require an appropriate character string. Wildcards are not allowed.
2. $S requires a numeric value (in bytes).
3. $D requires a date in the form yymmmdd (eg. 88Jul28), or the special values TODAY and TODAY-n (where n is a number of days prior to TODAY'S date).
4. $T requires a time in the form hh, hh:mm or hh:mm:ss where hh is hours (00 to 23), mm is minutes (00 to 59) and ss is seconds (00 to 59). Keep in mind that DOS recognizes seconds only as even numbers (13:30:31 is interpreted as 13:30:30).
5. $A requires a one- to four-letter combination of file attributes, which include:

R	Read-only
H	Hidden
S	System
A	Archive

All components of a Select specification must be separated by periods.

Examples: To select only files with today's date use:

```
($D.eq.TODAY)
```

You can combine SELECT phrases using '.and.' and '.or.' to separate them. In addition, you can use parentheses to group phrases, since in ungrouped combinations '.and.' is done before '.or.':

```
(($S.eq.0).or.($S.gt.10000)).and.($D.eq.TODAY)
```

which selects files with today's date and either a size of 0 bytes or a size greater than 10000 bytes.

Sort specifications:

A SORT is built using the following syntax:

```
(+ or -)FIELD
```

where + or – indicates an ascending or descending sort, and available sort fields include:

U	drive letter or Unit
P	full Path including drive letter
N	fileName without extension
E	filename Extension
F	entire Filename
S	file Size in bytes
D	Date of last modification
T	Time of last modification
M	date and time of last Modification

Multiple SORT specifications are allowed, and need not be separated. If you wish to separate them, use spaces.

Format Specifications:

FORMAT specifications control output displays. Use the following syntax:

```
"$n"
```

in which n is one of the following codes.

$U	drive or Unit letter
$P	full Path including drive letter and '\'
$I	dIrectory including '\' but not the drive letter
$N	fileName without extension
$E	filename Extension
$F	entire Filename
$S	file Size in bytes
$D	Date of last modification
$T	Time of last modification

$M	date and time of last Modification
$A	file Attributes
$$	dollar sign '$'
$B	vertical Bar '¦'
$C	Closing square bracket ']'
$G	Greater than sign '>'
$L	Less than sign '<'
$O	Opening square bracket '['
$Q	eQual sign '='
$R	carriage Return

The $S code is a total of 8 characters long when displayed.

You can also enter character strings to be included in your output display. For example,

```
"$N$E size=$S"
```

lists only the name, extension, and size of each file. It also puts the string ' size=' between the extension and size, so the output might look like:

```
README.DOC size = 1023K.
```

Certain FORMAT specifications can be further qualified using the following options enclosed in brackets:

$P and $I can be qualified with either a [+] or [-] indicating whether the path display is given a trailing backslash (\). A plus ('+') indicates a trailing backslash (default), and a minus ('–') indicates none.

$N and $E can be followed by [*w*], which is the desired width of the field. If *w* is negative the result is left justified. For example:

```
$N[-8] $E[-3]
```

formats the output with an 8-character filename and 3-character extension, justified left.

$D can be qualified using the following codes:

d	Date (1 through 31)
dd	Date with zero, if needed (01 through 31)
ddd	Abbreviated day (Mon)
dddd	Unabbreviated day (Monday)
m	Month (1 through 12)
mm	Month with zero, if needed (01 through 12)
mmm	Abbreviated month (Jan through Dec)
mmmm	Unabbreviated month (January through December)

yy	Two-digit year (94)
yyyy	Four-digit year (1994)
h	Hour (1 through 12 or 23)
hh	Hour with zero,if needed (01 through 12 or 23)
m	Minute (0 through 59)
mm	Minute with zero, if needed (00 through 59)
s	Seconds (0 through 59)
ss	Seconds with zero, if needed (00 through 59)
i	One-character AM or PM indicator (a or p)
ii	Two-character AM or PM indicator (am or pm)

Examples: The specification phrase:

```
$D[dddd mmmm d, yyyy]
```

produces

```
Sunday July 22, 1989.
```

Or this command line:

```
$D[mm-dd-yy]
```

produces

```
07-22-89
```

The leading character of the i code affects the case of the indicator. Hours are treated as military time unless the i code is present, as in this specification:

```
$T[hh:mm:ss]
```

which produces

```
23:40:18
```

While this command:

```
$T[hh:mm II]
```

produces

```
11:40 PM.
```

Options:

/E	Execute with Verification (short for /EV).
/EL	Execute and List (list each line).
/EQ	Execute Quietly (do not list lines).
/EV	Execute with Verification.

/P	Pause when screen fills.
/V	Verbose, lists specifications before executing command.
/VV	Verbose with Verification, lists specifications and prompts for confirmation before executing command.
/W	Wide display (list across width of the screen)
/WP	WordPerfect (output restricted to WordPerfect files)

This program is not public domain but *shareware.* To register, send a check or money order for $30 to:

William J. Claff
7 Roberts Road
Wellesley, MA 02181

Massachusetts residents add 5% sales tax.
Boston Computer Society members deduct 10% before tax if any.

ADDCOMM.EXE — David Foley — Shareware

Purpose: Allows you to define the address of your COM ports in the DOS lower-memory segment. Useful for machines whose BIOS doesn't support COM3 and COM4 ports by default.

Syntax: `[d:] [path]ADDCOMM [port] [address]`

Remarks: In many older machines including early 80386-based systems, the BIOS would set up only COM1 andCOM2 for DOS. Newer serial cards and modems allow you to define COM3 and COM4 on the cards, but these machines won't allow DOS to see these additional ports unless you place the corresponding address in low DOS memory.

ADDCOMM will place this information in the correct location for you and will also display the current address values for any COM ports that are installed in your system. By placing the ADDCOMM statements in your AUTOEXEC.BAT file you can have the machine load the correct values without having to intervene. ADDCOMM is not a TSR and will not require any overhead memory to set up your ports for AUTOEXEC or the DOS prompt.

Example: ADDCOMM COM3 3E8 will tell DOS to address COM3 at address 3E8.

ADDCOMM.EXE is Copyright 1989–1991 by Foley High-Tech Systems.

This program is not public domain but is "shareware" and part of the Foley Hi-Tech Systems ExtraDOS collection. To register send a check or money order for $19.00 to:

Foley Hi-Tech Systems
ExtraDOS Registration
172 Amber Drive
San Francisco, CA 94131
(415) 826-6084

ALARM.EXE ALARMSET.EXE — Thomas A. Lundin — Shareware

Purpose: ALARM provides a memory-resident on-screen alarm clock Hour, half-hour, and programmable alarms are available, with programmable tunes.

Syntax:

```
ALARM
```

enables the alarm.

```
ALARMSET [options]
```

sets the alarm.

The available options to the ALARMSET program are:

-x	Clock disableenable
-c	Chimes onoff
-a	Alarm onoff
-k	Clock display onoff
-p	Clock position topbottom
-e	Date display onoff
-rN	Repeat alarms N times
-l	List the current alarms

-sFILENAME	Set alarms from
FILENAME	(default=ALARM.DAT)
-tFILENAME	Load topofthehour tunesfrom FILENAME
-hFILENAME	Load halfhour tunes fromFILENAME

-mFILENAME	Load alarm tunes from FILENAME
-dMM/DD/YY	Set the alarm date
-vXX	Video attribute (hex value XX)
-?	List the available ALARMSEToptions

Multiple options can be used with ALARMSET as long as each one is separated by a space.

Remarks: The ALARMSET -s option will load the alarms from ALARM.DAT (or from a specified file, if you gave one). ALARM.DAT must reside in the current subdirectory, or in a subdirectory that is part of your PATH command. When alarms are set, they are automatically enabled, even if you disabled them previously with the -a option.

ALARM.DAT is an ASCII file that contains the alarm dates, times, and messages that the program will use. Up to 10 alarm times can be programmed for one date (30 alarm times in the registered version), but your ALARM.DAT file can contain alarms for as many dates as you want. Each alarm is entered in the following format:

```
MM/DD/YY  HH:MM AM¦PM  Your message here!
```

The first item in the line is the date the alarm will be loaded. If the alarm date matches the current date when the ALARMSET program is run with the -s option, the alarm line will be set; otherwise the line will be ignored. You can set a daily alarm by entering the word DAILY in place of a specific date. You can also set alarms to recur on any day of the week, such as MONDAYS, TUESDAYS, WEDNESDAYS, THURSDAYS, FRIDAYS, SATURDAYS, and SUNDAYS, by typing in the appropriate word in place of a specific date. The ALARMSET program must be run each day in order to update the day-of-the-week and specific-date alarms; only the DAILY alarm will carry over without intervention.

Each item in the alarm line must be separated by one or more spaces. The optional message can be up to 40 characters long. (See the sample ALARM.DAT file for examples.)

If you enter an alarm time that is on the hour or half-hour, the alarm tune will not sound, so be sure to set your alarms for something other than :00 or :30 minutes.

ALARM is distributed as shareware. It is not free software. If you continue to use this program beyond a 30-day trial period, you are required to register it. The registration fee for this version is $20 per copy. Upon registration, you will receive the most recent version of the program with an expanded 30-alarm capacity. Make checks payable to Thomas A. Lundin (U.S. funds and drawable at a U.S. bank). Please send your registrations to:

Thomas A. Lundin
16267 Hudson Avenue
Lakeville, MN 55044

(612) 431-5805 (nights and weekends)

ANSCOLOR.EXE — Patrick Kincaid — Shareware

Purpose: Changes your screen colors.

Syntax: `ANSCOLOR [n]`

Examples: `ANSCOLOR`

will display the color menu

`ANSCOLOR 17`

will change DOS output to green

`ANSCOLOR 17C`

will change DOS output to green after doing a clear screen.

Notes: In BAT files you can use ANSCOLOR before an ECHO command, and that line (and all following) will come out in the color of your choice. It can really liven up messages!

ANSCOLOR requires that you have loaded ANSI.SYS in your CONFIG.SYS file at boot time. See your DOS manual if this isn't clear to you. Also, there are a number of shareware replacements for ANSI.SYS that can speed up your display considerably.

Author's note: When you register this shareware program, the author will donate 50% of your registration fee to a worthwhile nonprofit organization that is trying to make this a better world to live in. If you find ANSCOLOR to be of use to you, please register it for the princely sum of $10. Thanks!

Copyright © 1988, 1991 by Patrick Kincaid. Please send shareware fee of $10 to:

Patrick Kincaid
618 Douglas Drive
Mill Valley, CA 94941

ANSICTRL.DOC | Paul Golder | Shareware

Purpose: ANSI Control provides a convenient method for controlling screen colors and screen modes. Cryptic and unforgiving ANSI control codes are replaced with descriptive, plain-English command options.

Syntax: `ANSICTRL [option] [option] /nc`

Options for setting screen colors are entered as:

```
foreground or f[color]and/or background or
b[color]
```

in which the foreground (f) option sets foreground color, and background (b) option sets background color. Available colors include:

black	or	bla
red	or	r
green	or	g
yellow	or	y
blue	or	blu
magenta	or	m
cyan	or	c
white	or	w

Enter screen mode options using this syntax:

```
screen [mode]
```

Available modes include:

```
RESET or RES
```

Resets bold, reverse, and blink to normal. Also resets the screen colors to white on black.

```
BOLD or B
```

Sets the foreground color to high intensity.

```
REVERSE or REV
```

Reverses the foreground and background colors.

```
BLINK or BL
```

Sets the foreground color to blinking.

```
CO40
```

Sets the screen mode to color, 40 columns.

```
CO80
```

Sets the screen mode to color, 80 columns.

```
BW40
```

Sets the screen mode to monochrome, 40 columns.

```
BW80
```

Sets the screen mode to monochrome, 80 columns.

The /nc (no clear) option disables screen clearing after an ANSI Control command is executed. By default the screen is cleared after each command. Also, the screen is always cleared after executing screen width commands.

Remarks: To view the ANSI CONTROL help screen, at the DOS prompt type:

```
ANSICTRL
```

and press Enter.If ANSI Control doesn't recognize the options entered, the help screen is displayed.

Examples: Using the screen color options are relatively obvious. Entering:

```
ANSICTRL foreground red
```

sets red as the foreground color, then clears the screen. Use caution not to set the same colors for foreground and background. If you do, simply enter:

```
ANSICTRL screen reset
```

The /nc option is especially helpful in batch files. For example, the following batch file displays a red, blinking warning whenever you enter FORMAT from the DOS command prompt.

```
@ECHO OFF
ECHO YOU ARE ABOUT TO FORMAT THE DISK IN DRIVE %1
ECHO
ANSICTRL /NC FCOLOR RED
ANSICTRL /NC SCREEN BOLD
ANSICTRL /NC SCREEN BLINK
ECHO WARNING ALL DATA WILL BE DESTROYED !!!
ANSICTRL /NC SCREEN RESET
```

```
ECHO
ECHO Press Ctrl-Break to exit or,
ECHO
PAUSE
ECHO
FORMAT %1
```

Notes: To use ANSI CONTROL you must first install ANSI.SYS. To do this, include the following line in your CONFIG.SYS file:

```
DEVICE=(path)ANSI.SYS
```

ANSI CONTROL Version 2.1 © 1991–1992 by Paul Golder.

This program is *freeware* and may be used and distributed, but not modified or sold for profit without author consent.

BL.COM — RSE Incorporated — Shareware

Purpose: BriteLine highlights the line where the on-screen cursor appears. You can select the highlight color and change cursor size. If turned off, BriteLine highlights the cursor line after two minutes of inactivity.

Syntax: `BL [options]`

The following options are available:

- `/D` Disables the automatic turning on of BriteLine after 2 minutes of inactivity.
- `/U` Uninstalls BriteLine.
- `/R` Changes highlight bar to red (black is default).
- `/C` Eliminates "flicker" on CGA screens.

Once the program is loaded, press Alt-O to activate the program. When the program is active, pressing Alt-O again deactivates it.

Remarks: BriteLine works only in text modes. It automatically deactivates during graphics modes.

Registered users are given a wider range of color and cursor options with the included configuration program.

If the cursor line flickers as you enter keystrokes, it is probably because the host program is writing data at that line in a different color. There is really no fix for this, other than deactivating BriteLine.

Using the /C option may slow your computer significantly.

 To become a registered user and receive the benefits thereof, send the registration feeof $15 and $1 for shipping ($5 overseas), plus $1 extra if you need a 3.5-inch disk, to:

RSE Inc., Dept. PT
1157 57th Drive SE
Auburn, WA 98002

Thank you for trying our programs!

BLANKS.EXE — F. M. de Monasterio — Shareware

Purpose: BLANKS is a DOS-based, resident utility that blanks the screen after a selectable time interval without keyboard, mouse, or video activity; an interval as short as 1 minute or as long as 60 minutes can be selected.

Syntax: `BLANKS [/SWITCH1/SWITCH2.../SWITCHn]`

Command Switches

These switches allow for the modification of the default (preselected) or of an already selected resident configuration, or the execution of one of the nonresident services provided by the program (e.g., display of a Help panel, adjustment of display brightness, etc).

Switches can be specified in any order, and they must be separated by any character between space (ASCII 32) and backslash (ASCII 47). They are not case-sensitive, e.g., /AM = /Am = /aM = /am. An invalid specification of a switch may result in the switch being ignored without affecting program execution (along with a warning message) or in program cancellation.

`SWITCH ?`

This switch displays the Status/Usage/Help panels, which are described in more detail in the section below.

SWITCH Ax

BLANKs configures its settings on-the-fly for the video adapter type that is detected at the time the program is executed. This switch reconfigures the program parameters to satisfy the selected video adapter type for the primary or active video system (or the only system if no other adapter is present.

Valid specifications:

/AM

MDA configuration: IBM Monochrome Display Adapter and, in text mode only, HERCULES adapters HGC, HGC+, InColor etc.

/AH

HGA configuration: HERCULES adapters (HGC, HGC+, InColor) in text or graphics mode, but not in CGA emulation.

/AC

CGA configuration: IBM Color Graphics Adapter, MultiColor Graphics Array [MCGA], and compatible adapters.

/AE

EGA configuration: IBM Enhanced Graphics Adapter and EGA-compatible cards.

/AV

VGA configuration: IBM Video Graphics Array and compatible adapters.

/A-

Ignore prior forced configuration. Uses the configuration selected by BLANKs for the adapter detected at the time of (each) execution.

Note: Proper blanking may not occur with some video adapters that are not compatible with the corresponding IBM adapter "standard" at the register level. Erratic adapter operation may occur in such cases, and the program should not be used.

SWITCH Bn

Adjusts brightness of the display (VGA only). The brightness change step is specified by the sign and value of number <n> ranging from 63- to 63+.

/Bn-

(for 0 < n < 64): Decrease the brightness of the screen, reducing the contrast of the display.

/Bn+

(for 0 < n < 64): Increase the brightness of the screen, reducing the saturation of the display.

/B0

Restore screen to its original brightness as dictated by the settings of the monitor. Clears the screen.

Note: Brightness changes are additive. The sign of the brightness change must follow the value of <n>. Repeated use of the switch or the use of large-step numbers yields unreadable displays; use /B0 to restore display contrast. (Switch /B is a sticky parameter, as brightness changes remain in effect even if BLANKs is made quiescent or uninstalled.)

Defaults:

/B = /B+ = /B2+, /B- = /B2-

SWITCH /Tn

Timed blanking period in minutes. This is the interval that the program waits before blanking the screen in the absence of keyboard, video (BIOS mediated), or mouse (INT-33h mediated) activity.

/Tt

Enable a period of 5 seconds for testing purposes.

/T0

Disable timed blanking.

/T1-60

Enable timed blanking after an inactivity period of between 1 and 60 minutes; a selection of 61 or more defaults to 60.

Defaults:

/T = /T3; no switch on installation = /T3

SWITCH /U

Uninstalls the resident code from memory. This request is disregarded if the address of any of the interrupts intercepted by the resident has been modified since the program was installed. The revectoring indicates that another resident has subsequently hooked the same interrupt(s). Thus, the program cannot be uninstalled, because this would leave such interrupt(s) pointing to empty memory, and the program would then crash.

The program should be uninstalled only if it is the last resident to have been installed. In practice, however, it can also be uninstalled when any subsequently installed resident intercepts different interrupts; although this increases fragmentation of memory, the resulting "hole" is innocuous and can be used by DOS for other purposes (e.g., an environment block).

Remarks: BLANKS.EXE is run from the command line or a batch file.

The registered version of the program adds additional capabilities, including the ability to park a hard disk (if one exists) when the screen is blanked.

Executing the program with switch /? selected allows access to the Status/Usage and Help panels. (If a mouse pointing device driver, compatible with the Microsoft Mouse driver version 6.0 or higher is loaded and active, all of the services provided by these panels can also be activated by pointing the mouse to specific areas of the screen and clicking either button. The mouse driver state is saved prior to the display, to be restored later, if sufficient memory is available for the panel display.)

Upon completion, the program passes an errorlevel value that can be used to check (via ERRORLEVEL commands in a batch file) the outcome of program execution. The following errorlevels may be passed:

Value	*Nature of Error*
255	Cyclical redundancy check failure
255	CPU type cannot execute 286+ version
128	XMM not installed or XMS error in UMB load
64	Error in update of environment variable
32	Invalid password format
16	Invalid hot key combination
8	Unknown video adapter
4	Unable to uninstall resident
2	Invalid switch request
1	User <CTRL-BREAK> keypress
0	Successful execution

Some conditions generating errorlevels 1 through 128 may be additive, and the resulting error value may represent more than a single error.

BLANKS is copyright © 1988–1993 by:

F.M. de Monasterio
P.O. Box 219
Cabin John, MD 20818-0219

BRKBOX.COM — David Foley — Shareware

Purpose: Displays the status of a COM port inside your PC.

Syntax: `[d:] [path] BRKBOX [port] [U]`

where,

[port] is the serial port COMx. Valid numbers are 1 through 4.

[U] tells the program to remove itself from memory. This only works if BRKBOX is the last TSR installed.

Remarks: The status of the DTR, DSR, RTS, CTS, DCD, and RI pins, as well as the data rate, parity, number of data bits, and number of stop bits are displayed on the top right-hand corner of the screen. This information is sometimes useful when trying to debug a serial port or some associated communications software.

If no communications port is specified, the program defaults to COM1. To toggle the display on and off, use ALT-C. The program will start with the display toggled off.

BRKBOX can be uninstalled by entering it with the optional U parameter (if it was the last TSR loaded).

Examples: `BRKBOX COM1 monitors communications port #1.`

BRKBOX.EXE is Copyright 1987–1991 by Foley Hi-Tech Systems

This program is not public domain but is "shareware" and a part of the Foley Hi-Tech Systems ExtraDOS collection. To register send a check or money order for $19.00 to:

Foley Hi-Tech Systems
ExtraDOS Registration
172 Amber Drive
San Francisco, CA 94131
(415) 826-6084

CBEEP.COM DBEEP.COM — >>-Swift-Ware-> — Freeware

Purpose: CBEEP and its matching file, DBEEP, replace the standard beep sound in a program with a visible flash and message on the screen.

Syntax: `DBEEP`

Executing DBEEP from the command line will bring up a menu that allows you to select a program to "debeep" and install the beep replacement function, CBEEP, which is a TSR (terminate-and-stay-resident) utility. DBEEP actually modifies your application, replacing the code that calls the speaker with calls to CBEEP's routines. Therefore, it's a good idea to make a copy of the unmodified appplication, just in case something goes wrong. Once an application has been "debeeped," it can be run as usual, but all beep sounds are intercepted by the CDBEEP utility and converted to a screen flash and message. (CBEEP.COM must be installed for this to work.)

DBEEP.COM searches the original user's program and replaces all code that generates beeps with code that generates a software interrupt. Normally, interrupt 60H is used, but CHGINT.COM may be used to select another interrupt if 60H causes interference with other users of the same interrupt. CBEEP, DBEEP, and CHGINT should be placed in the same subdirectory, and then CHGINT should be run. That will display a menu allowing selection of an alternate interrupt number in the range 60H to 66H. You should be very careful about using interrupt 67H, as it is used for LIM EMS (an Expanded Memory manager) in all versions of DOS beginning with DOS 2.0, although only officially reserved by DOS in DOS 4.0 and above.

Remarks: In many cases, loading CBEEP.COM will in itself handle the interception of DOS and BIO's beep calls. Thus it is recommended that CBEEP.COM be loaded first, then run the program in question to see if the beeps are intercepted and replaced with the beep flash; if not, then load DBEEP.COM and follow the instructions to replace the beep with a beep flash in the target program.

CBEEP and DBEEP Copyright © 1991 >>-Swift-Ware->. All Rights Reserved. The program may be freely distributed, but not modified or sold for profit without my written consent. The user takes full responsibility for any damages resulting from the use of this program.

William Cravener and Dave Hickman
520 N. Stateline Road
Sharon, PA 16146
Fax: (412) 962-0866
CompuServe: 72230,1306

CFG.COM — Mark Treadwell — Shareware

Purpose: CFG.COM provides and "launches" many useful configuration utilities. It can be run both as a device driver (from your CONFIG.SYS file) and from the DOS command line. It does not remain resident and releases all memory on termination.

Syntax: `DEVICE[HIGH]=[d:][path]CFG` *`command [options]`*

from within CONFIG.SYS, or

`[d:][path]CFG CommandName [options]`

from the DOS command line or a batch file where *command* refers to the commands described below, and [options] refers either to individual command options or to command-line switches that are available globally.

Commands: The following configuration utilities can be run using CFG.COM. A "C" and/or "B" in parentheses indicates whether the utility can be run from CONFIG.SYS (C) and/or DOS or a batch file (B).

`ANSI`

(B) Determines if the ANSI driver is loaded in memory.

Exit ErrorLevels:

0 = ANSI is not installed
1 = ANSI is installed

`ASCII a b c ...`

(B) Reads decimal numbers *a b c* ... and writes the corresponding ASCII characters to DOS StdOut. This allows the output to be redirected as desired to create short temporary files or send printer control characters.

`Beep [m,n[;m,n]...]`

(C, B) Beeps the speaker, where m corresponds to a frequency in Hertz, and n corresponds to the number of 1/18 second increments that comprise the duration. If nothing is specified, the default sound is a C note for 1/6 of a second (1046,3). Multiple specifications beep the speaker repeatedly.

`Blink`

(C, B) Calls Interrupt 10H Function 10H Subfunction 3 to enable blinking characters on EGA and above. Any characters with intense backgrounds will start blinking.

`Border [Color]`

(C, B) Sets the color of the screen border.The conventions of the Cls command apply here, with these exceptions: If no color is given or an invalid color is specified, the current screen background color at the cursor location is used. If anything appears after the CommandName that cannot be parsed as a color, an error message is displayed.

`Break`

(B) Determines status of DOS extended Break checking.

Exit ErrorLevels:

0 = Break is off
1 = Break is on

CanCopy *filespec* [*d*:] (B) Determines if there is enough room to copy files to a disk, where *filespec* can use DOS wildcards and *d*: specifies a valid DOS drive. If *d*: is omitted, the default drive is used.

Exit ErrorLevels:

0 = No room to copy files or DOS file error
1 = Room to copy files

```
Cecho[/B¦/I][/C][/N]"F[on]B" Text
```

(C, B)Displays specified text on screen in specified colors.

The double quotes must enclose the color specification. The notes for the Cls command use of colors apply.

The /B switch calls the Blink function.

The /C switch is used to output a carriage return only at the end of the Text, returning the cursor to the first column for overwriting the previous output.

The /I switch calls the Intense function to enable intense backgrounds on EGA and above.

The /N switch is used to eliminate the final carriage return/line feed, leaving the cursor at the end of the String just displayed.

The displayed text starts with the first character after the closing double quote of the color; leading spaces are included. During execution from CONFIG.SYS, the Echo command line format applies.

```
Cls [F [on] B]
```

(C, B) Clears the screen, sets foreground and background colors.

The following colors may be used:

Black	Grey
Blue	Bright Blue
Green	Bright Green
Cyan	Bright Cyan
Red	Bright Red
Magenta	Bright Magenta
Yellow	Bright Yellow
White	Bright White

If any color in the right column is chosen for a background, the video display is reprogrammed to show intense background colors via blinking text. Some programs may subsequently reset this, causing all text on the screen to start blinking.

If ANSI is not installed, the screen is cleared using a BIOS window scroll. Afterwards, the screen colors may not remain permanent, depending on the behavior of the video adapter. If

ANSI is installed before CFG is run, CFG will detect it and use ANSI escape sequences to change system colors.

If no colors are given or if an invalid combination is used, the current screen colors at the cursor location are used. If anything appears after the CommandName that cannot be parsed as a color, an error message is displayed with a three-second WaitFor pause prior to continuing with the clear screen.

Cls sets the screen border (overscan register) to the same color as the background. Use the Border command if you want to change this. It also restores the cursor size to what it was initially since some ANSI clear screen routines change the cursor size.

```
ColdBoot
```

(B) Performs the equivalent of a power-on system reset.

All disk buffers that may not yet be written are flushed to disk via Interrupt 21H Function 0DH (Disk Reset) prior to system reset. The function jumps to FFFF:0000 after clearing the warm boot flag in the BIOS data area.

```
Color F [on] B
```

(C, B) Sets the screen color for output using ANSI escape sequences and without clearing the screen.

The notes on colors for the Cls command apply to the Color command except as noted here. ANSI.SYS must be installed. The Color command is designed to be used immediately after ANSI has been loaded into memory to set its default colors from white on black to what you desire. It may also be used to highlight the output of a specific program or group of programs that do not use the BIOS for output. Note that Color will not repaint the screen. It only sets the color of any future output made via DOS. Use the Cls command to reset the entire screen.

```
Cols
```

(B) Displays the number of columns currently set for the display.

The returned ErrorLevel is based on the value stored in the BIOS data area.

```
ComHide H¦R
```

(C) Hides and restores the serial port base addresses.

H and R stand for Hide and Restore.

ComHide hides the serial port base addresses by copying them to another location in memory. When restored, ComHide verifies the signature and checksum stored with the port addresses to ensure that they were not accidentally over-written while hidden, then copies the base addresses back to their normal location.

The default location for the hidden data is 7001:0000. This is below the 512 Kb boundary in the event that the machine only has that much base memory available, and high enough to keep it from being over-written during execution of other device drivers while the data is hidden.

`Compare [/C] string1 string2`

(B) Compares two specified character strings.

Exit ErrorLevels:

0 = Strings are not the same
1 = Strings are the same

Both strings must be a single group of characters, containing no separators.

The comparison is case sensitive, unless the /C switch is included.

`ComSwap a b`

(C, B) Swaps the serial base port addresses for the two serial ports specified, where a and b are the numbers of the serial ports to be swapped. Valid numbers are 1, 2, 3 and 4.

Use ComSwap if you need to shift port addresses prior to loading software device drivers. This function may not have any effect on programs that use hard-coded port addresses. This function does not shift hardware IRQ values. The contents of the port addresses are not checked during the swap.

`CoProc`

(B) Identifies the Intel CoProcessor installed, if any.

Exit ErrorLevels:

0 = No coprocessor installed
1 = 8087
2 = 80287

3 = 80387DX or 80387SX
4 = 80486DX or 80487SX

`CPU`

(B) Identifies the Intel Microprocessor installed.

Exit ErrorLevels:

0 = 8086/8088
1 = 80286
2 = 80386DX or 80386SX
3 = 80486SX
4 = 80486DX or 80487SX

This routine uses the Intel recommended technique for properly determining what type of CPU is installed in the system on which it is run. The identification code will determine which Intel microprocessor and Intel Math CoProcessor (if any) is installed in the system. If a 486 microprocessor has been recognized, the routine will determine if the CPU has a floating point unit (486 DX CPU, 487 SX MCP) or not (486 SX CPU).

Cursor *arg* ¦ *a b*(C, B) Hides, restores, and sets the size of the text mode screen cursor, where valid *args* are Default, Hide, Restore. Each *arg* may be abbreviated to its first letter, and a and b are decimal numbers of the start and stop screen scan lines for the cursor. The start and stop scan lines are numbered with line 1 starting at the bottom and increasing towards the top.

If the routine fails, error messages are displayed, and the cursor size is not changed.

The Hide option works by setting the "invisible" bit code using Interrupt 10H Function 1.

The Restore option works by setting the "normal" bit code. Some programs may modify this on their own. There are known bugs in these functions in some EGA BIOS 43 line modes.

The Default option returns the cursor to default values.

Video adapter BIOS' implement the cursor functions differently. You may need to experiment.

Date and Time Functions

`(All Batch-File Related)`

(B) Determines the return value for the appropriate function, as below:

WeekDay	(0–6)
Day	(1–31)
Month	(1–12)
Year	(0–119)
FullYear	(0–99)
Hour	(0–23)
Minute	(0–59)
Second	(0–59)
AM	(0–1)
PM	(0–1)

For WeekDay, an ErrorLevel of 0 corresponds to Sunday.

For Year, the ErrorLevel corresponds to the number of years since 1980.

FullYear gives the last two digits of the current year.

For AM and PM, an ErrorLevel of 1 is True, 0 is False.

`DESQview`

(B) Determines if Quarterdeck's DESQview is running.

Exit ErrorLevels:

0 = DESQview is not running
Else = DESQview version [(32 * major) + minor]

`DirExist [`*`d`*`:][`*`path`*`]`*`name`*

(B) Determines if a specified disk directory exists.

Exit ErrorLevels:

0 = Directory does not exist
1 = Directory exists

`Display`

(B) Determines the display combination code.

Exit ErrorLevels:

1 = MDA
2 = CGA
4 = EGA color
5 = EGA mono
6 = PGS
7 = VGA mono
8 = VGA color

11 = MCGA mono
12 = MCGA color

`DOSmajor`

(B) Determines the current version.

DOSminor
DOSversion

For DOSminor, the return ErrorLevel is 10 for DOS 3.10, 31 for DOS 3.31, etc.

For DOSversion, the return ErrorLevel is equal to 32*DOSmajor+DOSminor.

Note that DOS 4.01 reports itself as 4.00.

`Drive [/A]`

(B) Determines the current default drive.

Exit ErrorLevels:

1 = A:
2 = B:, and so on.

The /A switch causes an ASCII drive designator to be written to StdOut. If C: is the current drive, the function will write "C:" to StdOut and exit with an ErrorLevel of 3.

`DriveExist` *d*

(B) Determines if the requested drive letter *d* is a valid DOS drive.

Exit ErrorLevels:

0 = Invalid
1 = Valid

`DriveReady` *d*

(B) Determines if drive *d* is ready for access.

Exit ErrorLevels:

0 = Drive not ready
1 = Drive ready

The DriveExist function is called first. The function then installs a replacement DOS Critical Error Handler to trap the resultant error if the drive is not ready when Interrupt 21H Function 1CH (Get Allocation Information for Specific Drive) is executed.

```
DriveSize [/Dn] [d]
```

(B)Determines the size of specified or default drive, where *d* specifies the drive and *Dn* specifies block size (default is 100) in kilobytes.

Exit ErrorLevels:

0 = Invalid drive error
1–255= Blocks of space on the drive

The number of full blocks on the drive is returned. Partial blocks are ignored.

If more than 255 blocks are on the drive, the returned ErrorLevel will be 255.

```
DriveSpace [/Dn] [d]
```

(B)Determines the amount of free disk space on the specified or default drive, where *d* specifies the drive and *Dn* specifies block size (default is 100) in kilobytes.

Exit ErrorLevels:

0= No blocks available or invalid drive error
1–255 = Blocks of space available

If more than 255 blocks are available, the returned ErrorLevel will be 255.

```
Echo [/C] [/N] [Text]
```

(C, B) Sends a comment line to screen.

The /C switch is used to output a carriage return only at the end of the Text, returning the cursor to the first column for overwriting the previous output.

The /N switch eliminates the final carriage return/line feed, leaving the cursor at the end of text.

For batch file execution, the format characters described below are not required. Use Cecho to output text in a specific color.

Since DOS capitalizes everything in CONFIG.SYS during its parsing scan, a carat (^) is used as the default character to toggle between upper- and lowercase for the displayed string. If a carat is desired on the displayed line, two carats (^^) should be used on the input line.

A tilde (~) inserts a carriage return/linefeed sequence. To display a tilde, use two tildes (~~) on the input line.

If the first character of Text is a double quote, the displayed Text starts at the first character following the double quote. This allows for leading spaces and tabs.

If the first character of Text is not a double quote, the displayed Text starts at the first non-separator character following the CommandName. All leading spaces are removed.

```
EchoPause [/C] [/N] [Text]
```

(C, B) Suspends execution (until any key is pressed) after printing a specified prompt. This command uses the same conventions as the Echo command (above).

```
EGA25 [/C]
```

(C, B) Sets a 25-line color EGA screen. Performs a mode 3 reset of the display adapter using Interrupt 10H Function 0. This works on EGA in a display-independent way. The /C switch clears the screen after switching modes to set the screen color, provided ANSI.SYS is installed first.

```
EGA43 [/C]
```

(C, B) Sets a 43-line EGA screen and forces the use of the display adapter's internal 8x8 font.

Interrupt 10H Function 11H Subfunction 12H performs an adapter mode reset when it executes. This works on EGA in a display- independent way. The /C switch clears the screen after switching modes to set the screen color, provided ANSI.SYS is installed first.

```
EMSversion
```

(B)Determines the EMS driver version installed, if any.

Exit ErrorLevels:

0 = EMS driver is not installed or driver error
Else = EMS version [(16 * EMSmajor) + EMSminor]

```
Env TOTAL¦USED¦FREE¦STRINGS
```

(B) Determines size and use of the DOS master environment, where STRINGS reports the number of strings currently defined in the environment. The other commands are self-explanatory.

(TOTAL = USED + FREE), and */Dn* specifies the block size in bytes (default is 16).

This function returns information about the DOS master environment that is created through the /E switch on the SHELL line in CONFIG.SYS. All information is returned via ErrorLevel.

Note: This function uses information that is undocumented. The function uses verifications to try to ensure accuracy, but the data structures examined may change in future DOS versions.

`FileDTC  [d:][path]file1 [d:][path]file2`

(B) Compares the date and time stamps of two specified files. DOS wildcards are not valid.

Exit ErrorLevels:

0 = Command line error
1 = File1 is older than File2
2 = (Date1 = Date2) and (Time1 = Time2)
3 = File2 DOS error on opening
4 = File1 DOS error on opening
5 = (Date1 = Date2) but Time2 is older than Time1
6 = Date2 is older than Date1

`FileExist [d:][path]filename`

(B) Determines if a specified file exists.

Exit ErrorLevels:

0 = File does not exist
1 = File exists

This function is identical to the DOS "IF EXIST" batch file command.

`Files TOTAL¦USED¦FREE¦ORPHAN¦PREVIOUS¦MARGIN¦BLOCKS`

(B) Determines the size and usage of the DOS System File Table, which is created using a FILES command in CONFIG.SYS.

TOTAL reports all entries available in the SFT, including any that may have been created by later programs such as Qemm's FILES or *PC Magazine's* UMBFILES.

USED reports the number of entries currently in use. Typically, this will be 3 unless files have been orphaned.

FREE reports the number of entries available for use. This is equal to Total minus Used.

ORPHAN reports the number of entries that are orphaned, typically by redirecting the output of a resident program to the NUL device during installation. This number is a subset of the Used files.

PREVIOUS reports the maximum number of files opened since the computer was booted. Since DOS reuses entries after they have been closed, this value may be looked at as the "high water mark" of SFT use.

MARGIN reports the minimum margin that existed at the above "high water mark" of previous use. This is equal to Total minus Previous. This value is essentially how close the system has gotten to a DOS file error due to running out of file handles.

BLOCKS reports the number of blocks the SFT is divided into. A large number of blocks has little effect on performance, but may use up more memory.

Note: This function uses information that is undocumented. It has been verified to work accurately for DOS versions 3.0 through 6.0. The function uses redundant verifications to try to ensure accuracy, but the data structures examined may change in future DOS versions.

`FileSize [/`*`Dn`*

(B) Determines the number of blocks fully occupied by a specified file. Partial blocks are ignored. */Dn* specifies the block size (default is 1024 bytes or 1 kilobyte), and filename specifies the file.

Exit ErrorLevels:

0 = File error or file size less than one block
1–255 = Number of blocks

If there are more than 255 blocks on the drive, the returned ErrorLevel will be 255.

`FileText [`*`d`*`:][`*`path`*`]`*`filename`*` "String"`

(B) Performs a case-sensitive search of the contents of a specified file for a specified character string.

Exit ErrorLevels:

0 = String not present
1 = String present

```
GetKey [/F] ["String"] [[F]n]
```

(B) Gets any keyboard input or limits the allowed keys to those specified on the command line.

The /F switch causes GetKey to flush the keyboard buffer prior to execution. String is a series of characters (enclosed in quotes) representing valid keyboard input, and *n* represents function key numbers (which may be preceded by F).

Exit ErrorLevels:

With list = Position of key in list(1, 2, 3, etc.)
Without list = Scan code of key pressed
255 = Ctrl-Break/Ctrl-C pressed

Used without options, GetKey returns the scan code of a pressed key.

GetKey's optional key list provides additional functionality. If you supply a "String" or Fn argument, Cfg waits either until one of those keys listed has been pressed or until you break out of the command with Ctrl-Break or Ctrl-C. All other keystrokes are ignored.

GetKey is case-insensitive, so if either "Y" or "y" is pressed, the ErrorLevel is the same.

If you want the single quote included as a valid keystroke, enclose it in double quotes and vice versa for double quotes.

You can include the function keys (F1 through F12) in the GetKey list by listing the key numbers without quotes. They may or may not be further identified with a leading "F." Multiple function keys must be separated.

A special case is F0 which represents the Return or Enter key.

```
IACAfill String
```

(C) Writes up to 16 bytes to the Inter-Application Communication Area for communication between CONFIG.SYS and AUTOEXEC.BAT.

There are 16 bytes at address 0040:00F0 called the Inter-Application Communications Area (IACA). These bytes can be modified by any program, but few applications actually use them since any program can change them and they don't provide much storage.

The IACAfill command moves the command line String to the IACA. The String must be a single word. A space or carriage return will end the transfer.

The advantage of IACAfill is that it allows communication between CONFIG.SYS and AUTOEXEC.BAT. When managing multiple configurations, this will allow you to set a variable in each separate CONFIG.SYS file for appropriate action in AUTOEXEC.BAT. Use the IACAread function (see below) to read the string from the IACA.

`IACAread [/F] [String]`

(B) Reads up to 16 bytes from the Inter-Application Communication Area and writes them to DOS StdOut. /F flushes old data from the IACA, and String is an optional character string that precedes the one from the IACA when output.

IACAread functions by checking the IACA for a string and scanning the command line, then writing what it finds to StdOut. It then terminates.

Writing to StdOut allows you to use DOS command line redirection to place the temporary batch file where you want it(a RAM disk, for example).

You can easily write your own program to handle IACAread's output since no error is generated for lack of command line input to IACAread. IACAread simply writes the IACA to StdOut.

The IACA is not cleared by IACAread.

`Intense`

(C, B) Enables intense background colors.

Calls Interrupt 10H Function 10H Subfunction 3 to enable intense background colors on EGA and above. Any blinking characters stop blinking and display intense backgrounds.

`IsVol [`*`d`*`:]`*`VolumeName`*

(B) Determines if a specified volume exists on a specified drive.

Exit ErrorLevels:

0 = Volume does not exist
1 = Volume exists

`KeyFlush`

(C, B) Flushes waiting keystrokes from the keyboard buffer.

This function checks for available keys and repeatedly reads the keyboard until they are all cleared from the keyboard buffer.

`KeyPause`

(C, B) Pauses execution when the Shift, Alt, or Ctrl keys are pressed. Execution resumes when the key is released.

Exit ErrorLevels:

0 = Pause not executed
1 = Pause executed

Use EchoPause to display a customized pause message; use Pause for a standard pause message; use WaitFor for timed pausing.

`KeyPress`

(B) Determines if there are keys waiting in the keyboard buffer.

Exit ErrorLevels:

0 = No keys available
1 = Keys are available

`Locate` *`r c`*

(C, B) Sets the cursor position on an active video page, where *r* designates row number, and *c* designates column number. Top left is 1,1. Decimal numbers are required.

Exit ErrorLevels:

0 = No errors
255 = Input parsing error

`LptHide Hide|Restore`

(C) Hides and restores printer port base addresses.

Command line format:

```
LptHide or LptHide
```

This program is written specifically for the Iomega Bernoulli Box RCD.SYS driver. During RCD.SYS execution, it interrogates the printer ports to determine if there are any parallel port Bernoulli Boxes installed. Unfortunately, some printers respond to this interrogation by printing the interrogation sequence.

LptHide hides the printer port base addresses by copying them to another location in memory when the Hide command is used.

On restoration, LptHide verifies the signature and checksum stored with the port addresses to ensure that they were not accidentally overwritten during RCD.SYS execution. LptHide then copies the base addresses back to their normal locations.

Default location for hidden data is 7000:0000. This is below the 512 Kb boundary in the event that the machine has only that much base memory available, and high enough to keep it from being over-written during execution of other device drivers while the data is hidden.

`LptSwap a b`

(C, B) Swaps base port addresses for two specified printer ports, where *a* and *b* are the numbers of the printer ports to be swapped. Valid numbers are 1, 2 and 3.

`Memory  BASE¦EXTENDED¦EXPANDED¦MAIN k [/R]  [/Dn]`

(B) Determines available memory, where BASE executes BIOS Interrupt 12H to get the amount of contiguous memory installed in the system. For this option only, the /R switch does not change the exit ErrorLevel. It will always give the number of blocks of base memory. The default block size is 16 kilobytes.

EXTENDED checks the machine ID byte at F000:FFFE for 286 or better machines. CFG then executes Interrupt 15H Function 88H to get the amount of available extended memory. The default block size is 64 kilobytes.

EXPANDED checks for the existence of an expanded memory driver. CFG then executes Interrupt 67H Function 42H to get the number of free expanded memory pages. The pages are converted to kilobytes for reporting. The default block size is 64 kilobytes.

MAIN shrinks its own program memory to 0, then attempts to allocate FFFFH paragraphs to generate a DOS error returning the number of free paragraphs of memory. This will be the amount of memory available to a program run from the command line or a batch file. The paragraphs are converted to kilobytes for reporting. The default block size is 16 kilobytes.

The specified number is compared to the number of available kilobytes of the requested type of memory. If available memory is greater than or equal to that requested, an ErrorLevel of 1 is returned. If available memory is less than that requested, an ErrorLevel of 0 is returned; and

k is the number of kilobytes of memory required, /R generates a screen report and sets the exit ErrorLevel to the number of full available blocks, and /D*n* specifies the size of blocks in kilobytes.

If the screen report is not desired but the ErrorLevel is, redirect CFG's output to the NUL device.

Exit ErrorLevels:

Without the /R switch

0 = Requested amount of memory is not available or format error
1 = Requested amount of memory is available

With the /R switch

0 = Requested memory is not available or format error
Other = Number of blocks of memory available

`Mono`

(C, B) Sets display mode for a 25-line monochrome screen.

Performs a mode 7 reset of the display adapter using Interrupt 10H Function 0. This works in a display-independent way. Use this function only if a monochrome monitor is installed.

`Page [n]`

(C, B) Sets the active video display page, where *n* designates the desired video display page. If *n* is omitted, no page change occurs.

This function always returns an ErrorLevel corresponding to the current display page. For modes 0 and 1, pages 0–7 are valid. For modes 2 and 3, pages 0–3 are valid. If anything else is specified on the command line, no page change occurs.

Note that some programs write by default to page 0.

`Pause`

(C, B) Prints a screen prompt and suspends execution until any key is pressed.

The default prompt is "CFG 2.0 Pause—Press any key to continue . . .". Use EchoPause to display a customized pause message, KeyPause for optional pausing, or WaitFor for timed pausing.

`Protected`

(B) Determines if an 80286+ processor is running in protected mode. This function first calls the CPU function, then determines if the protected mode flag is set for 80286+ processors.

Exit ErrorLevels:

0 = Real mode
1 = Protected mode

`PrtScr [/F] [+¦-¦?]`

(C, B) Prints the current screen (using BIOS Interrupt 5) and/or controls print screen operations, where /F appends a formfeed to the output; + or – is used to enable or disable the BIOS function by changing its status byte, and ? reports the current status of the print screen interrupt.

Exit ErrorLevels:

0 = Disabled
1 = Enabled

Upon the receipt of an Interrupt 5 Print Screen on this status byte, if the byte indicates that a print screen is currently in progress, the BIOS aborts the new request. This provides control of Interrupt 5 without a memory resident program.

`RamDrive [/S] [/A] [d:]`

(B) Checks all or specified drives for the presence of RAMdrives, where /S command checks drives until a RAMdrive is found, /A writes the drive specification in ASCII format to DOS StdOut, and *d:* is the first drive to be evaluated (default is D:. The /A switch is functional only if the /S switch is specified.

Exit ErrorLevels:

Without /S switch

0 = Drive is not a RAMdrive
1 = Drive is a RAMdrive

With /S switch

0 = RAMdrive not found
Else = RAMdrive found (A:=1, B:=2,etc.)

This function identifies a RAM drive by searching for three characteristic features: The drive is nonremovable, has only one FAT copy, and has a cluster size of one sector. If the first is true, and at least one of the last two are true, the drive is considered to be a RAMdrive. The tests are not completely foolproof. The following are the RAMdrives tested to date:

YES: Microsoft Vdisk
NO: Qualitas 386disk

`Rem [Text]`

(C) Displays specified, descriptive comments during execution of the CONFIG.SYS file.

This allows the entry of remarks in CONFIG.SYS for all DOS versions without generating errors.

`RenDir` *`oldname newname`*

(B) Renames a specified directory.

Includes the complete path for both old and new directory names, unless the directory being renamed is a subdirectory of the current default directory.

Exit ErrorLevels:

0 = No errors
255 = DOS error or DOSmajor < 3

`ROMdate`

(B) Displays the date of the ROM BIOS. The displayed date is the string of ASCII characters found at F000:FFF5 in memory. Not all BIOS may have the date at this location.

`ROMmodel`

(B) Displays the model bytes of the ROM BIOS. The displayed bytes are in hexadecimal. If the system supports Interrupt 15H

Function C0H, then the model, submodel, and BIOS revision bytes of the ROM configuration table are displayed. If the system does not support this call, the machine model byte at F000:FFFE is displayed. The exit ErrorLevel is equal to the model byte.

`Row`

(B) Determines the number of rows in the current display mode. The returned level is based on the value stored in the BIOS data area.

`Share`

(B) Determines if SHARE.EXE is installed. This function executes Interrupt 2FH Function 10H Subfunction 0. Note that if DOS 4.01 SHARE was automatically loaded due to large disk volumes, file sharing is inactive until this call is made.

Exit ErrorLevels:

0 = Not installed, OK to install
1 = Not installed, not OK to install
2 = Installed
255 = Invalid DOS version

`Shift-AND [Alt] [Ctrl] [Shift]`

(B) Determines if specified shift keys are depressed. The routine will work with either of the paired keys on the keyboard. The requested keys are considered to be ANDed, meaning all keys listed must be depressed. The arguments may be shortened to just the first letter, but must always be separated by at least one space. Use the Shift-OR function to do an OR comparison of the shift keys. Use the ShiftState function for identifying individual shift keys.

Exit ErrorLevels:

0 = Some or none of the keys listed are depressed
1 = All keys listed are depressed

`ShiftLock [Caps, Insert, Num, Scroll]`

(B) Determines status of keyboard NumLock, CapsLock, ScrollLock, and Insert. Each key can be abbreviated using its first letter. Issued without a SubCommandName or with a wrong one, the function returns the ErrorLevels noted below. ErrorLevel values are cumulative. The ErrorLevel returned can range from 0 to 15.

Exit ErrorLevels:

With key(s) specified

0 = Lock state is inactive
1 = Lock state is active

Without key(s) specified

0 = No lock states are active
1 = ScrollLock is active
2 = NumLock is active
4 = CapsLock is active
8 = Insert is active

Shift-OR [Alt] [Ctrl] [Shift] (B) Determines if one of multiple shift keys are depressed. The arguments may be shortened to just the first letter, but must always be separated by at least one space.

Exit ErrorLevels:

0 = None of the keys listed are depressed
1 = At least one of the keys listed is depressed

`ShiftState`

(B) Determines which shift keys are depressed. The exit ErrorLevels are additive. The final ErrorLevel is the sum of the listed values for the keys which are depressed.

Exit ErrorLevels:

0 = None of the shift keys are depressed
1 = Right shift
2 = Left shift
4 = Right ctrl
8 = Left ctrl
16 = Right alt
32 = Left alt

`StacInst [d]`

(B) Identifies the presence of a Stacker device driver in memory and determines (optionally) if a specific drive is a Stacker volume, where *d* represents an optional drive letter to be checked. When run without command line arguments, the program reports if a Stacker device driver is loaded into the system's memory. The Stacker device driver consults an internal table to determine if the drive is a Stacker volume. If a removable disk drive is checked (such as a floppy disk or a Bernoulli), the drive must be mounted in order to provide a valid response. A reserved removable drive that does not have a volume mounted will return an invalid response.

Exit ErrorLevels:

Without argument:

0 = Driver not installed
Else = Driver installed (32*Major + Minor)

With argument:

0 = Not a Stacker volume
1 = Valid Stacker volume
255 = Invalid drive letter

Stacker version 2.01 driver will return an ErrorLevel of 65.

`Toggle [N[+¦-]] [C[+¦-]] [S[+¦-]] [/S]`

(C, B) Toggles the shift state of the keyboard NumLock, CapsLock or ScrollLock keys where N represents NumLock, C represents CapsLock and S represents ScrollLock, and + enables, and – disables the corresponding key. Without a + or – the key is simply toggled. Use the /S switch to write to the keyboard port to synchronize the keyboard LEDs of systems that have a BIOS that does not automatically perform the update.

`Tones [down] or [up]`

(C, B) Generates a rising (Upward) or falling (Downward) series of tones from the system speaker.

Typematic [*m*,*n*¦Fast]

(C,B) Sets the keyboard typematic and delay rates, where *m* designates the typematic rate (1–32) and *n* designates, in 1/4 second increments, the delay rate (1–4). Default is 20, 2.

The larger the number, the faster the rate. The Fast option is equivalent to options of 32,1, setting the fastest repeat rate and shortest delay.

Exit ErrorLevels:

0 = No errors
255 = Invalid value

`Verify`

(B) Returns status of DOS Verify option.

Exit ErrorLevels:

0 = Off
1 = On

`VGA25 [/C]`

(C, B) Sets screen display to 25-line color mode, where the /C switch clears the screen after switching modes, if ANSI.SYS is installed, to set the screen color. This function performs a mode 3 reset of the display adapter using Interrupt 10H Function 0.

`VGA43 [/C]`

(C, B) Sets a 43-line VGA screen. This function forces the use of the display adapter's internal 8x14 font. Interrupt 10H Function 11H Subfunction 11H performs an adapter mode reset when it executes.

`VGA50 [/C]`

(C, B) Sets a 50-line VGA screen, where the /C switch clears the screen after switching modes, if ANSI.SYS is installed, to set the screen color. This function forces the use of the display adapter's internal 8x8 font. Interrupt 10H Function 11H Subfunction 12H performs an adapter mode reset when it executes.

`VideoMode`

(B) Determines the current video mode. The returned value is based on the value stored in the BIOS data area.

`WaitFor [`*m*`:]`*s*

(C, B) Delays program execution for a specified period, where *m* specifies minutes and *s* specifies seconds. If only one number is included, it is assumed to be seconds. The default is one second. Pressing any key during the wait period cancels the wait. WaitFor checks the keyboard buffer at one second intervals for a keypress.

`WaitTo` *hh*`:`*mm*`[:`*ss*`]`

(C, B) Delays execution until a specified time, where *hh* is the hour (0–23), *mm* is the minute (0–59), and *ss* is the second (0–59). If the seconds are omitted, 0 is assumed. Pressing any key during the wait period cancels the wait.

Exit ErrorLevels:

0 = Timed out as requested
1 = Exited prior to timeout due to keypress
255 = Format error

`WarmBoot`

(B) Performs a keyboard (Ctrl-Alt-Delete) system reset. All disk buffers that may not yet be written are flushed to disk via Interrupt 21H Function 0DH (Disk Reset) prior to system reset. This function jumps to FFFF:0000 after setting the warm boot flag in the BIOS data area.

`Window r c w h [b ["F [on] B"]]`

(C, B) Draws boxes on the screen in specified locations and using specified colors, where *r* specifies the location of the top row of the box, *c* specifies the left column, *w* specifies width, *h* specifies height. 1,1 is the top-left corner of the screen, and b (0, 1, or 2) designates the number of lines in the border of the box. For example, a 2 indicates a double-line border, 0 indicates no border. Default is 0.

Color designations must be enclosed by double quotation marks and follow the same requirements as the Cls command. A value for b must be specified if colors are specified.

The smallest valid window is 2 characters in width and height. The area inside the border is blanked with spaces. Text can be added to the frame using the Locate and Cecho commands.

Remarks: The command names can be abbreviated using the first significant letters.

Switches are handled by CFG as follows: After the command line has been transferred to a local buffer and before CommandName parsing, the command line is scanned for any switches. If a valid switch is found, a program variable is set and the switch is blanked from the local command line by replacing it with spaces. Thus, a switch may be placed anywhere on the command line and still be found. Realize, however, switches will also be found in text strings (such as in Echo, Cecho, and EchoPause) where they may not be intended. This method greatly simplifies parsing and reduces potential confusion, despite its limitations.

Global options:

`/Dn` Divisor switch. Several commands let you specify a block size (*n*) for ErrorLevel reporting of results larger than 255. Valid values range from 1 to 65535. Each CommandName function has a default value.

`/E` Displays the exit ErrorLevel (DOS command line only, not available from CONFIG.SYS).

Generally, the exit ErrorLevel is 0 for off/disabled and 1 for on/enabled. Other values are given for each function. An ErrorLevel of 255 generally indicates an error occurred. Functions with no exit ErrorLevel specified always set it to 0.

`/?` Displays an abbreviated command summary (DOS command line only, not available from CONFIG.SYS).

CFG is freeware, or what is known as "zero-cost shareware." CFG is not what is generally called "public domain" software because the author retains the copyright. However, the CFG package can be copied, used, and distributed freely as long as CFG.COM, CFG.DOC, and CFG.ZIF are not altered and are distributed together, preferably in the original Zip file.

Mark Treadwell
1247 Foursome Lane
Virginia Beach, Virginia 23455-6819
Voice: (804) 497-3281
CompuServe: 73700,3344
Internet: 73700.3344@compuserve.com

CHGENV.EXE Version 2.0 — Peter A. Hyman — Shareware

Purpose: CHGENV (Change Environment) is a program designed to allow the user to easily change settings in the Environment. With CHGENV, the user may add to, delete from, or modify any of the SETtings currently in effect. CHGENV is particularly useful when a long environment variable (e.g. PATH) requires modification. The user need not retype the entire SET command with CHGENV, merely edit the setting. New to version 2 is the ability to only sort the environment.

Syntax: `CHGENV [-s]`

The -s option sorts the current environment in alphabetical order. The revised environement may be viewed with the DOS SET command.

With no options, CHGENV displays a copyright message followed by the location in memory of the MASTER copy of the Environment, its Maximum allowable length followed by the current length of all the environment strings in use. The Maximum length may not be exceeded.

Next, CHGENV will display all currently SET environment variables in ALPHABETICAL order. If more than 16 variables are set, a scroll bar will be displayed in the left margin.

There are only three operations which CHGENV performs, and three keys used to perform them:

INSERT KEY:	Add a New Environment Variable
DELETE KEY:	Delete Currently Selected Environment Variable
ALT-C KEY:	Change Currently Selected Environment Variable

Pressing Control-Break, Control-C, or ESCAPE immediately ends the program. Pressing F10 ends the session prompting the userto save the changes. Even if no edits have been made, the environment has been sorted and the Save Changes prompt will always appear. A highlighter is always visible. It indicates the currently selected Environment Variable. To move the highlighter, the UP or DOWN Cursor, HOME or END or RETURN Keys may be used to move about the screen.

CHGENV is distributed as shareware; it is not free software. If you continue to use this program beyond a 30-day trial period, you are required to register it. The registration fee for this version is $10 per copy. Upon registration, you will receive the most recent version of the program and updates to the product for the coming year. Please send your registrations to:

PETER A. HYMAN, INC.
148 Tennyson Drive
Plainsboro, NJ 08536
(609) 799-2638

CHK_VL.EXE — OE Consulting — Shareware

Purpose: Checks volume label.

Syntax: `CHK_VL label [d:] [> NUL:]`

where *label* is the Volume Label to check for. *d:*, if supplied, is the disk to check. If not supplied, CHK_VL checks the current disk.

Returns: Errorlevel = 0 if Volume Label matches *label*
Errorlevel = 1 if Volume Label does NOT match

 OE Consulting is a subsidiary of Ostroff Enterprises.

The CHK_VL program is being released as shareware. If you find it useful, please feel free to send $5 to the address below:

Mark Ostroff, President
OE Consulting
516 Harry Truman Drive
Upper Marlboro, Md. 20772

When you do, the author will also send you two other utilities:

SP_ENUF allows BAT files to check whether a disk has enough free space to perform an operation.

ALERT is an EXE that sounds the PC's internal speaker with an attention-getting dual tone. (ALERT is designed for BAT files or any other programs that can call EXE's but have no ability to sound the PC speaker in a multitone mode).

CMOS.EXE Version 1.3 — Timo Salmi — Freeware

Purpose: Reads and displays your battery backup system information.

Syntax: `CMOS [/bw]`

Black and White for LCD, e.g.,laptops

Remarks: Modern PCs have a battery backed-up CMOS memory which includes the backedup clock to store the date and time, and configuration information. This program displays that information in a window.

CMOS Copyright © 1992 Timo Salmi. All Rights Reserved. The program may be freely distributed, but not modified or sold for profit without written consent. The user takes full responsibility for any damages resulting from the use of this program.

Timo Salmi
Professor of Accounting and Business Finance
Faculty of Accounting & Industrial Management
University of Vaasa
P.O. BOX 297, SF-65101 Vaasa, Finland
InterNet address: ts@uwasa.fi (preferred)
Bitnet address: SALMI@FINFUN.BITNET

CMOSALAR.EXE Version 1.0 — Timo Salmi — Freeware

Purpose: Checks your PC's COMS battery for valid functioning.

Syntax: `CMOSALAR [/b] [/h or ?]`

`/h` give help

`/b` Batch mode, no header

Remarks: Modern PCs have a battery backed-up CMOS memory which includes the backed-up clock to store the date and the time, and configuration information. This battery usually lasts for several years, but eventually will lose power. The state of the battery can be checked by programming, since as long as the battery is giving power, a certain bit in CMOS memory is on; if the battery loses power, the bit will be off. This CMOSALAR.EXE program reads the CMOS information. If the battery bit is off, an alarm will sound. Likewise, if the clock current-off bit is on, the alarm will sound. The alarm can be turned off by pressing any key. One option is to put this program in your AUTOEXEC.BAT, where it will act as a sentinel.

CMOSALAR Copyright © 1992 Timo Salmi. All Rights Reserved. The program may be freely distributed, but not modified or sold for profit without written consent. The user takes full responsibility for any damages resulting from the use of this program.

Timo Salmi
Professor of Accounting and Business Finance
Faculty of Accounting & Industrial Management
University of Vaasa
P.O. BOX 297, SF-65101 Vaasa, Finland
InterNet address: ts@uwasa.fi (preferred)
Bitnet address: SALMI@FINFUN.BITNET

CPYDSK.EXE — Michael Ferrel, Rawls Frazier — Shareware

Purpose: Allows you to copy entire diskettes without extra swapping, even with a single drive. Program can be run from command line or menu display.

Syntax:

```
CPYDSK
```

to run from the menu interface, or

```
CPYDSK [s [[t] h]] [/[no]exact] [/[no]wait]
[/[no]sound] [/[no]auto] [/[no]mono] [/[no]relax]
[/[no]verify] [/nn] [/[no]check]
```

to run from the command line: where *s* is the letter of the source floppy (the default is A:), *t* is the letter of the target floppy (the default is A:), and *h* is the letter of the disk used to temporarily store source disk data (if needed). If not specified, the target drive will be the same as the source drive. The source floppy letter must be specified first on the command line if the temporary data disk letter is to be specified. (Default temporary data disk is the first hard disk drive found, usually C drive, or nothing if no hard disk present—see /auto below.) The other options are as follows:

```
/exact  Make an exact duplicate of the Source
(default is /noexact).
```

This corresponds to the *Fast or Exact* menu choice. /exact will make an exact duplicate of the Source diskette, just like the DOS DISKCOPY command does. /noexact will skip diskette cylinders that do not have data on them. In either case, if the Target diskette is unformatted, all tracks on the Target diskette will be formatted.

```
/verify Do a read-after-write verify of copy
(default is /noverify).
```

This corresponds to the *read-after-write* menu choice. If this switch is on, each cylinder written to the Target will be compared with that read from the source. Only those cylinders actually written are checked. If /noexact is in effect, then cylinders skipped are not checked. /noverify disables the verify check.

```
/wait   Wait at menu before starting diskcopy
(default is /wait).
```

This corresponds to the *Change options* menu choice. /nowait will skip waiting at the menu and prompt immediately for the Source diskette.

```
/sound
```

Use audible prompts (default is /sound). This corresponds to the *Audible prompts* menu choice. /nosound will disable audible prompts.

```
/auto   Automatically selects the hard drive
(default is /auto).
```

If this switch is on, the program will find the first hard drive letter and make that the default for temporary data storage. If the h parameter (above) is specified, this option is ignored. /noauto disables this switch and no hard drive will be selected unless the h parameter is specified.

```
/relax  Allow any disk for temporary Source data
(default is /norelax).
```

If this switch is on, the program will allow any disk type to hold the temporary Source data read during the diskcopy. This includes floppy disks and ramdisks that look like floppies. The program will not allow the temporary data disk to be the same as the Source or Target disks. /norelax forces the disk type for temporary Source data storage to be a hard disk. Copying will be faster with this option, if temporary disk storage is needed.

```
/mono   Turns off color display (default is
/nomono).
```

If this switch is on, the program displays in black in white only. Useful for composite monitors. /nomono will enable color display.

`/nn Make nn copies of Source (nn = 1 to 99) (default is /0).`

Normally, if all the Source data was read in one pass, the program prompts after each copy "Make another copy of this diskette? (Y/N)." This switch allows you to specify how many copies to make and skip this prompt (see, however, /check below).

Also, when set with this switch, the current copy count is presented after answering Y to the "Diskcopy another diskette? (Y/N)" prompt. The value shown can be changed or accepted as displayed. A change is made by typing a new number over old the value. If the new value is only one digit long and the old value is two digits (e.g., going from 15 copies to 3 copies), be sure to remove the second digit after typing the first one by pressing the space bar. Entering 0 as the new value will turn off the switch. Note that if all the Source data was not read in one pass, this switch is ignored for that copy. The copy count, however, still will be presented for acceptance or change after the prompt "Diskcopy another diskette? (Y/N)" since the condition that prevented one pass reading of the first diskette may change with next diskette (e.g., by changing settings on the menu or switching to a smaller diskette size).

`/check`

Checks to make another copy of source (default is if /0, /check; otherwise, /nocheck)

If this switch is set neither on nor off, then CPYDSK will prompt "Make another copy of this diskette? (Y/N)" only when /nn is not specified or set to /0. If /check is specified, then CPYDSK will always prompt "Make another copy of this diskette? (Y/N)" after all the copies specified have been made. This will be the case whether /nn is specified or not. /nocheck will cause CPYDSK to never prompt "Make another copy of this diskette? (Y/N)."

To enable a switch, type a / and at least the first letter of the switch. For example, /exact can also be entered as /e or /ex or /exa or /exac. (The switch /*nn* is different.) To disable a switch, type a /, the letters no and at least the first letter of the switch.

Notes:

1. Careless use of CPYDSK with commands such as ASSIGN or SUBST can lead to inadvertent writing on your source disk. Be safe. Put a write protect on your source disk.

2. If you don't have expanded memory but do have extended memory, installing a RAMdisk in extended memory will enable CPYDSK to use that extended memory, rather than disk space, and somewhat speed up the copy operation.
3. When using a disk for temporary source data storage, the program creates a temporary file named $CPYDSK$.$$$ to hold the data. Normally, that file is erased when the program quits or is stopped (by pressing <Esc> or <Ctrl>Break). If under some unusual circumstance CPYDSK should leave that file behind, you can erase it by entering:

```
DEL $CPYDSK$.$$$
```


CPYDSK is distributed as shareware. It is not free software. If you continue to use this program beyond a 30-day trial period, you are required to register it. The registration fee for this version is $10 per copy. Make checks payable to R. Frazier (U.S. funds and drawable at a U.S. bank). Please send your registrations to:

CPYDSK REGISTRATION
179 Westridge Dr.
Petaluma, CA 94952

DEGRAPH.EXE — William Meacham — Public Domain

Purpose: Converts text files containing line-drawing characters from the IBM Extended Character Set (ECS). Dashes, vertical bars, and plus signs in the converted files are substitued for IBM Extended Character Set (ECS) characters in the original files.

Syntax: `DEGRAPH [d:][path][filename]`

Remarks: If no filename is specified, the program prompts you for one.

Use DEGRAPH if your printer cannot handle the IBM Extended Character Set (ECS). DEGRAPH also converts blocks (hex 0B1H, 0B2H, and 0B3H) to the "/" character.

Original files are retained and given a .BAK extension.

Example: To convert a file named LINEDRAW.TXT in the \TEXT directory on the C: drive, use the following command:

```
DEGRAPH C:\TEXT\LINEDRAW.TXT
```

The converted file keeps the name LINEDRAW.TXT, while the original file is renamed LINEDRAW.BAK.

This program is in the public domain and may be freely used and distributed without restriction.

Wm. Meacham
1004 Elm Street
Austin, Tx 78703.

DMM.EXE Adlersparre & Associates Inc.

Purpose: DMM.EXE, or Dynamic Memory Control, loads and unloads device drivers and TSRs (terminate and stay resident programs) from conventional memory without rebooting. DMM is actually four programs that work in conjunction with one another:

1. The DMM program itself reports on memory usage.
2. The NOTE program is used to place a marker in memory that will be used by FREENOTE and LDEVICE. As many as 24 NOTEs can be placed into memory. These markers are used by LDEVICE to load drivers into the designated area(s) and by FREENOTE to clear the area(s).
3. LDEVICE is used to load device drivers from the DOS command prompt (instead of from CONFIG.SYS). With LDEVICE, drivers are loaded into memory at a point or points marked by one or more NOTE commands. You can use LDEVICE to load multiple devices at a single NOTE marker. You can also use driver or TSR options to load them into extended or expanded memory.
4. FREENOTE clears memory from an area or areas marked by one or more NOTEs.

Syntax: Use the following syntax when placing NOTE markers:

```
NOTE -p(nnnnnnnn)
```

where -p indicates a password-protected NOTE, and *nnnnnnnn* designates a case-insensitive password.

The command syntax for the LDEVICE utility is:

```
LDEVICE (path)(filename)(options)
```

in which path and filename specify the device driver or TSR to be loaded, and options are the user-specified parameters and switches for the driver or TSR being loaded.

The command syntax for the FREENOTE utility is:

```
FREENOTE  -p(nnnnnnnn) (-options) -nn
```

where -p is a password designated with the NOTE command, and -options is one of the following:

- `-a` clears memory from all areas specified by NOTE commands
- `-s` suppresses confirmation messages
- `-t` clears the network memory block and the last NOTEarea
- `-x` clears expanded memory allocated since the last NOTE
- `-K` clears memory except that designated by the last-entered NOTE.
- `-nn` is a number from 1 to 24 indicating the number ofmemory areas specified by NOTE that commands are to be cleared. If no number is specified, memory is cleared from the area designated by the last NOTE command.

Remarks: DMM.EXE requires less than 10K of memory to install. It works only with conventional memory, although later versions also support loading and unloading to upper memory blocks (UMBs).

Examples: To create a RAM disk in extended memory, then unload it when you finish the current task, and to password-protect your configuration, place a marker in memory using the NOTE command:

```
NOTE -p MYCONFIG
```

MYCONFIG is the password for this operation. Your next step is to create the RAM disk using the following LDEVICE command:

```
LDEVICE C:\DOS\RAMDRIVESYS /e
```

The RAM disk is created in expanded memory with default parameters, unless otherwise specified. When you finish your task, remove the RAM disk using the FREENOTE command:

```
FREENOTE -x
```

Adlersparre & Associates, Inc.
304-1803 Douglas Street,
Victoria, B.C., Canada V8T 5C3

DOSVER.EXE Version 1.1 — Chuck Steenburgh — Shareware

Purpose: DOSVER determines what version of DOS is currently running on the system.

Syntax:

```
DOSVER [n.n]
```

where [n.n] is the optional version to check for.

Examples:

```
DOSVER
```

returns an errorlevel based on the version of DOS currently loaded.

```
DOSVER 3.3
```

checks to see if DOS version 3.3, or higher, is loaded

Remarks: DOSVER returns two possible errorlevels, based on whether it is reporting the DOS version or checking for a specific version number. When entered without parameters, DOSVER returns an error level according to the chart below:

DOS Version	*Errorlevel Returned*
6.00	60
5.00	50
4.01	40
3.3	33
3.21	32
2.0	20

When entered with a version number on the command line, DOSVER returns the following errorlevels:

Errorlevel	*Meaning*
2	Loaded DOS higher version
1	Loaded DOS same version
0	Loaded DOS lower version

DOSVER also prints a brief screen message stating the DOS version in use.

DOSVER.EXE Version 1.1 Copyright © 1991 by Tay-Jee Software. DOSVER is distributed as shareware; it is not free software. Part of STEENBURGH'S STUFF (Mildly Useful Utilities). Copyright © 1991 by Tay-Jee Software.

The full set of utilities includes the following programs:

BATBOX:	Simple menu creation/input system
CHKDRV:	Checks disk drive status
CHKPRN:	Checks parallel printer status
CLK:	Displays time on screen
CURSOR:	Changes cursor shape
DOSVER:	Checks for DOS version currently running
INPUT:	Simple prompt/input system
KLS:	Colorful screen-clearing utility
LAUNCHER:	File selection/execution system
MUSIC:	Plays transcribed sheet music on the PC
RAND:	Random number generator
SKIP:	Prints blank lines from batch files
SOUNDER:	Wide range of noise-making options
SPACE:	File/disk space reporting utility
WAITFOR:	Timed pauses
WHENISIT:	Date/time-telling utility
WRITE:	Colorful output anywhere on screen
XD:	Create/switch directories at the same time

You may evaluate these programs for up to 30 days on a free-trial basis. After 30 days, you should register your use of these programs. The registration fee is $20, payable to the author at the address given below. For those registering directly with Tay-Jee Software, we offer a $5 cash discount. Please send your registrations to:

Tay-Jee Software
Post Office Box 835
Lexington, VA 24450
(703)464-5290
CompuServe: 72330,1776

FD.EXE — John E. Bean — Shareware

Purpose: FindDuplicates searches and locates duplicate files on specified drives. Located files can be tagged for deletion, viewed, printed, or renamed. Search targets can be specified from the DOS prompt or by using a convenient menu interface.

Syntax:

```
FD
```

will load the menu interface.

Set the options in the Find Duplicates dialog box, then choose OK. There are four fields in the dialog box. Press Tab to move forward among the fields, Shift-Tab to move backwards. The menu selections are:

Drives to Scan: Use this text box to enter the drive(s) you want to search. Multiple drive designations must be separated by commas. Use ALL to search all drives.

Include Read-Only: Includes duplicates of read-only files with located files. Turn this option off (no check mark) if you want Find Duplicates to ignore read-only files.

Look Inside Arcs: Looks inside compressed .ARC files for duplicate file names. Find Duplicates can delete files within .ARC files as part of normal delete operations, provided you specify the location of the ARC or PKPAK programs.

Look Inside ZIPS: Looks inside compressed .ZIP files for duplicate file names. Find Duplicates can delete files within .ZIP files as part of normal delete operations, provided you specify the location of the PKZIP program.

Once you have set your search options, specify a Search Method by checking one of the following choices:

Fast Full (all versions): Searchs all specified drives for duplicate file names. The /HEAP mode is used, which triggers an error message if you run out of memory. If you see it, choose another search method.

Fast Partial (registered versions): Searches all drives in /HEAP mode for file names falling within a specified range of characters, such as A thru D.

Slow (registered versions): Searches and lists duplicate file names that fall within one character at a time (or pass). Duplicate files with names beginning A through M, for example, are listed on the first pass, N through Z on the second, as shown in the table below. Between passes, you can delete and rename files as needed.

Pass	*Character Range*
1	A thru M
2	N thru Z
3	0 thru 9
4	! thru /
5	: thru @
6	[thru ~

Use the /PASS option from the DOS command line to specify a starting point for your search.

Slower (registered versions): Also searches in passes, using narrower search ranges for each pass, as shown below.

Pass	*Character Range*
1	A – D
2	E – H
3	I – L
4	M – P
5	Q – T
6	U – Z
7	0 – 4
8	5 – 9
9	! – @
10	: – @
11	[– ~

Slowest (registered versions): Searches in passes, each pass representing a single character.

Pass-Char	*Pass-Char*	*Pass-Char*	*Pass-Char*
1 — !	25 — 9	49 — Q	73 — i
2 — "	26 — :	50 — R	74 — j
3 — #	27 — ;	51 — S	75 — k
4 — $	28 — <	52 — T	76 — l
5 — %	29 — =	53 — U	77 — m
6 — &	30 — >	54 — V	78 — n
7 — ’	31 — ?	55 — W	79 — o
8 — (	32 — @	56 — X	80 — p
9 —)	33 — A	57 — Y	81 — q
10 — *	34 — B	58 — Z	82 — r
11 — +	35 — C	59 — [	83 — s
12 —	36 — D	60 — -	84 — t

13	—	-	37	—	E	61	—	]	85	—	u
14	—	.	38	—	F	62	—	^	86	—	v
15	—	/	39	—	G	63	—	_	87	—	w
16	—	0	40	—	H	64	—	‘	88	—	x
17	—	1	41	—	I	65	—	a	89	—	y
18	—	2	42	—	J	66	—	b	90	—	z
19	—	3	43	—	K	67	—	c	91	—	{
20	—	4	44	—	L	68	—	d	92	—	¦
21	—	5	45	—	M	69	—	e	93	—	}
22	—	6	46	—	N	70	—	f	94	—	~
23	—	7	47	—	O	71	—	g			
24	—	8	48	—	P	72	—	h			

Loading Find Duplicates from the Command Prompt

To specify search targets and other parameters, use the following syntax:

```
FD (options)
```

These are the available options:

```
/D=<drives>
```

Used to specify multiple drives or a drive other than the current one.

```
-3-/RO
```

Uses READ-ONLY files as search targets. *Use caution when deleting read-only files. In most cases, they're protected because they're important!*

```
/A
```

Uses files within compressed .ARC files as valid search targets.

```
/BW
```

Uses a black-and-white display. Use this option with laptop computers.

```
/Z
```

Uses files within compressed .ZIP files as valid search targets.

```
/VW=<File>
```

Specifies a file viewer other than the default VIEW.COM, which is included with this program.

```
/PARTIAL
```

Searches a partial list of files.

/SLOW

Searches for files in SLOW mode.

/SLOWER

Searches for files in SLOWER mode.

/SLOWEST

Searches for files in SLOWEST mode.

/PASS=<#>

Used only in SLOW, SLOWER, and SLOWEST modes; specifies the drive on which temporary files are stored. If nothing is specified, the drive with the most free space is used.

/HEAP

Loads programs and file information (including drive/subdirectory list, ZIP/ARC files list, list of all files, and duplicate file list) into available conventional memory, which is called "HEAP" in the programming language I use. This option is not available unless there is sufficient conventional memory available for use.

/DISK

Creates and uses temporary disk files to store all data except the duplicate file list in temporary disk files. Default drive is the drive with the most free space. This method is slower than /HEAP, but may be required for large amounts of files.

/SD=<Drive>

Specifies drive for temporary disk files (as specified with /DISK parameter). You can use this option to specify a RAM disk for maximum speed.

Using Find Duplicates to Manipulate Files

Duplicate file names are listed on screen, each line containing a separate file. The following functions can be invoked from this screen.

Key	*Action*
+ - T*	Tags highlighted file for deletion
– - U	Untags highlighted file
U	Untags highlighted file
SpaceBar	Toggles tag/untag for highlighted file
ALT U	Untags all the files

S	Displays status of duplicate file names
R	Renames the current file
P	Prints to DOS Shell
F1	Displays Help screen
F10	Erases tagged files
ESC	Exits Find Duplicates

Examples: To locate duplicate file names on drives C and D, enter:

```
FD /D=D,C
```

To locate duplicate file names beginning with the letter C, enter:

```
FD /PASS=35
```

To locate duplicate file names on drives C And D using SLOW mode and a black-and-white display, enter:

```
C:>FD /D-C,D /BW /SLOW
```


This program is not public domain but *shareware.* To register, send a check or money order for $15 to:

JB Technology Inc.
28701 N. Main St.
Ridgefield, Wa. 98642
(206) 887-3442

FONTHT.EXE — Eric Meyer — Freeware

Purpose: Changes the font height.

Syntax: `FONTHT nn`

Examples: `FONTHT`

gives instructions, version/date

`FONTHT nn`

changes to font height nn (7–20)

`FONTHT 0 or OFF`

reverts to normal for your system

```
FONTHT ?
```

displays current font information

Notes: Many people are aware that EGA/VGA systems can provide both a *standard* 25-line text screen and a *compressed* mode (43 lines on EGA, 50 on VGA). But these video adapters are actually capable of a wide range of font sizes, of which these are only two examples. Below is a table of the possibilities offered by FONTHT; the character height is given in *points* or scan lines, and the two *standard* combinations are marked with asterisks:

	Text Lines	
Font Height	*On EGA*	*On VGA*
7	50	57
8	43 *	50 *
9	38	44
11	31	36
12	29	33
13	26	30
14	25*	28
15	23	26
16	21	25*
17	20	23
18	19	22
19	18	21
20	17	20

It's often useful to see as much text as possible on screen at once; the 7-point font can display an entire page full of text. On the other hand, larger characters, such as the 20-point font, are very easy on the eyes. You can determine which size is the best compromise for your computing tasks.

When FONTHT changes fonts, the overlapping portion of the screen is preserved, but some text will have disappeared or been added at the bottom, which may make the display slightly confusing at first.

FONTHT and its documentation are © 1991 Eric Meyer. All Rights Reserved. They may be freely distributed, but not modified or sold for profit without the written consent of the author. (Exception: Libraries may charge up to $6 for a disk.) The user takes full responsibility for any damages resulting from the use of this program. For a disk with the latest versions of all my programs send $10 to:

Eric Meyer
3541 Smuggler Way
Boulder, CO 80303 USA
CompuServe [74415,1305]

FONTLODR.EXE | Will Temple | Shareware

Purpose: FONTLODR.EXE is a utility that loads soft fonts to LaserJet printers. It also can be used to create special effects—such as rotate, scale, mirror, reverse, and more—for your fonts.

Syntax: Run FONTLODR.EXE from the DOS prompt using the following command-line syntax:

```
FONTLODR FONTFILE (-options) (DEVICE ID)
```

where the FONTFILE name can contain DOS wildcards.

DEVICE specifies the output destination. It can be a file name, PRN, LPT1, LPT2, or LPT3. When specifying a file name you also must specify an extension or include a period after the name.

The ID parameter refers to the number assigned to each soft font. This number increments with every font sent.

The following options are available:

```
-[ ]
```

Specifies a character, characters, or range of characters to be included or excluded from the font. Characters can be listed individually with no spaces or delimiters (as in ABCDE); or a range of characters can be defined using a dash (as in A-Z). The backslash (\) character triggers the next character to be taken literally. For example, the expression "\-\\" between brackets specifies two characters: - and \.

```
-A:#
```

Rotates characters # degrees.

```
-AW:#
```

Adjusts weight of font to # (-7 to 7). Normal fonts have a weight of 0. Bold is usually 3.

-DOS:*command*

Executes a DOS command before the font is loaded.

`-F:#`

Fixes character pitch to #.

`-I/-UP`

Labels font, italic, or upright

`-M`

Specifies the mirror effect.

`-U`

Turns font upside down.

`-N:#`

Sets the narrow/thin effect, removes # dots from the font outline.

`-O:#`

Specifies outline effect. # is thickness (in dots) of the outline. Default is 1.

`-R`

Rotates font 90 degrees.

`-RBM`

Rotates bit map only. Rotates a font, but leaves its orientation unchanged.

`-S:#`

Scales font to # points. Scaling fonts down produces acceptable results. Avoid scaling fonts up.

`-SH:#%`

Scales font height by # percent.

`-SW:#%`

Scales font width by # percent.

`-WT`*`filename`*

Writes an ASCII text file of font information while loading the font. The file is given the *filename* specified. Use NUL. (include period) to write the file without loading.

`-W`

Reverses font to white-on-black.

`-AA`

Automatically adjusts the height of cell (black) when using the -W option.

`-C`

Clears printer settings with reset.

`-D`

Deletes all soft fonts.

`-E`

Loads permanent (default) font. Permanent fonts survive resets (-C).

`-T`

Loads temporary font. Font is erased by reset (-C).

`-P`

Designates primary font (accessed with Ctrl-0).

`-S`

Designates secondary font (accessed with Ctrl-N).

Remarks: When loading multiple soft fonts, specify a different ID number for each font.

Specify command-line options in any sequence you wish.

Example: Suppose you want to load a soft font that is compressed in an archive file. To decompress the file and load it with one command, use:

```
FONTLODR TR30.USP -DOS"UNZIP TR TR30.USP"
```

 This program is not public domain but *shareware*. To register, send a check or money order for $25 to:

Will Temple
PO Box 5548
Incline Village, NV 89450-5548
(702) 831-8418

FORK.EXE — Marc Perkel — Shareware

Purpose: Lets you split the output of a DOS piping command into two separate *streams.*

Syntax:

```
command ¦ [d:] [path] FORK>device > ¦target2>
```

or

```
command [d:] [path] FORK Filename¦ >target2
```

or

```
command [d:] [path] FORK/command2¦ >target2
```

where command is a valid DOS command that produces redirectable output, and target1 and target2 are either file or logical device names that can accept input from a DOS pipe.

Remarks: If you don't use redirection a lot, this may seem a bit obscure at first, but it's worth playing with. This gives you two outputs from a single source, like a tee fitting on a physical pipe. To print a directory using DIR > PRN, and also see the directory on screen, simply type:

```
DIR ¦ FORK >CON ¦ >PRN
```

Note that the argument immediately following FORK needs a > if the argument is a device, and a / if it's a command; it doesn't need the usual > if it's a file.

Examples:

```
DIR¦FORK¦SORT
DIR¦FORK¦UNSORT.TXT¦SORT >SORT.TXT
DIR¦FORK/MORE¦SORT¦MORE
```


Computer Tyme
411 North Sherman
Suite 300
Springfield, MO 65802
(800) 548-5353

FSN.EXE — Michael Babigian — Freeware

Purpose: Finds lost files on disk.

Syntax: `[d:][path]FSN [d:][path][filename][.ext] [[/search word]¦[//]]`

where:

`[d:][path]`

before FSN specifies the drive and path that contains the FSN command file.

`[d:]`

after FSN is the optional disk drive to search. If no drive is specified, the default drive is searched.

`[path]`

after FSN is the optional path to search. If no path is specified, the current directory is searched.

`[filename][.ext]`

is the optional file name and optional extension to search for. If specified with the [/searchword] parameter, only files matching the file name and extension will be searched. Wildcards are allowed.

`[/search word]`

is the optional key word you believe is present in the file to be located (the search word is not case-sensitive and cannot contain blanks or tabs).

`[//]`

a double slash will cause the program to prompt you for a search phrase, which *can* contain blanks. The search word or phrase is limited to 15 characters, including blanks.

Although the file mask and search word parameters are optional, one or the other must be specified. Running FSN without parameters causes a help screen to be displayed.

FSN does not decipher word processing file formats that encrypt text like WordStar (document mode), and will find only strings that actually appear on disk. FSN will not search through system or read-only files.

A statement BUFFERS=16 in your CONFIG.SYS file will improve FSN's search speed.

An FSN environment variable may be used to specify extensions that should not be searched (i.e., COM, EXE, etc.) For instance, at the DOS prompt or in your AUTOEXEC.BAT file type:

```
SET FSN=COM;EXE;ZIP
```

Also, to avoid searching files with no extension, make the first character in the environment string a semicolon. For example:

```
SET FSN=;COM;EXE;ZIP
```

You are limited to 12 characters following the equal sign.The example above contains the maximum available characters. (This is *only* a limitation in the 2.3 version and is removed with the purchase of the latest 3.1 version.)

Network files that are opened by other processes and do not allow read access will not be searched. Also, files containing locked records will be searched up to only the first locked record.

Examples:

```
FSN M?N*.D?C
```

The above example might produce a list of files like this:

MeN88.DoC
MaNager.DiC
MaN.DeC

```
FSN PAS
```

The above example is a special case. If you specify a file name without an extension or period, the file mask could be found anywhere in the name or extension or even straddling the period, such as:

myprog.PAS
setuP.ASm
PAScal.doc

```
FSN /10-8-65          (<- same as:  FSN *.*
/10-8-65 )
```

In the above example, FSN will bring up any file that contains the search word 10-8-65.

To speed the search process, you could specify a subdirectory to search in, and/or a file mask to search for. For example, if you know that the file name you're trying to find is in the \PASCAL directory and the file's extension is .PAS, you could use the following parameters:

```
FSN \PASCAL\*.PAS /DRAW_WINDOW(
```

FSN would only search files with a .PAS extension in the \PASCAL subdirectory and all subdirectories under \PASCAL. This example might find a Pascal source file with the procedure DRAW_WINDOW(1, 1, 10, 10, YELLOW, BLUE, WHITE, RED); inside.

```
FSN *.TXT //
```

In this example, FSN would search all files that end in .TXT, and would prompt you to enter a search string. The double slash is used if your desired search string contains spaces, or if the first character of your search string is a slash.

Michael Babigian
8663 Rubia Dr.
Elk Grove, CA 95624

ICK!.COM R.Randall Rathbun Shareware

Purpose: Retrieves cursor and screen colors.

Syntax: `ICK!`

Remarks: First, make sure that ICK!.COM and SETUPICK.EXE are in one of the directories in your path, then run the file SETUPICK.EXE and answer the questions.

Now you are ready to run ICK!. When you have a problem reading the screen for any reason, or you cannot find the cursor, just type ICK! and everything will be back to normal.

Lastly, please keep in mind that we do not answer questions from unregistered users of ICK! If you have a legitimate problem, however, we would like to hear about it. Please drop us a note at the below address. Enclose a SASE if you would like a reply of some sort.

Copyright © 1991,1992 R. Randall Rathbun.

This program is *shareware.* If you would like to register, please send $1, a formatted 3.5" disk (either 720k or 1.44MB), and a self-addressed envelope to:

R. Randall Rathbun
18602 Cheyenne Drive
Independence, MO 64056-2082

IL.COM — Robert Best and Garland Wong — Shareware

Purpose: IL.COM (Invisible Link) is a general purpose asynchronous communications program that can function in *background* mode. This means you can dial or transfer files over your modem while working in another program.

Syntax: `IL [COMM PORT] [d:\path\il.com]`

Loading IL.COM is a simple one-step process. From the command line, simply specify the communications port you are using and the location of the IL.COM file. Defaults are COM1 and the current drive and directory.

Once you've loaded IL.COM, use the following commands to activate the program and perform tasks:

Keystroke	*Command*
ALT–RIGHT-SHIFT	Activate Invisible Link
ALT–X	Leave Invisible Link, program stays memory-resident
ALT–Q	Exit and hang up (drop DTR) phone
ALT–P	Change communication settings
ALT–H	Hang up phone, return to current application
PG UP	Begin uploading a file
PG DN	Begin downloading a file
ALT–D	Dial a number using the directory
ALT–C	Clear the screen
ALT–M	Dial a number manually
ALT–R	Change the auto-redial rate
ALT–LEFT-SHIFT	Terminate background dialing, or activate the File Transfer Status screen

Remarks: Setting Communication Parameters Press Alt-P, then enter the number of the communication setting you want to use. The options presented use the following conventions:

With 8 data bits, 1 stop bit, and no parity:

Type 0 for 300 Baud
Type 1 for 1200 Baud
Type 2 for 2400 Baud
Type 3 for 4800 Baud
Type 4 for 9600 Baud

With 7 data bits, 1 stop bit, and even parity:

Type 5 for 300 Baud
Type 6 for 1200 Baud
Type 7 for 2400 Baud
Type 8 for 4800 Baud
Type 9 for 9600 Baud

This configuration will remain in effect until you change it or reboot the computer.

Setting The Auto-Redial Rate Press Alt-R. You are then prompted to enter a number between 0 and 9 corresponding, at five-second intervals, to a period between 10 and 45 seconds.

Dialing from the Directory Press Alt-D to activate the directory. Enter the number of the entry you want to dial. You can create a queue of up to 5 numbers. Each entry in the queue is indicated by the > character. Press Enter when you are finished. You are returned to terminal mode and dialing begins in background. The program notifies you with a beep and a message when a connection is made.

Editing the Directory With the directory displayed, type R to revise or edit entries. Type D to delete directory entries.

Terminating a Background Dialing Session Press Alt-LeftShift. If you are working in your foreground application, the program beeps and displays the message: BACKGROUND DIALING TERMINATED!

Uploading Files Press PgUp to start an upload. Enter a file name and description (optional) in response to prompts. Also, enter the appropriate command to be sent to the host computer. For example, enter U X FOO.EXE when sending the file

FOO.EXE to the host using the XMODEM protocol.

You can queue up to ten files to upload. In addition, you are prompted for a goodbye command.

Know that once a transfer begins, you are returned to the foreground program and locked out of the terminal. When the transfer is complete and the INVISIBLE LINK TRANSFERS COMPLETED! message is displayed, you can reactivate Invisible Link again. You can activate the File Transfer Status screen anytime during a transfer.

Downloading Files Press PgDn to start a download. Prompts ask you to specify a protocol, file name, and command to be sent to host. You can queue files for downloading. Simply enter multiple file specifications, then press Enter.

If you attempt to download a file that already exists, you are prompted if you wish to overwrite the existing file. After five seconds, the transfer begins and the file is overwritten automatically. This is to permit unattended transfers.

Once the transfer begins, you are returned to the foreground program and locked out of the terminal. You can return to the terminal when the transfer is complete. You can activate the File Transfer Status screen anytime during a transfer.

Activating the File Transfer Screen Press Alt-LeftShift anytime during a file transfer to view the status of the operation. When this screen is activated, you can abort the transfer of the current file by pressing Q. The program proceeds to the next file in the queue.

IL.COM aborts file transfers after ten consecutive errors. If there are multiple files in a queue, the program proceeds to the next file. Please note that the total error count tends to be higher than conventional communications, because you are transferring in background mode. The program is equipped with a robust error recovery system, so chances are the file was sent properly.

Leaving Invisible Link Press Alt-X to leave Invisible Link and return to the foreground application. Invisible Link remains in memory and can be reactivated by pressing Alt-RightShift.

Press Alt-Q to simultaneously hang up the phone and return to the foreground application.

Hanging Up the Phone Press Alt-H.

IL.COM is Copyright © 1987 by Robert Best and Garland Wong. This program is not public domain but is *shareware*. To register send a check or money order for $20 to:

Garland Wong
8663 Via Mallorca #86
La Jolla, Ca, 92037

INFOBAR — Philip Maland — Shareware

Purpose: A programming tool, InfoBar displays, in X and Y coordinates, the exact position of the on-screen cursor. Using InfoBar, you can define and measure on-screen boxes. The program also displays the current color and number of the ASCII character at the cursor position, number under the cursor, and the video offset.

Syntax: `INFOBAR [/C] [/U] [/?]`

where the following options are available:

`/C` Configures the hot key combination (default is Alt-1).

`/U` Uninstalls InfoBar

`/?` Displays a list of command-line switches

Once the program is installed, press the hot key to activate InfoBar. Use the normal cursor-movement keys to move around the screen. Also, press:

`C` To move InfoBar's cursor to that of the on-screen cursor

`R` To redisplay information about the last box measured

To measure a box, position the cursor in the top-left corner and press Return. Then position the cursor in the bottom-left corner and press Return again. A message box displays the numbers of total bytes, columns (X), and rows (Y).

Remarks: The number of total bytes in a box is handy for determining the amount of memory needed to save that portion of the screen for later restoration.

InfoBar v1.51 is copyright © 1990 by Philip Maland. This program is not public domain but is *shareware*. To register, contact:

Philip Maland
13511 51st Ave. W.
Edmonds, WA 98026
(206) 745-6713

GEnie: L.MALAND
CompuServe: 72020,3626
ProVision - Node 1
Sysop: Joel Bergen
(206) 353-6966
Home of Global War

IP.EXE (IMAGPRNT) — IMAGE Computer Systems — Shareware

Purpose: IMAGPRNT prints ASCII files and enhances the print quality of IBM, Epson, or compatible dot-matrix printers. IP.EXE contains 25 built-in fonts. It lets you embed within your files formatting codes for fonts, boldface, underline, italics, margins, and other print settings.

Syntax:

```
IP
```

invokes the full-screen menu mode. The full-screen menu will display instructions about how to move between selection fields and how to edit the contents of fields. Context-sensitive help also will appear near the bottom of your screen as you move from field to field. Make your selections as needed, then press F10 to begin printing.

```
IP  filename.ext [LPTx:]  [options] (x=1,2,3)
```

runs IP.EXE from the command line, with the following arguments:

filename.ext

specifies a file for printing. Using CON enables typewriter mode.

LPT*x*:

specifies a valid printer port. Default is LPT1.

Options:

`-E` For Epson 24-pin or compatible printers.

`-P` Preview mode. Displays the output on screen, provided your system's graphics card is Hercules, CGA, EGA, or VGA compatible.

`-+` Sets output for 136-column printer.

`-Cx` Sets the number of copies to x.

`-M` Sets print mode to double density for MX-type printers.

`-D` Sets print mode to draft quality.

`-O` Optimizes print speed by sending regular spaces instead of returning the print head to the left margin for each pass.

`-F, -G, -Q,` or `-L`

Sets print quality, from fast (F) to laser (L).

`-00...-24`

Specifies font number, from 00 to 24.

`-W` Prints a WordStar document file, resets bit 7 to remove unwanted characters.

`-#(filename)`

Sends output to a disk file (filename).

`-N` Disables the automatic reset of your printer.

`-Tn` Changes the *trigger<D> character within documents to n. The trigger character is used to signal formatting commands embedded within files.*

Backslash Commands Backslash commands are embedded within text files and specify print or formatting characteristics. For example, \I turns italics on or off, depending on its current state. These commands might toggle a setting, such as italics, or might be followed by a value setting.

Backslash commands are not printed, rather they are used only to send instructions to the printer.

Here's a summary of available backslash commands. You can embed them anywhere within a file. Do not enclose them in quotes and don't use spaces after them unless you need a blank space on the printout.

\00 ... \24	Selects font, 00 through 24
\F	Selects fast print mode (3 passes)

\G	Selects grouped print mode (1 pass)
\Q	Selects quality print mode (3 passes)
\L	Selects laser quality print mode (6 passes)
\B	Toggles bold attribute
\H	Toggles half-high attribute
\I	Toggles italic attribute
\U	Toggles underline attribute
\W	Toggles double width attribute
\N	Sets normal offset
\^	Sets Superscript offset
\V	Sets Subscript offset
\C	Cancels all character attributes and offsets
\>	Selects 10 characters per inch
\¦	Selects 12 characters per inch
\<	Selects CONDENSED (17.1 characters per inch)
\P	Selects proportional spacing
\S	Sets six lines per inch
\E	Sets eight lines per inch
\[	Starts straight-through mode
\]	Ends straight-through mode
\-	Sets soft hyphen (if formatting enabled with ".EN")

Formatting Commands Formatting commands also are embedded within text files, and also might be followed by a numeric value specifying the format option. Two factors go into building format commands:

- First, formatting must be enabled using the .EN command.
- Formatting commands are preceded by a period (.), which must be the first character on a line.

You do not need to use formatting if your word processor has already formatted the text, and you can use backslash commands without using the text formatting commands.

Here's a summary of available formatting commands:

```
.EN
```

Enables formatting. This command must be sent before any other formatting commands are recognized.

```
.PL x
```

Sets page length to x number of lines

`.PN x`

Sets page number to x

`.PR`

Prompts user for page range to print

`.PA`

Move to top of next page

`.OH string`

Defines odd-page header string

`.EH string`

Defines even-page header string

`.OF string`

Defines odd-page footer string

`.EF string`

Defines even-page footer string

`.SW x`

Sets widths of headers and footers to x

`.KI`

Kills all header and footer definitions

`.LI x`

Sets lines per inch to x (6 or 8 only)

`.LS x`

Sets line spacing to x

`.PP x`

Sets temporary indent for paragraph to x

`.WW`

Enables word wrap with justification

`.NW`

Disables word wrap

`.RR`

Sets a ragged right margin

```
.LM x
```

Sets left margin to x

```
.RM x
```

Sets right margin to x

```
.EE x
```

Sets extra left gutter on even pages

```
.OE x
```

Sets extra left gutter on odd pages

```
.TI x
```

Sets temporary indent for next line to x

```
.CE
```

Centers next line of text

```
.FP
```

Prints text buffer

```
.LF x
```

Inserts x number of line feeds

```
.ST
```

Stops printing before each page

```
.!! \?
```

Executes a backslash command (/?)

Remarks: Included in the IMAGPRNT archive file is a convenient text editor, IE.EXE. You can use it to create, edit, or preview files you want to print.

Use the -T option to specify a different command trigger. In this way, you can print a text file with previously embedded backslash commands. The backslash commands are included on the printout for your evaluation.

Some IMAGEPRINT options, such as Epson MX compatibility mode, Epson 24 pin printer mode and print previewing are not available with the full screen menu. Invoke these options directly from the command line.

IP.EXE and IMAGPRNT are © Copyright IMAGE Computer Systems 1985–1993. This program is not public domain but *shareware.* To register, send a check or money order for $45.95 to:

IMAGE Computer Systems
P. O. Box 647
Avon, CT 06001
(203) 678-8771

JP.COM — Robert L. Morton — Shareware

Purpose: JP.COM is a stand-alone or memory-resident manager for LaserJet printers. Use it to control page settings and font specifications. You can create setup files of configuration settings, then save and load them as needed.

Syntax:

```
JP
```

loads JP.COM from the DOS command prompt. Use command-line options to load it memory-resident (see below). When the program is memory-resident you also can, from the DOS prompt, activate the program and specify new parameters for it. When first loaded, the program displays a set of pull-down menus.

Remarks: The following menus are available from the JP.COM screen. Control characters are shown in parentheses.

```
Control (C)
```

Use this menu to reset your computer, run its self-test, and eject a page.

```
Job (J)
```

Specify settings for numbers of copies and offset.

```
Page (P)
```

Set margins, paper size, and so on.

```
Font (F)
```

Specify font characteristics, such as pitch, height, spacing, and so on.

```
Other (O)
```

Use these selections to print envelopes and files.

```
System (S)
```

Save and load setup files, install the program memory-resident, and uninstall.

You can access specific menus and perform operations from the DOS command prompt. To do this, add the control keystrokes to your command line. For example, use

```
JP SI
```

to load the program memory resident. In effect, adding the SI parameter pulls down the System menu and executes the Install selection. Here's a list of other control characters you can use from the command line:

Program	*Command Line*
Enter	^M
Esc	^[
Backspace	^H
F1	&;
F3	&=
Home	&G
End	&O
PgUp	&I
PgDn	&Q
Up Arrow	&H
Down Arrow	&P
Left Arrow	&K
Right Arrow	&M
Insert	&R
Delete	&S
^	^^
&	&&

Setting print options using JP.COM changes your LaserJet's settings. To keep printer settings current, JP.COM updates them:

- Immediately when you activate or run the program.
- Before an envelope is printed.
- Before a file is printed.
- When you exit.

So, if your word processor resets your printer, and you want to reactivate JP.COM's settings, all you need do is activate the program.

Remarks: The JPCONFIG.COM utility (included in the archive file) controls JP.COM configuration settings. To load this utility, enter this command at the DOS prompt:

```
JPCONFIG <Enter>
```

A menu appears containing the following selections:

LaserJet Model
Printer Port
Use Expanded Memory
Immediate Update
Activation Hot Key
Internal Fonts
Cartridge Fonts

If JP.COM is memory-resident, changes made using JPCONFIG are not invoked until the program is exited and reloaded.

JP.COM supports Hewlett Packard LaserJet II, IID, IIP, III, IIID, IIISi, IIIP, or compatible printers.

Examples: Presented here are examples of executing tasks by adding control characters to the command line.

JP CR^[^[	Resets printer.
JP JN5^M^[^[	Changes number of copies to 5.
JP PL1.5^MR1.5^M^[^[	Sets left and right margins 1.5".
JP FLI^[^[	Selects italic font.
JP OFSUP.DOC^M^[^[	Prints file SUP.DOC.
JP SSTEST^M^[^[	Saves current setup to file TEST.

JP.COM is Copyright © 1993 by Robert L. Morton. This program is not public domain but *shareware.* To register, send a check or money order for $24.95 to:

Morton Utilities
81-887 Tournament Way
Indio, California 92201
(619) 347-7563
70132,3707 COMPUSERVE

KBSYNC.EXE — John Goodman — Freeware

Purpose: Sets keyboard lights to agree with shift states stored in lower memory. Use this program to reset your keyboard after running KBTEST.

Syntax: `KBSYNC`

Remarks: The program displays keyboard status and the DOS prompt is returned.

This program is discussed in detail in Chapter Four.

KBSYNC.EXE is Copyright © 1993 by John Goodman. This program is *freeware* and may be freely used and distributed, but not modified or sold for profit without author consent.

John Goodman
6221 Choctaw Drive
Westminster, CA 92683-2105
714-895-3195

KBTEST.EXE — John Goodman — Freeware

Purpose: Makes a binary counter of keyboard shift lights (Num Lock, Caps Lock, Scroll Lock) to test their functioning.

Syntax: `KBTEST`

Remarks: The program cycles through the numbers, 0 through 7, on the screen. Keyboard lights display each number in binary notation. Caps Lock represents the most significant bit, Scroll Lock the least significant bit.

This utility is discussed in detail in Chapter Four.

KBTEST.EXE is Copyright © 1993 by John Goodman. This program is *freeware* and may be freely used and distributed, but not modified or sold for profit without author consent.

John Goodman
6221 Choctaw Drive
Westminster, CA 92683-2105
714-895-3195

KEYS.EXE Davy Crockett Productions Public Domain

Purpose: KEYS.EXE maintains up to 4 sets of character strings for the function keys F1 through F12. Optionally you may substitute Shift-F1 and Shift-F2 for F11 and F12 on keyboards with only 10 function keys.

Syntax: The character strings are sent to the ANSI.SYS driver with the proper control codes to reassign the function keys. So before you can run KEYS, the ANSI.SYS (from your original DOS disk) must be installed in your CONFIG.SYS file, using a command similar to this one:

```
DEVICE=C:\DOS\ANSI.SYS
```

To Use F11 and F12 In addition, the file, KEYSINT.COM (from the archive file), must be installed before ANSI.SYS recognizes F11 and F12 on an enhanced keyboard. One caveat: you must also have a recent version of IBM's BIOS chip or the function codes 10H & 11H are simply ignored. You can tell your version is outdated if the keyboard dies after installing a key set containing F11 and F12. Your only recourse is to use Shift-F1 and Shift-F2, or upgrade your BIOS chip.

To load KEYSINT.COM, enter the following command at the DOS prompt:

```
KEYSINT [User-Int]
```

in which [User-Int] is a number between 60 and 67 (these are Hex but you don't need the "H") that tells KeysInt which user interrupt to use to point to itself (so Keys can find it to enable/disable it). If a parameter is not supplied, KeysInt will use interrupt 63H.

Once ANSI.SYS and KEYSINT.COM (optional) are installed, you can load KEYS in two ways.

Loading the Menu Interface To load KEYS and edit/configure the program from a convenient, menu interface, enter:

```
KEYS
```

at the DOS command prompt. Use the arrow keys and Tab to move around the screen.

While in the menu interface you can also press Ctrl-R to save the current line temporarily, then write it to another location by pressing Ctrl-W.

Press Ctrl-D to duplicate all key assignments from the previous set to the current set.

When you have configured a key set, press F1 to install that set. Press ESC or Ctrl-C to quit the program without installing or saving the configuration.

Loading from the Dos Prompt To load a KEYS set directly from the DOS prompt, use the following command syntax:

```
KEYS [#] [ON/OFF][HELP][SHOW][DUMP][LOAD]
```

Use this table to configure your command lines.

[#]	# = 0,1,2,3 or [keyword] in the title
ON	Installs Key Set
SHOW	Show strings
OFF	Re-enables standard DOS functions
HELP	Displays Help screen
DUMP	Dumps key definitions to file KEYS.TXT
LOAD	Loads key definitions from file KEYS.TXT

Remarks: While KEYS.EXE allows you to as assign up to 30 characters for each function key, ANSI.SYS has an extremely small area for storing these assignments. If you overload this storage area, by assigning large numbers of characters for many keys, your results can be unpredictable. This is not a "bug" in the KEYS program but a limitation in the ANSI.SYS driver.

Use "!" to represent a carriage return. Use "@" to represent a blank space.

You can use environment variables as part of the character strings (e.g., EDLIN %M%!).

When in edit mode, press F10 to change the style of box around menu selections; there are four different styles.

Your keyboard reassignments may interfere with programs that use DOS interrupts to obtain keyboard input. KEYS will return the character string you have programmed instead of the actual function key. If you find a program that uses the function keys and the program does not respond when you press a function key (or it beeps at you), turn off reassignments with the command: KEYS OFF before executing the program.

KEYS.EXE is Copyright 1989 by Davy Crockett Productions. This program is public domain and may be freely used and distributed, but not modified or sold for profit without the author's consent.

Davy Crockett Productions
5807 Cherrywood Lane,
Suite #104
Greenbelt, Md 20770-1259

KEYSCOPE 1.1 — William Pierpoint — Freeware

Purpose: Reads and displays the scan codes generated by keystrokes.

Syntax: `KEYSCOPE`

Remarks: For most keyboards, two codes are generated by each keystroke, one on pressing, one on release. Keyscope shows you these codes, as well as the order in which interrupts 9h and 16h occur, keyboard status at the time of interrupt, and whether the BIOS on your machine suppports the enhanced (101-key) keyboard.

Either "bios" or "XBIOS" are displayed in the upper-right corner of the KEYSCOPE screen, XBIOS indicates an extended bios that supports the enhanced 101-key keyboard.

Each time you press a key, the following information is displayed: scan code, key code, interrupt, and status. Scan and key codes are decimal numbers, interrupts are hexadecimal numbers (a small h is appended to them), and the keyboard status byte is decoded into the following symbols:

Symbol	*Active Keys*
LS	Left Shift Key
RS	Right Shift Key
Alt	Alternate Key
Ctrl	Control Key
Caps	Caps Lock Key

Num	Num Lock Key
Scrl	Scroll Lock Key
Ins	Insert Mode

Press ESC when you are ready to exit the program. Technically, the program looks for scan code 129, which is the release scan code for the ESC key on almost all keyboards. If not, you may have to hunt around to find it.

Part of the KEYSCOPE program is ram-resident. The ram-resident code is released on normal exit. Should you happen to exit some other way, you should reboot your computer.

KEYSCOPE only runs with MS-DOS or PC-DOS version 2.0 or greater and in video modes 2, 3, or 7 (80-column text modes). If these two conditions are not met, KEYSCOPE will issue an error message and quit.

This program is *freeware* and may be freely used and distributed, but not modified or sold for profit without author consent.

Pierpoint Software
P.O. Box 2198
Camarillo, CA 93011-2198

LASTBYTE.SYS Key Software Products Shareware

Purpose: The Last Byte Memory Manager is a collection of advanced programs for managing upper memory (between 640K and 1 Mb).

Syntax: `DEVICE= [d:][path]LASTBYTE.SYS [/options]`

where the command line options are of the general form:

`<keyword>=<base>:<size>`

where *<keyword>* is one of the option keywords and may be abbreviated by its first letter, *<base>* is a four-digit hexadecimal segment address in the range A000 to FC00, and *<size>* is a decimal number in kilobytes.

There are two restrictions on these options:

1. The base must be exactly 4 hexadecimal digits, must lie at or above A000, and must be a multiple of 0020 (512 bytes), and
2. The size must be in the range 1–384 kb.

The "multiple of 0020" requirement is necessary to be consistent with the resolution that The Last Byte Memory Manager uses to organize high memory during initialization. However, this requirement is often affected by the much coarser resolution used by most memory controllers—each block of memorymust be either totally enabled or disabled. If any part of a block's address space is disabled by the presence of an adapter card, the entire block of memory is disabled and cannot be made available as High-DOS Memory.

Valid keywords include:

`BANKSWITCH=<base>:<size>`

Forces a region of upper memory that would normally be used as High-DOS memory to be made available as Bank-Switch memory.

CACHE=<*kbytes*>

Forces LASTBYTE.SYS to think that there is a memory cache between the CPU and main memory and to set its size. This option is usually not necessary; LASTBYTE.SYS normally will automatically detect the presence of a cache and its size.

Activating bank-switch memory causes the contents of a cache (if present) to be invalid; this is known as a "cache coherency" problem. If a cache is detected during installation, LASTBYTE.SYS checks to see if any portion of the upper address space is cached. If not, then no cache coherency problem exists. If the upper address space is cached, however, LASTBYTE.SYS will flush the cache on every access to Bank-Switch memory to prevent the cache from providing invalid data to the CPU. The cache is flushed by filling it from low memory. The <size> value is used to determine how much to fill.

`DOS=<base>:<size>`

Forces a region of upper memory that would normally be used as Bank-Switch memory to be made available as High-DOS memory.

`EXCLUDE=<base>:<size>`

Forces a region of upper memory unavailable as either High-DOS or Bank-Switch memory.

MOVE=VIDEOBIOS

Tries to move an EGA or VGA bios to a better location within the available upper memory in order to reduce fragmentation of free memory.

MOVE=MAINBIOS

Tries to move the main bios to a better location within the available upper memory in order to reduce fragmentation of memory. The ADDHOLES suboption MOVE=MAINBIOS,ADDHOLES will create seven holes in the residual 8k left at FE00 for a total of more than 3k.

MOVE=OVERLAY

This option is for chipsets in which the main bios shadow ram cannot be made read/write (ETEQ, OPTi, Intel, and some by VLSI). This option puts that ram in write-only mode, copies the video bios on top of the main bios initialization code at the beginning of the bios, then returns the ram to read-only mode. Then the old video bios region is converted to usable Hi-DOS memory.

MOVE=XBDA

This option relocates the Extended Bios Data Area (XBDA), if it exists, into Upper Memory. The XBDA is usually 1k reserved at the top of conventional memory by the main Bios. Not all machines use an XBDA, but if it exists, LASTBYTE.SYS will report 639k of Conventional Memory instead of 640k, and the advanced utility HIGHAPND will refuse to append any memory. Some machines may not operate properly with a relocated XBDA, so use this option with caution. (Note that some computer viruses also "steal" the top 1k of memory.)

PHYSICAL=<MemoryController>

Used to specify the memory controller determined by the CHIPSET program. The OVERRIDE suboption as in: PHYSICAL=82C212,OVERRIDE, disables any shadow ram relocation that may be in effect, regardless of your CMOS configuration menu setup. Many memory controller chips can relocate all or part of shadow ram to the top of (extended) memory. If LASTBYTE.SYS fails to install with the error message: "Shadow Ram memory relocated—Use OVERRIDE option" try adding the OVERRIDE suboption to the PHYSICAL option. The NOEMS suboption may be used in conjunction with PHYSICAL=LIM4EMS or EEMS to use the 64k page frame as High-DOS Memory, as in: PHYSICAL=LIM4EMS,NOEMS. The NOEMS suboption must be used in conjunction with PHYSICAL=LIM3EMS (i.e., PHYSICAL=LIM3EMS,NOEMS). Doing so disables other (normal) use of all expanded memory.

```
RESTRICT=<ab> <cd> <ef>
```

Address lines A15 and A16 are not latched in hardware design of the AT bus, and some 16-bit adapter cards do not properly decode these address lines, and may occassionally respond to a memory access that is directed at some other portion of the address space. This can cause erroneous data to be transferred, and often occurs during 8-bit DMA transfers between a floppy disk drive and upper memory near the address space occupied by an offending 16-bit adapter card. This phenomena only occurs when the two address areas are within one of three 128K regions in the upper area: A0000–BFFFF, C0000–DFFFF, and E0000–FFFFF. LASTBYTE.SYS automatically senses the presence of 16-bit adapter cards in each of these three regions and records this information within its resident image or use by its utilities. The RESTRICT option is provided to override this automatic detection of 16-bit adapters. Each of the three arguments (one per 128k region) should be replaced by either "0" (indicating no 16-bit adapters), or "1" (indicating the presense of a 16-bit adapter) and separated by commas. RESTRICT=1,1,0 would imply that one or more 16-bit adapters are located in the first two 128k regions of upper memory (A000–DFFF), so that when the companion /RESTRICT option of HIGHDRVR, HIGHTSR, or HIGHUMM is used, only High-DOS memory in the region E000–FFFF will be allocated.

```
SHADOW=<base>:<size>
```

This option is for those who want to forces a region of memory (presumably ROM) to be copied into shadow ram. The Last Byte Memory Manager will automatically copy the video bios and main bios to shadow ram if they aren't already shadowed. However, it will not do so for other adapter ROMs. This is because some controllers "hide" a small RAM by overlaying it in a portion of the same address space they declare as being filled with ROM.

Such a RAM is no longer accessible when the ROM is shadowed, usually causing the adapter to stop functioning.

```
?
```

Causes LASTBYTE.SYS to erase the screen, display a summary of what it finds in the upper memory area,

Remarks: Before you run LASTBYTE, you can—and should—verify it's compatibility with your system. Do this using the CHIPSET utility. Run it from the DOS prompt by entering the following command:

```
CHIPSET
```

If CHIPSET finds a compatible system, it prompts you to begin installation. For more detailed information on the CHIPSET program and system requirements, consult the file CHIPSET.

The installation menu provides a selection called: Creating a demo diskette. Choose this selection to create a bootable floppy disk with your system files as they might look after you've installed LASTBYTE for real. Use the demo disk to test your installation and configuration without changing the system files on your hard disk.

Once it's created, put your demo disk in its floppy drive and reboot your computer. Your system is booted from the new system files on the demo disk. If it fails, or you aren't thrilled with the results, remove the disk and reboot off your hard disk.

LASTBYTE.SYS provides access to upper memory by using shadow RAM, conventional RAM, or by mapping expanded memory (EMS) pages into upper memory.

Using LASTBYTE, you can free conventional memory by moving device drivers, TSRs, even the master environment (DOS FILES and DOS BUFFERS) into upper memory. Depending on your system configuration, you may also be able to extend total conventional memory to as much as 736k.

LASTBYTE also includes utility programs for creating and/or handling:

- RAM disks
- print spoolers
- command line recall (history) buffers

- expanded memory emulation
- TSR markers

Note: When your computer reboots, LASTBYTE.SYS pauses thirty seconds, then waits for a keystroke before continuing. (Eliminating this pause requires a registered version of the program.)

If your computer stops before displaying the sign-on box, or if it fails to operate properly after booting, there are two possible reasons (and solutions):

1. CHIPSET identifies the wrong memory controller.

   Run CHIPSET again, manually testing each menu option. Check to see if more than one chipset is identified. Make a note of each additional chipset. Then run install again, using the additional chipsets.
2. The Last Byte Memory Manager fails to recognize an adapter that uses some portion of the upper memory address space.

   If this happens, you'll probably need to use the EXCLUDE option on the LASTBYTE.SYS command line to disable the region of conflict.

As an alternative, you can always bypass LASTBYTE by holding down Ctrl-Alt-Shift during a reboot.

LASTBYTE Utilities

LASTBYTE's memory-management utilities are configured and loaded during installation.

HIGHDRVR is a device driver that is used to load other device drivers into upper memory. HIGHTSR is a program that is used to load TSR programs into upper memory. Both utilities use most of the same command line options.

The syntax for HIGHDRVR is:

```
DEVICE=[path]HIGHDRVR.SYS [options] filename
[options]
```

where *filename* is the name of the device driver to be loaded high, optionally prefixed by a drive and directory specification. The filename may be preceded by one or more options, and followed by options at the end of the command line as required by the particular driver to be loaded. Adding the /SIZE option to either HIGHDRVR.SYS or HIGHTSR.EXE as shown below:

```
HIGHTSR /SIZE PRINT /D:PRN
```

or

```
DEVICE=HIGHDRVR.SYS /SIZE ANSI.SYS
```

will display both the initialization and resident requirements after the software has been loaded and initialized. The larger of the initialization and resident requirements may be specified with the /SIZE option to force a "best fit" allocation. For example:

```
HIGHTSR /SIZE:17120 PRINT.EXE /D:PRN
```

or

```
DEVICE=HIGHDRVR.SYS /SIZE:12032 ANSI.SYS
```

Usually the resident requirement is less than the initialization requirement. If there isn't enough free High-DOS memory to satisfy the initialization requirement, but there is enough for the resident requirement, then you may still be able to load your software by adding a second parameter to the /SIZE option, as in:

```
HIGHTSR /SIZE:16208,5776 PRINT /D:PRN
```

or

```
DEVICE=HIGHDRVR.SYS /SIZE:12032,4820 ANSI.SYS
```

In this example, the initialization requirement is specified by the first parameter and is 16208 bytes; the resident requirement is specified by the second parameter and is 5776 bytes. Note that specifying the second parameter is not helpful unless the resident requirement is less than the initialization requirement.

When the second parameter is used, HIGHTSR first looks for a free area larger than or equal to the initialization requirement (the first parameter); if found, it simply loads the software in this area and the second paramter is ignored. Otherwise, HIGHTSR searches for a free area larger than or equal to the resident requirement (the second parameter), and which has "data" allocated immediately above it that can be temporarily moved to create enough free memory to satisfy the initialization requirement.

The /LOW option lets you load a memory-hungry driver or TSR low, where it can use as much memorya s it needs to initialize itself, then move the initialized (and smaller) program into upper memory, for example:

```
HIGHTSR /LOW APPEND
```

or

```
DEVICE=HIGHDRVR.SYS /LOW MYDRIVER.SYS
```

Warning: The design of some software may prevent the /LOW option from working properly. Don't use it unless necessary, and then only after you have tested it to be sure everything works as expected. (For example, it will NOT work with PRINT, SHARE, FASTOPEN, MODE, or HyperDisk.) The /NOENV Option (HIGHTSR only) All programs, includiing TSR's, are allocated two regions of memory when they are loaded: One is the area for the program itself, and the other is for a copy of the environment. Most TSR's don't make use of their environment, and some actually release it to the operating system rather than hanging onto it.

If HIGHMEM finds an environment block, the corresponding entry in the "Description" column will have the name of the TSR that it belongs to (such as "CLOCK.EXE") followed by the indication "[Env]". Occassionally, you may see a similar indication "[Dat]"; this is a data block explicitly allocated by the TSR for some unknown purpose.

If you see a block labelled "[Env]" in the output of HIGHMEM, then you can use the /NOENV command line option of HIGHTSR to release this block, even if the TSR didn't:

```
HIGHTSR /NOENV CLOCK
```

As noted earlier, some TSRs will release their environment anyway and so you may be tempted to load them without using the /NOENV option. This usually will create a "hole" in upper memory since the TSR's environment is almost always allocated just below the TSR itself. Use of the /NOENV option forces the environment to be allocated down in conventional memory (where it will be reclaimed later) so that the "hole" is eliminated.

HIGHUMM creates and manages Upper Memory Blocks (UMBs). Another LASTBYTE utility, HIGHMEM, displays your system's memory usage for your evaluation. Run it from the DOS prompt using this simple command:

HIGHMEM displays memory usage similar to the DOS MEM command. Bracketed numbers in the High-DOS column (e.g., "[141,136]") indicate free memory that is available for additional device drivers and TSRs. Bracketed numbers in the "Bank-Switch" column (if any) indicate free memory that can be used by some of the advanced utilities contained in the file TLB-A211.ZIP; this memory can be used to implement a RAM disk, a print spooler, emulated EMS memory, or TSR markers.

LASTBYTE.SYS is Copyright (C) 1990–92 by Key Software Products.

This program is not public domain but *shareware.* To register, send a check or money order for $29.95 to:

Key Software Products
440 Ninth Avenue
Menlo Park, CA 94025

LHA.EXE — Haruyasu Yoshizaki — Freeware

Purpose: Serves as a high-performance file-compression program.

Syntax: `[d:] [path] LHA command [/option] archive [.LZH] [path] [filenames]`

Valid commands are:

- a: Add files
- d: Delete files
- e: Extract files
- f: Freshen files
- l: List files (default)
- m: Move files
- p: DisPlay files
- s: Make a Self-extracting archive
- t: Test the integrity of an archive
- u: Update files
- v: View listing of files with pathnames
- x: EXtract files with pathnames

Valid options are:

`/a0`	won't archive files with hidden or system Attributes (default)
`/a1`	allows any file Attributes
`/c0`	Check timestamp before overwriting files
`/c1`	don't Check timestamp
`/h0`	no Header (default)
`/h1`	standard Header
`/h2`	extended Header
`/i0`	Ignore case of filenames (default)
`/i1`	don't Ignore case of filenames
`/l0`	don't display Long filenames
`/l1`	display Long names of files stored or to be stored in archive
`/l2`	display Long names of all files referenced by LHA
`/m0`	displays Message before overwriting files or creating directories
`/m1`	No Messages—assumes "Y" response to queries
`/m2`	no Message, but renames de-archived file with numeric extension
`/n0`	No indicator toggle—default shows progress and compression factor
`/n1`	No indicator—disables "ooo..." progress indicator
`/n2`	No indicator—disables filenames and compression rates
`/o0`	Old version (of LH) compatability—default is off
`/o1`	Old version (of LH) compatability—produces compatible output
`/p0`	Precise filenames off—will restore all files of a given name
`/p1`	Precise files on—will distinguish between files of the same name from different directories within an archive
`/r0`	Recursive mode off (default)

`/r1` Recursively selects a given file from any subdirectory

`/r2` Recursively collects all files from all subdirectories of the named directory

`/t0` Timestamp off—defaults to system clock

`/t1` Timestamp on—with a,u,f,m, and d commands, sets archive time and date to time and date of newest file in archive

`/w0` sets Work directory to current directory (default)

`/w1` path sets Work directory to path specified

`/x0` sets eXtended pathnames off

`/x1` sets eXtended pathnames on

`/z0` Zero compression is off—files are compressed

`/z1` Zero compression is on—files are stored but not compressed

`/z2` [ext] files ending in .ARC, .LZH, .LZS, .PAK, .ZIP, and .ZOO are not compressed—optionally, any specified extensions will also be exempted

`/-1` allows the character @ as a character in a file name

`/-2` allows either – or @ as characters.

Remarks: LHA lets you store files in a highly-compressed format, using an algorithm developed by Haruhiko Okumura. One or more files can be compressed into a single file, called an archive, which has a default extension of LHZ. The basic A, D, and E commands, respectively add, delete, and extract files to or from the archive. To add BIGFILE.TXT to an archive STORTEXT.LHZ, type LHA A STORTEXT BIGFILE.TXT assuming LHA is in your DOS path and you want to store the archive of BIGFILE.TXT in the same (and current) directory where BIGFILE.TXT resides.

The M command moves the specified files into the archive, erasing the originals. This can be useful for compressing files you only need look at occasionally, as it frees up disk space.

The L and V commands let you examine the contents of an archive, while the F, U, and T commands can be used to update and verify achives. Many other options let you use full pathnames, work with files in subdirectories of the specified directory, work with hidden or system files (by allowing any attributes), toggle an indicator of compression or extraction progress on or off, use special characters in filenames, and more. Of particular note are the /x1 and /r2 options, which let you store and extract complete tree structures. The /x1 option is also needed to create a self-extracting file that can have its output redirected at the command line—if you create an archive with /x1:

```
LHA A/x1 MYARC *.*
```

then create a self-extracting achive with:

```
LHA s/x1 MYARC.
```

You can then redirect the output of the MYARC.EXE as follows:

```
MYARC/e path
```

LHA.EXE is Copyright 1989–1991 by Haruyasu Yoshizaki. This program is *freeware* and may be freely copied and distributed, but not modified or sold without author consent.

LIST.COM Vern Buerg Shareware

Purpose: LIST.COM is a powerful utility for locating and viewing files. You can enter command-line file specifications, search for the specified files, then view the located files. A windowing feature allows you to view two files simultaneously.

Syntax: `LIST`

You can run the program by responding to prompts. DOS wildcards are valid. Or from the command line:

```
LIST [filespec...filespec] [/switches]
```

Use multiple file specifications (filespecs) if needed. If no file is specified, the program programs you for a specification.

The following switches can be invoked from the command line:

- `/E` Displays selected files from the end (last line) first.
- `/Q` Toggles on and off beep sounds to signal events. Q
- `/W` Sets the wrap feature on.

`/H` Sets Hex mode; files are displayed in hexadecimal notation.

`/F(text)`

Invokes a case-insensitive search of all selected files for the specified string (text).

`/T(text)`

Invokes a case-sensitive search of all selected files for the specified string (text).

`/#nnnn`

Sets the file display at record or line number specified (nnnn).

Remarks: Once the program is loaded and selected files are displayed, use the normal cursor movement keys to move around the display. You can also use the following commands to navigate the file list:

`Ctrl-PgDn or Q`

To move to the next file

`Ctrl-PgUp or Z`

To move to the previous file

`Alt-F`

To locate another file

`Alt-W`

To toggle the dual-window display

`Alt-G`

To go to the DOS prompt without exiting LIST

`Alt-H`

To toggle Hex mode

`+ or -`

To scroll down (+) or up (–) a number of lines specified in response to resulting prompt

`Ctrl-Home`

To move to a specifed line number

`Alt-T`

To expand tab characters into blank spaces

`Ctrl-Y`

To set a bookmark

`Alt-Y`

To move to the bookmark

The following search functions are also available:

`/ or S`

To invoke a case-sensitive search for a specified string

`V or '`

To invoke a case-sensitive search for a specified string, beginning from current position upward

`\ or F`

To invoke a case-insensitive search for a specified string

`^ or '`

To invoke a case-insensitive search for a specified string, beginning from current position upward

`F3 or A`

To find the next occurrence of the target string

`F9`

To find the previous occurrence of the target string

`Alt-A`

To find the next occurrence of the target string, continuing through all selected files until the string is found.

LIST.COM also provides capabilities for marking blocks of text, then saving the marked text into another file.

`Alt-M`

To mark the first line of the block

`Alt-B`

To mark the last line of the block

`Alt-D`

To save the marked block as another file (you are prompted for file name)

`Alt-U`

To un-mark text.

Finally, you can print listed files using these commands:

`Ctrl-P`

Prints the entire current file

`Alt-P`

Prints a marked block.

LIST.COM is Copyright © 1983–1992 by Vernon D. Buerg. This program is not public domain but *shareware*. To register, send a check or money order for $20 to:

Vernon D. Buerg
139 White Oak Circle
Petaluma, CA 94952

LJLAND.EXE TaxWare Shareware

Purpose: LJLAND.EXE prints text files in landscape orientation on any HP LaserJet or 100% compatible printer. The program also lets you specify print and formatting options.

Syntax: `LJLAND [option option ...] fileSpec1 [fileSpec2 ... ]`

The configuration screen is displayed and you are asked to confirm the settings and begin printing. If no options are specified, the default configuration is used.

These are the options that can be specified from the command line:

`/B[N]`

Sets binder format; use N to disable hole-punch markers.

`/C#`

Sets columns of text per page; # = 1..5; default = 2.

`/D[n]`

Sets duplex printing; the n parameter sets the bind mode: L=long/S=short/M=manual.

`/E`

Expands tabs # spaces (maximum total is 10).

`/FC or /FP`

Sets column (C) or page (P) format.

`/G#`

Sets the greenbar options, which print an alternate shade every #th line; default = 1.

`/H (text) or (@filename)`

Inserts headers. You can either enter header text or specify a file to be used as a header.

`/IT# or /IL#`

Sets the indent for top (T) and left (L) margins a specified number (#) of lines or columns.

`/J[n]`

Specifies a network print job, in which n is the print job configuration (optional).

`/K`

Keeps files together; allows more than one file on a single page.

`/L#`

Sets lines (10–66). Default is 66.

`/N#`

Inserts a line number at every #th (1–100) line. Occupies the first six spaces in numbered lines.

`/O[n]`

Specifies the output destination. The n value can be any valid LPT port, the "dry run" specification, or a file name.

`/P#`

Specifies the paper source: Use 1 for multi-purpose, 2 for manual, and 4 for lower.

`/Rn#-#`

Specifies the range (n) in lines or columns. Valid values for n include P for pages, L for lines, and C for character columns.

`/S#`

Sets tab stops every #th (1—10) column. Default is 8.

`/T`

Alone, this options disables titles. Or you can specify a title by entering text. You can also use the Header and Title Codes, shown below.

`/W[#]`

Sets the number of spaces (#) to indent wrapped lines. No # indicates no wrapping.

`/X#`

Sets number (#) of copies to print.

`/Zn`

Prints files in alphabetical order. Use /ZA to alphabetize all files, /ZF to alphabetize files according to file name first, then extension.

The LJLAND.EXE default configuration is:

- Column format, 2 columns
- The output port is LPT1
- Print on one side of the paper
- Up to 83 characters per column
- Up to 66 lines of text per column
- Tab stops at every 8th column.

You can use the following codes when building headers and titles:

`$PN` Prints the current page (column) number

`$PP` Prints the total number of pages (columns) in the document

`$FN` Prints the DOS file name

`$FD` Prints the file's creation/modification date—literal (May 5, 1992)

`$Fd` Prints the file's creation/modification date—numeric (5-5-92)

`$FT` Prints the file's creation/modification time—military (14:30)

`$Ft` Prints the file's creation/modification time—am/pm (2:30p)

`$TD` Prints today's date—literal (August 17, 1992)

`$Td` Prints today's date—numeric (8-17-92)

`$TT` Prints today's time—am/pm (10:15a)

`$$` Prints the dollar sign "$" (the only way to print it)

`$_` Prints the underscore character "_" (the only way to print it)

`$~` Prints the tilde character "~" (the only way to print it)

`$J` Prints the line left justified

`$JC` Prints the line center justified

`$JR` Prints the line right justified

`$MC` Prints the line split-centerd

`%%` Prints the percentage character

`underscore "_"`

Prints the space character

`tilde "~"`

Adds a new line (carriage return/line feed)

Remarks: Specify options first, then file(s) to be printed. You can specify multiple files. DOS wildcards are valid.

To get detailed help about any option, enter the following command at the DOS prompt:

```
LJLAND /? (option letter)
```

Examples: Enter the following command:

```
LJLAND C:\TODAY.LOG d:basprogs\*.bas
d:c_progs\*.c 05??89.LOG
```

The following files are printed:

- TODAY.LOG located at the root of the C: drive

- All files ending with the .BAS extension in the BASPROGS subdirectory of the D: drive
- All files ending with the .C extension in the C_PROGS subdirectory of the D: drive
- All files that match the pattern 05??89.LOG in the current directory, where ?? can be any two legal filename characters.

To print the files, MANUAL1.DOC and MANUAL2.DOC, in 3-column format, 60 lines of text per column, on the second parallel printer, and indent wrapped lines 8 spaces, use:

```
LJLAND /o2 /c3 /160 /w8 manual1.doc manual2.doc
```

 This program is not public domain but *shareware.* To register, send a check or money order for $29.95 to:

TaxWare
Attn: LJLAND
PO Box 2014
Provo, UT 84603-2014

LM.EXE — Mom and Pop Shop — Shareware

Purpose: The LaserMiser utility conserves paper by printing multiple-page images on single sheets on Hewlett-Packard LaserJet printer. The trial version that you are now evaluating prints:

- Two-page images on one side of a sheet of paper
- 80 bytes per line
- 72 lines per page image, consisting of: 1 heading line, 1 blank line, 70 data lines.

Syntax: `LM [d:][path][filename] [/options]`

where *d:\path\filename* represents the drive, path, and filename (DOS wildcards are valid) for the file(s) to be printed and /options is one or more of the following control options:

```
Lnn[T]
```

where *nn* is the number of lines to print per page (range 1 through 72), and T (optional) pauses printing after two pages so you can verify your results.

```
/P(+or-)
```

Enables (+) or suppresses (-) page breaks. Suppressing page breaks strips FormFeed characters from the input stream, decreasing the overall output. To prevent blank pages, LM.EXE will ALWAYS IGNORE a form feed in the input if it appears before any text.

Remarks: LaserMiser supports any LaserJet printer that can print the "Line Printer Compressed" (16.66 cpi) font in landscape mode. Users of the LaserJet, LaserJet Plus and LaserJet 500 Plus models must employ a suitable cartridge (A, B, C, G, H, L, V, Y or Z), or a downloaded font. LaserJet II users will find the appropriate font built in.

LaserMiser will work with any LaserJet "clone" and with any LaserJet emulation software that understands Hewlett-Packard PCL.

If you already use a program that is loaded using LM (such as Label Master, © simply rename LM.EXE to another .EXE file. Keep the name short if you like to use multiple parameters.

 This program is not public domain but *shareware.* To register, send a check or money order for $27 to:

Mom and Pop Shop
709 No. Juanita Ave.
Redondo Beach, CA 90277-2227

LOOK4.EXE — R. Michael Schiavone — Shareware

Purpose: LOOK4 finds and optionally brings any selected file to the current directory.

Syntax:

```
LOOK4 filespec [switch] [switch] [...]
```

where 'filespec' is a standard DOS file specification, including wildcards.

Command Line Switches

L	Start up LOOK4.EXE in the LOOK4 mode.
B	Start up LOOK4.EXE in the BRING mode.
S	Start up LOOK4.EXE in the BRING Selected files mode.
D	Use the default drive set for the search.
E	Include every fixed drive in the search.
F	Search the Floppy drive set only.
C	Use the current drive only.
I	Include floppy drives in the search.
N	No floppy drives to be used in the search.
R	Resets all start-up defaults to original specs.

All switches must be preceded by a minus sign (–) or by a division sign (/). All switch changes may be made permanent by including the command ~RECONFIGURE on the command line. The switches may be entered as upper case or lower case characters. They may also be combined.

Remarks: The default drive set used is your chosen drive set. If you wish to change this, you need only to specify a different drive set switch on the command line.

Your default (selected) set may contain whatever combination of drives you wish. When you do not wish to include all of your fixed drives in the default set, you would type:

```
C:\>LOOK4 MYFILE.* /e
```

If you wish to include your floppy drive system in the search path. This is accomplished by using the I switch on the command line like this:

```
C:\>LOOK4 MYFILE.* -i
```

You may tell LOOK4 that you want to use JUST your floppy drive system for a particular search by specifying the F switch:

```
C:\>LOOK4 MYFILE.* /F
```

You may also have LOOK4 one drive only by specifying the drive to use on the command line in this manner:

```
C:\>LOOK4 D:MYFILE.*
```

LOOK4 and BRING uses the same wildcards that DOSs DIR command uses, with one slight difference, if you type:

```
LOOK4 MYFIL
```

at the DOS prompt, LOOK4 interprets it as:

```
LOOK4 MYFIL*.*
```

Because of this, there is no need to type trailing "*.*" on any filespec, as LOOK4 adds it for you.

 LOOK4 is distributed as shareware. It is not free software. If you continue to use this program beyond a 30-day trial period, you are required to register it. The registration fee for this version is $10 per copy. Upon registration, you will receive the most recent version of the program with an expanded search capability. Make checks payable to Computer Interface Services. Please send your registrations to:

Computer Interface Services
1173 Cypress Point
Twin Lakes, WI 53181

A copy of the source code, along with a non-exclusive license to use it, is available for $25.00.

LPTX701.COM — Mark DiVecchio, Kepa Zubeldia — Shareware

Purpose: Intercepts data sent to a printer port and writes it to a disk file. The program redirects the BIOS interrupt 17h, the line printer interrupt. It will redirect the output of LPT1, LPT2, or LPT3 to a disk file; and all three redirections may be active at the same time. This version of LPTX also contains a pop-up window feature that can be used to control output redirection from within other applications.

Syntax:

```
LPTX701 {-1,-2,-3} {-c -o -a
<d:[pathname]filename>} [?] [-m] [-x] [-l] [-i]
```

Available command-line switches and options are explained here below.

```
{-1,-2,-3}
```

Redirects output sent to LPT1, LPT2, or LPT3. This option must appear first.

`-o` This switch instructs the program to redirect output to the file specified. If redirection is already active for the specified port, the previous file is closed first. If this option is not specified but a line printer port is, LPTX, by default, uses either the file name specified last or LPTXy.LST in the root directory of the default drive, and in which y is 1, 2, or 3.

You don't need to specify the complete path name every time you run LPTX. If no path is specified, the default directory is used. Also, because LPTX always saves the complete path; a file specified once can be located with successive commands using only the file name.

`-a` Performs the same function as -o with this exception: If there is a file with the same name already on the disk, the redirected output is appended to that file without user confirmation. In order for this to work properly, the file on the disk must NOT be terminated by a control-Z (1Ah). Otherwise you may not be able to see the text that will be appended after the control-Z.

LPTX will not put a control-Z at the end of its files. If you need a control-Z at the end, you can use the copy command, with the concatenation option (copy x+y z) to add a control-Z. See your DOS manual.

`-c` Closes the active redirection file and directs all further output to the line printer.

`-?` Displays a short help screen.

`-x` Ignores the DOS Critical Section Flag. Use this option only with great care, unusual results may occur.

`-l` Strips linefeed characters from redirected data.

`-i` Removes LPTX from the interrupt chain. This effectively inactivates the program; however, the memory which it occupies is not freed.

`-m` Activates monochrome attributes for the pop-up window. Use this option on monochrome monitors with graphics adapter cards. Load the program with this option, then press Alt-R to activate the window. Then specify port, printer, file, and so on.

If DOS is busy when you try to open the window, you will get no response. In these cases, hold down Alt-R until the window opens. You can only redirect printers to files that have been previously opened with the command line version of LPTX.

Pressing Alt-R while in graphics mode toggles the redirection of LPT1 instead of popping up the window. The program sounds two beeps to indicate LPTX is inactive, one beep if active (LPT1 is directed to disk file).

Notes: The options, -1, -2, and -3, are mutually exclusive. The options, -o and -c, also are mutually exclusive. If neither the -o or the -c option is specified, LPTX displays program status.

Remarks: LPTX requires DOS 2.0 or later. It has tested satisfactorily on DOS 3.1 as well.

LPTX tested satisfactorily with the following programs:

- dBase II,
- The ARC utility with the "p" option and output redirected to prn,
- Shift-PrtSc,
- DOS PRINT utility,
- Lotus 123,
- DIR > PRN

LPTX tested unsatisfactorily with the following DOS commands:

- TYPE
- COPY

By redirecting LPT2 or LPT3 to a disk file, you can, in effect, have 2 or 3 printers on your system, with LPT1 working normally, and LPT2 and/or LPT3 outputs going to disk files.

This version of LPTX counts on the PC having some "free time" in order to write the data to disk. The program gathers data into a large buffer and writes it to disk during timer interrupts and keyboard idle periods. DOS must not be in its critical section for the write to take place.

LPTX does not work with the DOS TYPE command, apparently because the critical section flag is always set when the timer interrupts occur. It should work with most user programs since the critical section flag is not set in user programs and therefore will not be set when timer interrupts occur.

If LPTX encounters any error during redirection, the operation is terminated and output is sent to the line printer. No error message is displayed, your only indication is a series of beeps. Four beeps indicate a DOS disk access error. Two beeps indicate an internal buffer overflow error. This prevents the current program from being destroyed. An error with LPT1 redirection does not shut down LPT2 or LPT3 redirection.

LPTX captures the int 17h interrupt vector. Problems may occur with print spoolers which also use this interrupt. To ensure that LPTX works properly, run it before you run your print spooler. LPTX should be transparent to the print spooler (but your print spooler may not be transparent to LPTX).

LPTX also captures the int 24h critical error interrupt vector. This is done only while LPTX is using the disk, and prevents peculiar error messages that may be generated by other programs being run. (LPTX beeps 4 times and clears itself if a disk error occurs).

Examples: To redirect LPT1 output either to file, LPTX1.LST, in the root directory of the default drive, or to the last named file, use:

```
LPTX -1
```

To close any active redirection file and redirect LPT2 output to a file named NEWPRINT.XXX on drive A:, use:

```
LPTX -o A:\NEWPRINT.XXX
```

LPTX701.COM is Copyright © 1987 by Mark DiVecchio and Kepa Zubeldia. This program is released for use in non-commercial environments. Commercial users are asked to register the program by sending a check or money order for $25 for each site (any number of users and computers) to:

Mark C. DiVecchio
10435 Mountain Glen Terrace
San Diego, CA 92131
619-549-4056
619-549-9833 FAX

LQCHAR.COM — Eric Meyer — Freeware

Purpose: A small, efficient utility for designing downloadable character fonts for Epson 24-pin or compatible dot-matrix printers. You can design each character individually on screen, create a file of the entire character sent, then send the file to your printer when you want to use your custom font.

Syntax:

```
lqchar FONTNAME (/P /U)
```

FONTNAME is the name of the font file. If you specify a name that doesn't exist, a new file is created. If you don't specify an extension, the .LQC extension is added automatically. If you don't specify a download option (see below) the font file is loaded into edit mode. The following download options are available:

`/P` Send the specified font file to the printer.

`/U` Send the specified font file to the printer and start using it.

If you are creating a new font, you are prompted to specify whether it is to be Draft or Letter Quality. Two font files, DRAFT.LQC and LETTER.LQC, are included in the archive file for your convenience.

Working with Fonts Once the LQCHAR editor is loaded, a box on the left displays the current character dot-by-dot. The character matrix is always 24 dot rows high; its width varies according to the print quality: 9 dot columns for Draft, 29 for Letter. Keep in mind that in Draft mode LQCHAR spreads out each dot by a factor of 3 so as not unduly to distort the aspect ratio.

Background shading indicates the vertical boundaries of a normal capital letter. The rows above are available for accents, those below for lowercase descenders.

Modifying Fonts Several commands can be used to modify the entire character set in some way. These include:

`<F1>`

Toggles print quality between draft and letter. That is, draft fonts are expanded into "skeleton" LQ font, LQ fonts are compressed into draft quality. For both procedures, retouching is needed. Expanding fonts leaves blank columns that need to be filled, compressing fonts deletes two of every three rows.

`<F2>`

Toggles font type between full and partial. A full font contains only the characters defined. Undefined characters won't print. For partial fonts, undefined characters are printed using the printer's resident font.

`<F3>`

Changes character pitch: pica, elite, or proportional. This selection alters character spacing only.

To modify individual characters, press the key of the character you want to change. The cursor moves into the display box. Move it with arrow keys. Use the spacebar to toggle the highlighted pin position on and off until the character is modified as needed.

There are also special commands available, including:

`<R,L,U,D>`

Moves the whole pattern RIGHT, LEFT, UP, or DOWN.

`<C>`

Inserts the pattern of another character in the file. Use this, for example, if you want to use the B character as a template when working on the R.

`<O>`

Inserts the pattern of the same character from another font file you specify.

`<B>`

Erases the character pattern.

`<P>`

Previews the character in hi-res graphics (EGA only).

`<F1,F2>`

Moves the current column up, down.

`<F3,F4>`

Moves the current row left, right.

`<F5,F6>`

Inserts, deletes a column.

`<F7,F8>`

Inserts, deletes a row.

`<F9,F0>`

Rotates character left, right.

Rotating characters changes their overall slant, and requires some thought. Be sure the character isn't too wide, and is roughly centered in the box, or parts of it will get truncated. Note that the rotation works in increments of 2 rows; thus moving the character up or down one row first can give a slightly different effect. Also, if you're going to rotate more than once, you should move the character up or down once each time in between to get the smoothest effect. (Rotation works best on LQ characters; its effects are a bit drastic for Draft mode.)

When you are finished making modifications, press ESC to access the control menu. Select:

`P` To print the font. The entire range of characters will be printed, with the standard font above (for comparison) and your new font below.

`C` To save the font file under a different name.

`S` To save without exiting.

`L` To load a font file.

`E` To save the font file and exit to DOS.

`Q` To quit without saving.

Remarks: LQCHAR should work with any 24-pin Epson LQ compatible printer, however the details of downloading fonts may vary among printers.

Upon saving, character patterns are automatically centered in the matrix.

You cannot save a save a definition that violates this rule:

No two adjacent pins in any ROW may be ON!

This is because pins can't fire fast enough to print twice in adjacent columns. You could send such a character definition to the printer, but the second dot wouldn't print as intended, so LQCHAR warns you beforehand to avoid mistakes.

```
LQCHAR.EXE is Copyright © 1988-90 Eric Meyer
```

This program is "freeware." It can be freely copied and distributed, but not modified or sold for profit without the author's consent.

Eric Meyer
3541 Smuggler Way
Boulder, CO 80303 USA
74415,1305 CompuServe

MAKE.EXE — Peter M. Perchansky — Freeware

Purpose: MAKE.EXE allows you to create an empty text file of a specified length. MAKE was created with the intention of guaranteeing a given amount of space on floppies and hard drives.

Syntax:

```
MAKE filename [length]
```

For example:

```
MAKE A:\JUNK\NULL.FIL 1000
```

will create 1000 byte file called NULL.FIL on drive a:\ in directory a:\junk

```
MAKE TEMP.TXT
```

will create a 0 byte file called TEMP.TXT in the current directory.

Remarks: MAKE.EXE is FREE! I offer no implicit or implied warranties. I debuged and tested MAKE using the above mentioned computers and operating systems. MAKE worked. I cannot promise MAKE will work on all makes and models of computers or operating systems. It should, but I cannot promise it.

Copyright © Peter M. Perchansky 1989 All Rights Reserved. The program may be freely distributed, but not modified or sold for profit without my written consent. The user takes full responsibility for any damages resulting from the use of this program.

Peter M. Perchansky
412-1 Springside, Drive East
Shillington, PA 19607
(No phone calls please)
CompuServe: 71301,344

MAM.COM — Marc Mulders — Shareware

Purpose: MAM.COM maps and manages memory allocation. Use it to display and view detailed reports of your memory configuration, and to "mark and release" portions of memory as needed.

Syntax: `MAM d: (/options)`

Use the following options to configure your MAM operation.

`d:`

Designates a drive on which to store MARK files. Mark files are hidden and temporary. The root directory of specified drive is default.

`/UMB`

Displays an allocation map of upper memory blocks (UMB)

`/SYS`

Displays map of system memory, with programs

`/NOPROG`

Displays map of system memory, without programs

`/HARDWARE`

Displays I/O port information

`/PAGE`

Pauses display when screen is full

`/L`

Lists all mark files

`/M### (comment)`

Makes a mark file ### (0–999) and adds comment (optional, displayed with /L)

`/E`

Erases all mark files

`/R###`

Restores memory to specified specified mark (###)

`/V###`

Restores memory and environment to specified mark (###)

Remarks: Because memory marks are written to a hidden file on the current drive's root, they memory (RAM) space.

MAM will attempt to identify inconsistent memory setups such as EMS page frames conflicting with installed ROMS or suspect programs lurking at the top of DOS memory (as many boot-sector viruses do).

 MAM is shareware; the requested fee is $20.

Marc Mulders
P. O. Box 2217
Northcliff
2115
South Africa
CompuServe ID: 76040,1420

MB.EXE — Sitting Duck Software — Shareware

Purpose: Provide a variety of useful functions from either the DOS prompt or within a batch file.

Syntax: `MB argument`

The following is a list of supported arguments, their proper syntax and an explanation of what the operation does. The meaning of the parameter TEXT$ is: Any group of ASCII characters in the range of 0 to 255.

```
BOX/BR/BC/ER/EC/CHARACTER/COLOR/C
```

Draws a box where BR is the beginning row, BC the beginning column, ER the ending row, EC the ending column where BR < ER, BC < EC and COLOR < 256. CHARACTER is either 1 or 2 indicating a single or double line box. COLOR is a single value representing the foreground and background colors. See the single color chart below. The values for BR, BC, ER and EC should be within the allowable limits as dictated by the lines/columns mode of your monitor. Appending /C to the argument clears the inside of the box to the background color specified in the COLOR argument.

Example: BOX/1/5/12/75/1/79 draws a single-line box with the upper left corner at row 1, column 5, the lower right corner at row 12 column 75 in bright white on red and not cleared.

```
CLEARSCR/BR/BC/ER/EC/COLOR
```

Clears an area of the screen where BR, BC, ER, EC and COLOR have the meanings as described above.

Example:

```
CLEARSCR/1/5/12/75/31
```

```
BLOAD/FILENAME$
```

BLOADS a file into video memory as the BASIC's BLOAD command. The area of video memory the file is loaded into is automatically determined by the monitor in use. This command is for "slide shows" of predetermined screen files made with Basic's BSAVE or a screen capture utility.

Example:

```
BLOAD/MAINMENU.SCR
```

```
FILLSCRN/BR/BC/ER/EC/COLOR/ASCII
```

Fills the screen with the character represented by the value ASCII. BR, BC, ER, EC and COLOR are as previously described.

Example: FILLSCRN/1/5/12/75/30/45 will fill the described area with dashes colored yellow on blue.

```
PAINT/BR/BC/ER/EC/COLOR
```

Paints the screen without disturbing the existing text.

Example:

```
PAINT/1/5/12/75/7
```

```
OCPRINT/ROW/COLUMN/TEXT$/COLOR
```

Same as PRINT, below, except that printing takes place slowly; one character at a time, for effect.

```
PRINT/ROW/COLUMN/TEXT$/COLOR
```

Rapidly prints TEXT$ in COLOR at the ROW/COLUMN. TEXT$ will be displayed exactly as entered, including quotes if used. Extended ASCII characters may be displayed. The routine writes to video memory; no line feed issued.

Example:

```
PRINT/5/1/display these words/31
```

```
CURSOROFF
```

Turns the cursor off. Be sure to turn the cursor back on at the end of the bat file.

```
CURSORON
```

Turns the cursor on.

```
LOCATE/ROW/COLUMN
```

Locates the cursor at ROW/COLUMN. Handy if you want to use the ECHO command. Printing by DOS will begin at the cursor position.

Example:

```
LOCATE/1/1
WAIT
```

Suspends operation and waits for a keypress.

```
CHIME/WHICHONE
```

Makes a chime-like tone. WHICHONE must be in the range of 1 to 10.

Example:

```
CHIME/7
SLEEP/SECONDS
```

Suspends operation until SECONDS seconds elapses.

Example:

```
SLEEP/4
STUFF/TEXT$
```

Stuffs text into the keyboard buffer, appending an <ENTER> keypress. To simulate pressing <ENTER>, simply use STUFF without parameters. TEXT$ CANNOT be more than 15 characters.

Example:

```
STUFF/Y
USCROLL/BR/BC/ER/EC/TIMES
DSCROLL/BR/BC/ER/EC/TIMES
LSCROLL/BR/BC/ER/EC/TIMES
RSCROLL/BR/BC/ER/EC/TIMES
```

Provides for scrolling of a selectedarea of the screen, either Up, Down, Left or Right, TIMES times.

Example:

```
LSCROLL/1/1/12/80/4
FADE/COLOR
```

Provides for a screen disolve to COLOR.

Example:

```
FADE/64
```

```
BIG/TEXT/CHR/R/C/COLOR
```

Prints large block text; 3 rows, 10 columns in COLOR color with ASCII character CHR.

Example:

```
BIG/Hello there/219/1/1/31
```

```
RECOLOR/OLD/NEW
```

Changes all instances of color OLD to color NEW.

Example:

```
RECOLOR/31/78
```

```
LIST/ROW/COLUMN/COLOR/X/word/word/....
```

Prints a vertical list of words (18max) starting at ROW, COLUMN in COLOR. There will be X rows between words.

Example:

```
VPRINT/1/1/HELLO THERE/2
```

```
CBUF
```

Clears the keyboard buffer.

Color Chart

Foreground	Background: Black	Blue	Green	Cyan	Red	Magenta	Brown	White
Black	0	16	32	48	64	80	96	112
Blue	1	17	33	49	65	81	97	113
Green	2	18	34	50	66	82	98	114
Cyan	3	19	35	51	67	83	99	115
Red	4	20	36	51	67	83	100	116
Magenta	5	21	37	52	68	84	101	117
Brown	6	22	38	52	69	85	102	118
White	7	23	39	53	70	86	103	119
Gray	8	24	40	54	71	87	104	120
Bright blue	9	25	41	55	72	88	105	121
Bright green	10	26	42	56	73	89	106	122
Bright cyan	11	27	43	57	74	90	107	123
Bright red	12	28	44	58	75	91	108	124
Bright Mag	13	29	45	59	76	92	109	125
Bright Brown	14	30	46	60	77	93	110	126
Bright White	15	31	47	61	78	94	111	127

For a blinking foreground, add 128 to the above values.

Remarks: The ONLY legal argument separator is the "/".
DO NOT use anything else. Either upper or lower case text is acceptable.
Remember, each line is to be prefixed with MB, followed by a space and the argument, i.e., MB BOX/1/1/12/80/1/31

DEMO.BAT is a batch file which demonstrates some of the routines and contains some important remarks.

Note: In order that MB can load and execute as quickly as possible, syntax and error checking are non-existent.
Make no errors and you will have no problems.

MicroMacroBat is distributed as shareware. It is not free software. If you continue to use this program beyond a 30-day trial period, you are required to register it. The registration fee for this version is $35 per copy. Upon registration, you will receive the most recent version of the program along with a printed manual and additional utility functions. Make checks payable to Sitting Duck Software (U.S. funds and drawable at a U.S. bank). Please send your registrations to:

Sitting Duck Software
P O Box 130
Veneta, OR 97487
(503) 935-3982

Overseas registration require an additional $5 postage.

Site licenses are available for MicroMacroBat. In order to legally distribute MB.EXE with your products, distribution licenses are also available. Because the execution speed of MicroMacroBat depends on the size of the MB.EXE file, licensees may ask that only the routines they require be included. Contact us at the above address for details.

MCBS.EXE — John M. Goodman — Freeware

Purpose: Lists the memory control block chains, in both high and low memory. Also lets you specify starting addresses for one or more chains depending on the options you select.

Syntax: `MCBS [L, U, B, D] [hex address(es)]`

in which the following options are available:

- `L` lists memory control block chains in low memory, one hexadecimal address can be specified as a starting point.
- `U` lists chains in high memory, two hexadecimal addresses can be specified as starting points.
- `B` lists chains in both high and low memory, two hexadecimal addresses can be specified as starting points.
- `D` same as L, only shows device driver sub-blocks as well, one hexadecimal address can be specified as a starting point.

MCBS.EXE is Copyright © 1991 by John M. Goodman. This program is *freeware* and may be freely used and distributed, but not modified or sold for profit without author consent.

John Goodman
6221 Choctaw Drive
Westminster, CA 92683-2105
714-895-3195

MDR.EXE — Hank Volpe — Shareware

Purpose: MDR.EXE (the Modem Doctor) runs tests on your modem and COMM ports.

Syntax: `MDR`

Once loaded, MDR.EXE runs from a convenient menu interface.When you first load the program, it automatically searches your system and identifies active COM ports. You are then prompted to log-in a port for testing. Logging in involves specifying a COM port and BAUD rate. The program then runs some initial tests on the uart setup and the modem microprocessor. The results are displayed. Press any key to enter the menu interface.

You can press ESC and not log-in a port, but the menus are inactive until you do.

After a port has been logged, the menus are available:

Log-in menu Gives you two selections. Auto Log-in performs the automatic port identification routine that is run when you load the program. Manual Log-in lets you specify a base address (hex) for a compatible uart, or you can assign a different IRQ line to an existing port.

Reg menu Performs register tests, which determine how your modem responds to and uses data flow control signals between your computer and the modem.

Carrier menu Simulates an on-line connection between your modem and itself. Sends all 8-bit characters to your modem in originate and answer frequencies to check for proper operation. Also, provides several modem drivers you can select to ensure compatibility.

Loopback menu This menu is available only in registered versions of the program.

Options menu Provides several selections. Interactive Mode sets up your modem as a communications terminal, through which you can send custom commands to your modem. Also lets you view, reset and print statistics reflecting tests currently run.

Setup menu Provides selections for the setup routine the program runs automatically when you load the program. Use them to specify port, BAUD rate, and test options. Also provides selections for creating and saving a custom color scheme.

MDR.EXE is Copyright © 1989–1991 by Hank Volpe. This program is not public domain but *shareware.* To register, send a check or money order for $19.95 to:

Hank Volpe
9510 Stone Oak Road
Baltimore, MD 21236

MH-RESTR.EXE MH-SYS.EXE — Micro House International — Freeware

Purpose: Restores all or parts of a backup of system information created with a companion utility, MH-SAVE.EXE.

Syntax: You can run MH-RESTR from a convenient menu interface by entering the following command at the DOS prompt:

```
MH-RESTR
```

You are prompted to specify the drive(s) you wish to restore and the name of the backup file.

You can also specify command-line parameters for MH-RESTR. These include:

`/b(filename)`

Specifies the full path and file name of the backup file.

- `/0` Restores physical drive 0.
- `/1` Restores physical drive 1.
- `/n` Disables the prompt for floppy insertion.
- `/m` Restores master boot record.
- `/t` Restores remainder of track 0.
- `/e` Restores extended partition tables.
- `/d` Restores DOS boot records.
- `/f` Restores file allocation tables (FATs).
- `/r` Restores root directories.
- `/a` Restores normal CMOS information.
- `/x` Restores extended CMOS information.
- `/l` Sets monochrome/LCD mode.
- `/u` Uses the BIOS function calls, instead of disk parameter tables, to determine drive geometries.

Remarks: Use caution when specifying command-line parameters for MH-RESTR, they are not always equivalent to those used with MH-SAVE.

Examples: The command line:

```
MH-RESTR /x /0
```

restores all information for drive 0, using the default backup file, HDRIVE0.IIB on drive A, provided it exists.

Or, this command line:

```
MH-RESTR /bB:MYBKUP.FIL /x
```

restores all information for drive D from the backup file, MYBKUP.FIL, on drive B. (The default is A.)

MH-SYS provides an enhancement for the DOS SYS command.

Micro House International
4900 Pearl East Circle, Suite 101
Boulder, CO 80301
(800)926-8299

MH-SAVE.EXE MH-ESDI.EXE MH-IDE.EXE — Micro House International — Freeware

Purpose: Saves vital information about your hard drive. Use MH-RSTR.EXE to restore backed up hard drives.

Syntax:

```
MH-SAVE
```

gives two choices:

- Save All Vital System Areas
- Select Which Areas To Save

It is strongly recommended that you save all vital system areas. MH-ESDI and MH-IDE report what ESDI and IDE drives know about their own characteristics and compare that information to the CMOS drive type and hard disk parameter table. The types of information saved by MH-SAVE are described below.

You can also -specify command-line parameters for MH-SAVE. These include:

`/b(filename)`

Specifies the full path and file name of the backup file.

`/0` Performs specified backup only on physical drive 0.

`/1` Performs specified backup only on physical drive 1.

`/x` Runs the program in batch file mode, menus and prompts are bypassed.

`/n` Disables the prompt for floppy insertion.

`/s` Shows space required for specified backup.

`/f` Performs a DOS format on the floppy before a backup file is written to it.

`/m` Saves master boot record.

`/k` Saves remainder of track 0.

`/p` Saves extended partition tables.

`/d` Saves DOS boot records.

`/t` Saves file allocation tables (FATs).

`/r` Saves root directories.

`/c` Saves normal CMOS information.

`/e` Saves extended CMOS information.

`/l` Sets monochrome/LCD mode.

`/u` Uses the BIOS function calls, instead of disk parameter tables, to determine drive geometries.

Remarks: For maximum security, it's good policy to put MH-SAVE in your AUTOEXEC.BAT file. Then, every time you boot your computer a backup of vital information is created.

By saving the information your system's hard drives need to function properly to a floppy diskette, you can increase your chances of restoring your hard drive in the event of a malfunction:

Master boot record The main partition table and master boot program, stored in the first sector of track 0.

Remainder of track 0 The rest of track 0, which may be used by the controller or other function.

Extended partition tables The partition tables and logical drive information for extended partitions.

DOS boot records The DOS boot records and BIOS parameter blocks for every partition.

File allocation tables The information describing the physical location of files on disk.

Root directory The root directory of every partition.

Normal CMOS The system's basic configuration (AT-standard CMOS) information

Extended CMOS Any extra CMOS information.

Examples: The command line:

```
MH-SAVE /x /0
```

saves all information for drive 0, using the default file name: HDRIVE0.IIB on drive A:. The /x options invokes batch mode, the backup is performed without menus and prompts. This is the command you can use in your AUTOEXEC.BAT file.

Or, this command line:

```
MH-SAVE /bB:MYBKUP.FIL /m /d /f
```

saves the master boot record and DOS boot record in a file, MYBKUP.FIL, on drive B. In addition, the diskette in drive B is formatted before the file is written.

MH-SAVE.EXE is Copyright © 1991–1993 by Micro House International.

Micro House International
4900 Pearl East Circle, Suite 101
Boulder, CO 80301
(800)926-8299

MKD.COM Version 3.2 — Micheal Pollard — Freeware

Purpose: A utility program to create a new directory and move to it, even if it is on another volume.

Syntax: `MKD directory_name`

Any and all donations will be accepted and appreciated. I am not out to make money on this. I just wrote these programs because I had use for them and there was no existing software available to do the job and now I hope someone else out there finds any or all of these programs useful.

If you decide to send me a few dollars, make checks or money orders payable to:

Michael Pollard
134 Garner Ave.
Waldorf, MD 20602

For help or info on this or any other Castle Software programs, call:

The 4th Dimension BBS
301-645-4366
SYSOP: MICHAEL POLLARD
CO-SYSOP: SCOTT MILLER

MRFILTER.EXE J. Gillespie Shareware

Purpose: An easy to use text file cleaning/sweeping utility.

Syntax: `MrFILTER <options> <source file> [output file]`

`-d` Use default settings. (-cew). Default is best first choice.

`-c` Control-chars removed except LF, CR, TAB, FF. Also removes DEL character.

`-h` Extended ASCII chars set removed.

`-e` False End-Of-File markers removed.

`-s` Strips high-bit. Prints result as 0d-127d.

`-w` Wrap long lines greater than 80 columns.

`-f` Fills removed characters with SPACE.

`-r` Report only. No output file created.

Example:

```
MrFILTER -d   junkfile.txt newfile.txt
MrFILTER -chf junkfile.txt newfile.txt
MrFILTER -r   junkfile.txt
```

Remarks: MrFILTER is designed to be used on any IBM PC, XT, AT, PS/1, PS/2 or compatible computer with any conventional memory size and any monitor.

MrFILTER has a set of options which will configure it to a specific problem. Fortunately, in most cases the default settings work fine. Once you enter the entire command string, MrFILTER reads the source file, screens each byte, and writes accepted data to an output file. The original file is not altered in any way. Incompatible options will not execute.

Written by J. Gillespie © 1991, 1992.

Blue-Moon Consulting
1209 Diablo Avenue
Modesto, CA USA 95358

License fee: $12

NAME.COM Version 3.2 — Micheal Pollard — Freeware

Purpose: A simple program to rename directories/sub-directories.

Syntax: `NAME old_directory_name new_directory_name`

Any and all donations will be accepted and appreciated. I am not out to make money on this. I just wrote these programs because I had use for them and there was no existing software available to do the job and now I hope someone else out there finds any or all of these programs useful.

If you decide to send me a few dollars make checks or money orders payable to:

Michael Pollard
134 Garner Ave.
Waldorf, MD 20602

For help or info on this or any other Castle Software programs, call:

The 4th Dimension BBS
301-645-4366
SYSOP: MICHAEL POLLARD
CO-SYSOP: SCOTT MILLER

NEW.COM — John R. Pulliam — Public Domain

Purpose: NEW.COM lists files created since a specified date. Default is 00:00 hours (midnight) of the current day.

Syntax: Use the following command syntax at the DOS prompt:

```
NEW1 or NEW2 /x (d:\path\filename.ext)
```

in which files created x number of days prior to the current date are listed and only files meeting *d:\path\filename.ext* specifications are listed. DOS wildcards are valid.

Remarks: NEW displays all files, including those with hidden, system, and read-only attributes. The NEW display also includes the volume label and directory, the number of files, the number of total bytes, and available space on the current drive.

There are two executable files:

NEW1.COM displays dates in mm-dd-yy format, for example, 11-26-94.

NEW2.COM displays dates in the dd-Mon-yy format, for example, 6-Jun-94.

You can use either file, or rename the file you prefer NEW.COM and use NEW at the command prompt.

This program is *freeware* and may be freely used and distributed, but not modified or sold for profit without author consent.

John Pulliam
1324 Cypress Bend Circle
Melbourne, Fl 32934
407/255-7690

NOBREAK.COM John Socha Freeware

Purpose: Turns off the ability to interrupt an operation via Ctrl-C or Ctrl-Break.

Syntax:

```
NOBREAK ON ¦ OFF
```

When NOBREAK is on, the Ctrl-Break and Ctrl-C processing is turned off. This can be useful inmaking an uninterruptible batch file, for example. NOBREAK OFF restores the normal processing of these keypresses.

NOBREAK.COM is Copyright © 1993 by John Socha. This program is *freeware* and may be freely used and distributed, but not modified or sold for profit without author consent.

John Socha
(206) 822-9300

NUM.EXE — John Socha — Freeware

Purpose: Converts a user-specified number into hexadecimal or decimal notation.

Syntax: Run NUM.EXE from the DOS command prompt using this command:

```
NUM (number) or (numberh)
```

in which number is a decimal number and numberh is a hexadecimal number. Decimal numbers are converted into hexadecimal numbers, and hexadecimal numbers into decimal numbers. The binary notation for both types of numbers is also given.

NUM.EXE is Copyright © 1993 by John Socha. This program is *freeware* and may be freely used and distributed, but not modified or sold for profit without author consent.

John Socha
(206) 822-9300

OPTICOPY.EXE OPTIMOVE.EXE — Paul Galbriath — Freeware

Purpose: OptiCopy is an optimizing file copier. OptiMove moves (copies then deletes the original) using the same optimization strategy.

Syntax:

```
OPTICOPY *.* B:
```

optimally copies all the files in the current directory to drive B.

```
OPTIMOVE C:\TMP\*.ZIP A:\MYDIR
```

optimally moves all ZIP files in C:\TMP to A:\MYDIR.

OptiCopy and OptiMove can work with more than one source filespec. For example, if you want to copy all ZIP, ARC, and PAK files from the current directory to drive A, you would type:

```
OPTICOPY *.ZIP *.ARC *.PAK A:
```

Remarks: OptiCopy and OptiMove attempt to minimize the amount of wasted space on each floppy disk. Using a special algorithm, OptiCopy is able to select which files to copy onto each floppy disk, very often with the result being that there are "0 bytes free" on the floppy disk after the copy procedure. (Try it and see!)

Note: OptiCopy and OptiMove do *not* compress files; they only selects files from a long list so as to minimize wasted disk space.

Copyright © 1991 Paul Galbraith. All Rights Reserved. This program is *freeware* and may be freely used and distributed, but not modified of sold for profit without the author consent.

Paul Galbraith
275 Alscot Crescent
Oakville, Ontario
L6J 4R5
(416) 844-3770
CompuServe: 72060,152

P64.EXE — Lambert Klein — Shareware

Purpose: A full-featured print manager, P64.EXE prints files and manipulates them using pull-down menus.

Syntax: To load P64.EXE, enter the following command at the DOS prompt:

```
P64
```

The menu interface is loaded. The bottom half of the screen displays your directory structure and its files. The current path and file information is displayed across the top of the screen. Click on the menu name or press the highlighted letter to activate menus. Make selections as needed. Margin settings can be changed using the Print>Margins selection or by clicking on the Margins box on the left of the screen.

Any operation you execute, such as printing or moving, is applied either to the current file or to any number of tagged files. Tag files in one of three ways:

1. Highlight the file name and press Enter.
2. Position the mouse cursor on the file name and click the right button.
3. Press Alt-M to toggle the Autotag feature. When on, the cursor automatically moves to the next file when a file is tagged.

Press Tab to tag or untag all files on the displayed screen. Scrolling beyond the screen untags all files.

Here's a summary of pull-down menus and the selections they contain:

`View`

Displays the contents of the currently highlighted file.

`Print`

Presents selections for setting margins, headers, redirecting to a file, changing the print mode (PMODE) and printing files.

`File`

Presents selections for moving, copying, and deleting files.

Remarks: You can tag multiple files and individually specify the number of copies for them. To do this:

1. Tag files. Move the cursor to the first tagged file.
2. Press Shift-3.
3. Specify the number of copies for the file.
4. Repeat steps 1 to 3 for all tagged files.

Setting Print Mode (PMODE) The PMODE selection controls the format for the printed output. You have four choices:

`0` Prints file "straight through" without stripping formfeed character.

`1` Prints file, skips over perforations, and adds a formfeed to the end of the file.

`2` Prints file the same as Pmode 1, strips excess blank lines.

`3` Prints file the same as Pmode 1, strips ALL blank lines.

To send the print output to a disk file, press Alt-S when the Settings dialog box is displayed. You can specify one filename, then send multiple outputs to it. Each output (file) is appended to the file you specify. If you are building an output file from multiple tagged files, turn the Filter ON to prevent unwanted EOF characters from being inserted.

Previewing the Output Pressing [Alt-P] displays the number of pages needed to print the current file in each print mode.

Inspecting the Ouput Press F8 or click INS (lower left corner) to view a report of a file's form feed characters, left margin setting, tab stops, and length of the longest line.

P64.EXE is Copyright © 1990–1993 by Lambert Klein. All Rights Reserved. This program is not public domain but *shareware.* To register, send a check or money order for $23.95 to:

Shareable Software International
PO Box 611
Wayne, MI 48184

800-622-2793 ORDERS
708-397-1221 VOICE
708-397-0381 FAX
76226,2652 COMPUSERVE

PAGES.EXE | Mark Ellis | Freeware

Purpose: PAGES counts the number of pages in a disk file. Use it to find the number of pages in doc files before printing them!For help, just type "PAGES" at the DOS prompt.

Syntax: `pages [path\]filename`

For registration, send $2 to:

Mark Ellis
465 Mitchell Ave
Elmhurst, IL 60126

PARK.COM — Marc Perkel — Shareware

Purpose: Parks the read/write heads on you hard drive in an unused "landing zone" to prepare the computer for moving.

Syntax: `[d:] [path] PARK`

Remarks: While many late model drives have a self-parking feature, it never hurt to be sure that your drive heads aren't doing a flamenco imitation on the drive media while you trundle the computer to a new office down the hall. PARK moves the read-write heads to an area of the drive that's not used for data storage, this safeguarding your bits from an accidental and deletrious jolting encounter with the heads while the computer is in transit. Run PARK and then turn off the machine. Powering up restores the read-write heads to their normal position.

 This program is part of the Computer Tyme DOS ToolBox. To register, ask for the BANTAM BOOK special price of $25 (Reg Price $60)

Contact:

Computer Tyme
411 North Sherman, Suite 300
Springfield, MO 65802
(800) 548-5353

PATHINC.EXE — Tony Tschanz — Freeware

Purpose: Adds or drops (PATH INCludes) directory names from the path environment variable.

Syntax: `PATHINC [-] [d:][\][path] [position to place in current path]`

Remarks: For Use in Batch files or directly from the command line. Will not increase the path if already defined previously. PATHINC can place new name near the front of path for speed.

Long path names slow down procedures and repeated "set path=..." statements in batch files could make the path name longer and longer. This quick utility may encourage users to adjust the path names more often or to juggle to what is appropriate for the currently running application. Unlike environment editing routines PATHINC works just as well from batch files as from the DOS command line. You may want to rename PATHINC.com to something shorter if you use it often (i.e. PI), then put it in a directory which is included in your path.

If you run 4DOS then delete PATHINC.COM so it will use the more complex (and less syntax checking) PATHINC.EXE. PATHINC.EXE will work for both DOS 6.0 and 4DOS, but PATHINC.COM is preferable for monogamous DOS 6.0 setups.

Examples:

```
pathinc c:\tools
```

```
pathinc c:\tools 2 >nul
```

(typical with arguments in batch files)

```
pathinc    ..    *
```

(places parent directory at end of path)

```
pathinc /h
```

(brief help)

```
pathinc
```

(no arguments prompt for a path name)

```
pathinc - c:\tools
```

(eliminates tools directory)

```
pathinc -    .
```

(eliminates current directory)

```
pathinc - 2
```

(eliminates 2nd name)

```
pathinc -
```

(prompts again for path name to exclude)

Notes: These programs were updated for DOS 5.0, but may run on lower versions too.

Contributions and suggestions for enhancements gratefully accepted. Fee for commercial use $6 (see address below).

Not to be sold for profit.

© 1992 Tony Tschanz
5549 SW Campbell Pl.
Seattle, Wa 98116

PCL2ENG.EXE — H. B. Herman — Shareware

Purpose: Interprets PCL 4 commands (sent to HP LaserJets) in files, displays each command and a plain-English description of its function.

Syntax: Use the following syntax to run PCL2ENG from the DOS command prompt:

```
PCL2ENG filename.ext (/P)
```

Add the /P option if you wish to print the commands.

PCL2ENG.EXE is Copyright © 1990–1993 by H. B. Herman. This program is not public domain but *shareware.* Registration is free, although updates may require a registration fee.

H. B. Herman
One Thornton Lane
Lee, NH 03824-4014

PLIST.EXE — Steven Q. Stulz — Shareware

Purpose: Prints ASCII files. Use it to print program source code, documentation, and other text files.

Syntax: PLIST is run from the DOS prompt using the following syntax:

```
PLIST (d:\path\filename.txt) (80, 137, 132, or
226)
```

in which (d:\path\filename.txt) specifies the file to print and the number that follows specifies the column-width of the paper:

`80` prints standard text on 80-column paper.

`132` prints compressed text on 80-column paper.

`137` prints standard text on 137-column paper.

`226` prints compressed text on 137-column paper.

Remarks: Page numbers are inserted at the top of each page. The date and filename are inserted at the top of the first page.

This program is not public domain but *shareware.* To register, send a check or money order for $7 to:

Steven Q. Stulz
1723 Baltimore RD NW
Lancaster, OH 43130
70662,3145 COMPUSERVE

PORTTEST.EXE MicroSystems Devolopment Shareware

Purpose: PORTTEST.EXE is a comprehensive diagnostic program for I/O ports. It can be used to identify ports, manipulate system tables, test ports, and resolve problems.

Syntax: The PORTTEST.EXE menu interface lets you run the program by selecting the option(s) you wish to execute. To load the menu interface, use the following command at the DOS prompt:

```
PORTTEST
```

You can also run PORTTEST with these command-line options:

`/p` Use the system's default print screen handler. Disables PORTTEST's character translation when doing a print screen.

`/m` Activates monochrome mode on color monitors.

`/i` Loads menu interface (default unless other options are specified).

`detectserial or ds`

Updates the serial ports table

`detectparallel or dp`

Updates the parallel ports table

`addparallel or ap`

Adds a parallel port to the table

`com#:(b, p, d, s)`

Set parameters for COM#

`addserial or as(b, p, d, s)`

Adds a serial port to the table, sets its parameters (optional)

`delete port#`

Delete COM# or LPT# from the table

`swap (portx porty)`

Swaps table addresses for port *x* and port *y*

Examples: To update the serial ports table, use:

```
porttest ds
```

To add address 0280 hex to the serial port table as the next logical COM port, use:

```
porttest as 280
```

To set baud rate, parity, data bits, and stop bits for COM3, use:

```
porttest com3:9600,n,8,1
```

To swap the table addresses of lpt1 and lpt2, use:

```
porttest swap lpt1 lpt2
```

PORTTEST.EXE is Copyright © 1990 by MicroSystems Development. This program is not public domain but *shareware.* To register, send a check or money order for $xx to:

MICROSYSTEMS DEVELOPMENT
4100 Moorpark Ave. #104
San Jose, CA 95117 USA
(408)296-4000
(408)296-5877 FAX

POST.EXE — F. C. Betts — Shareware

Purpose: Prints ASCII files to PostScript printers or files. User can specify formatting from the command line.

Syntax: Use the following command syntax from the DOS prompt:

```
[d:][path]POST[option value]
```

Multiple options can, and usually will, be specified. Use upper or lower case except for Font names (see below). The output filename must be different from the input filename.

The following options can be specified from the command line:

Option	*Value*	*Defaults*
Left Margin or L	Left margin in points	L 54
Top Print Line or T	Top line (from bottom) in points	T 720
Bottom Print or B	Bottom print limit in points	B 54
Column Tab or C	Column tab spacing in points	C 56
Typeface Size or P	Typeface size in points	P 12
Leading or D	Vertical line spacing in points	D 12
Typeface Font or F	Selected font for printing	F
Courier Scaling or S	X,Y scaling multipliers	S 1.0 1.0
Page Origin or X	X,Y coordinates (points)	X 0 0
Page Orientation or R	Page rotation in degrees	R 0

Remarks: Points refer to standard typographical measurements: 72 pts = 1 inch.

Scaling is done by the PostScript printer. Printouts can be enlarged and reduced for both X and Y coordinates.

Default X and Y (0,0) coordinates locate the bottom left corner of the page. You can move the page origin by specifying X,Y values in points. Remember that positive values move the page up and right. Any characters that extend beyond the limits of the page as a result of your changes will not print.

The most obvious use the Page Orientation option (R) is to use it to print in landscape mode. The page is rotated counter-clockwise by the number of degrees specified.

If you encounter problems, first check your printer connection.

Examples: To print a directory listing to a Postscript printer, use:

```
C>DIR ¦ POST > PRN
```

To convert a file, DOS.TXT, to a PostScript file, PS.TXT, use:

```
C>POST < DOS.TXT > PS.TXT
```

To print a file, SIDEWAYS.TXT, in landscape mode, set the top of the page to 540 points ((7 inches from bottom), move the origin to the upper left corner, and rotate the page by 270 degrees, using this command:

```
C>POST T 540 X 0 792 R 270 < SIDEWAYS.TXT > PRN
```

 This program is not public domain but *shareware.* To register, send a check or money order for $10 to:

F. C. Betts
c/o Veda Incorporated
Suite 200
5200 Springfield Pike
Dayton, OH 45431

PPPD.EXE Version 3.01 — R. N. Wisan — Freeware

Purpose: Batch file utility. Allows current drive:\directory and path to be pushed (saved) into and later popped (restored) from a file. It keeps its data in a file.

Syntax:

```
PPPD PUSH
```

or

```
PPPD POP [M]
```

M pops to the master environment as well as the current one.

Remarks: PPPD PUSH causes the current drive, directory and path to be placed in a file. Repeated PPPD PUSHes keep stacking the then-current drive, &c. in the file.

PPPD POP switches to the most recently PUSHed drive:\directory & path and removes it from the file. When it's popped all the data, it deletes the file.

By default, the path is popped into the current active environment, the one from which PPPD is called. This is what you normally require. If you run with an extra layer of COMMAND.COM or any other shell (like 4DOS or DESQview), and especially if you do a lot of switching shells (stepping through the DOS door in a program, for instance), you might want to use the M option. That makes PPPD pop the path into the master environment (the environment belonging to the lowest layer of DOS) also.

If something goes wrong (usually an attempt to pop from an empty stack file, but possibly insufficient room in the environment for the PATH string), PPPD exits, setting the DOS errorlevel thus:

`0` No error. Everything went well.

`1` Complete failure. No data file to pop, couldn't open data file to push etc. Path not popped.

`2` (M option only) Popped path into the active environment but couldn't pop it to the master environment.

`3` (M option only) Popped path into the master environment but couldn't pop it to the active environment.

`255`

Syntax error: (no PUSH or POP, Option other than M, &c.)

For most purposes, it's probably wise to make sure PPPD starts with a fresh stack file at boot-up. Put a line in AUTOEXEC.BAT to DEL C:\STACK3.PPD (or whatever you're using for PPPD's stack). On the other hand, if you make a point to PPPD PUSH just before you turn off the computer, PPPD POP in AUTOEXEC.BAT will bring the machine up just as you left it.

R. N. Wisan
37 Clinton St.
Oneonta, NY 13820
internet: wisanr@hartwick.edu

QUADRIVE.SYS — Ronald Q. Smith — Shareware

Purpose: QUADRIVE.SYS is a device driver which supports the 720Kb format on high-capacity (1.2Mb) 5 1/4" disk drives. The 720Kb format normally is available only on 3 1/2" drives. With QUADRIVE you can read, write, and format 5 1/4" disks as if they were 720Kb, 3 1/2" disks.

Syntax: Install QUADRIVE in your CONFIG.SYS file using the following command:

```
DEVICE=QUADRIVE.SYS /D:d1 [/D:d2] [/D:d3] [/D:d4]
```

The parameters d1 through d4 are physical device numbers for which you want 720KB support and must must represent 1.2MB drives and controllers. Keep in mind these are the physical drive numbers 0 thru 4 and not DOS drive letters A:, B:, etc. Thus if you have a single floppy drive, you would specify DEVICE=QUADRIVE.SYS /D:0.

Remarks: Once QUADRIVE is installed you can refer to the same drive by multiple letters. In a single floppy system, DOS assigns the letters A: and B: to the disk drive, and QUADRIVE will add D: or E:. This requires some caution. While DOS will carefully prompt you when switching between drives A: and B:, it is unaware that D: is also the same drive. So you won't be able to copy files from A: to D: as you won't be able to change floppies fast enough.

QUADRIVE actually supports any mixture of 160KB, 180KB, 320KB, 360KB, 720KB, and 1.2MB formats on the drive. QUADRIVE automatically adjusts for reading and writing all media formats. However, you cannot format a disk in any capacity other than 720KB.

The new 720KB format is identical in all respects except pysical size to the 3 1/2" 720KB format. In fact, DOS utilities such as FORMAT and DISKCOPY will believe that it is a 3 1/2" 720KB media. QUADRIVE will also allow you to read and write your Tandy and DEC 720KB diskettes that your new system doesn't support.

So, you can read, write, and perform any function that doesn't require formatting using the QUADRIVE drive letter, and you can do it using all of supported formats. If you use a function that requires formatting, you must use the QUADRIVE letter for 720KB diskettes and the DOS A: or B: drive letter for other formats. Functions that may require formatting are FORMAT, DISKCOPY, and BACKUP. DISKCOPY and BACKUP only require formatting if the target disk is not already formatted.

You can use DOS' DISKCOPY, DISKCOMP, and many other file-manipulation programs with the QUADRIVE drive. DISKCOPY and others include their own prompting capability and will notify you when to change diskettes if you use the same drive letter for both the source and the target.

However, due to limitations in DISKCOPY, and sometimes BACKUP, you may not be able to copy from a 720KB diskette to a previously formatted 360KB diskette without reformatting the target first.

Another limitation involves the DOS FORMAT command. FORMAT.COM does not allow a 720Kb format on a 1.2MB drive. You must use the QUADRIVE drive designation.

Any application that uses the BIOS directly, such as many backup utilities, will not be able to use QUADRIVE. Because the make calls to the BIOS directly, they bypass the QUADRIVE driver. So you may run into problems with non-DOS formatters, such as Central Point Software's PCFORMAT.

Just for your peace of mind: the 720KB capacity is inherent in the 1.2MB disk controller and in all 360KB floppy media. No drive or media specifications are being exceeded. This is just a format the Microsoft and IBM chose not to support.

Examples: You can repeat the same physical device number two or more times. This will assign multiple drive letters to the same drive just as DOS assigns both A: and B: to drive 0 if you don't have a drive 1. You will be prompted to change diskettes with the familiar DOS message when you change the drive letter.

Thus, if you have a single floppy system and used the following CONFIG.SYS statement, you will have four drive letters by which you may refer to the drive.

```
DEVICE=QUADRIVE.SYS /D:0 /D:0
```

For this to work properly, you must set the LASTDRIVE specification large enough to accommodate the new drive letters. When toggling between A: and B: or D: and E: you will see the prompt message. However, DOS thinks that A: and B: refer to a 1.2MB drive and that D: and E: refer to a 3 1/2" 720KB drive. So you will not be prompted when changing between A: or B: and D: or E:.

To register sent $20 to:

Ronald Q. Smith
11 Black Oak Road
North Oaks, Mn. 55127-6204
71620, 514 COMPUSERVE

REFORMAT.EXE Timothy C. Barmann Shareware

Purpose: REFORMAT.EXE changes the line length of ASCII (text) files. You can replace the original file or specify a new name for the reformatted file. You can also strip carriage return/line feeds (except those at paragraph ends) from files so they can be used by word processors.

Syntax:

```
REFORMAT
```

Then respond to prompts for filenames and line length. Or use:

```
REFORMAT source.txt [new.txt] line length
```

in which *source.txt* is the original file, *new.txt* is the replacement file (if not specified, the original file is replaced), and *line length* is the number of characters per line in the replacement file.

Remarks: Suppose your printer prints compressed type at 160 characters per line. You know you can save paper by printing an 80-character-per-line file with the longer line, but it would take too long to load your word processor and reformat it. REFORMAT will automatically change the line length to the length you specify.

Or if you have a text file you want to edit with your word processor. Set a line length of 0 (or enable STRIP CR/LFs) to strip all carriage return/line feeds from the file, except those that mark the end of a paragraph. You don't have to go through and delete them manually.

When finished, REFORMAT.EXE reports the number of lines in the new file.

A consideration when setting short line lengths: REFORMAT will truncate (shorten) words in a file that exceed the specified line length. Thus, is you specify a 10-character line for a file that contains the word, painstaking, it will appear in the reformatted file as painstakin*. The asterisk (*) denotes a program-shortened word. You also see a message displayed informing you this happened.

REFORMAT works best on text files without special formatting such as centered text.

Examples: To change LETTER.TXT to a new file, LETTER.FMT with a 65-character line, use:

```
REFORMAT LETTER.TXT LETTER.FMT 65
```

Or to change the line length of READIT.TXT to 80 characters without creating a new file, use:

```
REFORMAT letter.txt 80
```

REFORMAT.EXE is Copyright © 1993 by Timothy C. Barmann. This program is not public domain but is *shareware.* To register send a check or money order for $10 to:

Timothy C. Barmann
60 Tingley Dr.
Cumberland, RI 02864
72070,652 COMPUSERVE

SECHO.EXE Version 3.5 — Chris Lucksted — Freeware

Purpose: SECHO is a replacement for the DOS ECHO command, but Secho supports MANY formatting, color, and variable commands within each line to be echoed.

Syntax: `[d:] [path] SECHO \switch`

Note: You may use upper- or lowercase letters for all switches.

```
\a
```

Sets the audible alarm. There are no parameters, and it is a replacement for the bell.

`\B#`

Sets the background colors of ALL following output. The colors are listed below. The parameter for this command is one, and only one digit.

`\C`

Clears the screen. No parameters are used.

`\D`

Displays the current date on the screen, in the current colors. The format is "Sunday, July 22, 1988."

`\F##`

Sets the foreground color. It MUST be two digits. Again, see the list of colors below.

Available Colors

This is a list of Colors that Secho can use:

Foreground	*Background*
01 – Blue	1 – Blue
02 – Green	2 – Green
03 – Cyan	3 – Cyan
04 – Red	4 – Red
05 – Magenta	5 – Magenta
06 – Low Yellow (Brown)	6 – Low Yellow (Brown)
07 – Light Gray	7 – Gray
08 – Dark Gray	
09 – Light Blue	
10 – Light Green	
11 – Light Cyan	
12 – Light Red	
13 – Light Magenta	
14 – Light Yellow	
15 – White	

`\G` Displays, in the current colors, the current path you are in.

`\H#` Prints a number of backspaces. The parameter can be only one digit. If you need to backspace further, repeat the switch.

`\M` Prints out the free RAM in the system, in the current colors. No parameters.

`\P#` The pause command. It takes one parameter, which can be only one digit. If the number is between 1 and 9, it will pause that many seconds. If the number is 0, it will prompt the user to press any key, and wait for a keypress.

`\R#` Prints 1–9 carriage returns to the screen. The parameter can be one and only one digit long.

`\S` Outputs to the screen, in the current colors, the amount of free space on the current drive. It is in the format: 367,203 bytes. If applicable (for example, if the drive's free space is larger than one megabyte), it will also convert this to megabytes.

`\T` Outputs the current time, according to the system clock.

`\Wx1y1x2y2P`

The window command. It is a bit involved. The parameter is nine digits long, and the breakdown is as follows:

Digits one and two are the x coordinates of the upper left corner of the window.

Digits three and four are the y coordinates of the upper left corner of the window.

Digits five and six are the x coordinates of the lower right corner.

Digits seven and eight are the y coordinates of the lower right corner. Note, the coordinates MUST be 2 digits each, so if you want position 1, you MUST use 01.

Digit nine is the window style. If digit nine is a 1, the window will be drawn with double lines. If it is a 2, the window will be drawn with single lines. If it is a 3, the window will have double horizontal lines, and single vertical lines. If it is a 4, the window will have single horizontal lines, and double vertical lines.

`\Xxxyy`

This is screen positioning. It must have a FOUR digit parameter. The first two digits are the x value, and the second two are the y value.

`\Z`

Screen ZAP! This is another command I added as a special effect. It will cause the screen to fade out, then clear. Just like the \c command, but more fun to watch. Try it!

`\-string,i,j`

The repeat function. It repeats the text string j times. The first output of your string will be in color i, the second in i+1, and so forth. It cycles colors. When i reaches color 15, it reverts to color 1.

`\="string"`

Repeats string until the user hits a key. Remember to include the quotation marks around the string. The magic is that the string can be a full-fledged SECHO command line, (no double quotation marks, as that is the command's delimiter.)

`\_#`

The # in this command is replaced with a 0 or 1, to turn the cursor off and on respectivly. It's main purpose is to turn the cursor off for the \= " " command, so the screen will not have an annoying little blinking cursor on it.

`}filename`

Sets file mode, so that SECHO reads its commands from the specifed filename. This will only work if the } is the VERY first thing on the command line. Look at TEST.BAT to see it implemented. If you are going to output lots of data, doing it line by line from a batch file can be SLOW. The } command lets you create a file of Secho commands, which are read by Secho. This method is MUCH faster then normal command line mode, but also requires a data file. Look at TEST.BAT, and TEST.DAT for more information.

Finally, if you enjoy Secho, and use it a lot, please feel free to make a small ($10) donation. This donation keeps me developing Secho, and my other public domain projects. It will also get you on the mailing list for any future upgrades to the program. (Make sure you include your address.)

Send comments and donations to:

Chris Lucksted
104 Roanoke
Rochester Hills, MI 48309-1425

SEPARATE.COM Larry Shannon Freeware

Purpose: Program to separate the filename from the extent in a filespec.

Syntax: `SEPARATE filespec,var1,var2`

Remarks: filespec is the subject file specification. May include drives, paths, etc.

var1 is the name of an environment variable where the filename will be stored.

var2 is the name of an environment variable where the extent will be stored

Note: Commas are necessary, but there may be spaces around the commas.

Note that the environment variables must be set up ahead of time, that is, before the program is run. This may be as recent as the line above in a batch file, but in any event the variables must exist at the time the program is run.

var1 should set aside st least 8 characters, and var2 3 characters. If your environment is not big enough (default is 160 characters) see your DOS manual under the SHELL statement for exact syntax for your DOS version.

A simple procedure would be the following lines:

```
set filename=XXXXXXXX
set extent=XXX
SEPARATE config.sys,filename,extent
```

after SEPARATE is run, you will see that

```
filename=CONFIG
extent=SYS
```

These values may then be used in a batch file, e.g.:

```
set fname=XXXXXXXX
```

makes space for filename

```
set ext=XXX
```

makes space for extent

```
SEPARATE %1,fname,ext
```

get filename and extent from passed parameter (%1)

```
copy %1 c:\sub1\%%fname%%.BAK
```

copies filename with new extent .BAK)

```
set fname
```

delete the environment variables

```
set ext
```

RETURN immediately after =

Error returns:

Errorlevel	*Meaning*
0	All OK, normal exit
1	Wrong DOS version (need 3.0+)
2	No command tail entered (no parameters)
3	Could not decipher filespec
4	Couldn't find var1
5	Couldn't find var2
6	Insuficient parameters given
7	Filespec too big to fit in available room
8	Extent too big to fit in available room

Larry Shannon
5615 Truscott Terrace
Lakeview, NY 14085

SHO.EXE — Dwayne Melancon — Freeware

Purpose: Displays a graphic, "gas gauge" indicator of used and available disk space.

Syntax: `SHO [drive letter] [options]`

If no drive letter is specified, the current drive is default. The following options are available.

`/M` forces monochrome "colors" for better visibility on composite monitors and laptops. Monochrome monitors are detected automatically.

`/1` sets Megabytes = 1,024,000 bytes and Kilobytes = 1024 bytes.

`/2` sets Megabytes = 1,000,000 bytes and Kilobytes = 1000 bytes.

`/?` displays Help text.

Dwayne Melancon
10049 North Reiger Road
Baton Rouge, LA 70809

SIZE.EXE — Stanley Hirshen — Freeware

Purpose: Graphically displays the bytes of memory used and free.

Syntax:

```
SIZE
```

Graphics Mode, (CGA/Hercules) Pie Graph for Default Drive.

```
SIZE A
```

Graphics Mode, (CGA/Hercules) Pie Graph for Drive A.

```
SIZE /H
```

Calls Help Screen.

```
SIZE /M
```

Text Mode, Bar Graph Display for default Drive.

```
SIZE /M B
```

Text Mode, Bar Graph Display for Drive B.

```
SIZE [?] [?]
```

There are two (2) possible commands. You must leave a space between them. If the /M command is used it must be the first command. The drive designation is first if /M is not used.

This program is *freeware* and may be freely used and distributed, but not modified or sold for profit without author consent.

Stanley Hirshan
4643 Sextant Circle
Boynton Beach, FL 33438
CompuServe: 72145,306 - Genie: ADAM

SNR.EXE — Thomas A. Lundin — Shareware

Purpose: SNR.EXE is a multi-string search-and-replace filter that works on text and binary files (with hexadecimal input).

Syntax:

```
SNR (@)FILENAME.EXT EXT TABLENAME (/D)
```

where filename.ext specifies the path and name of the input file. You can use the "at" symbol (@) to specify an input file created with a redirected DIR command, which specifies multiple files. See example below.

EXT specifies the extension given to output files. By default, output files are given the same name. Be sure to use a unique extension here, data loss may occur otherwise.

TABLENAME specifies the path and file name of the translation file. Translation files contain one or more string "equations" used for conversions (see below). There are no restrictions on names and extensions for these files, although consistency is recommended.

The /D option specifies that the original input file be replaced with converted data. If this option is enabled, the file specified by EXT is used a a temporary file while the conversion is performed, then the program deletes and renames it automatically.

Remarks: SNR.EXE translates both text and binary files can be processed by the program, since SNR allows the definition of hex values in a search-and-replace equation. SNR will translate a file of any size that your system can handle.

On the command line, the EXT can be DOS device names CON, NUL, AUX, and PRN. Using any of these, an output file is NOT created on disk; rather, the output is redirected to the console (CON), nowhere (NUL), the rs232 port (AUX), or the printer (PRN). Using CON is handy for a quick preview of the conversion process before storing it to disk.

If you preview converted binary files to CON, be aware that occurrences of hex code 1A (DOS end-of-file) terminates the conversion display, perhaps prematurely. This premature termination will NOT occur when you store to disk.

Conversion Tables

Translation files are ASCII files consisting of conversion equations: up to 50 multi-character (m:n) equations (maximum 200 characters for each) and 256 single-character (1:1) equations can be used. Thus, a total of 306 equations can be used. Blank lines in conversion tables are ignored.

For example, to convert upper-case "A" to lower-case "a" use the equation:

```
A=a
```

Similarly, to convert the string "Now is the time" to "NOW IS THE TIME," use:

```
Now is the time=NOW IS THE TIME
```

Notice that spaces are significant characters in an equation.

You can also use equations to delete search text, by using an equation similar to this:

```
Now is the time=
```

You can also specify hex codes as search and/or replacement strings. Simply use a backslash (\) followed by one or two hex digits. Use hex codes to search or replace binary characters that can't be generated directly from the keyboard. For example, use:

```
\0d\0a\0d\0a=\0d\0a
```

To convert occurrences of two CRLFS to a single CRLF.

Three ASCII characters which MUST be specified as hex codes in an SNR equation, since they have special meaning in their normal ASCII form. They are:

Backslash (\), which must be entered as \5c.
Equals (=), which must be entered as \3d.
Asterisk (*), which must be entered as \2a.

Signal the end of a table by inserting "\\E" on a line by itself. This code is optional, but recommended, since it will prevent the table processor from inadvertently reading past the end of your equations (some word processors may pad their last blocks with garbage, which the table processor would attempt to read as equation data).

You can also insert comments into conversion tables, either as lines by themselves, or set off from an equation. For example:

```
\    This is a comment line by itself.
\    A comment consists of a single backslash
\    followed by one or more spaces.
\0d\0a=\0d\0a   \ this will ensure that existing
\ CRLF pairs are left untouched
\0d=\0d\0a      \ this equation will convert an
\ isolated CR  into a CRLF
a=\0d\0a      \ this equation will convert an
\ isolated LF into a CRLF
```

The order of your equations is inconsequential, since SNR automatically sorts equations by length when loading a table into memory.

For your convenience, the translation files ASC2EBC.SNR and EBC2ASC.SNR (converts ASCII to EBCDIC and EBCDIC to ASCII) are provided with the archive file.

Context Flag

You can use context flags to toggle between two different replacement strings for the same search string. A context flag has two states: on or off. The "off" state of the context flag is entered as *00. The "on" state is entered as *01. When the conversion begins the flag's state is OFF. The context flag is the last item entered in a search or replacement string. For example, to replace the string "ABC" with either "abc" or "XYZ," use the equations:

```
ABC*00=abc*01
ABC*01=XYZ*00
```

For example, if data from the input file looks like this:

```
ABCDEFG ABCDEFG ABCDEFG ABCDEFG
```

it would convert to this:

```
abcDEFG XYZDEFG abcDEFG XYZDEFG
```

Use context flags thoughtfully. Be aware that one equation may set the flag on, another may set if off, as determined by the order of search strings in the input file. For example, the table:

```
ABC*00=abc*01
ABC*01=XYZ*00
EFG*00=efg*01
EFG*01=ZYX*00
```

applied to an input file with the following data:

```
ABCDEFG ABCDEFG ABCDEFG ABCDEFG
```

yields these results:

```
abcDZYX abcDZYX abcDZYX abcDZYX
```

Notice the context flag in this example is being toggled by only two equations:

```
ABC*00=abc*01    <--- this one
ABC*01=XYZ*00
EFG*00=efg*01
EFG*01=ZYX*00    <--- and this one
```

See some of the sample .SNR tables included with the archive file for more examples of using context flags.

Bit Stripping

By default, SNR maps all input characters to 7-bit ASCII before running them through translation equations. This is handy if you're converting an old WordStar file and don't want to deal individually with the tagged characters. However, if you're dealing with files that make use of specific binary characters (examples: Word Perfect, XYWrite, others). you may want to prevent 7-bit mapping. To do this, enter the string:

```
\\L8
```

as the first line of a translation table.

An interesting side-effect of the bit-stripping feature is illustrated by the table STRIP.SNR included with the archive file. It contains NO equations at all (except for the \\E), and yet it will effectively remove the high-order bits from any file that it is run through. Try it!

Examples: To create an input file of all files with a .TXT extension, use the DOS command:

```
DIR *.TXT >DIRFILE
```

To convert a file TSTFIL.DOC to TSTFIL.TXT using the translation table named TST.SNR, use the following command:

```
SNR TSTFIL.DOC TXT TST.SNR
```

To convert a group of files listed in DIRLIST into files with a .p1 extension using the translation table named SAMPLE.SNR, use this command:

```
SNR @DIRLIST P1 SAMPLE.SNR
```

 To register, send a check or money order for $25 to:

Thomas A. Lundin
16267 Hudson Avenue
Lakeville, MN 55044

(612)431-5805 eves/weekends

STF.EXE | R.P. McCormick | Shareware

Purpose: Compares two ASCII text files side-by-side.

Syntax: `STF [file1] [file2]`

STF with no parameters brings up an arrow-key selectable menu of filenames. Use F8 while in this screen to change directory. ESC key or ALT-X returns you to DOS. After selecting the first file, you may either select a second file name or choose "No 2nd File" from the upper left.

STF with one filename will display that one file full width, or 80 columns wide on the text screen. 130 characters max on the graphics screen.

```
STF '?' or 'h' or 'H' calls the help screen.
```

Remarks: STF can be used to see if two files are identical, or if not, to pinpoint what is different between the two files. This should help to identify what changes you may have made between two revisions.

Allows comparison of WordStar files, but ignores imbedded control codes.

Files may be up to 132 columns per line.

Differences are "Highlighted" by dimming unequal lines on the right side: File 2.

While viewing the files, Function Keys work as follows:

`Esc` Return to File Name Selection screen.

`F1` Brings up a help screen.

`F2` Makes both files "Active." This is the default mode.

`F3` Selects File 1, the one on the left side.

`F4` Makes File 2 active.

`F5` Selects the default "text mode."

`F6` Shows the files in a graphic mode if a VGA adapter is present. In graphic mode more characters are visible, although smaller.

`Alt-B`

Toggles the "Ignore Blanks" mode. By default, a line with an extra space at the end, for example, will show up as different, although the text is otherwise dentical. Ignoring blanks, or spaces will allow them to appear equal. In "Ignore Blanks, Tabs are also ignored.

`Alt-D or ALT-U`

Searches for the first unequal line of text.Upper case and lower case letters are considered unequal.Think of D for "Different" or U for "Unequal." Repeat this command to find the next unequal line.

`ALT-F`

Prompts you to enter a search string of text on the upper Information bar. Then it Finds the first occurrence of the text string in File1, the one on the left. the line containing the match is dimmed, and the matching text is highlighted. Upper & lower case differences are ignored.

`ALT-A`

Is "find Again." Looks for next occurrence of the entered text string.

`Alt-S`

Turns the "sign bit" on or off. Some word processors use this eighth bit for formatting purposes. Removing it can make the text more readable while viewing. No permanent change is made to the file.

`ALT-X`

Exit to DOS.

`Left Arrow:`

Moves both files 10 columns to the left.

`Right Arrow:`

Moves both files 10 columns to the right.

The following commands affect only the selected "active" file(s). The active file(s) can be identified by a bright white square on the top line on the screen, above the text of the file.

Up Arrow:	Move Up one line.
Down Arrow:	Move Down one line.
Page Up:	Move up one screen page.
Space Bar:	or
Enter Key:	or
Page Down:	Move down one screen page.
Home:	Go to start (top) of file.
End:	Go to End of file.

After viewing the files, you may want to delete one of them. "Escape" back to the file selection screen, highlight the filename, and hit the "Delete" key.

Copyright © 1991,1992 by R.P.McCormick. This program is not freeware or public domain but is "shareware". To register

Please send $10.00 to:

R.P. McCormick
79 Rye Street
Broad Brook, CT 01016

SUBCOPY.EXE　　Anthony Abate　　Freeware

Purpose: SUBCOPY copies all files (hidden and standard) in the current subdirectory to one or more floppy disks as required.

Syntax: `SUBCOPY`

Remarks: SUBCOPY takes the tedium out of backing up a subdirectory from your hard disk that requires more than 360K. Never again do you need to remember "Which files did I copy so far?"

SUBCOPY is simple to use:

1. Install SUBCOPY somewhere on your hard disk that is in the directory search path.
2. CD down into the subdirectory that you want to copy.
3. Be sure you have enough FORMATTED floppies to hold all of the files in the subdirectory.
4. Type "SUBCOPY" and insert floppies in drive A as asked.

Notes: SUBCOPY copies both hidden and visible files from the subdirectory. However, the files that were hidden on the hard drive will be visible on the floppies.

SUBCOPY copies only files NOT nested subdirectories. If a subdirectory to be copied has subdirectories in it, these will have to be CD'ed into and SUBCOPIED individually.

Look for a future version of SUBCOPY that will give the option of treeing through nested subdirectories.

Copyright © 1987–1993 by Anthony Abate, Formation Inc. This program is *freeware* and may be freely used and distributed, but not modified or sold for profit without author consent.

Anthony Abate
43 Dove Court
Turnersville, NJ 08012

SWAP_LPT.EXE — Dan Likins — Freeware

Purpose: Swaps assignments among parallel ports LPT1-3. Also displays status of these ports.

Syntax: Run SWAP_LPT.EXE from the DOS command prompt using the following syntax:

```
SWAP_LPT [NORMAL] [1, 2, or 3] [1, 2, or 3] [?]
```

If no command-line arguments are specified, the status of LPT ports is displayed.

The NORMAL parameter restores default settings for LPT ports.

Use the [1, 2, or 3] arguments to specify swapped ports.

Use the [?] parameter to display a help screen.

Examples: For example, to swap LPT1 for LPT2, use:

```
SWAP_LPT 1 2
```

SWAP_LPT.EXE is Copyright © 1993 by Dan Likins. This program is *freeware* and may be freely used and distributed, but not modified or sold for profit without author consent.

Dan Likins
1-714-543-6573

TESTHEAD.EXE Joseph J. Tamburino Freeware

Purpose: A diagnostic tool, TESTHEAD fires each head (pin) on a dot-matrix printer and identifies each pin mark. If a pin is misfiring, it can be isolated.

Syntax: To run TESTHEAD, enter the following command from the DOS prompt:

```
TESTHEAD
```

You are prompted to specify an 8- or 24-pin Epson printer.

Remarks: This program supports only Epson-compatible computers, which encompasses nearly every printer made today.

This program is in the public domain and may be freely used and distributed without restriction. Address any questions or comments to:

Joseph J. Tamburino
7 Christopher Rd.
Westford, MA 01886
(508) 692-7756

TIMEPARK.COM   Sanford J. Zelkovitz   Public Domain

Purpose: Will park drive heads in given number of minutes (1–9).

Syntax:

```
TIMEPARK [n]
```

Where n is the number of minutes that you will allow before the disk parking takes place.

This program is public domain and may be freely used and distributed without restriction.

ALPHA COMPUTER SERVICE
(Sanford J. Zelkovitz)
714-898-0286

TOUCH.EXE   David Foley   Shareware

Purpose: A Unix-like utility to stamp a file's attributes with the current system date and time.

Syntax:

```
[d:] [path] TOUCH [filespec [filespec]]
```

Remarks: Touch is useful if you want to have a group of files with identical date and timestamps. Multiple filespecs are acceptable, as are wildcards within each filespec. If you need to set the time and date. to a different time and date than the system clock, you can write a short batch file to reset the clock to the desired time and date, then TOUCH the files. Aftgferward, be sure to reset the time and date!

```
TIME 12:00:00
DATE 5-01-91
TOUCH \myfiles\*.*
```

TOUCH.EXE is Copyright 1985–1991 by Foley Hi-Tech Systems. This program is not public domain but is "shareware" and a part of the Foley Hi-Tech Systems ExtraDOS collection. To register send a check or money order for $19.00 to:

Foley Hi-Tech Systems
ExtraDOS Registration
172 Amber Drive
San Francisco, CA 94131
(415) 826-6084

TPP.COM TechStaff Corporation Shareware

Purpose: A menu-driven DOS print utility.

Syntax: Use the following command to load TPP.COM from the DOS prompt:

```
TPP
```

Press F10 or Q to begin the printing process. Respond to prompts to specify a file to be printed and operational parameters. Before you print, a summary of your selections is shown. You can make changes by pressing the appropriate function key.

Press F6 or F7 to display a file list or change the current directory as needed.

TPP-TechStaff Page-Printer 1.02b, TechStaff Tools version 1.01. Copyright © 1989–1993 by TechStaff Corporation. All Rights Reserved. This program is not public domain but *shareware.* To register, send a check or money order for $19.95 + $3 s/h to:

TechStaff Corporation
PO Box 823
Watertown, MA 02272
617-924-0306

VORCOMP.EXE Voree Software Shareware

Purpose: This program performs the function of comparing two files for any differences, or of comparing two complete directories for differences in contents or differences in the common files.

Groups of files may also be designated for comparison by the use of wild cards. Complete subdirectory trees may be also compared. Hidden files, volume labels, and directory attributes may be included in the comparisons. Many options are available to control the type of comparisons performed, the display, and the generated ErrorLevel.

Syntax: To compare files:

```
VORCOMP file1 file2
```

If desired, the filenames may include a path to the files.

A file may be compared to another file with the same name in another directory from the DOS prompt with the following command:

```
VORCOMP file path
```

To compare directories:

```
VORCOMP path1 path2
```

The path may include a drive specification, if desired, or may be only a drive specification.

Any two groups of files may be compared by specifying the two groups:

```
VORCOMP group1 group2
```

where a group may be either an entire directory or a file description with ? and * wildcards.

Options

A variety of options are available for use with this program. These options may be in upper case or lower case. They may be used anywhere on the command line, either before, between, or after the file and directory names. The order of the options is not important, but in case of any conflict the rightmost option overrides earlier ones. Options usually consist of a forward slash and a letter. An exception to the above rule is the ErrorLevel option, which consists of "/E=" followed by some series of letters to indicate the types of error checking desired. See the "ErrorCodes" section below for more information. Two or more options may be combined into a series by using one slash and followed by all of the desired options. More than one series of options is allowed. If the "E=" option is included in a series, it must be used last in that series.

General-Purpose Options

The general-purpose options are the following:

`/Q` Quick—Causes the file data comparisons to consider the file sizes only, in addition to the time and attribute comparisons. The actual data within the files is not compared.

When this option is used, it is possible for two files to be different, even though they may have the same size, date, and attributes. The output display will indicate the ambiguity in the number of different files by using a "?" for the total or by adding a "+ ?" to the total.

`/H` Hidden—Causes hidden and system files to be included in the comparisons of two groups. When the /M or /S option is also used, this causes hidden and system subdirectories to be included in those functions.

This option is not necessary in order to reference a hidden file or directory when it is specified directly by name. The option is only required when it is desired to find hidden and system files and directories within some directory or within some group specified with wildcards.

`/M` More—Causes the comparison of two groups to include subdirectories and volume labels in the output display and totals. Of course there is no data comparison performed here, but the time and attributes are compared.

Directories are indicated in the display by being enclosed in corner brackets < >, and volume labels are indicated by being enclosed in square brackets [ ].

`/S` Subdirectory Tree—Causes the comparisons of two groups to also include comparisons within subdirectories with common names.

When this option is used, an output display is made for each directory or subdirectory compared. This is then followed by a grand total of all the compared directories.

If a group is specified with wildcards, this option will cause the same wildcards to be applied to all of the subdirectories in the tree.

Display Options

`/T` Totals Only—Suppresses intermediate display information and displays only the totals.

When the /S option is also used, this displays only the grand totals, and the totals if each individual directory in the tree is suppressed.

This option may be useful even if the display output is redirected to the NUL device with the > feature of DOS, because its use will result in greater speed.

The following four interrelated options control the output display when two groups are being compared:

/X First Group—This limits the display to files which are unique to the first group, but the totals will correctly include all files. However, if this option is used without either /C or /D below, then no actual data comparisons will be performed, just as if the /Q quick option above had been used.

/Y Second Group—This limits the display to files which are unique to the first group, but the totals will correctly include all files. However, if this option is used without either /C or /D below, then no actual data comparisons will be performed, just as if the /Q quick option above had been used.

/C Common Files—This limits the display to files which are common to both groups, but the totals will correctly include all files.

/D Different—This limits the display to files which are common to both groups and which have been identified as different, but the totals will correctly include all files.

Significant differences here include data differences, date and time differences, and attribute differences.

These four options are listed here together because they are interrelated. They may be used together in combinations. Other than the /C and /D conflict discussed below, the options are additive, in that the display output will reflect the composite of the options selected. The default combination is /XYC. The use of any of the options in this set cancels the default combination completely, and the display is strictly under the control of the options which are specified.

It should be noted that /C and /D conflict with each other.If they are both used, the later (rightmost) option will dominate and cancel the earlier option.

Pause Options

The display pause options are the following:

`/P`

Pause—Causes the output display to pause when the screen is full.

`/P=nn`

Pause—The same as above, plus the ability to specify a custom screen size and/or prompt size. 'nn' is the size of the screen in lines. The default screen size is 25 lines. If a different size screen is used, it may be specified here with the number lines. For example: /P=43.

`/P#`

Pause—The same as the above, except that the "Press any key to continue" message is backspaced out of the display, instead of being left on the screen.

`/P#=`

Pause—The same as /P# and /P= together. Follow this with the screen and/or prompt size numbers as above.

Error Codes

`/E`

Error Codes—This option is used to control the detection and reporting of differences which will be considered to be "errors." The option is followed by any number of specific error codes.

The following is a list of the error codes which generate error messages if the specified condition is satisfied.

`/E=N`

Never—This may be used as a dummy place holder.

`/E=X`

Unique First Group File—Error if there is a file which is unique to the first group.

`/E=Y`

Unique Second Group File—Error if there is a file which is unique to the second group.

`/E=C`

Common File—Error if there is a common file.

`/E=D`

Data Difference—Error if there is a common file which has different size or data.

`/E=T`

Time Difference—Error if there is a common file which has different date or time.

`/E=A`

Attribute Difference—Error if there is a common file which has different attributes.

`/E=O`

Order Difference—Error if there are any common files which appear in a different directory position in the two groups.

`/E=U`

Unique First Group Subdirectory—Error if during a /S tree search there is a subdirectory which is unique to the first group.

`/E=V`

Unique Second Group Subdirectory—Error if during a /S tree search there is a subdirectory which is unique to the second group.

`/E=W`

Common Subdirectory—Error if during a /S tree search there is a common subdirectory. Only applies during a group search.

When appended to any of the preceding codes, this reverses the logic of the previous code. For example, E=C' generates an error if there are NO common files.

The following codes may be used as an optional termination to control the way errors are reported. These are mutually exclusive and, if present, must be used last.

`/E` Report Errors, Redirectable, Silent—The error message, if any, is standard output.

`/E` Report Errors, On Screen, Bell—The error message, if any, is DOS error output, which will always display on the screen even if the standard output is redirected elsewhere by the > or >> feature of DOS.

`/E` Report Errors, On Screen, Bell, Press Any Key to Continue. The error message, if any, is DOS error output, which will always display on the screen even if the standard output is redirected elsewhere by the > or >> feature of DOS.

When more than one of the above error codes is used, they must be combined in one /E= option statement. If the /E= option is combined with other options, the E= option must be the last in the series. For example, /E=XYDTA compares two directories and identifies any difference in the contents as an error. If the /E= option is combined with other options, the E=option must be the last in the series.

When the program exits after the comparison, the ErrorLevel is set to represent the degree of error. No errors results in an ErrorLevel of 0. An error generated by the first error code, results in an ErrorLevel of 1. An error generated by the second error code results in an ErrorLevel of 2, and so forth. If more than one error code generates an error, the ErrorLevel is set to the largest position number of the error codes which generate an error.

VORCOMP is distributed as shareware. It is not free software. If you continue to use this program beyond a 30-day trial period, you are required to register it. The registration fee for this version is $8 per copy. Please add $1 for 3.5" disks; Wisconson residents must add sales tax. Registered users will receive a floppy disk with the official version of the software, a 24-page booklet-style reference manual, technical support, new-product notices, and low-cost upgrades. They will also receive a configuration program which will create custom versions of VorComp 1.1 with different default values for the options. The configuration program is not shareware, and its use will be restricted to those who register. Make checks payable to Voree Software (US funds and drawable at a U.S. bank). Please send your registrations to:

Voree Software
5894 Spring Valley Rd.
Burlington, WI53105
Phone: (414) 763-4522

ZIP.COM — Eric Meyer — Shareware

Purpose: ZIP.COM transfers files between two IBM PC compatible computers using a serial (null modem) cable. It can be used from the DOS command line or a batch file, or run from an interactive menu.

Syntax: Before you can transfer files, you must do three things:

1. Link both computers using serial null modem cable.
2. Install the ZIP.COM program on both machines.
3. Set ZIP's serial port setting to the correct port on both machines

Serial Null Modem Cables

Serial null modem cables are available, in various 9- and 25-pin configurations, from most good electronics stores. Ask for a "null modem" cable, meaning the transmit and receive data lines should be crossed, and the signal ground connected straight through. (The pin numbers depend on whether you have a small DB9 or large DB25 connector, see below.) No other connections should be needed; ZIP uses no hardware handshaking lines. (Note: ZIPDUP does require the DTR connections between pins 20/4 and 6.)

You can also build one yourself, using

```
    COMPUTER 1        COMPUTER 2
    DB9 or DB25       DB25 or DB9
pin  2        3 -------- 2      3   transmit and
     3        2 -------- 3      2   receive data
     5        7 -------- 7      5   signal ground
pin  4       20 -------- 6      6   required
     6        6 -------- 20     4   for ZIPDUP
     7        4 -------- 5      8   optional
     8        5 -------- 4      7   handshaking
```

As an alternative, any serial cable with a "null modem adapter" attached should work. If available, use a well shielded cable; high speed transmissions can be especially susceptible to RF interference.

Installing Zip.com

Once you've connected the cable, the same version of ZIP.COM must be installed on both computers. If incompatible disk formats prevent you from getting ZIP.COM onto the second computer, you can "clone" ZIP with the ZIPDUP utility (see below).

To install ZIP, simply ZIP.COM and its related files to the hard disk of both systems. For convenience, put them in a directory specified in your PATH statement. Then you won't have to make ZIP's directory current every time you run it.

To load the program, enter the following command on both machines:

```
ZIP
```

Setting the Serial Port

By default ZIP uses the COM1 port file transfers. If you are using another port, you must change the default port setting. To do this:

- Choose the Parameters selection from the menu interface
- Or from the command line, include a /1, /2, /3 or /4 to specify COMM ports 1 through 4.

ZIP.COM looks for COMM ports at these standard addresses:

```
COM1: 03F8h
COM3: 03E8h
COM2: 02F8h
COM4: 02E8h
```

Some computers (including PS/2s) use different addresses for COM3 and COM4; nonstandard port addresses can be specified in hexadecimal, but only by modifying ZIP.COM with the ZIPCFG utility.

The Parameters selection also lets you set transmission speed. ZIP normally works at its fastest speed, 115200 bps, which works well for most jobs. Certain environments might be sensitive, and a slower speed might help. In fact, ZIP can be slowed down all the way to 2400 bps, so that it might even operate over a good modem connection.

Make sure both computers are set for the same speed.

Use the following command line option to set the transmission speed from the DOS prompt:

```
/Bnnnn
```

In which nnnn is a valid transmission speed (115200, 57600, 38400, 19200, 9600, 4800, and 2400). To abbreviate you can leave out the zeros (for example: /B96).

The main menu lists the valid selections. Press the highlighted letter to choose a selection. Then follow prompts and provide data as required.

Running Zip from the DOS Command Prompt

All ZIP.COM functions also are available from the DOS command prompt. Build a command line including the appropriate options, then press Enter.

Sending Files

From the menu interface:

Select Send. Enter filename(s) and a destination directory in response to prompts. Default destination is the current directory on the receiving machine.

From the DOS command prompt, use the following syntax:

```
ZIP FILESPEC /[DESTDIR]
```

in which FILESPEC identifies the file(s) to be transferred and DESTDIR is the destination directory and is enclosed in quotes. DOS wildcards are valid for specifying files. You can specify multiple files individually, separated by commas.

You can also specify files by listing them, separated by spaces or carriage returns, in an ASCII file. Then, on the command line, use:

```
@Filename
```

as your FILESPEC.

Receiving Files

From the menu interface:

Select Receive. Enter the name of the directory in which you want to put the transferred file(s).

From the DOS command prompt, use the following syntax:

```
ZIP /R[DESTDIR]
```

in which DESTDIR specifies the directory. By default, files are received into the current directory. Files appear with their original names. Do not supply a filespec before the /R option; the sender determines the files to be sent.

Confirming Transfers

You can set ZIP to display confirmation prompts before it transfers files.

From the menu interface, after you have entered the names of files to be transferred, choose PROMPT.

From the DOS prompt, use the following command-line option:

```
/P
```

Backups and Overwriting Files

ZIP provides capabilities for reconciling the contents of directories which are duplicated (in whole or part) on both computers. By default, ZIP transfers all files specified, and overwrites existing files automatically. You can set the program to warn you in one of three ways.

From the menu interface:

Select Options to display a help screen describing the selective copy operations.

From the DOS prompt, use one of the following command-line options:

`/N` transfers only new files (cannot be used with /E or /T)

`/E` transfers existing files only

`/T` transfers only files created after a specified time stamp.

`/ET` transfers only existing files created after a specified time stamp (useful for making backups)

These options can be specified independently on either computer—but the settings on the sending (or active) end govern each transfer. You will see a note in the ZIP sign-on message, "Option /_," if an option is in effect.

Directory, Delete, and Log Commands

ZIP.COM also provides capabilities for performing simple maintenance operations without exiting the program:

From the menu interface:

- Choose Delete to remove files.
- Choose Directory to view the file list.
- Choose Log to change the current directory.

Server Mode

Server mode lets you control transfers from a single machine. Set the receiving machine to Server mode, then control operations from the sending (client) machine.

To enter Server mode from the menu interface:

Choose Server.

To enter Server mode from the DOS prompt, enter the following command-line options:

```
/S[DFLTDIR]
```

in which DFLTDIR specifies the default directory on the destination drive.

The server machine is now set to receive commands from the sending machine. Valid commands are described below.

Press Escape, ^C, or Ctrl-Break to exit server mode. You can also disable server mode from the sending machine by adding a /U option to a ZIP command line.

Fetching Files

You can send files to a server machine using procedures described above. You can also tell the server to send you files.

From the menu interface:

Select Fetch, then provide file specifications and a receiving directory as prompted.

From the DOS prompt, use the following command-line option:

```
FILENAME /F[DESTDIR]
```

in which FILESPEC specifies the path and directory of the file(s) to be fetched, and DESTDIR specifies the directory to which the transferred files are written.

Server Directory, Delete, and Log Commands

You can also display the file list of the server's current directory, delete files on the server machine, and change the current directory.

From the menu interface, enter a ">" before entering specifications for the Directory, Delete, or Log commands. You enter multiple specifications. For example:

```
Directory: \WORK\*.BAK  displays *.BAK files on the
client's /WORK directory.
Delete: >B:\BACKUP\OLD.FIL deletes OLD.FIL from
the server's /BACKUP directory
Log: \WORK\*.BAK >B:\BACKUP   displays *.BAK files
from the client's \WORK directory and sets the
server's directory to \BACKUP
```

As a convenience, you can also type a quote mark (") to log the same default directory for the server.

Log: C:\WORK >"logs C:\WORK on both client and server

Log: C:\WORK >D"logs D:\WORK on the server

From the DOS prompt, you can also specify the following command-line options:

/D[FILESPEC]	Displays directory listing on server
/K[FILESPEC]	Deletes (kills) filespec on server
/L[NEWDIR]	Logs new directory (NEWDIR) on server

Comparing Directories

You can selectively compare the contents of client and server directories.

From the menu interface:

Choose Compare, then enter file specifications and directories for comparison. Remember to use the > character to specify server directories.

From the DOS prompt, use the following command-line syntax:

```
ZIP FILESPEC /C[SRVRDIR]
```

in which FILESPEC identifies the file(s) to be compared, and SRVRDIR specifies the server directory.

ZIP displays two reports:

- Files on the client machine that do not exist on the server.
- Files on the server machine that do not exist on the client.

Files that appear on both ends are flagged with a "+" or "–" to indicate which appears to be the most (+) or least (–) recent version, according to the files' timestamps.

Using ZIPDUP to Clone ZIP

Use the ZIPDUP utility to send ZIP.COM to another computer over the serial cable. To clone ZIP with ZIPDUP:

1. Connect the cable, using COM1 or COM2 only. Also, the cable must have the DTR lines, as well as the data lines, connected.
2. Set up the receiving end: Make sure the MSDOS utilities DEBUG and MODE are available (either in the current directory or in your PATH); you will have to use MODE, and ZIPDUP requires DEBUG.

   Be certain that the last character of your DOS prompt is ">". (Yes, this actually matters!) If in doubt, type the command: PROMPT PG

   Then enter the following commands:

   ```
   MODE COM#:96,N,8,1      ("#" = 1 or 2 only)
   CTTY COM#
   ```

   The CTTY command gives control to the sending computer, via the COM# port. The receiving system will seem to "lock up," ignoring any keyboard input.
3. On the sending machine, enter this command:

   ```
   ZIPDUP ZIP.COM
   ```

   (Actually, you can omit the filename if it is "ZIP.COM"; otherwise, type it.)

   You will be asked to specify the COM port (again, 1 or 2 only) to which the cable is connected. When the transfer is finished, ZIP.COM has been copies to the current directory of the receiving machine.

Using ZIPCFG to Change Defaults

Another utility, ZIPCFG, sets configuration options according to individual requirements. To load the utility, enter the following command at the DOS prompt:

```
ZIPCFG ZIP.COM
```

To change defaults:

1. Select Edit from the menu. Configuration settings are presented in sequence. Make changes as needed.
2. Select Save to save your changes. Select Restore to return to original settings. Select Quit to exit without saving.

Remarks: ZIP does not use interrupts, so it should not conflict with the IRQ usage of other hardware or software. However, do not use ZIP while the specific serial port chosen is being used by another program.

Using any communications software in a multitasking environment often requires special precautions. ZIP, in particular, may need to be given a "non-swappable" or "foreground-operation" status, so that other tasks will not interfere with its operation. (Under DesqView, ZIP will disable multitasking itself. Under Windows, you must create a PIF file and give ZIP both background and foreground priority.) You may also need to set a slower speed for ZIP to work reliably.

This program is *shareware.* Commercial use requires a site license, starting at $50 for up to 20 copies; individual registration at $30 is encouraged, but not required, and includes support. This program may be freely distributed, but not modified or sold for profit without the written consent of the author.

To register, send a check or money order for $30 to:

Eric Meyer
3541 Smuggler Way
Boulder, CO 80303

Index

Installation Notes

To install the DOS Power Tools utility programs requires:

- DOS 6.0
- A hard disk with at least 3.2 megabytes of free space

Yes, you really do need DOS 6.0 (at least), and if you're not convinced by now that you need a hard disk, nothing we say here is likely to sway you.

You must run the installation program from whatever drive the first disk is physically in., so the first step is to type A: or B: or whatever to get to the appropriate drive. The syntax for the INSTALL.COM program is:

```
INSTALL d:\path
```

where *d:\path* is the target drive and full (absolute) directory path for the utilities. It is a required argument for INSTALL.COM—but then again, to get any useful work out of the utilities, you'll have to install them *somewhere.*

If, perchance, you have an overly vigilant virus-checking program (like VSAFE with all the options turned on), you may get a "Write error on drive A:" message. This is because the virus-checking program is trying to write *to* the floppy, which has been write-protected to protect it *from* being written to by ill-behaved programs (like viruses.) You can either turn off that part of your anti-virus program that tries to write to floppies, or defeat the write protection by cutting a notch.

INSTALL will prompt you for the second disk, and will verify that the files were successfully installed. While you can then run any of the individual utilities, which are documented in the last chapter, you can get a better overview of what's on the disk by starting the PTOOL program and using it to browse or run the other utilities.

If you need this software on 3.5" diskettes, the simplest course of action is to find a computer with high-density drives in both sizes and copy the all the files from each distribution disk to a corresponding 3.5" disk. Failing that, send us a check or money order for US $9.95 ($12.95 Canadian), along with your original 5.25" diskettes, your completed warranty card, and appropriate sales tax to:

Bantam Electronic Publishing
1540 Broadway
New York, NY 10036
Attn: DOS 6.0 Power Tools

and we'll send you a set of replacement disks by first-class mail.